DAKTAR II

DAKTAR II

Viggo Olsen, M.D.

MOODY PRESS

CHICAGO

Library of Congress Cataloging in Publication Data

Olsen, Viggo B.
    Daktar II / by Viggo B. Olsen.
       p.   cm.
    Includes bibliographical references.
    ISBN 0-8024-0431-6
    1. Olsen, Viggo B.   2. Missionaries, Medical—Bangladesh-
Biography.   3. Bangladesh—History—1971-   I. Title.
R722.32.047A3   1990
954.9'205—dc   89-13583
                                                        CIP

1 2 3 4 5 6 7 8 Printing/RR/Year 95 94 93 92 91 90

Printed in the United States of America

Dedicated to

the myriad patients who flow into Memorial Christian Hospital like an endless river of sorrow and pain—yet with a vibrant faith and hope that they will be healed.

They are Bengalis, tribal people, and Westerners.
They are also Burmese who slip across the border under cover of darkness to obtain treatment.
They are Tipperas, Murungs, Moghs, and Chakmas from the jungle-covered hills.
They are Muslims, Hindus, Christians, Buddhists—and animists, too.

They are the focus of our attention, our constant companions, our inspiration.
We salute them for their courage and willingness to travel great distances to receive our treatment.
They cause us sleepless nights, anxiety, and exhaustion—but when they speak again, see again, stand again, or walk again, they bring us pleasure and profound joy.

May we ever care for them wisely and well with skillful hands, keen minds, and immensely compassionate hearts.

Contents

Figures

Tables

Acknowledgments

I am thankful for this page, which allows me to express my immense gratitude to four special women. How I appreciate my wife, Joan, who collated stacks of letters, reports, articles, and pictures; spent endless hours at the computer keyboard typing manuscript; and gave me invaluable suggestions and advice. I am grateful, too, to Linda Arildsen, who also invested innumerable hours typing manuscript pages, who cared for many nitty-gritty details, and who also made important recommendations concerning the manuscript. I am thankful, as well, for Alice Dauchy and Margaret Nendick, who have spent large blocks of time packaging and posting our books for distribution through the mail. These four dedicated women worked the long hours voluntarily, motivated by faith—and by love for those unseen and unknown persons who would read the words we have put on paper.

Furthermore, I owe a particular debt of gratitude to four heads of state who shared with me their views—and their hearts' desires. They are:

- President Mohammad Ayub Khan
- Prime Minister Sheikh Mujibur Rahman
- President Ziaur Rahman
- President Hussain Muhammad Ershad

Mr. Q. J. Ahmed, recent Secretary of the Ministry of Defense of the Government of Bangladesh, helped me immensely by reading the whole manuscript and making valuable comments and suggestions. I am grateful to him for this—and for the many lessons I have learned from him through the years.

I am also indebted to my colleagues in Bangladesh. They not only approved this book-writing project, but also provided some of the pictures and spent long hours checking the manuscript. My special thanks go to Margaret Archibald, chairperson of the critiquing committee, and three others (Dr. Donn Ketcham, Dr. Jeannie Lockerbie, and Rev. D. Jay Walsh) who read through the whole manuscript and offered important recommendations and advice.

In addition, I say "thank you" to our mission president, Dr. Wendell Kempton. He was a constant encouragement to me throughout the long task of completing this book.

I am grateful to photographer Dan Watts, the head of Dan Watts Productions, who came to apply his skills in Bangladesh. Several of the photographs in this book are his.

I am also fortunate to have enjoyed the friendship and excellent cooperation of the manager, editors, and others at Moody Press. Our relationship has been thoroughly enjoyable and productive.

But my greatest debt is to that Giver of all good and perfect gifts who granted me the time, the opportunity, and the inspiration to complete this work—and without whose help this book would not be worth reading.

VIGGO OLSEN, M.D.

Preface

Bengalis. What a fascinating people!

Bangladesh. What an intriguing place!

Desh means country or land, so Bangladesh is the land of the Bengalis—or land of Bengal. Although the people have been around for three thousand years and more, the new nation has completed only one full decade of existence. This book focuses especially on Bangladesh's growing pains during that first decade of the infant nation—and the singular life-style and unusual experiences of our family during those ten years. There were good days and bad days, hilarious happenings and other incidents so heartbreaking that they caused us great sadness.

You will also encounter scattered episodes from the lives of our co-workers, but to do justice to their experiences and notable accomplishments would require several books. During that first decade Bangladesh was also *rawktodesh*—nation of blood—for it was a violent, bloody period in the history of the fledgling nation.

We, along with our team, have served the Bengali people for more than twenty-five years. In fact, our official agreement with the government states that our purpose is to *"serve* God and man in the People's Republic of Bangladesh." Our long residence and intimate association with the people have helped us to understand this nation and the roots of the terrible civil war that led to the birth of Bangladesh—from the blood and ashes of a shattered and torched East Pakistan. I have written about our experiences during those dark days in *Daktar/Diplomat in Bangladesh;*[1] the Bengali word *daktar* means medical doctor.

Even if you have not read that first volume, you will be able to follow this book easily, for in the preliminary chapters I have built in a bit of overlap between the two books. This summary of a few key events of the past, melded with much new material in the early chapters, will also be useful for those who have read the first volume, for it will serve as a reminder and a bridge tying the two books together. This taste of the past may also whet your appetite to read or reread *Daktar/Diplomat in Bangladesh*, which is now being freshly reprinted.

Because we know them we love the people of Bangladesh. As you meet them in these pages may you, too, come to appreciate and love them.

Muslim, Hindu, and Buddhist friends reading this story will find it easy to grasp—except for possibly two concepts. If you belong to one of these groups, please turn to page 575 and read the Appendix before going on to begin chapter 1. In the Appendix I have explained the two concepts, and I hope that explanation will enhance your understanding and appreciation of this book.

Now for the first decade of Bangladesh.

Prologue

1

Three Majors
with a Plan for a Coup

DATELINE: DACCA, Bangladesh; August 14, 1975.

Occasional rumbles of thunder echoed from the towers of black clouds cruising the dark sky—a typical monsoon season night in subtropical Bangladesh. Major S. Farook Reehman, tactical commander of the First Bengal Lancers Tank Battalion of the Bangladesh Army, reached his squadron office and tank garages by 10:00 P.M. that somber night. Those garages are located within the huge army base at the northern edge of Dacca, the nation's sprawling capital. Assembled by the tank garages were four junior officers and nearly three hundred soldiers; all were clothed in the distinctive black uniforms worn only by the officers and men of the elite Bengal Lancers, the only tank battalion in Bangladesh.

Major Farook barked an order, and his men began practicing their night loading, unloading, inspecting, and otherwise checking the thirty tanks that were squatting in the shadows inside the huge garages. They noted that two tanks were too sick to travel. Diagnosis: mechanical problems. Farook's junior officers and men were relaxed, for they were accustomed to joint night maneuvers with the artillery battalion twice a month; as yet they were unaware of the grim agenda planned for that cataclysmic night.

In stark contrast to his men, Major Farook was tight as a bowstring. Three nights earlier he had announced to his lone confidant, "I am going to do it on the 15th. I am going to knock off Mujib on Friday morning."[1] After months of observation, analysis, and plotting, the time had come for him to attack and attempt to kill Bangladesh's president, Sheikh Mujibur Rahman. Fifty-five-year-old Sheikh Mujib was not only the immensely powerful head of state, a leader who possessed exceptional charisma, but was also the founding father, the "George Washington," of Bangladesh. Even so, with colossal self-confidence, Farook felt sure his men would follow him in this bold coup attempt against Mujib.

A quarter-mile away at the unused, partially built new Dacca airport site a second major directed his troops in their preparations for the "joint maneuvers." Major K. Abdur Rashid, commanding officer of the Second Field Artillery Battalion, was the brother-in-law of Major Farook, his confidant and co-conspirator in this brazen coup attempt. Their secret had been so well kept that Rashid's four junior officers and three hundred men were also completely oblivious of what was planned for them that night. Major Rashid proceeded to deploy his eighteen artillery pieces at the deserted airport.[2]

At 11:00 P.M. the third major deeply involved in the plot arrived at the new airport site with four companions to join Rashid. Major Sharful Huq, nicknamed "Dalim," was really ex-major Dalim since being dismissed from the army a year before—with the full approval of President Sheikh Mujib. Dalim brought with him two other ex-majors and two majors who were actively serving in the army. After greeting Dalim and his companions, Rashid took them and three companies of his soldiers to the tank garages where Major Farook awaited them.

Farook gave his *salam* (greeting) to the six active and former majors. A reporter later wrote that at this point Farook, standing on a tank, gave a "fire-eating speech"[3] to fan the rage and motivation of the two battalions of men gathered before him. But Farook told me that it happened quite differently; he did not use a tank for a stage nor did he make a rousing speech.[4] As commanding officer of the operation he simply told the officers and soldiers the overall plan and expected them to follow his orders; amazingly, all agreed to take part in this dangerous, potentially nation-convulsing operation.

Next Farook gathered the officers around a table and laid out his carefully prepared map of Dacca. He first pointed out several secondary locations, which their troops and tanks would have to control. Then he indicated the primary targets—four private homes in slumbering residential areas of Dacca. These were the homes of

- The president of Bangladesh, Sheikh Mujibur Rahman
- Sheikh Mujib's brother-in-law and minister in his cabinet
- The nephew of Mujib, who was also a key political leader and the editor of a government newspaper
- Another of Mujib's relatives, who held a powerful Civil Service post

Major Farook next assigned assault teams to each of these main targets. Three majors and former majors were selected to lead a very large force in the attack on the house of Sheikh Mujib, while ex-major Dalim would direct a smaller group in the assault on the minister's residence. Two other relatively small teams were selected to carry out the attacks on the other two houses. According to Farook, he instructed the teams to kill only the four key political leaders, not their family members.[5] But they were given leeway to play it by ear and were instructed to destroy any forces that might oppose them on the way to their targets.

In the hours after midnight, while the angry, determined majors were making their final preparations, the generals were asleep in distant housing areas of the immense army base known as the cantonment. We, too, were asleep 240 miles south of Dacca at Memorial Christian Hospital, which was situated in a beautiful wooded locality named Malumghat in the District of Chittagong.

Presumably awake, however, were those manning the General Headquarters Field Intelligence Unit—just a hundred yards away from the busy coup staging area near the tank garages. But the intelligence personnel did not investigate or react in any way; they sensed nothing amiss, as Farook had cleverly planned, for this was the usual night for combined tank and artillery exercises.

Major Farook's main concern was Sheikh Mujib's private military force, the *Jatiyo Rakkhi Bahini* (National Security Force). This military group was quite separate from the Bangladesh Army and existed to protect Mujib and do his bidding. Three thousand Rakkhi Bahini soldiers were camped between the cantonment and the four target residences. The success of the whole operation depended upon neutralizing or diverting these three thousand pro-Mujib fighting men. Farook himself, with his tanks, would handle this part of the action. The gall of the man! He knew full well that he could not lay his hands on the shells for the tank cannons because they were under lock and key outside of Dacca.[6] Yet he was ready to try to intimidate three thousand well-armed troops with his twenty-eight tanks—and only the tanks' machine guns for firepower.[7] Perhaps he would surprise them as they slept, or maybe Rashid's artillery gunners could zero in on the Rakkhi Bahini camp if Farook needed their support.

By 4:55 A.M. the final planning and preparations were complete. Major Rashid's artillery pieces were in position with all their crews on the alert. At the tank garages Bengal Lancers, resplendent in their black uniforms, manned the tanks and crowded into some of the trucks and jeeps. Khaki-clad soldiers armed with rifles from Major Rashid's artillery battalion filled the other trucks. And the generals slept on.

At "first light" (5:00 A.M.) Farook boldly gave the signal that launched the "major's coup." As the truckloads of Muslim officers and men intent on killing their Muslim leaders began to inch forward, the hauntingly beautiful early-morning Muslim call to prayer from the cantonment mosque reached their ears. But there was no time for dawn prayers. The time for action was at hand.

Some minutes after the troop-filled trucks departed, Farook shouted to his tank crews, "Follow me!"[8] Immediately he mounted his lead tank and sped south on the main cantonment road. At the major crossroad within the cantonment he made a sharp right turn, then two or three minutes later passed through a gate into the old Dacca airport, which handled both civilian and military air traffic. He crossed the main runway and headed for the fields beyond it—the most direct route to the Rakkhi Bahini camp. As Farook's tank charged across the airport's empty fields he checked his watch—perfect timing! If the killer teams had encountered no resistance on the way, they should be in position at their targets ready to launch their assaults.

As he approached the far wall of the airport Farook glanced back to check his column. A jolt of adrenaline shot into his bloodstream! Only one tank was following him! Somehow twenty-six tanks had got lost in the shuffle. As he crashed through a small gate in the far wall he was agonizingly aware that it would be far more difficult—perhaps impossible—to bluff the Rakkhi Bahini with only two of his twenty-eight tanks. But it was too late now to change the strategy. This was it!

Wheeling around the corner of the Rakkhi Bahini barracks he was in for a second rude shock—which he later described in these words: "Suddenly I found a brigade of 3000 Rakkhi Bahini lined up six rows deep. They were battle equipped—steel helmets, rifles, packs, everything."[9] Meanwhile, we and the generals slept on. Just then, from the direction of President Mujib's house came the staccato sound of automatic weapons firing.

If we somehow had been on the sidelines observing this incredible series of events, dozens of questions would have instantly come to mind. Could Major Farook possibly succeed in bluffing three thousand well-armed fighting men, at the ready, with his two tanks? What had incited this handful of midlevel army officers to attempt this daring coup? What had precipitated their rage? Could these officers and their few truckloads of men possibly topple the present government and install a new one? If they failed, how many of them would hang? If they succeeded, who would take over as the new head of state? Why had the "poetic Bengalis," long thought to be a non-martial race, become so warlike, so violent? How would this cataclysmic event affect the beautiful Bengali people who had suffered too much already? And what would happen to our own American/Bangladeshi team and our work of serving God and man in the People's Republic of Bangladesh? If the coup were to succeed, would the new government push us and other foreign missions out? Such painful questions—painful because of our seventeen-year-long love affair with the people of Bangladesh.

2
Three Decisions
by a Couple Named Olsen

My love for the Bangladeshi people is inextricably intertwined with my love for a girl with shining eyes from Ohio—and for a Man from Palestine. In my twenty-second year I married the girl from Ohio, whose name is Joan. After our marriage I continued my studies as a medical student at the University of Nebraska College of Medicine. For three intense years we worked day and night, partied with verve, and enjoyed life together. At age twenty-four I graduated from medical college and received that long-awaited M.D. degree. Joan had played a vital part in the whole process —typing papers, working, and supporting me in many ways. I do love that girl!

After graduation we joyously drove the highways and turnpikes to New York City's Borough of Brooklyn, where I would be an intern for a year in the Department of Internal Medicine, Long Island College Hospital. There, during our twenty-sixth year, we met the Man from Palestine and entered into a remarkable relationship with Him. Born nearly two thousand years before, He was a figure both ancient and modern, for it was alleged that He was still alive. He had an unusual number of names and titles: the Galilean, the Messiah, Jesus of Nazareth, the King of Israel, the Prince of Peace, the Son of God, Christ the Lord, King of kings and Lord of lords, plus dozens of others.

At first He was a mystery figure to us. In fact, we initially tried to prove that He and His Christian religion were false. Our plan seemed reasonable enough. We knew that all ancient books are said to be filled with scientific errors. So we thought we could easily disprove Christ and Christianity by laying bare, with one sweep of an intellectual scalpel, the scientific errors in the Bible, the Christian's handbook. We discovered otherwise. The remark-

"I married the girl from Ohio"

able scientific accuracy of the Old and New Testaments, their historical validity, archaeological confirmation of Biblical events and places, the incredible fulfillment of numerous ancient prophecies penned centuries before, and many other varieties of evidence turned the tables on us. We became thoroughly convinced that our diabolical plan to disprove Christ and Christianity was a mistake.

The day came when we bowed our hearts before the Man from Palestine. Deeply believing in Him and His astonishing teachings in a personal way, we each accepted Him as our Savior and Confidant and acknowledged Him as Lord of the universe. What a dynamite experience! Glory seemed to fill the plain little apartment where we made that great faith decision. We had been converted from agnosticism to Christ—and it turned out to be a remarkably life-changing conversion.

Within weeks we discovered a Biblical command that was new to us and intriguing to consider:

> . . . present [surrender] yourselves to God as being alive from the dead . . .[1]

> . . . present [surrender] your bodies a living sacrifice, holy, acceptable to God, which is your reasonable service.[2]

Obviously, this act of presenting or surrender or dedication differed from our conversion experience. The day of our great faith decision had been a day of receiving, not giving. Through receiving Christ we had received various inestimable benefits: forgiveness of sins, a loving acceptance into God's family, the promise of happiness forever beyond the grave, and many other gifts. Although our hearts had overflowed with gratitude for these wondrous benefits, we did not at that time think to give Him anything in return. Now, however, that very gratitude impelled us to give God what He asked for, to surrender our lives unreservedly to Him.

"Father," we prayed, "we give ourselves to you—body, soul, and spirit. We yield to you our aims and ambitions and our plans for the future. We will do anything you say and go anywhere you ask. Use us for good and spiritual purposes and give us the guidance we will need each step of our lives."

Two years later, in 1954, I was serving as a naval medical officer on a jewel of an island in the South Pacific. As that tour of duty wound down Joan and I took time to carefully analyze career options open to me as a physician so that I could make application for the next phase of my medical education. For two weeks we listed options, considered them one by one, discussed, studied the Scriptures, and prayerfully sought the direction we would need to

Vic "received that long-awaited M.D. degree"

make the right decision. The guidance came clearly and forcefully—that we should prepare ourselves for foreign medical mission service.

Interestingly, our sense of calling was punctuated with two key provisos:

1. We should go some place where modern medical care was not available, a place where people died without the care of trained physicians and a hospital.
2. We should go to a locality with a great lack of Biblical teaching—an area where Christ's good news message was not known.

A third proviso involved future medical training—I must be thoroughly prepared so that I might properly represent my Creator and Lord with the best possible medical-surgical work.

We recognized that the events of those three life-changing years could be summarized in three words—words simple but vibrant with meaning because they so clearly described our experience:

1. Salvation
2. Surrender
3. Service

On the day of *salvation* we had accepted the Man from Palestine to be our Savior and acknowledged Him Lord of all. He lovingly saved us from lives of uselessness and an eternity of unhappiness and granted us life everlasting. Months later, on the day of *surrender*, we turned over our lives to God in a moment of dedication and commitment. Then His remarkable guidance came to us as never before. Two years later this guidance made clear to us that we should serve Him and that our *service* should be on some distant shore. And that service would monopolize the remaining years of our lives.

The tour of navy duty completed, we returned to New York City where I took a second internship—this time an internship rotating through several departments of immense Kings County Hospital. Next we traveled to Milwaukee, Wisconsin, where I would study to become a surgeon at Milwaukee County Hospital. That four-year surgical residency program extended from 1955 to 1959 and, by providing very broad and thorough general surgical training, prepared me to care for the sick and injured in some medically "empty" place on the other side of the planet.

While I was studying surgery we simultaneously studied the various countries of the world and the mission agencies serving in those lands. Because we were ignorant about these mission societies, we wrote to dozens of them and collated the details from their replies on huge flow sheets. Slowly, bit by bit, one mission board began to stand out for us above the rest—the Association of Baptists for World Evangelism, commonly known as ABWE. But this high-quality mission agency had no plan for a medical mission anywhere in the world that matched our two provisos. Sadly, we turned away from ABWE and began to restudy other excellent mission boards.

Then it happened! A lovely teenage girl, daughter of an ABWE missionary, became ill in the southern part of East Pakistan (now Bangladesh). This precious young person died because there was no surgeon who could operate and relieve her intestinal obstruction. Shattered by this tragedy, with deep emotion the governing board of the mission voted to open their field in southern East Pakistan to medical work. When that news reached us in 1958, we began reading about the land of East Pakistan, the eastern half of ancient Bengal.

Figure 1. Bengal in 1940

Bengali billboard

During undergraduate years we had heard vaguely of Bengal Lancers and royal Bengal tigers, but we were otherwise quite ignorant about this part of the world called Bengal. Now, freshly motivated, we studied the area with intense interest. On an old map published in 1940 before Pakistan came into being, we easily located in South Asia the country of India, sometimes known as *Hindustan* (place of the Hindus) or the Indian subcontinent. On the eastern flank of the subcontinent we found Bengal perched commandingly astride the Bay of Bengal (see figure 1).

This 80,000-square-mile province of India was inhabited primarily by the Bengalis, one of India's fifteen major nationalities. The Bengalis spoke —and deeply loved—their beautiful Bengali language. We were surprised to learn that most of the Bengalis in the western half of Bengal (West Bengal) followed the Hindu religion, whereas the majority of those who populated East Bengal were Muslims (followers of the religion of Islam, which had been founded by their prophet Muhammad).

By 1947 the Bengalis and other Indians had been ruled by the British for 190 years—and they despised being subject to those foreigners from a distant land. That year three cataclysmic events occurred simultaneously in India:

1. The British gave up their rule over India.
2. India became a sovereign nation.

3. Five Muslim-majority provinces and regions were carved out of India and named Pakistan, which was also declared a new and sovereign nation. Pakistan was created to be a homeland for Muslims of the Indian subcontinent.

In the process of creating Pakistan, Bengal was cut in two. Because of its Hindu majority, West Bengal remained part of India, but Muslim-majority East Bengal became a province of Pakistan. Newborn Pakistan was a geographical conundrum, for its four western provinces were separated from its one eastern province (East Bengal) by eleven hundred miles of unfriendly Hindu-majority India (see figure 2).

Nine years later, in 1956, Pakistan's four western provinces were unified into a single maxi-province called West Pakistan. At the same time the East Bengal province was renamed East Pakistan (see figure 3). The Bengali people were not happy about this name change, for they had a centuries-long attachment to the name East Bengal.

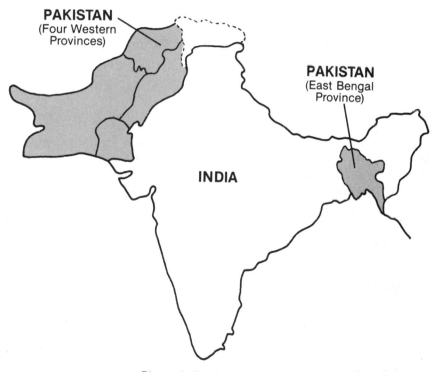

Figure 2. Pakistan 1947-56

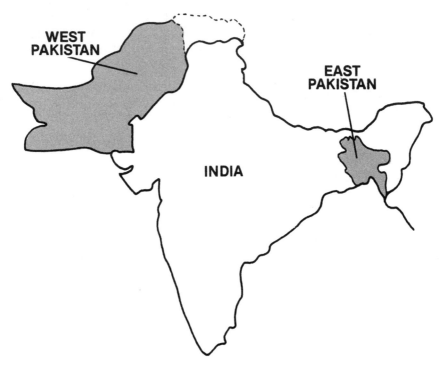

Figure 3. Pakistan 1956-71

While we read on about East Bengal/East Pakistan and the intriguing Bengali people, one question kept surfacing in our minds: *Will this be the place where we take our four children, live, and serve for the rest of our working lives?*

We and our four children:
LEFT TO RIGHT: *Mark, Lynne, Nancy, and Wendy*

3
Three Meetings
with a President Named Khan

As we continued to study—and face the insistent question—the people of Pakistan on the other side of the globe were embroiled in political turmoil. The nation had begun in 1947 with no desks, office equipment, or even paper clips. Confusion reigned. Pakistan's first head of state died within a year; his successor was assassinated three years later. The chaos of those early years had continued on throughout Pakistan's first decade. The Bengalis of East Pakistan were especially unhappy because Bengali influence was small in Pakistan.

From the beginning the relationship between East and West Pakistan had been strained. Because they were more experienced in business, government, and the military, and because they seemed to feel racially superior, the West Pakistanis increasingly took advantage of the Bengali people of East Pakistan. The Bengalis despised this condescending attitude, for they are a proud race with a distinguished background, an attractive culture, and a remarkably beautiful, highly developed language, which is precious to them.

They were also keenly aware of the galling inequalities between East and West Pakistan. The Bengalis always seemed to get less—less power, prestige, and *paisha* (money). And they were dismayed by the political shenanigans of clever, manipulative West Pakistani leaders, who governed the nation capriciously and ineffectively. The only things holding East and West Pakistan together, it seemed, were Islam and the daily interwing flights of the Pakistan International Airlines.

Throughout the 1950s conditions in politically unstable Pakistan became increasingly chaotic. Finally the angry, disillusioned Pakistan Army acted decisively. In October 1958 the army declared martial law and replaced the civilian president with Pakistan's top general, Mohammad Ayub Khan. This bloodless "October revolution" wrested the government from the hands of the politicians and placed it squarely in military hands. But could General Ayub Khan succeed when the politicians had failed to unravel the tangled threads of Pakistan?

He made a strong beginning. Ayub quickly lowered food prices to help the common man. He fired numerous corrupt and inefficient government officers and forced others to retire. He declared new laws to control the politicians who had made such a mess of the country. And he launched Pakistan on the path of impressive economic progress. For a time he would be considered by many to be Asia's greatest living statesman. We could not have guessed then as we read about President Ayub Khan's accomplishments that one day he would become a valued friend.

Then, in 1959, while Ayub was busy pressing his reforms, back in the United States we also were busily finalizing important decisions. Through our studies we had learned much about East Pakistan—and the Bengali people who lived there. Further, we had discovered that the southernmost section of the country, where the ABWE mission now wanted to establish a hospital, was particularly neglected and needy. This area seemed to perfectly match the two provisos attached to our original sense of calling several years earlier. So when the ABWE board approved thirteen basic principles of medical missions,[1] which we earnestly espoused, everything clicked. Confident in our sense of guidance we took the plunge and were accepted by ABWE to establish a medical mission in desperately needy southern East Pakistan (now Bangladesh).

In 1960-61 our preparations for overseas service involved raising grants and monthly funds to construct and operate a hospital, plus recruiting doctors, nurses, technicians, teachers, builders, and church workers. With the recruitment completed and substantial funds in hand, we departed from the United States and proceeded by ship to England where I studied tropical medicine for several months. Then, on the twelfth day of January 1962, aboard Indian Airlines flight 401 we took off from Calcutta, India, on the final leg of our journey to Chittagong, East Pakistan. When the stewardess learned that we were going to Chittagong to stay, eyeing our four children she exclaimed, "But why would you want to go there to live? That's the end of the world!"

End of the world or not, we loved bustling, brawling Chittagong, the major city in the area where our team served (see figure 4). It was East Pakistan's second largest city and the major seaport, a fascinating cultural crossroads highly susceptible to strikes and urban uproar.

Chittagong Port

Dacca street scene

Figure 4. The two major cities of East Pakistan

Then we visited Dacca (spelled "Dhaka" in later years), the capital city located in the center of the country (see figure 4). There we discovered the Governor's House, the High Court Building, the Secretariat, army headquarters, and other upper-echelon government offices. Dacca was the nerve center of East Pakistan—and the prime spot for riots, coups, and other kinds of skullduggery. It was precisely because Dacca was the seat of power that Farook and his dissident majors launched their bold coup attempt there.

Chittagong City was the gateway to the southern finger of East Pakistan, which pointed south toward Burma (see figure 5). Our mission particularly served the multitudes of this fascinating region. This finger was made up of two of the province's seventeen districts:

1. Chittagong District—a long, narrow, shoestring coastal plain fronting on the Bay of Bengal.
2. Chittagong Hill Tracts District—a hilly, jungly interior district lying side by side with Chittagong District. Here many of the intriguing non-Bengali tribal people lived in their scattered villages.

Figure 5. Southern districts of East Pakistan

Morning mist in the Hill Tracts

Tribal village in Chittagong Hill Tracts

Colleagues who arrived in the late 1950s had established two centers or stations in Chittagong District:

1. Chittagong City Station
   • The station at Chittagong City was a center of administration and church work.
2. Hebron Station
   • The station at Hebron had been established primarily to serve the non-Bengali tribal people of the Hill Tracts.
   • Hebron Station lay at the tip of a slender corridor of Chittagong District, which followed the winding Matamuhuri River and projected deep into the Chittagong Hill Tracts (CHT) District (see figure 6). In later years, when the government ordered all foreigners to stay out of the CHT, we were able to continue our tribal work at Hebron Station because it was located in Chittagong District.

About fifty million people inhabited the 55,000-plus square miles of Iowa-sized East Pakistan when we arrived in 1962;[2] this made it the most densely populated nation in the world (with the exception of city-states like Singapore and Hong Kong). The population was extremely homogeneous, for nearly everyone was Bengali:

1. Bengalis	98%
2. Non-Bengalis	2%
Tribal people	
Immigrants	

Hebron Station

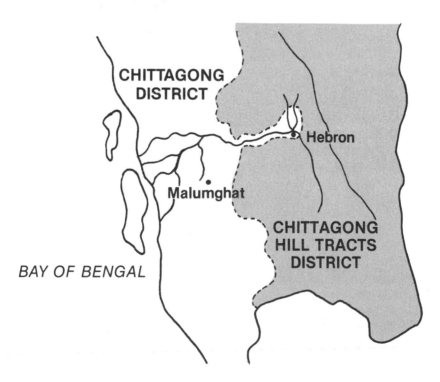

Figure 6. Hebron Station at the end of a narrow corridor of Chittagong District which extends into the Hill Tracts

Bengali men wearing lungis

Young women wearing saris

The burqa is worn by Muslim women

Bengali girl in traditional dress

We found the *Bengalis* to be short, slim, hospitable, volatile folk. Most Bengali men wear a shirt with a *lungi* (full-length sarong) or Western-style pants. Most Bengali women wear the *sari*, a graceful, attractive, full-length garment, with a blouse; others wear a sarong and blouse. Many Muslim women, when they leave their homes, cover themselves with a long, usually black, sacklike *burqa*, which extends from the top of their heads to their feet. This Bengali version of the veil was designed to protect Muslim women from the eyes of rude men. The women themselves can see only with difficulty through a small opening or two peepholes; this limited visibility makes crossing a busy street a dangerous exercise. Also, we saw many Bengali children who were appealing enough to steal your heart away—pretty little girls and boys whose impish eyes were alive with mischief.

We soon discovered that the *non-Bengali tribal people* look very different from the Bengalis. They are more oriental in appearance, often looking rather like the Chinese or Burmese. More than a dozen tribes inhabit the Chittagong Hill Tracts, each with its distinctive language, dress, and culture. Other tribes inhabit hilly, jungly areas along other borders of the nation. Tribal men are often called hill men because they inhabit the hilly regions. The major tribes within reach of our two stations were these:[3]

1. Chakma	(Buddhist)	170,000
2. Mogh (Marma)	(Buddhist)	90,000
3. Tippera (Tripura)	(Animist-Hindu, Christian)	50,000
4. Murung (Mru)	(Animist)	20,000

We found the *Chakmas* to be the most educated of the tribal people of the Chittagong Hill Tracts; a few of them even had college degrees. The *Moghs* (rhymes with logs) came originally from the neighboring Arakan District of Burma; they spoke a dialect of Burmese and some could read the curious Burmese script.

The *Tipperas* espoused an animism tinged with Hinduism; in the previous few years hundreds of them had become Christians, and we had helped them to establish a number of congregations and churches. The animistic *Murungs* were the most aboriginal of the hill men. The first Murungs I saw impressed me with their powerful physiques and colorful appearance; on that day, however, I had no way to know how important and precious these scantily clad jungle people would one day become to me.

The *non-Bengali immigrants* in Bangladesh were chiefly Urdu-speaking Muslims who had migrated to the area from India after

Smiling Bengali girl

Bengali boys with impish eyes

Chakma young woman   *Mogh man*

the creation of Pakistan in 1947; because they were Muslims they had opted to move to Muslim-majority East Bengal rather than remain in Hindu-majority India. Since many of them had migrated from the Indian province of Bihar, all such immigrants were commonly known as "Biharis"—even if they actually came from Indian provinces other than Bihar. They looked much like Bengalis.

Religiously East Pakistan was a strongly Muslim-majority land. These are the 1961 census statistics for the religious groups of East Pakistan:[4]

1.	Muslims	80%
2.	Hindus	19%
3.	Other	1%

In the years that followed, the percentage of Muslims gradually increased to 87 percent at the expense of the Hindus. The Christians numbered only about 150,000 people—less than one-half of one percent of the total population. In the Christian community nearly half were Protestant and the rest were Roman Catholic. Most of the Protestants were Baptists related to Baptist missions from Great Britain, Australia, New Zealand, and the United States.

In this vibrant, pulsating tapestry that was East Pakistan my wife, Joan, and I, alongside our dedicated colleagues, began to serve the people in many different ways.

Tippera girl

A colorful Murung man

After settling in, we surveyed extensively to find just the right location for the hospital we had come to build. We found that site on the countryside sixty-five miles south of Chittagong City. This spot perfectly matched the two provisos attached to the original sense of calling which had come to us eight years earlier:

1. We should go to an overseas area with a great medical need—a place where people died without proper medical and surgical treatment.
2. We should go to an overseas region with a great lack of Christian teaching—a locale where Christ's good news message was not known.

First, modern medical facilities were lacking in southern Chittagong District and multitudes tragically died without effective treatment. A new Bengali acquaintance graphically confirmed this sad state of affairs when he exclaimed, "We don't even have enough quack doctors here!" Second, Christ's gospel was unknown in the area, and the Christian population numbered absolute zero. Memorial Christian Hospital would be constructed in the center of a medical and Christian void.

Later, I discovered a historical reason for the existence of this Christian vacuum. In 1793 the father of the modern missionary movement, William Carey, had come as the first missionary from England to Bengal.[5] He and his British baptist colleagues had effectively established their teaching in Bengal as far as the city of Chittagong (see figure 7). Twenty years later Adoniram Judson, the first American missionary, reached Burma, the country just south of East Bengal.[6] The sphere of influence of Judson and his co-workers extended to northern Burma (see figure 7). Although both missions made sporadic efforts to permanently establish the church and Christian truth in the hiatus between their works, none of those efforts had taken root. Because the outreaches of Carey and Judson had never effectively interfaced, we found no Christians in the area when we arrived. We would be the twentieth-century pioneers who would attempt to fill the gap between the works of those two nineteenth-century forerunners.

During 1962-63 we and our team members studied the Bengali language and obtained a marvelous building site in the sub-county of Dulahazara, a lovely wooded spot named Malumghat. There the builders on our team constructed Memorial Christian Hospital, a center of healing and spiritual light and the base of our medical mission. Many call our medical center "Dulahazara Hospital" or "Malumghat Hospital" because of its location. The word *Malumghat* means "Port of Perception" or "Anchorage of Understanding." True to its name, it is a river port where large country

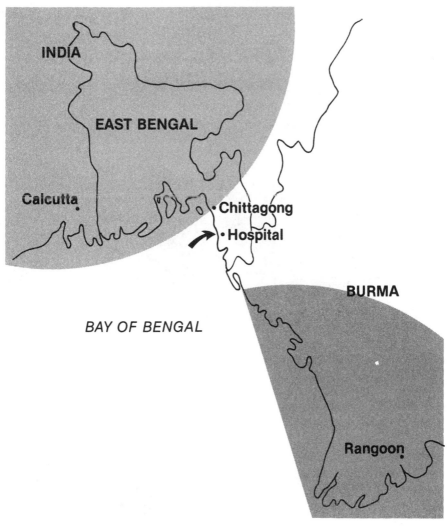

Figure 7. Hospital in area between circles of influence of W. Carey in India and A. Judson in Burma

boats anchor and load—and it has become a place of new understanding for many since our arrival. At Malumghat we serve not only Bengalis but also the tribal people of the nearby Chittagong Hill Tracts.

During the 1960s we occupied our newly built hospital, cared for the multitudes who came to us, and discussed spiritual truth with interested people. We enjoyed many unusual and unforgettable life experiences—and suffered some heartaches, too. Four events from that era were particularly germane to our lives later on during the first decade of Bangladesh (1972-82):

Memorial Christian Hospital,
"a center of healing and spiritual light"

Country boats at Malumghat

Mr. Q. J. ("Jalal") Ahmed   *Mrs. Shakina Ahmed and daughter Bitu*

1. We developed a warm relationship with Mr. Q. J. ("Jalal") Ahmed and his family; they became dear friends as well as patients. Jalal, then deputy commissioner (chief officer) of Chittagong District, was instrumental in our obtaining the superb Malumghat site for our hospital. In the years that followed he enjoyed a meteoric rise in government service, quickly becoming a Dacca-based senior civil servant. Because we were like brothers, and because he believed in the importance of our medical mission, Jalal found ways to help us again and again.

2. We learned from experience that the nation's Muslims spoke Bengali differently from the non-Muslims (Hindus, Buddhists, Christians). Or, to put it another way, there is a standard Bengali and also a Muslim Bengali way of speaking the Bengali language. Because standard Bengali evolved from the ancient Hindu-flavored Sanskrit language, it also contains many Hindu-flavored words—along with many other words that are religiously neutral. So when the Muslim conquerors came eight centuries ago, they retained the neutral words but cast out the Hindu-flavored words—and replaced them with their own beloved Arabic and Persian words. These are the vocabulary words that make Muslim Bengali distinctively Muslim. Here in diagram form is what happened:

Standard Bengali
− Hindu-flavored words
―――――――――――――
Neutral Bengali words
+ Arabic & Persian words
―――――――――――――
Muslim Bengali

Muslim Bengali dictionaries

3. I was fascinated by this Muslim Bengali vocabulary but, surprisingly, I could find no dictionary of these words on the market. So for my language student research project, with a big assist from Joan, I produced and published *A Muslim Bengali to English Dictionary*.[7] This small, bright-red volume was the first such pocket dictionary in East Pakistan.

4. While doing the dictionary we dreamed that one day we would be able to produce the New Testament, and possibly the whole Bible, in this special Bengali as a gift to the multiplied millions of Bengali Muslims in East Pakistan and adjacent India. They revere the New Testament of Jesus, the Psalms of David, the Pentateuch of Moses, and other Biblical books as Muslim Holy Scripture—in addition to the Koran of Muhammad. We began the work with the fascinating fourth book of the New Testament known as the Gospel According to John. Our starting point was a new standard Bengali common language translation being done concurrently by our own colleagues Lynn Silvernale and Mrs. Bashanti Dass.

Also during the 1960s Pakistan's president, Ayub Khan, experienced both satisfaction and sorrow. His economic and other programs produced highly visible results during the so-called Decade of Development (1958-68).[8] But our Bengali people of East Pakistan were not impressed. They complained bitterly that most of the development benefited the people of West Pakistan, not the Bengalis. They claimed that the ubiquitous West Pakistani entrepreneurs who conducted business in East Pakistan made big profits, then sent the money to their accounts in the west wing—and they bemoaned the economic loss to East Pakistan caused by this flight of funds. Furthermore, they hated martial law rule and demanded democracy.

President Ayub was responsive for he, too, wanted to establish democracy in a careful, step-by-step fashion. So he set the wheels in motion for an election for president to be followed by elections for members of a parliament (congress).

Nineteen sixty-five began with presidential elections. President Ayub not only had ordered them, but also had himself become a candidate. We listened in snatches to the Radio Pakistan election returns throughout election day. The final compilation of votes from East and West Pakistan showed Ayub to be the winner with 63 percent of the votes. The next step would be parliamentary (congressional) elections.

Though the elections greatly enhanced Ayub's prestige internationally, many of our Bengali friends complained that the presidential election was technically a vote for electoral college members who would really elect the president; to them that amounted to a limited franchise. They felt cheated to be denied full adult franchise, with each person's vote counting directly for his or her candidate of choice. Of course, that would not have affected this particular election because Ayub had decisively won both the popular and the electoral college votes.

About this time the people of East Pakistan began to rally around a dynamic, highly visible Bengali leader named Sheikh Mujibur Rahman; he was the head of an increasingly popular political party named the *Awami* League (People's League). Presenting facts and figures about the marked inequities in power and wealth between East and West Pakistan, he relentlessly blasted the Pakistan government with tough, angry speeches in Dacca and throughout the country. He punctuated his speeches with the bold rallying cry *"Joi Bangla* [Victory to Bengal]!" And the hundreds of thousands who came to hear him would answer exuberantly with their own thundering *"Joi Bangla!"*

When I asked a thoughtful Bengali friend why Mujib had become so popular, he replied, "Because he is one of us, he understands us—and he understands the problems we are having with those domineering West Pakistanis. Not only that, he also has come up with a six-point formula to relieve our grave problems and give us justice." Mujib's six points were music to Bengali ears. If the government would ever accept these six carefully crafted demands, Pakistan would be drastically changed:

- Voters would enjoy full adult franchise.
- The nation would not only become a parliamentary democracy, but also most of the power would reside in the two provincial (state) governments rather than in the central (federal) government.
- The financial imbalance between the people of the two wings would be corrected and the flight of money from East to West Pakistan stopped.
- East Pakistan would have a military force of its own.[9]

Mujib, with his overpowering charisma, had become the chief antagonist to the incumbent government and to President Ayub Khan.

From 1965 to 1970, while these political dramas were taking place, I met three times with President Ayub. The places of meeting, the reasons for meeting, and the subjects discussed were markedly different each time. Our first meeting in 1965 was completely unplanned.

Soon after his decisive election victory, the president crossed India to visit our own neighborhood in East Pakistan to support his party's congressional candidate from the area. Unexpectedly, we were invited to an outdoor breakfast for President Ayub under a festive red-and-white-striped *shamiana* (canopy). The hundreds of people milling about were filled with a sense of awe and excitement. Suddenly a messenger hurried over to us and said breathlessly, "Come quickly! The president is calling for Dr. and Mrs. Olsen."

As we approached the breakfast table Ayub stood and welcomed us. "Thank you so much for joining me for breakfast. I want to hear more about the hospital you are building here." He graciously seated Joan beside him, and we enjoyed a delightful two-hour breakfast with this president of the world's fifth largest nation. After breakfast we proceeded to the forest to hunt the wild and elusive jungle fowl, one of the famous species of Bengal. That morning during our first time together we developed a warm friendship with Ayub which lasted throughout his lifetime.

We wondered at the unusual series of circumstances that initiated that friendship. Had it happened for some unknown purpose? "The day will come when we will know for certain," Joan predicted. And she was right.

For many months all the mission societies had found it more and more difficult to obtain visas for their personnel; a visa is an approval to enter a foreign country stamped into a traveler's passport. The situation deteriorated even further in the summer of 1966. Visa applications for all new personnel were being rejected by the government, and we veteran workers were offered only six-

Vic and Joan at breakfast with President Ayub Khan

month single-entry visas in place of the usual four-year multiple-entry visas. The change made a normal one-year furlough in the United States impossible and would very severely complicate our children's annual school schedule. Here was a serious problem, which we feared might soon lead to the outright expulsion of mission personnel.

Later, when we learned that President Ayub Khan had again crossed India to spend a week in Dacca, East Pakistan, we decided to go to the top. All our other strategies had failed miserably. A friend and neighbor Mr. Fazlul Karim Choudhury, the elderly Muslim patriarch of our area, offered to speak to his friend President Ayub on our behalf. Together we flew to Dacca and made our approach to the president. His voice quavering with emotion, the old gentleman described to Ayub how the hospital team had saved the lives of many of his people who used to die untreated. Then he explained our severe visa problems and asked, "Mr. President, what fairness—what justice—is there in that?"

With a puzzled expression Ayub responded, "It does indeed seem strange."

Then the old gentleman said something unexpected. Although his facts were quite wrong, he made a telling point. "I have heard," he said, "that missionaries in West Pakistan are facing no such problems, only those here in East Pakistan. I'm sure you do not love our East Pakistan any less than the west wing."

Servant fanning the elderly patriarch,
Mr. Fazlul Karim Choudhury

"Of course not!" Ayub shot back, "I will look into this immediately." And he did delve into our problem quickly and aggres-
sively. Wonderfully, Ayub cut through all the obstacles and
granted our every request.

Months earlier we had wondered why the unusual sequence of
events had brought us to the breakfast table with President Ayub.
This second meeting with him made the answer clear. Our acquaintance with the president, plus the help of a faithful friend—a-
long with volumes of earnest prayer—produced four-year
multiple-entry visas worth a million dollars apiece to us. And this
stunning visa victory ultimately helped other missions, too, at this
critical juncture in the history of missions in Pakistan. King Solo-
mon certainly knew what he was talking about when he declared,
"The king's heart is in the hand of the Lord, like the rivers of water;
He turns it wherever He wishes."[10] "Thank You, Father!"

But the masses in East Pakistan did not feel that their problems were being solved. Emboldened by Sheikh Mujib and his
now-famous six-point program, the people of East Pakistan became more forceful in their protests. In mid-1966 their demonstrations were so massive and so militant that eight hundred were
arrested and eleven were killed by police firing. Mujib was

promptly incarcerated in the Dacca Central Jail where he remained for the next eighteen months.

As soon as he was released from the civilian prison in 1968, the army immediately clapped Mujib in military solitary confinement in the Dacca Cantonment. He and thirty-four others were charged with conspiracy. The government claimed that they had plotted with Indian officials to create an armed revolt aimed at leading East Pakistan to secede from Pakistan.

Later in the year President Ayub Khan became extremely ill; his private physician told me that he had suffered from pulmonary embolism (blood clot to the lung). During the weeks of his illness when he was most vulnerable, the Bengali movement against his government gained unstoppable momentum. From December 1968 through February 1969 the angry people of East Pakistan rioted so violently and so often that they paralyzed the government's administration of the country. The upheaval during that three-month period became known as the "great mass upsurge."[11] East Pakistan had gone berserk!

Then we heard a poignant radio speech by President Ayub in which he announced his decision not to be a presidential candidate in the upcoming election. The next day he canceled the conspiracy trial and released Sheikh Mujib from the military prison. Thousands of Bengalis accompanied Mujib in a joyous, ecstatic victory procession from the cantonment down the main streets of Dacca. As the news spread like wildfire out into the districts, millions of Bengalis rejoiced.

The next month President Ayub invited politicians from both provinces of Pakistan to a round table conference. Despite his own convictions regarding the need for a guided democracy with a strong president, he had decided to bow to the will of the people and agreed to establish full parliamentary democracy and to dismantle his electoral college in favor of full adult franchise. In the new parliamentary system the prime minister would be the powerful leader and the president a figurehead.

Most of the politicians were more than satisfied when President Ayub agreed to these two demands. But Sheikh Mujib wanted more. He would be satisfied with nothing less than agreement on his full six-point manifesto. Having made two great concessions already, the central government would not agree to the other points. The government feared that East Pakistan might try to break away and become an independent nation if it were given so much autonomy.

Mujib returned to East Pakistan to report that the Pakistan government was unwilling to accept some of his six points. Once more tumultuous riots and strikes completely paralyzed East Pakistan; the police were simply unable to maintain law and order. At last, defeated by Bengali public opinion and the sheikh who had molded it, on March 25, 1969, President Ayub Khan stepped down. And—déjà vu—he turned the country over to the commander of the Pakistan Army, a general named Yahya Khan, who promptly placed the country under military rule to restore law and order. What a heartbreak for Ayub who had worked so hard for Pakistan —and who had set the wheels in motion to improve East Pakistan's position.

During the hot season of 1970 I flew across India to Rawalpindi, the capital city of Pakistan at that time. I planned to care for some mission business and meet Ayub Khan; this would be our third meeting. I knew he would appreciate the visit of a friend, for I was aware that many so-called "friends" had deserted him after he stepped down from his position as head of state. But it seemed to me that a friend is most needed when reverses come and the going gets rough.

When I learned that Ayub would be out of town for two or three days I concentrated on completing mission business. The final morning I was in Rawalpindi I telephoned again and talked with his secretary, who informed me that Ayub had returned from his trip. When I requested an appointment the secretary responded, "I am sure he will want to see you. Please wait just a moment; I will check with him about the time." A moment later he returned and suggested 3:30 P.M.

"I am sorry, " I answered, "I should be flying across India toward Dacca at that time. I am scheduled to leave the city this afternoon."

"Wait just another minute, please. We will try to work out another time for you to come." A minute later he was back on the line saying, somewhat apologetically, "I fear that this may be inconvenient for you, but is there any possibility that you could come now?"

"That will be just fine with me," I responded. *"Inshallah* [if God wills], I will be there in thirty minutes."

Hailing a cab I returned to my room, buffed the dust from my shoes, picked up a newly purchased inexpensive paperback book from my bedside table, and slipped it into my briefcase. The book, entitled *The Man Jesus*[12] and written in readily understandable English, was a compilation of New Testament passages on the life and teachings of Christ arranged chronologically. As the waiting taxi eased out into the traffic and crossed town I spent some minutes in earnest prayer, asking the Father for ability to encourage my friend and also for a natural opening in the conversation to discuss spiritual truth with him.

My taxi pulled up in front of a large, attractive mansion. I entered the outer office just on time, and in a moment the secretary ushered me into Ayub's reception room. His genuinely warm smile and outstretched hand projected his pleasure at having an old friend come to call.

"Hello, Doctor," he said, "I am so glad to see you after a long time. Thank you for coming." As my slim surgeon's hand gripped his broad soldier's hand in a firm handshake, I returned his greeting. Because he could not speak Bengali and I did not know Urdu, we talked in English, mine American-style and his precise, British-flavored English. He was a westernized person of the East, as I was an easternized man of the West.

Animatedly we discussed his recent three-day trip, old times, and the agonizing political pressures he had passed through. He was touched to learn that someone cared about his anguish and distress. He thanked me. Ayub continued, "You would be interested, Doctor, to know that I have been reading the Bible recently."

"What portion have you been reading?" I asked, sensing instantly that the answer to my prayer was at hand.

"I have been reading in the first book, mostly, the book called Genesis. I find very fascinating the passages about the creation of this world, the creation of the first human beings and animals, and the life-histories of various prophets."

Ayub Khan

"I am pleased to hear about your studies," I said. "I am especially intrigued by the fact that you who have been reared in an Islamic culture are sincerely reading the Bible, while I who grew up in a Christian culture started my study of the Bible trying to prove it unreliable and false."

His curiosity piqued, he asked, "What possessed you to start on such an impious study?"

"I will answer your question and take it a step further to explain how this study ultimately led to our coming to East Pakistan. It all started this way. After my wife Joan's parents experienced a great deepening of their Christian faith, they pressed us, also, to believe. Being scientifically inclined and trained, I felt that religion was outmoded and untrue. It seemed to me that weak people had manufactured a god to help them out of their troubles and somehow, someday, take them to an imaginary heaven on the other side of this life. Finally, however, we made a bargain with Joan's parents that we would study their seemingly unscientific religion if they would agree to respect our final decision once our study was completed. We all agreed to this proposal."

Although he did not speak, Ayub's expression made clear that he was intrigued by this bargain. He nodded for me to continue.

"Being skeptics, we began by considering the most basic question of all. *Is there a Deity (a God, an Allah) who created this earth and our universe?* We knew from scientific studies that our planet and the universe surrounding it had not always existed; some immense power had brought them into being in ages past. But was that creative energy the power of God or just some gigantic cosmic explosion? We soon recognized that this creative power must have been an intelligent power, for the universe is filled with indications of order, pattern, and design. Unintelligent power, like a hydrogen bomb exploding in the heart of a city, produces chaos and rubble and destroys design.

"Or, to put it another way," I continued, "suppose we could place all the mechanical parts of a Pakistan Army tank (nuts, bolts, screws, washers, piston rings, valves, carburetor, fuel pump, tread sections, gauges, guns, etc.) into a gigantic cement mixer, mix them up, and throw them out upon the ground. We could throw them on the ground again and again for a lifetime, but never would all the pieces just happen to fall together in the form of a tank. Each time the pieces would look like a pile of junk.

"On the other hand, if an intelligent mechanic assembled the many pieces one after another, he could produce a perfectly functioning tank. The difference? The power of the giant mixer throwing the pieces on the ground is raw, unintelligent power. But the power of the mechanic who assembles the pieces in the correct pattern and design is intelligent power. In the same way, we saw that it required an intelligent power to put together the innumerable pieces of this vast universe—billions of stars and galaxies, this planet, plant life, animal life, and human life—into their trillions of intricate patterns and designs. That intelligent power men call God or Allah or Khoda.

"Then we analyzed more deeply the nature of God and soon decided that He must be more than just cold, impersonal, intelligent power. Two observations made this clear to us:

1. The finest thing about human beings is not our human anatomy or physiology, or even our intellect, but our soul, spirit, personality, and our ability to love and show mercy and kindness.
2. And because the Creator cannot be less than the creature He brought into being He, too, must possess personality, spirit, and the ability to love others and show mercy to them."

"Yes," Ayub said firmly, "I, too, believe that God is real—and that He is a Creator who cares for us."

"We were now ready," I continued, "to consider a second important question: *Did the Creator reveal Himself to the human race through any sacred Scriptures?* We studied the Scriptures of various groups for a long time. In most of them we failed to find the scientific accuracy, historical accuracy, or the moral tone that would be marks of God-given revelation. But in the Bible we found all these impressive marks of inspiration. We had expected to find many scientific errors in the Bible because all ancient books are said to be filled with such errors. We discovered, instead, that these Scriptures somehow avoided the superstitions and scientific errors of many other ancient books. We were impressed, too, with the historical accuracy of the Bible, which was confirmed again and again by the scientific work of archeologists. Also, we were influenced by the unexpected unity and consistency of the Bible's sixty-six books written over many centuries. The completeness of the message and the inexhaustibility of the contents had their effect upon us, as did the changed lives of believers in ancient days and in our day.

"Furthermore, we discovered that hundreds of prophecies, including prophecies of a Messiah-Savior to come, were literally and precisely and remarkably fulfilled hundreds of years later. During those weeks of intensive study we discovered more than enough evidence to convince us that the Old and New Testaments of the Bible were God's Word given to mankind. No wonder, Your Excellency, that Jews, Christians, and Muslims revere the Bible's Old Testament, for therein are the Holy *Taurat* [Pentateuch] and Holy

Zabur [Psalms]. No wonder that Christians and Muslims both recognize the *Injil Sharif* [Holy New Testament] of Jesus as sacred Scripture, the Word of the living God."

"Yes," Ayub responded, "along with the Holy Koran, we Muslims do revere the Holy *Taurat, Zabur,* and *Injil.* Please go on. What happened next in your study?"

"Now that we were sure about the existence of God and were developing confidence in the Holy Scriptures, we quickly confirmed truths well known to you and me:

- By a remarkable miracle of God, without any human father, Jesus the Messiah was conceived in a virgin's womb.
- He grew up to become a beloved teacher and a mighty prophet.
- He had power to lovingly heal the sick, give hearing to the deaf, speech to the dumb, sight to the blind, and even raise the dead to life.
- Because He is the perfect expression of God to man, He is rightfully called *Kalematullah,* the Word of God.
- He led a truly sinless life, a perfect life which is beyond our capacity to live.
- He is coming back to earth someday to set up His kingdom."

With conviction Ayub accurately responded, "Yes, we Muslims find all of these points in the Holy Koran and believe in them."

"We found further details," I continued, "about the power and person of Jesus in the Holy Scriptures:

- He inherited from His mother, Mary, a human body and human personality—He was thoroughly human.
- In the absence of a human father, He obtained from God the divine nature and power; in the Holy New Testament it states that 'God was in Christ reconciling the world [of people] to Himself.'[13] He was more than a prophet. And isn't the logic of this concept clear? To communicate successfully with jungle fowl like those you hunted near our hospital in 1965, I would have to enter into a jungle fowl body and learn the language of jungle fowl. Similarly, God indwelled the human body of Jesus the Messiah and communicated with the people of His day in their own language.
- We should not be surprised that in Christ deity is united with humanity, because the ancient prophets made clear that the Messiah-Savior would have this dual nature, that He would be more than a prophet.

- We found several passages of Scripture which taught that ages before He worked as a village carpenter in Palestine, He was involved in the construction of the universe. Other passages speak of His existence through the countless ages of eternity before His birth.
- He came into this world not only to love us and teach us and help us, but also as a Savior to save us from our many sins. In fact, at the time of His birth an angelic being announced,

> For there is born to you this day in the city of David a Savior, who is Christ the Lord.[14]

- We learned further that He is not only qualified to save us because of His sinless life, but also because He died on a cruel Roman cross, not to pay the penalty for His sins but to pay the penalty for ours. Another passage in the New Testament states that

> God demonstrates His own love toward us, in that while we were still sinners, Christ died for us.[15]

- But death could not hold Him; a number of passages teach that on the third day He arose again from the dead—to prove that all His claims and teachings were true. Then he appeared to His twelve disciples, ate and drank with them, and later gathered with a crowd of more than five hundred of His followers.

"As we carefully studied these and many other passages in the Holy Scriptures, my friend, we became convinced that Jesus the Messiah is who He claimed to be, more than a prophet—deity united with humanity in a single personality."

President Ayub replied, "Some of these last points are new to me. I will have to study them further and give them much thought. But what was the final outcome of your studies in the Bible?"

"Finally, we tackled a third question: *What do I have to do to obtain the salvation, forgiveness of sins, and life everlasting that Jesus the Messiah died to give me?* Prior to our investigation of the Holy Scriptures, we presumed that religion taught such benefits could be gained by doing enough good works to satisfy God. Imagine our surprise when we read,

> *Not by works of righteousness which we have done,* but according to His mercy He saved us. . . .[16]

> [God] has saved us and called us with a holy calling, *not according to our works*, but according to His own purpose and grace. . . .[17]

"We were confused. If we could not gain salvation and eternal life by doing good works, then what did we have to do? Further studies made it clear. To gain the benefit we had to believe the record and, by faith, receive Christ the Lord into our lives as the Savior He came to be. Some of the key passages explained it this way:

> Believe on the Lord Jesus Christ, and you will be saved. . . .[18]

> But as many as received Him [Christ], to them He gave the right to become children of God, to those who believe in His name.[19]

> For whoever calls upon the name of the LORD shall be saved.[20]

"This act of faith, we learned, instantly gains the new believer certain religious benefits that men and women long for:

> Forgiveness of sin
> Loving acceptance by God
> Right standing with God
> Salvation from punishment after death
> Happiness forever after death

"But there is more! Beyond these basic benefits, we learned that God grants other remarkable gifts to the new believer, including a new inner life (eternal life) and a new inner strength to overcome evil, to live honorably, and to love and help others.

"Finally the day came when we found our skepticism vanquished. We were convinced that God was real, the Holy Scriptures were true, and that Jesus the Messiah was more than a prophet, that He was deity united with humanity. And we recognized that He was also the Savior who had died in our place, paid the penalty for all our sins, and who desired to save us and grant us eternal life. Furthermore, we had learned that our destiny and salvation depended not on our good works but rather on our faith in Him. As I sit with you just now, I vividly remember the evening that I believed—that I accepted Jesus the Messiah as my very own Savior and Lord of lords. And the great inner miracle happened just as the Scriptures had promised."

"What a remarkable story!" Ayub Khan exclaimed. "That means, then, that you are a convert."

President Ayub's statement was unusually perceptive; not one in a hundred Pakistanis would have made that comment. Pakistanis and Bengalis feel that you automatically belong to the religion into which you are born. They would say that from birth I was a Christian because I was born in a Christian family in a Christian country. But Ayub Khan recognized that I was a convert—from agnosticism to faith in Christ the Lord. His comment told me that he had clearly comprehended, step by step, the explanation of my personal spiritual pilgrimage.

"Yes," I responded, "and I promised that I would tell you not only about our impious study and its outcome, but also how our newfound faith ultimately moved us from America to East Pakistan. Our conversion brought us wondrously close to God and gave us so much happiness and peace of mind that we ultimately surrendered our lives to Him to serve any place on planet Earth where He might send us. His guidance came and pointed us to one of the neediest regions in the world, the two southern districts of East Pakistan."

I sensed emotion in Ayub's voice as he said, "I do thank you, Doctor, for telling me that wonderful story! You have given me much to think about."

As he spoke I was opening my briefcase. "My friend, the timing of this appointment finally came up so quickly that there was no time to go out and find a suitable gift for you. I wish I could have done that. I did, however, bring you something which I purchased previously for my personal study. Although it did not cost a large sum of money, I can tell you that it is incredibly precious and valuable." With those words I removed from the briefcase the two-dollar paperback book *The Man Jesus*. As I placed the book in those soldier-statesman's hands, I explained that the book was a careful compilation of passages from the Holy New Testament on the life and teachings of Christ.

As he looked at the cover and turned to the table of contents President Ayub said, "How can I thank you enough for this valuable book! You were so kind to bring it for me."

Although we talked about other things during the remainder of our time together, Ayub repeatedly thanked me for the little book. In fact, I have never before or since had anyone express so much gratitude and pleasure for the gift of any kind of book. Three or four times he broke into the conversation to again express his thanks. And when I stood to leave, his final words were, "I want to thank you once again for bringing me this book. I will not only continue to treasure it, but I promise you again that I am going to read every word of it. *Khoda hafez* [God be with you]!"

4
Three Attacks
in a Province Called East Pakistan

During 1970-71 East Pakistan was battered by three fierce attacks. An unprecedented natural calamity first struck the populous province. On November 12, 1970, when this monstrous cyclone, armed with a forty-foot tidal wave, smashed into the southern shores of East Pakistan, about *half a million* people perished within minutes! Houses, crops, flocks, and herds by the hundreds of thousands were also destroyed. This—*planet Earth's greatest natural calamity of the century*—instantly attracted worldwide attention.

Despite the desperate need for massive immediate aid, the Pakistan central government responded lethargically and minimally. This niggardly response by the government greatly angered the devastated Bengali people, but it became a political boon for Sheikh Mujib, who was stumping for the upcoming parliamentary (congressional) elections. In the final three weeks before the elections, he moved about the country thundering that this neglect by the central government of Pakistan demonstrated conclusively the need for greater political autonomy in East Pakistan.

On December 7 the stunning election results brought elation to the Bengalis, for in the new Parliament Sheikh Mujib and his Awami League gained 98 percent of the seats allotted to populous East Pakistan.[1] That constituted an absolute majority of East plus West Pakistan seats (160 out of 300 seats)—*and meant that Sheikh Mujib would become the next prime minister of all of Pakistan.* Mujib had won big and, paradoxically, had set the stage for something even more disastrous than the juggernaut cyclone.

The people of West Pakistan were appalled that their new leader would be Sheikh Mujib, a Bengali. But Pakistan's President Yahya Khan had no choice but to announce that the National Assembly (Parliament) would meet in Dacca on March 3, 1971. What a triumphant day that would be for the Bengalis! With an absolute majority in the National Assembly they could include every one of their precious six points in a new Constitution and gain vastly increased autonomy for East Pakistan. They were jubilant. In fact, they had already prepared a draft of the new Constitution they intended to approve.

But suddenly President Yahya canceled the March 3 meeting of the Parliament, then three weeks later ordered the Pakistan Army to attack and subdue the people of East Pakistan. Before midnight on March 25 the boom of artillery and the stuttering sound of machine-gun fire rocked the capital city. Scores of fires crackled ominously, exposing hundreds of ghastly killings as the flames leaped high into the night sky. The Pakistan government had turned loose its army to kill Bengalis and to bring the "unruly province" of East Pakistan to its knees. The terrible crackdown of Pakistan's troops on the defenseless people created a nightmare of terror in East Pakistan.

The next day, March 26, 1971, the secretary of the Chittagong District Awami League defiantly announced from the Chittagong radio station *the independence of the new nation of Bangladesh*.[2] His words seemed to be little more than whistling in the dark. A day later, from the same Chittagong radio station, a young army major named Ziaur Rahman also declared the independence of Bangladesh—and brashly proclaimed himself the head of state.[3] Because Major Zia's announcement aired at a time of day when it was heard by a much larger audience than the earlier broadcast, he was widely credited as the first to announce the independence of Bangladesh. The people were thrilled by his bold declaration. Later he adjusted his proclamation to affirm that Sheikh Mujib was the real president of independent Bangladesh.

In the days and weeks that followed, the West Pakistan Army systematically and viciously killed hundreds of thousands of Bengalis. Sheikh Mujib himself was captured immediately, flown to West Pakistan, and imprisoned to await trial and execution. Thousands of villages were burned to the ground and tens of thousands of Bengali women cruelly and purposefully violated to dilute and alter Bengali blood lines. *Ten million* Bengalis ran from their homes and crossed the nearest border to become refugees in India. Strangely, the U.S. government failed to express outrage at these war crimes and almost seemed to be supporting the Pakistanis, despite their shocking attack on the Bengalis of East Pakistan.

Our team members remained as long as possible, but ultimately we were told by our government to evacuate. Three of us remained behind, Dr. Donn Ketcham and I at the hospital and Rev. Reid Minich in Chittagong, to help our stricken Bengali brothers and sisters and to protect our hospital and other mission property. During this brutal civil war we had enough adventures to last a lifetime—and to fill a book or two.[4]

During the first week after the holocaust began, courageous Bengalis were resisting the Pakistan troops with *das* (machetes), bamboo staves, bricks, bare hands, and the force of numbers. Simultaneously, Awami League leaders slipped across the borders of blood-drenched East Pakistan to safety in neighboring India to regroup. Two of them, Tajuddin Ahmad and Amirul Islam, made their way to India's capital city, New Delhi, to obtain help from India's prime minister, Mrs. Indira Gandhi. When she agreed to

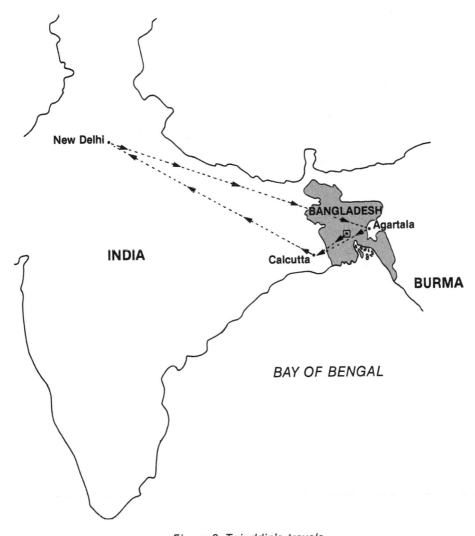

Figure 8. Tajuddin's travels

provide assistance, Tajuddin precociously declared himself the first prime minister of Bangladesh and Sheikh Mujib the president; Mujib, of course, would have to be president in absentia, for he remained incarcerated in the West Pakistani prison.

On April 10, 1971, Prime Minister Tajuddin spoke words of encouragement on tape to be broadcast into Bangladesh later in the day. That same day the Indian Air Force flew him to the Indian town of Agartala, just across East Pakistan's eastern border (see figure 8). There, in room number five of the Agartala Circuit House, he met with the other four senior Awami League leaders.

Then, while their people were bleeding and dying inside East Pakistan/Bangladesh, they haggled for three days over who would hold which prestigious position in the new provisional government of Bangladesh. The four senior officers were incensed with Tajuddin because he had stolen a march on them by meeting with Indira Gandhi and then declaring himself prime minister.[5]

In the end, Tajuddin won out and retained his position and title. Another leader was selected to be vice-president, while the other three senior Awami League notables became cabinet ministers over various ministries of the embryonic "shadow government." The newborn cabinet than appointed a retired army officer, Colonel Osmani, to be the commander of the surviving Bengali soldiers and young guerrilla fighters training in India. After their three days of rancorous discussions these leaders were flown by the Indian Air Force to Calcutta, India's largest city and the capital of the province of West Bengal (see figure 8). There, forty miles from the border of their homeland, they began to further organize the provisional government of Bangladesh.

From the beginning factionalism was a problem. Prime Minister Tajuddin, the vice-president, and two of the cabinet ministers headed the pro-Indian faction of the Bangladeshi leadership. Associated with them were others including Amirul Islam, who had escaped from East Pakistan with Tajuddin. He was a British-trained attorney, an elected member of the Parliament, and he had played an important part in drafting the Bangladesh Proclamation of Independence.[6] Incidentally, years later Amirul and his family became our patients and friends, and he became our legal adviser.

The fifth and last cabinet minister was Khandaker Mushtaque Ahmed, the minister of foreign affairs and head of the right-wing, pro-Islamic, pro-American faction; this anti-communist group feared that overdependence on India would result in excessive control by the India-Soviet axis. Associated with Mushtaque were two of his close friends; this group of three became known as the "Mushtaque triangle." Mark the name Mushtaque, for four years later he would skyrocket to sudden and unexpected prominence.

The Mushtaque triangle also attained a certain notoriety in 1971 during the Pakistan Army crackdown, when they negotiated secretly with American officials to derail the Bangladesh independence movement.[7] Apparently Mushtaque and one or more front men had eight clandestine meetings with American government representatives in India to agree upon terms to halt the breakup of Pakistan. Mushtaque and the United States favored a loose tie between East and West Pakistan, with maximum autonomy for each of the two provinces, rather than the full independence of East Pakistan. When his fellow-ministers discovered Mushtaque's secret flirtation with the Americans and the West Pakistanis, they were incensed. Consequently, they isolated him and his two cohorts and frustrated their plan to maintain a link with West Pakistan.

In early July 1971 President Nixon's right-hand man, Henry Kissinger, visited West Pakistan. After he participated in some meetings, it was reported that he fell ill and was resting at a mountain retreat very near the high school that Wendy and Lynne, our two oldest children, had attended. But something quite different was really happening. While a fake motorcade traveled the winding road to the mountain retreat, the Pakistan government secretly flew Mr. Kissinger behind the bamboo curtain to Peking (Beijing in later years) to carry out far-reaching negotiations with the Chinese government. His successful visit set the stage for President Nixon's momentous trip to China and the initiation of a surprising new relationship between the two giants, capitalist United States and communist China. Pakistan was the key intermediary in this new connection, for she was friendly to both sides.

The breathtaking news of the Kissinger secret trip and the opening of China to the United States suddenly threw new light on the U.S./Pakistan/Bangladesh enigma. We could now understand why President Nixon and Henry Kissinger had seemed so uncompassionate toward burning, bleeding Bangladesh and so supportive of vengeful, murderous Pakistan. The United States vitally needed Pakistan to play the intermediary role in the secret China initiative—and this initiative was so supremely important to American leaders that they would allow nothing to interfere with it. In fairness it must be said, however, that American officials did use "quiet diplomacy" behind the scenes to press Pakistan to moderate its behavior in Bangladesh.

By August 1971 Bengali young men, trained in India to be guerrilla fighters, began trickling back into East Pakistan. The main group of them was called the *Mukti Bahini* (Liberation Force). Each week, as more and more of these Bengali freedom fighters slipped back into East Pakistan, they began to inflict increasing damage on the Pakistan Army and Navy. In addition, they fought groups of their own Bengali countrymen who were radical Communists striving to create a frankly communist Bangladesh. These "red guerrillas" fared poorly against the Mukti Bahini and against the Pakistan Army.

Whereas the first attack on East Pakistan had been a vicious cyclone, and the second an attack by the murderous Pakistan Army, the third was essentially a counterattack—by the Indian Army and Bengali freedom fighters. From November 20 onward, inside the borders of Bangladesh Indian troops were fighting secretly alongside the Mukti Bahini guerrillas. Then on December 4 the Indian Army poured across the borders into East Pakistan, along with more Mukti Bahini forces, and powerfully counterattacked the Pakistan Army (see figure 9).

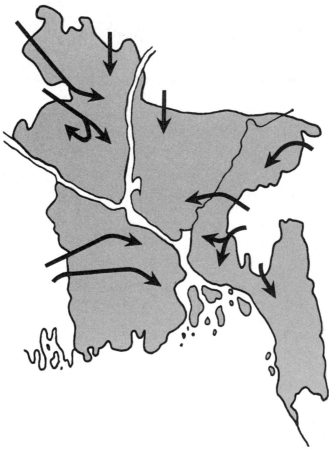

Figure 9. Incursions of the Indian Army and the Bangladesh freedom fighters in East Pakistan/Bangladesh in late 1971

New Bangladesh flag flying at Malumghat

Finally, on December 16, 1971, the defeated Pakistan Army's commanding general surrendered. With that surrender East Pakistan died a tragic, horrible death, and from its ashes arose a new and independent nation called Bangladesh—land of the Bengalis.

On that same December 16 at our Memorial Christian Hospital at Malumghat the flag of independent Bangladesh was raised briskly to the top of the hospital flag pole. In the center of the green flag was a red circle containing a golden map of Bangladesh. As barefooted Bangladeshi freedom fighters fired volleys of shots into the air the exhilarated hospital crowd over and over joyously shouted, "*Joi Bangla* [Victory to Bengal]!"

The next day West Pakistan's leading politician, Z. A. Bhutto, took over the West Pakistan government from thoroughly disgraced President Yahya Khan; thereafter, the former West Pakistan was termed simply "Pakistan." Then, learning that their Sheikh Mujib was still alive in Pakistan, the Bengalis were intoxicated with joy. And—you guessed it—they filled the streets with yet another massive and passionate demonstration.

That same day thousands of Bengali young men, quislings who had tacitly or actively cooperated with the brutal Pakistani regime against their own people, quickly declared themselves to be Mukti Bahini. The true freedom fighters, who had risked their lives for their country, scornfully spoke of these false Mukti Bahini as the "Sixteenth Division"—because they suddenly became freedom fighters on the sixteenth of December, the day the Pakistan Army surrendered.

But for some notorious Bengali collaborators this ruse did not work. A flamboyant Mukti Bahini commander named Khader "Tiger" Siddiqi and his men bayoneted some of those collaborators in cold blood in front of a crowd of Dacca spectators. A French photographer's famous photo of that gruesome scene won a Pulitzer Prize that year.[8]

For the first week of independence, Bangladesh wandered aimlessly in a political fog without leaders or government. Meanwhile, Prime Minister Tajuddin and his cohorts irresolutely remained in Calcutta, hesitant to face the Indian Army and the freedom fighters in Dacca. They well knew that the Mukti Bahini resented them for sitting comfortably in Calcutta while the Bengali guerrilla fighters were sacrificing and dying on the breast of their motherland. Would self-proclaimed Prime Minister Tajuddin be able to establish his authority in Dacca, or would the Mukti Bahini reject him?

Finally, after nearly a week of indecision, Tajuddin and his ministers took the fateful trip to Dacca. They were immensely relieved when no one challenged their right to govern. Yet the newborn government functioned fitfully and anemically in the absence of the beloved and powerful Mujib. How Bangladesh needed Sheikh Mujib!

While Bangladesh was in the throes of this turbulent, traumatic change of leadership in 1971, our mission in the United States enjoyed a peaceful and orderly transition of leaders. Missionary statesman Dr. Harold T. Commons had wisely and skillfully led the mission for thirty-six years, ably assisted by Rev. Edward C. Bomm who had served as treasurer and special assistant to the president. As Dr. Commons stepped down, the ABWE governing board unanimously chose Dr. Wendell W. Kempton, an astute administrator with a fine track record, as the next president; what a wise choice they made! Not only did these three men possess impressive administrative skills but, more important, they were spiritually-minded men who each had a heart for the work —and a heart for people.

Also in 1971, ABWE moved from rented offices in Philadelphia to its own beautiful new building across the river in Cherry Hill, New Jersey. As 1971 drew to a close the mission's prospects for the future looked far brighter than the outlook for Bangladesh.

Bangladesh: The First Decade

5
1972: Relief and Reconstruction

I have already written about some events that occurred during 1972 in the earlier book.[1] So in this chapter I will touch on those incidents only when necessary and usually in much less detail.

The new year dawned in brand-new Bangladesh with continuing euphoria and the daily influx of untold thousands of ragged Bengali refugees from India. India provided railway cars and trucks to assist in the return of these ten million refugees, one of the most massive migrations in human history.

During the first week in January the new government took over Pakistan International Airlines facilities and *voilà!*—a new airline named Bangladesh *Biman* (aircraft) was born. Also during that first week, left-leaning Prime Minister Tajuddin unceremoniously dismissed right-wing Mushtaque as foreign minister but did allow him to remain in the cabinet as minister of a more minor ministry. In this way Tajuddin punished Mushtaque for his dalliance with the United States and Pakistan to derail the Bangladesh independence movement. Mushtaque brooded over the insult—and never forgot it.

While government officials were struggling to get organized, the people thought and talked incessantly about their imprisoned leader, Mujib. *Will the Pakistan government release him or execute him?* they wondered. Then when the news finally reached Bangladesh that Bhutto would free Mujib, countless thousands poured out into the streets of Dacca and other cities in tumultuous, ecstatic celebrations. In Dacca truckloads of jubilant people clutching huge portraits of Sheikh Mujib shouted, *"Joi Bangla!"* and, "Sheikh Mujib *zindabad* [Long live Sheikh Mujib]!"

Across the ocean in the United States, on January 5 newspapers throughout the country unexpectedly carried bold front-page headlines like those in the Chicago *Sun Times*:

SECRET TEXTS RAISE LID ON
KISSINGER POLICY AGAINST INDIA IN WAR[2]

Syndicated columnist Jack Anderson had obtained and released to the press three secret documents, minutes of meetings of a special section of the National Security Council. In the special section meeting in the White House Situation Room on December 3, 1971, significant statements had been made by the assistant to the president for national security affairs, Henry A. Kissinger:

> The President [says] that we are not being tough enough on India. He has just called me again. He does not believe we are carrying out his wishes. He wants to tilt in favor of Pakistan.[3]

In the December 4 meeting Dr. Kissinger stated that he would not want to suggest the release of Mujib.[4] And concerning economic aid, President Nixon had ordered that cutoff of aid was to be directed at India only, not Pakistan.

There for the world to see were the clear-cut policy statements that the *United States had tilted away from India and incipient Bangladesh toward Pakistan*, despite Pakistan's appalling attack on the Bengalis. How distressed many American citizens were to learn that their government had tilted toward the killers, not the victims! This revelation was so sensational that Anderson won a Pulitzer prize for his journalistic coup.

During the previous year a number of Dacca-based U.S. State Department officials, including American Consul General Archer Blood, also had sharply disagreed with the official U.S. position. In fact, nine months earlier in April 1971 he had led twenty American consulate officers in sending a remarkable cable from Dacca to the State Department in Washington. The cablegram was entitled "Dissent from U.S. Policy Toward East Pakistan" and concluded with these forceful words:

> Private Americans have expressed disgust. We, as professional public servants, express our dissent with current policy and fervently hope that our true and lasting interests here can be defined and our policies redirected.[5]

Consul General Blood later won the American Foreign Service Association's coveted Herter Award for his intellectual courage and creative dissent.

In the early morning hours of January 8 in the city of Rawalpindi, Pakistan's President Bhutto dispatched Sheikh Mujibur Rahman and one of his close associates to England aboard a special Pakistan International Airlines jet. The flight touched down at

London's Heathrow Airport at 6:30 A.M., and Mujib was taken immediately to posh suite 112 of Claridges Hotel to prepare for a hastily arranged press conference. For Mujib, who had been held in tight solitary confinement in Pakistan for the previous nine months, it was a modern-day Rip Van Winkle experience. He had only a vague notion of what had happened in Bangladesh during the months of his imprisonment, for he had been denied visitors, letters, newspapers, and radio. As he ambled about the suite admiring the flowers and peering out the big windows at the traffic, he reveled in his new freedom.

The acting head of the Bangladesh Mission to Great Britain did his best to give Mujib an instant update on what had transpired during the previous bloody months in Bangladesh. But very soon the newspapermen began to arrive for the press conference. One reporter, London's *Sunday Times* correspondent, was an old friend. Mujib welcomed him warmly and confided, "I have a big scoop for you. We are going to keep some link with Pakistan but I can't say anything more till I have talked it over with the others. And . . . don't you write anything till I tell you."[6] Apparently Pakistan's Bhutto, during a meeting just before Mujib's flight to London, had convinced him that retaining a loose connection with Pakistan would somehow work to the advantage of the people of Bangladesh.

"Are you mad?" the correspondent replied. "Don't you know what's happened in Bangladesh? After what the people have gone through they will lynch you on the streets of Dacca . . . if you so much as utter one word about a link."[7] Then the telephone calls began pouring in—from Prime Minister Tajuddin in Dacca, Prime Minister Indira Gandhi in New Delhi, and many others. In short order Mujib learned more details of the slaughter that had occurred in Bangladesh and of the new nation's impatience as it awaited his coming to set everything right.

At the press conference Sheikh Mujib issued a jubilant statement to the crowded room full of expectant journalists:

> Today I am free to share the unbounded joy of freedom with my fellow countrymen.
>
> We have earned our freedom in an epic liberation struggle. The ultimate achievement of the struggle is the creation of the independent sovereign [Bangladesh], of which my people have declared me President while I was a prisoner in a condemned cell awaiting the execution of a sentence of hanging. . . .
>
> I now appeal to all states to extend recognition to the People's Republic of Bangladesh, to enter into diplomatic relations with us and to support her immediate admission to the United Nations.[8]

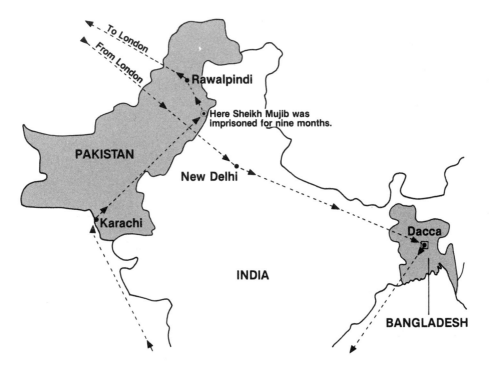

Figure 10. Sheikh Mujib's travels and imprisonment in 1971-72

Early the next morning an exuberant Sheikh Mujib took off from London aboard a British RAF jet to arrive triumphantly in New Delhi, India, at 8:06 A.M. for a brief four-hour stop (see figure 10). During a twenty-one-gun salute he was warmly greeted by the Indian president and by Prime Minister Indira Gandhi. A guard of honor snapped to attention while a band struck up the national anthems of Bangladesh and India. At the airport ceremony Sheikh Mujib gave a brief but moving speech to the assembled throng. He concluded with these words:

> When I was taken away from my people, they wept; when I was held in captivity they fought; and now when I go back to them they are victorious. I go back to the sunshine of their million victorious smiles.[9]

The RAF plane took off at midday and at 1:20 P.M. touched down in Dacca, the capital of Sheikh Mujib's beloved Bangladesh. In an incredible, thrilling, tumultuous moment he stepped from the plane into the view of a million of his ecstatic followers. My colleague Jay Walsh was present at the Dacca airport to observe

that climactic reentry. Bedecked with dozens of garlands of chry-
santhemums and surrounded by students and Mukti Bahini guerrillas, with difficulty Mujib proceeded to the official reception line
composed of senior government officials lined up beside a long red
carpet. Finally, after shaking hands with these officials, he greeted
the Indian generals and senior diplomats from various countries.

When the airport ceremony was concluded, Sheikh Mujib
climbed into an open truck, which took him slowly, inch by inch,
through a throbbing, undulating sea of shouting, singing, dancing
Bengalis. After two and one-half hours the truck finally reached the
meeting place at the Dacca Race Course. His fifteen-minute speech
was turbulent, emotional, and punctuated by tearful outbursts:

> At the outset I remember those innumerable Hindus and
> Muslims of Bangladesh who embraced martyrdom. I pray for the
> salvation of their departed souls. . . .
>
> My Golden Bengal, I love thee! I appeal to all countries of
> the world. There is no road in my Bangladesh. There is no food.
> My people have lost their homes. They are like street beggars to-
> day. I want your help.
>
> Once again I appeal to you to recognise Bangladesh. . . .
>
> You wanted me to come. I have come. The order of my [exe-
> cution] was passed. A grave was also dug. I was all prepared to
> die. I said, I am a man, a Bengalee and a Muslim. . . . I will em-
> brace death smilingly. But I will never pray for mercy to
> them. . . .
>
> It is ironical that in the name of Islam the Pakistani army
> killed the Muslims of this country and dishonoured our women. I
> want to tell you in clear and unambiguous terms that ours will be
> a secular, democratic and socialist country. . . .
>
> While I was returning after my release from Pakistani pris-
> on, Mr. Bhutto requested me to try to maintain some sort of loose
> tie between the two countries if possible. I told him that I could
> not say anything unless I returned to my people. Now I wish to
> say: Mr. Bhutto, live in peace. Bangladesh has achieved indepen-
> dence. If anyone ever dared to snatch our freedom Mujib would be
> the first to lay down his life for the preservation of
> independence. . . .
>
> Today I cannot speak any longer. I will address you again
> when I recover a little. Let us all pray for the salvation of the de-
> parted souls. *Joi Bangla! Bangladesh-Bharat bhai bhai* [Bangladesh
> and India are brothers]![10]

The next day, despite jet lag, President Sheikh Mujibur Rahman presided over an informal meeting of his cabinet, which
passed the Provisional Constitutional Order of Bangladesh. This
order contained rules for a parliamentary democracy and estab-

lished a body called the Constituent Assembly, which would produce a new constitution. Interestingly enough, this Provisional Constitutional Order was drafted in the office of a legal firm, the Law Consultants. I have often sat in those same offices visiting our legal adviser Mr. Amirul Islam. Amirul, along with another attorney and a future president of Bangladesh, drafted this Provisional Constitutional Order.[11]

The world watched with keen interest and reacted positively to these steps toward democracy. A closer look at the Provisional Constitutional Order, however, revealed one strikingly undemocratic feature. Although the Constituent Assembly was set up to produce a constitution, *no legislative power was given to this body.* This meant that Mujib not only held executive powers, he also had dictatorial legislative powers to make all the laws through presidential orders (POs); during the first year of Bangladesh he made about 150 very basic laws by means of those POs. The government was not at that point set up in such a way that he could practice what he had preached about democracy for so many years.

Soon Sheikh Mujib resigned from his largely ceremonial post as president and took the oath of office as prime minister of the new cabinet. He felt he must be where the action was, and the prime minister's post was the action post in the new parliamentary system.

On January 13 Prime Minister Mujib presided over the cabinet in its first formal meeting. The cabinet ministers decided that the national anthem would be *"Amar Shonar Bangla* [My Golden Bengal]"* written by a famous Hindu Bengali Nobel Prize-winning poet—to the discomfiture of many orthodox Muslims. Also, the cabinet modified the design of the national flag. Because no country's flag contains a map of that nation, the golden silhouette of Bangladesh was removed, leaving only the red circle on the green background. The red circle represents the rising sun of independence and signifies the end of darkness after a long, bloody struggle. The green ground speaks of the youthful vigor of the people and the lush greenness of rural Bangladesh.[12]

At this stage the country was filled with thousands of armed Mukti Bahini freedom fighters. Becoming restless, many began to use their weapons to harass fellow citizens and rival groups. Mujib called for all these groups to turn in their weapons, but it seemed unlikely that he could successfully defang them all.

Back in the United States we, too, found January 1972 to be an active month. I phoned a friend, Bangladeshi ambassador M. R. Siddiqi in Washington, to discuss our need for entry visas to Bangladesh. He explained that he could not issue visas until the United States granted diplomatic recognition to his nation. Before I could

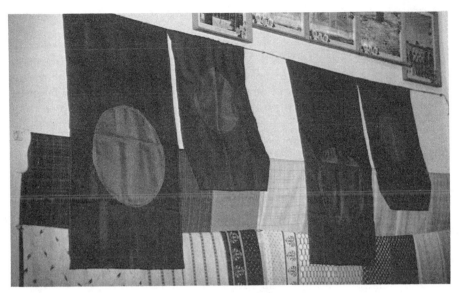

Bangladesh flags

respond he continued, "Dr. Olsen, don't worry about your visa. I am making an official notation that *we will reserve Bangladesh visa #1 for you in recognition of your service to our country.* We deeply appreciate your love for Bangladesh and our people." Great news indeed! Could it be that the visa problems of Pakistan days would be gone forever?

Ambassador Siddiqi then explained that he had been called by Sheikh Mujib to return to Bangladesh to become minister of trade and commerce in the new cabinet. The next Bangladeshi ambassador to the United States would be Enayet Karim; I was well acquainted with Mr. Karim, another fine and competent diplomat.

On January 14 our mission's president, Wendell Kempton, and treasurer, William Pierson, and I proceeded to the U.S. State Department Building in Washington, D.C. The time had come to speak up for Bangladesh. Our appointment, set up by a high-level contact of Dr. Kempton's, would be with top State Department officials responsible for Pakistan/Bangladesh issues. We met Christopher Van Hollen, deputy assistant secretary of state for Near Eastern and South Asian affairs, and two other key officers.

We expressed our gratitude to these fine men for the outstanding job they had done in keeping tabs on our team during the dangerous days of the war and answering many phone calls from our worried loved ones. Then I continued, "We hope our government will quickly provide generous humanitarian aid to the people of Bangladesh." The State Department officials assured us that legislation would soon be passed granting large amounts of monetary aid to the new nation.

Then we discussed the touchy question of diplomatic recognition of Bangladesh. Our three hosts mentioned various obstacles to recognition, especially the presence of Indian soldiers in the country. Ultimately they asked for my ideas on the subject; I spoke strongly in favor of recognizing Bangladesh as soon as possible. Among the several points I advanced, one argument unexpectedly made the most impact: the fact that we, as Americans living in Bangladesh, would find our rapport with the people and government upset and our work hampered if America should delay recognition. At this, Mr. Van Hollen responded, "That point is very important to us, and it will be carefully considered during our future discussions on the subject." We were grateful for the opportunity to speak on behalf of the infant country—a newborn nation, which we loved like a child of our own.

Also in January, with the concurrence of my own mission I began wearing a second "hat." At the request of Medical Assistance Programs (MAP) in Wheaton, Illinois, I accepted the position of MAP's first acting medical director. MAP is an organization set up to receive valuable donations of medicines and other supplies from pharmaceutical companies, which it then sends to dozens of mission hospitals around the world. Our hospital in Bangladesh had benefited greatly from this fine program, and we had served as MAP representatives in Bangladesh. Shortly after I donned this new hat, MAP president Dr. J. Raymond Knighton suggested that we travel to Bangladesh together and determine what we might do to help the damaged nation. Great! Comparing our schedules, we decided to leave in mid-February.

Later in January, publishers began approaching me about writing a book, so we began carefully considering their proposals. That same month I gave three addresses at Wheaton College, a well-known Christian college with high academic standards situated in Wheaton, Illinois, the town where we lived. I spoke twice to the student body during the annual missions conference and once to the faculty; as a result, the campus was buzzing with interest in the new nation of Bangladesh.

On February 21, Martyrs Day, Bangladeshis remembered the students and others who had died for the Bengali language movement twenty years before when West Pakistani officials had attempted to replace Bengali with their own Urdu language as the official language of the country. The people were thrilled to observe this Martyrs Day in newly independent Bangladesh.

Later in the month a high-powered commission was established to rehabilitate the Bangladeshi women who had been dishonored by the Pakistani soldiers during the civil war; this was necessary because the violated women had been rejected by their families, who considered them defiled and unclean. We applauded the government's compassionate move. A few days later the Bangladesh cabinet decided that its members, the cabinet ministers, would receive a salary of only 1,000 *takas* ($125) per month.

On the U.S. side of the planet, also, February was a busy month. Although I was unaware of it at the time, on February 2 Senator Edward Kennedy, chairman of the Judicial Subcommittee on Refugees and Escapees, was holding official hearings on Bangladesh issues in Washington, D.C. Among the various Americans giving testimony was Christopher Van Hollen, deputy assistant secretary of state, whom we had met in Washington two weeks earlier and whom we had encouraged to speedily recognize Bangladesh.

During those hearings, Senator Kennedy entered into an interesting dialogue with Mr. Van Hollen, which established, among other things, that until the United States granted diplomatic recognition to Bangladesh, our American consul general, although physically in Dacca, could not discuss with the leaders of the new nation vital political matters affecting the United States, Bangladesh, Pakistan, India, the Soviet Union, and other countries.[13]

A few days after the hearings I telephoned the South Asia desk of the U.S. State Department to tell them that I would be flying to Bangladesh to consult with Prime Minister Sheikh Mujibur Rahman to work out a program for helping distressed people in the southern end of the country. Simply as a courteous gesture I added, "If there is anything I can do to be of help to you in Dacca or Chittagong or in my meeting with the prime minister, I would be glad to do so." Just two days before I departed for Bangladesh, the State Department surprised me by calling back.

"We have decided," the spokesman said, "that we would like you to do something for us in Dacca—convey a message to the prime minister of Bangladesh."

"What is the message?" I wanted to know. After he outlined the three-part message, I agreed in an instant to convey it to Mujib —with pleasure!

On February 14 I departed from Chicago's O'Hare Airport, linked up with Ray Knighton in London, and with him headed for Calcutta, India.

The next day, while we were still in Calcutta preparing to fly to Bangladesh, a watershed event was taking place in Dacca, an event that would affect the lives of the tribal people of the Chittagong Hill Tracts (CHT) for decades to come.

At the turn of the century under the British, the simple tribal people had enjoyed a special protected status that prevented more sophisticated Bengalis from migrating into the CHT and exploiting them. In addition, the British had granted the tribespeople considerable autonomy by dividing the CHT into three circles, each governed by a tribal king or chief. Also, all the CHT police were tribesmen. In 1900 this special, compassionate system of administration had been enshrined in a book known as the *Chittagong Hill Tracts Regulation*, but more commonly called the *Hill Tracts Manual*.

After the CHT became a part of Pakistan in 1947, the situation deteriorated drastically. The Pakistan government promptly replaced the tribal police with Bengali and West Pakistani policemen. Then, in flagrant violation of the 1900 *Hill Tracts Manual*, the government assisted thousands of Bengali settlers to migrate to the sparsely populated Hill Tracts; this influx naturally led to frequent altercations between the Bengalis and tribals. Later the Pakistan government constructed the huge Kaptai Dam in the CHT far upriver from Chittagong City. When the water rising behind the dam finally crested, the beautiful new Kaptai Lake extended much farther than anyone had anticipated—to form the largest man-made lake in Asia. The water destroyed the homes of 100,000 tribespeople and submerged 40 percent of the best farmland in the CHT (see figure 11).

In late 1971, when the CHT became a part of newly born Bangladesh, the tribal people fervently hoped for an improvement in their situation. Instead, their suffering soon increased—at the hands of the Mukti Bahini, who had marched into the Hill Tracts to punish any tribals guilty of collaborating with the Pakistan oc-

Beautiful Kaptai Lake

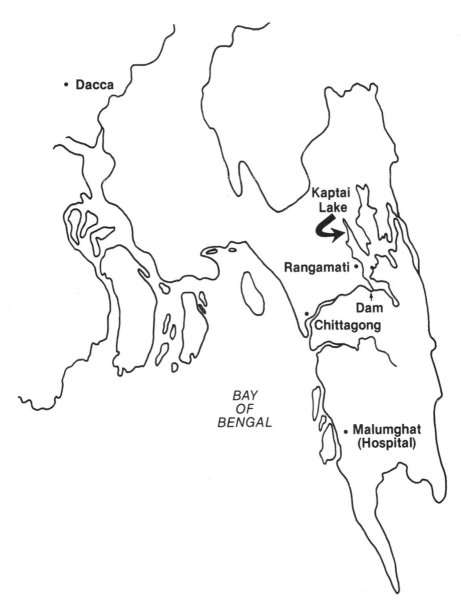

Figure 11. Kaptai Lake and Dam

cupation army. Sadly, the Bengali freedom fighters went berserk, even killing innocent tribal people who came forward to greet and receive them.[14]

On February 15, 1972, in Dacca, while Ray and I were about to fly from Calcutta to Dacca, the Chakma tribal leader M. N.

Larma led a delegation of tribals to Prime Minister Sheikh Mujibur Rahman to protest the recent killings by the Mukti Bahini in
the CHT. Then he presented to Sheikh Mujib a memorandum containing these four demands:

1. The CHT should be an autonomous region of Bangladesh
   with its own legislature.
2. The three tribal *rajas* (kings) should be allowed to continue
   as heads of the three circles in the CHT with full administrative powers.
3. The new Constitution should contain all the provisions of
   the 1900 CHT *Hill Tracts Manual,* which would restore the
   special protected status of the tribes in the Hill Tracts.
4. The new Constitution should contain a provision guaran-
   teeing that no amendment to the Constitution affecting the
   citizens of the CHT could be made without the consent of
   the people of the CHT.

Sheikh Mujib's reaction was sharply negative; he rejected the
tribal leaders' request for autonomy.[15] Although he had struggled
for years to gain autonomy and social justice for the people of East
Pakistan, he was adamant against allowing the tribal people of the
CHT any such self-government. He agreed only to allow the three
tribal rajas to continue—with much-reduced authority. Mujib's
adverse response changed everything for the hill men. Before 1972
closed a group of tribal activists secretly began to organize a guerrilla force to fight for their rights; these guerrilla fighters were
named the *Shanti Bahini* (Peace Force).

With our work in Calcutta finished, Ray and I took the hourlong flight to Bangladesh. My pulse quickened as we landed at the
Dacca airport where we were met by two of my colleagues from
the hospital. Jay Walsh, from Michigan, was Field Council chairman (team leader) that year. Bob Adolph, a laboratory technologist, had planned and organized Memorial Christian Hospital's
excellent clinical laboratory. How fine it was to be with them
again!

We soon met with our friend former Ambassador Siddiqi, now
minister of trade and commerce in Sheikh Mujib's cabinet. Next
we visited both the minister and the secretary of the Ministry of
Health and Family Planning. These three top-level officials
promptly granted several extremely important concessions and
supplied the necessary letters of approval on the spot. Never in
Pakistan days had we accomplished so much in such a short period
of time.

Bob Adolph and Jay Walsh with Sheikh Mujib

The next afternoon, February 19, at 5:15 P.M. we met the renowned Prime Minister Sheikh Mujibur Rahman, the beloved "George Washington" of Bangladesh. When I introduced Ray, Jay, Bob, and myself he received us graciously and gave us seats in a semicircle around him. He seemed alert and vigorous. I explained that we were American medical workers from Memorial Christian Hospital and MAP who were prepared to help the people of the southern region of the country. Then, without difficulty, I gained his approval to tape-record our discussion.

The instant I turned on the recorder Mujib began to expostulate in staccato, emotional bursts of words about what had happened in Bangladesh while he was a prisoner in West Pakistan. "The barbarous Pakistan Army destroyed my economy," he began. "They destroyed my hospitals; they destroyed my schools; they destroyed my communication systems; they destroyed my food *godowns* [storehouses]; they destroyed about three million people; they burned about thirty million houses. Although I was away then, you were present here. You know everything! Now we need all kinds of help. We need medicines. There are no medicines left in my country."

At the mention of medicines I explained that already we were preparing for shipment several hundred thousand dollars' worth of vitamins. Sheikh Mujib expressed his gratitude, then pressed on with his tale of grief. "But my people have no food. What will my people do with only vitamin tablets? If they don't get food twice a day, a hundred medicines won't help them. And also the monsoon is coming. My people require shelter." In a few moments, Mujib had outlined the three major priorities—medicine, food, and housing.

Then, suddenly, his mood changed and he said with great intensity, "You told me about the American people; I have nothing against them. People in general have supported my cause. They have exposed Pakistani barbarism all over the world. I owe my thanks to them." As he continued his voice began to rise and his eyes flashed with anger. "Your administration—the Nixon administration—however, knowing everything how it is happening in Bangladesh, was giving help to the Pakistani army, weapons to kill my people. I don't know whether the American people know it or not. If they know, I think they will revolt against the Nixon government, against Nixon's reactionary policy which has blackened the face of America."

His rising crescendo made it clear that it was time to give him the new and special message from the United States government, the message I had been requested to bring because the American Consul General's lips were sealed until the U.S. granted diplomatic recognition to Bangladesh.

After explaining about the telephone call I had received from the State Department, I delivered my message: "First, Your Excellency, the State Department sends to you its warm regards and

It was time to give him the special message

best wishes. Secondly, they want you to know that the U.S. government will do its utmost to provide maximum humanitarian relief and rehabilitation to the war-affected people of Bangladesh. Thirdly, I am to tell you that the matter of diplomatic recognition of Bangladesh is now under very active consideration by the U.S. government and the question will be settled as soon as possible." What a moment to savor! How I enjoyed bringing to the Bangladeshi head of state the first word that American diplomatic recognition was finally under active consideration—diplomat's jargon for "it won't be long now."

Later, when the message from the U.S. government was announced to the cabinet, that warm message stabilized the shaky relations between the two countries until America officially recognized the Government of Bangladesh several weeks later.

As the interview continued, Jay told Sheikh Mujib about a letter prepared by our mission team and sent to President Nixon. The letter described what we had seen during the occupation period and recommended generous humanitarian help and early recognition of the Government of Bangladesh. Later in the interview Jay mentioned meeting Mujib's wife in Dacca shortly before his release from the prison in West Pakistan.

During the last half of our talk, Sheikh Mujib had more to say about the shocking Pakistani attack upon his people and the reactions of various nations to that tragedy. "It is genocide!" he exclaimed, "clear and simple genocide. Do you know that the young boys have been taken to Kurmitola and had their blood taken out? ... Do you know that your administration had given [the Pakistanis] arms at that particular time? Can you show your face to the world? ... Do you know that India stood by us giving shelter to ten million people? The Russians have given great hope to save my country. I tell you that we have all respect and love for these Soviet people and Great Britain and India. ...

"This is international politics. If this is not genocide then what is genocide? Why did you [Americans] enter the Second World War, taking the risk? Why did you support Great Britain and other countries against Germany? You people have declared, 'We are going for humanity and democracy.' Is that why you have given money and weapons to the Pakistani army? What democracy and humanity is it when my people have been killed? Three million people have been killed—innocent women, innocent girls, old men of ninety. Their houses were burned, and when they came running out they were shot. Now my people keep bringing me the bones of the victims; *lakhs* and *lakhs* [hundreds of thousands] I am getting now. Can you understand my sentiment? ...

"My people have nothing against the people of America, believe me. But it is impossible—we cannot conceive—we cannot imagine—how the Nixon government has behaved against the people of Bangladesh. They have no human—I'm sorry! But I can say that from the human consideration also they should stop giving arms to Pakistan."

Sheikh Mujib predicted many problems for the now-truncated nation of Pakistan. And he ventured an optimistic prediction, in fact a farfetched prediction, about the future economy of Bangladesh. "But so far as I am concerned," he declared, "my economy will be sound if I can only face this crisis. Within one year my country's economy will be better than any economy anywhere in the world! I have my jute, I have my tea, I have my fish, I have my *piaz* [onions], I have my forests, I have my sweetwater fish, my saltwater fish. If I can develop it, then I have no difficulties in future. My people will be happy."

At the end he asked us to do what we could to help his new nation. We closed the turbulent meeting with the appropriate sentiments in Bengali. Throughout the interview, the prime minister had spoken forcefully, with great emotion. We heard and felt his bitter reaction to the Pakistan Army, which had let loose a reign of terror in his land—and to our American government, which had "tilted" toward Pakistan. But we were astonished at Mujib's perception that, while Pakistan's economy would break down, the Bangladesh economy would outstrip all the world's other economies within a year.

The next day we traveled by road south toward Chittagong. Signs of warfare were everywhere visible: blown-up bridges, burned-down villages, blasted tanks, and shattered buildings.

Blown-up bridge

Our food relief program had expanded greatly

From Chittagong we traveled on to Malumghat. Although it was dark by the time we reached the hospital, someone spotted our car and people came running from all directions. What a wonderful reunion it was, with Bengali and American brothers and sisters! I was home.

We listened to our colleagues' fascinating adventures during the final days of the war. I marveled at our food relief operation, which had expanded greatly since Dr. Donn Ketcham and I had initiated it in the early days of the Pakistani crackdown; ours was the first food relief operation the Pakistan Army had allowed in the country. When we visited Hindu friends in the nearby villages, some whose lives we had saved fell to the ground and clutched me by the feet.

Then we met with our team in a Field Council meeting and described our discussion with Sheikh Mujib. We explained the priorities Mujib had thrown out to us: medicine, food, and houses before the torrential monsoon rains would sweep over the land four months later and inundate multitudes who had no roofs over their heads.

Although they were mentally and physically exhausted, our ABWE team responded magnificently during those meetings. Despite the heavy pressure of caring for thousands of seriously ill, malnourished patients, they agreed that we should try to mount a massive relief operation in our southern section of Bangladesh. There was no other organization situated as well as we were to provide help to the people of this area. Since our existing mission team already was greatly overworked, we would have to recruit many new hands and raise hundreds of thousands of dollars as soon as we returned to the United States.

Back in Dacca, during our final discussion with Commerce Minister Siddiqi I presented to him a beautiful Bible with his name inscribed upon it as a token of our esteem. He seemed delighted to receive it and thanked us warmly. Then I conveyed to him the message from the U.S. government I had presented to the prime minister. He responded that Mujib had already told him about it. He was genuinely delighted, for as a democracy-minded former Bangladeshi (shadow) ambassador to the United States, he had a pro-American mentality. At the end we thanked this grand friend for his many kindnesses and departed.

On our flight back to the United States, despite our exhaustion our thoughts raced a mile a minute. We discovered, however, that we were departing with more questions than answers. How could we organize a program of house-building, supply of medicines, and expanded food relief in the brief time available to us before the monsoon rains would pour down on Bangladesh? How could we possibly recruit 15-20 men and women in 15-20 days to donate two or three months of work between mid-March and mid-June? Where would we obtain the hundreds of thousands of dollars required to launch such a project?

Presenting a Bible to Commerce Minister Siddiqi

On the last day of February 1972 Sheikh Mujib announced a stringent law to control properties abandoned by the fleeing Pakistanis. But later the people complained that these valuable industries and businesses were then turned over to largely unqualified members and protegés of the Awami League party. And as a result of the inexperience and incompetence of some of those managers the country suffered great financial loss. Production plunged to record low levels, and we heard allegations that much equipment and raw material were secretly sold and smuggled out of the country to India.[16] How disturbing! We grieved like parents over the suffering of the infant nation.

March 1972 was a whopping month for us and others interested in Bangladesh. The Soviet Union was particularly active in promoting its relationship with the new country; it donated a squadron of MiG aircraft and jacked up its embassy staff to ninety people. And, while communist propaganda films were being shown on Dacca television, Mujib and the Soviet head of state signed a joint communiqué in Moscow expressing broad agreement on world affairs. The Soviets' stance during the Pakistan civil war was now paying them handsome dividends. Later in the month they volunteered to clear mines and sunken ships from Chittagong harbor so that this main seaport of Bangladesh could resume its vital function.

On March 7 the Bangladesh government issued the *Jatiyo Rakkhi Bahini* (National Defense Force) Order. Thus the Rakkhi Bahini was born as a militia separate from the army and controlled directly by Sheikh Mujib rather than the Ministry of Defense; these men were trained not by the Bangladesh Army, but by the Indian Army and wore the Indian-Army-style green uniform. Many soldiers and other Bangladeshis were disturbed by this order setting up a second military force parallel to the Bangladesh Army. Why didn't Mujib, instead, simply issue an order to strengthen the existing Bangladesh Army? Presumably he did not trust his army.

Several days later the final farewell dinner for the commanding general of the Indian troops signaled the terminus of the Indian military presence in the country. By mid-March the Indian Army had withdrawn from Bangladesh, and on March 17 Indian prime minister Indira Gandhi arrived in Dacca and addressed a mammoth public meeting. Two days later she and Mujib signed the twenty-five-year Indo-Bangladesh Treaty of Friendship and Cooperation. That treaty contained a provision calling for joint military action in case of a threat to the security of either of the countries.

Across the ocean, American politicians were striving to make up for lost time. In early March the U.S. Senate Committee on Foreign Relations held hearings on the question of the recognition of

Bangladesh. Senator Frank Church, presiding officer of the hearings, made a strong case for speedy recognition. He spoke of Sheikh Mujib's "sweeping victory at the polls in Pakistan's first free elections," which indisputably established him as the popular leader of the seventy-five million citizens of the land.[17] And he emphasized further that the Bangladesh government met the three requirements of statehood: a defined territory, a government in administrative control, and the consent of the people governed.

Senator Church concluded his statement with these words:

> In summation, the case in favor of U.S. recognition of Bangladesh is compelling. So is the recognition, I might add, of our own blunders. We should never have "tilted" toward Pakistan over the last 12 months and during the recent war on the subcontinent. It is time to make amends; to change course; to extend the hand of recognition to this new democratic government in Asia.[18]

The fruition of those hearings came two weeks later when the U.S. Senate unanimously passed a resolution stating that the president of the United States should recognize Bangladesh as an independent nation and should recognize the government of that country. By mid-February the U.S. government had decided to give serious and positive consideration to the matter of recognition of Bangladesh. A few days later, at their request, I had passed that information along to Prime Minister Sheikh Mujib in Dacca. Then, in March, the U.S. Senate, having the constitutional responsibility to advise the president on foreign policy matters, had recommended that he grant diplomatic recognition to Bangladesh. It shouldn't be long now.

On March 26, 1972, the people of Bangladesh observed their first Independence Day. Just one year before, on the fateful night of March 25-26, the Pakistan Army had begun killing Bengalis; hours later Bengali spokesmen defiantly proclaimed the independence of Bangladesh, a declaration that seemed very hollow at the time and during the following nine months of Pakistani occupation. But now that hoped-for independence was real.

During that first Independence Day celebration, Mujib announced the government's decision to nationalize major industries including jute, sugar, cotton, steel, fertilizer, oil, and gas; he was beginning to make good on his promise of socialism.

March 1972 was an active month for the governments of Bangladesh, India, the USSR, and the U.S.—but it was a frantic month for us. On March 1, following our quick trip to Bangladesh, MAP's Ray Knighton and I had only an earnest desire to help our stricken Bangladeshi *bhai-bon* (brothers and sisters)—but we had no money, no manpower, and no method of operation. During the first three days of March we chalked out a program of supplying medicines, food, and utensils and constructing four thousand houses. Because MAP was registered as a voluntary agency with the U.S. Agency for International Development (USAID), Ray flew to Washington to present to them our application for funds. He requested an early decision—the monsoon rains would not wait, not even for the powerful U.S. government.

While USAID studied our application, we considered how and where to recruit fifteen to twenty strong men willing to drop what they were doing to serve in Bangladesh for two or three months between mid-March and mid-June. We decided that Christian colleges would be the most likely source of such dedicated personpower. We contacted several such colleges that were closely related to our mission only to find that they operated on the semester system; they were keenly interested but unable to provide any students for us. Only students attending a college operating on the quarter system could give a quarter, then make it up during the following summer quarter.

Even as we began contacting various colleges, rumors about a possible project in Bangladesh spread from student to student at nearby Wheaton College. The messages about God's work in Bangladesh in the college's missions conference apparently had struck fire in the hearts of a number of young men and women. And Wheaton College had just shifted from the semester system to the quarter system! Many students began telephoning MAP and knocking on my door; soon we had more applications for the "Bangladesh Brigade" than we could accept. In our selection process we chose young men and women who were not only physically healthy, mentally alert, and emotionally strong, but also who were earnest Christians deeply dedicated to Christ and His purposes. What a wise decision that turned out to be!

Sixteen of our team of twenty-four were students from Wheaton College, while the large Walnut Ridge Baptist Church of Waterloo, Iowa, provided the doctor, the mechanic, and two nurses. Even though President Nixon had signed the Bangladesh foreign aid bill, deliberations about our project seemed to bog down in Washington. I sensed that the obstruction or hang-up might be connected with the reaction of someone either in Washington or Dacca—or both. Finally, wonderfully, we received a clear-cut verbal yes from USAID officials; they promised to send a written contract as soon as possible. The project was on.

So on March 27 at Chicago's O'Hare Airport we ran the gauntlet of reporters and television cameras to take off on the first leg of our journey to Bangladesh. Four days later we arrived in Dacca in the early morning hours of April 1. After completing various for-

The "Bangladesh Brigade" arrived in April

The standard village home

malities in Dacca, we headed for Malumghat and arrived on April 4, the very day the American government granted diplomatic recognition to Bangladesh. That recognition would facilitate our work.

We elected to construct the "standard village home." Only three building materials were required: giant bamboo for the uprights, ordinary bamboo to be split and woven into walls, and sungrass for the waterproof roof. Every villager knew how to use these materials and how to construct the standard village home. Not a single skilled worker would be required. And every Bengali villager would feel at home living in this type of house.

Because we needed a newly required approval from the Bangladesh government, and because I could find no available trucks in Chittagong, I flew on to Dacca. During four days there I obtained a letter of approval for the project; the letter additionally instructed the Chittagong DC to provide me with some government trucks. Also, a United Nations official agreed to loan me six UN trucks. And in the USAID office I learned that the written contract had come granting nearly a million dollars for our Bangladesh Brigade projects. On April 14 I returned to Chittagong feeling great.

The next morning I awakened and, according to my custom, opened my Bible. It is a worn yet colorful book, for various passages are underlined with my own six-color marking system; many of the margins are "decorated" with a blizzard of notes from my daily morning meditations and study. For some days I had been reading each morning in the Old Testament books of Ezra and Nehemiah, written by those two men who traveled to a distant, beloved land to do some building for God. Because that was exactly what we were doing, I reasoned that I could learn something from those books, and that any needed guidance might easily come through reading them.

At that point I had a need for guidance regarding how best to organize our work in the field. If I made the wrong decision we would fail, for there would be no time to regroup—time was too short. For ten days I had been mentally toying with several options. That April morning as I opened and read the third chapter of the book of Nehemiah, two clues simply leaped out of those pages at me—clues that showed me precisely how the work in the field should be organized. "Thank You, Father!"

The chapter, often considered a somewhat tedious passage, simply listed various groups of people working together, side by side, rebuilding the wall of the city of Jerusalem. The clues I noted were these:

1. A number of groups (teams) worked simultaneously on separate sections of the wall.
2. Each team did the total job from beginning to end on its section of the wall (as opposed to teams of skilled specialists carrying out special tasks on every section of the wall).

In the same way, I concluded, we should send out a number of two-man teams to work simultaneously in different areas; each pair would consist of an American and his Bengali interpreter. Second, each team would complete all facets of the work from beginning to end in its assigned areas.

Back at Malumghat we put this plan into operation by assigning twelve two-man teams to specific villages. Each team surveyed the area, kept the records, ordered the basic materials from our supply department, counted out the materials to the recipients, and paid daily wages to each villager to buy food so that he and his family could eat while he constructed his house.

Jay Walsh did a tremendous job of heading up the supply department. His work involved organizing contractors to cut down the bamboo and sungrass deep in the jungle-covered Hill Tracts and seeing that they reached a river landing where our trucks could pick them up.

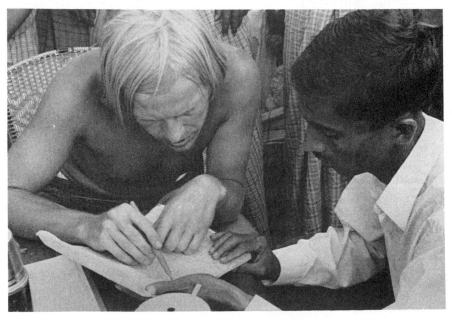

We sent out twelve two-man teams

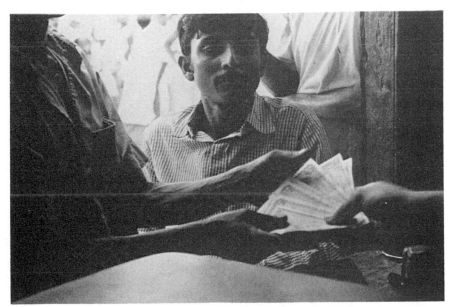

Each team paid daily wages to the villagers to buy food

Ours was a complex, mammoth undertaking. At the height of the project more than fifty thousand people were working—cutting bamboo and sungrass in the jungles, floating the materials down the long, winding rivers, transporting them to the villages, and actually building the houses. But the work was producing a veritable crop of bright, fresh-looking bamboo houses sprouting up all over southern Chittagong District. Even though we knew we had hit upon a dynamite system, the final count amazed us; we had far surpassed our goal of four thousand houses. *In fact, we had constructed or carried out very major repairs on more than ten thousand houses!*

Also, we spent a portion of our grant for needed utensils for several thousand families, and MAP sent nearly $2 million worth of donated medicines, plus tens of thousands of dollars worth of garden seeds and foodstuffs. MAP also sent thousands of dollars for in-country rice purchase. Somehow we had put together a $3 million project to help the people of southern Bangladesh. "Oh, thank You, Father!"

In early June 1972 most of our Bangladesh Brigade team departed from Malumghat to return to the United States. As a dozen of us traveled together on our way out of the country, we were pleasantly surprised in Dacca to receive an invitation from the U.S. Consul General (the chief American diplomat) to a reception in our honor. We attended the reception with pleasure.

Villager working on roof

A veritable crop of bright, fresh-looking bamboo houses

Part of Bangladesh Brigade with the American Consul General

After greeting everyone, the Consul General stood up in front and amazed us as he spoke: "They say that confession is good for the soul," he began, "and I have a confession to make to you." Then, remarkably, this top-level representative of the world's most powerful nation confessed to us that he had been very much against our project. He explained, "I did everything in my power to block your project. I was in Washington at the time and made a maximum effort to stop you." *So,* I thought, *that was the obstruction in Washington that had prevented the final "yes" decision for so many days.*

The Consul General went on to give the reasons for his negative reaction. Then he continued, "Now I have made my confession to you—but I want to say one thing more. I also owe you an apology. You have confounded me. None of the things I feared have actually happened. Not only did you achieve your goal, but you far surpassed it. I cannot conceive how you did it, but what you have done is a remarkable victory for America and our foreign aid program in Bangladesh. I not only offer you my apology, but I want to congratulate you on your marvelous work. Every report I have heard of you and your work has been outstanding. I am proud of you, and your country is proud of you." Out of the corner of my eye I noticed a few broad smiles and a few young men swallowing hard.

We thanked the Consul General for his kind comments, for the refreshments, and the reception, then headed for the airport. The gentleman was right. An ordinary group of young people probably would have failed miserably. But I had brought to Bangladesh an extraordinary group of young men and women deeply committed to the task of sincerely helping the distressed people of southern Bangladesh—and thoroughly dedicated to their Lord. Our Consul General had no way to know that our group possessed this extra spiritual dimension. But on the front lines it made the difference.

There were other, less positive, developments in Bangladesh in April 1972. Many among the people were convinced that some prominent members of the Awami League party had become involved in the smuggling of foodstuffs and other illegal activities. So in early April more than 25,000 shouting, screaming Bengalis participated in a mass meeting, the first significant public opposition to Sheikh Mujib's government since the birth of Bangladesh. The speaker was Maulana Bhashani, the ninety-year-old leader of a left-wing political party. He denounced looting and dishonesty by Awami League members and students. He called for a genuinely free press and thundered, "I warn the Awami League that if they do not stick to the right path, their dream will be shattered by the people."[19] His short speech was interrupted again and again by deafening applause. We were surprised that the independence euphoria was wearing so thin this soon.

A week later Sheikh Mujib was reelected head of the Awami League political party and also leader of the Constituent Assembly; usually different people fill these two posts to prevent an undue monopoly of power, but Mujib was all-in-all during those days. The Constituent Assembly formed a thirty-five-member committee to draft the new Constitution for the country; the committee functioned impressively, completing its task in just seven months' time.

In mid-April the prime minister declared that horse racing and drinking of liquor would no longer be allowed in Bangladesh; these prohibitions were based upon Islamic teaching and were much appreciated by sincere Muslims. But by mid-May, four months after liberation, we could see that many were becoming steadily more disillusioned. In addition, the authorities seemed to be unable to control the widespread smuggling of rice to India, which was forcing food prices up in Bangladesh.

By June the likelihood of a severe famine worried everyone. The UN secretary general appealed to member governments to rush relief to Bangladesh, and he assured Sheikh Mujib that 2 million tons of food grains would be sent in an effort to head off the famine. Despite the suffering of the people, smuggling, hoarding, and misuse of relief goods continued driving the prices of staple items ever upward. In a mammoth public meeting in Dacca, Prime Minister Mujib warned hoarders to cease their antisocial actions within fifteen days; later in the month he again warned against the misuse of relief goods. But these warnings had zero effect. The people claimed that the warnings failed because many of the culprits were Mujib's own Awami League men.

On June 13, 1972, the day after my arrival in America following the Bangladesh Brigade project, I traveled to Washington, D.C., to pick up the special visa that had been promised. The "Bangladesh Mission"—the shadow embassy—was gone and inscribed upon a bright new name plate I saw the words "Bangladesh Embassy." There Ambassador Enayet Karim awaited my arrival. After warm greetings and a few minutes of conversation, the friendly ambassador graciously presented to me the special visa—Bangladesh Visa #001—in recognition of our service to his nation. The visa had been promised by the first ambassador, Mr. M. R. Siddiqi, the promise recorded in an official document, and now the visa was being granted by Enayet Karim.

As he handed back my passport stamped with the new visa he again expressed his appreciation for our team's work in Bangladesh. And I accepted the visa on behalf of our mission and staff, for our service to the people and our reputation are based on the combined work of our outstanding team members. The ceremony was simple but warm and meaningful to both of us. Afterward, I shared with him my impression of the current situation in Bangladesh and conveyed a verbal message to him from Commerce Minister Siddiqi.

Ambassador Enayet Karim presenting Visa #001 to Vic

In early June in Dacca, the communist party held its first public meeting in eighteen years, for during the Pakistan era the party had been banned and forced underground. Through the years the communist party and other leftist parties kept splitting over doctrinal fine points until there were several such parties. (If you are interested in the details see table 1.)

These several leftist parties used classical communist techniques in East Pakistan/Bangladesh: strikes, riots, agitation against "Western imperialism," infiltration of popular political parties such as the Awami League, agitation of the populace against poverty and bad working conditions, demonstrations to preserve the heart language of the people, and so on. They gained hundreds of converts, especially among college and university students.

Although the Communists were pleased with their improved position, they were dissatisfied that the Bangladesh revolution had stopped short of bringing in a full communist government. Later they were further disappointed when Sheikh Mujib selected twenty-three Awami Leaguers—and no Communists—to make up his cabinet. Their only consolation was his continuing advocacy of socialism as one of the four main principles of the new government.

There were wide differences within the broad-based Awami League (AL) party itself. Some members leaned to the political right, were pro-Western, and believed in democratic principles and private enterprise. Other AL members were more centrist in their views. Still others leaned leftward, were pro-Moscow, and believed that socialism offered the most hope to Bangladesh. And during 1972 an overt split occurred in the AL Student League—between center-of-the-road students on the one hand and a radical, pro-Chinese leftist group on the other. Later this radical group would split off to form its own new political party.

According to July newspapers, three AL workers in various parts of the country had been killed by "miscreants." Such reports cropped up again and again in the months that followed. The word "miscreants," we discovered, was a euphemism for radical, pro-Peking Communists who were bent on revolution.

In August Bangladesh sent its official application for United Nations membership to the UN secretary general and Mujib followed up with special letters to the members of the UN Security Council requesting their support. On August 23 at the UN headquarters India, the Soviet Union, Yugoslavia, and Great Britain urged the UN Security Council to admit Bangladesh as a member of the UN. Two days later, however, China cast its first-ever UN veto—against the Bangladesh application for UN membership. China was still tilting toward Pakistan and away from the Soviet Union, India, and Bangladesh. What irony! China, who used to complain so bitterly when vetoes kept her out of the UN, now

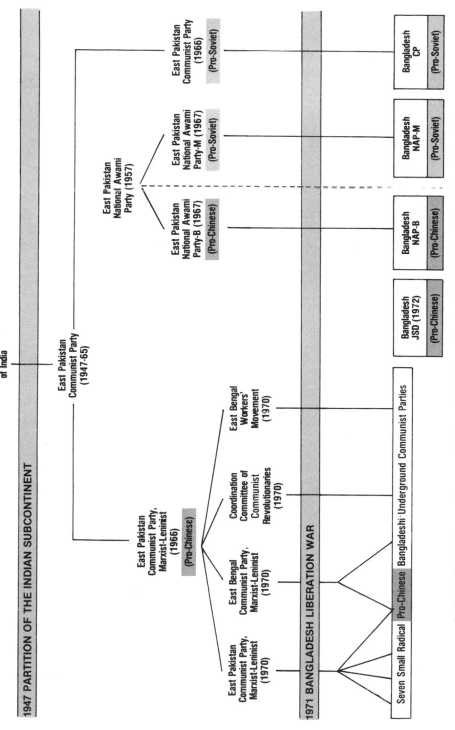

Table 1. Evolution and fragmentation of leftist parties in East Pakistan/Bangladesh to 1975

vetoed the acceptance of Bangladesh. Of course, this China veto caused acute embarrassment to the radical pro-Peking Communists in Bangladesh.

On the first day of September the Bangladesh government ordered law-enforcement agencies to take strong measures against smugglers, hoarders, and the radical left terrorists. The killing of several more Awami Leaguers in various parts of Bangladesh made it clear that stringent measures were necessary. One AL leader, who had been shot and injured by these leftist terrorists, was shot a second time as he lay in his hospital bed.

September brought an exciting development to the Bengali Christians in southern Bangladesh. On Sunday, September 17, 1972, nine months after the birth of the nation, a new church was born at Malumghat. Although we and Bengali and tribal Christians had worshiped together and functioned as a church congregation from our earliest days at the hospital, it took time for the numbers to grow and for the group to prepare its constitution and other church documents in Bengali. I remember spending dozens of hours helping with these documents and leading the church group during periods when no "reverend" was available on station. Although all of our mission team members played various roles in the establishment and development of the church, Mel Beals and Jay Walsh were especially involved, and Mel was responsible for guiding the final stages of development.

The newly formed, independent, indigenous church promptly selected its Bangladeshi leaders and conducted its first communion service. Christian truth and the Christian church had finally become established in the "great Christian vacuum area" between the circles of influence of William Carey and Adoniram Judson! We hoped the church's roots were deep and strong enough to withstand any storms or pressures the turbulent future might spawn.

In early October the frazzled government finally deployed the Bangladesh Army and Navy to the border areas to help the police and border militia stop smuggling, which had become steadily more flagrant. These armed forces were empowered to take stern measures to bring smuggling to a halt. That was a strong and positive step.

During the final three weeks of October the Constituent Assembly worked over the draft of the Constitution. The only opposition member in the Assembly was not at all cowed by his lonely status or by the fact that he was a Hindu. He spoke up boldly, criticizing various aspects of the proposed Constitution bill.

On the last day of October the young, radical pro-Peking Communists who had split away from the Awami League student orga-

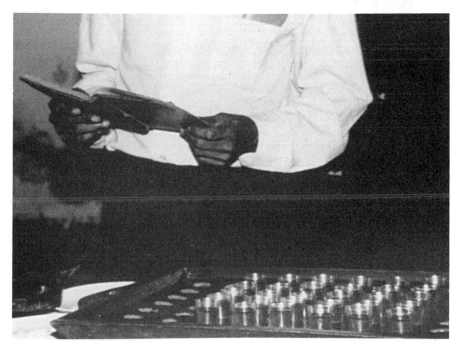

Communion service

nization did the expected—they formed an official political party called the JSD party or the *Jatiyo Samajtantrik Dal* (National Socialist Party). The JSD was an open party, not an underground group, and would oppose the Awami League in the ongoing political debate and in further elections.

On December 15 the speaker of the Constituent Assembly announced its dissolution, and the Constitution of the People's Republic of Bangladesh came into effect. The preamble of this fascinating document began this way:

> We, the people of Bangladesh, having proclaimed our Independence on the 26th day of March 1971 and, through a historic struggle for national liberation, established the independent, sovereign People's Republic of Bangladesh;
>
> Pledging that the high ideals of *nationalism, socialism, democracy* and *secularism*, which inspired our heroic people to dedicate themselves to, and our brave martyrs to sacrifice their lives in, the national liberation struggle, shall be the fundamental principles of the Constitution;
>
> Further pledging that it shall be a fundamental aim of the State to realise through the democratic process a socialist society, free from exploitation. . . .[20]

Some other provisions worthy of mention were these:

> 3. The state language of the Republic is Bengali. . . .
> 6. [The] citizens of Bangladesh shall be known as Bangalees.[21]

Interesting! Although racially the great majority of the people are Bengalis speaking the Bengali language, politically both Bengali *and non-Bengali* citizens would now be known as Bangalees. Henceforth we could call most of the people *Bengalis* (as members of the Bengali race) or we could call them *Bangalees* (as citizens of Bangladesh). Understandably, the non-Bengali tribal people, proud of their own heritage, bitterly resented being called Bangalees.

Various important fundamental rights were guaranteed:

> 28.(1) The State shall not discriminate against any citizen on grounds only of religion, race, caste, sex or place of birth.
>
> 41.(1) Subject to law, public order and morality—
> (a) every citizen has the right to profess, practise or propagate any religion;
> (b) every religious community or denomination has the right to establish, maintain and manage its religious institutions.[22]

On December 16 the new nation celebrated a gala occasion—the first anniversary of its victory over the Pakistan occupation forces. The next day the president, the prime minister, and the members of the cabinet each took a fresh oath of office under the new Constitution. On the following day the president inaugurated the Supreme Court of Bangladesh.

What had been accomplished during that first year of the infant nation? The government had succeeded in attracting an unprecedented amount of foreign interest and aid—$1 billion worth, the largest amount of foreign aid ever showered on a country in a year's time. The United States gave by far the greatest single contribution, $313 million. Through all this help much of the country's shattered infrastructure (bridges, roads, railways, and so on) had been repaired and the impending famine averted.

Ten million refugees were received back from India, and most of them were housed. The government ordered land reforms and made provision to rehabilitate the Bangalee women violated during the war. A Constituent Assembly was formed and produced an excellent democratic Constitution in record time. Also, Bangladesh gained the diplomatic recognition of most countries of the world and became a member of a number of international bodies—but not the UN. These were praiseworthy accomplishments.

There was, however, a flip side of the first-year coin. *Newsweek* magazine, in a year-end article, detailed some of the negatives:

> Bangladesh today is far from recovery. Both the political and economic landscapes remain very much in need of reconstruction and popular frustration is rapidly outrunning expectations. . . .
>
> Murder, robbery and general lawlessness are still rampant. Shortages of raw materials and spare parts are crippling the economy. In some parts of the country, the textile mills are just barely running and buses and trucks are grinding to a halt for lack of spare parts. Everywhere the cost of living has soared; in many places, rice prices have doubled or even tripled. Normal consumer goods are available only in the black market, which is kept supplied by commodities smuggled in from India.
>
> One cause of the trouble is that the Awami League party . . . has proved weak and indecisive in running the country. . . . Trained Bengali technocrats and civil servants are also in short supply and many of the brightest of them are still trapped in West Pakistan. They are being detained as virtual hostages for the return of the 90,000 Pakistani prisoners of war held in India. . . .
>
> And there has also been gross misuse of relief. . . . Food and medicines simply disappear, often to be sold in India and Burma.
>
> Aside from purging several dozen Awami League members and ordering the border closed to smugglers, Mujib has yet to take a strong stand against corruption among his supporters. "He is too loyal to his followers to crack down on them," says one of Mujib's associates.[23]

Despite many pressures our own mission team had enjoyed a productive year. Our American and Bangladeshi staff had all survived the war, with the exception of Shudhir Barua, a Bengali religious teacher who died of illness, not injury. The Bangladesh Brigade project, a smashing success, had warmed the hearts of thousands of Bangalees in our end of the country and provided homes for up to one hundred thousand of them. In the wake of the project the church had reached out with Christian love and teaching to hundreds of interested people, and some had decided to follow Christ. The Christian congregation in our area had matured to become a full-fledged, properly organized, fully independent indigenous church.

In addition, output of compassionate medical care had greatly expanded because our MAP project brought massive supplies of high-quality medicines to us at a time when most hospitals in the country were out of medicines. And a new "Heart House" program, established by nurse Mary Lou Brownell, effectively assisted and trained widows and other homeless women who had no means of support. As the first year of independence drew to a close, we were pleased with the performance and progress of our mission, but troubled by the turmoil and distress throughout the land.

Heart House ladies

Key Events of 1972: Summary

January
- Secret government papers detailing the U.S. "tilt" toward Pakistan make headlines around the world.
- Sheikh Mujibur Rahman returns triumphantly to Bangladesh.
- The Bangladeshi national anthem is selected and the national flag revised.

February
- Prime Minister Sheikh Mujib refuses to grant any autonomy to tribal people of the Chittagong Hill Tracts.
- Olsen/Knighton take a fact-finding trip to Bangladesh.
- We have a turbulent meeting with Prime Minister Mujib—and meet with our mission team.

March
- The Indian Army departs from Bangladesh.
- Bangladesh and India sign the Treaty of Friendship and Cooperation.

April
- Our Bangladesh Brigade begins its mission of mercy in southern Bangladesh.
- The U.S. government accords diplomatic recognition to the government of Bangladesh.
- First public outcry against the Mujib government occurs.

June
- The Bangladesh Brigade completes construction or major repairs of over 10,000 bamboo and sungrass houses.
- Life-saving medicines and food are flown in by MAP and we distribute them to the people.
- Visa #001 is presented by the Bangladesh ambassador in Washington.

July
- First public meeting of the communist party in eighteen years is held.

September
- A new independent, indigenous church is formally established at Malumghat.

October
- The Bangladesh military is deployed to the borders to help the police and border militia crack down on smuggling.
- The new JSD political party is formed; this far-left radical party advocates a communist takeover of the government through armed revolution.

December
- The new Bangladesh Constitution is adopted.
- Our Malumghat food relief operation continues to help the starving—and the "Heart House" program trains needy women in sewing and crafts.

Figure 12

6

1973: Elections and *Daktar*

Nineteen seventy-three began explosively—violence marred New Year's Day! The student front organizations of two pro-Soviet, leftist political parties brought out a procession in front of the United States Information Service (USIS) building in Dacca. Scrawled on its walls were bitterly hostile anti-American slogans and the communist hammer and sickle. The students marched and shouted to protest the resumption of American bombing of communist North Vietnam. When police unexpectedly opened fire on the procession, two students were killed and six were injured![1] With this action the government also shot itself in the foot, for the killing of these boys created a furor throughout the land.

We were surprised at this extreme response to a student demonstration. First of all, the police are always ordered to exercise great restraint when students are on the march. Secondly, the two pro-Soviet political parties behind the demonstration considered themselves allies of the Awami League government which had declared them the only other "patriotic" parties in the country. In reaction to this tragic incident the opposition complained loudly that the Awami League was becoming increasingly high-handed and intolerant of all other political parties, even its allies.

On January 4, while addressing a public meeting, Prime Minister Sheikh Mujib declared emphatically that there would be no all-party government. He meant by this that he would continue to preside over an all-Awami-League government and would not allow pro-Soviet or pro-Chinese Communists to have seats in his cabinet. Certainly he would not let leaders of the rightist orthodox Muslim religious parties be a part of his government, because a year earlier he had banned those parties and jailed thousands of their members for collaborating with the hated Pakistan military occupation force. Since most fundamentalist Muslims did not

want to see Pakistan break up, many of them had supported the
West Pakistan Army even though it was attacking their own East
Pakistan (Bangladesh).

Meanwhile, the Bangladesh Election Commission selected fif-
ty-five symbols (such as a boat, sheaf of rice, umbrella, and so on)
which would be used by the various political parties. Each party
would need a symbol so that illiterate voters (80 percent of the
population) could properly cast their votes in the upcoming parliamentary (congressional) elections.

Despite progress on the domestic front, thousands of Bangalees—and Pakistanis—remained stranded far from home:

- 93,000 Pakistani soldiers and civilians were held as prisoners of war in India.
- 300,000 Bangalee soldiers and civilians were detained in
  Pakistan.
- 280,000 Pakistanis and *Biharis* (pro-Pakistan, Urdu-speaking, non-Bengali Indian Muslim settlers) who desired to
  move to Pakistan were stranded in Bangladesh.

At first, Sheikh Mujib had proclaimed that his government
would prosecute as war criminals all the Pakistan military prisoners of war held in Indian POW camps since their defeat thirteen
months before. Later, recognizing that it would be logistically impossible to bring tens of thousands of soldiers to trial, Mujib's government drastically reduced the figure to a mere fifteen hundred.

The Bhutto government in Pakistan, of course, was adamantly
opposed to these war crimes trials; Bhutto's political future depended on his getting the Pakistani soldiers safely back home. Furthermore, Bhutto was not willing to receive all the Biharis. What
would he do with them? How could Pakistan absorb so many when
many native Pakistanis could not find employment?

Meanwhile, in Chittagong the Soviet salvage crew reported
that they had cleared the shipping channel of all mines deployed
there by the Pakistan military during the war. Even so, their work
had just begun. They still had twenty-nine bombed, sunken ships
to cut up and remove from the jetty areas before their assignment
would be complete. What a pile of trash that would make! Many
Bangalees were disturbed about the Soviets' intense interest in the
port of Chittagong—and apprehensive that they would persuade
the Bangladesh government to allow the Russian Navy to use Chittagong Port as a permanent base of operations.

During February newspapers continued to report murders
and other terrorist activities caused by "miscreants,"[2] the government code word for radical, pro-Chinese Bangalee Communists

Sunken ship at Chittagong Port

(Maoists) who were attempting to launch a bloody revolution. Ordinary armed robbers also were on the prowl. Two of our Malumghat colleagues, Jesse and Joyce Eaton, in their February 1973 newsletter described the pervasive terrorism in the neighborhood of our hospital:

> Although Bangladesh has commemorated its first year of independence with great fanfare, much of its sought-after independence remains in the hands of the criminal element. Because some of the freedom fighters refused to relinquish their arms in the cities, and especially in the rural areas where the majority of our missionaries live, an unchecked spirit of lawlessness prevails. Organized gangs loot and kill at will. Hijacking of private cars occurs in broad daylight. Protection money is easily extracted after one threat and an incident. In the wake of the growing fear many of the local villagers are coming to us with their money, valuables, and best clothing for safekeeping. We desperately need your prayers for wisdom and that our God will protect our national believers and us.

Political parties and their frenetic activities dominated February, the final month before parliamentary elections. When the parties announced their nominated candidates for each of the three hundred election districts in the country, each candidate began moving about his district making speech after speech extolling his and his party's virtues. We felt right at home seeing politicians smilingly mingling with the people and haranguing the crowds over noisy PA systems. We and other lovers of the democratic process were delighted to see this democracy in action.

In America elections focus essentially on two parties, the Republican and Democratic parties. In Great Britain four parties dominate the political landscape. In Bangladesh, however, the situation was far more complex. Bangalee political commentators wrote about dozens of political parties spanning the spectrum from far right to far left; several of these parties were often mentioned (see table 2 if you are interested in the details). Only a handful of these, however, would participate in the upcoming elections, since seven of the small far-left communist parties were underground groups and because the five rightist Islamic parties were still banned from politics for their pro-Pakistan sympathies.

The remaining parties vigorously presented their various manifestos to the public. The party in power, the Awami League (AL), emphasized nationalism, democracy, socialism, and secularism (separation of religion and politics). The two moderate, pro-Soviet communist parties (CPB and NAP-M) espoused principles so similar to those of the AL that the public did not take them seriously; they were derisively called "the B team of the Awami League." The Maoist JSD party took the most radical stance; this new and highly visible party loudly proclaimed that there must be a violent revolution to establish a frankly communist government.

Even the tribal people of the Chittagong Hill Tracts (CHT) participated in the political process with their own political party,

Using a rickshaw-mounted loudspeaker
to announce a political meeting

FAR LEFT	LEFT	CENTER	RIGHT	FAR RIGHT
9 RADICAL PRO-CHINESE COMMUNIST PARTIES	**2 MODERATE PRO-SOVIET COMMUNIST PARTIES**	**PARTY IN POWER**	**2 PRO-ISLAMIC, ANTI-COMMUNIST PARTIES**	**3 ISLAMIC FUNDAMENTALIST PARTIES**
1. National Awami Party-B (NAP-B) 2. Jatiyo Samajtantrik Dal (JSD) (= Nat'l Socialist Party) 3.–9. Seven small radical leftist underground parties	1. National Awami Party-M (NAP-M) 2. Communist Party of Bangladesh (CPB)	1. Awami League (AL)	1. Muslim League (ML) – 3 factions 2. Pakistan Democratic Party (PDP)	1. Jamaat-i-Islami 2. Jamaat-i-ulema-e-Islam 3. Nizam-e-Islam
			(ALL BANNED FROM 1972 TO 1976)	
FOR 1. Establishing a Communist government—by violent revolution 2. Socialism 3. Secularism (separation of religion and politics) 4. China	**FOR** 1. Establishing a Communist government—by peaceful means 2. Socialism 3. Secularism (separation of religion and politics) 4. USSR and India 5. Awami League to some degree (socialism, secularism, pro-Soviet and pro-India stance)	**FOR** 1. Nationalism 2. Democracy 3. Socialism 4. Secularism (separation of religion and politics) 5. India and USSR 6. Islamic countries (with Muslim majorities like Bangladesh)	**FOR** 1. Orthodox Islamic religion 2. Making Bangladesh an Islamic republic 3. Democracy 4. Private enterprise 5. Pakistan 6. America—in its tilt toward Pakistan and its democracy	
AGAINST 1. Private enterprise (capitalism) 2. Center and right parties 3. Pro-Soviet left parties 4. Each other—because of small, Communist doctrinal differences 5. America—and other capitalist countries 6. USSR and India	**AGAINST** 1. Private enterprise (capitalism) 2. Rightist parties 3. The 9 radical pro-Chinese Communist parties 4. China 5. America—and other capitalist countries	**AGAINST** 1. Including leaders of other parties in the AL government 2. Rightist parties 3. The 9 radical pro-Chinese Communist parties 4. China 5. America, to some degree, because it tilted toward West Pakistan during the brutal civil war in 1971	**AGAINST** 1. Secularism (separation of religion and politics) 2. Awami League—the party in power 3. Left and far left Communist parties 4. Communism and socialism 5. China and USSR 6. Hinduism and India 7. 1971 breakup of Pakistan, which produced independent Bangladesh 8. America—in its tolerance of drugs, alcohol, gambling, free sex, etc.	

Table 2. Major political parties in Bangladesh in 1973.

the CHT United People's Party. This party had been formed the year before by two brothers named Larma. The ideology of the party was mixed with leftist and centrist members, but all were pro-tribal nationalists. Of course, their fifteen-point manifesto centered around tribal autonomy for the CHT. This declaration was so popular with hill men that, on election day, M. N. Larma would be elected a member of the Bangladesh National Assembly (Parliament) by a landslide. Although the CHT United People's Party had formed an armed wing called the *Shanti Bahini* (Peace Force), they were holding it in check. "Let us see if our representative will be able to accomplish anything on the floor of the new Parliament," the tribal leaders said to one another.

In innumerable public meetings the various opposition leaders shouted out their bitter complaints and charges against the Awami League government in power. These were their claims:[3]

1. The government is unable to stop the upward spiral of prices; the cost of rice and other basic commodities has doubled in the first year of the new nation's existence.
2. The government is unable even to ensure basic law and order; murder, thievery, armed robbery, kidnapping, and rape are commonplace.

The price of rice doubled

3. The Awami League government is powerless to stop smuggling, hoarding, black marketing, and other social crimes —because its own people are the main culprits.
4. The Mujib government is inefficient and completely unable to manage the industries which it has nationalized; this causes further severe loss of national wealth.
5. The government is guilty of massive, unprecedented corruption which is destroying the country.
6. The Mujib government is taking unfair advantage of the opposition in the election campaign by shamelessly using government vehicles, helicopters, and government television, radio, and newspapers to promote its party's candidates.
7. The government has made the independent nation of Bangladesh a client state of India.

These harsh complaints, focused by the impending elections, shocked and disturbed us, for we continued to love this infant nation which had begun with such high hopes and with so much unity and esprit de corps. Now, fourteen months later, the fabric of the nation seemed to be disintegrating. What a disappointment!

For months the political killings had been continuing throughout the land. An article in a leftist newspaper claimed that during the twelve months between February 1972 and February 1973 seven hundred Awami League workers and five hundred opposition party workers had been murdered.[4] Radical pro-Chinese Communists seemed to think it was open season on Awami League workers, and the Awami League government security forces were killing the radical Communists in return.

At this point we were in the United States on home leave, which would continue throughout the year. In early February a young couple came to our house in Wheaton, Illinois, to talk. They were medical student David Clutts and wife, Kathy. After a warm discussion and a meeting of the minds, they decided to spend the elective quarter in his senior year of medical college at our Bangladesh hospital. That short-term experience turned out to be so positive that they further committed themselves to lifetime medical mission service. After Dave completed his surgical training they ultimately joined our mission, then raised the necessary funds to replicate our type of medical mission in Togo, Africa. Dave always drew a chuckle, during his months of fund-raising, when he began his address with, "I'm a left-handed surgeon named Clutts!"

During February in Bangladesh grenade blasts punctuated the news. Enemies of the Awami League exploded a powerful grenade in an AL public meeting on a large island near Chittagong City; six persons died. Even closer to home, in the sea resort town of Cox's Bazar thirty miles south of our hospital, someone pulled the pin and threw a live grenade into a crowded theater lobby. Soon the terribly injured patients were arrayed in our emergency room and corridor to receive the care they urgently needed. More blood! More senseless tragedy!

During the same month another injury case entered Memorial Christian Hospital; he should have come eighteen months earlier. The village schoolteacher wept as he recounted how the Pakistan Army had attacked his village in 1971 and torched the village houses. Risking his own life, he had raced into his burning house and rescued his wife and five children. The price he paid?—severe third-degree burns to his hands, arms, face, and chest. Over the ensuing months thick blotches of scar tissue inexorably bound his fingers and deformed his hands, rendering them almost useless. He could no longer eat rice the "normal" way—picking it up between fingers and thumb. He was forced to eat with a spoon wedged precariously between rigid, claw-like fingers.

Our physiotherapists began working to increase the mobility of his crooked fingers. Then surgeon Donn Ketcham skillfully ex-

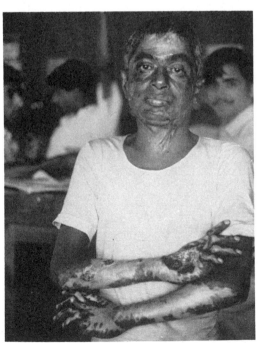

The brave village schoolteacher

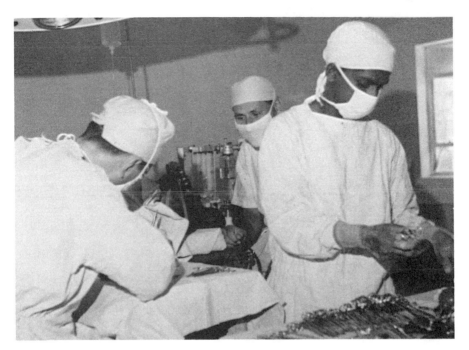

Dr. Donn Ketcham excised the ugly scars

cised the ugly scars, releasing the fingers; finally, he carefully covered the raw tissues with skin grafts. The operations were successful. When the brave village schoolteacher returned to his home, he left with a smile on his face and a deep faith burning in his heart —and he could eat with his fingers again like normal people do.

While these personal dramas were playing out at the hospital, election fever continued to build around the country. The government party (Awami League) effectively used its highly developed grass-roots network to promote its candidates. At the same time, the other parties were also making an enormous effort and particularly large crowds were attending the leftist opposition parties' rallies.

Finally, the calendar announced March 7—election day! With the politicians' speeches still ringing in their ears, more than 19 million Bangalees trudged to their polling stations and cast their votes. More than 15 million of the voters were illiterate, so they had to select the symbols of the parties for which they wished to vote. The vote was running strongly in favor of the boat, election symbol of the Awami League.

In about thirty of the three hundred election districts, however, opposition candidates were said to be defeating the AL candidates; some of those men were experienced, well-known, highly visible opposition leaders who, if elected, would be able to speak powerfully and persuasively in the new Parliament. But then, according to critics, the Awami League leaders opted for overkill—they set up a central control room in Prime Minister Mujib's official government office block. When losing AL candidates frantically telephoned, the control team dispatched AL civilians and the Rakkhi Bahini to control the voting.[5] Whether or not these allegations were accurate, the opposition made a poor showing, winning only 9 of the 300 seats. Obviously the electorate still had more faith in Sheikh Mujib and the Awami League than in the opposition.

Because of their large majority, the Awami League was granted all 15 of the additional seats reserved for women. This 15, plus the 291 seats gained in the election, gave them a total of 306 seats in the new Parliament. Here are the lopsided results of Bangladesh's first parliamentary elections:[6]

Awami League	306
Independent candidates	6
JSD Party	2
Bangladesh National League	1
Total:	315

Also in March, in the United States we completed a personal project that had required immense effort—writing a book about our life in East Pakistan and the birth of Bangladesh. While we were in the States during our furlough in 1966, and again in 1971, there had been pressure to write such a book but no time to do so. By early 1972 four publishers were encouraging me to write the story and wanting to publish it. But I kept thinking, *Me? Write a book?*

On the eve of my departure for the Bangladesh Brigade project, three men from the Moody Press of Chicago came to our home to make a proposal. They offered to utilize for our book a substantial special budget which the press had put aside for extensive promotion of one major book in the upcoming year; the press had never before established such a large fund to promote a single book. What a bonanza for a green author who had never written a book—and who had not yet penned one word of this one!

I responded that we would carefully consider the proposal and, to counterbalance my inexperience, I would collaborate with an experienced writer named Jeanette Lockerbie. Jeanette was a dear friend, wife of a beloved pastor, and mother of our mission co-worker Jeannie Lockerbie. During the Bangladesh Brigade project Jeanette visited Bangladesh. She rode with me in jeeps and huge

UN trucks, and over the roar of the engines we discussed which publisher to select.

"Jeanette," I suggested, "it seems to me that Christian people usually write for each other. But that does not provide information or help to the rest of the country or the rest of the world. I would like to write this book primarily for secular readers and only secondarily for the Christian community."

Jeanette responded, "I couldn't agree with you more, Vic. And, among the interested publishers, probably prestigious Harper and Row could promote the book most effectively to the secular world. On the other hand, Moody Press has promised the large promotional budget, which is a great advantage."

"I did discuss with Moody Press this point of promotion outside the religious/inspirational market," I remembered aloud, "and they suggested a way to accomplish this. The chief editor explained that once the hardcover and deluxe paperback editions were selling well through their outlets, they could grant rights of publication to a secular publisher for a mass paperback edition. Another point appeals to me about Moody Press, Jeanette. The profits they make on the book will not go into some executive's swimming pool, but will be used to pay tuition for young men and women to study theology and missions and Christian education at the Moody Bible Institute. We would have a part in that if we went with Moody Press."

We continued to prayerfully mull over the pros and cons of the various publishers. Some days later, sitting in the Chittagong airport, we finally decided to go with Moody Press. This decision was right on target, too, for the results of working with this press surpassed our fondest expectations.

Back in Wheaton, after the Bangladesh Brigade project was completed, Joan and I began pulling together old letters, diary notes, magazine articles, and other sources of information. We paused often to revel in the recollections of great life experiences. And we decided to put all our income from the book into our work of caring for the sick and injured of southern Bangladesh; it seemed the perfect use for these profits.

Again and again we were interrupted by telephone calls from pastors and others wanting meetings, articles, and so on. Interest in our medical mission in the new nation of Bangladesh was running high. *With all these interruptions, how will I ever get this book written?* I wondered. The next day my frustration eased when our friend and landlord, John Thorne, ensconced me in a beautiful nearby private office without a telephone—a haven away from phone calls and other interruptions. Bless that man! Each noon and evening, after hours of productive work, I would cross the street to our home, pick up the calls which had come in, and respond to them in an orderly fashion.

I remember vividly the morning I started page one of *Daktar/ Diplomat in Bangladesh*—usually called *Daktar*. Suddenly I was acutely aware of the commitment which I had made to the press, the huge responsibility of turning out this book, the large promotional budget which had been set aside for it, and my own total lack of experience. I felt like absolute zero—and that's pretty low. I remember, as though it were yesterday, bowing to pray, "Oh, Father, what have I gotten myself into? I don't really know how to do this. The task is far beyond me. Please keep me from messing it up and producing a fiasco. Please inject some ability into me and help me to do this well. Let me produce a book that will actually help people—change some readers' lives out there. Father, without your help I cannot do this." Then the fear eased off and, little by little, peace of mind came. The first word became the first paragraph became the first page—and the manuscript was launched.

I know other people use quite different techniques to produce books. But my system worked for me. Joan collated and organized all the notes, articles, and letters chronologically. I perused that material, then jotted down what I wanted to cover from each year's activities. Next I dictated the book, page by page and chapter by chapter. It was better to do this than expect someone to decipher my doctor's handwriting—the typist might have needed a pharmacist to translate it into English.

A friend and expert typist Lillian Smith transcribed the dictation, producing triple-spaced pages. A day or two later I refined those pages by writing additions or corrections between the lines and in the margins. Next Joan checked the manuscript and made wise suggestions for improvements which I would also add in the margins. Then, from the hashed-up manuscript Lillian would type the second draft of each chapter. Finally, after letting it cool for a few days, I would read this draft carefully several more times, then pencil in a few refinements to produce the final draft of the manuscript.

Because of a production deadline, we delivered each chapter as it was finished to the chief editor at his nearby home in the evening. The next day his checking editor reviewed the chapter and sent it off to the printer for typesetting. We also sent copies of each chapter to Jeanette Lockerbie and our colleagues in Bangladesh for any additional points or suggestions. At the end we selected and delivered appropriate pictures and maps to the editor to illustrate the text.

Because we were enthusiastic about the project, we were full of ideas about every aspect of the production of the book. We made suggestions about how to improve the cover art, where to place the pictures, how to promote the book, and so forth. The editors and the marketing staff humored us and were unfailingly courteous—they could have been annoyed at our becoming so involved. Only later did we learn that a press usually deals with the various details of production with little or no author involvement.

We were relieved when we finally completed the last chapter of the manuscript and turned it over to the publisher. The next steps were up to the artists, printers, and promoters.

Meanwhile, one of our Bangladesh co-workers also had completed a book which was published about that time. Jeannie Lockerbie's book *On Duty in Bangladesh*[7] focused on the wartime experiences of our Chittagong contingent as they struggled to serve the people of their city who were caught up in the maelstrom of civil war. Because Jeannie's book was beautifully written, interesting, and popular, it sold many copies.

By April 1973, on the other side of the world, the 93,000 Pakistani soldiers and civilians had been held in custody as prisoners of war in India for sixteen months. And they were sick and tired of it. For several months the governments of Pakistan and other countries had been pressing India and Bangladesh to release the POWs from their Indian prison camps. Even the usually shy, veiled Muslim wives of the prisoners had been vigorously agitating for the release of their husbands. A *Newsweek* article detailed their strategy:

> Following the pattern set by their American counterparts, the wives of the Pakistani prisoners have taken up their husbands' cause—placing full-page ads in the Western press, touring the U.S. and Europe and buttonholing every foreign newsman they can find to tell their story. As one young wife put it: "I want my husband back now. The Indians are using him to achieve political aims, and political decisions can take years. What will our children do? What will we do?"[8]

Stung by this agitation, India's prime minister sent a special envoy to Dacca to convince Sheikh Mujibur Rahman and other Bangalee leaders to back away from conducting war crimes trials involving hundreds of Pakistani soldiers. The Bangalee leaders listened—and agreed to scale down their demands. Here, then, is the deal, the Indo-Bangladesh Joint Declaration, which they offered to the Government of Pakistan:[9]

1. Bangladesh would prosecute only 195 Pakistani prisoners of war for serious war crimes.

2. India would send these 195 prisoners to Bangladesh for trial.
3. India would send the rest of the 93,000 Pakistani military and civilian prisoners back to Pakistan.
4. Bangladesh would send to Pakistan the 280,000 Pakistanis and pro-Pakistan, non-Bengali Indian Muslim settlers (Biharis) who desired to leave Bangladesh.
5. Pakistan would allow all 300,000 Bangalees who had been detained in Pakistan to return to Bangladesh.

The Government of Pakistan began to consider this sweeping proposal—but again threatened to prosecute Bangalees in Pakistan if any of the Pakistani POWs were put on trial. Then, in the early morning hours of May 6, Pakistan security forces swooped down and rounded up several thousand Bangalees to sequester them in uncomfortable internment camps. Simultaneously, the Pakistan government initiated an international campaign to influence world opinion against the Bangladesh/India determination to continue holding the Pakistani POWs and ultimately try 195 of them for war crimes.

At last Pakistan responded to the Indo-Bangladesh Joint Declaration: Pakistan refused the proposal, refused to grant diplomatic recognition to Bangladesh, and reminded India and Bangladesh that they were guilty of breaking the Geneva Convention rule about releasing POWs without delay once a war is finished. However, despite their negative reply, the Pakistani leaders carefully left the door ajar for further negotiations.

In April, on the American side of the globe I continued giving addresses to thousands of people about our work of serving God and man in the People's Republic of Bangladesh. During the first week of April I addressed the Executive Club in beautiful Oak Brook, Illinois. These upper-level executives listened with interest to the description of the birth of Bangladesh and our adventures during those dark days; some seemed to listen even more intently to the spiritual points in my message.

Three days later I met Dr. John Jess, the founder, director, and radio minister for the Chapel of the Air radio broadcast; he kindly requested me to come to their studio and prepare four taped messages for their radio audience. I was delighted to do this because the Chapel of the Air was a fine program, broadcasting over 180 stations throughout the United States and abroad.

That same afternoon, after taping the messages, I flew to Philadelphia, then proceeded to Cherry Hill, New Jersey, to address the ABWE Board of Directors. The following morning I slipped over to Washington, D.C., to meet the current Bangladesh ambassador to the United States. He was an alert, intelligent, well-dressed Bengali gentleman who seemed to represent his country well in Washington. We had enough time together to become very well acquainted.

Meanwhile, problems escalated in Bangladesh. Many were wondering whether there would be sufficient food to feed the people during the rest of 1973. The UN secretary general announced a serious shortage of food in the country and encouraged the worldwide community of nations to help fill the gap to prevent starvation in Bangladesh. The aged leader of the leftist NAP-B political party embarked on a hunger strike to protest high prices and shortage of food—shades of Mahatma Gandhi!

By this time the people were blaming India, and to a lesser extent the Soviet Union, for the food shortages, high prices, and other problems—despite all the assistance these countries had rendered to the Bangalees during the brutal crackdown by the Pakistan Army. Simultaneously, anti-Americanism was easing as millions of U.S. dollars poured into Bangladesh to rehabilitate the nation. In fact, the hammer and sickle and anti-American shibboleths scribbled on the white walls of the USIS building had been painted over and replaced by new slogans: "Running dogs of Russia and India, quit Bengal!" and "Agents of Russia and India, go home!" How fickle desperate people can be as they cast about for scapegoats!

At this point in time a handsome college student from a Buddhist village appeared to talk with our church leaders and mission personnel in Chittagong City. What a fascinating story he related! A year earlier he had received some literature distributed by church members; inside a pamphlet he found a sheet advertising the Bible Correspondence School. "The word of God was so sweet to me," he explained, "that I studied course after course until all ten were completed. According to their promise the school authorities then awarded me a free Bengali Bible."

He continued reading and regularly visiting a Christian friend to gain further instruction. Finally, convinced by the Holy Scriptures, he placed his faith in Christ the Lord. I could relate to that, because years earlier I had been convinced by the same Scriptures and had made the same faith decision. He continued to read his new Bible avidly; that, too, mirrored my own experience.

In the meantime, his family and the members of his village were making preparations for an annual Buddhist religious festival; this involved preparing special foods for the feast and erecting a costly idol. The young man, uneasy now because he was convinced that idolatry was wrong, continued his reading of the life history of Noah as recorded in the book of Genesis. By the time the religious ceremonies began, he was gripped with three truths: *sin is an offense to God—divine judgment is coming—time is short.* Seeing his family members and neighbors bowing before the vividly painted clay idol, he suddenly lost control. Seizing a stout stick, he began furiously beating the statue and broke it into a thousand unsightly pieces!

The frenzied crowd, shouting death-threats, seized the young man, bound him, and imprisoned him in a village hut. Outraged by his son's behavior and shamed before family and friends, his father announced that the village council would hold a religious trial in three days. The young man tolerated the three days of insults, abuse, and danger with exceptional calm. Then, on the night before the trial a wild-eyed mob surged into the improvised jail. But suddenly they were diverted by a mysterious fire which broke out in the building next door; they rushed out to fight the flames. When his would-be assailants finally returned, drained by their exertions, they asked their prisoner if he knew anything about the timely fire. He responded, "Perhaps the true God has spared me for some special work."

The next morning he was brought before a council of priests, charged, tried, convicted, and sentenced to be handed over to the civil authorities for imprisonment. Offered the usual opportunity to make a final statement, he boldly and eloquently explained to the council the reason for his actions and the truth of his new faith. His passionate words were more a sermon than a statement. Then all was quiet. Someone whispered, "He is right. If there is a true Creator-God, to bow down before a statue made of clay is wrong."

The council members, suddenly uncomfortable with their judgment, debated the issue further. Wonder of wonders, the sentence was overturned, and the father agreed to pay half the cost of the idol whereas the rest of the villagers would take up a collection for the other half. The young man departed to receive further instruction in the Holy Scriptures. Although we would have advised him to handle his newfound faith in a less explosive way, we marveled at the power of the Scriptures in a young man's life—and at his last-minute deliverance. "Thank You, Father!"

Simultaneously, the same Scriptures were influencing the minds and hearts of a more primitive people, the Tipperas, in a more remote area. The sixty-thousand-strong Tippera (or Tripura) tribe lived in scattered villages in the forest- and jungle-covered hills of the Chittagong Hill Tracts District. Religiously these hill people espoused an animism tinged with Hinduism; they sacrificed fowl and animals to appease evil spirits and seemed to be well acquainted with Satan whom they (and Bengalis) call "Shoi-

Tippera village house

tan." Some of our team had worked with the Tipperas for years and helped them to establish many churches and congregations.

For several weeks three Tippera leaders had been touring from village to village in the hills, teaching and preaching and discussing Old and New Testament truths. And again the Scriptures were powerful—forty Tipperas made the great faith decision and were baptized in mountain streams to give open, vivid testimony to their new faith.

In May and June, in the United States the Moody Press promotion of our book *Daktar* burst upon the scene. They had promised a strong promotional program—they kept their word. The inspirational/religious market was their first target. Full-page ads in various magazines reached a readership of several million. Posters, flyers, and point-of-purchase displays were sent to thousands of book stores. The highly regarded magazine *Christianity Today* selected *Daktar* as a Book-of-the-Month Club selection, while various radio broadcasts offered the book over the airwaves. I had to put aside time to appear on radio and television shows and, later, to hold autograph parties at various book stores. Through all these means a keen interest began to build around the country.

In June the first ten thousand copies of *Daktar* rolled off the presses. Because they had all been sold prior to that time, the sec-

Tipperas were baptized in mountain streams

ond printing began rolling immediately; the publisher told us that this was an unprecedented experience for them. On several daily radio programs across the country dramatic readers began to read the book through from cover to cover on the air. Another organization, the Moody Literature Mission, sent copies of *Daktar* to the president of the United States and his staff, to every senator and congressman, and to every Supreme Court justice. We were pleased to learn that orders kept pouring in, so that more and more printings rapidly succeeding each other were necessary to keep up with the demand. "Thank You, Father!"

Across the seas in Bangladesh July 1 was important for two reasons:

1. It marked the end of the 1972-73 fiscal (financial) year.
2. It marked the beginning of the government's official First Five-Year Plan (1973-78).

An analysis of the 1972-73 fiscal year uncovered very little to be happy about. The year's negatives, however, were many:[10]

- Rice production was less than 10 million tons; that left a huge food gap, for the people needed 12-13 million tons of food grains to survive that year.

- To make up the food grain deficit, the government had to purchase 2.8 million tons of rice and wheat from abroad (at a cost of $320 million).
- Even with this large expenditure the share of food grains for each person was only 15.5 ounces per day compared to the availability of 17 ounces per day three years earlier.[11]
- The industries which the government had nationalized and begun operating lost $39 million.

July 1 also marked the beginning of an ambitious exercise in planning the economy of Bangladesh; a document called the *First Five-Year Plan (1973-78)*[12] detailed the program. The plan was produced by an elite and powerful agency of the government called the Planning Commission which had been established by Sheikh Mujib and his cabinet within five weeks of the birth of Bangladesh. The top planners were Bangalee economists who had trained at Harvard University.

The *First Five-Year Plan (1973-78)* was a surprisingly detailed, sophisticated document. It was no small accomplishment to produce such a plan during the chaotic postwar period with inadequate statistics at hand. The plan had a basic philosophy: to implement a socialist transformation of the economy.

The agents to produce this change would be first, the political leaders and second, a huge cadre of devoted, idealistic political workers highly trained in the principles of socialism. These low-paid "socialist missionaries" would live among the people to educate and inspire them to build the socialist society. Knowing how tough it is to recruit any kind of missionaries and to carry out successful missionary service, it seemed unlikely to us that the government would ever be able to find, train, and utilize such a large and selfless band of workers.

Here were some of the objectives of the First Five-Year Plan (1973-78):

- Proceed toward socialism by establishing more and more government-owned corporations and industries
- Gradually reduce dependence on foreign aid to finance the budget
- Increase the output of goods required by the common man (rice/wheat, edible oil, sugar, kerosene, clothing) and maintain reasonable prices for these essential items
- Gradually reduce the rate of population growth

All these measures were aimed at reducing poverty and improving the lot of the ordinary people, a very commendable goal.

But we frankly could not see how these objectives could be achieved short of several major miracles.

During July severe law-and-order problems flared throughout the country. In one area government forces apprehended two hundred ultraleft Communists fomenting revolution, arrested them, and captured their large store of arms and ammunition.

Then on a hot and humid Wednesday afternoon reports reached our team at Memorial Christian Hospital that a very large group of *dacoits* (armed bandits) had raided a nearby bazaar and were proceeding toward the hospital. These robbers were armed with powerful automatic weapons left over from the 1971 war. There would be no police protection, for the nearest police station was several miles away and had no telephone. In addition, the police were few in number and poorly armed and, because they had no vehicles, they had to travel on foot or by public bus. (How can a cop fight crime without transportation and a suitable weapon?) The hospital and staff houses containing valuable instruments and equipment were tempting targets to the dacoits.

In the evening a long line of buses and trucks stopped in front of the hospital, the drivers not daring to pass through the nearby forest area where the bandits lurked. If these dacoits should decide on an under-cover-of-darkness attack with their automatic weapons, there would be little our staff could do to resist them.

The church's midweek prayer meeting was very well attended; Bangalee and American Christians prayed with earnestness! That night many of our people bedded down on their flat roofs to avoid being hit by ground-level fire. During the long, tense night some slept, many did not. Then, as the first fingers of dawn light caressed the dark sky, our watchmen quickly passed the word that the forty or more ferocious bandits had decided during the night to bypass the hospital, then slipped off through the forest. "Thank You, Father!"

At about that time Joan and I traveled to Dallas, Texas, to participate in the huge annual convention of the Christian Booksellers Association (CBA). Moody Press set us up in a comfortable hotel, scheduled press conferences, and erected an impressive display at the conference center. I had to hustle to produce a substantial news release in time to meet the press.

The CBA extravaganza with press conferences, addresses, and elaborate displays covering many thousands of square feet of the gigantic conference center was aimed primarily at those selling inspirational/religious books. These booksellers came from all over the United States, Canada, and elsewhere to be informed about the hundreds of new books available and to be inspired to go back home and sell them. When the *Daktar* cover was selected by the appropriate CBA committee as the best cover for the year, we were grateful for the artist who had produced it.

On the night of July 17 I gave an address at the Moody Press *Daktar* reception. Because of the effective promotion and the high interest in our team's compassionate medical mission to the infant nation of Bangladesh, the place was packed; we gave away hundreds of autographed copies to those who attended. True to their word, Moody Press had launched an effective promotional effort.

But things were not so rosy back in Bangladesh; our team was struggling with new visa problems. Shades of East Pakistan days! Three months earlier, without warning the government began to reject the visa applications of our newly appointed mission personnel. Administrators Jay Walsh and Reid Minich then approached key officials in the capital city; they soon learned that the government's visa rules had hardened to stifle any further increase of foreign personnel. Old hands and replacements would continue to have their visas renewed, but new hands would be scrutinized with great care and only rarely be granted visas. Jay and Reid submitted an official appeal, explaining that our new people who had been rejected were coming to replace former workers who had left the field. This approach was successful and the visa rejections were reversed.

During the last week of July in Pakistan a different kind of negotiation was taking place; Indian negotiators met with their Pakistani counterparts in the capital city of Pakistan. The subject? Pakistani soldiers imprisoned in India, Bangalees stranded in Pakistan, and Pakistanis and Biharis stuck in Bangladesh. In these meetings India had to represent Bangladesh, as well, since Sheikh Mujib steadfastly refused to sit down with the Pakistanis until they granted diplomatic recognition to his country. This stance, of course, kept him on the sidelines throughout the intricate negotiations.

After a seventeen-day break the discussions were resumed in the Indian capital of New Delhi. The negotiators finally succeeded in hammering out the highly important "Delhi Agreement" which provided solutions for most of the pressing humanitarian problems:[13]

1. Nearly all the 93,000 Pakistani POWs would be released from India to return home to Pakistan; only 195 POWs would remain in Indian hands awaiting their war crimes trials in Bangladesh.

2. The 300,000 Bangalees detained in Pakistan would be released to return home to Bangladesh.
3. Any Pakistanis stranded in Bangladesh would be free to return to Pakistan.
4. The Urdu-speaking non-Bengali Biharis who wished to move to Pakistan would not be the responsibility of Pakistan. However, Pakistan would accept some of these Biharis based on humanitarian considerations.
5. After completion of this three-way repatriation, there would be further discussion about the fate of the 195 Pakistani prisoners of war. But Bangladesh would only enter into the discussion on the basis of "sovereign equality"; that meant diplomatic recognition by Pakistan.

Although Mujib still had control of the 195 POWs held in Indian camps, we noted that Pakistan's Bhutto continued to hold his own trump card—diplomatic recognition of Bangladesh. The Delhi Agreement had left these two critical points hanging. It looked like there might be some further horse-trading. In the meantime, special planes began ferrying the stranded populations to their home countries.

During this period the so-called "Muslim Bengal"movement was producing an identity crisis in Bangladesh. The ruling Awami League government always had espoused "secularism"—a nonreligious government as opposed to an Islamic republic. This was their brand of "separation of church and state."

In the summer of 1973 Islamic fundamentalists and other pious Muslims began to actively oppose the AL secularism. Because their right-wing political parties had been banned, these zealous men were not allowed to hold mass meetings or rallies; instead, they fanned out to the tea shops, the bazaars, and the mosques talking face-to-face with farmers, laborers, students, teachers, civil servants, and others. They spoke about the importance of Islam to the great majority of Bangalees, and they railed against secularism, Hindu India, and Indian influence. Essentially they were stirring up the Muslims of Bangladesh to re-emphasize their Islamic heritage. In time the movement became successful enough to influence the actions of Bangalee heads of state and, eventually, to force the secularism provision out of the Constitution of Bangladesh.

But from the revolutionary left the pressure was even more intense. So in September, to obtain more and sharper teeth against these Maoists, the government submitted to the National Assembly the Constitution's Second Amendment Bill, 1973. One year earlier, even twenty years before, no one could have imagined that an Awami League government would push a bill with such restrictive provisions:[14]

1. Persons could be jailed without a trial.
2. The President could declare a "state of emergency" if he felt that a grave emergency existed; during a state of emergency the fundamental human rights guaranteed by the Constitution could be suspended.

The opposition was shaken. They protested that these were the very points that the Awami League had militantly fought against throughout the twenty-four years of its existence. Among the Bangladesh Constitution's most enlightened provisions had been the guarantee of all fundamental human rights and the promise that no one could be held by the police in the absence of a proper trial. Those great democratic principles would be lost if the National Assembly were to enact the Second Amendment.

The handful of opposition members in the National Assembly spoke vehemently against the amendment on the grounds that it would diminish the nation's precious democracy. They pointed to the existing laws which seemed quite adequate to deal with any internal and external disturbances. Ultimately, the opposition members walked out of the National Assembly session in angry protest against the "repressive" Second Amendment, whereupon the Awami League legislators passed it without opposition. They were obviously reacting to the deadly attacks by the radical Communists.

Also in September, Mujib realized his ambition to bring Bangladesh into the Nonaligned Movement. This movement is a haven for nations, particularly developing Asian and African nations, who prefer to join neither the Western bloc led by the United States nor the communist bloc led by Soviet Russia. They feel that taking the nonaligned stance enables them to maintain their independence and freedom of action—and often to obtain foreign aid from both sides. On September 3 the foreign ministers of the Fourth Nonaligned Summit Conference meeting in Algiers approved the Bangladesh application for membership. Three days later Mujib flew to Algiers where he attended the summit meetings, addressed the gathering, and held a series of private meetings with the leaders of several nations. He was quite pleased with the week's developments.

In the United States we also were pleased with positive developments. Sales of *Daktar* continued strong. In September it jumped into the top ten of the National Religious Bestsellers list of hardcover books. Of course, we and Moody Press were delighted. Then their sister organization, the Moody Literature Mission, sent copies to 2,500 Christian physicians and dentists to read and to share with interested colleagues.

In mid-September I traveled again to Dallas, Texas, for an appealing assignment. Highly regarded Dr. Richard DeHaan, a noted Bible teacher and television producer, had invited ABWE president Dr. Wendell W. Kempton and me to tell their huge "Day of Discovery" television audience about God's work and our work in the new nation of Bangladesh—and about *Daktar*. At the Dallas Channel 4 studio, just before the videotaping, we discussed two or three questions the host might ask to get the program moving in the desired direction. To keep the telecast from seeming canned and to give it life, I purposely did not reveal to anyone the climax point which I had in mind, or the visual aid I had in my pocket to illustrate my point of focus. I hoped that object would not prick me in the leg and draw blood.

As the videotaping began I quickly sensed the skill of the two cameramen and their smooth teamwork as they faded back and forth between each other's cameras and instinctively moved to find strong angles of view. After Dr. Kempton's warm, empathetic remarks about ABWE's interest in Bangladesh and concern for the hurt and struggling people, I talked in some detail about the establishment of our medical mission there, about the thousands of patients we care for each month, about our Bangladesh Brigade mission of mercy, and about the growth of the church among Bengali and tribal people. The program host asked about *Daktar*. I explained the idea of the book and something of its content.

Finally he asked, "Dr. Olsen, why did you decide to cross the ocean to serve the people of Bangladesh?" In response I told about our conversion from agnosticism to Christianity and the wondrous *salvation* we had received. I spoke then of the second step, the *surrender* of our own wills and aims and ambitions into the Father's hand so that we might do His will and carry out His purposes rather than our own. Thirdly, I continued, came the ultimate guidance about what our *service* should be.

"Let me illustrate," I said, removing from my pocket a shining, stainless steel scalpel with its razor-sharp blade glinting in the studio spotlights. All eyes instantly fixed on the scalpel. A sense of expectancy hung in the air. The cameraman on my right quickly zoomed in to focus with exquisite accuracy on the scalpel in my hand; it was a stunning shot. Then I proceeded to use the scalpel as an illustration of that three-fold rule of life which was the basis of our sense of calling to serve God and man in the People's Republic of Bangladesh. When I finished speaking, all was quiet for a moment, then the denouement and the program was complete.

Later we sat in the control room to watch the sound engineer mix together the various facets of the total program. Seated at his console he prepared several reels of film on separate spindles. The stock opening scenes and title, which had been filmed in Florida,

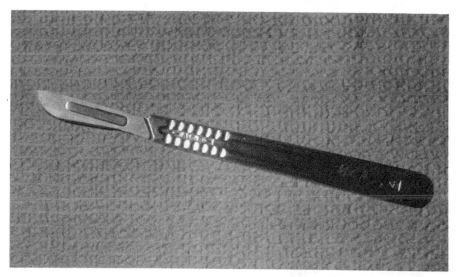

A shining scalpel

flashed on the main console. Then from another reel, taped in Chicago, he dubbed onto the master tape a vocal musical selection. The instrumental music, incidentally, had been taped in London to obtain high quality at reasonable expense. Then he put onto the master our major segment of the program, produced in Dallas for Dr. DeHaan whose headquarters are in Grand Rapids, Michigan. Florida, Chicago, London, Dallas, Grand Rapids—yet the whole program fit together like hand in glove. The sound engineer greatly impressed us with his skill—and reminded us that the divine Engineer eagerly desires to mix together each of our innate skills and spiritual gifts to produce beautiful, harmonious lives which will bring joy to Him, help to others, and satisfaction to us. He does just that if we allow Him to—if we surrender our lives to Him and act on the guidance He gives.

In the Middle East, October witnessed another war between Israel and the Arabs, especially Egyptian and Syrian Arabs. Of course, Sheikh Mujib was sympathetic with his fellow-Muslims in Egypt and Syria. Although he had no money or munitions to send to the front, Mujib did send a unique gift—100,000 pounds of Bangladesh's finest tea for the refreshment of the Arab troops. That thoughtful gift, like a kind of ill-fated boomerang, strangely rebounded months later to strike terror into Mujib's heart and to place him in mortal danger!

In mid-October, while Mujib paid a weeklong visit to Japan, I traveled to Canada to minister to people and to talk about *Daktar*.

Les Tarr, a popular and experienced Toronto Star journalist, met me at the Toronto airport. He had an engaging personality and had such high regard for our medical mission to Bangladesh that we were immediately on the same wavelength. He had set up the ambitious schedule which was to fully occupy me for the next several days. That whirlwind tour included a physicians' conference, a ministers' conference, a college convocation, a seminary chapel, church meetings, and media appearances on radio and CBC's Channel 5.

I returned to Chicago in time for the American College of Surgeons annual meeting; this provided highly important updating which would pay off during our next four-year term of service in Bangladesh. Unknown to me at the time, I would be flying urgently to Bangladesh much earlier than I had anticipated because of a shocking, unexpected happening. Also in Chicago I learned that *Daktar* continued in the top ten of the National Religious Bestsellers list—in fact, it was rising in the ratings.

In Bangladesh, to further combat the growing threat of the radical leftists pressing to overthrow the government by force, officials announced clemency for nearly forty thousand right-wing fundamentalist Muslims who had been jailed in 1972 as collaborators with the Pakistan Army. Presumably a massive infusion of rightists into the society would help counterbalance the aggressiveness of the radical leftists. Despite this act of clemency to individuals, however, the government refused to withdraw its ban on the several rightist political parties.

November in the United States witnessed continuing encouraging sales of *Daktar*. The fifth large printing rolled off the presses —and the book had jumped to number three in the National Religious Bestsellers list. And we were pleased that some churches were declaring "*Daktar* Sundays" to collect funds to give the book to all the physicians in their communities or cities.

Encouraged by the month by month rise in the ratings, we blithely suggested to the Moody Press directors that they increase their promotional efforts during the pre-Christmas season when many people would be purchasing books as gifts. We felt no inhibition about promoting the book, since the profits would be used to help our needy patients. "Maybe," we said, "if you put on a big push in December, that will keep the momentum going and possibly move *Daktar* up in the ratings."

Their response was not what I had hoped for. "That is exactly what we would like to do, but the year's promotional funds are exhausted. So we are afraid that our hands are tied."

"Who has the authority to grant extra funds from next year's budget at this critical time?" I asked.

"Only Dr. George Sweeting, the president of the whole Moody Bible Institute system, including Moody Press."

"Why don't you go to Dr. Sweeting and ask him to treat this as a special case and adjust the budget?"

"Sorry, but we are not free to just go to the president about such a matter. We have a chain of command here."

"Well then, do you have any objection if I go to discuss it with Dr. Sweeting? I am not part of the chain of command." Although this would be highly irregular, all agreed to the plan.

On a brisk winter morning in late November I came in from the cold into the warmth of Dr. Sweeting's office. Much of the warmth emanated from the personality of this able, gifted president of the entire Moody Bible Institute system. After discussing a few other matters, we got down to the business at hand.

"Your press," I explained, "has just exhausted the promotional budget for our book at exactly the time that funds are needed for the pre-Christmas push. Some effective promotion these last four weeks before Christmas could conceivably move the book higher in the ratings. As soon as the paperback version comes out, of course, hardcover sales will immediately fall off. So it is now or never. And I have an idea about a way to stimulate sales which will cost very little."

"Let's hear it," he replied.

"You have WMBI and several other Moody radio stations in other cities —and many other stations around the country pick up material from you. If we could obtain a few positive comments from Christian leaders who have read the book, they could be broadcast around the country as spot announcements at very little cost."

Without hesitation Dr. Sweeting exclaimed, "We'll do it! Let us select the names of some Christian leaders who may have read *Daktar*, and I will notify them by telegram today that our Walter Carlson will call them on Tuesday with his tape recorder patched into the phone. And he will be ready to receive any comment about the book they might care to make. How's that?"

"Perfect! Perhaps you and I can also make a spot announcement or two. Now for the names of those we want to contact."

We selected ten names. Then Walter, a well-known broadcaster and newsman in the Chicago area, succeeded in contacting seven of the ten men; the other three were out of town or out of the country. All seven had read the book and made favorable comments. Dr. Sweeting and I prepared our spot announcements. Then the Moody stations and other stations around the country began broadcasting these spots, sometimes bombarding the air waves every hour on the hour throughout the pre-Christmas season. We would not know until January if we achieved our goal.

As December drew to a close the United Nations Relief Operations in Bangladesh (UNROB) finally began to wind down its massive relief program which had helped to put the infant nation on its feet. Although UNROB was departing, other voluntary agencies and mission societies would remain to help the people. By the end of December Bangladesh had enjoyed independence for two years. During that period the nations of the world had given the new country a staggering $1.3 billion! The generous United States easily topped the list of donors.

Despite the immense amount of aid and assistance given by friendly nations, 1973 had been a bad year for the people of Bangladesh. Inflation had fueled high prices and, in effect, had decreased their earning—and eating. The continuing breakdown of law and order had not been reversed despite the recruitment of tens of thousands of new police, the deployment of special forces, and extensive forays by the police and army which scoured many areas of the country with so-called "combing operations." The government was certainly trying hard. But the problems were daunting; during a previous five-month period radical leftists had attacked sixty police stations to seize any weapons stored in their armories.

For our medical mission December 1973 was a landmark month. I say "landmark" because the government finally granted to us a perpetual lease on eighteen additional acres of land which we urgently needed for expansion. Originally we had been granted twenty-five acres; after careful consideration we had selected sixteen acres beside the highway for the hospital and nine acres a half-mile west at the riverside for our housing site. This left an empty area between our two blocks of land like a thick slab of cheese between two halves of a bun (see figure 13). We had reasoned that this arrangement would give us the best chance to obtain this additional land someday if it were needed. The acquisition of this intervening land ten years later suggested that our guidance factor had been right on target. In addition, Jay Walsh's friendship with the secretary of the Awami League party played a key role in our obtaining the land so expeditiously; the helpful secretary endorsed the application, giving it added weight.

About this time Jay also initiated a new approach to applying for visas. Instead of each mission member making a separate visa application himself or herself, each year Jay submitted a single ap-

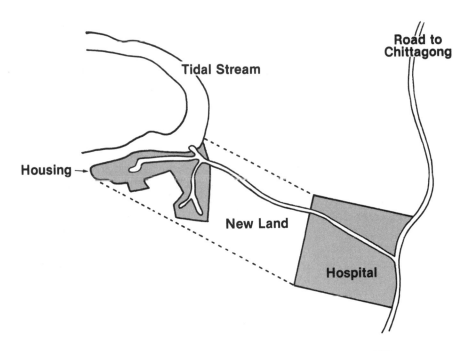

Figure 13. Additional Malumghat land acquired in 1973

plication with all the names listed. This streamlined the whole process and was a great improvement over the old system.

At this point we had two families, the Benedicts and the Webers, serving at our Hebron Station up the Matamuhuri River. Willard Benedict had been a successful pastor in New York City; after his wife died he married Donna Ahlgrim, one of our experienced single workers. They had courageously reopened this rather primitive station after it had been closed for years. George Weber was a new theological teacher from Pennsylvania with a heart for the tribal people and a winsome sense of humor. His wife, Shirley, was a mother, homemaker, and nurse.

These two families would be joined by Pat Barkley from Ohio, after she completed language school. She would be the primary school teacher for the Benedict and Weber children; her teaching would make it possible for the families to serve effectively at this isolated interior station.

In mid-December a worried George Weber brought his wife, Shirley, from Hebron Station to the hospital for emergency care. The result: a miscarriage. On December 21 after Shirley had recovered, the Webers with their eighteen-month-old daughter, Lori, linked up with Willard and Donna Benedict and their three small children (Buddy, Scotty, and Donnal) to return upstream to Hebron; joining them was schoolteacher Pat who was eager to visit Hebron for a few days. Relishing the sunshine and blue skies, the five adults and four children chatted, laughed, and enjoyed a picnic lunch as the newly repaired Evinrude outboard motor smoothly propelled the thirty-foot boat up the winding Matamuhuri River. It was an idyllic scene.

But danger was brewing as water quietly filled the bow of the boat through an opening where the caulking had worked loose. When the bow had settled a bit in the river, water suddenly began cascading over the prow to fill the front half of the sinking boat. Quickly Willard jumped into the river, followed by Shirley who scrambled over the stern clutching baby Lori. Well aware that their catastrophe was happening at the deepest part of the river, George revved the engine and turned briskly toward shore. But the long narrow craft promptly overturned and the woven bamboo canopy floated loose; Donna, her three preschoolers, and Pat were trapped under the canopy.

Pat, with a boy under each arm, struggled free of the canopy and made her way to the shore. But Donna could neither swim nor touch bottom, so she hung on to the canopy with one hand while trying to keep Donnal's head above water with the other. Finally, Willard and a boatman pushed the canopy, and the precious cargo

The Webers and Pat

Hebron's thirty-foot boat

clinging to it, to shallow water. The Benedict family was out of danger.

Meanwhile Shirley Weber, who could barely swim, was struggling in deep water to stay afloat and keep her baby's head above water. But she was losing the battle—she could not keep Lori's face out of the water and the child was drowning in her arms. Just then George reached them and swam with little Lori to the overturned boat; Shirley, gasping, managed to struggle to the boat on her own. Quickly the men pushed the boat to shore and the Weber family was also safe. The bedraggled little band stood on the river bank dripping, weeping, and thanking the Father for seeing them through the danger. How fortunate that Pat had joined the group for a vacation visit to Hebron! Without her help Buddy and Scotty Benedict might have been lost.

And what of the cargo? Gone were fifty eggs, fifty pounds of potatoes, eighty pounds of tomatoes, and many other things. With the help of passing boatmen, however, some items were recovered from the river bottom, including the engine and a briefcase filled with 6,500 takas ($800) of Hebron Station money. Limp, dripping taka bills later festooned the Benedict house while salvaged rice, flour, sugar, books, and pillows were drying out in the winter sun. Although he said nothing at the time, one of the involved boatmen was so shaken by the close call that he began thinking deeply about the fleeting nature of life—and what happens to a person when life is over. Seven years later he finally resolved his fears by making the great faith decision.

During the final week in December I traveled to Illinois for "Urbana '73," a gigantic student missions conference which attracted students from every state in the union and some foreign countries. For five days the throng of students took over an immense university campus. The displays were intriguing and the sessions inspiring. As MAP medical director, my duty was to conduct a seminar for the medical and nursing students and other health care professionals in attendance; I enjoyed every minute of that assignment. And the outcome was positive. Many of those attending made decisions to serve in overseas medical missions; one of them later joined us as a short-termer in Bangladesh. As a result of the total conference, over eight hundred students made commitments to foreign mission service.

As 1973 faded out, one last shock hit home. On December 30 at Memorial Christian Hospital my friend and fellow-surgeon Dr. Donn Ketcham was stricken with a hammer of pain in the center of his chest. Donn well knew that the crushing pain, his sudden perspiration, his pale skin and bluish fingernails, and his thin, rapid pulse spelled heart attack! But, on the other side of the world, we knew nothing of this until the new year.

Key Events of 1973: Summary

January
- The police fire on leftist students, killing two.
- The Soviet salvage crew clears the last mines from the channel at Chittagong Port, then begins dismantling sunken ships.

February
- The Awami League (AL) gains a landslide victory in the parliamentary elections.
- We complete writing *Daktar/Diplomat in Bangladesh.*
- The "Indo-Bangladesh Joint Declaration" offers a plan for the repatriation of Bangalees, Biharis, and all but 195 of the Pakistani POWs; Pakistan rejects the proposal.

April
- The UN recruits the nations of the world to send foodgrains to avert a famine in Bangladesh.
- Tippera Christian leaders make a fruitful tour in the CHT.

July
- Production figures for fiscal year 1972-73 are depressing.
- With high hopes the government launches its first Five-Year Plan.
- Severe law and order problems plague the land; Malumghat Hospital is threatened by armed robbers.

August
- The "Delhi Agreement" (between India and Pakistan) effectively addresses most of the humanitarian concerns of Bangalees and Pakistanis stranded in enemy territory. The repatriation of these soldiers and civilians begins.
- The "Muslim Bengal" movement gains momentum.

September
- The new Parliament passes the Constitution's Second Amendment Bill—over the vehement protests of the opposition.
- Bangladesh joins the Nonaligned Movement.

October
- The Bangladesh government releases 40,000 fundamentalist Muslims (who had been jailed for collaborating with the Pakistan Army) to counterbalance the radical leftists who are killing AL leaders to further their revolution.

December
- *Daktar* climbs on the National Religious Bestsellers list.
- Our mission obtains eighteen more acres of prime land at Malumghat.
- The Hebron team has a close call on the Matamuhuri River when their boat overturns in deep water.
- Dr. Donn Ketcham is stricken with a heart attack at Malumghat.

Figure 14

7

1974: Floods and Famine

The year 1974 brought tension and pain not only to Bangladesh but also to many other countries of the world. America suffered the unforgettable trauma of the Watergate scandal which climaxed in the resignation of President Richard Nixon. And the exploits of awesome Henry Kissinger, who had graduated from the National Security Council to become secretary of state, continued to be bigger than life.

For us January brought good news. The momentum of *Daktar* sales and the promotion in December had actually pushed it up in the ratings. Excluding the Bible, *Daktar* had become the number one best seller on the National Religious Bestsellers list.[1] And it remained there for many weeks. "Thank You, Father!" Of course, we were pleased. Simultaneously, a proposal for a film about our medical mission came from the head of an excellent film production company.

On January 11 I taped an interview for Chicago's radio station WGN. We completed the taping—but the questions kept coming. Apparently intrigued by some point which had spiritual significance to her, the host probed further. Surrounded by the hurly-burly of a busy radio station, we discussed spiritual issues for an hour or more. As she reacted warmly to our Lord's good news message, I encouraged her to go home or some other quiet place where she could settle the matter, invite Him into her life, then go out and put her new faith to work.

With everything going so well, I was not prepared for the telephone call that evening which instantly erased my sense of well-being and replaced it with anxiety. ABWE's president, Dr. Wendell Kempton, called to tell me that Dr. Donn Ketcham had suffered a heart attack at Malumghat! "Vic," he continued, "could you possibly go out there to help? You are badly needed!"

"The answer is yes," I replied, "subject to Joan's agreement. If I have any different thoughts after discussing it with her, I'll call you back. Otherwise, I will depart as soon as possible. Thanks for the call."

I was soon on my way across the Pacific to Manila where I was met by dear friends and colleagues Russ and Nancy Ebersole. As my connecting flight did not leave until the next day, I spent much of the afternoon touring a private school called Faith Academy. After a two-hour meeting with the school superintendent and a careful look at the lovely facilities, I was satisfied that this would be a fine place for our Mark and Nancy to attend high school after we returned to Bangladesh in the spring. For two years we had been deeply concerned about locating a truly suitable high school for them in Asia; suddenly I had found it and that concern had evaporated. On the path of duty I had stumbled onto the solution to our problem. "Thank You, Father!"

The next day I departed from Manila headed for Hong Kong. As I clicked my seat belt in place, a young American woman found her assigned seat occupied by another person. To avoid confusion the stewardess directed her to another seat—next to mine. She was weeping, for she had just said good-bye to her husband, a U.S. Navy man. Little by little, as we talked, Helen regained her composure. I discovered that she was a person with an open and ready heart, quite attuned to spiritual issues. It seemed so natural to share my faith with her and explain some of the wondrous benefits of following Christ the Lord. Halfway to Hong Kong she bowed to pray silently and made the great faith decision. More tears—but of joy this time. I spent the last half of the journey explaining basic truths important for a new follower of Christ to understand. We were so absorbed in our conversation that we hardly touched the dinners put before us. In my next letter home I asked Joan to send appropriate books to help her grow in her newfound faith.

In Hong Kong I went shopping for an electrocardiograph (ECG) machine; I felt a strong sense of urgency about doing so. If our hospital's two older models both happened to be out of order, we would find it difficult to guide Donn through his post-heart-attack period. I purchased a sturdy, well-designed, Japanese portable model that could easily be carried as hand luggage. Three days later I would learn that my inner urge to purchase this ECG machine must have been inspired.

The next day I flew into Dacca, Bangladesh. As soon as possible I visited with Mr. Q. J. ("Jalal") Ahmed and his family. What a delight to be with this beloved family who are as close as brother and sister to Joan and me. Jalal was disheartened by the situation prevailing in his country. He explained that the nation was passing through three stages: disappointment followed by disillusionment, which was rapidly turning to despair.

That evening I flew from Dacca to Chittagong to be received at the airport by most of our ABWE team. All the kids came running out on the field, and I was inundated with little arms and legs and sweet words of welcome; I was glad that I had candy bars for each of them in my suitcase. How we all enjoyed each other's company during a welcome party that evening. There were so many things to talk about.

Jay and Eleanor Walsh drove me to Malumghat the next morning. They were veterans who had served in Bangladesh even longer than Joan and I had. Jay was not only an administrator, but also a theological teacher and head of the tribal work; as Jay and I were both involved in administration and both connected to the tribal program, we often worked together. Eleanor was a fine pianist and nurse who majored on being a homemaker and caring for their seven children. As we arrived at the hospital Bangladeshi co-workers converged from all sides—Shorno, Shubash, Meri, Goni, Momin, and many more. I was home!

Then I visited Donn and Kitty Ketcham. Donn was medical director that year, a responsibility each doctor has to shoulder in his turn. Donn, a skilled surgeon, had been extremely busy until the day of his heart attack—at age forty-two. Kitty is a homemaker and artist; she used her fine artistic talent to benefit various mission departments.

Donn had recovered from the acute symptoms of his heart attack and was resting at home. He looked fine. When I checked his

Jay and Eleanor Walsh

Dr. Donn Ketcham, surgeon

Artist Kitty Ketcham

pulse, however, I found it to be very irregular. How fortunate that I had purchased the new ECG machine! Both of our hospital machines were, in fact, out of order. I attached to his limbs and chest the leads of the neat new Fukuda portable and obtained a vivid, clear tracing. As I feared, the ECG revealed numerous extra beats —and they were a particularly dangerous type of beat that seriously increased his chances of complications or even sudden death. We prescribed appropriate medication and more rest. Wonderfully, that drug so quickly controlled the troublesome extra beats that I could soon start Donn on an aggressive exercise program. "Thank You, Father!"

Also during the last week of January, an old friend came to talk. Robichandro Tippera, a respected Christian member of the Tippera (or Tripura) tribe, was working as a *darwan* (watchman) for the hospital. This Christian layman, however, had a heart for his fellow hill men and an intense concern for their spiritual welfare. He wanted them to know God's love, to stop worshiping trees and rivers, and to cease making useless animal sacrifices to appease the evil spirits. Furthermore, Robi possessed two gifts. First, despite being illiterate, he could teach and preach Biblical truth quite skillfully using a set of large, vivid picture cards. Secondly, he could fluently speak Mogh, the tribal trade language, and even

Robichandro with his picture cards

teach and preach in it. Hill people from all the tribes could understand this trade language; even Murungs (also called Mrus), the most aboriginal of all the tribals, could understand Mogh. His eyes sparkling, Robi began to pour out his story:

"You may have noticed that there are quite a few Murungs staying on the hospital property. Because of famine in the Chittagong hills they came here to get work. I saw my opportunity. Even though I am a Tippera and cannot speak their Murung language, I knew they would understand me if I taught them using the Mogh language. So I began my teaching sessions.

"Night after night, when the day's work was done I explained God's Word to six Murung men. I taught them about the foolishness of worshiping objects and explained the wonderful story of Christ and His love for them, and the true sacrifice of Himself that He made for them. Night after night I preached to them—but there was no response. Finally, after more than two weeks, three Murung men said they wanted to follow Christ."

Robi then explained how he took the three scantily-clad Murungs (Menshai, Adoi, and Changkaw) aside to talk further. Earnestly they said, "We believe. List us as Christians."

But, wanting to be completely sure about their sincerity, Robi responded, "No, think some more about whether or not you are really serious about this. There is no value in being *mukh* (mouth) believers."

"We have thought about it for quite a few days," the Murungs expostulated. "We agree with your words that we have sinned. We have made blood sacrifices, and we have worshiped rocks and trees. Now we are putting all that behind us and will follow the true path you have taught us. We will be Christ's Murungs."

Still wanting to be absolutely certain of the sincerity and stability of their change of heart, Robi declared, "But you must think about it for three more days."

During those three days fifteen new Murungs emerged from the forests and jungles of the Chittagong hills to obtain work at Malumghat and to hear this fascinating new message. Each night Robi preached his heart out to them in the dim light of a flickering oil lamp. On the third night, skillfully using his brightly-colored pictures and his fluency in the Mogh language, he taught them about the birth of Christ and about His good news message. Just as Robi neared the end of his riveting sermon, Menshai Murung leaped to his feet to cry, "Let me say something to my Murung brothers."

Passionately, in his own Murung tongue, Menshai testified to the truth and beauty of this new message, how superior it was to their old ways, and how he personally had come to believe in the message and in Christ who had given Himself as the ultimate blood sacrifice. That night five more Murung men decided that they would follow Christ.

Then, when Robi did not act quickly enough on their request to be considered true believers, the three original Murungs decided to talk over their situation with the head of the mission's Tribal Committee, Jay Walsh. This was the first news any missionary had heard about these fascinating developments; Robi had been carrying on his work completely on his own initiative. Jay listened attentively, sensed the Murungs' deep sincerity, and felt that there was no question about the reality of their faith. By then Robi, too, was satisfied. What a memorable story! That night he began to teach the Murungs new truths that would foster their love for God and their spiritual growth.

Daily hundreds of patients were coming to the Outpatient Department for attention and dozens for admission to the hospital. One man with a markedly distended abdomen had been seriously ill for three weeks before coming to the hospital. After a careful medical history and physical examination I was sure that his duodenal ulcer had perforated, allowing the contents of his stomach to pour into his abdomen. I presumed that a substantial abscess had developed. After preparing him for surgery with intravenous fluids and large doses of antibiotics, I took him to the operating room and explored his abdomen—my first operation in many months. I hit a gusher! More than three quarts of pus burst forth from the dangerous abscess. He would be all right now.

Other ominous pockets of infection were threatening—and snuffing out—lives throughout the land. I speak of the radical pro-Peking Communists who were still busily attempting to foment revolution in Bangladesh. Because they had not gained enough strength to launch a frontal attack on the army or Rakkhi Bahini, they continued to assassinate Awami League leaders here and there and to attack buses, launches, and police outposts. They had murdered more than eighteen hundred people during the previous year.

In Dacca near the end of January, an unpleasant incident happened involving Major Dalim, one of the three army majors who would play leading roles in the attempt on Mujib's life eighteen months later.[2] Dalim, his attractive wife Tasmin, and many others from the upper crust of Dacca society were enjoying a wedding reception at the Dacca Ladies' Club. Both Dalim and his wife and their families were very close to Sheikh Mujib and his family. Because Dalim's mother had died when he was a child, he looked to Mrs. Mujib as his mother substitute. "I lost my mother when I was a boy. Now you are my mother," he had told her.[3]

G. G. Mustafa was also very close to Mujib—and also present at the reception. He was not only the powerful boss of the Awami League's Dacca City machine, but also the chairman of the Bangladesh Red Cross. For some reason or other, a relative of Mustafa's who was with him at the reception insulted Tasmin. Dalim reacted, and in the scuffle that ensued Mustafa's strong-arm men roughed up the major and his wife. Then, when Mustafa took Dalim and his wife to Mujib's house, Dalim complained bitterly about the verbal and physical insults. But Mujib showed him little sympathy, insisted that they all cool down, and made Dalim and Mustafa shake hands. He then passed candy to everyone. Dalim was furious!

Meanwhile some of Dalim's fellow officers filled two trucks with troops, raced around town looking for Mustafa's toughs, and finally broke into his house and ransacked it. Although Dalim claimed he had nothing to do with vandalizing Mustafa's house, Mujib was angry with him and his fellow officers. But he took no action at that time.

February 1974 was an important month jam-packed with activities. On the first Saturday, after my ward rounds were completed, Robichandro Tippera and I jumped into a jeep, drove on the main highway two miles south to Dulahazara bazaar, then turned left on a fair-weather road heading toward the Chittagong hills. For two miles the road proceeded through flat rice land, then plunged sharply down to the flowing waters of a river shallow enough to ford by jeep, because this was the dry season. Shifting into four-wheel drive, I accelerated down the hill and slammed into the water, sending sheets of spray shimmering and sparkling in the bright sunlight. Although the muddy bottom sucked greedily at the heavy-duty tires, the four powerful, grinding wheels readily conquered the mud. Our jeep emerged from the water dripping, then roared up the far bank and buzzed merrily along for another mile before the road petered out.

We parked the jeep and walked the last mile through fields and wooded slopes to Hargaza Village, which straddles the boundary line between Chittagong District and the Chittagong Hill Tracts District. Hargaza was a Mogh (Marma) tribal village. Here nine families had decided to follow Christ in the wake of the Bangladesh Brigade project; a mile further in a neighboring village (Headman Village) five other Mogh families also had determined they would be His followers.

We enjoyed the company of these tribal Christians, who could interact easily with us because of Robi's expertise in the Mogh language. And we had a long talk with the Buddhist *carbari* (village leader) who agreed that teachers were welcome to come to instruct the Christian group. We promised that we would return the next week to begin this training program.

I spent the next afternoon talking with two Bengali men from the offshore island of Kutubdia. Daniel had migrated to the hospital years before and, through an unusual mystical experience, had become an earnest follower of Christ the Lord. Thereafter he had suffered much persecution. On one occasion I had to rescue him from a tumultuous mob of eight hundred people. However, none of this had deterred his quiet, steady spiritual growth. The other man, a carpenter, still lived with his family on Kutubdia Island. He, too, had become a follower of Christ. The two men reported excitedly that through their discussions and sharing they were able to have a positive influence on a handful of men on Kutubdia.

In Dacca the winter session of the National Assembly continued on into February. Early that month the Assembly passed a law called the Special Powers Act.[4] This strong act empowered the government to imprison a person to prevent him from committing a crime (preventive detention), to control the media, and to curtail the freedom of association of Bangalees. Severe penalties were stipulated for hoarding and dealing in the black market. And a whole new set of courts (special tribunals) were created to try offenses under this act. Later in the year this strict legislation was made even tougher. The opposition parties protested indignantly that the Mujib government was destroying the country's democracy with these restrictive laws.

On the same day that the Special Powers Act was passed the secretary general of the Islamic Conference arrived in Dacca to invite Bangladeshi leaders to attend the Islamic Summit meetings, which would convene in two to three weeks in Pakistan. Bangladesh forthrightly declined on the grounds that Pakistan had not yet granted diplomatic recognition to Bangladesh. But there was some indication that other Muslim nations might apply pressure on Pakistan's Bhutto to recognize Bangladesh.

Two days later I received a small patient with an unusual injury. The ten-year-old Muslim boy had been attacked by a *sambar* (large deer) that had been kept chained up as a family pet. The lightning thrust of the deer's antler had impaled the boy, leaving two penetrating wounds in his right lower chest. A soiled, bloody cloth was wrapped around the dirty chest wounds; air was sucked noisily in and out of the wounds with every breath. The boy was very short of breath and lay gasping and groaning with his eyes tightly closed. I noted that he was extremely pale from severe chronic anemia—and his abdomen was rigid and tender.

Pet sambar

I cleaned and bandaged the boy's wounds in a special way to prevent any more air from being sucked into his chest. But, because his blood donors unaccountably disappeared for several hours, I could not begin his surgery until the evening. During the operation I expanded his lung, then trimmed and sutured the vicious chest wounds; I also explored his abdomen to confirm that the antler had not penetrated that far. Within a few days our little patient was well and able to return home, where I am sure he kept his distance from the rambunctious sambar.

Two days later two special people were married. Shabitri, because of a difficult family situation, had lived for several years with nurses Mary Lou Brownell and Becky Davey. Mary Lou and Becky had experienced the usual joys and trials of raising a teenager. During the wedding festivities Becky served as the mother of the bride. The bridegroom, Gonijan, was a member of the Tippera tribe. Because he was a brilliant student and because some missionaries had helped finance his education, he had completed high school and graduated with an excellent record. I had led him to Christ as a teenager on the verandah of our home. And, during several years of training, his spiritual growth was so rapid and his spiritual maturity so outstanding that he had been elected as one of the three pastors of the church in the Malumghat area—and later became the senior pastor. This was notable because Bengalis tend to feel superior to tribal people and would not ordinarily select a tribesman to be senior pastor of a primarily Bengali church.

At 10:00 A.M. the ladies carried out the traditional ceremony of washing the bride with yellow water. As usual, the women soon began hilariously chasing one another and splashing yellow-colored water upon each other until all were drenched. By 1:00 P.M. they had cleaned up the mess and began dressing the bride and painting intricate patterns on her face. An hour later the wedding took place in the elaborately-decorated hospital chapel. Outside, a Bengali sign announced "Happy Wedding." The chapel was packed. The lovely ceremony included admonitions from Scripture, prayer, the signing of official papers, and the exchange of vows, rings, and garlands. The bride was so happy she found it difficult to look suitably somber. Of course, whatever her religion, every Bengali bride is expected to look sad and tearful because leaving her father's house permanently is so distressing to her. The festivities were capped off by a wedding feast in the evening.

Next morning the observance of the Lord's Supper (Communion) was especially moving to me. First of all, we had delayed celebrating this ordinance at Malumghat until the national church had been officially formed and established; church formation had occurred during our home leave. This, then, was the first time that I had received the Lord's Supper at Malumghat. And the pastor who served me the bread and the cup was Gonijan. What a vivid example of the value of training young men to become capable leaders! Incidentally, there is no grape juice in Bangladesh; so the tiny cups contained a tropical fruit juice made from bottled concentrate, the closest available substitute.

That afternoon Robichandro Tippera and I returned to the Mogh villages. But this time we just greeted our Hargaza friends,

Becky Davey, "mother of the bride"

Gonijan, the happy bridegroom

Shabitri, looking "suitably somber"

The old Mogh headman

explained that we would return later, then hiked on to Headman Village to meet with the Christian group there. Entering the village, I immediately spotted the old headman sitting in a chair on an elevated area; he was ancient. A headman is a more important dignitary than a carbari, because he is the head of a *mouza* (subcounty), which contains more than one village. We met him and various Christian and Buddhist heads of households, then conducted an informal teaching service, which all attended.

I was impressed with Robi and his presentation. At more sophisticated Malumghat, where he is surrounded by educated Bengalis and Americans, he is quiet and reserved. But when he stepped into this tribal village his personality changed instantly. He became strong, confident, and forceful—he was the teacher! His interesting message touched on several themes, including the concept of eternal life.

Next it was my turn. I spoke in Bengali and Robi interpreted in Mogh. "Robichandro," I began, "has mentioned to you the matter of everlasting life. I, too, want to emphasize the high importance of this special life which goes on forever. So let me read to you a small section of the Holy Scriptures, a section that is the favorite passage of people of many tribes and nations throughout the world:

> "For God so loved the world that He gave His only begotten Son, that whoever believes in Him should not perish but have everlasting life."[5]

I explained the passage. Knowing that the Buddhist listeners considered life a dismal affair, and knowing that they were struggling and longing for the cessation of all desire (even the very extinction of life itself in the nothingness of *nirvana*), I described the peace and gladness to be enjoyed in that eternal life beyond the grave—in the somethingness of a place called heaven.

Then I shifted gears. "As we walked into your village," I continued, "I immediately noticed your highly respected elderly headman. And this thought struck me: *He is a very aged man. I wonder whether we will be able to return to this village enough times before he leaves this world for him to properly understand and obtain eternal life.*"

At this, a peculiar, wide-eyed expression came over the old headman's face. Standing shakily, he stepped down from the elevated area where he was seated, tottered over to where I was standing, then fell to the ground before me. Clutching my feet he repeated again and again, "Eternal life. I must have it! Help me to find it!"

I was shaken by this unexpected turn of events; because I knew little of Mogh culture, I cast about in my mind for the best way to handle this situation. First, I helped the old gentleman gently to his feet and back to his chair; then I explained Christ's good news message to him from two or three different angles until I was sure that he understood it. Finally I said, "I can see that you are very moved, my friend, but I want you to do something. Every day this next week I want you to think about what you have learned, then decide definitely if you are ready to become a follower of Christ. Face the fact that you may suffer persecution for following Him. When we return in seven days you can settle the matter."

The old gentlemen thanked me profusely and, as we left, the Mogh Christians pointed out a possible location for a "Jesus house" (church building). Then we walked back to Hargaza Village, taught the group there, and returned to Malumghat tired but exhilarated.

The next morning I was up very early to tackle another busy Monday. Outside the Outpatient Department I carried out the painful *triage*—an old French word meaning "There is no way we can take care of all of you patients today, so I will have to pick out the sickest ones." The triage involved selecting the two hundred most seriously ill patients, then telling the others to return the following morning. That night, exhausted after the very busy day, I finally had time to slow down a bit—and feel very lonely for Joan and my children. Just then, on the Rangoon, Burma, radio station someone began to sing, "I am so lonesome for you, darling, and you know that letters have no arms." He done sung a mouthful!

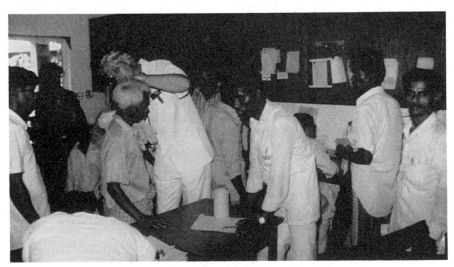

Another busy Monday—Vic in the OPD

On Wednesday, our main elective surgical day, I took a Muslim teenager to the operating room; her abdominal tumor made the emaciated girl look about thirteen months pregnant. Then the incision. A great white watermelon-sized tumor, growing from the left ovary, filled her abdomen. After removal, the fluid-filled tumor tipped the scales at twenty-three pounds and contained nine quarts of liquid. The family was euphoric to learn that she would get well and be able to marry and, probably, also to bear children.

The next Sunday morning the sun rose bright and clear over Malumghat. After the morning church service I met with the Murung tribals at Robi's request. We sat down on the ground in a shady area and a dozen Murung men took their seats in a semicircle around us; some of the group were new Christians and others had arrived recently to hear this new, exciting message. A middle-aged man had confided to Robi that he was eager to hear but would not want to make any decision until his sons came.

Just then another dozen Murung men, including the two sons, arrived fresh from the hills and jungles of the Chittagong Hill Tracts. They had been on the trail for two or three days. These Murungs were a wild, handsome group of men encumbered only with G-strings and packs on their backs. Each man's four-foot-long hair was expertly wound in a bun on top of his head and either skewered with a giant comb or covered by a turban. Some of them had colored their cheeks and foreheads with red dye. The long hair, painted cheeks, and the jungle flowers jutting from the holes in their earlobes made them look almost female from the neck up —but their deep chests, strong legs, and powerful muscles affirmed that they were men indeed.

The newcomers joined the semicircle around us. With Robi interpreting, I reminded the sizable group of jungle men about their own venerable legend that the Murungs in ancient times had been granted scriptures by the great spirit, but those scriptures were written on a banana leaf and, sadly, a cow ate them. "But I am happy to tell you," I continued, "that the true Creator of the earth, sky, sun, and the jungle birds, animals, Murungs, and all the tribes of the world has given His true Scriptures to all men, and these Scriptures have survived to this day. In fact, I have a copy in my hand this morning." The giant combs and turbans bounced as they nodded and turned to look at each other with approval.

Opening the pages of the New Testament in my hand, I read several of the key passages that emphasized the existence of God, His mighty power to do good, and His ability to control the evil forces that afflicted them; then I read other selections that laid out Christ's good news message of forgiveness of sins. More bobbing turbans and combs. I suppose an onlooker would have thought it a strange sight—an American surgeon speaking in Bengali to

Murung young man

Turbaned Murung man

bronzed Murung tribesmen, using a Tippera interpreter who conveyed the message in the Mogh language. Some were hearing the timeless message for the first time. And some believed. "Thank You, Father!" I had appreciated this opportunity to teach these tribal men, an experience Jay Walsh often enjoyed.

That afternoon Robi and I retraced our jeep trip through the fields and across the river to the two Mogh villages, Hargaza and Headman Village. We entered Headman Village with an inner sense of high drama and anticipation of learning what the old headman had decided after reflecting coolly for a week about whether or not to follow Christ—after seven days of counting the cost.

One look at the old gentleman's face told me that his decision was affirmative. He explained that he had not agonized at all over the decision, but was prepared to tolerate any persecution that came along. It would be a small price to pay for gaining eternal life. As we prayed together the old gentleman uttered a prayer of repentance and faith, then thanked the Giver of every good and perfect gift for granting him a new forever-life. In the teaching meeting that followed, the old headman announced to his people, "I've been a Buddhist for many long years, but Buddha never did a thing for me. Today I have put my faith in Christ the Lord, and I hope all the rest of you will do likewise." Some months later the

The headman uttered a prayer of repentance and faith

old gentleman went on to glory; I look forward to getting to know him better some day.

Prior to the second Islamic Summit meetings, Arab delegations arrived in Pakistan and began to pressure Pakistan's Bhutto to grant diplomatic recognition to Bangladesh. On February 21 delegates of several Arab countries then flew to Dacca to convince Mujib to drop his plan to try the 195 Pakistani POWs. This would trigger Pakistan's diplomatic recognition of Bangladesh and allow Bangladesh to afford reciprocal recognition to Pakistan. Then Mujib could lead his delegation to the Islamic Summit Conference in Lahore, Pakistan. Apparently Mujib privately agreed to this proposal, but made no public announcement of his intention to drop the war crimes trials. The next day Bhutto proclaimed Pakistan's diplomatic recognition of Bangladesh, a decision hailed by world leaders. A day later, Mujib and his delegation flew to the Islamic Summit meetings; in Lahore Mujib embraced Bhutto and invited him to visit Bangladesh.

On that weekend, as the Islamic nations were meeting, Jay Walsh, Daniel, and I took a fascinating trip to Kutubdia Island. We traveled by jeep thirteen miles north, then turned left on a dirt road for twelve miles toward the ocean (see figure 15).

Daniel and Vic en route to Kutubdia

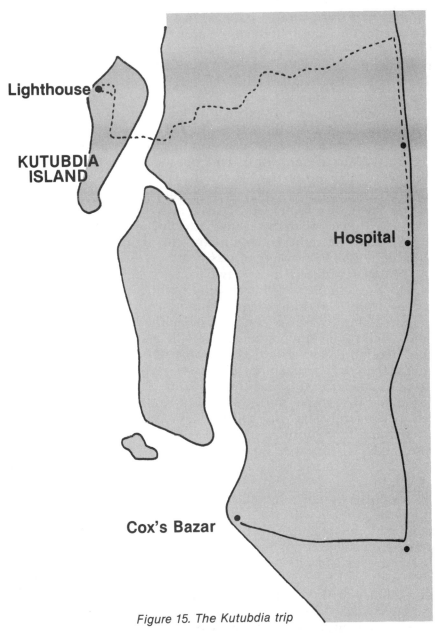

Figure 15. The Kutubdia trip

We passed through beautiful high hills, then descended to low land where the road finally stopped. We walked a mile, then rented a sampan to cross the three-mile channel between the island and the mainland; our sampan trip lasted more than an hour. A mile or two walk took us to the home of the high school principal who also served as chairman of the Kutubdia branch of the Awami League political party. The hospitable principal received us warmly, fed us, then took us by motor rickshaw to a major bazaar in the northern part of the island. In the large crowd there to greet us I noticed familiar faces of some who had come to us as patients. Then we met "county" officials, teachers, and other assorted dignitaries. They made an official request that we establish a clinic or small hospital on the island.

At sundown we were taken for a long walk to see the imposing lighthouse located by the sea on the northwest side of the island. This ancient structure had been standing for fifteen years when the U.S. Civil War began, for it had been constructed in 1846. We climbed to the top of the lighthouse and enjoyed a breathtaking view of the ocean and much of the island. With the wind blowing in our faces, Jay remarked, "This really brings back memories. When we first came to this country in 1960 our ship was approaching the coast at night; the light from this lighthouse was the very first bit of East Pakistan that we saw."

We then walked a mile or two from the lighthouse to the home of our friend the Kutubdia carpenter. While his wife and children served us an elaborate dinner, many local dignitaries and other visitors came to see us and get acquainted. Then the carpenter said, "Tell my neighbors and these officials the story about Jesus the Messiah." So we told the people about another carpenter, Christ the Lord, and explained his wonderful good news message. To our knowledge this was the first time that foreigners had ever explained this gospel on the island of Kutubdia. Later that night we met several men who had been impressed by the teaching of Daniel and the Kutubdia carpenter. We slept that night on rock-hard beds.

The next morning I saw many patients, and we enjoyed substantial breakfasts at three different homes. People told us about the recent visit of a religious crook named Jinn Fakir. A *fakir* is a religious person who goes about begging; this one apparently claimed to be in contact with the *jinn* (spirits) and may have used ventriloquism to simulate a conversation with them. Jinn Fakir had succeeded in bilking the people out of 12,000 takas ($1,500); they were still furious about it. After warm good-byes we retraced our journey to Malumghat and slept long and hard that night.

A few days later I was called from my ward rounds to do some unexpected surgery—on three cows who had been slashed by the *da* (machete) of their owner's enemy. While onlookers chortled we knelt on the ground to suture the lowing creatures' lacerations. That afternoon I saw upper-class private patients from Chittagong City and elsewhere. No one can tell what a day will bring forth at Malumghat.

As February drew to a close I managed to send Joan roses for her birthday by cabling a helpful friend in the U.S. At the same

The Kutubdia carpenter

time our new American personnel in Chittagong were plugging away at their Bengali language lessons. Among them were Dr. Dick and Carol Stagg, dear friends from Toledo, Ohio. I was not sure whether they were encouraged or discouraged to discover a myna bird speaking quite fluent Bengali—and a dog who could roll over in both English and Bengali.[6] Learning Bengali is no small task, for the grammar is complex, the vocabulary immense, and there are over 40 basic letters in the alphabet plus more than 250 combination letters.

The next week I crossed the highway in front of the hospital and hiked a mile to the area called *Cha Bagan* (tea garden). No tea had grown there for decades, but a new crop of houses dotted the wide area. Our hospital had purchased more than twenty-five acres of this land to divide into plots for sale to our employees. We loaned them money to purchase plots and build their mud-walled, tin-roofed houses. Then through payroll deductions they could pay off their "mortgages" in less than ten years and own their houses and land outright. That beats the thirty-year mortgages that Americans must repay. Through this program valued workers could come from other districts and become rooted in the land near the hospital. Thus these Bangalee co-workers could remain in the area and carry on their church and possibly the medical mission in the event that we foreigners ever had to leave Bangladesh.

Mud-walled house in Cha Bagan

I was thrilled to see the attractive new houses, each on as much as an acre of land. As I visited friends in the various homes, I noted their pride of ownership and their neat, prolific gardens. Also I noticed a high, flat, empty area overlooking much of Cha Bagan and thought immediately, *What a beautiful place for a church building! There must be one here someday.* The church members having their own church building on their own property near their homes could only strengthen the church and be a great improvement over meeting in the hospital chapel. In the months that followed church leaders selected that exact site, and the church building in Cha Bagan ultimately emerged from idea-land into reality.

The weekend merged into another pressure Monday—crowds in the Outpatient Department and the wards overflowing with inpatients. On my ward rounds I found an anxious Maulvi Idris at the bedside of his tetanus-racked son. A *Maulvi* is an orthodox Muslim who has been educated in a *madrassa* (Muslim religious school). Maulvi Idris is principal of the senior madrassa ten miles away in the town of Idgaon. He is a kindly, warm-hearted, soft-spoken, white-haired gentleman, a fine person and a good friend. I comforted him and prayed that his precious child might survive; ultimately that prayer was answered—affirmatively.

In the afternoon I sutured up the knee of another anxious man—he had fallen for an instant while being chased by a raging bull elephant in the jungle a few miles away. He was fortunate to escape, for elephants usually win such races.

On March 7 I awakened at 5:45 A.M. with no sleep left in me. So I focused on a project which had been given to me by Moody Press—adapting chapters 5 and 6 of *Daktar* into a separate, small book to be called *The Agnostic Who Dared to Search.* This book would tell the story of our spiritual pilgrimage. For some time I had been unsure how best to adapt these chapters. But as the dawn light filtered into my room that morning I could see in an instant just how to do it.

Later that day two other good things happened. After being starved for mail throughout a twenty-one day postal strike, the strike finally ended and I received a great letter from Joan—dated a month earlier. Later in the day an unexpected short-term surgeon named Dr. Everett Sugarbaker and his youngest son, Steve, arrived out of the blue. Everett was a first-rate surgeon who had invented surgical instruments and written excellent scientific papers, which I had read over the years. We had never received the cable announcing the time of his coming.

The next morning I took Everett on detailed rounds of all the patients. The staff obligingly had all the patients' X rays ready, our notes on the charts were up-to-date, and most of the patients were doing quite well, despite the seriousness of their operations and illnesses. At lunch he spoke of his reaction to all that he had seen and finished with "I'm impressed!" Apparently he expected to find a more primitive level of care in backward southern Bangladesh.

Because I had the weekend duty, I was awakened at four o'clock Saturday morning to send a note advising the midwife how to handle an obstetrical problem. As I wanted to test a new camera in various situations, still clad in my pajamas I set up a tripod and

Roof pour—the endless circular human chain

took multiple pictures of the luscious full moon. Later in the morning I photographed Murungs and others doing the "pour" of the roof of the new women's residence. Bearing pans of wet concrete on their heads, the men made an endless circular human chain clambering up the bamboo ladders, dumping their headpans of concrete, then climbing down for the next refill.

That night two emergency cases required attention. I first had to operate on a Hindu child with a severely fractured skull; her uncle had viciously thrown a club at a pesky chicken, but hit her instead. I closed out the night's surgery by taking a Muslim woodcutter to the operating room; the powerful jaws and teeth of the fierce bear that had attacked him in the forest had broken the woodcutter's right arm and left leg.

The next day, after the Sunday services, I suggested to Everett Sugarbaker that he come to the operating room at 2:00 P.M. to see a case different from any he had ever seen. The patient was an elderly woman whose nasal cavities had become infested with maggots. As I plucked wriggling maggots out of her nose one by one with a surgical forceps, Everett readily agreed that he had never before seen such a case. Using my camera he photographed the procedure for me. During his time with us Everett did his own share of interesting cases and we enjoyed good surgical camaraderie and spiritual fellowship.

The next weekend a jeepload of us traveled fifteen miles to visit a Bengali village. Our invitation had come from Dr. Q., the minimally-trained physician of that village. For more than a year he had been avidly studying Biblical materials given to him by church members. Fascinated by Christ and His teachings, he had become His disciple. He invited us to his village to share with his neighbors the truths which he had found so compelling.

Awaiting us was a huge crowd of villagers and area political leaders—plus local religious priests, who appeared somewhat skeptical about the whole affair. Dr. Q. stood and addressed the throng on religious subjects for a while. Then his effusive introduction ended with some embarrassing hyperbole: "Dr. Olsen," he announced, "is the number two doctor in the world!" (I forgot to ask him who was number one.)

In my address I simply explained my own spiritual pilgrimage from agnosticism to Christian faith with an emphasis on the identity of Christ the Lord and His good news message. Then Jesse Eaton, our hospital administrator, made some excellent comments on related topics. Later we answered many questions and interacted with a number of individuals; I particularly enjoyed talking with the religious priests and responding to their questions. We returned home that night tired but happy about the new friendships we had made.

The next week I received a letter from Joan about a man wide-ly known for his beautiful reading of various books on the air; he had begun the reading of *Daktar* over a dozen radio stations across the U.S. Joan's letter included these poignant words:

> Today Myron Canaday read the end of chapter 6 and some of chapter 7. I was quite touched that the story of our baby's death was read on the air exactly on the twenty-second anniversary of his dying. The Lord and I were the only ones who knew about it. It really meant something to me, for it seemed quite apart from the laws of chance. Sort of a memorial.

And I remembered vividly the devastating day our firstborn infant son had died; I would have given anything I possessed that day to save his life.

The next morning I admitted to the hospital a newborn infant who was unable to swallow his feedings properly. As I could not pass a catheter down to the baby's stomach, I knew he had been born with an obstruction in his esophagus (swallowing tube). X rays confirmed the diagnosis, so I started the wheels rolling so that we could operate on him within twenty-four hours.

The next morning I still did not have a parental consent to operate on the baby. The mother was there, but a Muslim woman in southern Bangladesh has no right to sign an operative permit, even on her own baby. When the father finally came, I noticed that he, like Idris, was a *maulvi*. After I had carefully explained the seri-ousness and urgency of his baby's problem and the need for him to sign the consent and donate a unit of blood, I was amazed at his harsh response. Unlike Maulvi Idris, he showed no sympathy or concern for his dying son. Well aware that it spelled certain death for the lovely baby, he adamantly refused to sign the consent or donate blood. His attitude and manner were so insufferable that I could not restrain myself from giving him a tongue-lashing—which is quite the opposite of our usual approach. Inwardly I justi-fied myself with the recollection that even our Lord had sternly rebuked the very religious but wrong-minded Pharisees; there is a place for occasional righteous indignation.

Joan's late March letters commented on the Kodachrome film I had been sending to her for processing. One box of slides she had whimsically entitled "Moons and Maggots." When the children saw this group of pictures they exclaimed, "Oh, Mother, look at all those pictures of the full moon; Dad is really lonely for you. But yuch! Look at the weird things he picks out of people to keep him-self busy."

We continued to observe striking signs of the progressive breakdown of law and order. In early April relatives excitedly brought in a forty-year-old Bengali man with ten holes in his body. During an attack by armed robbers he had been hit with five bullets from a high-powered automatic weapon; the bullets passed right through his arms, legs, chest, and liver. Although in English we say he was "hit with five bullets," the Bengali idiom is "he ate five bullets." He must have been really hungry—for trouble. Twice on the operating table his heart stopped beating—cardiac arrest! But we succeeded each time in getting it restarted. We were all thankful when he survived and ultimately made a good recovery.

During that same week a two-man team arrived to take ten thousand feet of moving picture film that would then be used to produce a film about our various activities. Jim Ferguson, the producer, and photographer Jerry Calloway were both fine men who fit right in with our team. They filmed almost continuously for ten days and I spent hours dictating information about the land of Bangladesh and our work among its people so that the script writer would have ample facts.

On Palm Sunday Jerry and Jim filmed the moving baptism ceremony of the first four Murung believers. By then these jungle men had taken seriously the Biblical teaching that if a man has long hair it is a dishonor to him; they had whacked off most of their four-foot-long tresses. Their mentor Robichandro did the baptizing while Bengalis, Americans, and other Murungs looked on. What a memorable occasion!

Jim Ferguson, film producer

Jerry Calloway shooting footage

Robi baptizing Menshai Murung

On their way out of the country the film team ran into an unexpected snag with a senior Chittagong Customs official. The three-striper pointed out, "Our checklist of all this photographic equipment you brought into the country is in the hands of an officer who is at home in bed. So I see no way to help you get the necessary clearance for it. What can I possibly do?"

I replied, "You can trust me and believe my declaration that the list which we have is the true duplicate of the missing list. After all, friend, you have known me for years." Smiling, he accepted our list, checked the serial number on only one camera, then passed the whole pile of equipment. Jim and Jerry departed—and they were smiling, too.

While the two men had been filming our work in Chittagong District, 240 miles to the north the sudden chatter of automatic weapons terrified the students and faculty of venerable Dacca University. Trigger fingers did not ease until seven blood-drenched university students lay dead! They were all members of an organization of young Awami Leaguers—slain, not by radical Communists, but by a rival group of young Awami Leaguers.[7] So the senseless killing of young people had reached a new level of insanity, and Bangladesh continued to be *rawktodesh*—nation of blood.

On April 9, 1974, the foreign ministers of Bangladesh, India, and Pakistan meeting in New Delhi, India, signed the historic "Tri-

partite Agreement" concerning the soldiers and civilians who had
been detained in Pakistan, India, and Bangladesh.[8] The three foreign ministers first noted that nearly 300,000 persons already had
been repatriated to their home countries over the previous seven
months since the signing of the Delhi Agreement. Regarding the
unwanted Bihari settlers in Bangladesh, the Pakistan side had finally agreed to receive certain categories of them. This would leave
about 250,000 Biharis stuck in Bangladesh but longing to move to
Pakistan, in addition to the 400,000 who had opted to remain in
Bangladesh.

Regarding the 195 prisoners of war remaining in Indian POW
camps, Pakistan's Bhutto appealed to the people of Bangladesh to
forgive and forget the mistakes of the past in an effort to promote
reconciliation. Furthermore, a representative of Pakistan said that
his government deeply regretted any crimes that might have been
committed. In response to this apology and the appeal of Bhutto,
the foreign minister of Bangladesh declared that his government
had, as an act of clemency, decided not to proceed with the war
crimes trials. This was a bit humiliating for Bangladesh, because
for over two years the government had repeatedly promised that
the guilty Pakistani soldiers would be tried and convicted for their
war crimes.

By this time Donn Ketcham had recovered from his heart attack and was able to see patients, so I began packing my bags. My
last day at Malumghat was an elective surgery day. The first case,
a nephrectomy (kidney removal), went smoothly. When I opened
the abdomen of the next patient, I found that tuberculosis had attacked and obstructed his intestine. Very few American surgeons
have ever seen such a case, for in America tuberculosis is well controlled. At the operating table I relieved the obstruction, then put
the patient on a regimen of strong anti-tuberculosis medications,
which ultimately cured him. That afternoon another of my patients, a quack doctor from Cox's Bazar, brought his version of payment: four chickens, two stalks of bananas, eggs, cookies, and
candy. How I would miss these great people until Joan and I could
get back three months later!

The next day I was off to Dacca. There I attended a reception
for newly arrived Davis Eugene Boster, the first full-fledged American ambassador to be posted to Bangladesh. The U.S. government
had by then upgraded the American consulate to a full embassy.
We had a good talk, and he requested a copy of *Daktar*. And I enjoyed a warm chat with Mr. and Mrs. Dan Newberry; Consul General Dan had been the ambassador's predecessor. The Newberrys
loved our team and the hospital; in fact, they had been visiting
Malumghat when Donn Ketcham's heart attack struck.

John Sircar

The next day I spoke with John Sircar, manager of our Literature Division, who had been accepted for theological studies in India. He was in Dacca trying to obtain approval from the Bangladesh government to spend the necessary weeks in India. The next morning I went with John to the Ministry of Education to request a recommendation letter to take to the immigration office.

"I am sorry," the officer said, "but I cannot help you. It is almost impossible for a Bangalee to get approval to leave the country and spend more than fifteen days in India. My only suggestion is that you try somehow to get the approval and signature of one of the ministers."

As we walked out I noticed that John was dejected. But he brightened up immediately when I told him that I had an appointment that very night to examine and prescribe for a minister. In the evening I met the food minister, who turned out to be Amirul Islam, the lawyer and Awami League member of Parliament who had escaped to India with Tajuddin during the 1971 war, and who had participated in drafting the Declaration of Independence and the Bangladesh Constitution. This was our first meeting. After a careful medical history, I examined him, made the diagnosis, prescribed medication, and had a lengthy discussion with him and his wife about his diet and related matters. They seemed grateful.

The next morning in the minister's office he kindly endorsed our application to the immigration office in his own handwriting and signed it. His notation began, "This is Dr. Olsen, Medical Director of Memorial Christian Hospital, who also treated me for my ailment. . . ." This letter worked like magic in the immigration department, and John was given his passport without delay and granted permission to study in India. "Thank You, Father!"

On another occasion I met the minister at a party at the home of Jalal Ahmed. While we were talking, Jalal's teenage daughter Bitu came up to greet us. "Bitu," the food minister exclaimed, "you are looking so thin!"

Without a second's hesitation she replied with a little smile, "True, Uncle; it is because you are not providing enough food for us."

On the day of my departure from Bangladesh I was up early to fly to Calcutta, India, then Bangkok, Thailand. Over the next three days I had stops in five other countries; then on April 30 I arrived in Chicago where Joan and the children met me at the airport. What a joyous reunion!

On that same April 30 many other glad reunions were taking place far away in the land of Pakistan. On that exact day the last of the 93,000 Pakistani POWs who had been imprisoned in India arrived home. Three days later the Pakistan government declared a special public holiday to celebrate the return of the POWs; this holiday they called "Thanksgiving Day."[9]

In the impressive pile of mail that had accumulated on my desk during my three months in Bangladesh I found the first copy of the paperback edition of *Daktar*. This was the deluxe paperback, which was larger than an ordinary mass paperback book and contained all the pictures; it was beautifully printed, and we were pleased. The smaller mass paperback edition would appear in the book stores, airports, pharmacies, and other outlets at a later date.

During that first week in May we began our countdown to complete that longer-than-usual furlough and return to Bangladesh for our third four-year term of service. So much to do during our last two months in the U.S.! Also during that week Joan, along with our daughters Lynne and Nancy, attended a church mother-daughter banquet. Lynne, a high-school senior, had a part in the program. Sitting at a desk on a stage decorated as a college room, she read a loving tribute letter she had written as a surprise to her mom. It was a moment for Joan to treasure always. When they returned home I could tell that Joan was feeling emotional, so I took her out for a long ride to talk.

The moving tribute letter, and the lovely mother-daughter time together had thrown into bold relief the fact that very soon our family would be scattered to far-distant spots on the globe, and we two would resume our work in Bangladesh—in a completely empty nest. Wendy would remain in the U.S. to work and Lynne to begin university. And, en route to Bangladesh, we would be dropping Mark and Nancy off at Faith Academy in the Philippines, for there was no suitable English-medium high school in Bangladesh. We commiserated together, sharing the anguish of the impending separation—by far the toughest part of foreign mission service!

Back in Bangladesh the Soviet salvage team finally completed clearing the bombed and sunken ships from the jetty areas of Chittagong Port; that would allow both imports and exports to increase greatly. And the Soviet crews would soon be returning to Russia.

May was also a big month for the Bangladesh military, for Mujib ordered the army into action to help the police and Rakkhi Bahini shut down the ubiquitous smuggling and terrorism. During the month these forces seized large amounts of smuggled goods and 7,700 weapons; they also arrested nearly 2,000 radical Communists, armed robbers, and smugglers.

Major Dalim, who fifteen months later would be a key player in the plot to kill Mujib, had been sent to Comilla, a town halfway between Dacca and Chittagong. When he and fellow officers captured some notable smugglers who claimed to be members of the Awami League,[10] they were so incensed that they allegedly bound

Bangladesh military seizes smuggled goods

the ankles of one smuggler and dragged him through the streets of Comilla. When Mujib learned of the officers' unprofessional conduct and their humiliation of the prisoner, he ordered the generals to discharge them—and Dalim became ex-major Dalim. Although the unpredictable Sheikh Mujib later helped set Dalim up in a business as a gesture to his family, Dalim's anger was not allayed.

In late May in Chicago Joan and I enjoyed attending the awards dinner of the Society of Midland Authors. This society presented its Distinguished Service Award for *Daktar*. While the master of ceremonies was describing the book in a generous way, I remembered vividly my "absolute zero" state and my intensely earnest prayer eleven months earlier: "Oh Father, what have I gotten myself into? I don't really know how to write this book. This task is far beyond me. Please keep me from messing it up and producing a fiasco."

"Thank You, Father!"

A few nights later we had as guests in our home Bob and Janice Goddard. Bob was a talented medical student with an earnest interest in medical missions. At their request we arranged for them to work at Malumghat during his senior year elective quarter; once there, they loved the people and the country. Years later Bob did another short-term stint at Malumghat, became a specialist in general surgery, and ultimately came with his family to work with us and serve the people of Bangladesh for a number of years.

During the first week in June Joan and I flew to Toledo for our final bittersweet visits with Joan's dad and mom before our return overseas. Then we traveled to Cedarville College in Cedarville, Ohio. At commencement, while I stood on the platform receiving an honorary degree, Joan, who was seated in the audience, was asked to stand. How I loved and appreciated her in that moment, as I remembered her loving ways and her intelligent, sacrificial input into our life's work. I could not keep from giving her a salute; despite the black robes and the dignity of the moment, from the platform I threw her a kiss.

From Cedarville Joan returned home, and I traveled to Dallas, Texas, where I was met by my friend film producer Jim Ferguson. Jim introduced me to Mal Couch, president of the film company, and I also met scriptwriter Marshall Riggan and read his script for our film.

The script was beautifully and artistically written. Some portions would be spoken by a professional narrator, whereas I would narrate other sections. After viewing several hours of Bangladesh footage, Jim and Marshall asked me what I thought. I replied, "The footage is lovely. And I want to congratulate you on the beautifully written script; I really like it. In fact, I have only two reservations.

First of all, my first-person sections don't always sound just like the words I would normally use, so I would like the opportunity to revise them a bit so they sound more natural. Secondly, it seems to me that the film, beautiful as it is, needs a more coherent spiritual message."

The men, especially Marshall, were dubious about the idea of rewriting sections and attempting to tie in a message. They feared that the script would lose its artistic integrity, and that the changes might seem artificial or inappropriate. I said, "How about our giving it a try? What do we have to lose? I think there is a way to do it that would not only preserve the script's integrity, but maybe even strengthen it."

I spent parts of the next day and on into the early morning hours refining my parts of the script. The next morning, after only three hours' sleep, I recorded the rewrites. In the final section I included the message I wanted to get across. It fit in quite naturally as an analogy of the East Pakistan-West Pakistan civil war. East Pakistan, oppressed by the cruel and powerful Pakistan Army, was powerless to liberate itself. It required the help of soldiers from an alien country (India) to free the people; thousands of Indian young men gave their life's blood to liberate the Bengalis. This all resulted in the birth of a new nation—Bangladesh.

In the same way, we members of the human race are oppressed and enslaved by our faults and failures. Yet we, too, are powerless to liberate ourselves. But one day a young Man came out of the alien cosmos to our planet Earth. Here He gave His life's blood to pay the penalty for human sin and to free us from sin's oppression. And when we make that great faith decision, not only are we liberated, but a new life is born within us—and we become new people.

Fortunately, Marshall and Jim were happy with the rewrites. They seemed especially pleased about the final analogy and satisfied that it maintained—and even enhanced—the artistic integrity of the film. The final work on producing the film was not completed by the time we departed from the U.S. We finally viewed it, with pleasure, months later at a screening in the Philippines.

By the second quarter of 1974 the fragile economy of Bangladesh was being squeezed by several powerful forces like the coils of a Hill Tracts python crushing a delicate fawn. The United Nations relief operation with its massive funding had ceased. Two years of severe worldwide inflation had hit struggling Bangladesh below the belt. Smuggling of rice, jute, and relief goods to India continued on an unprecedented scale, causing an enormous loss of national wealth. And the people angrily complained about continuing mismanagement of the nationalized industries and widespread corruption. It is no wonder that in June Finance Minister Tajuddin announced that the nation's economy had almost broken down. Bangladesh badly needed help from some wealthy nations; that meant the oil-rich Middle Eastern countries and the Western democracies.

While Americans celebrated their Independence Day on July 4, Bangladesh's National Economic Council made decisions that the U.S. and other free-enterprise-loving nations could appreciate. They declared a moratorium on nationalizing industries. Also, they decided to return some nationalized industries to their previous owners, to allow Bangalee businessmen to begin investing sizable sums in private business ventures, and even to open the door for foreigners to invest in Bangladeshi firms. These "capitalist" changes were anathema to the leftist, socialist forces. Three days later six left-leaning cabinet ministers resigned.

Soon Mujib again ordered the armed forces out of the barracks to help the police and Rakkhi Bahini round up smugglers, armed bandits, and radical communist terrorists. As a part of that operation Major Farook Reehman led a squadron of his First Bengal Lancers to areas south of Dacca. There they captured the most ruthless *dacoit* (armed robber) of the area. The man maintained that he was a member of the Awami League and, under questioning, he confessed that he had killed twenty-one people—and claimed that he had carried out the killings on Sheikh Mujib's orders.[11] Major Farook apparently took this claim at face value—he was dumbfounded.

During that same period, one of Farook's fellow majors was commanding another squadron of Bengal Lancers in an area north of Dacca. There they arrested and questioned three hoodlums. One of them cracked under interrogation and confessed their involvement in a gruesome murder of a bride, a bridegroom, and their taxi driver. The hoodlum also implicated his boss, the chairman of the local branch of the Awami League.

When the major went to arrest this chairman, he reportedly offered the major a huge bribe (300,000 takas), saying, "Don't make it a public affair; you will anyway have to let me go, either today or tomorrow. So why not take the money and forget about it?"[12] The indignant major refused and took the chairman to civil authorities in Dacca for trial. But a few days later the chairman was released —allegedly on direct orders from Sheikh Mujib. Again, the majors believed the allegations of their informants.

This incident was more than Farook could stomach; it was the turning point for him. Embittered, he declared, "It seemed as if we were living in a society headed by a criminal organisation. It was as if the Mafia had taken over Bangladesh. We were totally disillusioned."[13] It was then that Farook decided Mujib would have to be assassinated so that a new and better government could be installed.

In July, Sheikh Mujib received a gift—a worrisome, unwelcome gift. Egypt's President Anwar Sadat, grateful for the planeload of Bangladeshi tea that Mujib had sent for his troops during the Arab-Israeli war, had developed a liking for Mujib. Knowing that Bangladesh had only three ancient, decrepit tanks, he sent Mujib thirty Russian T-54's from the clutter of tanks he had parked in the desert around Cairo; Sadat also sent 400 rounds of ammunition for the tank cannons.

Mujib accepted the gift very reluctantly, for he did not really trust his army, and this would give the armored corps immensely increased strength. Yet he could find no way to refuse Sadat's generous gift. The best Mujib could do was to order his generals to keep the 400 rounds of tank ammunition under lock and key. His instincts were correct, for a year later those very tanks would bring him face to face with grave peril.

On July 10 we said our heart-wrenching good-byes to Wendy and Lynne at Chicago's O'Hare Airport, then flew to my parents' home in Tucson. After two days and more painful good-byes we flew to San Francisco, then out across the Pacific to Faith Academy near Manila. There we helped Mark and Nancy to settle into their rooms and met their new boarding parents; the next day school began. My time was spent being with the children, speaking at their high school chapel hours, and addressing the fine, responsive Filipino students of our mission's theological college in Manila. We also orchestrated a birthday party for Nancy before our last good-byes—before we headed for our empty nest in Bangladesh.

We flew on to Hong Kong, then across Southeast Asia to Dacca. Flying with us were Dr. John and Tense Bullock, new team members who were entering Bangladesh for the first time. John was a skilled orthopedic surgeon and Tense an excellent artist. From the air we could see that Bangladesh was inundated with flood waters; Dacca looked like an island in an immense ocean that stretched as far as the eye could see. Because of unprecedented monsoon rains the land was in the grip of the most serious deluge in the country's history. The devastating floods continued throughout July and August, destroying a huge amount of rice, wheat, vegetables, and livestock. This was yet another major setback for the already reeling nation.

Because of economic collapse Bangladesh had run out of foreign currency to purchase food and other items from foreign markets. Sadly, the government was forced to cancel a contract for a month's supply of wheat scheduled to arrive in October. With crops so badly damaged and this contract canceled, what would the people eat in the fall? Bangladesh officials began traveling the world to obtain financial aid to attempt to stave off an autumn famine.

Our hosts in Dacca were dear friends Mark and Ida Tucker. Mark was a competent, warm-hearted American engineer in charge of the physical plant of the Cholera Research Hospital. And Ida was a gracious, always-hospitable homemaker. Their elegant home was a haven away from the hassle and red tape of government offices, the drenching rain, and oppressive humidity. After visits to the police and immigration officials, I obtained multiple-entry visas for the Olsens and Bullocks to cover the upcoming year, then the Bullocks headed for Malumghat.

Next I tackled one of the hospital's extremely serious new problems. The Chittagong Customs officials had stopped honoring the hospital's duty-free status and were demanding payment of tens of thousands of dollars of Customs duty and sales tax on the hospital goods lying stacked in the Customs warehouses. But the hospital was facing a financial crisis and could not possibly pay these huge sums.

Because the Customs Department answered to a high-powered body called the National Board of Revenue (NBR), I would have to negotiate with them to try solving the hospital's

Mark and Ida Tucker with their children, Brian and Marsha

Gene Gurganus teaching a Bible class

problem. I discovered that a key, high-ranking member of the NBR was ill; when I was asked to treat him, I readily agreed and examined him at his home. Later, I met him in his office, along with his two deputies. The outcome of those meetings and negotiations was outstanding. The excellent letter from the NBR to the Chittagong Customs officials ordered them to "allow clearance of all such goods received as gifts by Memorial Christian Hospital, Chittagong, free of Customs duty and sales tax. . . ." This would save the hospital those tens of thousands of dollars, since all of our goods were purchased with donated funds. "Thank You, Father!"

The next day we flew to Chittagong. When I presented the new NBR letter to the Chittagong collector of Customs, orders flew and officers began to jump to quickly release the urgently needed hospital shipments.

Our first evening in Chittagong we enjoyed a lovely reception given by our Chittagong team members. We had quite a crowd of co-workers in Chittagong at that time, including veterans, Bengali language students, and short-termers. The veterans included Gene and Beth Gurganus, senior personnel from North Carolina. Gene was a faithful, effective theological teacher and founder of the mission's popular Bible Correspondence School. While Gene worked with the emerging church, Beth cared for her children and home.

Lynn Silvernale was a nurse from New York State with a high language aptitude and training in theology, linguistics, and piano. Because of the urgent need for a readily understandable Bengali Bible, the medical team in the 1960s had released Lynn to head up

Lynn Silvernale with Mr. Dores and Mrs. Dass

the standard Bengali common language New Testament translation project. She promptly teamed up with competent Mrs. Bashanti Dass to begin this important work; later they were joined by
a capable Bengali gentleman named Mr. Polycarp Dores.

Jeannie Lockerbie from Canada and New York City was a
nurse with literary skills, long experience in children's work, and a
lovely voice. She was deeply moved by the dearth of Christian literature in Bangladesh and longed to do something about it. Recognizing the overall importance of Jeannie's vision, the medical team
had released her to establish the mission's Literature Division. She
then moved to Chittagong City to begin this daunting task.

Joe Massey from Wisconsin was an able theological teacher
with many Bengali friends—especially the leader of a mystical Islamic sect (Sufi sect). His wife, Mary, was a mother and homemaker. Absent from his post was Reid Minich from New York State,
another capable theological teacher and also an administrator who
looked after an immense number of nitty-gritty details. At that
point, he was in the U.S. convalescing from an illness.

Studying the Bengali language were several career workers
who would later locate in one of our three stations as soon as they
completed their studies. Those who would remain to serve in Chittagong City were Jack and Margaret Archibald from Illinois. Jack,
trained in business, bookkeeping, and theology, would become an
administrative officer and theological teacher. Margaret was a

mother, homemaker, and primary school teacher with musical skills.

Ron Perrine from Michigan was trained in theology and Biblical studies and would have a part in the Bible translation project. His wife, Cheryl, was a homemaker and mother of two active boys. Sue Breckley from New York State would devote herself to teaching missionary children in Chittagong City.

Language students who later shifted to the Malumghat Hospital station were the Staggs, the Fidlers, and Jan Wolfe. Dr. Dick and Carol Stagg were from Ohio where Dick had been a family practice physician with expertise in giving anesthesia. Carol was a mother, homemaker, and nurse with writing and secretarial skills.

Dave Fidler from Michigan was an X-ray technician and equipment maintenance expert. Darlene, his wife, was a medical secretary turned mother and homemaker. Jan Wolfe from Pennsylvania was a capable nurse who looked forward to serving in the hospital.

And one family would join those serving at Hebron Station. They were Dave and Doris Totman from New York State. Dave was a theological teacher planning to work with the tribal people. Doris was a nurse involved in homemaking and care of her new baby. It was great to relax and enjoy time with these dear friends.

My first working day in Chittagong I visited the controller of imports and exports to tackle another severe problem. He and I were well acquainted, for I had examined his son three months earlier. I learned that, although his son was improved, the controller himself was now ill. I heard his symptoms and ordered the necessary tests.

The problem we faced was this. His office was no longer permitted to honor a previous important agreement, which had allowed the hospital to import materials without a separate permit for each shipment; in that agreement we had been granted a "blanket import permit" that automatically covered all the shipments. Because I would have to negotiate the case in Dacca, I requested a

Jeannie Lockerbie and literature worker Mrs. Bisswas

Reid Minich

copy of the blanket import letter that had granted us this valuable concession in the first place. Unfortunately, that letter had been lost or destroyed during the Pakistan Army occupation. However, the controller graciously gave me an affidavit verifying that there had been such a letter.

As I was about to leave another officer said, "Oh yes, by the way, the government has just levied a new tax on imports; unless you get an exemption you will now have to pay a 20 percent import tax on all the goods you import." What a shocker! That meant that the hospital would have to pay additional thousands of dollars in new taxes—another crisis! I would also need to tackle this new problem as soon as I could get back to the capital city.

Arriving in Dacca, I placed two requests with the Ministry of Commerce:

1. Renewal of our blanket import permit
2. Exemption from the new 20 percent import tax

The officer sent me to negotiate part of the matter with a related department—and also to gain the approval of the Ministry of Health. More red tape.

That night I enjoyed the American ambassador's reception for some visiting dignitaries. I met a number of people there, including the Bangladesh government's secretary of health. He was the officer who had granted us some important concessions shortly after the birth of Bangladesh. I thought, *How fortunate! I'll approach this friendly secretary tomorrow, and maybe he'll give me the approval that we need on the spot.*

When I met the health secretary in his office the next morning, I felt that everything had been orchestrated just right and that his endorsement was in the bag. Imagine my surprise when he said, "I am sorry, but I will not give you that endorsement—until you enter into an official, written bilateral agreement with our ministry. We are now requiring this of all health care organizations."

What a jolt! But then, as I considered his unexpected response further, another thought came to me. *Maybe this is for the best. Why can't we go for new concessions beyond any we have enjoyed before? Possibly this will allow us to obtain money-saving concessions for our personnel, as well as for the hospital. Since we are being forced to enter into this agreement, we might as well shoot for the moon—and see what God will do for us and our patients.*

The Ministry of Commerce had favored us far more than the Ministry of Health. That afternoon I picked up two great letters. One letter extended our blanket import permit until the end of the year, giving me time to negotiate for a permanent settlement of the matter. The second letter exempted us from the 20 percent import permit tax, saving the hospital those thousands of dollars. "Thank You, Father!"

I then flew back to Chittagong, where I presented the key letters to the controller of imports and exports. The letter worked wonders. The next morning Joan and I left Chittagong to drive south in the pouring rain to Malumghat. There we drove excitedly through the hospital's front gate—we were home!

We were met by co-workers who exclaimed, "Welcome! It's great to see you. And are we ever glad to have you back! During June and July we were down to a skeleton crew."

That skeleton crew had included a handful of veteran career workers—a hospital administrator, several nurses and a school teacher. Jesse Eaton, from New York State, was the hospital's administrator/business manager and an excellent theological teacher. His wife, Joyce, was a mother, homemaker, and nurse. Becky Davey, from Washington State, one of our original medical team, was a highly trained nurse and supervisor of the nursing staff. She was so versatile that she became involved in many other phases of the work and was especially concerned that church leaders be thoroughly trained.

Millie Cooley, of Michigan, was an experienced operating room nurse who naturally fit into the same role at Malumghat. Because she had a special interest in the Bengali nurses and nurses' aides, some became her friends and she conducted Bible study sessions for them. Gwen Geens came from New York State to serve on the wards, where she worked with the Bengali nurses and supervised patient care. And she cheerfully took over supervision of the pharmacy, which was not an easy task. Shirley Harkness, an experienced primary school teacher, came from the upper peninsula of Michigan to devote herself to teaching the missionary children.

This little group of veterans had depended heavily on several short-term workers who had "come to the kingdom for such a time as this." Among them were two short-term doctors. One was Dr. John ("Jake") Jaquis, a family practice physician who had just completed his third invaluable short-term stint at the hospital.

The second doctor, a general surgeon, had arrived in a timely fashion. The day after notices were sent throughout the countryside announcing, "Except for emergencies the hospital will be closed until the return of Dr. Olsen," Dr. Charles Engel and his wife, June, arrived out of the blue. Immediately fresh notices were sent out, notifying the people to disregard the earlier ones; the hospital would remain open. Back in the U.S. the Engels had made a commitment to God that if a certain piece of their land sold quickly, they would do something special for His work. When the land

Nurse Millie Cooley

Teacher Shirley Harkness

Bob Adolph

sold immediately and someone told them of the hospital's urgent need, they said to each other, "This is it!"

In August and September the furloughing veterans who were so badly needed to help keep the ship afloat returned. Two of these were Bob and Barb Adolph. As part of the original medical team, Bob had set up the hospital's excellent laboratory; he was also involved in the theological education of church leaders and young men of the church, and he headed up the camping program. Barb was a mother, homemaker, and primary school teacher.

Mel and Marjorie Beals also returned about the same time. Mel was a theological teacher who worked closely with the church at Malumghat. Also, he had a vision for getting church members involved in gardening and agricultural projects to help them become financially stable; this would allow them to better educate their children and to build a strong, solvent church. Marge was a mother and homemaker who taught a Bengali Sunday School class and prepared literature pieces.

Jean Weld, a nurse-midwife, returned from Minnestota and plunged back into the work. Although she cared for some obstetrical cases, her main focus was the Outpatient Department (OPD). Because she was tall and willowy, with eye-catching red hair, she stood out strikingly when surrounded by dozens of shorter, black-haired Bangalees. She would be on deck for only a few months, as she was engaged to be married in December.

Mel and Marge Beals   *Nurse Jean Weld*

We were among those who returned in August. And a few days later Dr. Joe and Joyce DeCook, from Michigan, drove in to begin their second term of service; Joe was an experienced obstetrician/gynecologist with an engaging sense of humor that often lightened up heavy moments. He initiated the important Audio-Visual Department at Malumghat and was actively involved in theological teaching, too. Joyce was a mother, homemaker, fine violinist, and nurse who played an active role on the Bible Translation Committee.

Other veterans who returned about that time were Larry and Jane Golin. Larry was not only a theological teacher but also a newly licensed physiotherapist. Larry was eager to build up the hospital's Physiotherapy Department, and he would continue his work on the Translation Committee. Jane was a nurse who cared for a busy household, including two Bengali girls whom they ultimately adopted.

We were delighted to be enjoying and interacting with this crowd of co-workers, most of whom were already dear friends. I had played a small part in introducing a number of them to the work of Malumghat Hospital. But it is God who did the recruiting and gave that deep inner sense of calling that makes a person stop short, change direction, resign his or her employment, and travel to the ends of the earth to serve Him and the needy people of the land.

Then a letter from Dr. Donn Ketcham updated us on his situation. I had referred Donn to heart doctors in Milwaukee, Wisconsin, for special tests and X rays to determine if heart bypass surgery might help prevent further cardiac problems. The X rays indicated that he needed the surgery, so he was scheduled to be operated on in September by a noted pioneer cardiac surgeon who had come up behind me in the same surgical residency program where I had trained.

Next Joan and I went to work cleaning our house, unpacking our belongings, hanging our curtains, and putting our stove and

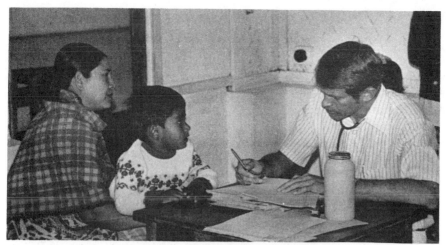

Dr. Joe DeCook talking to a patient

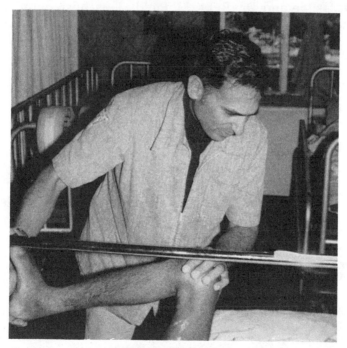

Larry Golin doing physiotherapy

refrigerator in working order. After a solid week's work we still had half-filled steel drums scattered around in the living room and on the front porch.

One evening a little Hindu haircutter came to talk. Although he belonged to one of Hinduism's lower castes, he had a heroic middle name—Ram. His namesake was one of the most prominent of the Hindu gods. "Remember the talk we had three months ago?" he began.

"I do remember; we talked about important things," I replied.

"Yes, and I have been thinking about our religious discussion all these weeks and waiting for you to return. I have come to tell you this evening that I am ready to follow Christ." Then, after discussing his decision further, we knelt together beside the shiny black steel drums and I heard Ram's simple prayer of faith. His face glowed at the thought of sins forgiven and a new station in life—being a part of God's family.

We were delighted to get acquainted with two new physicians, Dr. Peter and Dr. Reba McField. This husband-wife team had a name that sounded Scottish or American, but in fact they were both Bengalis. During the 1971 war they had barely escaped from the Pakistan Army, briefly took refuge at Malumghat, then traveled to Burma with some of our Bengali staff and stayed there for the duration of the war. There Peter deeply believed in Christ the Lord, which greatly pleased Reba who was a pastor's daughter and the first Christian woman in the country to graduate from

Drs. Peter and Reba Mcfield

medical college. When the war was over, they had returned from Burma to newborn Bangladesh and signed on to be part of our medical team.

On the last surgical day of August, Dr. Peter and I both had surgical cases to do. Peter was making solid progress on his surgical skills, and that morning he did a rather complicated hernia operation, needing no help from me. The next day we admitted six soldiers who had been injured in a jeep accident. Although Peter and I worked side by side, it took quite a bit of time and effort to patch them all up.

That evening I operated on an elderly gentleman. Always interested in surgical goings-on, Peter and Reba came over to see the last part of the case. Afterward we enjoyed coffee, cake, and conversation together. Peter told us about his visit to the government officer who was second in command of the whole Cox's Bazar Subdivision. He explained, "The second officer likes the hospital, and he was really affected by reading your book *Daktar*. Not only that, he told me about some of his personal problems and said that I should pray for him. So I said, 'Yes, I will. In fact, I will pray for you right now.'" So, there in the government office, Peter had prayed for the Muslim officer in his warm, earnest way. As he told us the story, Peter's eyes were shining, and he was smiling and filled with the joy of living.

How fortunate we were to have Dr. Peter and Dr. Reba! You could count on one hand the number of earnest Bengali Christian physicians in this Muslim-majority land, yet we were privileged to have two of them. I could see Peter as the hospital's first Bengali medical director. The staff loved him, and he had gained the respect of the people of the countryside. He was warm-hearted, intelligent, and gaining increasing medical and surgical expertise as he worked with us day by day. Because he was only thirty-four years of age, he would have many years to serve his people and his church in important ways.

I went home, tumbled into bed, and fell into a deep sleep. At 3:15 A.M. I awakened groggily to an insistent rapping on my bedroom window. The note handed through the window by the watchman had been scrawled hastily by the night nurse:

Dear Doctor: Please come now. Dr. Peter condition serious.

What could this mean? Alarmed and perplexed, I dressed in seconds and roared off to Peter's house on my motorcycle.

Peter was lying unconscious, limp, gray, and cold, with no pulse. Was he dead? No, not quite—he was breathing slightly. But, as Reba gasped something about two previous heart attacks, Peter's breathing suddenly stopped. Instantly I began CPR and we quickly rolled him to the hospital on a patient trolley. The electro-cardiogram showed a massive heart attack, a rarity at our hospital. Despite CPR, oxygen, medications, and other measures, his heart suddenly stopped beating—and Peter was gone. I was numb with grief.

As dawn approached, I did my best to comfort Reba, and we laid Peter's body out for viewing. Then we passed the word of Peter's death to the staff and to the church folks.

By then it was time for the Friday morning chapel service. Peter usually led the service each Friday, so I took his place. The chapel was packed with mourning, weeping staff members. Peter's death on a Friday, after three years of serving in the hospital, reminded us of another young Man who died two thousand years before after three years of serving and teaching the people—a Man whose death we also remember on a Friday. We looked at a passage of Scripture that contained the phrase "He being dead still speaks," and we contemplated what Peter's life—and death—were telling us. Many staff members made important inner spiritual commitments during that chapel meeting.

The next morning, during a moving two-and-a-half-hour memorial service, many spoke and gave testimony to Peter's character and influence on their lives. That afternoon we slogged through the rainy-season mud carrying Peter's homemade coffin to the burial site. Pastor Dewari spoke beautifully. Then, during a hymn, Peter's elder brother suddenly arrived from his distant home. Someone brought Peter's three-year-old daughter through the crowd to the edge of the open grave as they fitted the lid on the coffin and noisily nailed it down. It seemed cruel to make her watch this just inches away—but that is age-old Bengali custom.

While men threw earth into the grave over the coffin, the monsoon rains poured down on the miserable, shivering crowd. *What a contrast this scene is with the vista Peter is enjoying in glory,* I thought. *Maybe by now he has met his namesake, the apostle Peter; they both loved fishing. Oh, why did this fine man with so much to give his people have to die? I just don't understand. But I'll see you later, dear friend.*

The next day Joan and I hastened to Dacca to negotiate and, hopefully, sign an official agreement between the mission and the Ministry of Health of the Bangladesh government. Only by signing this agreement could we reclaim all the hospital's lost concessions and possibly gain new benefits for our individual workers which would save additional thousands of dollars. That was particularly important just then, because the hospital was still strapped financially and the shipments of our many returnees and new workers were piling up at Chittagong Port—and would be stuck there until

Pastor Dewari spoke beautifully

Dr. Peter's grave

we could see what import concessions the government might grant our personnel.

During the first week of September I wrote the first draft of the proposed agreement, then had it appraised by Jalal and our legal adviser Amirul Islam. They made wise suggestions about how to refine some of the wording. I incorporated their suggestions and my own new insights into the next draft. Then, after further study and discussion, I wrote up the official version, and Joan typed a beautiful final draft.

On September 11 I submitted our proposed agreement to the secretary of the Ministry of Health. Because the agreement contained clauses involving ten separate ministries, I would have to negotiate with three or four or five officers of each of these ministries. That taxing job took exactly two months and required more than 150 meetings with government officers. In many of those meetings intense negotiations took place. Most of the major ministries rejected our proposals the first time around which, of course, compounded my problems and intensified the negotiations. For a full thirty days the Muslim holy month of Ramzan (Ramadan) further complicated this work, because fasting from dawn to dusk is difficult and tends to make people—including government officers—tired out.

I was consulting Jalal each morning to gain his insights and background information on the upper-echelon officers I would be meeting. His input was vital, and he soon suggested that, for our convenience, we move in with his family for the duration of the negotiations. So we did move in, and their hospitality knew no bounds. The two months were punctuated by highs and lows, but ultimately the high points prevailed. There were five especially memorable days:

On September 14 the Ministry of Health agreed that I could hand-carry copies of the agreement and their cover letter to each of the ten ministries that would have to approve sections of the draft. This would bring me into immediate contact with key officials in each ministry and facilitate my negotiations.

On September 26 the important Ministry of Finance approved significant sections of the agreement. That was a major victory.

On October 1 I was scheduled for a critical noon meeting with the powerful National Board of Revenue (NBR). I had just finished two weeks of sometimes difficult negotiations with NBR officers; one seemed to be for us and the others against us. I learned that one officer had written a sharply negative note in the file. The chairman of the NBR was taken aback when I requested an opportunity to appear before the board. He said, "That's not the way the board operates—but we'll see."

I awakened that October 1 morning with a keen sense of the high importance of the day. Never in history had the NBR granted "privileged person" status and income tax exemptions to mission society members; I was asking for the impossible. I decided to prepare myself for the critical meeting with a morning of study, quiet contemplation, fasting, and earnest prayer. I have never been into fasting in a ritual, legalistic sense—nor in a spooky or magical sense. But on a few crucial days in my life I have put aside food to focus on prayer, meditation, and the Scriptures—and invariably found that the combination heightened my inner strength and prepared me for the crisis at hand. This was one of those days.

When Joan went to the breakfast table, Jalal and his wife, Shakina, asked, "Where is he?"

"He is in the bedroom. We can go ahead and eat; he won't be taking breakfast this morning."

"Why not? What's the matter with him? Is he sick?"

"No, he is well. He has just decided to fast and pray and meditate this morning to prepare himself for this extremely important meeting today."

"Oh, my!" Shakina Ahmed sighed. Joan later reported that something about the episode seemed to deeply impact our friends. Apparently they were intrigued by the idea of a spontaneous, voluntary, from-the-heart putting aside of food to focus on more urgent and important matters.

It was good that I was well prepared for any eventuality, for the NBR was stacked against us. Unfortunately, the only member of the board who favored our request was away that day. The chairman was an enigma, but I knew that the other three officers were against granting us additional concessions. The board members discussed the issues for nearly an hour before I was allowed in. I noticed at a glance that their faces were tight, grim, unsmiling; I knew I was in for a rough ride. "Why should we grant your personnel exemption from paying income taxes?" one asked tersely.

"Because, gentlemen, you have kindly granted that privilege to other expatriate experts—and our service is no less valuable than theirs." I was speaking of experts of the UN, Ford Foundation, and other groups.

"Why do you feel that we should give your personnel 'privileged-person' status and exempt them from paying Customs duty on their personal effects?"

"Sirs, there are four reasons why I feel that you should do so. First of all, you have already granted such privileges to other foreign experts, despite the fact that they serve for only a few months or a year or two. On the other hand, most of our experts are so dedicated to the people of Bangladesh that they give their lifetime services to your country.

"Secondly, the qualifications of our experts are equal to or greater than the qualifications of those already receiving these privileges. Thirdly, these other foreign experts receive a handsome salary for their services. But our personnel receive an ordinary, maintenance type of salary. And the final reason is this: the money our members will save by duty-free clearance of their goods does not go into their pockets or bank accounts; rather, the money is channeled into our projects which help the poor and needy. This is important, because our medical projects are currently in financial distress. Gentlemen, you have given these privileges to various expatriate experts and diplomats for years. Why should you not grant the privileges to our highly qualified personnel who give their lifetime services to devotedly serve your people?"

The queries kept coming—question after question. But the terseness eased, and the faces were softening.

"What salary are you paid?" I gave the figure. "Oh, that's not a salary; that's a maintenance stipend. I am sorry I raised objection to the income tax exemption," one key officer said.

Then the chairman asked, "How much liquor and cigarettes do you import?"

"We all know that is an important question," I replied, "because so many privileged foreigners import liquor and cigarettes duty free up to the limit allowed for themselves, their wives, and even for their babies, then sell them on the black market for huge sums. I know that you are all disturbed about those who behave that way. But we are different. None of our personnel ever imports one bottle of liquor or one package of cigarettes. This is another reason why they are so deserving of privileged-person status."

At that, the super-negative officer suddenly leaned forward and asked intensely, "Do you mean that you and your people do not drink liquor or smoke for religious reasons, like us Muslims?"

"Exactly," I responded, "and here is the reason why. The *Injil Sharif* [Holy New Testament], which both you and I revere, teaches that our bodies are temples of God. What right have we to damage and destroy them?"

The change in the man was as remarkable as it was instantaneous. Apparently he had thought that all Christians were drunkards and cigarette addicts and illegally sold items to the black market; after all, he reasoned, Americans do these things and they must all be Christians, because America is a "Christian" country. Apparently my simple recital had completely changed his view of this. Addressing his chairman, he said apologetically, "Sir, we have only granted their hospital benefits in the past, but maybe we should agree to this proposal and grant their medical workers and administrators privileged-person status."

And that's exactly what happened. For the first time, members of a mission society were given these unique privileges. "Thank You, Father!"

Another memorable day—October 29. For more than a month I had been carrying on sticky negotiations with the Ministry of Commerce. After they had rejected my initial proposal, I made a strong appeal. In this ministry, also, one officer was particularly negative. But on this climactic October day his superior officer brushed aside every one of his objections and gave us all that we asked for—including the blanket import permit, which then became a part of our official agreement with the government. It was thrilling to sit there and watch it unfold before me.

One day I made a house call to treat the wife of an NBR officer. I was quite unaware that his lively sons had been watching each day on Dacca television the ongoing saga of *Gulliver's Travels*, a story about the Englishman Gulliver who wound up in a land inhabited by tiny Lilliputians, to whom he seemed a giant. The two small boys met me at the door, took one look, then shouted excitedly to their mother inside, "It's Gollivar! It's Gollivar!" Their mother had planned a more sedate reception, but I quite enjoyed the one I got.

By the second week in November the many negotiating sessions were completed, dozens of immensely valuable concessions obtained, and the final draft of the agreement typed up by Joan. Finally, on November 11, while America was honoring its veterans of foreign wars, I walked into the office of the secretary of health —feeling a bit like a veteran of foreign wars myself. To make the occasion a "signing party," he thoughtfully served tea, Coca Cola, and bananas. Precisely at 3:05 P.M. he signed the agreement on behalf of the Government of Bangladesh, and I signed on behalf of our mission. Then two other high-ranking officers signed as witnesses. Whew! "Thank You, Father!"

During those two months of intense negotiations there were other developments, too. On September 13 in Milwaukee, Wisconsin, the cardiac surgeon opened up Donn Ketcham's chest, held his damaged heart in his hand, then went to work. The operation was especially difficult, but finally he successfully completed three bypass channels. But in the early hours after surgery Donn's condition seriously deteriorated; he was hemorrhaging internally. The surgeon had to reoperate on an emergency basis to stop the bleeding. But from then on Donn made steady progress and finally resumed his active, busy life. "Thank You, Father!"

A few days later in mid-September, Bangladesh became the 136th country to be admitted into the United Nations. Opposed by Pakistan and China for two years, Bangladesh had struggled long and hard for this recognition, so Sheikh Mujib savored the triumph. A week later he flew to New York to address the UN General Assembly. Then, after the key to New York City was presented to him, he proceeded to Washington, D.C., to meet American president Gerald Ford.

Although it is customary for the American government to receive heads of state who attend the UN for the first time, American officials had shown little enthusiasm about Mujib's visit. Not only did he have a mere fifteen minutes with President Ford, but Secretary of State Henry Kissinger was conspicuous by his absence. Also, instead of the usual luncheon hosted by the president or secretary of state, Mujib was offered only a luncheon to be hosted by a minor cabinet official.

Mujib's foreign minister complained that "the level of protocol treatment accorded during the Prime Minister's visit to Washington . . . reflected a clear degree of coolness. This was apparent from the fact that there was only a brief meeting with the President and a marked absence of the usual hospitality extended on such occasions."[14] Apparently Mr. Kissinger was still miffed at Mujib for the embarrassment he had caused him and America's client state (Pakistan) by winning the civil war and gaining independence. Mujib had hoped for a warm reception and greatly increased food aid; sadly, he obtained neither.

Although the monsoon rains and floods began to abate in September, the notorious "famine of '74" had struck with full force. For two months the newspapers had been reporting sporadic starvation deaths around the country, but now deaths due to famine had become epidemic. The government announced that it would set up "gruel kitchens" in the country's 4,300 unions (subcounties) to feed the starving people. Newspapers declared that the famine was caused by the floods, but that was far too simplistic. Perhaps the real "formula for famine" would look something like this:

> Habitual poverty + no savings + breakdown of the national economy + cessation of emergency funds from abroad + spiraling prices + destruction of crops by devastating floods = FAMINE.

Another event in September intrigued observers of the political scene. Sheikh Moni, the nephew of Sheikh Mujib, leader of the youth league of their party and editor of a government-controlled newspaper, began proclaiming widely that the system of parliamentary democracy had failed the nation. Therefore, the country

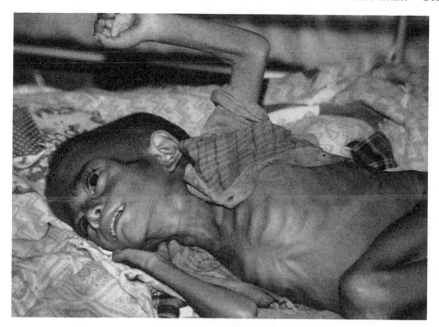

*The famine of '74—
starving baby*

needed a "second revolution," which would have to be led by Mujib. We wondered what his angle was—and what kind of revolution he had in mind. It sounded pretty suspicious to me.

In the autumn of 1974 Major Farook Reehman continued to analyze how best to bring down Mujib and his government. He had secret meetings from time to time with several disgruntled army majors and others. Some of these officers talked about Communism and setting up Marxist cells among the soldiers. But when it came to ideology, Farook felt at a disadvantage, for hc had never been a student of politics and ideologies. So, in his characteristic direct way, he set out to rectify this deficiency by reading book after book on politics, government, and Communism. After reading the philosophies of Chairman Mao, Ché Guevara's diaries, and other leftist pieces, he felt that Communism was not the answer. He explained, "The only conclusion I came to was that they had their own problems and had tackled them in their own way. But this was not a solution for Bangladesh. There was nothing I could find in any textbook or anywhere which fitted our situation."[15]

For a while Farook searched for some way to sidestep actually assassinating Mujib. He considered the pattern of the overthrow of Sukarno in Indonesia; Sukarno had been deposed and retired to a palace. But he soon decided that would never work in Bangladesh.

Either the Rakkhi Bahini would overwhelm his small force to re-capture Mujib, or the Indian Army might come in to rescue Mujib. And if the Indian Army did reenter the country, India might be tempted to annex Bangladesh. So Farook reverted to Plan A. He put it like this: "In a way Sheikh Mujib signed his own death warrant because of his love affair with India. We could not put him away like Sukarno. I was convinced there was no alternative. Sheikh Mujib had to die."[16]

In October a team of Bangalee officials departed Dacca for Paris to attend the upcoming meeting of a newly created group called the Aid Bangladesh Consortium. For two years Bangladesh had resisted the formation of such an aid club, preferring to deal with aid-giving countries on an individual basis. But with their economy nearly moribund, the Bangalees finally had to give in and work with the Consortium, which promptly demanded a devalua-tion of the Bangladesh taka and new rules further favoring private business. The Aid Consortium, headed by the World Bank, includ-ed representatives from seventeen non-communist countries and nine international funding organizations. In the October meeting they raised $600 million for Bangladesh. Later in the year this in-creased to $950 million, which put Bangladesh back in the running for awhile.

The flow of events made clear that Mujib had apparently be-come somewhat disenchanted with socialism and dependence on the India-Soviet axis. India also was suffering from famine that year and Russia from a severe shortfall of grain, so neither country could bail Bangladesh out of her famine and economic chaos. For these reasons Mujib had been making increasing overtures to Washington. This new pro-Americanism made me remember sit-ting beside Mujib two and a half years earlier and listening to him harshly vilify the U.S. government; time does change things. Then during October Mujib and his government busily prepared for the scheduled visit of U.S. Secretary of State Henry Kissinger later in the month.

For a long time Kissinger had apparently nursed negative feelings about the emergence of Bangladesh in general and Sheikh Mujib in particular. One of his former staff assistants put it this way:

> [One of Kissinger's most senior confidants told me] there had been three nemeses of American foreign policy in the Kissin-ger era. These were the three "most hated men" on Kissinger's "foreign enemies list." He said they were Allende, Thieu and Mu-jib. . . . Kissinger certainly perceived the Bangladeshi events as a

personal defeat. . . . It didn't create any great shift in the balance of power, but it was an extraordinary embarrassment.

Mujib's welcome-back as an exiled persecuted leader, I think, was probably the most embarrassing single event in American foreign policy since Castro rode into Havana on a tank. . . .

It certainly was perceived as a major political setback for the Administration. It spoiled things badly for awhile. . . .

It is the only place the Administration has been under public fire in the Congress or in the press. It is the only place where Kissinger's diplomacy is seen to be ineffectual and where no magic could be made to work. It is the only place where American interests have been reversed and where there is an obvious Soviet inroad, and obvious Soviet advantage.[17]

On the eve of Henry Kissinger's arrival Mujib made the ultimate gesture toward his powerful American guest—he dropped left-leaning, pro-Soviet Tajuddin from his cabinet. Kissinger arrived in Dacca on October 30 for his brief visit, which lasted less than twenty-four hours. After a two-hour meeting with Mujib, he reacted politely and told the waiting reporters that their prime minister was a man of "vast conception."[18] He said that he was honored to meet Mujib, for he had rarely met a man who was the father of his nation. These generous comments and the pledge of an extra 100,000 tons of grain seemed to strengthen Mujib in his shift toward Washington. The next day warmly pro-American newspaper articles lauded Kissinger's visit, and ten days later the press trumpeted the beginning of the Bangladesh-U.S. Friendship Society.

Not to be outdone, members of the Soviet embassy and the two pro-Soviet leftist political parties intensified their contacts with Mujib and his advisors, especially Sheikh Moni. This was their message: The deterioration in Bangladesh has proved that parliamentary democracy has failed. The government should scrap the parliamentary system in favor of a one-party state. *As in Soviet Russia?* I mused when I learned of this. *So that was what Mujib's nephew Sheikh Moni had in mind with his talk of a second revolution.*

During my several weeks in Dacca I had examined quite a number of patients—Jalal's family members, friends, and servants, cabinet ministers and their loved ones, shopkeepers, secretaries of the government, a senator, a beggar, relatives of an army general, poorly paid government clerks and typists, officers of the National Board of Revenue, and others. Even the very negative NBR official requested medical attention, and I was happy to help him.

Also during that period I treated a Japanese gentleman, the distinguished director of the Bangladesh branch of a famed Japanese company, for high blood pressure. The correct dose of one of the medications I prescribed was one-half tablet twice daily. He returned a week later complaining that he was dizzy, his thinking was fuzzy, and he found it difficult to write. I was baffled! Only after long questioning did he finally admit that he was taking a *full* tablet of his medicine *three* times a day—triple the prescribed dose. I asked him why he was taking such large doses of the medication. Looking at me coyly, he said, "Am I a child, that I should take half a tablet of medicine? Besides, it is easier for me to take three tablets daily, one with each of my meals." With some difficulty I finally convinced him to take his medication exactly as prescribed. He did so, and very soon his head cleared up.

By this time our friend Jalal had been retired from government service quite prematurely; apparently he and the existing government were not on the same wavelength. Feeling that he would be a tremendous asset to the American embassy, I decided to notify the ambassador that Jalal might be available. First, I wrote a letter of recommendation, which was quite a task because Jalal had a long, distinguished, star-studded record of serving his country. During my appointment with the ambassador he first asked about the outcome of our negotiations with the Bangladesh government. When he heard the provisions of our agreement, he congratulated us on the results.

Then I learned that the embassy actually was looking for a competent Bengali to fill a vacant post. I told him about Jalal and explained, "I just happen to have a recommendation letter with me." The ambassador promised to study it and said they would interview him. Later, after highly successful interviews, Jalal was given the job. At the end of my letter to the ambassador I had listed five things I thought Jalal could do for the embassy. Although his job description covered other areas, within a few weeks he was contributing in all five of those dimensions.

After the climactic signing of our November 11 agreement with the government, I remained in Dacca to attempt to resurrect the Hebron land case. We were trying to purchase additional acreage at our Hebron Station, but over a ten-year period the case had become hopelessly tangled in red tape. At the Home Ministry I requested action on the file, but there was no response—because the file had disappeared. The troubled officials searched intensely for several days, but could never locate the file; they suspected foul play by someone else who wanted that land. But they were kind enough to open a new file and list what they could remember of the missing papers.

My next stop would be the Ministry of Land Administration. I decided to start at the top of the chain of command—the minister. Another minister, whose wife was under my care, kindly made the appointment. Apparently he said a good word on our behalf, because the minister of land administration was very friendly and helpful. He minimized the bureaucratic maneuvering and on a banner day, November 27, signed the paper granting us rights to the new Hebron land. Even then, it took years to complete the endless formalities at the local level; Jay Walsh and Momin, our hospital public relations officer, bird-dogged the many details through to the end.

During that same week our mission in Chittagong City celebrated a special occasion—the official formation of a church. I flew from Dacca to Chittagong for a day to participate in this important event. The steering committee had organized the day to include a baptismal service, speeches by several members, a history of the development of the congregation, joyous singing, and a preaching service. My assignment was to give a charge to the seven deacons of the new church. All this was followed by a great feast to wind up this highly significant day, another milestone in God's work in Bangladesh. "Thank You, Father!"

November was harvest month for the main, rainy-season rice crop. Although the floods had destroyed thousands of tons of the precious rice, the farmers carefully and successfully harvested a partial crop, which quickly eased the famine for a while. Then the government closed the 5,862 gruel kitchens and tried to get back to business as usual. Government officials announced that 27,500 citizens had died because of the famine, but unofficial estimates exceeded 100,000 starvation deaths.

Also in November rumors were rife in the capital city that someone might try to overthrow the Mujib government. And a foreign reporter later claimed that, beginning in November, certain unknown Bengalis began a series of secret meetings with U.S. embassy officials to feel out how the United States would react in case a coup should bring down the present government. These allegations were categorically denied by an embassy political officer.[19] Later, Majors Farook and Rashid also disavowed making any such contacts with the U.S. embassy.

At the end of November we flew to Chittagong with a profound sigh of relief; that difficult Dacca chapter was over. During my negotiations in Dacca many shipments of team members' personal effects had piled up at Chittagong Port. I went immediately to the office of the traffic manager of the port, enjoyed the tea he served, and presented to him a copy of the new agreement. He immediately canceled the thousands of dollars worth of storage fees, for the agreement contained such a provision. Now the shipments could be cleared free of Customs duty and sales tax and, one by one, trucked down the pike to Malumghat. The next day I traveled the same road. How great to be home again!

On the first Monday in December I made ward rounds with Dr. John Bullock, took over his patients so that he could begin his language studies, then plunged back into hospital work. That Monday, as usual, was extremely busy, for the Outpatient Department is closed on weekends. After the day's work was done emergencies kept coming, so I operated on into the night and finally fell into bed exhausted at 3:00 A.M.

The next day the new first-year Bengali language class began for the first time at Malumghat. The students were Dr. and Mrs. John Bullock from California and nurses Alice Payne and Karen Carder. John, the experienced orthopedic (bone and joint) surgeon, and Tense had flown into Dacca with us, then reached Malumghat some days ahead of us. The timing was right, for some difficult orthopedic cases came in shortly after their arrival, and John soon had a thriving orthopedic practice—which, of course, he had to set aside when language classes began. Tense was a mother, homemaker, and artist; with her fine artistic talent she would be an asset in various facets of the work.

Karen Carder was a seasoned nurse who had worked with a plastic surgeon in Ohio. She looked forward to doing surgical nursing at Malumghat — but later a visiting doctor had other plans for her. Alice, who hailed from Indiana, was also an experienced nurse; she hoped to serve at our Hebron Station. But the first priority for all four was learning the complex but beautiful Bengali language.

A man nicknamed Putul (doll) was the Bengali course teacher and Joan the teacher/supervisor. *"Kaw, khaw, gaw, ghaw"* soon emanated from the classroom as the students tackled the first letters of the Bengali alphabet. Within two years they would be proficient enough in Bengali and would understand the culture of the people well enough to begin full-time hospital work.

The following day I was called from the operating suite to see a battered young man lying like a rag doll in the arms of his relative in a bicycle rickshaw. No respirations, no heart sounds—he was dead! Minutes earlier he had argued with a bus conductor over twenty *paisha* (three cents), then jumped from the moving bus and fell under its heavy, crushing wheels. *What a tragic, bitter commentary,* I thought, *on the expression "life is cheap."*

Before the week was over two patients flew in from Dacca, one the wife of a National Board of Revenue officer. It was possible to help her with medicine and the other lady with surgery.

Then the Mogh king, head of the southern one-third of the Chittagong Hill Tracts, came bringing his chief Buddhist priest for treatment. The priest, arrayed in his striking yellow robes, appeared on the outside to be reasonably tranquil. But on the inside a raging peptic ulcer burned, causing him much pain. He responded beautifully to treatment, and we had valuable discussions about spiritual issues important to us both.

During the first week of December Major Farook, impatient with talk—talk—talk, devised a new and daring plan to assassinate Sheikh Mujib in his helicopter.[20] Farook discussed the plan with his secret group and an air force squadron leader who was flight control officer in Dacca at the time. Farook, who knew there were short periods of radio silence between the helicopter and control tower when a helicopter flew from one control zone to the next, suggested that the squadron leader himself fly Mujib on his next trip, shoot him during a moment of radio silence between zones, then drop his body into the nearest river. In the meantime, Farook and his forces would capture Dacca. But Major Farook could not get the cooperation he needed to carry out the plot.

Farook was frustrated. He could not seem to find anyone he could depend on to act, and Dacca was filled with rumors that Mujib was about to make some move that would give him absolute power over the country. So in mid-December Farook decided to formulate a new plan that he himself could control. First he listed all the persons who might conceivably react against his attack and frustrate the plan. But his calculations revealed that it would take more than a brigade of troops to control everyone on his long list. Because he did not have that many soldiers at his disposal, little by little he began to whittle down the list by crossing off individuals who he decided might not have power or courage enough to react against his plot. He finally narrowed his list to just four names.

Every night Farook would write his lists, draw his diagrams, then carefully burn every scrap of paper. He could not afford to risk being discovered because, as he explained, "I had my wife, children, father and mother with me in the cantonment. All our lives were at stake."[21]

Across the cold Atlantic another life was at risk that December—the life of Hebron Station's Willard Benedict. Because he was plagued by prolonged Chittagong perihepatitis pain, we had sent

Willard to the U.S. for an intensive medical workup. That pain turned out to be his best friend, for the sophisticated medical testing uncovered a large tumor growing in his liver—in addition to the perihepatitis. So on December 11 Willard was wheeled into the operating room; there a skilled surgeon removed the tumor along with three-fifths of his liver. Although the operation was long, difficult, and bloody (44 units of blood), the result was excellent. Willard survived to become a pastor in the state of Florida. "Thank You, Father!"

A week before Christmas we flew to Dacca to receive Mark and Nancy flying in from their high school in Manila for Christmas vacation. We were thrilled to see them exit from the plane. Mark was easy to spot, looking handsome with his profusion of yellow curls and loud plaid sport coat. And Nancy, with her snapping brown eyes, looked beautiful. Later, we flew to Chittagong, then drove down to Malumghat, arriving after midnight. At 1:30 A.M. Nancy, after greeting all her waiting friends, was busily putting all her clothes in her drawers and pinning up pictures on her bulletin board. "I have to live in my room a little before I sleep in it," she explained. During their three weeks at home we celebrated a joyous Christmas and relished life together. Mark majored on hunting, bringing home for the larder as many as fifty birds in a single day.

On December 16 Bangladesh celebrated its third birthday with subdued fanfare. In the beginning Sheikh Mujib had asked for three years to set things right and bring stability and happiness to the people. Although the three years had passed, the people complained that they were poorer, hungrier, more sick and emaciated, and more threatened by armed robbers than ever before. How discouraging! The December 16 holiday was called "Victory Day," but neither the government nor the people were feeling very victorious.

As 1974 drew to a close, Mujib and his government made an unusual move. They issued the Emergency Powers Ordinance proclaiming an official state of emergency and a suspension of the fundamental rights of the people.[22] We could not understand the reason for this ordinance, for most of its restrictive provisions were already in force through previous tough laws. How puzzling! Bangladesh's third year had been a difficult one, and it ended on a note of confusion.

Key Events of 1974: Summary

January
- I take an urgent trip to Bangladesh—for 3 + months.

February
- The aged Mogh headman decides to follow Christ.
- Pakistan recognizes Bangladesh—and vice versa.
- Mujib attends the Islamic Summit meetings in Pakistan.
- We take a fascinating trip to Kutubdia Island.

March
- A visiting film team shoots 10,000 feet of film.
- The first four Murung believers are baptized.

April
- The "Tripartite Agreement" is signed; Bangladesh pardons the final 195 Pakistani POWs.
- The American consulate in Dacca is upgraded to the American embassy; then the first U.S. ambassador arrives.
- The deluxe paperback *Daktar* reaches the book stores.

May
- We attend awards dinner of The Society of Midland Authors.

July
- The Bangladesh economy is nearly moribund.
- Major Farook Reehman decides to assassinate Mujib.
- Egypt sends a gift of thirty Russian tanks to Bangladesh.
- We return to Bangladesh for our third term of service.
- Unprecedented floods inundate the country.

August
- *Negotiation #1:* we regain hospital's duty-free status.
- *Negotiation #2:* we regain import permit concessions.
- The government orders us to sign an agreement with them.
- Our young co-worker Dr. Peter McField tragically dies.

September
- *Negotiation #3:* negotiation regarding the "agreement" begins.
- Bangladesh finally is admitted into the United Nations.
- The "famine of '74" strikes; tens of thousands die of starvation.

October
- The new Aid Bangladesh Consortium raises money to prop up Bangladesh's economy.
- Secretary of State Kissinger visits Dacca for a few hours.

November
- I sign excellent agreement with the Bangladesh government.
- *Negotiation #4:* we gain additional land at Hebron.
- "Jalal" Ahmed takes a position with the U.S. embassy.

December
- Joan and I resume our work at Malumghat.
- Mujib suddenly declares a "state of emergency" and suspends the fundamental rights of the people.

Figure 16

8
1975: Mrus and Coups

The year began with an early-January announcement of the rules spawned by the Emergency Powers Ordinance. Many of them were a rehash of previous regulations that had controlled the press and listed the prevalent crimes—only this time the rules ordered the *death penalty* for smugglers, hoarders, black-marketeers, and others.[1] The opposition labeled it another case of overkill—and that was not meant as a pun.

Again provision was made for arresting anyone whom the government suspected might someday commit a crime (preventive detention). The first person arrested under this rule was an unlikely candidate. He was an acquaintance, Moudud Ahmed, a highly trained lawyer, law partner of our attorney, and general secretary of the Committee for Civil Liberties and Legal Aid. As secretary of this committee, his duty was to speak out against any government actions that diminished the democracy of the nation or the fundamental rights of the people, especially the opposition. Some claimed that his only "crime" was criticizing the government so convincingly that he was sometimes quoted in the foreign press. We could not know then that later he would be released, resume his law practice, become a highly respected author, and ultimately become a prime minister of Bangladesh.

On the personal side, during the second week in January a Bengali hunter who had affection for us brought a fresh sambar skin and part of the meat so that we could all enjoy a venison curry. Later our family relished a last picnic on the Cox's Bazar beach, celebrated Mark's birthday several weeks in advance, then sent Nancy and Mark back to Manila to resume their studies. What a delightful three weeks of Christmas vacation we had enjoyed together!

As our children were departing, another family with four children unexpectedly arrived at Malumghat. Things had become uncomfortable for the Kutubdia carpenter because some of his relatives and neighbors disliked him and his religious views; so he had come bringing his wife and four children from Kutubdia Island to our area. We helped them find a suitable place to stay, and the carpenter began plying his trade at the hospital and nearby areas.

In mid-January a middle-aged patient came to Malumghat from a very northern district of the country. He was a Brahmin (highest caste) Hindu with cancer of the tongue. We frequently see cancers of the tongue, mouth, and throat because many Bangalees smoke cigarettes and also chew betel nut—a bad combination that causes tissue damage and sometimes results in cancer. These patients usually come to us so late that the cancer can no longer be removed by surgery. But the Brahmin was different; he had come fairly early. I operated, removing the right half of his tongue, mouth, and a portion of his right neck. We were pleased when he survived the extensive surgery, made a good recovery, and returned to his home.

Also in mid-January we welcomed Dr. Dick Stagg (who had completed his language study in record time), his accomplished wife, Carol, and their three pretty daughters. While they began settling in, Joe DeCook and I and our nursing staff continued to receive the many patients who rolled in to Malumghat as though brought by an unending conveyor belt. That day Joe operated on a patient with acute abdominal pain; he found thirty ounces of fluid due to the perforation of an ulcer in the intestine caused by typhoid fever. An hour later I operated on another patient with an acute abdomen; I also found exactly thirty ounces of fluid caused by typhoid perforation. There was only one difference—this patient had *two* perforated typhoid ulcers.

The next day 120 miles to the north in Rangamati, the capital city of the Chittagong Hill Tracts, an unusual young man had a tragic accident. His name was Debapriyaw Roy; he was a prince of the Chakma tribe and a member of three tribal royal families. Because he was popular, handsome, personable, and a star soccer player, he had been elected "Mr. Rangamati" two years in a row. And as he was intelligent, too, he had been offered the opportunity to go to Moscow for university studies. Because of all these positives, people felt that he was well named—Debapriyaw means "beloved of a god."

But suddenly everything changed for Deb on that idyllic, sun-splashed day in Rangamati. Caught up in the pleasure of the moment, he and a friend raced about town on his new motorcycle. As Deb accelerated down a hill, suddenly, unexpectedly, an old man walked slowly out into the path of the oncoming cycle. Deb swerved confidently, but in that instant the old gentleman turned and darted back toward the roadside. The cycle struck him a mortal blow, and Debapriyaw was thrown from the cycle and knocked unconscious. Onlookers folded his tall, limp body into a motor rickshaw—the worst thing they could have done—and carried him to the very primitive Rangamati Hospital. When he regained consciousness Deb was terrified—he could feel nothing from his chest down, his legs were paralyzed, and his arms were partially paralyzed. But that day at Malumghat we knew nothing of him or his anguish 120 miles away.

At that point in time I had as patients two children requiring plastic surgery. The eleven-year-old girl, the niece of a member of Parliament (senator), had a lumpy, bumpy, long, irregular tumor of the scalp extending down into her neck. This tumor, called a hemangioma, was made up of very large abnormal blood vessels and could be relieved only by surgery. Dick Stagg took time off from his settling in to give the anesthesia. Because of the many blood vessels, there was considerable bleeding during the operation, but transfusion of a unit of blood compensated nicely for that; the result was excellent.

The six-year-old boy had quite a different problem. He had been born with deep clefts down the middle of both hands and feet, making them look something like lobster claws. The operation on each hand was nearly identical. First the incision, then removal of obstructing bone, next repair of the cleft, then constructing a web between the fingers, and finally applying the special bandage. At the first dressing change, when little Nurul saw his new hands for the first time, a huge smile lit up his little face—and I was pleased, too. Later we would also repair the boy's feet.

My physician colleague Joe DeCook was one of our idea men. And that January he floated two of his best ideas. Recognizing the importance of using more audio-visual technology, he began the use of a lapel microphone on those giving health lectures at the hospital and others teaching and preaching in the church and chapel services. In this way, over several years, the Audio-Visual Department collected a large library of immensely valuable lectures and messages on audiocassette.

His second idea evolved into the "Women's Mite" program. Hundreds of church women's groups in the U.S. were recruited to make small donations to the hospital and to pray earnestly for the work of our team. Because so many groups were involved, the many small donations added up to substantial contributions. And the multiplied prayers of hundreds and hundreds of women played their vital part in the many wonderful happenings at Malumghat.

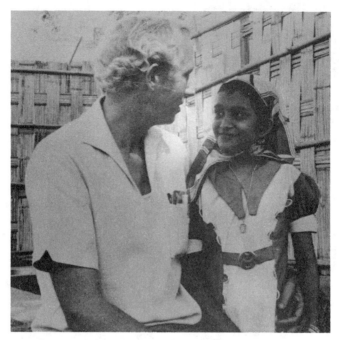

Senator's niece with scalp tumor

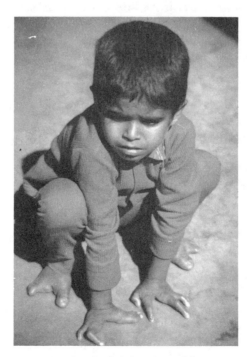

Boy with cleft hands and feet

Periodically Joe wrote informative and entertaining letters to these donors, keeping their interest high.

That January I focused on a new and satisfying assignment. Because Jay Walsh was in the U.S. on home leave, at his request I was assigned by the Station Council to supervise our work among the tribes of the southern Chittagong Hill Tracts (south of the Matamuhuri River). At the same time George Weber, located at our Hebron Station, would supervise the tribal outreach into the central portion of the Hill Tracts lying north of the Matamuhuri River.

A month earlier I had begun by gathering together a close-knit team of three tribesmen:

1. Gonijan was an educated member of the Tippera tribe and a pastor of the Malumghat church.
2. Robichandro was also a Tippera and the sparkplug of the new movement among the Murungs.
3. Menshai was one of the first new Murung believers; he possessed excellent speaking ability and a sense of calling to bring Christ's good news message to his people.

On the first day of the new year we had sent Robichandro and Menshai on a trek to six villages in our southern Chittagong Hill Tracts. Now, three weeks later, Gonijan and I listened intently to their report. In all, they had visited five Murung villages and one Tippera village.

The first Murung village gave them a mixed reception. More than half the families, who had recently become Christian believers, received them warmly. But some of the others mocked Robi and Menshai during their first teaching session, claiming that they already called on Shagrama, who seemed to embody their hazy conception of God. For three nights Robichandro faithfully continued his teaching, and members of one family decided to follow Christ. Three nights of teaching in the second Murung village also produced some results. The village *carbari* (leader) and his family members believed.

Then the men traveled on to Leukrang Murung village where Robi again began three nights of teaching. But after the first night he decided that Menshai had gained enough experience to give the message. When Menshai rose and spoke strongly and movingly in his Murung tongue, Leukrang Carbari himself and his family members placed their faith in Christ the Lord.

The next Murung village was filled with sadness and mourning, for a mother of three had just died of fever and throat pain (probably caused by diphtheria). A family member sadly explained, "We called on Shagrama to save her, but there was no result; she died anyway."

Robi replied, "For months you have heard about God from the new believers in your village. And for months you have refused to open your hearts to Him, so it will do you no good to call for Him when trouble comes. If you keep calling me to your house, but never allow me to come in, you make me feel sad and rejected. And that is how you are treating God. Now this poor woman has missed out on going to God's beautiful heaven because of her unbelief."

"Those are hard words, Robi," cried the dead woman's mother-in-law.

"Also I must tell you," Robichandro replied, "if you keep on refusing to believe, you, too, will miss out on God's heaven and go to a sad end like your daughter-in-law." Aroused by this conversation, everyone came to attend the evening meetings and listened intently to the teaching. The result? Members of four families believed, including the dead woman's husband and mother-in-law. Ultimately, all in this village became followers of Christ.

Finally, the two men trekked long and hard over high trails deep into the Hill Tracts to reach the last Murung village, which consisted of twenty-two houses. Because no Christian teacher had ever reached that distant village before, all were animists. As he taught, Robi quickly sensed that something was wrong. He stopped and began to ask questions. He soon discovered that some of these primitive people were confused, thinking that his picture-card visual aids were paper idols. Robi hastened to clear up this misconception, then taught far into the night, knowing that the next day they would have to depart. The teaching sparked some interest, so the leaders said, "Your words are good. Also, we heard a rumor that the headman of our *mouza* [subcounty] has believed. So please come back someday and tell us more."

Gonijan and I were impressed by this moving recital. The next day we met again so that we could learn the names of other competent tribal men whom we might possibly challenge to share in the trekking and teaching in the Chittagong hills. From this list we selected some names, and a few days later Robi and Menshai again headed for the hills to contact these men and continue their village outreach.

While Robi and Menshai had been engaged in their January trek, a drama of a different kind was taking place in Chittagong City. The central figure in this incident was a young man who had grown up to become an activist; as a student he had flirted with Communism and became a labor organizer. One day, some Christian literature came into his hands; he read it with great interest. Fascinated by some of the concepts, he searched until he found a Christian who wisely and carefully explained the way of life to him. Soon he became a follower of Christ, and began calling himself Samuel. Ultimately he became our co-worker in the New Testament translation project.

During the third week of January the Awami League leadership engaged in three days of official party meetings. Sheikh Mujib, the party's all-in-all, took a particularly forceful stance. Although he criticized the opposition, he blasted his own party men and officials even more strongly for their corruption. And, along with this drumbeat of criticism, he kept emphasizing that some sort of radical change in the government would be required to rescue the country from its doldrums and disintegration. He was so insistent and so dominating that no one felt like arguing with him—or even questioning him too closely about exactly what he meant by a radical change. At the close of the meetings the party officials simply empowered Mujib "to take such steps as are necessary to resolve all the outstanding problems of the country."[2]

Just four days later Mujib took the first giant step. He moved with unbelievable brashness to make drastic changes in the carefully designed, much-admired Constitution of Bangladesh—and the very nature of the government itself. He picked Saturday January 25 to introduce to the Parliament the Fourth Amendment to the Constitution. That day there seemed to be implicit in his commanding presence something that deterred anyone from opposing what he was doing. And so, *without any debate*, the immensely important Fourth Amendment Bill was quickly and quietly passed into law in less than an hour's time.

Remarkably enough, one section of this constitutional amendment ousted the existing president of the country and declared Sheikh Mujib the new president—making an election superfluous. Another provision in the amendment ordered that the oath of office would be given to the president, not by the country's chief justice as usual, but rather by the speaker of the National Assembly, who was close at hand. So there in the Parliament Building, shortly after the bill was passed, the speaker hastily administered the oath of office to the nation's new instant president. Because it all happened so quickly, and because the Supreme Court does not meet on Saturdays, there was no legal challenge to this unprecedented series of actions. Then the new system—and the new president—were presented to the nation and to the world as a *fait accompli*. What an incredible Saturday morning!

But why did Mujib decide to switch from being prime minister, the action post, to president, which was a figurehead position? Because this new amendment converted Bangladesh from a parliamentary democracy to an autocratic system; in this new "presidential" system the prime minister's authority was sharply reduced, whereas the president became the all-powerful chief executive of the republic. Here are a few other changes wrought on that amazing Saturday morning:

1. The legislature (National Assembly) was no longer the most powerful organ of the Bangladesh government; President Mujib was now supreme.
2. The judiciary (judges and courts of law) was no longer independent and protected from intervention by the executive branch of government; President Mujib now had broad new powers, even over the judges and courts.
3. Sheikh Mujib was now authorized to dissolve all existing political parties and establish a single national political party under his own control.[3]

These are only the broad outlines of the sweeping changes brought in by the Fourth Amendment; for those interested in further specifics, I have summarized additional details in table 3. Although for months the unpredictable Mujib had seemed securely in the Western nations' orbit, he had suddenly changed course once again. The Soviets—and his nephew Sheikh Moni—had convinced Mujib that a single-party semidictatorship was Bangladesh's only hope.

As soon as the National Assembly passed the Fourth Amendment, Mujib addressed the body. His extemporaneous speech was rambling and punctuated by angry words. One by one he explosively ticked off the woes and problems afflicting the country and the tragic circumstances of the people. And he justified the Fourth Amendment as the only way to bring order out of such chaos; for a dangerous disease strong medicine is required. This, then, was Mujib's "second revolution."

We were stunned when we read the next day's newspapers. Sheikh Mujib had not only devoted his life to the struggle for democracy, but he had spent years in prison because of his passionate belief in the democratic process. He had given innumerable speeches extolling the virtues of democracy. He had struggled against Pakistani leaders because they did not share his views about full, unfettered democracy. And he had established the nation of Bangladesh and its Constitution squarely on the principles of parliamentary democracy. But suddenly, in an hour's time, he had dismantled the whole system. Mujib's about-face was so drastic that our minds could hardly take it in that first day we learned of it.

The following day he began to utilize his extensive new powers. In quick succession, a council of ministers was sworn in, the National Assembly session was abruptly adjourned, and the office of the radical leftist JSD party newspaper was seized. Mujib had mounted his new "Fourth Amendment steed" and was galloping off into the future.

During that last week in January at Malumghat Jalal Ahmed's wife, Shakina, with her daughter Bitu, dropped in out of the blue —quite literally. They arrived by government helicopter to enjoy a two-week visit with us and to allow Shakina to have her medical checkup. That same week we received surgeon-in-training Dr. Jack Sorg with his wife, Sandy, and two little daughters. They had come to work with us for the next six months and would live with us in our home. Ultimately, they became career workers with our organization and replicated our style of medical mission along the Amazon River in South America. We were delighted to have friends Shakina and Bitu Ahmed and the enjoyable Sorg family with us.

Then our attorney, the former government minister Amirul Islam, arrived at Malumghat to visit us and have his medical examination. With him was his handsome young son, who was also to have a routine checkup. Although the child had no complaints and looked fine, I examined him thoroughly. And, as often happens, thoroughness paid dividends. A laboratory test revealed that the boy had developed childhood diabetes. For both father and son the trauma of this news was compounded by the shock of learning that the boy would require daily insulin injections—and Amirul must learn how to give them. At the same time, Shakina Ahmed's daughter Bitu also needed to learn how to give her diabetic mother daily insulin injections. When I told Amirul and Bitu that I would teach them how to give the injections, they agreed to "take a stab at it."

"Here, take this syringe," I began. "Now put the needle on it, like this, but be careful not to touch the shaft of the needle. Next you'll practice on these oranges, and when you can give the orange a smooth injection, it will be easy to do it for your patients. No, don't push it in slowly. That is too painful—even the orange will complain about that. Pop it quickly through the skin, almost like throwing a dart. Yes, that's right. Now you're getting it."

A week later I was summoned to the Outpatient Department by these hastily scrawled words: "Can you come now? A VIP is here to see you." The VIP turned out to be a fascinating person, a triply notable minister of the Bangladesh government:

1. She was the only woman in Sheikh Mujib's new council of ministers (cabinet).
2. She, a Buddhist, was the only non-Muslim minister.
3. She was also the queen mother of the Chakma tribe.

I could tell in an instant that Mrs. Benita Roy was worried. She came right to the point. "Doctor," she said in perfect British-

Table 3. Effect of the Fourth Amendment on the Bangladesh Constitution

	Original Bangladesh Constitution	Fourth Amendment Changes
Chief executive officer	The prime minister was the chief executive of the republic, while the president was but a figurehead.	The president, with immense new powers, replaced the prime minister as chief executive of the nation, whereas the prime minister had a much diminished role.
Executive branch of government (the president, prime minister, cabinet ministers, and their ministries)	The prime minister, president, and vice-president were elected by members of the National Assembly (Parliament). The chief executive officer (prime minister) was accountable to the Parliament. The cabinet of ministers was responsible to the Parliament.	Mujib was declared president by the Fourth Amendment; future presidents would be elected by the public. The president was empowered to appoint his vice-president, prime minister, and council of ministers—and he could dismiss them at his own discretion. The powerful president, as chief executive officer and head of state, was accountable to no one (except that he was subject to impeachment by a three-fourths majority vote of the Parliament). The council of ministers was responsible to the all-powerful president.
Legislative branch of government (the National Assembly = Parliament)	As the most powerful branch of the Bangladesh government, the Parliament was sovereign and supreme. The executive branch of government (the prime minister, president, cabinet ministers and their ministries) were accountable to the Parliament. The members of Parliament elected the chief executive officer (prime minister) from among their own ranks. The Parliament had full authority to pass laws, and no one had the power of veto over those laws.	With his new sweeping authority, the president became more powerful than Parliament—he was sovereign and supreme. The prime minister and council of ministers were now accountable to the president—and the executive branch of government was no longer accountable to the Parliament. The Fourth Amendment declared Sheikh Mujib the chief executive officer and head of state (president); future presidents would be elected by the public. The president now held the power to veto any new law made by Parliament—and he also had the authority to dissolve the Parliament. These provisions gave the president effective control over the Parliament and greatly diminished the significance of the legislative branch of government.

Table 3. Effect of the Fourth Amendment on the Bangladesh Constitution (cont.)

	Original Bangladesh Constitution	Fourth Amendment Changes
Judicial branch of government (the judges and courts of law)	The separate and independent judiciary was insulated from control by the executive branch of government (so that it could fairly resolve disputes between citizens and the executive branch). The Supreme Court had the authority to protect and enforce the fundamental human rights granted by the Constitution to the people. The Supreme Court had the authority to appoint the judges of the lower courts. Judges could be dismissed only through a process of impeachment. The chief justice administered the oath of office to the president, speaker, and deputy speaker of Parliament.	The president now had broad new powers over the judiciary, making it subservient to the executive branch of government. The authority to enforce fundamental rights was withdrawn from the Supreme Court. The president now had the authority to appoint all judges. Now the president was authorized to remove any judge, including the chief justice, at his discretion. The speaker of the Parliament administered the oath to the president, then the president administered the oath to the speaker and the deputy speaker.
Political parties	Multiple political parties each had the right to create platforms and sponsor candidates for elections.	One-party political system—the president was empowered to dissolve all existing political parties and establish a single national party. The elected members of Parliament would lose their seats unless they joined this new party.

style English, "I have a serious problem, and I need your help. My grandson, Debapriyaw Roy, was terribly injured three weeks ago in a motorcycle accident at Rangamati. We transferred him to a hospital in Chittagong City, but he is getting worse, not better. He is paralyzed and has a high fever—he is dying. Doctor, will you receive him here and try to help him?" She was not weeping, but there were tears in her voice.

"Of course we will receive him. Bring him as soon as you can," I replied. "We will prepare a room for him immediately, and all will be ready when he arrives. His case sounds very difficult, and I cannot guarantee the outcome, but you may be sure that we will do our best to help him."

"Oh, I do thank you, Doctor. Because of your words I will return home with a lighter heart. Thank you very much."

Hours later twenty-year-old Chakma prince Debapriyaw arrived. He was alert, spoke Bengali and Chakma fluently, and was taller than most Bangladeshis; also, he could read English quite well and could speak it somewhat, but preferred to converse in Bengali. He explained the details of his motorcycle accident and all that had happened since then. His legs were still completely paralyzed and his arms and hands partly so. He could feel virtually nothing from the chest down. He was feverish and had a massive, ugly, infected bedsore just above his buttocks. The cause of all this? The lowest vertebra in his neck had been broken and displaced, damaging the nerve tissue of his spinal cord.

Our team swung into action—we drew blood for laboratory tests, took X rays, put a sterile catheter in place, started powerful antibiotics, placed him on a special mattress, and began changing his position hourly. Physiotherapist Larry Golin began applying the appropriate exercises daily. Then I took Deb to the operating room, drilled two holes in his skull, and inserted special stainless steel tongs so that we could apply traction to his damaged neck vertebra.

From the operating table we shifted him directly to a special turning bed that would allow him to be face down part of the time, make it easier to treat his bedsore, and prevent the formation of other bedsores. We were making some progress. By this time his fever was gone and his general condition improved, but the lost sensation and the paralysis had not changed—and probably would not change, because his spinal cord was so badly damaged and because he had come to us so late.

Later that day we had a visit from our friend Shahabuddin, son of the elderly Muslim patriarch of our area, the old gentleman who had interceded on our behalf with President Ayub Khan. Our friend had come to invite us to dinner to celebrate his fourth wedding anniversary. After she served him tea Joan asked, "Shahabuddin, have you ever heard of our American custom of giving particular kinds of gifts for wedding anniversaries, depending on which anniversary it is?"

He replied, "I have never heard of that."

"Here, let me show you the list in this book."

As Shahabuddin read the list, a big smile crinkled his face and he exclaimed, "I can see that this list was prepared by a man for us men. See, the first year's gift is paper—then cotton, leather, wood—I should give her a wooden gift this year. But Bengali wives always want a new silk *sari* and some gold jewelry on these occasions. Definitely, this list was made by a man for us men!"

In mid-February Major Farook wrote two crucial words in his diary: "OFFENSIVE PHASE."[4] This soldier-talk meant that he was now ready to launch his coup at any time. His cryptic phrase signaled the end of three long months of intense surveillance and planning. Each night during that investigative phase, Major Farook had removed his jackboots and uniform, then donned a gray-checked *lungi*, dark top, and sandals as a convenient disguise. Then he traveled by bicycle rickshaw to the upper-class Dhanmondi Residential Area where he dismounted on the main road. There he would blend with the crowds and stroll into Road 32, the location of Sheikh Mujib's house.

Squatting in the shadows by the lake across the road from the house, Farook appeared to be just an ordinary passerby, but his sharp eyes recorded all the comings and goings because, as he later explained, "I had to check Mujib over personally for a period to see exactly what were his movements, his habits, what he did, where he went. I had to firmly establish the pattern of his life."[5] Fortunately for Farook, some of his own First Bengal Lancers troops provided the military night guard at Mujib's house. So Farook often stopped in to check on the vigilance of his soldiers—and to chat innocently with them about the movements of family members and visitors to Mujib's house.

Leaving the house, Farook checked the flow of traffic in the area and noted any possible snags to the future movement of his troops and tanks. Then he would proceed on to carry out his nightly surveillance at the homes of his other targets—the influential relatives of Mujib. Because he could not risk requisitioning military maps of the area, he had to make do with a small city map put out by the Tourist Bureau.

Farook's long hours of work, added to the extreme danger of the scheme, produced anxiety and quite severe stomach pains. His physician admitted him to the military hospital and gave him a tranquilizer because, as he told Farook, "You are suffering from extreme tension; you are concentrating too much on something."[6]

Farook soon left the hospital because he could not afford the mental fuzziness the tranquilizer caused; he knew he needed a clear mind during those critical days. By mid-February his strategy was complete; he was now ready to kick off the "offensive phase" as soon as the time seemed right.

A few days later two of our experienced personnel returned from home leave. Nurse Mary Lou Brownell had first come to the country even before we did. She had operated effective clinics in Chittagong City and at Hebron Station before there was any Memorial Christian Hospital. And later it had been her vision to establish Malumghat's beautiful Heart House program, which involves training destitute women in sewing and handicrafts, including making attractive dolls, so that they can support themselves and their children.

Linda Short was as short as I am tall; we cut quite a figure whenever we stood side by side. Linda had returned to continue her valuable work of teaching Bible classes to Christian women —and to begin a new program of teaching illiterate Bangalee women to read. Because of Linda, the program of training church women considerably antedated the program of training the men. She was also a tireless and welcome visitor to Bangalee homes.

Linda Short

We read in the February 25 newspapers that Sheikh Mujib had exercised the power granted to him by the shocking Fourth Amendment to dissolve all political parties and create a single new nationwide political party. This new national party he named the *Bangladesh Krishak Sramik Awami League* (BaKSAL)—in English, the "Bangladesh Farmers'/Laborers'/People's League." But we and the public had to wait nearly four months to learn the BaKSAL party's organizational setup, platform, and leaders' names. However, the public's expectation was high that honest, competent leaders would be selected to guide the new party.

During the final week in February Robichandro Tippera and Menshai Murung returned with three prospective tribal teachers/preachers. We enjoyed long, detailed discussions together, and I quickly learned to appreciate the three new Tippera men—Shadijan, Shotish, and Gonochandro.

Each of these men explained that he had given much prayerful consideration to the idea of trekking the hills to proclaim Christ's good news message to more and more tribal villages. They had discussed the proposition in depth with their families for, among the tribes, decisions tend to be made more by families than by individuals. Their family members had agreed to the plan and sent them off with their blessing to be servants of the most high God. I found myself greatly moved by their recital, for I knew that their wives and children were making real sacrifices. The men would be paid from the tithes and offerings given by the tribal churches into their tribal church fund.

Also during these meetings, we decided to build at Malumghat a tribal guesthouse and teaching center so that we could properly receive tribal patients and tribal leaders who came in for training. Then, on the final day of our tribal meetings, I gave the men a session on how to wisely help an interested person turn to Christ and begin following Him. In concluding this session I added, "I know that tribal people tend to make important decisions as families rather than as individuals. And that is a fine system. But it is important when a tribal household decides for Christ that you question each one to be sure that each person really understands and has opportunity to pray a personal prayer of faith. You should aim to produce good, strong, genuine, believing people who will no longer worship trees and rivers—and no longer make blood sacrifices to Satan and the spirits."

Then Gonochandro spoke up and explained this last point far better than I had. "Yes," he said, "we want tribal believers who are like the inside core of a great tree which is hard as a rock. Insects can attack and eat the bark and outer layer of such a tree, but they cannot touch the hard inner part."

By this time, at the hospital Debapriyaw's condition had stabilized. His infections were controlled, his nutrition was improved, and the bedsore was clean, but his numbness and paralysis were unchanged. His tragic condition had stimulated a great outpouring of sympathy from the hospital staff. Christian staff members prayed earnestly for him in the hospital chapel services, in their church services, and in their homes. Yet his situation seemed so hopeless. Then one day, suddenly, normal sensation began to return to his body—first his chest, then his abdomen, thighs, legs, feet, and toes. And a few days later he wiggled one big toe, then the other! The news went around the hospital like wildfire—and we all rejoiced with Deb. "Thank You, Father!"

The hospital staff's prayerful interest and the careful, competent, compassionate care which Debapriyaw was receiving from the whole medical team made a tremendous impact on him and his family. They began asking questions about why our staff members were so helpful and loving. "Is it their Christian religion that makes them so kind? What are the teachings of the Christian religion, anyway?"

Day by day I would answer these and other questions and explain Christ's good news message to Deb, his mother, and his friend. We gave them Scriptures in Bengali and someone loaned Deb a copy of *Daktar*. I noticed he was reading these books avidly,

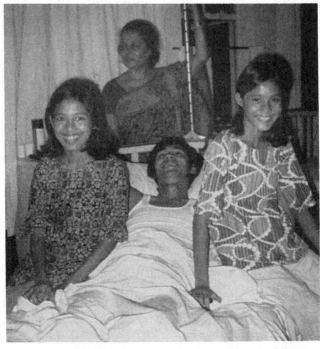

Deb with mother and younger sisters Ring and Ting

especially when his turning bed rotated him into the face-down position. His eyes were just the right distance from the books placed on the floor, and when his weakened arms became weary, his little sister Ring patiently turned the pages for him. Later, we were able to transfer him back to a standard hospital bed.

The questions, answers, discussions, and reading all had an increasingly positive effect. One morning, after examining Deba-priyaw and writing his orders for the day, I said, "Well, Deb, do you have any more questions about your treatment or about these spiritual issues you have been asking about?"

"No, Doctor, I think you have answered all my questions."

"So what have you decided about Christ the Lord? Have you concluded that His words are true?"

"Yes, I do believe His teachings are true."

"Well, then, are you going to accept Him as your Savior and Lord?"

"Yes, I am ready now."

"Would you like to do so in a private way or here with your family and friend?"

Deb glanced at them and nodded his head almost impercepti-bly toward the door; they slipped quietly out of the room. Then he prayed a heartfelt prayer of repentance and faith, finishing with these words, "Oh, God, I do accept into my heart your Son Jesus as my Savior and Master. Please save me from my faults and sins, and thank you for loving me so much—and for helping my hurt body to improve. Amen." Then I prayed for Deb and his family, commit-ting them to God's loving care. It was a deeply moving moment for both of us. Within hours Deb's mother also made the great faith decision. "Thank You, Father!"

During the first quarter of 1975 we again noticed an increas-ing number of ragged, poorly-nourished patients in our Outpatient Department. Famine had returned to stalk the land. I guess it was predictable, for the previous winter's harvest had been small due to crop damage by the unprecedented 1974 floods. Now that scanty harvest had been nearly consumed, rice prices were up again, and we noticed the lean, haunted look of hungry people all around.

Fortunately, our many wonderful supporters in the United States and Canada and new friends in Germany and Holland gave sacrificially to our famine relief fund. This allowed us to do three things:

1. Feed starving patients and pay their medical expenses
2. Purchase bulk quantities of rice from the market, then re-sell to our staff at a price they could afford
3. Purchase a substantial acreage of land to put into rice pro-duction for the future benefit of our patients and staff

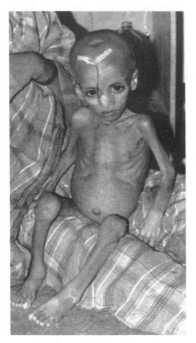

Malnourished child

The specter of starvation finally eased after an excellent spring rice harvest and the arrival of delayed shipments of grain from abroad.

About this time I admitted a young woman with a swollen, tender neck and a history of swallowing a crab claw a week before —she must have been really hungry! The claw was firmly stuck in her esophagus (swallowing tube). Under anesthesia I inserted a special lighted pipelike instrument (esophagoscope) through her mouth into the esophagus. Because the claw was tightly stuck, I had to remove it piecemeal with a long forceps. Happily, she made a good recovery.

On the following Sunday afternoon I heard a soft knock at our front door. Responding, I found a crowd of seven people. So I invited them in, and after they were seated Daniel and a former Hindu named Indra introduced Indra's five relatives: his two daughters, brother, brother's wife, and a more distant relative. I soon learned that for some weeks Daniel and Indra had been explaining Scriptural truth to them. While we sipped tea together they asked me their final questions and were satisfied with the answers. It was obvious that the five were ready to place their faith in Christ the Lord—and they did so. Later they departed looking very pleased.

In mid-March Farook's brother-in-law and co-conspirator, Major Rashid, took leave from his gunnery training course in India to visit Dacca. Farook briefed him on the results of his many nights of surveillance and on his refined tactical plan for the killing of President Mujib. Because both majors recognized that they lacked the stature and experience to assume the presidency, they discussed at length whom to elevate to that position if their coup should succeed. Their first choice was the respected Major General Ziaur Rahman (General Zia), the second-in-command of the Bangladesh Army.

So man-of-action Farook succeeded in getting an appointment with General Zia on the evening of March 20. Major Farook knew that he could not address such a shocking subject head-on with the deputy chief of army staff without the risk of putting himself in jeopardy. He later explained how he had gingerly approached this sensitive topic: "Actually we came around to it by discussing the corruption and everything that was going wrong. I said the country required a change. Zia said, 'Yes, yes. Let's go outside and talk,' and then he took me on the lawn.

"As we walked on the lawn I told him that we were professional soldiers who serve the country and not an individual. The army and the civil government, everybody, was going down the drain. [I said,] 'We have to have a change. We, the junior officers, have already worked it out. We want your support and your leadership.' "

Zia replied, "I am sorry; I would not like to get involved in anything like this. If you want to do something you junior officers should do it yourself. Leave me out of it."[7]

According to one report, another person also approached General Zia about that time regarding the same subject; he allegedly represented Minister of Commerce Mushtaque Ahmed. Mushtaque was the minister who had secretly communicated with the U.S. government in Calcutta in 1971 to frustrate the breakup of Pakistan and the full independence of Bangladesh. Now he reportedly sent one of his men to convince Zia to lead a military putsch against Mujib. Zia listened but also declined to become involved in his proposed coup.[8]

During the third week in March all the members of our mission congregated at Malumghat for our biannual Field Council meetings. There were excellent station reports and committee reports. Dr. Joe DeCook, writing the Medical Committee Report, was able to relate that the hospital's financial crisis had eased. This was due largely to increased funding from West Germany's generous Christoffel Blindenmission. Joe, in his inimitable way, also reported on a new staff house building project:

> In an attempt to beat the impossible cost of building materials, and yet provide enough housing for our Bengali staff, we felt we should try mud construction. No sooner had we made that decision, than some men digging on our property came up with a momentous find—they struck mud! In fact, it turns out to be the basic foundation of our whole property. Working with our seismographs and geological charts, we were impressed to discover that from ages past God in His foreknowledge had placed here just for our use at this time an extremely rich deposit of mud. Currently four family dwellings are under construction with this new "brown gold."

The next day I had a visit from Oncherai Tippera, whom I had not seen for a long time. Oncherai was a born leader, one of the very first Tippera Christians in the central Hill Tracts, and the leading Tippera Bible/theology teacher. He talked about three disturbing problems currently plaguing the tribal people. First, the communist Shorbohara party members had become very active in the Chittagong Hill Tracts and were causing no end of trouble. They demanded food from every village they entered—and because they were armed, they got it. They carried Chinese weapons, pictures of Chairman Mao, and copies of Chairman Mao's world-famous red book.

Second, for a week the Rakkhi Bahini had been announcing in the tribal bazaars that fifty tribal men from each *mouza* (subcounty) must volunteer for military training. The result? Many

Mud house under construction

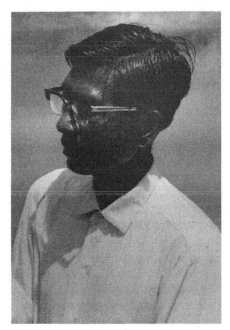

Oncherai Tippera

Mogh men were fleeing across the border into Burma, while Tipperas and others were crossing into India.

And third, he talked about hunger, for the famine was striking the hills as well as the plains. "Doctor Shahib," he explained, "A few years ago rice was only one taka per *sher* [two pounds], but now a sher costs eight takas! On top of that, Bengali dacoits have attacked four of our villages and taken all the food and the womenfolks' ornaments. Many Tipperas are already reduced to eating jungle potatoes [roots], and at least three have died of starvation. I fear that one out of every four Tipperas may die in the next month or two unless they get some help."

"Oncherai," I replied, "I am shocked to hear your report. We will do everything we can to help with food—and we will redouble our prayers for the hill people." He was relieved and grateful.

The next day I met with our other tribal teachers and leaders who confirmed the seriousness of the famine conditions in the hills. We decided to provide some food to prevent starvation deaths and seed rice to ensure the next harvest. We also decided that Gonochandro Tippera would begin to work out of Hebron Station since it was much closer to his home. Shotish Tippera would live in a Mogh village long enough to improve his knowledge of the Mogh language, while Shadijan Tippera would move into a Murung village to begin learning the Murung language.

And that very day we were reminded to rejoice about the progress among the Murung people when new Murung believers arrived from the hills, bringing in the first tithes and offerings for their church fund and the salaries of their teachers. Like the poor widow in the Scriptures, they gave to their Lord out of extreme poverty.

Also by the third week in March, Debapriyaw had gained further function in his legs; he could now flex his knees and ankles. Real progress! He was more comfortable, too, for Dr. Jack Sorg had closed the open bedsore by a plastic surgery operation.

During that same week we operated on a young woman whose face had been smashed in an automobile accident. Interestingly enough, none of the standard X rays of her face had revealed any broken bones. But when the swelling subsided I was able to detect several fractured facial bones by simple physical examination, and a special X ray confirmed these findings. At the operating table we located the various fractures and wired the bones together. Also, I discovered that the floor of the orbit of her left eye was so badly shattered that the eye had sunk downward; this I had expected to find, for she had complained of double vision. So I manufactured a new orbital floor, using a plastic mesh material that supported her eye very nicely. Within three weeks she looked much better and her vision was perfect. Months later, while Joan and I were shopping in New Market in Chittagong City, I felt a gentle tugging at my sleeve. There was my patient—and her face looked very pretty.

Meanwhile, Mujib was still crafting the government's "new face." On March 26, the fourth anniversary of Pakistan's brutal attack on Dacca and Bangladesh's declaration of independence, he made a wide-ranging speech that laid out more facets of his second revolution.[9] He announced these overall objectives: stop corruption, increase production, initiate effective family planning, and build national unity.

Mujib then announced an impressive program to decentralize the administration of the country:

1. The country's twenty-one districts would be abolished.
2. Then the sixty-one subdivisions would be transformed into sixty-one new districts. Each new district would be run by a governor (rather than by a deputy commissioner). This powerful governor, assisted by a district council, would not only operate the day-by-day administration of the district, but also he would control the police, the army, the Rakkhi Bahini, and the border militia in his district.

Shadijan Tippera

First tithes from Murung tribesmen

3. The 465 subdistricts known as *thanas* (counties) would be upgraded into important centers of local administration. Courts would be established at this subdistrict level so that the public would not have to travel all the way to courts in the district towns to obtain justice.
4. At the village level, each of the nation's 68,000 villages would have a large cooperative with compulsory membership. These multipurpose groups would promote cooperative farming and marketing, and would help put idle, hungry men to work.

Also in his speech Mujib explained these other unique aspects of his second revolution:

- The Bangladesh Army would be transformed into a "people's army." Instead of fighting enemies of the country, it would be utilized constructively in building the nation.
- With the new one-party political system and the changes in the government, corruption would be completely eliminated.
- Everyone in the society would work harder, which would automatically increase production.

Although there certainly seemed to be merit in decentralizing the administration, Mujib's picture of a totally hard-working, corruption-free society seemed unrealistic. How could reorganizing the administration of the country suddenly transform the basic nature of those members of the society long involved in cheating, smuggling, hoarding, political assassination, and other forms of crime and corruption?

At 4:30 A.M. on Easter Sunday we were awakened by singers from the church who were serenading the various households. Two hours later I opened the sunrise service in the lovely hospital garden, bright with poinsettia bushes, surrounded by church members, hospital staff, and interested patients and their relatives. Some were illiterate, others literate, and yet others were highly literate. Among them were Christians, Muslims, Hindus, Buddhists, and animists.

I knew that it would require an innovative approach to hold the interest of this diverse audience and make the Easter message live for them. So I read the appropriate Scripture passages from the manuscript of the readily understandable standard Bengali New Testament. Then, using some very large and beautiful pictures, I showed and explained the thrilling events of that first Good Friday and Easter Sunday. Next I focused on several particular

Part of Easter sunrise service congregation

pictures, then attached a one-word Bengali title to each picture in turn. Those several words then became the outline for the Easter message I wanted to present.

Later I learned that the Stagg family's houseboy was so moved by the events of the first Good Friday and Easter that he wept all the way back to their house. I was not surprised, for those were the events that had shattered my own agnosticism, brought me to faith, and so changed the course of my life.

By the end of March Major Farook was feeling steadily more frustrated. He had failed to gain the support of General Zia, and his trusted co-conspirator, Major Rashid, had been posted to a town far from Dacca near the Indian border. Forgetting for the moment his long nights of surveillance and careful planning, on a sudden impulse he decided on a whole new scheme to assassinate Mujib. He went to his friend, an air force squadron leader, and said, "What about taking off in some MiGs and doing a bit of strafing on his house? I'll surround the house, and you can control the whole thing with your aircraft."[10] Amazingly, the squadron leader agreed, and they scheduled their off-the-cuff operation for the next day at dawn. But, when Farook laid out the plan before his secret group, not one agreed to fall in with it.

Now Major Farook was really upset. None of his plans had succeeded, and he had relearned the lesson that others were often undependable. Then he decided on a new tack. He began feigning complete loss of interest in killing Sheikh Mujib. As he put it, "I told everybody to forget it. I withdrew completely from all discussions so that they would think that I had cooled down. I believe in tactical surprise. The idea was to let the others believe that I had gone to sleep."[11]

Then in April the two majors got a break. Through an unexpected series of circumstances Rashid obtained a transfer to Dacca. His transfer made him the commanding officer of the Second Field Artillery Unit. Now Farook had someone whom he could trust in a position to help him. Major Rashid soon approached army headquarters with the suggestion that his artillery unit join the First Bengal Lancers Tank Battalion's night training exercises. When the army brass agreed to this proposal, Farook and Rashid were delighted. The cantonment population and the neighbors had already become accustomed to the rumble and clatter of tanks on alternate Thursday nights —and soon they became used to seeing the artillery together with the tank forces during these night maneuvers twice a month. The stage was being set.

Major Farook had decided to wait until July or August to strike, because then the country would be converted into a swamp by the relentless monsoon rains. Hopefully, this would discourage India from deciding to send forces to bolster Mujib's BaKSAL party and government. Farook put it this way: "If India does anything and we are forced into a civil war then the monsoon is the one season they will be badly tied down. If everything fails, at least we will have the protection of the monsoon."[12]

Farook's plan to wait for the monsoon season gained some unexpected metaphysical support. In early April Farook came to Chittagong on army business; because his stomach pain continued to trouble him, his wife took the skeptical Farook to confer with a famous Muslim holy man named Awndho Hafiz (blind holy man). Hafiz had never seen anything, for he had been blind from birth. But he was reputed to have mystical powers, including the ability to "see" into a person's mind. The two men, as different as night and day, sat side-by-side on a cot in the holy man's quarters. He took Farook's hands in his own and held them quietly. Finally Blind Hafiz said to Farook, "I know you are going to do something very dangerous. Do whatever you have to do, but if you do not follow the principles I give you, you will be destroyed."[13]

The three principles that Farook must observe were these: he should carry out his task to serve the cause of Allah and Islam, not for personal gain; he should have courage; he should choose the correct timing, which meant waiting at least three months.

Farook was stunned and impressed by Blind Hafiz, his seeming knowledge of what was in Farook's head, and the delay he suggested that fit in perfectly with his own sense of timing.

By early April Joan and I were gearing up to press on with our special Bengali common language New Testament translation project. Samuel, the young man from Chittagong City, had moved to Malumghat to be the main Bengali translator. Several other men were available in the area to help with checking the translation. I had some long sessions with them, explaining the principles of our translation project and how the work should be done. They seemed quite enthusiastic about sharing in the project that would ultimately give to the vast Muslim community the gift of the precious Holy Scriptures.

Also during that first week in April, I met again with our tribal team. Shotish reported that ten days in a Mogh village had doubled his proficiency in the Mogh language. Shadijan explained that the Murung language was very difficult, but he had learned *ek ana* (one sixteenth) of it. And, teaching in rudimentary Mogh and "hill Bengali," he had helped three Murung families come to faith in Christ. Robi reported that he and Menshai Murung had visited a very warm and receptive Murung village; there the members of five families had decided to follow Christ the Lord. Menshai had remained to give these new believing families further instruction.

During their trek Robi and Menshai had also reached ten Murung villages to notify the leaders that there would be a special seminar for them at Hebron Station. For months George Weber had been doing a tremendous job of teaching spiritual truth to Tippera leaders in a monthly seminar program; these sessions were in addition to the annual tribal Bible school. Now George, with the help of tribal teachers, would hold the first of many seminars for Murung leaders. His program greatly strengthened the tribal Christian leaders in both the central and our southern Hill Tracts regions.

Shotish Tippera

Menshai Murung

The next morning we distributed food and seed-rice money to a number of tribal village heads. Their next move astounded—and melted—us all. Deeply influenced by Biblical teaching on tithing (giving one-tenth) they insisted on *giving a tenth of their relief money into their church fund!* The impact of the lesson that those simple impoverished tribal men taught me that day has never left my heart.

Also during April our tribal leaders told me about another group of Murung Christians who lived in Hill Tracts villages far to the north of us. I learned further that one of these northern Murung Christians, Shintai Murung, was a song leader who knew some Murung language hymns. Here was the key to teaching hymnology to our new Murung congregations. A few days later our men brought Shintai to Malumghat, where we hired him for a month to begin teaching spiritual songs to our Murung churches in the southern Hill Tracts.

By then, Joan's Bengali language students had learned how to read and sing Bengali hymns; they were making solid progress, despite various obstacles. She had developed excellent grammar drills and comprehension exercises, which were a great help to the students. However, Joan had lost her good Bengali instructor, who had moved away from the area. And her letter home that week vividly described some of her difficulties in finding a suitable replacement:

> It has been a frustrating week in many ways for me, for I was working with a language teacher applicant who drove me and all the students right up the wall. He doesn't understand enough English to know what is going on, and he doesn't thoroughly understand the spelling and grammar of Bengali (but bluffs it). And he is of the school of thought which makes him jump down the throat of anyone who makes a mistake—which is not the way we approach it at all!

At that point in time we were hearing rumors that two discharged employees were working together behind the scenes to stir up trouble against the mission staff. Then we received an anonymous warning that Linda Short should stop giving literacy instruction and holding Bible studies in the Cha Bagan Christian village. She did not take this threat too seriously, but a week later between the hospital and Cha Bagan a boy hurled a stone at her, then scampered away—the stone struck her in the face. Naturally, Linda was momentarily shaken by the experience. No one at Malumghat had ever been "stoned" before.

That same day Dr. Q. came to the hospital. Suddenly, at the roadside six young men seized him and began to beat him savagely. Then they forced him into a waiting motor rickshaw where three men inside pommeled him while three others hung on the outside. As the vehicle raced to the south one assailant put a revolver to Dr. Q.'s head and demanded money; he was surprised to get 8,432 takas, much more than Bangalees usually carry. After two miles of abuse they stopped at Dulahazara bazaar, then threw Dr. Q. on the ground where they battered and kicked him unmercifully, breaking his glasses. One assailant grabbed a large, heavy log and jammed it into his chest and abdomen, all the while verbally abusing him. "We're going to kill you," they screamed in his face.

Simultaneously, Jesse Eaton and Mel Beals came running to say that Dr. Q. had been beaten in front of the hospital and taken away. We leaped into a car and headed south. Within three minutes we reached Dulahazara bazaar, where we saw a huge crowd. With brakes screeching and a cloud of dust flying, we jumped from the vehicle and dived into the crowd. The assailants fled in all directions and there, lying at the roadside, was dirty, disheveled Dr. Q. with the heavy log on his lower chest.

We hoisted the log off his body, then helped him to his feet and into the car. Then we picked up a witness at Malumghat and drove directly to the nearest police station. After statements were taken and a case opened, we drove to Cox's Bazar to notify the subdivisional officer, who promptly ordered the police to surround the culprits' houses at night and arrest them.

That evening I reexamined Dr. Q's injuries, treated him, gave him a hot shower and a hot meal, then settled him down to sleep at our house. The next morning we had breakfast together, and he fearlessly returned to his home. The police had failed to capture any of the assailants during the night.

By the next week life at Malumghat had returned to near normal. I operated on Shankor, a high-caste Hindu teenager. He had been ill for months with a severe chronic infection of his left tibia (main lower leg bone). An aggressive, radical operation would be needed to cure him. This surgery I call the "S-S-S operation." The three S's stand for sequestrectomy-scraping-saucerization. With the patient under anesthesia I removed a long piece of the tibia bone, exposing the marrow cavity. It looked like a junkyard, with scattered pieces of riddled, dead bone (sequestra) protruding from clumps of infected tissue. I first pried out the loose pieces of dead bone (sequestrectomy), then curetted out every speck of infected marrow (scraping). Finally I sculptured the tibia bone so that its cavity was wide open and saucer-shaped (saucerization). After closing the soft tissues we took Shankor to the recovery room where he promptly went into shock due to loss of blood and fluids; this was easily rectified by a blood transfusion.

After some days of treatment with powerful antibiotics Shankor was able to go home. Each time he returned for his checkups, he would ask more questions about spiritual issues, for he had become greatly interested in what he had read and learned during his time at Malumghat. I enjoyed answering his intelligent questions. Some months later, with the approval of his older family members, he decided to follow Christ. This made his healing complete because, wonderfully, his terribly infected tibia was by then completely cured. Shankor then began to teach Scriptural truths to friends in his village and developed quite a band of disciples.

In mid-April 1975 a serious longstanding dispute between Bangladesh and India came to a head. This controversy swirled around India's construction of a barrage (damlike structure) across the mighty Ganges River at a place called Farakka, just eleven miles upstream from the Bangladesh border (see figure 17). The purpose of the barrage was to divert Ganges water into a south-flowing Indian river to flush out the silt deposits in the channel of Calcutta Port. Of course, Bangladesh was concerned that she would lose lifegiving Ganges water, especially during the dry sea-

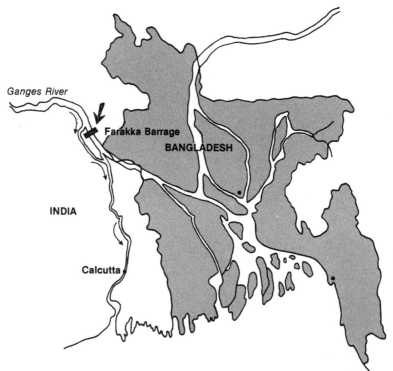

Figure 17. The Farakka Barrage—diverting Ganges River water away from Bangladesh toward Calcutta Port in India

son, to the great detriment of the western third of the country. The Indian government had begun constructing the Farakka Barrage fourteen years earlier. Finally, in April 1975 the barrage was commissioned, and the Indians began a forty-one-day test of withdrawing Ganges water and diverting it toward Calcutta. The people of Bangladesh were highly apprehensive about the loss of Ganges water during this long dry-season period.

That week I admitted to the hospital a sixteen-year-old Muslim girl who was apprehensive about a personal problem; she had an unusual puffy, pillowy-feeling tumor of her lower face, jaw, and neck. She was eager to get married, but who would marry her with this tumor disfiguring her face? Previous surgery and X-ray treatments elsewhere had been unsuccessful. At the operating table I found the soft mass to be made up of hundreds of small connecting sacs filled with fluid. But when I punctured one sac, fluid drained from the whole tumor and it collapsed. This made it impossible to see and remove the infiltrating fingers of the tumor.

Fortunately I had a trick up my sleeve. I injected a special blue dye into the main body of the tumor, and immediately the dye flowed from one sac to the next until it stained each tiny sac and projection of the tumor. This allowed me to clearly see and painstakingly excise every bit of the tumor, even that part that had penetrated to her mouth. Later she also required a special skin graft operation. Because the operations ultimately succeeded, her appearance was so improved that the last obstacle to marriage was removed. A few months later she attained her heart's desire—she became a bride.

Later in May our tribal teachers and Shintai Murung returned from their month of Bible/theology and hymnology teaching in several Murung villages. Seated in our living room, they gave a fascinating report. Robi had preached the first night in the "Jesus house" (bamboo and sungrass church building) of the large Rao Headman Village. The team rejoiced when twelve men and women (six couples) responded to his invitation to follow Christ.

Each day that week the team had a special training session for those six couples and their families. And each night Shintai Murung taught singing to the Jesus-house congregation. He found it tough going to teach these primitive tribespeople who had never sung before. It took them six days to learn two hymns. In the next village the people laughed at the idea of singing songs—but in six days they, too, successfully learned the same two hymns.

Meanwhile, in each village Shadijan Tippera concentrated on learning more of the Murung language; he discovered that he picked up the most by playing and talking with Murung children. He succeeded in mastering several of Shintai's Murung songs, as well. The men also discovered that the Christian group in a distant

A Jesus house

Murung village had constructed their own Jesus house and a second village would complete theirs within a week or two. They were delighted.

Then I asked Shintai how he had liked his monthlong project of teaching Murung hymns. He replied that this had been the most thrilling experience of his life; never before had he been able to serve God by doing this kind of "missionary" work. Then I put a microphone in front of him and asked him to sing some of his songs. Knowing nothing about microphones and recordings, Shintai was mystified, but he sang the haunting melodies beautifully.

When he had finished I rewound the tape and switched the recorder to play from the room speakers. In a moment, seemingly out of thin air, Shintai heard someone singing the same Murung songs he had just sung. How confusing! Then suddenly he recognized that somehow, unaccountably, his own voice was singing the hymns. Slowly a huge smile erased his startled look, and he began to sway with the rhythm of the music. When we explained to him the recording process, he was enthralled with this new discovery. What stories he would have to tell when he returned to his jungle village!

Later that week two tribesmen came from the Hill Tracts with a unique item for sale: a fifteen-foot golden-headed python. I purchased it to obtain its skin, to provide meat for the Murungs' cooking pots—and also to have a taste of python curry myself. I placed the huge lethargic reptile back into its covered carrying basket, put it in our screened roof-room for the night, and tied the cord around its neck loosely to a post. The tailor who was working for Joan for a few days slept in the same room. He was a bit apprehensive, but I calmed his fears with the words, "Oh, don't worry. He's very sleepy; he just lies there in his basket."

Sometime after 11:00 P.M. we awakened to an insistent rapping at the front door. There stood the tailor, shivering with fright. "It's loose," he blurted out. "That snake is out of its basket!" Rubbing my eyes, I climbed the stairs to the roof-room and with very little struggle coiled the python back into its basket. I tied the cord hanging from its neck this time more tightly to the post and replaced the lid on the basket.

"There!" I said reassuringly. "Now you should be able to sleep soundly through the night." Somewhat relieved, the tailor lay down on his bedroll.

In the morning he appeared again at the door, looking bleary-eyed and haggard. He had not slept a wink all night. "After you left," he grumbled, "that snake snored loudly all the rest of the night. How could I possibly sleep with all that racket right next to me?" Oh-oh! The python must have strained against the cord and tightened it around his neck.

Later that morning a number of children and others came to see the unusual python with the golden-colored head lying in the grass of our front yard. As before, it lay quietly, lethargically, unresponsively. Sandy Sorg came with her small daughter to view it at very close range and then returned to the house. Just a moment later the Golins' playful German shepherd bounded out their door and directly toward the listless reptile. Instantly the scene changed! With a flash of motion the python's spring-steel body rose, and he struck the oncoming dog full in the face—and clamped his jaws down fiercely. The terrified dog jumped into the air, howling and crying, for she had left a piece of her cheek in the big snake's mouth. We were all astounded and shaken by this split-second attack, never dreaming that our sleepy snake could react so quickly and violently. What if one of the children had stimulated the same reaction?

Robichandro supervised two Murungs in killing and skinning the snake. I received the skin and a bit of the meat, while the two tribesmen joyously took the bulk of the meat, a delicacy in Murung-land. And Robi got the one small part he wanted—the python's gall bladder. When I naively asked him about his choice, he explained patiently that he could sell the gall bladder for a very good price to a *kobiraj* (traditional eastern doctor), who would use it to make "strong medicine." Both tribals and Bengalis alike well knew that the gall bladder of a python could be turned into a powerful aphrodisiac. And the python curry? It tasted very firm and rubbery. Joan called it "awful stuff," but I think it might have been tastier if the cook had simmered it an hour or two longer. Maybe next time.

Mark and Nancy loved being home again. Mark soon went to work as a trainee in the Physiotherapy Department at the hospital. And Nancy, who had been introduced to free verse in a poetry class at school, presented me with a copy of that afternoon's poem, a whimsical memory of her very early years:

The Prayer

Before each meal my father says the prayer;
Everybody must close his eyes and you may not—
    —under any circumstances—
         peek.
That is naughty.
Especially if you peek at your sister across the table,
Because that will make you laugh—
    —and that's even worse than peeking.
But one lunch I peeked.
And I saw gravy running—
     —very slowly—
       —into my corn.
How could I save my corn? —How?
Maybe if I block it with my fork. . . .
But what if Daddy says "Amen"
    ——right when I get the fork in my hand?
Then everybody would open his eyes and see . . . Oh, no!
Please, Daddy . . .
    Hurry, Daddy . . .
     —It's almost there . . .

A few days later our second daughter, Lynne, arrived for her summer vacation. With Lynne was her school friend Cheryl Vanderlaan. They had successfully completed their first year of pre-nursing studies at Biola University in southern California. How wonderful it was to have them home! If only Wendy had been able to come, too, our family circle would have been complete.

About that time the painters came to paint the inside walls of our house. Joan had decided on a sandalwood color for the living room and dining room. Because she is skillful with pigments she helped Sayed, the paint team supervisor, mix the color to perfection. As the painters completed the sandalwood walls, Joan overheard one of the men chuckle and comment to his fellow worker, "Amazing! The memshahib could have any beautiful color she wishes, but she wants *mud*-colored walls like ours."

India's central intelligence agency, known as the Research and Analysis Wing (RAW), habitually kept close tabs on developments in neighboring Bangladesh. This was easy enough because RAW had a network of spies in key positions throughout the country. During the first quarter of 1975 RAW agents picked up clues that a coup attempt might take place, and they noted that some other countries' intelligence agencies were becoming increasingly active. RAW apprised Mujib of their suspicions, but he paid no attention.

Then in mid-June, RAW operatives picked up the names of Major Farook and Major Rashid and seemed to know that there had been a meeting with General Zia. One of these men had written or drawn something on a scrap of paper, then thoughtlessly thrown it in a wastebasket. A RAW agent cleverly obtained the piece of paper and sent it on to his headquarters in India.

The writing or diagram on the piece of paper convinced the RAW high command that a coup was definitely in the offing. Alarmed, the RAW director himself (R. N. Kao) slipped into Dacca, posing as a betel nut exporter. He was driven directly to a rendezvous point to meet with Sheikh Mujib. Mujib, however, was rather amused at the cloak-and-dagger atmosphere of the hourlong meeting and did not take the intelligence seriously. Even though Kao gave him the names of the suspected connivers, Mujib responded, "These are my children, and they can do me no harm."[14]

Also in June, the new authoritarian government closed down twenty important daily newspapers in the four major cities of the country. Only two Bengali language dailies and two English language dailies survived; two of these already were government newspapers, and the other two were promptly brought under government control. The editor of one of these major newspapers was Mujib's nephew Sheikh Moni. Several hundred smaller daily, weekly, and monthly newspapers also were banned.

A few days later the government officially delineated the country's sixty-one new districts and again announced that these districts would be run by governors whose names would be made public at a later date. These governors would be appointed by Mujib in time to receive their briefing before beginning their new duties on September 1. That they would be appointed by the president was highly significant, because it meant that the deputy commissioners (Civil Service professionals) would be replaced by non–Civil-Service governors (politicians). After being in the driver's seat for more than two hundred years, the Civil Service officers were not at all pleased with this new development.

On July 3 Major Farook wrote in his diary in bold red letters, "START WORK."[15] This meant that he and Major Rashid would actually begin implementing their plan, step by step, to carry out the coup against Mujib. Farook later explained, "From that point, as the Americans say, all systems were Go. . . . Suddenly I had crystallised in my mind that I would not wait longer than the 15th of August."[16] In fact, Farook decided tentatively that the early morning hours of Friday, August 15, would be the ideal time to strike, for their mid-August after-dark tank and artillery exercises would take place the night of August 14/15.

But Farook kept this tentative date to himself. In fact, to prevent any possible chance of a leak, he did not even share it with Rashid. He and Rashid merely agreed that they would have to strike before September 1 when the 61 new governors would begin operating the 61 new district administrations, police forces, and military units. It was essential to act before that date because, as Rashid explained, "In that case the situation would have become very difficult to control because instead of being centralised in Dhaka you will have 61 different places where your enemy is spread."[17]

While Farook and Rashid were coming ever closer to their D-day, our hospital operation was again facing unexpected financial pressure. The new government suddenly had declared valueless all one-hundred-taka bills and ordered that they be turned in. Because these were the nation's largest currency notes, people with illegal gains from the black market and smuggling operations kept their money squirreled away in the form of one-hundred-taka bills. But the hospital, also, was caught in this surprise move and had to turn in one-hundred-taka notes worth $30,000. Theoretically, the government should immediately replace this legally imported money with lower denomination bills. But, in fact, they announced that they would issue bonds for the amount, which could not be redeemed for eight long years.

This money problem greatly complicated life for our overworked hospital administrator, Jesse Eaton. But with the bitter came some sweet. Bob Nusca, an experienced businessman from Kalamazoo, Michigan, arrived to devote two years to working with the business management of the hospital. Rather than continue his employment in the U.S., he and his wife, Jimmie, preferred to devote their lives to serving God and the people of Bangladesh. Jimmie, a skilled homemaker, took over the supervision of the guesthouse. She was particularly expert at sewing and was soon deeply involved in helping the women trainees at Heart House learn sewing and crafts. In addition, she gave piano lessons and taught home economics to the upper grade American girls.

Jesse Eaton, hospital administrator

Bob Nusca and hospital bookkeeper

By then Mark and Nancy's long vacation at home was drawing to a close. Nancy had performed valuable service as my typist. Mark had enjoyed life playing soccer, hunting, being with Bengali friends, and learning something about physiotherapy. And he had spent hours helping Debapriyaw with his physiotherapy program. By then Deb had regained enough strength in his legs that he could laboriously walk fifty yards wearing leg braces and using crutches; the rest of the time he would sit in a chair or a wheelchair. He studied the Scriptures hour after hour to learn all that he could about his new faith—and he thought deeply about how to bring the glorious truths he had learned to his Chakma people. When he became sufficiently accustomed to his crutches and braces, we sent him home to his family in Rangamati.

Shortly before Mark and Nancy returned to Manila, Joan traveled ahead to Dacca to obtain new passports and new Philippine visas for them. But unexpectedly she ran into a serious snag. Just a few days earlier the Philippine government had issued a new rule stating that student visas would no longer be granted to foreign students under age eighteen. Later, after the children and I arrived in Dacca, we consulted further with the Philippine consul general, then decided to take the bull by the horns. I would fly with Mark and Nancy back to Manila on the strength of twenty-one-day tourist visas, then attempt to negotiate a solution to their problem on the spot.

As soon as we arrived in Manila they returned to their classrooms while I studied how the Philippine government was put together and crafted a strategy of how to approach the proper officials. But after several days of meeting lower-, middle-, and upper-echelon officers in the Immigration Department, the situation looked extremely bleak. None of them could find any exception, loophole, or way around the new rule that student visas could not be granted to foreign students under eighteen years of age.

"Oh, Father," I implored, "show me what to do. Give me a new insight about how to approach this complicated problem." Then the thought came, *I should check with officials of the ministry overseeing the Immigration Department—and also other departments in any way related to the Immigration Department.*

More fruitless visits to these offices followed. And time was running out, for I had to return to Bangladesh by the time the DeCooks departed for their annual vacation. Finally, late in the afternoon of my last day in Manila I requested the last officer to give his deepest thought to finding some way that we might resolve this serious problem. He leaned back in his government-issue chair, concentrated for a while, then said slowly, "I do seem to vaguely recall seeing a memorandum—years ago—which specified that *American* children living in other Asian countries could be granted a special type of visa which would allow them to study here in the Philippines."

He called for a clerk, described the memorandum, and set him to work trying to find it. *Oh, Lord, this is it!* I cried out inwardly. *The office closing time is nearly here, and I leave Manila tomorrow. Do help this clerk to find the file where this paper was put so many years ago. It's now or never!* After searching many files fruitlessly for more than half an hour, the file clerk suddenly returned just at the office closing time with a triumphant smile on his face—and the precious memorandum in his hand. The issue date of the memorandum was thirteen years earlier. The principal of Faith Academy was with me, and he, too, was ecstatic because this document solved similar problems faced by thirty other students of the school. "We thank You, Father!"

The next morning I flew back to Bangladesh and reached Malumghat in good time. One of the first surgical cases awaiting my return was a precious little two-year-old Muslim boy who had suffered from urinary problems for nearly a year. I had to remove a large stone from his bladder. At the time of his discharge from the hospital the family found they had not brought enough money to pay the small bill, so they left the mother's nose ring as security until they could come back with the money.

As the month of July wound down Major Rashid began his task of selecting and recruiting a new head of state to replace President Mujib in the event that the coup should succeed. He quickly decided against choosing any opposition party leader, for that would infuriate the Awami League—and the nation's 25,000 well-armed Rakkhi Bahini, who could easily overcome a few hundred coup-makers. The Indian army might even cross the border to support these pro-Mujib forces. So Rashid began looking for a suitable Awami Leaguer to take over for Mujib. Soon he settled on Mushtaque, the right-wing, pro-Islamic, pro-American cabinet minister who four years earlier had held secret meetings in Calcutta, India, with U.S. agents about frustrating the breakup of Pakistan. Here was a practicing Muslim who was anti-communist and pro-democracy, and who would appreciate the value of the armed forces. Mushtaque was the logical choice.

Wearing civilian clothes Major Rashid arrived at Mushtaque's house in Old Dacca on an evening in early August. In an upstairs room the two men conversed for nearly two hours. Wisely, Rashid worked up to his subject slowly and cautiously. Finally he asked, "Can the nation expect progress under the leadership of Sheikh Mujibur Rahman?"

"No, they cannot," Mushtaque replied.

With this much encouragement Rashid then inquired, "Will there be any justification at this stage if somebody takes a decision to remove Sheikh by force?"

Then Rashid heard the reply he was waiting for. Mushtaque reportedly answered, "Well, probably for the country's interest it is a good thing. But it is also very difficult to do it."[18]

Then Mushtaque raised the question about who might take over for Mujib if he were removed from the picture. Rashid responded that anyone removing Sheikh Mujib had to have a replacement in the wings ready to take over—and that this replacement would have to be an experienced person who could handle the political aspect of a new regime. Major Rashid departed feeling elated that he had found an excellent replacement for Mujib; he was sure that Mushtaque had read between the lines of his cautious comments and comprehended exactly what he was talking about.

While the coup preparations in Dacca were gaining a frightening momentum, we continued to be busily involved with the joys and rigors of caring for the sick and injured at Malumghat. One of these, our Hindu mailman, sustained a terrible injury in a motor rickshaw accident. His right hip was dislocated backward, while his left hip was seriously broken and dislocated forward. He was in deep shock. Immediately we manipulated one hip, then the other, to reduce the dislocations. Later I stabilized the fractured hip in surgery by inserting a stout nail. Ultimately all these injuries healed, and Shadhan resumed his mailman's duties.

The man in male ward bed thirteen was also an injury case. He claimed that he had sustained his gunshot wound in a land dispute, but the police told us quite a different story. They explained that he had killed a wealthy man in a town twenty miles away, then had stolen the man's two very tight gold rings by cutting the two fingers off. The robber had been shot while trying to escape. The police kept him under tight armed guard in the hospital until he recovered sufficiently to be discharged.

At the beginning of the second week in August Farook's mind was filled with his tactical plan, for his anti-Mujib countdown would reach its climax in just one more week. Despite his preoccupation, on August 12 Farook hosted a gala party at the Dacca Golf Club to celebrate his third wedding anniversary. He was painfully aware that he might not live to celebrate another anniversary, so he made the most of the occasion.

Farook and Farida looked handsome as they circulated from group to group, greeting their guests and receiving their gifts and best wishes. The weather was exceptionally good for a monsoon season night. While the military band played popular Bengali music, the strings of colored lights stretching from tree to tree gave the whole affair a festive ambience. Farook appeared so carefree and happy that no one could possibly have guessed the deadly plan that he carried in his heart.

When the guests finally departed and only family members remained, Farook took his brother-in-law Major Rashid aside and announced with quiet intensity, "I'm going to knock off Mujib on Friday morning."

Shocked, Rashid protested, "Are you mad? It's too short notice. We don't have officers. We don't have equipment. How can we do it?"

His mind made up, Farook replied, "It's my decision; I have the tactical plan ready. I'm going ahead even if I have to do it alone. You can keep away if you want. But remember, if I fail they will surely hang you, also."

Rashid thought deeply for long seconds, then answered, "All right. . . . But we must talk. I need to bring in some more officers."[19] Later, in a private place, they had their talk and laid out the final parameters of the plan.

The next afternoon (August 13) Major Rashid slipped into Old Dacca again for another meeting with Mushtaque, a short meeting this time. He inquired whether Mushtaque had any plans to travel outside the city or outside the country in the next several days. Mushtaque replied that he had no travel plans and would definitely be in Dacca.[20]

Next Rashid began considering how best to recruit some additional officers to help lead the attack against the four houses. Then inspiration struck! Why not recruit ex-army officers who were angry at Mujib for having them dismissed from military service? He immediately telephoned ex-major Dalim.

That night the two men met at Major Rashid's house in the cantonment. Rashid gave Dalim a general briefing on the scheme to assassinate Mujib and his three close associates. Dalim readily agreed to fall in with the plot and suggested the name of another former major who might also be willing to join them; he then departed to find him and bring him back to Rashid's house. Later, after he was briefed, the second ex-major also was positive about joining the plot; the next day they succeeded in recruiting a third ex-major.

While Rashid was busily recruiting ex-officers, Major Farook's wife, Farida, traveled to her parents' home in Chittagong City. The following morning (August 14) she hired a motor rickshaw to take her to the home of Blind Hafiz. Farook's instructions were ringing in her ears:

Tell him I'm going to do it on the 15th. That I'm doing it in the cause of Islam and the State, with faith in Allah that what I am doing will benefit the people. Tell him also that I'm not doing it for personal desire or ambition. I am prepared to follow the path of Allah, whichever way He wills. I want him to tell me if I'm doing wrong or right or if there is anything else I must do.[21]

Farida entered the blind mystic's simple quarters, put her hand in his so that he could sense the emotions he could not see, then gave him Farook's message. After long contemplation of the message, Blind Hafiz gave his answer for Farook. Speaking in Urdu he intoned, "His [Mujib's] time has run out. Do what you have to do but do it very secretly."[22] Then he advised that Farook and his fellow officers pray earnestly for Allah's help in their attack. In addition, he gave Farida verses from the Holy Koran that Farook should periodically recite and think about to keep his mind fixed on the task. At the close of the interview he reassured Farida that he had placed Farook and his fellow officers in Allah's hands. "It's His will. He will take care of them."[23]

Sheikh Mujib did not return home from his office until 8:30 P.M. that fateful night. He found his ten-year-old son Russell (named for British philosopher Bertrand Russell) excited and happy, for Russell had been chosen to be one of six boys who would garland Mujib the next morning at Dacca University prior to his major presidential speech there.

According to one reporter, Mujib was feeling pretty happy himself. He had succeeded in hamstringing his opposition by outlawing all the opposition political parties. He had established control over the judicial system and the news media. The organization of his monolithic BaKSAL party was complete, with all its officers in place. And in less than three weeks his sixty-one hand-picked governors would be at the helm of the sixty-one new districts. Also, the army and other militias would be split into sixty-one groups to integrate with the new district set-up and perform productive work at the district level. Furthermore, Mujib was savoring a special secret which pleased him immensely: his supporters had arranged that the next day at the university he would be declared by public acclaim "President for Life." No one could touch him now![24]

A little later that night Majors Farook and Rashid slipped out into the cloudy, thunder-rumbling darkness to reach their respective battalion headquarters areas by 10:00 P.M. Waiting for Farook in the tank garages were four of his junior officers and nearly three hundred soldiers, all dressed in the unique black uniforms that marked them as troops of the First Bengal Lancers Tank Battalion; they were proud men who regarded themselves as the *crème de la crème* of the Bangladesh Army.

Farook was tense, for he knew a dozen different ways his tactical plan could go awry. But he was exhilarated, too, because the carefully mapped-out night of action had finally come. He put his troops to work doing their standard night check of the twenty-eight operating Russian-made T-54 tanks and carrying out their loading and unloading exercises.

At the same time, Major Rashid transported his eighteen recently imported 105 mm. howitzers a quarter-mile away to the half-constructed, deserted new Dacca airport; there he positioned the artillery pieces and their crews around the perimeter of the site. Rashid's men had no idea about the catastrophic plan for that night's activities; they expected only another routine night of joint maneuvers.

At about 11:00 P.M. ex-major Dalim and the two other former majors arrived an hour late at the new airport; with them were two majors completely new to the plot. These five men also were unaware that the tanks and troop-filled trucks would roll that night. Rashid greeted the men, then took them and three companies of his soldiers by truck to meet Major Farook at the tank garages.

Their arrival was the signal for Farook to tell the officers and troops his bold plan for the night's work. According to him, there were no speeches—no histrionics. He simply explained the plot, then began issuing commands.[25] His explanations and orders were remarkably effective; all the officers and troops present were convinced by his words and joined in the preparations for the highly dangerous attack on Mujib and his cohorts.

Then Farook gathered the officers around the table in his squadron office and laid out the worn tourist map of Dacca City. He identified several locations that their tanks would need to control while the assault teams carried out their lightning attacks.

Then he pointed out the primary targets. These were the homes of four men:

- Sheikh Mujibur Rahman, the president of Bangladesh
- A. R. Serniabat, Sheikh Mujib's brother-in-law and minister in his cabinet
- Sheikh Moni, the nephew of Sheikh Mujib, who was also a top officer in Mujib's new BaKSAL party and the editor of an influential government newspaper
- Another Mujib brother-in-law who was a powerful administrative head in the Bangladesh Civil Service

Each house would be attacked by assault teams of varying size. Farook requested ex-major Dalim to lead the large team attacking Sheikh Mujib's house. But Dalim refused this assignment because he and his family had such a long-standing friendship with Mujib and his wife (Dalim's so-called mother substitute); however, Dalim did agree to direct the assault on Minister Serniabat's residence.

Instead of Dalim, then, three other majors were selected to lead the main attack on the house of Sheikh Mujib. Next Farook picked a reliable junior commissioned officer named Risaldar Moslemuddin to lead the assault on Sheikh Moni's residence and a non-commissioned officer to lead the troops attacking the fourth house. According to Farook's testimony, he specified that only the four men should be killed and Mujib's two older sons captured; all other family members were to be spared.

Farook himself would handle the most difficult and dangerous part of the operation—controlling the Rakkhi Bahini, Mujib's own militia, which had been especially created to protect him and carry out his orders. Three thousand Rakkhi Bahini soldiers were stationed between the cantonment and the four principal targets; their barracks were located less than two miles, as the crow flies, from Sheikh Mujib's house. To subdue those three thousand well-equipped fighting men Farook would have to pull off a substantial bluff—because the shells for his tank cannon were locked up in an ordnance depot away from Dacca. At least he had ammunition for the three machine guns aboard each tank.

At 12:30 A.M. Major Farook ordered the quartermaster to issue ammunition to the troops and uniforms to the ex-majors. Because the inexperienced quartermaster had never operated under battle conditions before, he laboriously began counting out the ammunition to each soldier and listing the amounts in his journal. It was taking an age. Impatiently Farook scolded, "Look, in wartime you don't do it this way! In an emergency like this you open the locks and the men take the ammunition they need. If we fail, nobody will be bothered about your books. If we succeed, we will sort out all your books afterward."[26]

The units were supposed to be ready by 4:30 A.M. But the issue of ammunition and other items was not quite complete by then, since more than 500 soldiers had to be supplied. The officers were getting jittery, but Farook calmed them with the words "What difference does it make? Whenever we are ready, we will move."[27]

By 4:55 A.M. all preparations were finally complete. Major Rashid's eighteen artillery pieces were in position at the deserted new airport with their crews ready to fire if they should be called into action; a nineteenth howitzer would be taken into the city to provide additional firepower at Mujib's house. At the tank garages 275 Bengal Lancers clothed in black crowded into the tanks and into a number of trucks and three jeeps. Then about 140 other khaki-clad soldiers from Major Rashid's artillery battalion filled the remaining trucks; they were armed with rifles.

At "first light" (5:00 A.M.) Farook ordered the tank engines started; then he gave the signal for the assault teams to move out, and the "majors' coup" began to roll. As the column of troop-filled trucks pulled out, Farook heard the *azan,* the enchantingly beautiful early morning Muslim call to prayer, from the cantonment mosque. His mother had given him life on a Friday just at the time of the azan, but this Friday morning the sonorous call from the mosque might rather be heralding his death. In his heart he really did not expect the coup to succeed; he did not think he would survive the operation.[28]

Farook waited some minutes to allow the attack teams time to reach their target areas. Then he gave the order to the tank commanders, "Follow me!" and sped south in the lead tank on the main cantonment road.[29] When he reached the major crossroad in the cantonment, he made a sharp right turn and charged toward the old, still-in-use airport, which was separated from the cantonment by only a brick wall (see figure 18). He drove through a gate into the airport, crossed the main runway, then roared south on a taxiway to the fields beyond, for this was the quickest route to the Rakkhi Bahini camp. As Farook's tanks lumbered across the airport's fields he checked his watch. Excellent! If the assault teams had encountered no opposing forces on the way, they should be in position at their targets.

It was then that Farook glanced over his shoulder to see only a single tank trailing him. He was shocked to the core of his being, because he had fully expected to see a long column of tanks strung out behind him. But by the time the bulk of the tanks had reached the crossroad in the cantonment, they could not see that the first two speeding tanks had turned right—and, as the Russian-made radios in the tanks were defunct, there was no radio communication between tanks. Presuming that the two lead tanks had continued south, they had passed the crossroad and proceeded south out of the cantonment into Dacca City. Now what was Farook to do? He really needed all those tanks to help him cow the Rakkhi Bahini before the tanks scattered to strategic points throughout the city.

Always decisive, Major Farook instantly concluded that he must go ahead, anyway, and attempt the bluff with his minicolumn of two tanks—and no shells for the tank cannon. He crashed through a small gate and brickwork of the airport's far wall, pulverized some trees, and swung around into the Rakkhi Bahini parade grounds—to find all three thousand battle-equipped Rakkhi Bahini troops standing in formation. The fat was in the fire now!

"What am I supposed to do?" the tank driver asked.

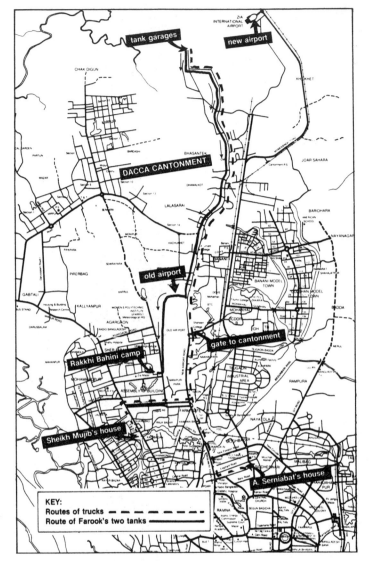

Figure 18. August 15, 1975. coup in Dacca—routes of trucks and tanks

"You just drive past them six inches from their noses, and if they start anything just steer right and run over them. Gunner, you keep the gun pointed straight at them. And you other chaps, look brave!"[30]

As the two tanks trundled slowly and menacingly down the long column of Rakkhi Bahini troops lined up six rows deep, not a soldier stirred. By then the troops could hear the frenzied chattering of automatic weapons off in the distance in the direction of Sheikh Mujib's house. Wonder of wonders! Farook had actually succeeded in bluffing the three thousand armed troops—with his two tanks and empty cannons. These were the very tanks that Mujib had so feared that he hesitated to receive them as a gift from Egypt's president Anwar Sadat; his fears had been well founded. Having coolly intimidated the Rakkhi Bahini troops, Major Farook ordered his two tanks to head for Mujib's house on Road 32.

Minutes before Farook and his tanks had departed from the tank garages for their gut-wrenching confrontation with the Rakkhi Bahini troops, the long column of troop-filled trucks had filed out of the cantonment, then proceeded south a mile or so to a corner called Farmgate. There Dalim with one truck and two jeeps split off toward Minister Serniabat's house on Minto Road. The rest of the trucks turned right and headed toward the upper-class Dhanmondi Residential Area. Then one truck peeled off toward Sheikh Moni's residence and another toward the quarters of the other Mujib relative. The bulk of the force pressed on to Sheikh Mujib's house on Road 32.

As soon as the troops tumbled out of their trucks, the artillery crew set up their howitzer beside the main road and quickly aimed it toward Mujib's residence. The troops divided into three groups:

1. An outer or perimeter cordon circling the half-mile area around the house (this ring of soldiers, with heavily armed checkposts, had orders to prevent anyone [friend or foe] from going to Mujib's house)
2. An inner cordon to prevent anyone from escaping from the Mujib house
3. The actual assault force, which numbered nearly a hundred armed men

The assault group surprised the police posted outside the boundary wall; they surrendered immediately. Then the astonished Bengal Lancer sentries quickly allowed their fellow Lancers to pass through the gate. The officers called for Sheikh Mujib to come out of his house. At first there was no resistance from the house, so the attacking soldiers were at ease and confident. Then, suddenly, Mujib's son Sheikh Kamal stepped out on a balcony and began firing a powerful automatic weapon; two attackers were killed and three fell injured. Mujib's bodyguards also began shooting from the house. The assault team quickly took cover behind the boundary wall.

Just then the artillery officer decided to fire his first shell at the Mujib residence; it fell far short and exploded in the lake behind the attacking troops, upsetting them even further. The next shells sailed high over the house, killing and injuring people four miles away. An officer raced over to the artillery crew and ordered them to stop shooting. The only good they had done was to fool the Rakkhi Bahini, still at their camp, into thinking that the tank cannon were able to fire.

In the meantime, President Mujib hurriedly telephoned the Rakkhi Bahini camp, but could get no response, for by then all at the camp were under the control of Farook's two tanks. Then he desperately telephoned army headquarters and called for immediate help. In response the director of military intelligence came at once with five trucks of fighting men, but when he was cut down by Farook's outer-perimeter soldiers, these men raced away.

By that time the assault force had opened up with heavy firing on the house; Sheikh Kamal was killed on the balcony, and soon the bodyguards were also dead. That allowed the tense marauders to enter and comb the house from bottom to top. A major named Mohiuddin headed up the main staircase to find Mujib; halfway up, he suddenly saw him standing commandingly at the top of the stairs. Mujib was dressed in a gray-checked *lungi* and white *kurta* (long shirt), and his right hand held an ever-present pipe. Mujib barked, "What do you want? Have you come to kill me? Forget it! The Pakistan army couldn't do it. Who are you that you think you can?"[31]

Mohiuddin was so dominated by the confident presence and powerful personality of Sheikh Mujib that he just kept repeating, "Sir, please come. Sir, please come."[32] But Mujib's wife was pulling him back, and Mujib also was refusing to leave the house; he was gaining a little time with his courageous performance. Then more attackers barged up the staircase, including ex-major Nur. Although some writers reported that Risaldar Moslemuddin returned from Sheikh Moni's house to assassinate Mujib, Farook emphasizes that could not have happened. He states clearly that Nur pulled the trigger.[33] And the mercurial Mujib was dead. Then the attacking troops, enraged by their casualties and now completely out of control, cruelly slaughtered Mujib's family members—his wife, his younger brother, the two new brides of the adult sons, little Russell, and later the remaining older son. The operation had turned into a shocking and cold-blooded massacre of the whole household.

The fourth assault force could never find its target, so that relative of Mujib escaped unharmed. But at the residence of Mujib's nephew Sheikh Moni the attacking team, led by Risaldar Moslemuddin, quickly dispatched Moni and his pregnant wife, who leaped in front of her husband to protect him.

And in another part of town at the home of Mujib's brother-in-law, Minister Serniabat, an appalling bloodbath was taking place. The attacking forces under Dalim, firing crazily and indiscriminately, killed the minister, his son (age 11), two daughters (ages 10 and 15), a grandson (age 5), a nephew, a maid, a houseboy, and a family friend. And they wounded the minister's wife, daughter, daughter-in-law, and five houseguests. Without even checking to see whether or not Serniabat was dead, Dalim raced off to the radio station. All this was quite contrary to Farook's orders.

Those who escaped injury were the minister's thirty-year-old son, Abu Hasnat, Hasnat's two young daughters who had hidden behind a sofa, and four family friends. Hasnat's escape was particularly remarkable because the attackers were specifically searching for him. But while he was in an out-of-the-way upstairs loft looking for ammunition for his Sten gun, the marauders killed his cousin in a case of mistaken identity. Later, taking some of the other survivors, Hasnat slipped out and appeared at the nearby home of an American diplomat. The upset American immediately called Jalal, who worked with him at the U.S. embassy, and asked, "What do I do with these people?"

Jalal counseled, "Make them comfortable overnight. I will pick them up and move them first thing in the morning when the situation has cooled down a little."

Meanwhile, Major Farook had left the subdued Rakkhi Bahini still standing in formation and had taken his two tanks to Mujib's house. He found ex-major Nur at the outer perimeter looking distracted and disturbed—because he had been forced to kill Mujib himself and because his troops had gone out of control.[34] Farook ordered Nur to return to the house to control his soldiers. Then he commanded the other officers to remain at the house and not touch anything until the new government's security forces arrived to take charge of the premises.

Farook then rumbled along the main streets of Dacca collecting his widely scattered tanks. Then he shifted to a jeep and returned to the Rakkhi Bahini camp. As he put it, "All twenty-eight tanks were following me like sheep. We entered inside and the twenty-eight tanks halted right in front of the Rakkhi Bahini headquarters with their twenty-eight exhausts pumping toward their headquarters—pup-pup-pup-pup-pup! And that was finished."[35] He had quickly reassembled his tanks to maintain control over the Rakkhi Bahini and to be ready for any other forces that might attack him.

While all the shooting and carnage were taking place Major Rashid tackled his assignments. He awakened his friend the air force squadron leader to tell him what had happened and request him to stand by to support the coup with his aircraft if he were needed. But the airman refused to cooperate without an order from his superior officers. Rashid then hurried to Road 32 where he learned of the massacre of sixteen members of Mujib's family, plus the other innocents who happened to be in the wrong place at the wrong time. He was dismayed because he well knew that news of the wanton killing would badly damage the coupmakers' reputations at home and abroad.

Next Rashid drove to the cantonment, where he faced the generals and the colonels—his senior officers—to ask them to support the coup and the new government. Although they were angry, upset, and noncommittal about supporting the coup d'état, they took no action against him.

Then at 6:00 A.M. on the radio Rashid heard these unexpected words:

> This is Major Dalim. Under the leadership of Khandaker Moshtaque Ahmed the armed forces have taken over. In the greater interest of the country, this step has been taken. Sheikh Mujibur Rahman has been detained and his government has been toppled. The country is now under martial law and will become the Islamic Republic of Bangladesh.[36]

Rashid was flabbergasted. Ex-major Dalim was out of line; he had no business making that radio announcement. Now Rashid would have to pick up Mushtaque posthaste and get him to the radio station immediately.

Mushtaque, alerted by the sound of Rashid's jeep and the clatter of a tank in front of his house, looked out the window. He was unnerved to see the tank cannon pointing in his direction, and more so when a disheveled Rashid and two soldiers armed with Sten guns burst into the room. But when they politely saluted him he was greatly relieved and went with them. Upon reaching the radio station to announce his ascension to the pinnacle of Bangladesh authority, he did not seem at all surprised to find two old friends waiting for him—the other two members of the "Mushtaque triangle." It appeared that these two men were also very much involved in Mushtaque's part of the coup.

Mushtaque then demanded that the chiefs of the army, navy, and air force be brought immediately to the radio station. He insisted that they support him as head of a martial-law government, but with a civilian cabinet. These military chiefs conferred among themselves for a while, agreed to Mushtaque's terms, and then, one after the other, they stood up to the microphone and swore allegiance to Mushtaque's new government.

Only then, at 11:15 A.M., did Mushtaque broadcast his own message. He explained that Sheikh Mujib had been killed in a military coup that was a historical necessity, for there was no other way to change the corrupt and unpopular government. He hailed the majors and their men as heroes and called them children of the sun who had opened up the golden gates of opportunity for the people. There was an Islamic religious tinge to the speech. And he ended, not with *"Joi Bangla,"* but with *"Bangladesh zindabad* [Long live Bangladesh]!"*—a more Muslim type of expression. The Islamic flavor of Mushtaque's speech seemed to confirm ex-major Dalim's initial pronouncement that Bangladesh would indeed become an Islamic republic.

The commanding general of the army complimented Mushtaque on his well-organized speech. Mushtaque allegedly replied, "Do you think it was all done in a day?"[37] Those listening took this as further evidence that Mushtaque had been involved in the plot for a long time.

Reflecting on this disturbing series of events I could see many contrasts, as well as parallels, between the assassination of Sheikh Mujib and the equally brutal killing of Christ the Lord two millenia before. Early on, both were looked upon as messiah figures, saviors of their people. But later, when the majors decided that Mujib had failed in his mission to alleviate the distress of his countrymen, they plotted to remove him by assassination. Jesus the Messiah, on the other hand, succeeded brilliantly in His mission of showing us what God is like, giving us exalted teaching, and opening up a way of forgiveness and life everlasting. In fact, it was this success that drew people to Him, but created hatred in the hearts of jealous religious leaders and caused them to hatch the murder plot against Him.

Many were involved in the coup against Mujib—an intimate in his inner circle (Mushtaque), a religious figure (Blind Hafiz), soldiers, army officers, and others. Similarly, the coup against Christ the Lord was fostered by a person from His inner circle (Judas Iscariot) and was accomplished by the religious leaders of His day; finally, Roman soldiers mocked Him, tortured Him, took Him to the killing grounds outside of Jerusalem's city walls, and spiked Him to a cross. There it was an army officer who was so awed by the midday darkness that descended upon Jerusalem, the violent earthquake, and Christ's behavior as He hung there dying that he exclaimed, "Truly this was the Son of God!"[38]

In his extremity Mujib had picked up a telephone and desperately called for military help, but the three thousand nearby Rakkhi Bahini fighters and thousands of Bangladesh Army soldiers and police were impotent to protect him. How different was Jesus' approach! Although more than twelve legions (tens of thousands) of angels were available to Him, He never put in the call. Here is a quotation of His own words on the subject:

> Or do you think that I cannot now pray to My Father, and He will
> provide Me with more than twelve legions of angels? How then
> could the Scriptures be fulfilled, that it must happen thus?[39]

So the major purposes of His coming to planet Earth were to fulfill
the ancient prophecies and to die—for the sins of every needy
member of the human race. He Himself described the unique, voluntary nature of His action in these words:

> Therefore My Father loves Me, because I lay down My life that I
> may take it again. No one takes it from Me, but I lay it down of
> Myself. I have power to lay it down, and I have power to take it
> again. . . .[40]

Both men died a bloody death. Mujib fell on his stairway, his
white *kurta* drenched with blood and his lifeless right hand still
clutching his pipe. Our Lord bled, too, from the wounds of thorns,
spikes, and a vicious spear thrust. But, somehow, His blood was
instantly recognized to be sacred and indescribably precious. This
was true because He was a perfectly holy Person who willingly
gave His blood—and His life—as a sacrifice for us all.

The majors made clear that the purpose of the killing was to
save the nation, which, they felt, was deteriorating under the leadership of Mujib. The purpose of Christ's death also was to save the
people—not only for time but for eternity, as well.

But as far as the effectiveness of the assassinations is concerned, there was a world of difference. The killing of Sheikh Mujib
completely failed to save the people of Bangladesh; the poverty
and misery and sadness continue. But Christ the Lord's death was
eminently successful. It paid the death penalty for all human evil
and sin. And it certainly worked for Joan and me—and for myriads
of Americans, Bengalis, Murungs, Tipperas, Chakmas, and millions
of other people around the world. Through His sacrificial act we
gained the miracle of forgiveness—the guilt is gone. And with forgiveness came peace of mind and the joy of a life worth living.

The body of Sheikh Mujib was taken by army officers in a helicopter to his ancestral village. There the villagers were forced to
make hurried funeral arrangements. The officers were told they
could join the burial prayers only if they were ceremonially clean;
they stepped back and did not participate. Sheikh Mujib still lies
in that grave; no mausoleum or memorial befitting the "father of
the nation" has ever been erected over his grave. Soldiers were also
involved with the burial place of Christ. They guarded the tomb
where His body lay. But, despite the guards, today that tomb is
empty. He rose from the dead that first Easter Sunday morning to

show how different He was from other buried and entombed leaders, and to convince us that all His beautiful teachings are true.

At 6:00 A.M. on August 15 in Dacca, Americans as well as Bangalees heard ex-major Dalim's radio announcement about the coup
and the fact that Bangladesh would become an Islamic republic.
The U.S. embassy was the first agency to broadcast this news
abroad. At the same time, Jalal had to carry out his dicey operation—removing the hunted Abu Hasnat group from the American
diplomat's house and transferring them to a place where they
could survive. This he did with characteristic skill and aplomb, despite the military checkpoints and roving patrols.

The new government quickly closed the Dacca airport and
shut down most communications with the outside world. Later
that day Mushtaque appointed a vice-president and a cabinet
made up of ten ministers from the previous cabinet. However, he
carefully excluded Tajuddin and the other three ministers who had
opposed him during the 1971 Calcutta days; although four years
had passed, his antagonism toward them had not abated. Some of
the ministers he summoned were apprehensive about coming, not
knowing what to expect, so armed soldiers had to bring them.
When all had arrived, Mushtaque convened the first cabinet meeting on the spot.

Across the subcontinent Pakistani leaders were delighted that
conservative, pro-Pakistan, pro-Islamic Mushtaque had become
the new head of Bangladesh. That same evening Prime Minister
Bhutto announced that Pakistan had recognized the new government in Dacca. He further stated:

> As a first and spontaneous gesture to the fraternal people of
> Bangladesh, I have decided to immediately despatch to Bangla-
> desh as a gift from the people of Pakistan 50,000 tons of rice, 10
> million yards of long cloth and five million yards of bleached mull
> [soft, sheer cloth]. . . .
> We respectfully urge the State members of the Islamic Con-
> ference to accord recognition of the Islamic Republic of Bangla-
> desh and we appeal to all countries of the Third World to do
> likewise.[41]

I was not surprised that Pakistani leaders were so effusive toward the new government, for Mushtaque had long been pro-Pakistan—and their nemesis, Mujib, who had led the movement that
ultimately tore East Pakistan from their grasp, was now gone. The
next day Saudi Arabia and Sudan, two countries who had never
before considered Bangladesh sufficiently Islamic under Mujib to

grant their diplomatic recognition, recognized the new regime in Dacca. Apparently they did so because of the broadcast that announced that Bangladesh would now be an Islamic republic.

Also on the day after the coup, while Mujib was interred in his ancestral village, his family members were buried unceremoniously in a Dacca graveyard without the benefit of proper graveclothes or the usual religious rites—a sacrilege to devout Muslims.

Interestingly, there were no riots, processions, or other public outbursts in response to the assassination of the "father of the country." The opposition claimed that the people were so fed up with the country's deterioration that they had no heart to react against the coup.

Majors Farook and Rashid were headquartered with Mushtaque at President's House as his special assistants and, as such, they were not subject to the discipline of the generals. Mushtaque quickly promoted the two men to the rank of lieutenant colonel.

During the last week in August President Mushtaque arrested his four main pro-Mujib rivals. They were Tajuddin and the other senior ministers of the Bangladesh provisional government in Calcutta who in 1971 had put the clamps on his negotiations with the U.S. government to halt the breakup of Pakistan. And Tajuddin, Bangladesh's first prime minister, was the one who in Dacca had demoted Mushtaque from being minister of foreign affairs to a lesser ministry. These rivals would now pay for their past deeds and for their pro-Mujib, pro-Indian, pro-Soviet sympathies.

The next day, as a result of pressure from Farook and Rashid, President Mushtaque appointed General Zia as the new commanding general of the Bangladesh Army. But to maintain some control Mushtaque placed above Zia his new defense adviser, General Osmani, who had commanded the Bangladesh Army and guerrilla forces during the 1971 war.

While these earthshaking events were taking place in Dacca during the last half of August, life went on as usual for us at peaceful Malumghat. I operated on a young man with leprosy suffering from weakness and paralysis of one hand and arm. Despite his taking strong antileprosy medicine, a lump appeared on one of the main nerves of his arm and some of his hand muscles became weakened and wasted. At the operating table I discovered that the leprosy germs had produced an actual abscess in the nerve. Very unusual! I opened the nerve's thin, filmy covering, removed the abscess material, then injected a special cortisone solution into the nerve above and below the damaged area. This treatment did the trick. Over a period of time sensation and good strength returned to the affected arm and hand. Both the young man and I were elated with the good result in an unusual and complicated case.

Nurse Joan Voss

Also that week, newcomers arrived at Malumghat. Joan Voss was a competent nurse who had worked devotedly with us for a time as a part of the Bangladesh Brigade. Now she had returned as a career worker to practice her specialty, obstetrical nursing, and oversee the operating room.

A short-term husband-wife team, both experienced school teachers, arrived at the same time. They were Duane and Linda Cross. Duane would supervise the small group of high school students, and Linda would teach the upper primary grades. Later an unexpected medical problem of Linda's would cause us considerable concern.

As August was winding down our Lynne and her friend Cheryl's vacation was also rapidly drawing to a close. They had successfully completed the hospital nurse's aide course and conscientiously and compassionately helped care for patients on the women's/children's ward. They had also learned how to assist in the operating room. Several times Lynne had scrubbed in and helped me with complicated cases; for a young woman who had not yet attended nurse's college, she had become surprisingly skillful. Before leaving Malumghat Lynne hosted a lovely birthday lunch for Gita, her childhood Bengali friend. And we had an early birthday celebration for Lynne as well. Despite the heavy workload, we always managed to fit in family celebrations and fun times.

At the end of August the Mushtaque government canceled Mujib's scheme to divide the country into sixty-one new districts headed by politicians rather than Civil Service professionals; these civil servants were greatly relieved that the program was dropped in the nick of time. On the last day of the month Mushtaque was heartened by China's recognition of his new government. This was highly significant, for Peking had steadfastly refused to afford diplomatic recognition to the Mujib regime. This was so because the government of China disapproved of Mujib's strong alliance with India and the Soviets. The Chinese leaders naturally appreciated Mushtaque because his political alignments paralleled their own.

The same Sunday that Peking recognized the new Dacca regime an unusual-looking man bicycled up to the hospital at dusk. Long-haired, barefooted Peter W., a Dutch hippie, sported an undershirt and a Bengali *lungi* topped off with a battered hat. Dr. Dick Stagg greeted him and learned that Peter was on his way to Cox's Bazar. Seeing that he needed accommodations for the night, Dick invited him to stay at Malumghat and arranged a comfortable room for him in the guesthouse.

Later, Peter joined our Sunday evening English language church service. He listened with interest to Joan Voss's upbeat report about her yearlong preparations to return to Malumghat and

Peter W.—in search of truth

the Crosses' story of their sense of calling to come to teach the children of the Malumghat team. Afterward, as I chatted with Peter during the welcome party for our new co-workers, I could see that he was greatly enjoying the warmth and love and family feeling of the group. Neither of us could know then that four nights later we would meet again—in an unexpected way.

The next day we cleaned house, packed hurriedly, then departed to begin our annual vacation. As the hospital receded in the distance the constant pressure of feeling responsible for hundreds of sick and dying patients began to ease and be replaced by a rising euphoria. We were on vacation! Joan, Lynne, Cheryl, and I chattered and munched cookies all the way to Chittagong. There, after dinner, we were accosted by a pitiful beggar lady, so we gave her some money and shared our last box of cookies with her. After a night's rest we spent the next day at the giant lake behind Kaptai Dam; a long speedboat ride was the highlight of the trip.

Back in Chittagong City we attended our mission's Thursday evening prayer and Bible study meeting. We were surprised to walk in and find Peter W. sitting there. He was more trimmed and tidy than when I had last talked with him, and he seemed to have a knowing look on his face; I noticed again how piercingly blue his eyes were. After the meeting began we were surprised again to hear the meeting leader call on Peter to say a few words. His "few words" became quite a few words, for he had a lengthy and fascinating story to tell.

As a young man in Holland he had spent four years studying in a monastery. But just before finishing the program to become a full-fledged priest, he decided that was the last thing in the world he really wanted to do. So he ran away from the monastery, jettisoned all the religious teaching he had learned, and began dabbling in behavior that he knew was wrong. He could not return home because that would be too embarrassing—and because his draft board was looking for him. Finally he tired of fast living, longed for some kind of spiritual reality, and decided to search for that reality in the Eastern religions.

At that point Peter jumped on his bicycle and began pedaling toward Asia. Whenever he ran out of money he would stop and work for a while as a carpenter, then peddle on. He remained in Turkey for some time to examine the religion of Islam. He studied awhile, then decided to continue his journey to learn about other religions.

Soon he was on the road again, pedaling to India, where he spent time in Amritsar, the holy city of the Sikh religion. He decided against Sikhism because of its militancy and because for him it did not ring true. He cycled on until he reached the Hindus' foremost Krishna temple, where he began to learn about Hinduism.

But later, he said, when a priest told him to donate fifteen rupees so that his name could be written on a holy wall, he was disgusted.

He cycled on farther and farther eastward across India into Nepal, where he studied under Buddhist priests high in the Himalaya Mountains. Again he was disenchanted because he did not sense true love within the hearts of these holy men, and, to him, their teaching lacked logic.

Hearing that the new nation of Bangladesh was suffering and needed relief and rehabilitation assistance, he cycled down the Himalayas and onward, day after day, until he reached Dacca. There he visited the offices of various relief agencies, but was turned off by what he called an attitude of superiority. He cycled on south to Chittagong—and further disappointment. Not knowing what else to do, he pedaled farther south toward Cox's Bazar; there on the long, beautiful oceanside beach he would relax and think things through for a while.

It was then that the approaching darkness had forced him to turn in at Malumghat, join the Sunday evening service, and share in the congenial reception that followed. After enjoying the refreshments and meeting the team members one by one, he had a final chat with Bob Nusca. Bob said, "Here, let me loan you this book for the night. It's called *Daktar* and was written by Dr. Olsen, whom you met a while ago. I think you'll enjoy it."

Back in his room Peter began to read. Despite his long day he was wide awake and read for many hours. He focused particularly on the early chapters detailing our own convoluted spiritual pilgrimage. He noted our skepticism and unbelief, some of the great evidences for the validity of the Christian faith that we had discovered, the ineffable love of Christ the Lord, and the satisfying logic of His way of life. Finally, he closed the book and said to himself, "That's it! That's what I've been searching for all these years. That's the truth I'm going to follow!"

The next morning Peter noticed Tense Bullock eating breakfast in the guesthouse dining room; this would be Tense's last breakfast at the guesthouse, for she and John would be moving into their new house that day. Peter joined Tense at the breakfast table with the words, "It doesn't seem right for a lady to eat alone, so I will come and sit with you." Soon he was telling her how the night before he had finally found the truth he had been searching for so long—that life had opened up for him in a new way.

"Peter," Tense exclaimed, "that's wonderful news! I am so happy for you." Then she emphasized to him the importance of clinching his new insight by talking directly to God and accepting Christ. She went on to explain, "Peter, I am handing you this banana. But it will only be yours if you actually reach out and take it; similarly, it is important for you to receive Christ as your own Savior and Lord. Why don't we kneel down together right now? You can tell God about your new faith and invite the Lord Jesus into your life—and I will thank Him for all He's done for you."

"And that," Peter said to us in the Chittagong meeting, with his blue eyes sparkling, "is what happened. This has been the biggest week in my life!"

Instantly, I remembered my heartfelt prayer uttered that day I began writing *Daktar*: "Please keep me from messing it up and producing a fiasco. . . . Let me produce a book that will actually help people—change some readers' lives out there." He had answered that earnest prayer. "Thank You, Father!"

"What a fascinating story! What are you going to do now, Peter?" I asked.

He replied, "I must now return to Holland and give myself up to the authorities. They are searching for me because I evaded military service; I may have to go to jail. Anyway, I must do what's right, and I must explain to my family about all I have learned and about my new faith."

The next day we wished Peter Godspeed and flew to Dacca and then Bangkok, Thailand. For five days in Thailand Joan, the girls, and I went sightseeing, lounged on the beach, took boat rides, ate in a top-of-the-building revolving restaurant, and generally enjoyed life and each other. Then came the tearful good-byes as we sent Lynne and Cheryl back to the U.S. after a great summer together. Two hours later Joan and I flew out of Bangkok for the Philippines where we would spend the rest of our annual vacation with

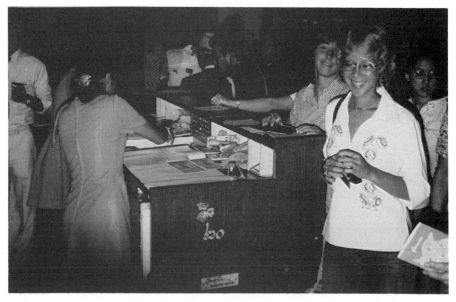

Cheryl and Lynne at Bangkok airport

Mark and Nancy; during that period they would have a ten-day break.

We arrived at Faith Academy in time to watch Mark and two dozen other fellows on a hot, muggy afternoon run over hill and dale in a very long cross-country race. Giving it all he had, Mark crossed the finish line fourth. One look at him was almost more than his mother could bear, for his face was ghastly white, and he was completely drained. I have seen dead bodies that looked better. But he soon recovered—and so did his mother. A week later, after exams, the school holiday began. We spent the ten days together at a beautiful mountain retreat at a colorful town named Baguio.

After another round of good-byes, Joan and I flew out of Manila and arrived in Dacca to find the Customs officers wearing party clothes. We had arrived on the major religious holiday that culminates the Muslim monthlong period of fasting. Because the officer was in a festive mood, Customs clearance went exceptionally smoothly. We stayed that night with Jalal and Shakina Ahmed.

Jalal was eager to discuss a highly important matter connected with a new policy of the Mushtaque government. This policy was not directed toward the pro-Mujib Civil Service officers who had escaped to India during the 1971 Pakistan Army crackdown; rather, it affected those top-level officers who had remained at their posts during the military occupation. They did so because Civil Service professionals are taught to serve whatever government comes along and because they felt that they could help their people during extremely trying times.

Jalal was one who had remained at his post—and he did provide exceptional help for the people of Bangladesh during the Pakistan Army's cruel oppression over them. As secretary of the Ministry of Railways, Highways, and Inland Water Transport, he developed such an impressive food distribution plan that the skeptical U.S. government ultimately released millions of dollars worth of foodstuffs to help hungry Bangalees. As good as his word, despite immense wartime obstacles, Jalal got the food to his people.

But after the birth of Bangladesh, because Mujib was angry with all the officers who had remained at their posts during the Pakistan Army occupation, he dismissed some of them and assigned others to dead-end positions. From those no-win postings Jalal and others finally had been prematurely retired. Then Jalal, with my encouragement, had taken the position with the American embassy.

But now the Mushtaque government, feeling positive toward these competent officers and urgently needing their high-level administrative skills, was pressing them to return to government service. However, because Jalal had suffered in the dead-end post and was happy at the U.S. embassy, he was very wary about agreeing to reenter government employ. He had been awaiting our return so we could brainstorm in depth about his two options. On into the night we discussed every conceivable pro and con that we could think of. As a result, he finally decided that it would be prudent to leave the decision in the hands of the American ambassador. He would be in the ideal position to know whether Jalal could best serve his people through government service or by continuing with the U.S. embassy, which also assisted the people of Bangladesh in many important ways. Later, the ambassador reluctantly decided his only choice was to release Jalal because his government needed him so urgently.

Although September was vacation month for us, it had been a period of intense activity for Mushtaque and his new government. On the first day of the month he had scrubbed Mujib's carefully crafted BaKSAL political party. The next day he arrested one of Mujib's men, the Dacca City political boss/Red Cross head, who was charged with corruption and scandalous misuse of relief goods. Then Mushtaque began lifting the bans on various newspapers.

In mid-September the new Mushtaque government released a "white paper" on the serious economic situation facing the country. Among many other substantial economic problems, the nationalized industries had sustained a loss of tens of millions of takas during the previous year because of incompetent management.

Interestingly, the paper stated that the nation's ideology would continue to be based on the four pillars of the Bangladesh Constitution: democracy, nationalism, socialism, and secularism. Secularism? The canny Mushtaque had waited this long to reveal that the radio announcement by ex-major Dalim—that Bangladesh would become an Islamic republic—was not accurate. But the mistaken announcement had played a valuable part in gaining the diplomatic recognition of Pakistan, Saudi Arabia, and the Sudan. Although Mushtaque was a devout Muslim, he felt it prudent to maintain secularism, which would to some extent mollify the Indian leaders and many Bangladeshis.

By this time human nature was asserting itself inside President's House. Farook and Rashid were becoming more and more dissatisfied with Mushtaque; it seemed to them that he was getting all the credit for the nation's "historical change," while they were more and more looked upon as just the men who did the killing. And, to the army generals, the two freshly commissioned lieutenant colonels were becoming insufferable as they continued to operate outside the normal army chain of command and rode around town in a Mercedes from the president's motor pool. So it was not surprising that some high-level army officers began plotting their downfall.

Throughout October Mushtaque made announcements calculated to please the army and the people. On the fiftieth day of his new regime he announced that ten months later political parties would again be allowed to function and prepare for parliamentary elections to be held in early 1977. That was a positive and popular step. Then his government ordered that the Rakkhi Bahini be disbanded and absorbed into the Bangladesh Army; this, of course, strengthened his position with the army generals.

In mid-October the Mushtaque government released another white paper—on the pervasive corruption in the Bangladesh Red Cross Society. Then Mushtaque called a special meeting of all the members of the National Assembly (Parliament). Because they were virtually all Awami League men who had heartily supported Mujib, only two-thirds of them showed up, and a number spoke out forcefully against the "murderers of Sheikh Mujibur Rahman." From Mushtaque's point of view that meeting was a failure.

There was plenty of work awaiting us at Malumghat in early October after our month in Bangkok and the Philippines. Also, new team members had come: X-ray technologist and "Mr. Fix-It," Dave Fidler, and his wife, Darlene, had completed their language study and settled in at Malumghat. Dr. Walter and Frances Griffeth had also arrived and would be living with us. Walt was a highly trained agronomist who would work with Mel Beals and advise how best to develop the land purchased for rice production. Fran would do secretarial work, which would be an immense boost for Joan, myself, and others.

Long before, our household goods had arrived from the U.S., including some whitish vinyl floor covering. Finally I took time to cover some of our dark, stained concrete floor with the vinyl. When we completed the second bathroom floor and stood back to inspect it, the workman who was helping me exclaimed, "It looks like the Taj Mahal!" Since then that bathroom has retained its new title.

At that point our special Bengali New Testament translation project was in severe jeopardy. Samuel, our Bengali translator, who had been doing excellent work, was about to leave us for a higher-paying job in Chittagong City. He had not found it easy to live away from the city in our Malumghat society. Because of his somewhat proud manner he had quickly alienated many Bengalis and Americans. He was the only one out of hundreds of medical workers, patients, and neighbors who wore a necktie to his daily work. Then, when he received a lucrative job offer, he decided to take the job and return to the city where he felt more comfortable.

Agronomist Dr. Walter Griffeth

The loss of Samuel would be a severe blow to our translation project, for he was highly competent at his work and we could see no one equally capable on the horizon. Despite his foibles, and despite the fact that he constantly kept us in hot water, we would miss him. We admired his devotion to God, his love for the Scriptures, and his immense capacity for work. And as we had worked with him, taught him, and advised him we had seen some signs of progress and spiritual growth in his life.

Just at that time a stranger arrived at Malumghat. He was a Bengali Christian religious teacher from neighboring India who had enjoyed a long association with a mission society well known to us. Because he had outstanding preaching and teaching skills, he was invited to give messages in the hospital chapel and in the church. Not only did he capture the hearts of the people by his public ministry, but also through his sincere interest in the problems of many individuals.

Samuel was deeply impressed with Awjit's teaching, character, and compassion, all honed by many years of training and living and growing as a follower of Christ. And Awjit took a special interest in Samuel, listening for hours to his ideas, feelings, and plans. He got the picture. Finally Awjit leveled with Samuel: "My brother, I have much love for you in my heart. But I must tell you that you need to make some changes in your Christian life. You need to stop being so proud, as though you were superior to others;

our Lord Jesus really was superior, but He lived a life of beautiful humility. Take off your necktie! Be with the people here as one of them. And why don't you forget this idea of leaving your important translation work to go to the city to take a job? There you will serve some company only to make money. Here at Malumghat you are getting enough money—and you are able to serve God and help provide the Scriptures for millions of people. Why give up an opportunity that is great and valuable for something that is poor and ordinary?"

The next day Awjit departed. And Samuel arrived for work —without his necktie. He had decided not to take the job in Chittagong, but would remain and see the New Testament project through to completion. "Thank You, Father! Thank You for bringing a wise Bengali brother from another country to Malumghat at just the right time to touch Samuel's life for good."

Spiritual truth was touching the lives of others at Malumghat, too. Recently eleven new people had joined the church and three young men, each nicknamed Babul, had decided to follow Christ. And the church was on fire, teaching and preaching at a fishermen's village some miles distant. Also, our bookrooms at Malumghat, Cox's Bazar to the south, and another town to the north were busily selling inspirational and religious books to many interested people.

By the end of October there was a widespread expectation that a fresh coup was in the offing. But who would lead this countercoup was anyone's guess. Would it be Awami League forces, or radical leftists like the JSD party, or Islamic fundamentalists on the far right, or General Zia, or some other army brass? It turned out be the latter.

On the afternoon of November 1 four army officers huddled over a quiet table in a Chinese restaurant near the Dacca soccer stadium to plot out a countercoup against President Mushtaque, Farook, and Rashid. The two senior officers were the chief of the general staff, Brigadier Khalid Musharraf, and the commander of the Dacca Brigade, Colonel Jamil.[42] The following night they would attack President's House and take over the government; simultaneously they would arrest General Zia and seize control of the army, as well.

This November 3 coup (1975's second coup) began to unfold just after midnight when Colonel Jamil quietly withdrew the three hundred troops guarding President's House. While the troops were silently stealing away, inside the stately President's House President Mushtaque was discussing the coup rumors with key aides. Soon after this meeting broke up, a flustered police officer caught

Rashid in the hall to report that the soldiers guarding them had "run away."

Rashid instantly notified President Mushtaque and Farook that the countercoup had begun to roll, then frantically telephoned for help to General Zia, the chief of the air force, General Osmani, and others; only Osmani ultimately came to help out. As the tank engines rumbled to life, hundreds of crows sleeping in the nearby trees began cawing raucously and flying wildly about, adding to the general confusion. Then Farook slipped out into the night to assign eight tanks located near the radio station to defensive positions in the city and to prepare the crews to resist the countercoup.

Simultaneously, a Bengal Lancer killer team (led by Risaldar Moslemuddin) headed for the Dacca Central Jail—to exterminate Tajuddin and the other three top Awami League leaders whom President Mushtaque had imprisoned. The killer group reached the jail and, after the prison director made several telephone calls, were finally admitted to the prisoners' cells.[43] There the other three AL leaders were brought into Tajuddin's cell, where all four were executed in cold blood by automatic weapons' fire. These brutal jail-slayings wiped out the last of the old top-level Awami League leadership—and would shock and sicken the Bangalee people when the news leaked out. An investigative reporter later claimed that President Mushtaque, Farook, and Rashid had these leaders killed to prevent any resurgence of the Awami League.[44] But all three men denied any complicity in the murders.

While the jail killings were going on, and while infantrymen of the Dacca Brigade were taking their positions around President's House, a detail of soldiers was sent to place General Zia under house arrest. The young captain in charge of the detail pointed his weapon at Zia, the commanding general of the army, and said anxiously, "Sir, you are under arrest. Please don't do anything."[45]

As soon as the Dacca Brigade completely encircled President's House, coup-leader Brigadier Khalid telephoned Rashid inside and advised him to surrender. Rashid harshly refused and averred that he would fight to the death. A few more minutes of verbal sparring did not change Rashid's mind. By then the halls and grounds of President's House were filled with clamor as Rashid and his men raced about preparing to resist attack.

At daybreak two Bangladesh Air Force MiGs thundered over President's House, forcing President Mushtaque and others to take temporary shelter in the basement. Next, an Air Force helicopter began circling over the house and the tanks in the courtyard. The pressure was on.

Then, as the eastern sky continued to brighten, five military men arrived from the cantonment to present coup-leader Brigadier

Khalid's demands. President Mushtaque refused these demands and told the military messengers to notify Brigadier Khalid that he was resigning from the presidency as of 6:00 A.M. The soap opera had begun.

After two hours the messengers returned with a slightly revised set of demands. But Mushtaque refused to receive them because he was no longer president. So the officers tried to present the demands to General Osmani, but he also refused to accept them on the grounds that he was no longer defense adviser to the president, for there was no president. The messengers carried this baffling news back to the cantonment.

Then at midmorning the inspector general of police telephoned an officer at President's House, his friend, and confided to him that during the night the four senior Awami League leaders had been slain in the jail. For some unknown reason, that officer did not announce the jail killings to others at President's House. Meanwhile, Farook waited impatiently for word from Rashid to attack. Instead, Rashid called him back to President's House for urgent consultation with himself and President Mushtaque.

The three men then decided that if the surrounding troops captured Farook and Rashid, they might be in great jeopardy because they had assassinated Mujib and his family. Mushtaque felt they should leave the country immediately; at his request Brigadier Khalid supplied an airliner so that Farook, Rashid, and fifteen other officers involved in the August coup against Mujib could fly with their families out of the country. They departed that afternoon for Bangkok, Thailand; ultimately, most of these officers went into exile in Libya. Of course, the enlisted men of the Bengal Lancers Tank Battalion and the Second Field Artillery Battalion who had carried out the August coup against Mujib were shattered to see their officers depart. Who would help them and protect them now from the current countercoup?

The next morning (November 4), General Zia, who was still under house arrest, prudently resigned to save his life. His resignation opened the way for Mushtaque to appoint Brigadier Khalid as commanding general of the army. So Mushtaque scheduled a cabinet meeting to take place after evening prayers to finalize Khalid's appointment and to reestablish himself as president of the new countercoup regime. At that moment, an intelligence officer rushed in to loudly report the cold-blooded jail murders of the four senior Awami League leaders (which had happened thirty hours earlier). The impact of this terrible news created pandemonium in the room. Mushtaque immediately called an emergency cabinet meeting.

Very soon the cabinet appointed three Supreme Court judges to investigate the jail killings. Then the cabinet members animatedly discussed the flight of the majors, General Zia's resignation, and the choice of his successor as commanding general of the army.

Just then Brigadier Khalid's co-conspirator, Colonel Jamil, with five armed officers burst into the cabinet room. While frightened cabinet ministers scurried this way and that, a young major stood over President Mushtaque, who had tumbled to the floor, and pointed an automatic rifle at his head. Quickly General Osmani interceded for Mushtaque imploring, "Don't do anything. This is madness. You will destroy the country."[46]

Then a furious Colonel Jamil raged at President Mushtaque, "You have killed the Father of the Nation. You have killed the four leaders in jail. You are a usurper. Your government is illegal. You have no right to stay in power. You must resign immediately."[47] Again the young officers pushed forward, brandishing their weapons. Once more General Osmani pushed them back. Amid the terrifying uproar Mushtaque wisely resigned on the spot.

This quieted the situation enough for the ministers to sit down and consider who would replace Mushtaque as president. Colonel Jamil suggested that the chief justice of the Bangladesh Supreme Court, an honest nonpolitical figure, would be the best choice. Finally all agreed to this proposal and sent for him. Chief Justice Sayem did not arrive at President's House till after midnight; only after much persuasion did he reluctantly accept the presidency.

While these events were taking place at President's House during November 4, Awami Leaguers throughout Dacca were overjoyed to learn that the majors responsible for killing their Sheikh Mujib had flown away to Bangkok. Pro-Mujib groups then declared the day "Mujib Day" and organized processions, which began at different corners of the city and converged upon Mujib's house on Road 32; there they chanted slogans and covered the house with garlands of flowers. Significantly, coupmaker Brigadier Khalid's mother and brother, longtime members of the Awami League, led the main procession.

Also, throughout the day India's government radio and press extravagantly praised the developments in Bangladesh. And on the next day, November 5, Dacca was shut down for half a day to bury the four Awami League leaders who had been killed in the jail. With all this sudden emphasis on Sheikh Mujib and his murdered Awami League colleagues, the public assumed that the present countercoup was designed to bring back pro-Mujib forces and resurrect Mujib's system of government. Many were convinced that India was behind the whole thing.

Ready to take advantage of this public perception were two anti-Indian groups: the far-right Muslim fundamentalist parties and the extreme left-wing JSD party. Both groups showered a snowstorm of leaflets and posters on the military cantonments and major cities of the country on November 5 and 6. These papers charged that India was behind Brigadier Khalid's countercoup and warned that if he succeeded in bringing back the Mujib system, Bangladesh would be destroyed.

The sparkplug behind the leftist agitation was retired Lieutenant Colonel Abu Taher, the ardently communist head of the JSD party's military wing. His ultimate aim was to create a revolution that would change the Bangladesh Army into a copy of China's so-called People's Army—and turn Bangladesh into a communist state. To those ends he had been working secretly for more than a year to establish cells of his Revolutionary Soldiers' Organization throughout the battalions of the Bangladesh Army. Then, on that critical November 5 and 6, he preached to his revolution-minded soldiers that to realize their demands they should rise up not only against Khalid, who had finally declared himself the commanding general of the army, but also against all the officers—"class war" he called it. This rhetoric had strong appeal for the leftist soldiers affiliated with the JSD cells, as well as to the men of the Bengal Lancers and the Second Field Artillery Battalion who were feeling fearful and vulnerable without the protection of their former commanders, Farook and Rashid.

Next, in reaction to the November 3 coup, the November 7 countercoup exploded; this was 1975's third coup. Inspired by a freshly fired hatred of their officers, in the early hours after midnight hundreds of *sepoys* (common soldiers, enlisted men) rose up as a body, broke into the armories, swiftly armed themselves, and fanned out through the Dacca Cantonment chanting in rhyming Bengali:

> *Sheepai, sheepai, bhai, bhai. Offisharder rawkto chai* [All we soldiers are brothers. We want the blood of officers]!

Seeing that the sepoys meant business, scores of officers slipped over the cantonment walls and disappeared hurriedly into the busy city.

In short order the troops took over the cantonment, then rescued General Zia from his four days of house arrest. Without even giving him time to change from his pajamas, they bore him on their shoulders to the nearby headquarters of the artillery battalion. These leftist sepoys calculated that right-wing General Zia would be so grateful to them for rescuing him that he would grant their revolutionary demands. For a long time Zia embraced the cheering sepoys and shook their hands. Then he called for some loyal officers who could help him begin to bring order out of the chaos.

By 1:30 A.M. another group of sepoys had taken over the Dacca radio station and announced repeatedly throughout the night that the sepoy revolution was in progress and would continue under General Ziaur Rahman. With each announcement, more people poured out of their houses into the streets to celebrate with the troops. Because these people were convinced that India, through Brigadier Khalid, was bringing back the Mujib system of government, they applauded the sepoys as liberators. Together the people and the soldiers danced in the streets, shouted slogans hour after hour, and cheered Bengal Lancers' tanks piled high with sepoys. It was a heady, exciting night of celebration—like a Bangalee Mardi Gras.

About 5:30 A.M. leftist Abu Taher showed up at the cantonment to embrace Zia and congratulate him. But Taher, like the sepoys, also had a hidden agenda for General Zia. He hoped to get him up in front of a large gathering of sepoys where he would present their twelve demands—really, the JSD party's twelve demands. He knew it would be difficult for Zia to stand before the sepoys who had rescued him and refuse their petition. These twelve demands included the following:

- Higher pay and better housing for the soldiers
- Abolition of the hated "batman system," which required sepoys to act as personal valets for officers
- Equality among soldiers and officers
- Strengthening of the leftist cells of the Revolutionary Soldiers' Organization in every unit of the army
- Supervision of the cells by a Central Revolutionary Soldiers' Organization, which General Zia would have to consult before making decisions

In order to carry out his scheme, Taher urged Zia to go with him to the radio station. But other officers, sensing Taher's clever ploy, refused to let him go. Instead, they summoned technicians from Radio Bangladesh to record Zia's message.

General Zia's brief speech was a winner. In a strong, sincere voice he explained that he had taken over as the chief martial law administrator (CMLA), which seemed to mean that he had become head of the government. He emphasized that his military government would be nonpolitical and temporary, for his purpose was to restore democracy to the people through free and fair elections. He encouraged the people to work together unitedly to get the country moving again. And he closed with the words "May Allah help us all.''[48] The public was greatly reassured by this straightforward address given by a distinguished military man who had fought heroically in 1971 to bring Bangladesh into being—and whom many remembered as the first person to announce the independence of Bangladesh in 1971.

At this point Brigadier Khalid knew that the jig was up; his short-lived coup had failed. He and some of his men drove quickly out of the army camp, but the mutineers were in hot pursuit. A few minutes later the Khalid group was cornered near the tall, gray-as-death Parliament Building; there they were gunned down by their pursuers.

At 11:00 A.M. that morning (November 7) General Zia chaired a key meeting in the cantonment. Here it was decided that Mushtaque would not be brought back as president, but that Chief Justice Sayem would continue in that capacity—and also become the chief martial law administrator (CMLA). Zia diplomatically agreed to give up that post, which he had claimed during his early morning radio broadcast; he and the heads of the air force and navy would be deputy CMLAs.

That afternoon Abu Taher tried once again to pressure Zia to go along with his demands. At the Dacca radio station, surrounded by exuberant soldiers, he handed to Zia a paper listing the twelve demands. Seeing that openly refusing these demands would create a furor, Zia tactfully signed the paper—but a little later when he made his second radio speech of the day he mentioned nothing about the twelve demands. He did, however, find another way to partially appease Abu Taher; he released two important fellow JSD leaders from prison that day.

The next day (November 8) the sepoys, who had chanted that they wanted the blood of officers, vented their blood lust by killing a dozen or more of them. Many more officers then fled the cantonment and conveniently disappeared, until less than a third of the officers remained at their posts. Those unnecessary killings made clear that getting rid of Brigadier Khalid and restoring General Zia were the bare beginnings of the communist JSD-inspired sepoy revolution.

The next day Abu Taher and the other JSD leaders whom General Zia had just released from prison called for continuing the revolution to take over the army, then the country. They were becoming rapidly disillusioned with Zia, who was not obediently falling in with their radical communist demands and plans. So they deluged the military cantonments with thousands of new posters and leaflets, which urged the soldiers to continue their rebellion to force compliance with all their demands.

On November 9 General Zia holed up in army headquarters with his loyal troops protecting him and his staff from the mutinous sepoys, still thirsty for the blood of more officers. Not sure in the beginning which battalions and regiments were most deeply infected with revolutionary fervor, Zia held his position and prudently bought time to gain a clear picture of the overall situation. One by one, he granted the sepoys' legitimate demands: he canceled the "batman system" and gave them improved housing, better equipment, and increased pay. Over a two-week period those concessions gradually took the steam out of the insurrection. Because many of the involved sepoys were far more interested in pay and housing than in a communist takeover, the revolution gradually fizzled out and the tension in the cantonment eased.

Then General Zia picked up information that outside the cantonment in the city JSD leaders were plotting yet another counter-coup to take place on November 24. And if that coup were to succeed, the whole army command system might be destroyed, producing such complete chaos that the Indian Army might be strongly tempted to intervene. So, at that point, Zia decided to counterattack. On November 23-24 he ordered a special unit of combat police to crack down on the JSD leadership. In a lightning move Abu Taher, his older brother, and other top JSD leaders were quickly arrested. And Zia broadcasted a stern warning: "We shall not allow any more disorder . . . we shall not tolerate any more bloodshed."[49]

As November drew to a close an advisory council (cabinet) was constituted to help the president and the three military chiefs operate the martial law government; the powerful General Zia himself took over responsibility for the most important ministries. He also disarmed some army battalions and created a new division unreservedly loyal to him.

While these back-to-back November 3 and November 7 countercoups were taking place in Dacca, at Malumghat we followed the confused reports with keen interest. In the beginning it was quite unclear what was really taking place; only later did enough facts emerge to produce a clear picture of the momentous happenings in the capital city (see figure 19).

Then on November 8, while enlisted men were shooting their officers in Dacca, twenty-two miles north of Malumghat a group of farm laborers also initiated a shootout—with local landowners. The rice in the fields, not politics, was the issue there. Soon three bleeding men were brought to the hospital. We quickly assessed their injuries:

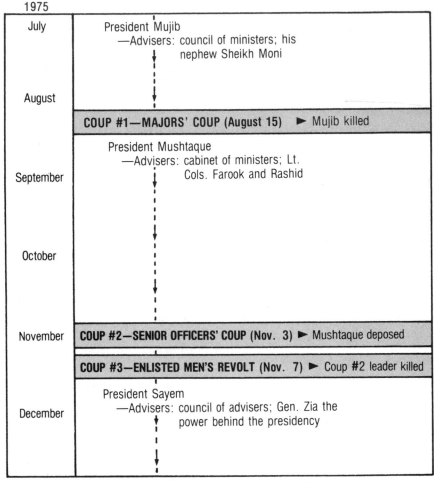

Figure 19. The three coups of 1975

- First patient—shot through the liver and right lung
- Second patient—shot in the lower abdomen and legs
- Third patient—bullet injury to the groin resulting in severe hemorrhage

The surgery on the third patient was particularly interesting. After giving three units of blood I opened the injured groin, controlled the bleeding, and removed the slug, which had damaged the mainline artery that supplies blood to the whole thigh and leg. Using arterial clamps and special very fine suture material I succeeded in closing the hole in the artery. Later the senator from that area came to Malumghat to give us special thanks for saving the lives of the injured men, especially the one who was his son.

In mid-November another prominent Bangalee also came to the hospital to give thanks for the cure of his beloved mother whose broken thighbone had healed nicely. He was the artist Delwar Hussain, and he presented me with one of his paintings as a tangible expression of appreciation. I noted that this surrealistic work, done in earth-tones, had been shown abroad—and carried a price-tag equivalent to sixteen thousand takas ($2,000). I thanked him for this generous gift created by his own hand, then asked him to explain the meaning of the picture. He replied, "You will have to decide yourself what is the meaning of the picture for you."

"I will enjoy doing that, but tell me, what is the most usual interpretation of the picture?"

"Well, the upper part of the picture is sometimes considered to represent paradise, while the lower portion pictures the earth."

"In that case," I replied, "I will take that ethereal vertical line which touches both paradise and earth to represent the Holy Prophet Jesus, for He is the cosmic connecting link between heaven above and earth below. He came from heaven's glory to walk on planet Earth for a few years. Then He offered up His magnificent life a sacrifice for all and returned to heaven so that we earthly creatures might believe, then one day leave our dead bodies behind to join Him in paradise."

"That's beautiful!" Delwar enthused, "I will have to tell my friends about your unique interpretation; they will be fascinated by it."

Then Joan drove home with the painting. There our *mali* (gardener) carried it into the house for her. Seeing him looking curiously at it, Joan explained, "This picture was just given to my husband by the artist who painted it. People have been discussing what the picture is and what it means. What do you think it is?"

The *mali* looked at the valuable painting for a long minute, scratched his head, and finally replied, "Well, Memshahib, to me it looks as though some little children put their hands in the dirt outdoors and went like this [smearing motions] all over it." Then, when Joan told him the amount on the price tag, he just shook his head and smiled, as though to say, "Maybe so, but it doesn't look like much to me."

Also in November, I debriefed our four tribal Bible/theology teachers regarding their recent two-week trip into the Hill Tracts. This time, instead of going two by two, each man had gone alone in a different direction to broaden their coverage of the villages. The men were all smiles, rejoicing over new believers, new Jesus houses, and other positive spiritual results. Three of them, however, had also encountered problems.

Vic with Shadijan, Robichandro, and Shotish

Menshai Murung had talked with a man who was about to become a believer, but began to think, *If I do follow Christ, I will no longer be able to do blood sacrifices when sickness comes, and this will make my wife very angry with me.* So he said to Menshai, "Not now. Later I will believe."

In one of his villages Shadijan Tippera faced opposition from the disciple of a Buddhist priest. This disciple insulted him and declared loudly that the monkey kingdom will bring about the end of the world. But when Shadijan asked him who created the world, the stars, and all the tribes of men, the disciple had no idea and could give no answer; the crowd laughed at him. Then the discomfited man listened quietly to Shadijan's exposition of the majestic Biblical creation narrative. At the end the Buddhist disciple blustered, "Oh, you Christians stole our Bible!" And the crowd laughed again.

Robichandro Tippera, who had been prevented earlier by a headman from baptizing new believers in his *mouza*, reported on the outcome of our appeal. Robi had presented the letter which I had written to the headman. While he was studying the letter, Robi explained, "Listen, in your Buddhist religion you have religious duties like shaving your head and putting on yellow robes. Likewise, we have two Christian religious observances we call baptism and the Lord's Supper. And, as Dr. Olsen's letter says, the law of Bangladesh is clear that everyone must be free to practice his religion." Convinced by the logic of the speech and the letter, the headman gave Robi his written approval. An hour or two later, in a nearby Murung village, Robi baptized Nang Doi Murung who had been waiting several weeks for this special occasion.

During the last week of November Joan heaved a sigh of relief, for her all-consuming task of supervising the first year Bengali course had come to an end. She was more than satisfied that the many hundreds of hours devoted to the task were well spent when her students passed their final examinations in good style. Now she would have much more time for the New Testament translation project—and to just live a little.

Also during the last week in November a two-year-old Bengali child made headlines around the world. That little girl was the last case of smallpox in Asia. In fact, except for a few smallpox cases in an isolated area of wartorn Ethiopia, she was the last case in the world. Later, the carefully organized World Health Organization program succeeded in eradicating smallpox in Ethiopia, too, making planet Earth completely smallpox-free. That was an impressive accomplishment.

By December the situation in Dacca had calmed down considerably. The new government honorably decided to pay compensation to the former owners of industries that had been confiscated and nationalized by the previous government. Furthermore, the

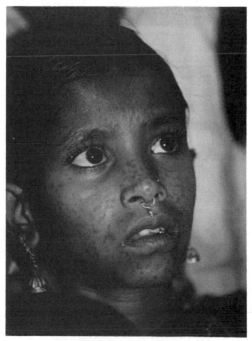

Bengali girl with smallpox scars

government passed regulations that allowed private businessmen to launch quite substantial industries and businesses valued up to 100 million takas each. These measures to stimulate the economy through private enterprise were applauded by the Western democracies.

Then, on National Day, President Sayem reiterated the military government's pledge to improve the law and order situation and ultimately to hold democratic elections. So 1975, a year of excruciating trauma for the struggling nation of Bangladesh, closed on a somewhat upbeat note.

Key Events of 1975: Summary

January
- Joan supervises the Bengali language class; I care for the sick and direct the tribal program.
- The Fourth Amendment passes, creating a near-dictatorship; this is Mujib's "second revolution."

February
- We hospitalize Debapriyaw Roy, the injured Chakma prince.
- Mujib replaces all other parties with his BaKSAL party.
- New tribal teachers join the tribal outreach team.

March
- Debapriyaw improves and decides to follow Christ.
- Famine conditions return to Bangladesh.

April
- We give food money to starving tribals; they tithe it.
- We resume the special Bengali NT translation project.
- The Farakka Barrage problem comes to a head.

June
- Indian intelligence (RAW) alerts Mujib to an impending coup; he disregards the warning.

August
- *Coup #1—the "majors' coup."* Mujib and others are killed.
- President Mushtaque takes over and appoints General Zia commanding general of the army.

October
- Mushtaque disbands the Rakkhi Bahini and announces future elections.

November
- *Coup #2—the senior officers' coup (on Nov. 3).*
- General Zia is placed under house arrest.
- Four imprisoned senior AL leaders are killed in jail.
- Farook, Rashid, and other officers responsible for coup #1 flee from Bangladesh.
- Chief Justice Sayem replaces Mushtaque as president.
- *Coup #3—the sepoy revolt (on Nov. 7).* Radical leftist enlisted men kill the leader of coup #2 and other officers, then free General Zia from house arrest.
- Radical leftist JSD party leaders fan the flames of revolt, aiming for a communist takeover of Bangladesh.
- General Zia quickly breaks with these radicals and puts down their escalating revolution.
- President Sayem continues as head of state—but Zia is the "power behind the throne."

December
- The Murung movement is alive and well; new Murung believers have built several village "Jesus houses" (churches) during the year.

Figure 20

9

1976: Militant Majors and Ragged Refugees

As 1976 emerged from blood-drenched 1975 we were well aware that it would be a busy year. It was my turn to be medical director of the hospital, a responsibility that would be added to several other taxing and time-consuming duties. But we could not know then that we would also be devoting much time and energy to helping hundreds of ragged, desperately needy refugees who would straggle into our area—and into our hearts—during 1976.

Early in the year an articulate, intelligent young man from a nearby village was coming to grips with the claims of Christ the Lord. He had been the first person from his village to graduate from high school; that made him a "matriculate" in the parlance of Bangladesh. Because of his education and leadership abilities, his peers admired and looked up to him. We trained him in our Outpatient Department and, because of his skill and other qualities, he soon became a top physician's assistant. For months he had also been learning all he could about Scriptural truths, and one day I noticed him watching, quite wistfully, a public baptismal service. Then one of our Bengali co-workers developed a warm friendship with him and soon helped him to make the great faith decision; this seemed to enhance his many good qualities.

January also marked the beginning of a fund-raising effort —"Project Heartbeat for Bangladesh." We had a need for an infusion of $300,000 for construction of buildings on all three stations, repaying funds advanced by the Home Board for previous construction, and a number of other highly important projects. Jay Walsh, still on home leave in the United States, would head up the project. ABWE president Wendell Kempton would also become personally involved, and we would all add our prayers and emphasize the project in our newsletters, which reached thousands of people. Time would tell what amount would actually come in during the year.

By early January the new martial law regime also had a need to deal with several major problems confronting them:

1. An unstable army fragmented into different groups with conflicting ideologies
2. Extreme left-wing radical Communists still attempting to take over the country by armed revolution
3. Pro-Mujib forces maneuvering to regain control of the nation
4. A prickly Indian government next door
5. Exiled coupmakers Farook and Rashid pressing to return to Bangladesh from Libya
6. Economic collapse
7. A destructive population explosion

We followed with keen interest the steps taken by the new martial law government to combat these several enemies of progress. General Zia was responsible for controlling the divided army—no easy task. One rift separated those troops who had fought during the 1971 civil war (freedom fighters) from those who had been stuck in West Pakistan during the fighting; these "repatriates" were now back in Bangladesh. Further divisions existed among the democracy-minded, pro-U.S., pro-Islamic soldiers on the right, the pro-Mujib men in the middle, and the cells of extreme left communist revolutionaries. *Of all the armies in South Asia, only the Bangladesh Army was riddled with far-left revolutionary troops.* In addition, there were personal enmities and divisions among various high-level army officers. So General Zia, himself a moderate right-winger, could only attempt to suppress the turbulent leftists and deal with mutinies and coup attempts as they came along.

The most active radical leftist groups in the Bangladesh society were the JSD party and the Shorbohara band; the Shorboharas focused much of their effort in the Chittagong Hill Tracts, while JSD party members created chaos throughout the country. To counteract these revolutionaries the government in early January began to create a 12,500-man special combat police force under the direction of the tough secretary of the Ministry of Home Affairs.

Devoted, militant followers of slain Sheikh Mujib created a third problem for the government. Khader "Tiger" Siddiqi, the pro-Mujib freedom fighter whose men had publicly bayoneted several collaborators shortly after liberation, took two thousand fighting men across the border to India. There he persuaded Indian officials to give him arms and sanctuary so he could harass the Bangladesh government. Early in 1976 Tiger Siddiqi began attacking Bangladesh border posts; later in the year he started infiltrating his men back into Bangladesh to carry out disruptive sabotage operations.

Bangladesh was displeased with India for providing this sanctuary—and for other reasons, too. Smuggling, which worked to India's advantage, had severely damaged the Bangladesh economy because Bangladeshi smugglers exchanged life-sustaining rice for poor quality Indian luxury goods. Furthermore, India was still completely intransigent about the Farakka Barrage dispute. Despite the objections of Bangladesh, India continued withdrawing Ganges water at the maximum rate, knowing full well that it was the dry season. There was very little that Bangladesh could do to obtain the needed water or to soothe this rocky relationship.

Meanwhile, Lieutenant Colonels Farook and Rashid, sitting impatiently in Libya, were trying to get General Zia's attention through the mail. But, even though they shared his right-wing ideology, he definitely did not want them back in Bangladesh. He considered them too aggressive, too controversial, and too likely to start trouble if things didn't go their way. Because of these concerns he not only did not answer their letters, but also he arbitrarily retired them from the army. Since the army was their whole life, the two officers were dismayed by this stroke.

The new government took some quite concrete steps to tackle the sixth problem—economic deterioration. Already by January the government had stopped the nationalization of industries and passed laws to stimulate private business. As men who favored democracy and private enterprise, the new officials determined to take further steps to encourage businessmen and get the country's industries moving again.

But the nation's public enemy number one was the exploding population. Already the world's most densely populated country, Bangladesh was becoming more jam-packed every month. And trying to grow enough food to feed everyone was a losing battle. Even if the nation could produce 2 percent more rice every year, the food shortage still would not ease—because the population was increasing 3 percent a year.

Previous governments had made only token efforts to tackle this devastating problem. But during January the new government sponsored an extensive survey of the public attitude about family planning; 20 percent of the people surveyed said that they would utilize family planning methods if they were made available. This survey was the beginning of a significant effort to attempt to control the staggering birth rate in Bangladesh. Within four months the government trained and deployed 6,000 male and female family planning assistants who fanned out across the country to teach the people how to prevent pregnancy.

As we observed these various prudent steps of the new government we were encouraged. And we felt positively euphoric when the new leaders decided to pay back to the hospital the $30,000 that the previous government had confiscated in the form of one-hundred-taka notes; other foreign charitable organizations also benefited from this ethical policy.

At this point the Bangladesh Bible Society was breathing down our necks about receiving the manuscripts for the special Bengali Gospel of John and for the Scripture story books known as New Readers' Selections. So my cooperative and generous medical colleagues agreed to shoulder extra duty to free me temporarily to work nearly full-time on the translation project. Thus began a month-long period of all-out effort to complete these manuscripts.

Despite the extreme pressure of the translation project, I did take time to debrief our tribal leaders about their January treks. Three of them had worked together teaching in the first Murung village. There one man had reacted warmly to their message, but he was troubled, too. He explained, "If I should be the only one to believe, I may fall back someday into unbelief."

To that Shotish replied with some of his own wisdom: "But if I plant one banana today, a year later there will be many bananas."

By late January Joan and several other American co-workers were down in bed with flare-ups of a virus disease that we call "Chittagong hepatitis" or "Chittagong perihepatitis." We named this new illness because it had not yet appeared in medical texts. We theorized that the offending virus attacks the capsule covering the liver (and sometimes the capsule of the spleen) causing pain in the upper abdomen and a "sick all over" feeling. This unusual illness hit first at Malumghat in 1967-68, striking down 85 percent of our American staff and their families; we were even forced to close the hospital for a while. Now, in early 1976, a flare-up of new and recurrent cases attacked about a dozen Americans and some Bangalees, too. Although this time some of them complained of new symptoms in addition to the usual ones, we were sure it was the same basic disease caused by the same virus.

As far as Joan was concerned, the illness was not all loss; she was soon able to do sedentary work while resting in bed. This allowed her to devote many hours to the final checking of the special Bengali Gospel of John and New Readers' Selections. With her big boost we completed the manuscripts by mid-February, and Samuel delivered them to the Bible Society in Dacca for printing and selling throughout the country. Great! Then Joan began teaching (from her bed) a little basic Bengali to our short-term workers.

In February I operated on a tragic little three-year-old boy. He had been born with his lower abdominal wall and the front part of his bladder missing; of course, this caused urine to drain into his clothing all the time. Because there was not enough tissue left to create a new bladder for him, I implanted his ureters (tubes carrying urine from the kidneys) into the lower bowel. This gave him immediate control and stopped the soiling of his clothes. He and his family were immensely relieved. Later, another of our surgeons closed the gap in his abdominal wall.

By mid-February coupmakers Farook and Rashid were fed up with their exile in Libya. So Rashid wrote a long letter to General Zia detailing their problems and requesting permission to return to Dacca. He also asked for fifteen thousand British pounds to cover travel expenses and threatened to come to Dacca, anyway, if he did not receive a reply within three weeks.

Zia was disturbed enough by the threat in Rashid's letter to send a senior army officer all the way to Libya to discuss the matter face-to-face with Farook, Rashid, and other officers who had been involved in the assassination of Mujib. He requested them to remain outside Bangladesh and offered them attractive diplomatic assignments in various Bangladesh embassies abroad. But Farook and Rashid rejected these offers, insisting that they were eager to get back to their home country. When the senior officer agreed to try to help them, Rashid gave him a handwritten note addressed to General Zia which stated in part:

> We sincerely place our loyalty and owe allegiance to you personally and to the government. . . . We genuinely feel disgraced regarding our coming out of the country on the night of 3rd/4th November, 1975. We are eagerly interested to go back to the country to wash off that unfortunate disgrace and to solve our problems. Once we are back to the country we place our devoted services at your disposal for the betterment and glory of our nation.[1]

Rashid gave Zia a month in which to respond.

By the time the senior officer returned to Bangladesh to deliver Rashid's note, General Zia was embroiled in another problem involving disgruntled army men; mutinous leftist troops in the Chittagong Cantonment were angrily demanding better quarters like those the officers enjoyed. This minimutiny was suppressed by force, as was a flare-up in the Dacca Cantonment earlier in the

month. The rebellious radical sepoys continued to prove themselves a thorn in Zia's flesh.

But the men of the Army Engineers Battalion headquartered
two miles north of our Malumghat Hospital were attending to
business. By February they had made considerable progress on the
road they were constructing deep into the nearby Chittagong Hill
Tracts. For several reasons their job was difficult. The up-and-
down terrain was a constant challenge, and they even had to make
their own gravel—by means of a machine that crushed rocks into
small pieces. They had completed seven miles of paved road
which, ultimately, would pass quite close to our Hebron Station on
its way to a very interior town named Alikadam.

On the evening of February 27 the Army Engineers sepoys finished a hot, dusty, exhausting day's work. After cleaning up they
rested, ate dinner, and talked awhile until bedtime. Then they bedded down in their rough-built bamboo and sungrass shelters and
quickly fell asleep.

Shortly after midnight, when the soldiers were deeply asleep,
militant Shanti Bahini tribesmen slowly and silently surrounded
the camp. When every man was in position, according to a prearranged plan the tribal attackers ignited one of the bamboo houses;
it burned furiously. Then, as the groggy soldiers stumbled out of
their shelters into the light of the blazing house, the tribal guerrilla
fighters let loose with automatic weapons. Sepoys fell like trees in
a raging cyclone; some scrambled for their lives into the surrounding underbrush. It was a minimassacre—taking place just nine
miles from Malumghat (see figure 21). Six soldiers were killed on
the spot and five were seriously wounded.

In the early morning hours the officers of the Army Engineers
began bringing to us their injured soldiers. One of them, whose
right hand had been shot off, lay in his bed sobbing, "I wish I had
died. Oh, why do I have to live?" After several hours of blood transfusions, surgery, plastering, and setting up traction, we had the injuries of the five shattered men under control. Later, to free up our
beds, as soon as a sepoy recovered sufficiently the army would
transfer him by helicopter to the military hospital in the Chittagong Cantonment. The army commanders and we were relieved
that all five patients survived.

That same week a visiting member of the Bawm tribe, a nomi-
nal Christian, heard enough teaching at Malumghat to make him
question whether or not he had ever really placed his faith in
Christ. "That is a simple problem to solve," I explained to him,
"You can easily talk to God, tell him that you now clearly understand Christ's good news message, mention that you are unsure of
how you stand, and tell Him that you want to settle the matter

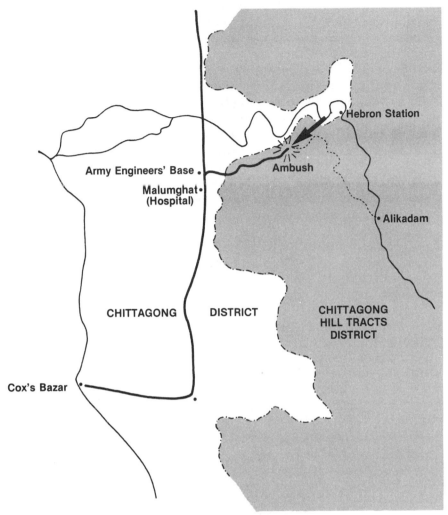

Figure 21. New military road to Alikadam (partially completed)

right now." He did just that and the next day left Malumghat with a spring in his step. How simple it was to replace nagging doubt with reassuring certainty!

During this time we had visiting us for a few days Sam Logan, an American Ph.D. engineer who was also a senior medical student. He scrubbed in with me on a few surgical cases, and I invited him to come along on an interesting and unusual boat trip we had scheduled for the weekend. Although he was eager to go, he politely declined. I was not surprised, for I knew he had developed an instant interest in one of our beautiful nurses, Karen Carder, who had been a member of Joan's language class. That weekend would be Sam's last at Malumghat, and he and Karen really needed to spend time together. The outcome of that weekend? An understanding—later engagement—then marriage—years later a lovely family of four sons—and short-term stints at Malumghat Hospital.

So leaving Sam behind, John Bullock, his son David, and I drove south to Teknaf, the southernmost town on the mainland. After a night of rest at the attractive Teknaf government rest house we were up at 5:45 A.M. to sail to tiny St. Martin's Island. This island was the absolute southernmost bit of Bangladesh territory and the country's only coral island (see figure 22).

Across the channel we stepped off the big motor-and-sail-driven country boat onto the three-square-mile island, which was home to about fifteen hundred people. We were taken first to the home of a prominent local man. Knowing that we would be thirsty and unsure of the safety of the local water supply, he sent his servant shinnying up a tall coconut tree to bring down some *dab* (green coconuts). Another servant opened each coconut with a blow of his sharp *da* (machete) so that we could drink the refreshing, germ-free juice inside.

Next we paid our respects to the priest at the mosque and the headmaster of the madrassa who were eager to discuss religious matters; we answered their questions about Scriptural teaching and left them some reading material for further study. Bangalees

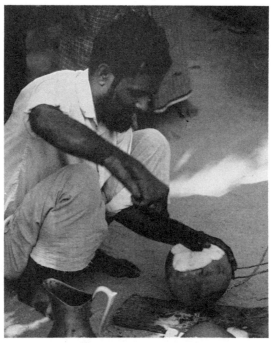

Opening green coconuts

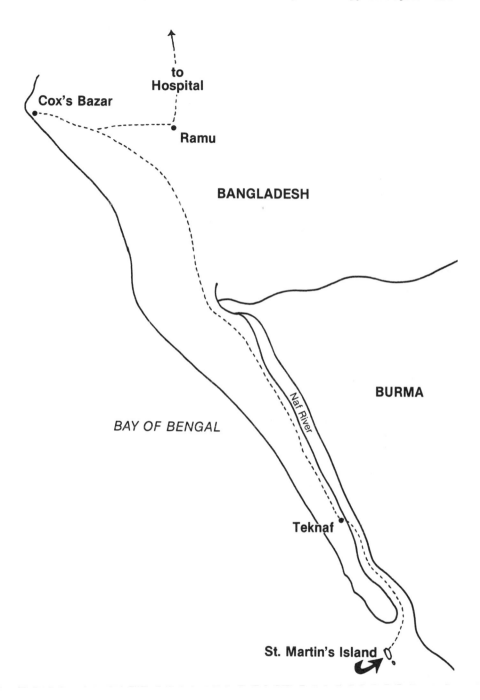

Figure 22. Trip to St. Martin's Island

love to discuss religious subjects—especially if they have been cooped up on a tiny island for months. Not wanting to be left out, the primary school headmaster and the chief of police also requested literature to read, so we obliged them. At every stop there were sick people, and we were glad for the opportunity to examine and prescribe for them because there was no trained physician on the island.

In the afternoon our trip back to the mainland was quite rough, for the wind was sharp and the waves high. We enjoyed dinner at the home of the local Union Council chairman, then returned to the Teknaf rest house to sleep. The next morning sick people began arriving. After talking to these patients and examining them, we wrote prescriptions for some and advised others to go to the hospital for X rays or laboratory tests.

Later a government Civil Service officer who observed the patients receiving care commented, "You certainly will have nothing to fear at *kiamot* [Judgment Day], because you do so much good for poor people."

"But, my friend," I replied, "in the Holy *Injil* [New Testament] it is written,

> For by grace you have been saved through faith, and that not of yourselves; it is the gift of God, not of works, lest anyone should boast.[2]

"So I don't think I will boast about doing good works when kiamot comes. Rather, it will be wiser to depend upon the grace of God and my faith in Jesus the Messiah." That new concept led to a lively and interesting discussion. Later that afternoon we drove back home.

On March 23 the American ambassador came to Malumghat. Mr. and Mrs. Davis Boster toured the hospital and our campus for an hour or two. The hospital beds were full, the Outpatient Department was booming, and in the two schools the Bangalee staff children were reciting in Bengali, the American children in English. Impressed by the size and drawing power of our medical mission, Ambassador Boster exclaimed, "I had no idea what a large operation we had going here!" He also seemed surprised at the number of Americans serving in this heretofore neglected part of the country.

By the end of March Farook and Rashid were getting more and more restless in Libya. And General Zia had failed to respond to their hand-carried letter within the stipulated time. Rashid allegedly described their rather extreme reaction to that affront in

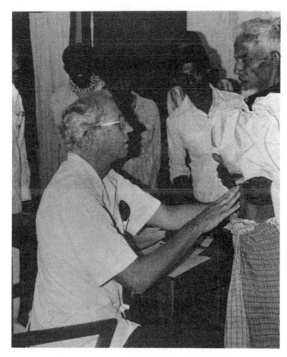

The next morning sick people came

these words: "We felt ourselves completely free to do all things possible to overthrow the government and eliminate General Zia."[3] So much for their wholehearted loyalty and allegiance to General Zia and the existing government.

To activate their ambitious plan required excellent telephone contact with their friends in Bangladesh. So Farook flew out of Libya to Frankfurt, Germany, to improve his chances of a clear telephone connection with Dacca. In Frankfurt he made his calls and also picked up news that the head of the Bangladesh Air Force was in London at the Portman Hotel.

So Farook hurried off to London where he had three meetings with the air force chief. He learned that his old outfit, the First Bengal Lancers Tank Battalion, had been divided, losing half its men and tanks to form a new armored regiment, the First Bengal Cavalry. This new regiment was deployed about twenty miles from Dacca at the Savar Cantonment (see figure 23). Then General Zia had transferred the remaining Bengal Lancers a hundred miles from Dacca across the mighty Brahmaputra River to the cantonment in the town of Bogra (see figure 23). Farook further learned that the tanks at Savar were involved in training maneuvers early every morning. Instantly he fantasized about the possibility of

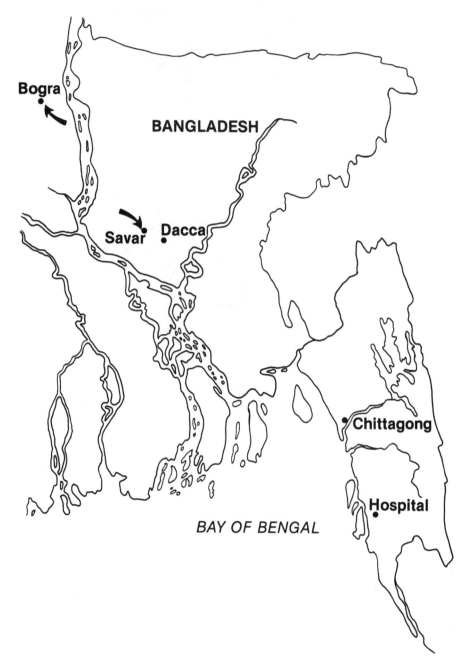

Figure 23. Location of Savar and Bogra, where tank battalions were based

some morning leading that group of tanks into Dacca to overthrow General Zia.[4]

On his return to Libya Farook learned that during his absence Rashid had received a letter from the Bangladesh government containing both good news and bad news. The good news was approval for Rashid and his family to return to Dacca for a while to discuss the problems of the exiled "majors"; Farook's wife could also go along to visit her children who had been left behind in Dacca. The bad news? Farook and the other exiles were not permitted to go along on this trip. But the two coupmakers were elated that Rashid could visit Dacca, as he could then secretly lay the groundwork for a fresh coup d'état.[5]

During the final week in March, at Malumghat I again debriefed our tribal leaders. They reported that the infuriated Bangladesh Army and police were combing the Hill Tracts to apprehend the militant tribal guerrillas who had killed the Army Engineers sepoys. Despite the increased danger of military action, our tribal teachers had carried out two successful treks during March; as a result, more than a dozen tribespeople had decided to follow Christ, and our men had joyfully participated in the dedication of a new Jesus house.

One day during that week doctors Joe DeCook and Dick Stagg asked me, as the team's general surgeon, to examine short-term teacher Linda Cross who had been suffering with abdominal pain. The results of the examination and the abnormal blood count spelled appendicitis. Soon we three doctors had her in the operating room, and I removed her severely inflamed appendix. Although the adjacent tissues were also infected, powerful antibiotics should prevail; we expected Linda to be OK.

Several days later she was getting along well enough that I flew to Dacca to care for urgent hospital business and attend a translators' conference. But the following day, unknown to me, Linda became ill with fever and pain in the area of her incision. Dick and Joe rehospitalized her and adjusted her treatment. But the next morning she was worse, and the doctors feared that she might have to be reoperated for a possible bowel obstruction. So they set the wheels in motion to somehow try to contact me in Dacca. *But even if our message does reach him in Dacca, how will he possibly get back here quickly enough to help resolve this problem?* they wondered.

Later that morning in Dacca I was called out of a translation conference session to learn that a message had come through about the deterioration in Linda's condition and that I should get back to Malumghat pronto. But how? Then I discovered that possibly an oil company's helicopter might be flying south that day. I checked on this rumor immediately and was soon "whirlybirding" over the southern half of Bangladesh, then across a channel to a landing on large Hatia Island in the Bay of Bengal (see figure 24).

An hour later we took off again, crossed the upper part of the bay, then followed the main road south to Malumghat where the staff was praying earnestly for some special or miraculous way for me to reach them that afternoon. The pilot circled our area once to pick out the best landing spot. Then, skirting the trees and electric wires, he set the chopper down right on our hospital property. By

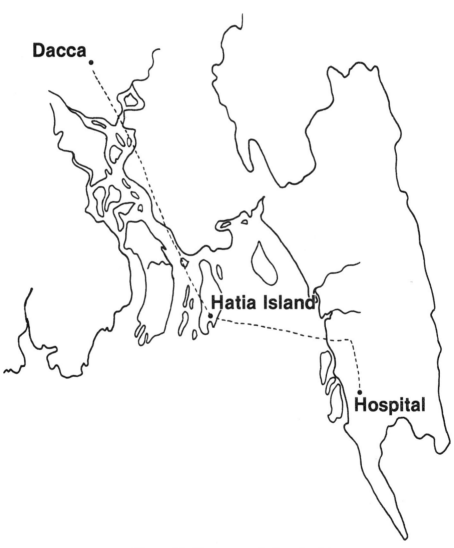

Figure 24. Emergency helicopter trip

then a crowd of hundreds had gathered, the curious attracted by the noise, as well as our staff and church people who sensed the answer to their prayers was at hand. As I leaped out they gave a great cheer, then the pilot quickly lifted his craft up and away.

I went directly to the hospital to consult with Joe and Dick and check Linda. After examining her and considering the situation we decided that the virulent germs responsible for the infection of Linda's appendix and surrounding tissues were resistant to our antibiotic; this had allowed infection to increase in that corner of her abdomen which, in turn, had a paralyzing effect on her intestinal tract. So we decided not to operate, but rather to shift to other antibiotics to combat the infection. Over the next few days Linda's pain eased and her intestinal tract began functioning properly again. We were relieved at her progress, but vigilant to detect any other complications that might crop up.

By April Joan's sharp recurrence of Chittagong perihepatitis was slowly improving, but she was still at bed rest. So to redeem the time she began to study New Testament Greek, using books we had available. This knowledge would be extremely valuable to our translation team for it would immediately open a number of important reference books to us. She studied from a detailed and rather difficult textbook written by a British author. Working full-time with her usual bulldog tenacity, she completed the first semester's material in less than two weeks, then pushed on immediately into the second semester's work.

Meanwhile, I took Nancy's cat, Munchkin, to the operating room and performed a sterilization operation—using surgical gloves, gowns, the works. The surgical technicians found it hilarious. But the last thing we needed at that time was a litter of kittens.

Because of health problems nurse Millie Cooley went on early home leave; she had put in countless hours of effective work in the hospital and we would miss her. Fortunately, experienced, capable Gwen Geens returned from furlough to step into the gap, and short-term nurse Ruth Yocom also was able to handle a substantial load. In addition, we had with us short-term medical student Dan Nelson and his wife, Carol (a nurse), who were also a big help.

In April Farook and Rashid left Libya. Rashid flew to London where ex-major Dalim was staying; there he successfully recruited Dalim to join their plot. Then Rashid telephoned army officials in Dacca and succeeded in gaining permission for Dalim, also, to travel to Bangladesh.

The next day Farook, disregarding his orders to remain in Libya, flew to Singapore to await developments in Bangladesh. With him was one of his Bengal Lancers three-man teams led by Moslem-

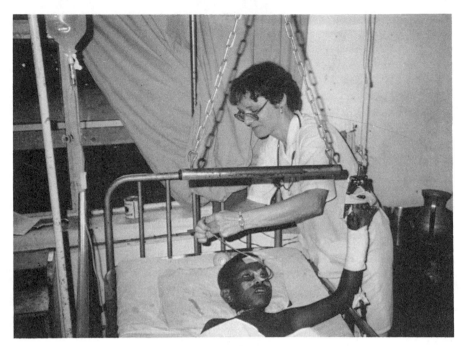

Nurse Ruth Yocom

uddin—the intensely loyal men who in August had assassinated Sheikh Moni and in November had murdered the four top Awami League leaders imprisoned in the Dacca Central Jail.[6]

Several days later Rashid flew to Dacca where he was met by relatives, friends, and Farook's parents; intelligence officers were scattered unobtrusively about to keep a close eye on Rashid's reentry to Bangladesh. That same evening he had a long meeting and meal with General Zia, who was friendly and listened sympathetically as Rashid explained the loneliness and problems of the Bengali exiles in Libya. Then Zia asked specifically about Farook and his whereabouts. Rashid responded that Farook was in Libya. But Zia replied sternly that he had been informed that Farook had flown to Singapore and that this information had come from "reliable sources, including Americans."[7] At this, Rashid was embarrassed—and upset—for it was clear that Zia's intelligence forces were keeping close tabs on him and Farook and suspected them. This would make his task much more difficult.

For the next two days Rashid was an extremely busy man. Between meetings with the military high command about the problems of the exiled Bengali officers in Libya, Rashid secretly and skillfully began inciting the men of his old Second Field Artillery Battalion, the new tank battalion at nearby Savar, and even the Bengal Lancers Tank Battalion in faraway Bogra.[8] And he organized a group of soldiers to appear at the airport to welcome Farook and his three-man team when they would fly into Dacca—a brash violation of their orders.

The next day, when Farook's flight from Singapore reached Dacca, the band of soldiers received him, then took him immediately to Savar where over two thousand troops exuberantly welcomed him. The nucleus of that mass of sepoys was made up of men from his old tank battalion who were now stationed in Savar; they had co-opted hundreds of infantrymen to join them in receiving Farook, their old commander. Military intelligence soon reported to General Zia that the soldiers had cheered, chanted, and hoisted Farook triumphantly on their shoulders. Hearing this, Zia quickly decided that putting Farook in irons for returning to Bangladesh against orders would cause a tremendous uproar among the sepoys, so he reluctantly left him free to roam in Savar and Dacca.

By this time the capital was buzzing with excitement about the return of the two militant former majors; then, when ex-major Dalim flew into Dacca two days later, the tension heightened even further. And the troops that Farook and Rashid had previously commanded were becoming increasingly insolent to their current officers. They did not hesitate to leave their barracks to meet with Farook and Rashid, who, reportedly, continued to agitate these sepoys to rebel.[9]

Then on April 27 General Zia's authority was sharply challenged by the Bengal Lancers Tank Battalion in far-off Bogra. The Lancers troops boldly sent word to Zia that he must send Farook to Bogra to see them; otherwise, they would advance on Dacca with their tanks. Zia reacted to this challenge by sending an infantry regiment to control the river ferry landing, since the Bogra tanks could cross the wide river only by ferry (see figure 23). Along with this sensible defensive action he made a second, more risky, move; he sent Farook to Bogra with instructions to quiet the Bengal Lancers troops. This was like sending a tiger to tell leopards not to attack villagers' flocks. For Farook the opportunity was almost too good to be true; now he would be able to incite his old troops in Bogra as he had in Savar.[10]

As he rode into the Bogra Cantonment Farook looked dashing in his new jet-black Bengal Lancers uniform. Instantly his old troops, the men who had helped him assassinate Sheikh Mujib, crowded around and excitedly welcomed him. Their officers urged Farook to help calm down the soldiers, not stir them up. But Farook, bent on launching another coup, ignored their words. Instead, he aroused the sepoys to rebellion against General Zia and the present government. He shouted, "Bogra is not the place for us. Dhaka is where we belong. We will go there!"[11] Soon the Bogra Cantonment was seething.

While Farook was inciting the troops in Bogra, his three-man team continued haranguing the men of the new tank battalion at Savar. For General Zia the situation was rapidly getting out of hand, so he had no choice but to act immediately and forcefully. That evening he sent a military guard unit to surround Rashid's house, making it impossible for him to go out or for anyone to enter.

The next morning the guard unit escorted Rashid to General Zia at army headquarters. Zia explained first that he appreciated Rashid and Farook for convincing President Mushtaque to make him commander in chief of the army after Mujib was killed. But now, he said, the situation required that they and the other coup-makers who had originally left the country remain abroad for some time. Zia would provide them with excellent positions in Bangladesh embassies in various foreign countries to make their exile more pleasant. And Rashid must leave the country immediately. Despite his protests, army officers put Rashid—and Dalim—aboard a flight to Bangkok two hours later.

General Zia then ordered infantry regiments to surround the rebellious troops at Savar and the Bengal Lancers Battalion in Bogra. One day of deadlock passed, then a second. By the third day it was clear to Farook at Bogra and his men at Savar that the encircling infantry would not break ranks to join their rebellion. Then General Zia sent Farook's father and sister by helicopter to Bogra to persuade him to give up the mutiny and quietly leave the country again with his three-man team. Finally a deflated Farook, seeing he had no other choice, reluctantly gave in and departed from Bogra.

Naturally, the Bengal Lancers sepoys were fearful and angry, for they knew they would have to stand trial for the mutiny, while Farook would escape punishment and live abroad. Throughout the night the troops argued among themselves whether to surrender or to attempt the coup—to go for the "revolution." But, even as they argued, their officers deserted them and quietly slipped off into the night to join the surrounding infantry officers.

The next morning the revolutionary soldiers, despite the loss of their officers, decided to attempt the coup led by their noncoms. As the tanks moved out, the encircling infantry let loose with fierce fire from heavy machine guns. Shaken by this stiff resistance, the noncoms fled, and the sepoys surrendered. As the Bogra mutiny was winding down, Farook and his team of three flew off to Libya.

Later, in Dacca, Zia's government put the mutinous sepoys on trial; ultimately some were executed and others jailed. Eleven weeks later Zia decommissioned the First Bengal Lancers, and the famous battalion then passed out of existence. With forceful action and a bit of luck Zia had put another coup attempt behind him.

While the abortive coup was cooking in Dacca, Linda Cross developed further unexpected complications of her severe appendicitis. By the time Farook was making his triumphant flight into Dacca, Linda was suffering from the fifth significant complication of her illness—a kidney infection that as yet showed no sign of responding to the antibiotics we had available in Bangladesh. That evening we held a three-doctor conference and decided to send Linda and Dewey back to the U.S. on the next available flight; there additional antibiotics and facilities would be available if required for her treatment. Medical student Dan Nelson and his wife, Carol, would fly with them to give any assistance needed. Joan and I would accompany both couples to Dacca on the first leg of our flight to the Philippines for our son Mark's high school graduation.

On a cloudy afternoon we six flew from Cox's Bazar to Chittagong, then took off again for Dacca. Soon we were in the teeth of a raging storm that tossed our small airliner around the sky like a leaf in a wind tunnel. The passengers were terrified, and I noticed some anxious orthodox Muslim priests fingering their prayer beads with tremulous hands and reciting audible prayers. Dewey, concerned about his sick wife, was perspiring freely. This was certainly not what Linda needed!

I wondered why the pilot didn't face reality and turn back to Chittagong. Just then a European left his seat and stumbled to the cockpit; a few minutes later the plane laboriously turned in the face of the furious wind and headed back toward Chittagong. The European? He turned out to be an airline pilot on vacation; he and the Bangladeshi pilots in consultation had decided that they could not risk going any further toward Dacca.

Back at Chittagong, the pilot made a careful approach and an excellent landing. By then Linda's temperature had climbed to 103.2 degrees. We spent the night in a hotel, then enjoyed a beautiful, smooth flight to Dacca early the following morning. I was encouraged to find Linda's temperature down that morning. Then the Crosses and the Nelsons boarded their connecting flight and headed for New York City. Only later did we learn that Linda had no fever or other problem throughout the flight—or even in the United States. Our strong treatment had finally taken hold and conquered the last complication, and no additional treatment was ever necessary. "Thank You, Father!"

The next day, before we departed for Bangkok I heard about the mutiny in progress at Bogra. We decided to continue with our vacation plans, anyway; whether the mutiny succeeded or failed, Bangladesh would probably still be there a month later when we returned. Of course, we were completely unaware that ousted Rashid and Dalim were on the same Thai International flight with us until we boarded the plane and heard other passengers excitedly talking about them.

On to Manila. As we arrived there Mark, Nancy, and friend Bruce Ebersole met us at the airport and put a lovely, fragrant jasmine-flower garland around Joan's neck. How wonderful it was to see our precious children and friend again! We stayed with the generous, hospitable Ebersole family. Russ Ebersole was our mission's coordinator for workers in Asia, including Bangladesh. Nancy Ebersole, a former member of our Bangladesh team, was a busy wife, mother, and homemaker. She and Russ were wonderful to our Mark and Nancy; their home—and hearts—were always open to them. This was an immense comfort to us in far-off Bangladesh.

Mark's high school graduation was a very special occasion, and we were proud of him. Two Ebersole sons also graduated, so after an all-night graduating class party, their house was strewn with sleeping forms the next day. Then we drove the winding mountain road to beautiful Baguio; after a delightful vacation there, we four flew back to Bangladesh.

Back at Malumghat, Mark and Nancy quickly settled into their rooms and got together with their old friends. Mark decided he wanted to learn the work of a surgical technician that summer—plus enjoy plenty of good hunting and play as many games of soccer as he could. Nancy would again do some secretarial work

The hospitable Ebersole family

Mark and Nancy home for the summer

and learn more about how to cook—especially nutritious things like fudge and brownies.

While we were especially happy with two of our children home, the government and people of Bangladesh were particularly unhappy with neighboring India over the Farakka Barrage problem; India was continuing to withdraw water from the Ganges River at the maximum rate. This loss of huge amounts of precious Ganges water was substantially reducing the water available for drinking, irrigation of fields, navigation of vessels, and generation of power in the entire western third of Bangladesh; also, there were adverse effects on fishing, livestock, forestry, and public health. In addition, salt water from the ocean was pushing ever further up the disturbingly low river, wreaking further havoc. But, because of India's tough stance, countless meetings with Indian officials had been useless.

In mid-May General Zia vented his frustration over this damage to his country at the forty-two-nation Islamic Foreign Ministers' Conference held in Turkey. He explained the Farakka problem to the assembled Muslim foreign ministers and succeeded in gaining their unanimous support. At the same time in Bangladesh Bhashani, the aged left-wing "red *maulana*" (priest), led a long march to the Indian border near Farakka to protest India's continued withdrawal of Ganges water. Of course, this dramatic act hit the front pages of the newspapers in Bangladesh—and in India.

At Malumghat our medical workload escalated again as Dr. Dick Stagg and his family returned to the United States for their first yearlong furlough. Also departing for home leave were the Webers from Hebron Station and the Eatons from Malumghat. Bob Nusca and Linda Short would take over for Jesse Eaton in the hospital business office. And the Totmans, who had joined the Webers at Hebron Station the previous year, would carry on the tribal seminar training program and other work that had been initiated previously at Hebron.

During May we opened a new department in the hospital—the Brace and Limb Shop. Physiotherapist Larry Golin, in consultation with orthopedic surgeon John Bullock, had worked for months obtaining materials and equipment from abroad, finding space for the shop, and hiring a trained technician. This shop would greatly benefit our many patients with bone and joint problems and those requiring amputations.

At this point, a dying man was brought in from Cox's Bazar; he was a Hindu artist/sign painter suffering from a hemorrhaging duodenal ulcer. He was pale from loss of blood, and his pulse was weak and rapid. While his wife was giving blood, I opened his abdomen, controlled the bleeding, and carried out a procedure to cure the ulcer.

The following morning at his bedside, the wife thanked me profusely for saving her husband's life. And I thanked her in return for donating the blood which had played such an important part in keeping him alive. As they were religiously minded people, I explained that what she did for her husband was a beautiful picture of what Christ the Lord has done for all of us. Because of her love she gave blood to save her husband's life. Similarly, because of His divine love the Lord Jesus offered His blood—and His very life—to save us and give us new life. Soon they both decided to be His followers. About that time others were making this great faith decision, as well, and several people were preparing for baptism and church membership.

By then Mark had begun his training program to become a surgical technician. In the beginning he learned the names of the various instruments and how they are cleaned, packed, and sterilized in the Central Supply Department. Next, he began scrubbing in on operations and soon became a skilled technician. This left him weekends, evenings, and the early morning hours for other activities, including playing soccer and hunting trips.

The artist and his wife

One morning he brought in for our larder a brilliantly colored wild jungle rooster with long spurs above its feet. Also tied on the back of his motorcycle was a strange-looking animal, which had charged Mark's companion before they brought it down. The twenty-five-pound creature had a pig-like snout, bristly fur, fierce fangs, and long, vicious claws. When we looked it up in our book of Indian animals we found a picture of the beast that is called a "hog-badger." Two Murung men skinned the badger; although they eat almost anything that moves, the Murungs drew the line at the smelly badger meat. So, along with some money for their labor, Mark gave them each a bar of Dial soap to help them wash away the clinging odor.

In early June I flew off to Dacca, on the hospital's behalf, to obtain government permission to import pain-killing medicines and to obtain relief from a new rule that ordered a government factory to stop selling intravenous fluids to non-government hospitals. These approaches were both successful, giving me a free mind and heart to enjoy meeting our daughter Lynne as she flew into Dacca to spend the summer at home. She looked beautiful to me as she stepped off that plane.

As we flew back to Malumghat together she told me that I almost met a flight that had no Lynne on it. Two days before her departure she had stopped at the travel agent's office to double-check that her reservation was secure—only to learn that the cost of her ticket had escalated $600 and her reservation was not confirmed. She quickly phoned from California to the president of our mission society on the East Coast and explained the problem. "Dr. Kempton," she asked, "will the mission approve that extra $600 or will I have to stay in the U.S. this summer? And, if it is approved, how will I get the money or another ticket in time?"

"Don't worry, Lynne," Wendell Kempton replied, "You definitely cannot stay in the U.S.; you have been away from your family far too long already. And if there is any difficulty in getting the Finance Committee approval in time, I will pay the amount from my own account. And we will find a flight that will get you to Bangkok in time to catch the plane from there to Dacca; I want you to be on that flight so your dad and mom will not be disappointed or worried."

Then that fine, thoughtful man, despite his hectic schedule, personally spent the rest of the morning tracking down a flight with a seat available that would get Lynne to us on time, then arranged to send the ticket to her within twenty-four hours. "Thank You, Father, for a loving president and a compassionate mission board who really care." Then, at Malumghat, Lynne had another joyous reunion—with Joan, Mark, and Nancy. She was home! And just in time, too, for the next day the road was closed by monsoon flooding.

In spite of the rains, we were quite busy at the hospital. For three weeks I had been preparing a seriously ill patient for surgery. He was a forty-three-year-old Muslim contractor from the city of Chittagong who had been vomiting for more than a week before he came to us. He had a long history of duodenal ulcer and freely admitted that he was an alcoholic; this was quite unusual, for Muslims are forbidden to drink and there are very few alcoholics in the Muslim community. Alcohol is especially damaging to the stomach, duodenum, liver, and pancreas; at the operating table I found a severely inflamed pancreas with a very rare pancreatic abscess. After quickly carrying out a procedure to cure the duodenal ulcer, I drained the pus from his abscess. After this he made good progress and, finally, a full recovery.

We continued, also, to make steady progress on our special Bengali New Testament translation project, as did the standard Bengali (SB) translation team in Chittagong City. There was a close interrelationship and interaction between our two teams:

1. We made a detailed check of every verse of the SB translation, then submitted to the SB team suggestions for refinements and improvements.

2. Then, when the SB text was finalized, we worked from it to produce the special Bengali version. To do this we revised it to a more formal written style and substituted the beautiful words and phrases appreciated by the immense Muslim community.

We were pleased that the work on the standard Bengali translation was done with care. Team leader Lynn Silvernale had a good grasp of the original Greek text and up-to-date principles of translation, and Mrs. Dass and Mr. Dores came up with fine colloquial renditions in readily understandable Bengali. Greek scholar Dr. Phil Williams had come three separate summers to check the translation for accuracy against the Greek original. Bible Society experts, other members of our mission, and Bengali reviewers from various parts of the country also had participated in the checking process.

Finally, a respected linguist/translator had come from the U.S. to do a linguistic check on portions of the translation—and to teach a valuable course in cross-cultural communication. On his final day at Malumghat he came to me to say that he questioned the wisdom of doing the special Bengali translation. Was I hearing correctly? Evidently something or someone had raised doubts in his mind about the validity of the project. Although we had no doubts about the high importance of the translation, this reaction was certainly painful and disheartening.

But others in the neighborhood were suffering far more severe pain. About fifteen miles north of Malumghat, in broad daylight armed robbers attacked a young man and looted his house. They shot him at point-blank range with a revolver. Upon his admission to the hospital I found powder burns on his face and a bullet wound just above his right collarbone; the bullet had gone right through and out his back. Instantly we began to type and cross-match blood for transfusions while I took him directly to the operating room. As soon as my incision opened two layers of tissue, furious hemorrhaging began. I put my thumb in the hole, stopped the bleeding by pressure, and called for Dr. DeCook to scrub in; who better than a Hollander to put his finger in the dike? Then, with Joe's thumb in the hole, I removed most of the collarbone to give me room to work and control the heavy bleeding. The bullet had cut a path between a large nerve trunk and the mainline artery to the arm, leaving "cookie-bite" holes in both the artery and the nerve; the main vein was also lacerated and bleeding. I succeeded in repairing these structures and, after several months of physiotherapy, the young man had regained much of the strength and feeling in his arm.

By now both Lynne and Nancy had mild recurrences of Chittagong perihepatitis, which would keep them campused for a month or so—and give them plenty of opportunity for long talks together. One night during this period Joan and I drove to Cox's Bazar for the evening. While we were gone Mark and the girls discovered the cat sparring with a small yellow-banded krait in our bedroom. They were well aware that the krait is a dangerous snake, even more poisonous than a cobra. So Mark put the cat outside. Then, keeping his distance, he began heaving my sandals and shoes at the snake; finally, one black dress shoe made a direct hit and crushed its head as it was weaving crazily against the closed bathroom door. Joan's reaction when we returned? "A krait! How scary! I'm so thankful you are all safe! This certainly confirms my policy of 'never trust the bare floor in the dark.'"

In mid-1976 danger of another type drove a pitiful group of refugees to our area. They were Bengalis who had been born and reared across the southern border in the neighboring Arakan District of Burma (see figure 25); thus they were Burmese citizens.

In that district a million Bengali Muslims lived side-by-side with another million Burmese Buddhists; the Burmese were racially different and more oriental in appearance. This community of Bengalis had lived there in northern Burma for centuries. As long as anyone could remember there had been bad blood between the two groups, for they were racially and religiously poles apart. Recently these Bengalis had run from persecution, beatings, and killings committed by the Burmese police and military, abetted by their Buddhist neighbors; they then escaped to safety across the border into Bangladesh.

The several hundred refugees settled in a hilly area about five miles from the hospital on the borderline between Chittagong District and the Hill Tracts District (see figure 25). They were a poor, ragged group, camped out in simple shelters made from boughs of trees; their water supply was unsafe, and malarial mosquitoes pestered them mercilessly. To survive, the men cut firewood in the nearby forest and sold it in the local bazaar.

The leader of the group, a middle-aged man named Mr. U., brought several of his subleaders to meet us and get acquainted. When we learned about their sad plight, our hearts went out to them, and we wanted to do what we could to help. So we taught them about malaria prevention and helped them dig a well which would supply safer water. Later we obtained from the Salvation Army tins of high-protein biscuits, which we distributed to them weekly. And, of course, we provided medical treatment for the many who became ill.

Mr. U. was an interesting man with a certain wisdom and sweetness of spirit despite his desperately poor circumstances; in

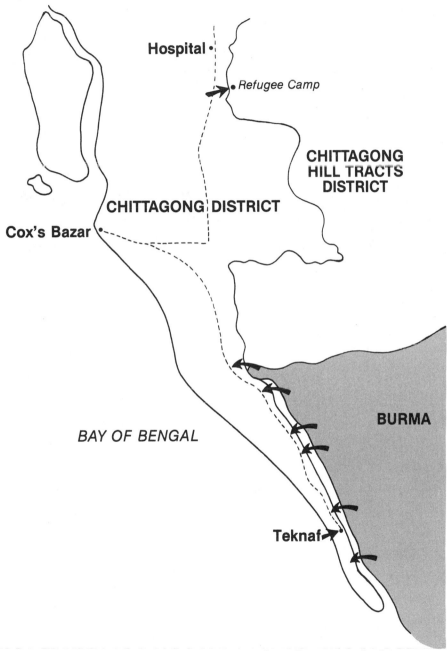

Figure 25. Influx of fleeing Bengali refugees from Burma—and refugee camp near the hospital

Simple leaf shelters made from boughs of trees

Burma he had owned a house and land, but as a refugee in Bangladesh he had nothing. He expressed keen interest in learning all he could about "the highly respected Jesus." I asked him the reason for this interest, to which he replied, "I once got a small booklet that told about the prophet Jesus; since then I have always wanted to learn more about Him." So I gave him some simply written Bengali pamphlets and booklets, for he was not highly literate.

At the end of June the American ambassador telephoned our Chittagong office to pass on a message inviting me to attend a special bicentennial party at his residence on July 5. So Mark and I flew to Dacca a day early to share in the daylong Fourth of July celebration and barbecue at the American Club. Then the next day, representing our mission team, I attended the ambassador's reception. Because it was America's two hundredth birthday, the celebration was elaborate and festive. In addition to enjoying the occasion, I met various top-level Bengali officials including the current strong-man, General Zia.

While we were enjoying these festivities in the capital city, a few miles away in the bowels of Dacca Central Jail a deadly serious secret trial was taking place. On trial were twenty-two communist revolutionary soldiers and a dozen of their civilian mentors, leaders of the far-left JSD party. Chief among the accused was Abu Taher, a former lieutenant colonel and the spark behind the November 7 sepoy rebellion several months earlier. Never before in Bangladesh or Pakistan history had a trial been held inside a prison. Machine guns behind sandbagged walls guarded every entrance. Obviously the government feared an attack by radical leftists. The defense attorneys were required to take an oath of secrecy, and newspapers were prohibited from covering the proceedings.[12]

There was a certain irony to this trial. Those enemies of General Zia who had arrested him in the November 3 coup were now free. But those who had freed him in the November 7 countercoup were now the accused in this secret trial ordered by Zia himself and the present government. Ironic or not, the government considered it necessary because, after freeing Zia, these radical communist men had continued to kill army officers, promote revolution, and attempt the violent overthrow of the government.

The charges against the accused were mutiny and treason. Abu Taher made a lengthy statement before the military tribunal emphasizing his distinguished military credentials, his heroic part in the liberation war, his love for his country, and his success in launching the sepoy rebellion that had freed General Zia from house arrest. He claimed that Zia had requested his help and thanked him for it when the sepoys rescued him, but later Zia had turned against him for his continuing revolutionary activities.[13]

When the depositions were finally completed the military tribunal declared the accused to be guilty, sentenced most of them to long terms in jail, but imposed the death penalty on Abu Taher. Only then were the government newspapers allowed to write about the trial, and their July 18 headlines boldly declared, "TAHER TO DIE."[14]

Two days later Amnesty International sent a cable from London to President Sayem requesting a fresh trial in an official courtroom outside the jail; that same day Sayem rejected this request for a retrial. So Abu Taher was hanged at 4:00 A.M. the next morning, a severe blow to the communist revolutionary movement.

Also in July, the annual figures were totted up for fiscal 1975-76, a surprisingly good year for the Bangladesh economy despite the coups, countercoups, and many other problems. New, tough measures taken by Sheikh Mujib before his assassination and by the subsequent martial law government had begun to bear fruit, and good weather had smiled upon the farmers. As a result, they enjoyed a bumper crop. The industries improved their output as well. Because of these favorable factors the price of rice and other items actually decreased in 1976, making poor people very happy.

Later in July the government held a second secret trial. This time the accused were six additional radical leftist JSD leaders and a foreigner who was aiding them in their revolutionary activities; he was a Dutch journalist and relief worker named Peter Custers. All seven men were declared guilty and sentenced to fourteen years imprisonment. However, after appeals by leaders of various nations, Custers was pardoned and deported to his own country.[15] His experience strengthened our long-standing determination never to become embroiled in the politics of our adopted land.

While the government meted out punishment to its enemies in the nation's capital, at a village a few miles from Malumghat armed robbers viciously battered the two village watchmen, a father and his eighteen-year-old son. The father suffered such severe brain damage that it was impossible to save him. The son also sustained severe blows to the head, but he was conscious and his condition was serious but stable. We have our nurses examine such patients hourly, day and night, to be sure their condition does not deteriorate. Thirty-six hours later, about 11:00 P.M., those checks showed that something was going wrong. The duty nurse immediately sent for me, and I found the boy was becoming stuporous with increasing weakness on the right side of his body. This spelled epidural hematoma—bleeding inside the skull causing pressure on the brain. Immediately I wrote preoperative orders and sent for surgical technician Mark Olsen to come to assist in the operation.

Joan received the message and awakened Mark, who was tired out from a long hunting trip that afternoon. She shook his sleeping form calling, "Mark! Mark, wake up! Your dad needs you at the hospital to scrub in on an emergency case."

Mark lifted his head from the pillow in a daze and protested sleepily, "Oh, Mom! I can't!"

"I'm afraid you'll have to, Mark. You're needed. So get dressed now; I have a Coke and some chocolate cake ready for you on the table."

Mark was revived by the time he reached the hospital, and we began the operation about midnight. Eighteen-year-old Mark first helped me place sterile drapes around the shaved head of eighteen-year-old Hossain. Next the scalp incision, followed by a drillhole through the skull, which confirmed the presence of a huge clot of blood pressing on the left side of the boy's brain. Then I opened a large window in the skull and carefully removed the massive blood clot, which covered the whole left side of the brain and depressed the brain surface nearly an inch. Next came the tedious job of stopping the many bleeding points and giving the brain time to re-expand.

Suddenly, right in the midst of this, the lights went out! It took thirty minutes to get a generator started to provide emergency electricity—more blood loss. Then, with dogged determination, we resumed our tiring work. Finally, at sunrise, we had all the bleeding controlled and placed the last stitch in the scalp at 7:00 A.M. Mark had been a tremendous help, for during the summer he had become a competent technician. And although we were both exhausted, we felt exhilarated from working together all night to save the boy's life.

A few hours later the young patient regained consciousness. Then over the next three days his right-sided weakness disappeared, and on the sixth postoperative day I removed his sutures and sent him home. Mark was there to wave good-bye, for a bond of friendship had developed between the two boys. Although their cultural backgrounds were as different as night and day, they had two things in common: their age and the dangerous ordeal they had passed through together.

In late July Dr. Donn and Kitty Ketcham returned from the United States accompanied by short-term surgeon Dr. Byron Sheesley and his wife. Byron would be a boon to me and our patients while Donn and Kitty were getting resettled at Malumghat. Donn's heart surgery had definitely helped him, for he was vigorous and quite well enough to make his usual excellent contribution to the work. A few days later Jay and Eleanor Walsh also returned to give the work at Malumghat a further strong boost.

In August General Zia represented Bangladesh at the eighty-five-nation Summit Conference of Nonaligned Nations held in Sri Lanka. At this conference, also, he successfully presented his grievances against India for the severe problems caused by the Farakka Barrage and the diversion of Ganges water away from Bangladesh. He gained the widespread sympathy of many of the nonaligned nations. Back in Dacca government officials then decided that, since they had gained the support of so many nonaligned and Muslim nations during the year, they would now try to take their case against India to the United Nations. That should make India's Indira Gandhi sit up and take notice!

Toward the end of August Mark completed his work as a surgical technician in the hospital, for he would soon be traveling to the U.S. to begin his university studies. This gave him extra time for some final games of "football"—the Bangladeshi name for soccer, Mark's favorite sport. He had been captain of his high school team in the Philippines, and throughout the summer he had played on the hospital's soccer team in the surrounding towns and villages. Near the end of August the hospital team was scheduled to play a college team in a distant town. So Mark, with a Bengali team member on the back of his motorcycle, drove nearly fifty miles over the rough road to the game.

The two teams were well matched, both having several good players. Sometime during the first half Mark was involved in a scramble in front of the opposing goal. When a teammate kicked

Mark, captain of his soccer team at Faith Academy

the ball up in the air toward the goal, Mark leaped high to hit the ball into the goal with his head. At that moment the goalie, a stocky, powerful fellow, came rushing out of the goal to intercept the ball. His head crashed into Mark who was stretched out full-length up in the air; the goalie's head plowed into Mark's upper abdomen, knocking the wind out of him. He crumpled to the ground. The referee stopped the game for a few minutes, then play resumed; despite sharp abdominal pain, Mark kept on playing because he did not want to leave his team a player short. By the end of the first half he was suffering, and by the end of the game the pain in his abdomen had become intense. Yet he was not aware that he had sustained a serious injury and was bleeding internally.

It was dusk when the game was over. Leaving the others to enjoy post-game refreshments, he and his friend mounted the motorcycle for the trip back. On the way home every bump, every jolt of that forty-seven miles was agony. After the first thirty-two miles of the nightmare trip Mark thought that he could go no further. But he gritted his teeth and said again and again to himself, "Fifteen miles—fifteen miles—only fifteen miles to go." And he kept on pounding down the road.

Nearly an hour before Mark reached home a friend and neighbor arrived at the front door. Forty-five-year-old Momin was the hospital's public relations officer. He had a special place in his

Momin

heart for Mark, for he had often been his hunting companion and mentor, and they had enjoyed many adventures together. When Joan invited him in, he asked if Mark had returned from the soccer game. Then he sat down nervously in the living room to wait for him. Joan offered him tea, but he refused and then alternately sat and paced about restlessly. It was obvious that he was agitated and worried about Mark. He later explained that, although he had never felt any concern about Mark's previous soccer or hunting trips, he felt some special strong premonition that this time something was wrong. Because of this foreboding he had come to the house just after 7:00 P.M. to check on Mark.

In the meantime, our son's harrowing journey continued. The next few miles were only a blur. How easily he could have passed out and crashed that dark night as he continued to bleed internally! Later, he had no recollection of the last six miles of his pain-wracked, mentally fogged ride.

At last we heard Mark's motorcycle coming into the carport. Momin shot from his seat and ran to the door, calling, "Mark, my boy! Are you all right?" Then, seeing Mark walking unsteadily, he added, "What's the matter with your leg?"

Mark groaned, "No, Momin—I'm not good. Not good at all! It's not my leg—it's my stomach!" He was pale, perspiring, and doubled over with pain. When I laid him gently on a bed to examine him, he winced as a lightning pain struck his left shoulder and he began to tremble violently. His abdomen was hard as a board and tender throughout, especially in the left upper corner. I was sure he had ruptured an organ, probably his spleen.

Immediately I called for the other two surgeons, Donn Ketcham and Byron Sheesley, to come and check my findings while I arranged a shot of morphine for Mark. Then we drove Mark to the hospital, took X rays, and prepared him for surgery. By then the morphine was easing his pain—and I had time to pray, "Thank You, Father, for bringing our precious son home safely through the dark night." A little later Mark's pain was so effectively eased by the morphine that he got up to walk home; someone put him back on the gurney.

Because we had two other excellent surgeons on the scene, there was no need for me to operate on my own son. Instead, I would sit by his head and be a father to him. As we wheeled him into the operating room, surgical technician Mark lifted up his head to check that all the proper instruments for a splenectomy were there on the tray. Then, deciding he didn't want to give any of his fellow technicians the satisfaction of sewing up his skin at the end of the operation, he said to Donn Ketcham, "Hey, Uncle Donn, you close—OK?" And Donn agreed.

Once the incision was made it was easy to see that Mark's spleen had been torn and that was the cause of the bleeding. So the surgeons removed his spleen, took out his appendix for good measure, and closed the incision. Then our wonderful nurses began giving Mark careful around-the-clock nursing care; with their heavy schedules this was not easy for them to do, but they would have it no other way. Mark's "Aunt El" (Eleanor Walsh) began attending him as soon as he reached his room. So Mark began to recover from his injury and surgery.

The following morning about 6:00 A.M. Momin roared into our carport on his motorcycle. He had gone first to the hospital and learned that Mark's spleen had been removed. And he had one burning question as he came to the front door: "Just tell me one thing. Can you live without your spleen?" He was immensely relieved when I explained that Mark could live quite nicely without his spleen, because other organs of the body take up its functions. I could easily answer Momin's question, but I have never obtained a clear answer to another question that filled my own mind just then—how did Momin sense that Mark was in danger that night? Neither Joan nor I, Mark's own parents, had any premonition of his peril. Very strange. At any rate, Mark went on to make a fine recovery. And like David Livingstone, who left his heart in the soil of Africa, Mark Olsen left his spleen in a jar in the laboratory of Malumghat Hospital in Bangladesh.

Not long before Mark's injury another little drama began to unfold. Mark's fellow surgical technicians, all Bengali young men, kept teasing him about getting married. "Mark, when are you going to get married? Do you have anyone in mind?"

After several days of these persistent questions, Mark finally had replied, "Oh, I'm already married." Immediately they pressed him for the name of his supposed wife. Pulling a name out of the air, Mark responded, "Why, her name is Julie." Imagine his surprise when, a few days later, a short-term orthopedic surgeon named Dr. Jabaay arrived at Malumghat with his attractive teenage daughter named—you guessed it—Julie! Then when this real Julie offered to donate blood for Mark's surgery, went to the laboratory to have her blood tested, then fainted in the process, the surgical technicians said to each other, "Maybe Mark isn't kidding us. Maybe he really is married." Later, Mark had some difficulty trying to set the record straight and convince his friends that this pretty Julie was not really his wife after all.

By the time Lynne had recovered from her Chittagong perihepatitis it was time for her and Mark to fly off to California; Lynne would continue her prenursing course at Biola University, and Mark would begin his studies at the same institution. We drove to Chittagong, gave Mark a day's rest there, then flew on to Dacca. After our semifinal good-byes the children disappeared into the Customs checking section of the cavernous airport.

We then slipped around to the VIP lounge where we had been invited to have a last meeting with the American ambassador, who was about to leave Bangladesh to take up his new post as ambassador in Guatemala. This gave us an opportunity to tell him good-bye and also to spend final minutes with Lynne and Mark who would wait to board the plane just across a low fence from the VIP area. I thanked Ambassador Boster for his many kindnesses to us and congratulated him on doing such a fine job, for he had been an excellent ambassador. He graciously replied, "I am humbled hearing that from you, because I know your degree of dedication to the people of Bangladesh."

Then we had some final minutes with Lynne and Mark before the inevitable good-byes—and all the deep feelings that accompanied them. There were last kisses, last hugs over the fence, some tears, then we sent our dear children off across Southeast Asia and the Pacific Ocean to their university in the United States.

In the VIP area we also saw Admiral Khan fly in from New Delhi where he had been negotiating with Indian officials about the Farakka Barrage problem. He was angry because the meetings had been a complete failure, and Prime Minister Indira Gandhi had castigated him for complaining to the members of the Nonaligned Nations and for scheduling further complaints before the United Nations. Would this sticky Farakka problem never end?

Joan and I went back to Jalal's house to spend the night. Because of the heavy pressure applied by the Bangladesh government, Ambassador Boster finally had agreed to release Jalal from his post in the U.S. embassy so he could return to government service. He was promptly made the secretary of an important ministry. At Jalal's house we met the Japanese ambassador and the Japanese director of the giant Mitsui Company in Bangladesh. They had come to sign an official agreement with the Government of Bangladesh. Jalal signed on behalf of the government, the Japanese dignitaries on behalf of the Mitsui Company, and I signed as a witness to the official protocol. Then Joan helped serve the refreshments provided by Jalal's cook.

After our return to Malumghat, Robichandro Tippera and his bright son Awshai came to talk over the boy's educational program. During our discussion I learned that Awshai was very warm toward spiritual matters but had never yet specifically placed his faith in Christ the Lord. He did so that day and savored the same joy and peace of mind that Bengalis or Americans or any others experience. Then he departed to live out his new faith in his daily school life.

We were always up early on Sunday mornings because the Sunday school class of eight- to ten-year-old Bangalee children

Jalal signing the official agreement

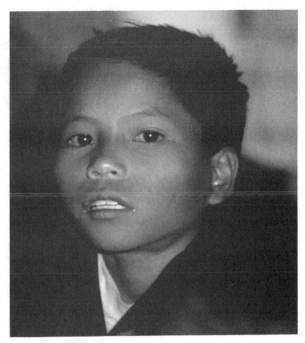

Awshai

met at our house. Marge Beals had long been involved with the class, but Chittagong perihepatitis had plagued her for months. So Joan and Alice Payne were enjoying leading this group of two dozen bright boys and girls. Ultimately, most of these children decided to follow Christ; among them were future leaders of the church.

In September nurse Becky Davey went down with Chittagong perihepatitis. Because Becky is so versatile, her illness left a big gap in the work. She was a veteran, part of our original team, which had designed and begun the hospital. During the years when we used a "matron" system at the hospital, she was the matron (head nurse) because she had special training and qualifications in nursing administration. Also Becky was a capable teacher of nursing and Bible/theology subjects; sometimes she even helped out efficiently in the hospital business office. During other periods she supervised the operating room and learned how to competently give general anesthesia. And through the years Becky learned so much about the treatment of many of the patients who came to us that later she became supervisor of the Outpatient Department and all the physicians' assistants who worked there. Fortunately, she recovered from her illness after just a few weeks and returned to her duties.

By this time the Kutubdia carpenter, who had shifted his family from the island to our area, was well settled into the Cha Bagan

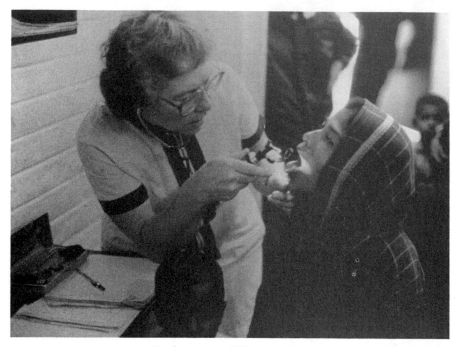

Becky Davey, OPD supervisor

village near the hospital. He had taken advantage of available loans for land and house construction, then built a fine, strong, mud-walled house. Later, he and his family had planted an impressive garden of vegetables, pineapples, bananas, and other fruits. Yet there were pressures. Because his personality was aggressive and somewhat abrasive, the carpenter was not finding it easy to gain new friends and integrate smoothly into the community.

In mid-October an injured child was brought to us. The doctors whom the family consulted in Chittagong City could not solve the problem, so they brought the child to Malumghat. The little boy had jumped onto a sharp bamboo spike, which had penetrated right through his foot. But the spike had wedged so tightly between two bones that no one could pull it out. After anesthetizing the child I had to actually chisel away portions of both bones to free up the bamboo so we could remove it. The little tyke made an uneventful recovery—and learned from his ordeal that it pays to "look before you leap."

During October we again gathered for our annual Field Council meetings. Our three stations and various committees reported progress on all fronts. As a Field Council we gave special recognition during these meetings to two people:

1. To Lynn Silvernale for more than ten years of work to bring the standard Bengali common language New Testament close to completion
2. To Jay Walsh for spearheading Project Heartbeat for Bangladesh. (More than $400,000 ultimately came in for the various important projects.)

Also, there was notable progress in the theology/Bible training programs for church leaders and members. The women's program, spearheaded by Linda Short, had successfully completed the first year's courses. The men's program, initiated by Jesse Eaton, was pushing hard to try to catch up. And at Hebron Station Dave Totman was launching a three-year Tribal Bible Institute curriculum to replace the monthly seminar program. Training national leadership for the churches had necessarily become a high priority item in the mission's work.

In late October I flew to London, England, to be a speaker in an international conference. At the conference center one day, suddenly a tall, beautiful, blond young woman came running up and threw her arms around me. Instantly conversations near me ceased, and people turned to stare. It was my eldest daughter, Wendy. I was dumbfounded. What a happy, wonderful surprise! But I was not surprised to find out later that her coming had been engineered by ABWE president, Dr. Wendell Kempton. Wendy and I had not been together for more than two years, so we talked non-

Dave Totman teaching in the Tribal Bible Institute

stop about everything under the sun. Wendy's unexpected appearance was the best part of the whole trip.

For four days the conference organizers attempted to obtain an overhead projector for some of the visual aids I wanted to use in my presentation, but to no avail. The rules and regulations and the power of the British unions made it impossible to simply rent an overhead projector, bring it to the auditorium, and use it for a meeting. So I readjusted my message to fit the circumstances, and the results were positive, anyway. Then Wendy and I had several more days to be together, do some shopping, visit friends, and chat about old times—and the future, too. At last I flew back to Bangladesh, leaving her in London to spend a few more days with friends.

Back at Malumghat, Joan and I talked for hours, sharing our adventures. While I was gone she had completed a college credit correspondence course in Biblical Greek; because of her previous studies in the subject six months earlier, she was able to complete the course in a few days of steady work. Also she had an interesting visit from a French lady who had married a Bengali man abroad and returned with him to live for a time in Bangladesh. She was a spiritually needy person, very receptive to Joan's teaching and explanations. With evident relief she placed her faith in Christ the Lord and determined to follow Him.

Nurse Alice Payne

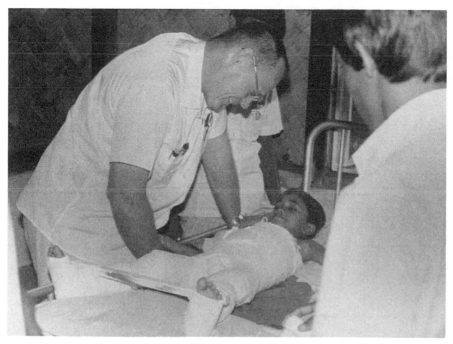

Dr. John Bullock, orthopedic surgeon

By mid-November nurse Alice Payne had completed her Bengali II course; she promptly went to work competently caring for patients on the wards and in the Outpatient Department. By then John Bullock had also completed his Bengali II studies.

When John and Alice were told that they and their class had an exceptionally good grasp of Bengali grammar, they gave Joan and all her carefully-constructed grammar drills the credit. Then John began his valuable work as an orthopedic surgeon in the hospital. As soon as Tense completed her studies she focused on her artwork and Bible teaching of women and children; she skillfully used puppet dramas to get her points across to delighted audiences.

During November in the United States the 1976 presidential campaign reached its climax with the election of Jimmy Carter as the next president of the United States. During that same month in the U.S., Bangladesh representatives were striving to gain a victory over India in the Farakka Barrage issue at the United Nations in New York City. Several weeks earlier they had won a procedural triumph by getting the case placed on the agenda of the main UN General Assembly with preliminary study by the powerful Special Political Committee. One day Bangladesh presented its case before

Artist Tense Bullock

this special committee; the next day India presented its rebuttal, claiming that the Farakka issue was a bilateral problem between two nations and insisting that the UN had no business getting involved. Discussion and debate by the committee members were then scheduled for the following week.

But during that week Bangladesh continued lobbying the representatives of various countries. The Bangladesh delegates made good use of a film entitled "Ganges-O-Ganges" made by Bangladeshi film makers; this film showed some of the severe damage caused by the loss of Ganges water during the dry season. The visual impact of the film helped Bangladesh representatives to convince various countries of the justice of their complaints.

Then several friendly countries helped Bangladesh draft a resolution that both Bangladesh and India could accept. So this compromise resolution was approved by the special committee and finally adopted by the UN General Assembly. In the resolution both countries agreed to meet speedily at Dacca to attempt to resolve the impasse, and they pledged to abide by the principles of international law. Only time would tell whether India had really become more sensitive to Bangladesh's problems and would agree to share the Ganges water more fairly.

On the last day of November General Zia, who had always been the power behind the new government even though he was only one of three deputy chief martial law administrators, openly became the head of the nation's military government. He took over as the chief martial law administrator (CMLA); this made him effectively the head of the government, yet left to President Sayem certain more ceremonial presidential functions.

On the same day that Zia took over, eleven political leaders, including former president Mushtaque, were arrested for harmful activities against the state. Later Mushtaque was tried by a martial law court for corruption and misuse of power while in office; he was convicted and sentenced to five years in prison.

The next day General Zia, in his new role as visible head of the government, made a policy statement. He emphasized the need for national pride, self-reliance, and an increased pace of development in the villages where most Bangladeshis live. His words were well received by the people.

In early December in Chittagong City, a British missionary looked out his window and saw a buff-colored envelope lying on the green lawn. He eased out of his chair, ambled outside, and picked up the open envelope. Although it was not a normal cable envelope, it had a cablegram inside—addressed to Dr. and Mrs. V. B. Olsen. The brief cabled message stirred him to action; he quickly jumped into his car and took the cable to those in our Chittagong office. They, in turn, immediately sent a messenger by bus to bring the cable to us.

The messenger found me in the hospital staff men's quarters where I was talking with a Christian young man and two friends of his who were on the verge of deciding to follow Christ. As the discussion proceeded back and forth I opened the cablegram. Shocking news! Joan's beloved father had passed away four days earlier. My impulse was to jump up and race back to our house to tell her the news. But then it struck me that Dad Baur wouldn't have wanted it that way. He would have said, "Now, Vic, don't let this cable interrupt what you're doing. Just carry on and help these men of Bangladesh get right with God. It is far more important that they join me here in heaven someday than that Joan learn about my homegoing just now."

So I tucked the cable in my shirt pocket, dismissed the messenger, and rejoined the conversation. When all questions were answered to their satisfaction, the two men said, "Yes, now we are ready to become followers of Jesus the Lord." So each, in his own words, prayed a prayer of acceptance and faith which sealed and settled the matter for him.

In the afterglow of their earnest prayers I explained, "One of the great satisfactions for you will be a lifelong assurance that you have eternal life and that there is a place reserved for you in heaven itself in the presence of God." Then, taking the cable from my pocket, I opened it and continued, "While we were talking just now, I received the unexpected news that my beloved father-in-law has died. But, because of that wonderful assurance, I know that he is now in the glory where life is better than he has ever known. And the same will be true for you and me someday." This spontaneous, unexpected illustration of assurance about afterlife was deeply moving to the two men.

Then I went quickly home to give Joan the news. How we wished we could have been in the United States to comfort and help sustain Mom Baur at the time of the funeral, but that was not possible. When Dad Baur was buried we had been half a world away and not even aware that he had passed on. That is one of the hard things about the life of foreign mission service. But we remembered his wonderful ways and his great influence on our lives—and we thanked the Father for him. And we thanked God, too, that the lost cablegram floated to the lawn of a friend in Chittagong who knew us, could read English, and who knew where our Chittagong City office was located.

By this time Chakma prince Debapriyaw Roy had been back with us at Malumghat for several months. He not only needed further physiotherapy to gain optimum improvement, but also he wanted to study Biblical and theological courses. In addition, Deb needed a way to make a living, so Bob Adolph and his staff trained him to become a competent laboratory technician. Deb was psychologically up and down during those months. It was not easy to walk with crutches and braces, and he watched soccer games at the hospital with profound wistfulness, knowing that he would never play again. At one point, leaving the troubles of this earth behind and entering the joys of a heavenly home began to look so good to him that he contemplated suicide. In fact, he tentatively picked out December 12 to be the day he would end his life.

But as he studied powerful passages of Scripture and learned great concepts of theology, and as he reflected on the importance of influencing his Chakma nation for Christ, he was buoyed up and, at last, canceled his ill-conceived plan. Instead, he elected to be baptized on that December 12 as a vivid, open declaration of his faith to all who would be there to watch. Because he could not walk down the rough hillside with his crutches, he was carried in his wheelchair down the slope and into the water of a pond. There Pastor Gonijan administered to him the ancient ordinance of baptism while the church members and many others looked on. They were witnessing a celebration of life triumphing over death—in more ways than one. Then Deb was carried back to the shoreline, wheelchair and all, beaming with inner satisfaction and joy. "Thank You, Father!"

Deb's baptism

The next day at Hebron Station a young man from a Buddhist family named Khoka also followed his Lord in the ceremony of baptism. After counting the cost for several months he had gained courage to take the step, well aware that some extremist villagers might react negatively. One evening two weeks later, Khoka came to the Totman house at Hebron, explained that some village men had told him to appear at the Buddhist temple, and requested that Dave go along with him. Doris was apprehensive as the two men walked out into the darkness, but she gained some inner strength when her eyes fell on a Christmas card that had arrived from the United States just that day. On it were written words from the Biblical book of Isaiah:

> Fear not, for I am with you; be not dismayed, for I am your God. I will strengthen you, yes, I will help you, I will uphold you with my righteous right hand.[16]

Arriving at the temple, the American and the Bengali removed their shoes to show respect for a religious sanctuary. As they stepped into the pitch blackness inside Dave felt a chill ripple through his body. Then from the dark corners of the temple several of the extremists began to lash out with sharp questions:

The rustic Buddhist temple near Hebron

"Khoka, what was the meaning of the ceremony you carried out at the river?"

"What is this new faith of yours, anyway?"

"What are the beliefs of this religion?"

"Are you ready to recant?"

Khoka gave a good account of himself and the foundational truths of the Christian faith.

Then they began to fire questions at Dave. Having been well trained, he had no difficulty replying to the various theological questions. As one man struck a match to light a cigarette, Dave recognized a "friend" whose friendship had faded under the circumstances. When Dave began laying out Christ's good news message and explaining His unique sacrifice, the interrogation ended as abruptly as it had begun. Relieved, the two men returned to their homes; when Doris saw Dave coming up the path, she also breathed a deep sigh of relief.

But this was only the first crisis for Khoka. A few nights later he suddenly awakened as his door was battered down and the dark shadows of several men poured into his house. Fear clutched his heart as they seized him and dragged him off into the surrounding jungle of the Hill Tracts. The next morning the news reached the Totmans that Khoka had been kidnapped. Dave approached a local leader, who demanded money for Khoka's release. At that, Dave decided to back off and take time to ponder the pros and cons of what to do—and give the Father a chance to tip His hand.

Just at that point agronomist Walter Griffeth and his wife, Frances, arrived at Hebron from Malumghat to spend a couple of days with the Totmans. It was New Year's Eve. After discussing Khoka's predicament the four Americans, one after the other, prayed earnestly for their missing brother and pleaded for wisdom to know what to do. Even as they were praying they heard a knock on the door. Dave arose and walked to the door, where he heard the night watchman excitedly announce, "Brother Khoka is here! Brother Khoka is here!" A bedraggled Khoka entered quickly, and he and David embraced each other. Then Khoka told his remarkable story to those who had just been interceding for him.

"Several tough men broke down my door and dragged me out of my house into the jungle," he began. "They kept beating me and told me that I must give up my religious belief. But I said that I could not do that. Then they beat me some more. Finally, one ringleader gave the order to shoot me. But at that instant a mysterious tribal man appeared from out of the darkness and snapped, 'Stop! This man has done nothing wrong. Shoot me instead!' Those who had kidnapped me were so shaken by the sudden appearance of this unknown tribesman and his bold words that they backed off and disappeared into the forest. And I ran here as fast as I could." So the Isaiah passage had been true for Khoka, too:

> . . . . I am your God. I will strengthen you, yes, I will help you, I will uphold you with my righteous right hand.[17]

Key Events in 1976: Summary

January	• Militant pro-Mujib forces attack Bangladesh border posts from sanctuaries in India.
	• The government addresses the population explosion: it conducts a survey and trains 6,000 family planning workers.
	• Chittagong perihepatitis strikes again; Joan and others are laid low.
February	• We submit special Bengali Gospel of John for publishing.
	• Zia quells army mutinies in Dacca and Chittagong.
	• The Shanti Bahini tribal guerrillas attack Army Engineers nine miles from Malumghat; we treat the casualties.
March	• The American ambassador visits Malumghat Hospital.
April	• I take an urgent helicopter trip from Dacca to Malumghat.
	• Former majors Farook, Rashid, and Dalim return to Dacca; they incite troops in three cantonments to rebel.
May	• General Zia crushes the rebellious troops and deports Farook, Rashid, and Dalim.
	• The Islamic Foreign Ministers Conference supports Zia on the Farakka issue.
	• Malumghat Hospital opens a new Brace and Limb Shop.
June	• Ragged refugees from Burma establish a nearby camp.
July	• I attend the U.S. ambassador's bicentennial party —America's 200th birthday is enthusiastically commemorated.
	• *Trial #1* of radical leftist soldiers and JSD party leaders; JSD's Abu Taher draws the death penalty.
	• *Trial #2*: more radical leftists (including a Dutch national) are convicted and sentenced.
August	• Some non-aligned nations support General Zia on the Farakka issue.
	• Mark Olsen is operated on for a serious soccer injury.
October	• Wendy Olsen surprises me at a London conference.
November	• Bangladesh takes the Farakka dispute to the UN.
	• Zia becomes chief martial law administrator = head of government; President Sayem remains the head of state.
December	• 1976 is another banner year for the Murung tribal program; the Murungs build more Jesus houses.

Figure 26

10
1977: Translation Triumphs and Visa Crisis

Because the cool season (November to February) is the most delightful time of year in Bangladesh, many do their traveling during those months. So during the 1976-77 cool season Mr. Edward Masters, the new American ambassador, along with his wife and two children, came to visit our team, inspect the hospital, and see the sights in southern Chittagong District. After they toured the hospital and the whole Malumghat campus, we presented to Mrs. Masters some attractive dolls created by the Heart House ladies. The ambassador spoke appreciatively of the hospital and staff— and the high quality of their humanitarian service.

Later that day Jalal and I hosted the Masters family at the charming Enoni Forest Rest House nestled among pines and palms on a lovely secluded stretch of beach a few miles south of Cox's Bazar. I have rarely seen such a beautiful setting. The welcome sign was neatly lettered, the weather balmy, and the beach perfect. Our afternoon together was simply delightful. Before departing we made the expected notations in the official guest book. I found Ambassador Ed Masters very personable and friendly, and before the year was over he extended himself mightily to help us in a time of extreme crisis.

That evening we spent an equally pleasant time at another forest rest house located at the rubber plantation near Ramu (twenty miles south of our hospital). There we were joined by the Walshes, the Nuscas, and Joan to view a tribal cultural show. We were welcomed grandly by an elephant with an intricately painted head who knew how to trumpet a welcome and raise his trunk in a smart salute.

Jalal had also organized Mogh entertainers who sang, danced, and played various instruments. One of these consisted of differ-

U.S. Ambassador Masters signing the guest book

*Joan, Ambassador Masters and family,
and Jalal at the tribal cultural show*

Tribal musician playing brass gongs

Murung playing small pipes

ently pitched brass gongs arranged in a circle; the player sat in the center and struck the gongs with mallets. When the music was fast he had to spin like a dervish to hit some of his notes.

With Robichandro's help I had engaged a Murung tribal troupe for the evening. The Murungs had been dancing the shuffle centuries before it hit the discos. And as they performed their "plain vanilla" version of the shuffle, they played on unique bamboo pipes of varying size and pitch; their tones had a characteristic organ-like quality. It was a night to remember.

In early January ex–lieutenant colonel Farook Reehman, still exiled in Libya and feeling increasingly lonely for his family and friends in Bangladesh, flew into Dacca. He hoped to slip through airport security again, but this time it was not to be. Military intelligence officers promptly spotted and arrested the bold Farook there at the airport. Later he was tried before a martial law court on charges of carrying an unauthorized firearm and of impersonating another man. He was found guilty and sentenced to five years in prison.[1] General Zia's patience with him had finally run out.

At Malumghat I returned the supervision of the tribal work to Jay Walsh, the usual head of the mission's tribal outreach. I found that change quite wrenching, for I had come to love these simple, hardy jungle men and women and to treasure my working relationship with Tippera teachers Robichandro, Shotish, and Shadijan, and with Menshai Murung. My two years of guiding them, encouraging them, teaching them, and working hand-in-hand with them had been one of life's great adventures. During that period

Jay Walsh teaching Murung tribesmen

several hundred Murungs and scores of Tipperas had come to Christ and had established more than a dozen congregations in their primitive villages in the jungles of the southern Chittagong Hill Tracts. Happily, I would retain a connection with the tribal work by continuing to serve on the Tribal Committee.

To facilitate our work with the tribal people and the care of tribal patients, we had built at Malumghat a tribal guesthouse. The central room of the T-shaped structure was the chapel/auditorium room where they worshiped, sang their plaintive, minor-keyed hymns, studied the Scriptures, and discussed tribal matters. Radiating from that central assembly room were three wings, one each for the Tipperas, the Murungs, and the Moghs. The tribal people were thrilled to have their own guesthouse at the hospital.

Later in January Chakma prince Debapriyaw Roy took a vacation from his studies at Malumghat to help our Literature Division team with book sales at the annual fair in Rangamati, the capital city of the Hill Tracts and Deb's home town. Jeannie Lockerbie, head of the Literature Division, and her staff set up an attractive book display in a rented stall at the fair; because Deb was so well-known and well-liked in Rangamati, his support of the book sales was a real plus. His grandmother, the cabinet minister and queen mother of the Chakmas, visited the bookstall at Deb's request. When presented with a copy of the Bible she announced to the crowd, "We should all give our lives sacrificially to our nation as Christ gave His life sacrificially and unselfishly for the people of the world!" Hmm. She must have gained this insight from her talks with Deb or from her own reading.

In early February two highly important land purchases took place. First, the church at Malumghat bought from the mission the beautiful piece of high land in Cha Bagan that had caught my eye two years earlier. There they would build their own church building on their own property near the homes of the majority of the church members. A big step forward!

Then on February 9 administrative officer Jack Archibald, on behalf of the mission, completed the endless formalities for our purchase of a beautiful piece of land in Chittagong City. On this plot the mission would build a substantial building to house the Literature Division, the Standard Bengali Bible Translation Division, administrative offices, and some apartments for American staff. This would cut expenses immediately and in the years to come because urban rents and land values were skyrocketing. Jeannie Lockerbie spearheaded the project and, with the help of other team members, raised most of the capital for this building; the Heartbeat for Bangladesh promotion provided the final $80,000.

Jack Archibald with administrative assistant Monendro

During this period at Malumghat we enjoyed the three-week visit of dentist Dr. Charles Garabadian and his wife, Audrey. They had been stimulated to come by reading *Daktar*. Chuck provided valuable dental care for the American and Bangalee hospital staff during his short visit. Moved by their experience at Malumghat, they volunteered for career service with us. But, sadly, sickness came along and made it impossible for them to come.

By this time we were crushingly involved in two aspects of the Scripture translation projects. First of all, we were working day and night to help our colleagues on the standard Bengali team carry out the final check of their common language New Testament; in fact, I took two weeks of my annual vacation to free me from hospital work so that I could do my share of the final checking.

Although we were working flat-out on this last check of the standard Bengali translation, I had to take time to try to put out a new fire threatening to consume the special Bengali translation project. A number of new members had been voted onto the Executive Committee of the Bangladesh Bible Society, the organization that would print and market our two new translations of the New Testament. But some of these new Executive Committee members were strongly against producing a translation of the Scriptures that used vocabulary more appreciated and treasured by their non-Christian neighbors than their own church people.

I understood perfectly what was going through their minds. Their churches were tiny minority islands surrounded by an overwhelming sea of the majority religious groups. In that environment many Christians, who were struggling to maintain their identity and their culture in Bangladesh, felt a keen sense of social disadvantage. Furthermore, they were not attracted to the special Bengali words cherished by the Muslim community, so they insisted, "We should not be producing this special Bengali translation of our Holy Christian Bible; it is not right."

So in mid-February, armed with an overhead projector and some carefully prepared overhead slides, I headed for Dacca to address the new Executive Committee of the Bangladesh Bible Society. I had been requested to do so by the head of the Bible Society and the rest of the paid staff, who were very enthusiastic about the project. They, of course, felt frustrated that the new Executive Committee was balking at the special Bengali translation (which had been fully endorsed by previous executive committees).

The day before the meeting, some of the committee members were unexpectedly called out of town. Interestingly enough, those called out of Dacca were the ones who most strongly opposed the translation. To the rest, a bare quorum, I presented the reasons for the project and the importance of it. They reacted positively to this explanation and voted unanimously that the Bible Society should carry on with its plan to publish both of our mission's New Testaments. "Thank You, Father!"

Then I asked for a chance to talk with those who had been absent from the meeting as soon as they returned to Dacca. So the Bible Society staff arranged a dinner meeting, which gave me an opportunity to explain the project to those most vociferous against it. I brought out passages of Scripture that emphasized our responsibility to do good to those around us and to share God's Word with the multitudes. Then I presented the results of our research projects, which showed clearly that many Bengalis understand material written in special Bengali better than that written in standard Bengali—and millions certainly love and appreciate it more deeply. And I reminded the church leaders that the New Testament was not only Christian Scripture, but also Muslim Scripture, for Muhammad, the prophet of Islam, had declared this to be so. The translation would especially be our gift of love to the millions of Muslim friends and neighbors around us.

Then came the question and answer time. Some of the initial questions were sharp, even hostile. But because there were good answers to each of these questions, the give-and-take of the session soon became more congenial and positive. Finally, the men expressed their opinion that the project should proceed as planned. I was impressed with these church leaders and their open-mindedness, and pleased with their final conclusion.

March 1977 was a month of elections in South Asia. In Pakistan they created strikes and rioting. But an even greater shock wave struck neighboring India a few days later. The voters of the world's largest democracy threw out Prime Minister Indira Gandhi and her Congress party, which had ruled India for the thirty years of its independent existence. Mrs. Gandhi's new authoritarian policies had simply alienated the Indian people. At the ballot box they struck back—and elevated to power a new prime minister named Desai, the head of the brand new Janata party. He was something of an ascetic who ate mainly fruits and yogurt; he also publicly extolled the benefit of drinking one's own urine. This stunning change in the Indian government would have its inevitable impact on relations between India and neighboring Bangladesh; the result turned out to be quite positive.

By the time of our half-yearly Field Council meetings in early April a new short-term nurse, Becky McGregor, had come to join us for a year or two; she did a fine job filling the gap left by Jan Wolfe, who had gone on home leave. The Fidler family also departed for their first furlough.

In mid-April a literacy workshop at Malumghat culminated two years of growing interest in teaching the illiterate. Linda Short, Marge Beals, Bob and Barbara Adolph, Jeannie Lockerbie, Lynn Silvernale, and Mrs. Bashanti Dass all had early involvement in the literacy work. Jeannie had made contact with Dr. Robert F. Rice, the head of Literacy International, who ultimately had conducted a literacy workshop in Dacca. Lynn and Mrs. Dass arrived at that Dacca workshop to discover they would have to do the lion's share of translating three literacy primers and a teacher's manual; they succeeded and turned the manuscript over to our Literature Division for publication.

Even though they now had printed literacy primers, those who had been attempting to teach illiterate people to read were certainly having their troubles. Some of the students were so inexperienced at trying to learn anything that they could not seem to make progress. One lady tried to write on the blackboard with her pencil and in a notebook with the chalk. So the mid-April seminar was meant to train the teachers how to surmount such obstacles.

The instructor for the literacy seminar, Dr. Rice, had an excellent grasp of his subject. He explained the design of the literacy manuals and how to really use them effectively. Then he set up practice situations, answered innumerable questions and, in the end, gave a final exam. By the last day of the seminar a number of

Nurse Becky McGregor

Refugee child in relief sweater

our Bengali and American team members were eager to contact an illiterate person and begin teaching him or her how to read Bengali—and those who were already involved were keen to apply their new knowledge.

By this time the nearby camp of Bengali refugees from Burma had increased to over a thousand people. Before Christmas our ladies had sorted hundreds of used sweaters, which we gave to the refugees to protect them from the biting winter cold. They had suffered much sickness and, surprisingly, because they were so weak and helpless, some people from our locality had taken unfair advantage of them. This angered me and made me even more eager to help them, for they were desperately needy people. So we continued to encourage the refugees, care for their sick, and distribute to them the nutritious Salvation Army high-protein biscuits that were helping them to fight malnutrition. They were deeply grateful for every little thing we did to assist them.

I talked with the refugee leaders every week or two, especially Mr. U., one of the principal leaders. He continued to ask questions about spiritual matters and soaked up the answers like a sponge. And he often requested more literature about Biblical subjects. Just then we received the initial shipment of a new pamphlet we had carefully researched and designed. This pamphlet about Jesus the Messiah was entitled *The Remarkable Prophet;* it contained a number of passages of Scripture arranged in six categories with each category filling a single page. I presented to Mr. U. our first copy of the new pamphlet the next time he requested something to read.

Also during April the new Government of India, in order to improve the prickly relationship between India and Bangladesh, sent a high-level team to Dacca to sort out the Farakka Barrage problem. But the meetings were soon deadlocked, as had happened so many times before. Finally General Zia himself had a three-hour session with the head of the Indian delegation. Apparently some heavy-duty negotiations took place, for the two men came up with a basic agreement satisfactory to Bangladesh—with the fine points to be worked out later. Zia had proved himself to be a persuasive negotiator. Although this agreement was phenomenally good news, months were still required to work out the details.

At this point General Zia was the commander-in-chief of the Bangladesh Army and the chief martial law administrator of the military government, with President Sayem carrying out various presidential functions. But it was not long before Sayem made an important official announcement:

> I, Abusadat Mohammad Sayem, because of my failing health, am unable further to discharge the function of the office of President. I do hereby nominate Major General Ziaur Rahman to be the President of Bangladesh and hand over the office of President to him.[2]

President Sayem certainly did have health problems and needed an operation, but also he had been pressured to resign by some of his own senior cabinet officials who preferred to see General Zia run the country.[3] So on April 21, 1977, General Zia took over as president of Bangladesh, while continuing to hold his other powerful positions.

The next day President Zia addressed his people over a nationwide television and radio hookup. He declared his faith in democratic principles in these words:

> I and my government believe in full democracy and are determined to restore the government of the elected representatives of the people in due time.[4]

Then he promised that elections would be held in December of the following year and declared that he would amend the Constitution to change a few provisions that were widely disliked by the people.

Very soon President Zia did make the constitutional changes he had promised:[5]

1. He canceled "secularism" (separation of mosque and state) as a fundamental principle of the Constitution; secularism had always been one of Sheikh Mujib's four cardinal principles and was also an integral part of the constitutions of India and the United States. He replaced secularism with the phrase "absolute trust and faith in Almighty Allah." However, this fell short of declaring the country a full-fledged Islamic republic.
2. He defined the word "socialism" in the Constitution to mean "economic and social justice"; this toned down the Marxist implications of the word.
3. He guaranteed that there would be no nationalization or requisition of private property without compensation.
4. He added these new emphases to the Constitution: the participation of women in national life, the developing of friendship with other Muslim nations, and the promotion of local government institutions.

Of course, those on the religious right and those who favored private enterprise were very pleased with these changes.

Zia also decreed that citizens of Bangladesh would henceforth be called "Bangladeshis"—rather then Bangalees. This certainly made sense and greatly pleased the tribal people, who had long resented being called Bangalees.

Back at Malumghat I operated on an infant with a grotesque problem. Issuing from the top of the baby's head was a huge skin-covered mass as large as the head itself. This tumor was filled with fluid and also contained a piece of malformed brain tissue passing into it through a hole in the infant's skull. At the operating table I had no difficulty removing most of the mass, but I found it impossible to tuck all of the abnormal brain tissue inside the skull—there was space for only three-fourths of it. Yet I had to find a way to close the incision or the baby would die of infection. So I decided to stimulate the excess brain tissue with a mild electric current to see whether or not it exerted any control over the baby's arms or legs or vital signs; when there was no response to this stimulation, I could only assume that the abnormal piece of brain was non-vital. Then, still with some trepidation, I cautiously removed it. Although the baby's pulse and respiration became irregular for a moment, that problem quickly passed and my little patient made a fine recovery. Whew! "Thank You, Father!"

At the end of April the Translation Committee had its last meeting to finalize the text of the remaining books of the standard Bengali New Testament. Our crash program of final checking and settling that text had come to an end. The next day we recovered

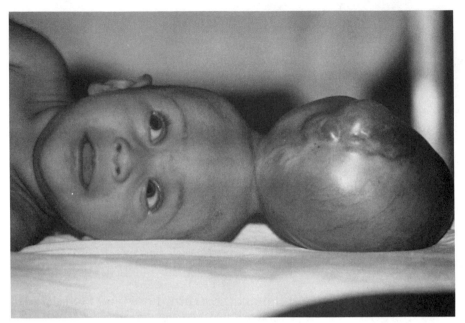

Infant with a grotesque tumor

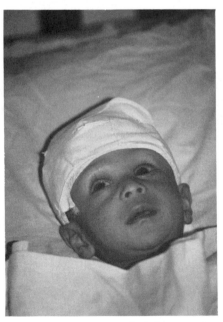

Infant after removal of the tumor

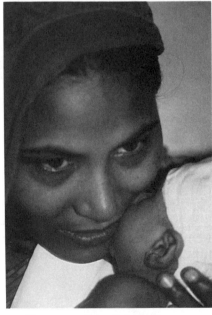

Happy mother after the surgery

The Translation Committee had its last meeting

from our exhausted state enough to enjoy a victory dinner and, especially, to congratulate Lynn Silvernale, Mrs. Dass, Mr. Dores, and Samuel (who had helped them from time to time) on their historic accomplishment. Now Lynn and Mrs. Dass could travel to Dacca to proofread the final printed text as it came off the press.

And we, also, had some traveling in mind. The next day Joan and I headed for our Nancy's high school graduation in Manila. The graduation ceremonies were lovely, and Nancy was a beautiful, happy graduate. She had done well and developed special expertise in the field of photography. One of her pictures won first prize in the fine arts contest, and her portfolio of pictures, garnished with one of her poems, was marked A + + +. Her teacher said to us, "Nancy takes pictures with her heart!"

Our Field Council and Translation Committee had decided that I should now be freed from medical/surgical work as much as possible to give me more time to guide the special Bengali common language translation of the New Testament to completion. To decide is one thing, but to make this plan work out in practice required some fresh manpower—short-term surgeons who would come to do my share of the medical and surgical work. So we began to publicize this need through our newsletters and through a front-page article in the mission's magazine. Wonderfully, we soon began to receive applications from American and Canadian surgeons willing to provide the necessary relief.

In mid-April another very special pair of short-term workers arrived in Chittagong City. Harold and Marie Wolters were both in their seventies; Harold had suffered so severely from heart disease that he had required coronary bypass heart surgery. So he had no illusions that he would necessarily return to the United States alive. In that context, his good-byes to his children and grandchildren were touched with a special poignancy. Harold was to supervise construction of the mission's new literature/translation/administration building in Chittagong City, while Marie would keep the account books for that operation. Their spiritual maturity and expertise turned out to be a great benefit to our Chittagong team.

In the month of May yet another short-term couple had a personal adventure in a distant land. After a pleasant vacation in Malaysia, Bob and Jimmie Nusca boarded the train for the long twenty-four-hour trip back to Bangkok, Thailand. They settled down for the night in their berths, hoping for a night of rest as the train made its way through the Malaysian darkness. They were soon asleep, but about 1:00 A.M. Bob was awakened by an acute pain in his right lower chest. He shifted and squirmed in the cramped upper berth, then got up and paced the aisle, all to no avail; the pain only became more severe.

Could this be a heart attack? Bob wondered. *If so, there is not much I can do about it. Here we are in the middle of nowhere, hurtling through the night with no medical help of any kind available.* By this time, the pain had become quite unbearable. "Lord," Bob gasped in anguish, "I am really in serious trouble, and there is nothing I can do. It is all up to You. Please take this pain away until we reach some place where I can get medical help—or just take me home to heaven." Within seconds, the excruciating pain simply vanished.

Harold and Marie Wolters—serving God in retirement

Bob Nusca back at work—
with orders of the day for ambulance driver Babul

Back at Malumghat, which temporarily lacked a surgeon, Bob remained comfortable for days. Then—just after surgeon Donn Ketcham and a short-term surgeon arrived—the severe pain suddenly recurred. Bob quickly notified one of the doctors. The diagnosis? Acute gall bladder attack requiring surgery. As Bob was wheeled into the operating room he remembered his middle-of-the-night prayer on the train: "Please take this pain away until we reach some place where I can get medical help." Now he was in that place—and the surgeons were there, too. The operation involved removal of the inflamed gall bladder and plucking out two dangerous stones from the bile duct. The surgery was a success —and the timing of each phase of the episode had been perfect. "Thank You, Father!"

Throughout the month of May President Zia traveled from city to city and village to village preaching his nineteen-point program for the salvation and development of Bangladesh. This effort prepared the populace to vote for or against him and his policies in a so-called referendum on May 30. The referendum question was simple:

> Do you have confidence in President Major General Ziaur Rahman and in the policies and programmes enunciated by him?[6]

Nearly 99 percent of the voters voted "yes" to this question. And there was a much larger than usual voter turnout. So some complained that there must have been government pressure on people to vote. But, in fact, the vote showed President Zia, his actions, and his policies to be highly popular. And, even though he was not pitted against another candidate, the referendum gave his presidency added legitimacy.

On the first day of June general surgeons began to arrive to relieve me so that I could focus more exclusively on the New Testament translation project. The first surgeon was Dr. Ross Gillman from Canada; he and his wife, Ellen Marie, would be with us throughout the month of June. As soon as they arrived the local government land officer was brought in with a hemorrhaging duodenal ulcer. While operating on him I was able to demonstrate to Ross how our operating room and staff functioned.

Later, when I took him with me on ward rounds to acquaint him with all the patients, he was amazed to find that five of them had tetanus, a disease rarely seen in the United States. Bangladeshis call it the "bow (arch) disease" because the violent muscular spasms and contractions cramp the victim's back into the shape of a curved bow. One of these cases was a newborn infant. Another was a twelve-year-old boy who had contracted the terrible disease when a local priest circumcised him with an unclean knife. Ross shook his head, then expostulated, "Whew! Your spectrum of patients is a far cry from what I see in Canada."

As soon as Ross was oriented enough to take over my work, I began forging ahead in the translation—and helping the Burmese Bengali refugees who were still being troubled by some of the local people. One elderly refugee woman had been beaten and a young woman abducted. Then the oppressors beat up a main refugee leader near the hospital; while I was treating him for his injuries, he explained that he could not stand the pressure any longer and would be leaving the area. He expressed thanks for our kindnesses to him and for giving him an opportunity to learn something about the highly respected Jesus. Puzzled, I replied, "But you have never requested any teaching on spiritual subjects."

"That's true," he responded, "but you have explained much to my friend Mr. U. and he, in turn, has taught everything to me." Later that day I spent more time with this man, and he decided to be a disciple of Jesus the Messiah.

That same evening Mr. U. appeared, and immediately I sensed something determined about him. Cutting the usual formalities to the bone, he declared, "I want to become a disciple of the highly-respected Jesus; kindly help me." This unexpected request caught me off guard. But I quickly recovered from my surprise and began questioning him to be sure that he clearly understood about Christ and His basic message. Then we knelt together there in my living room, and he prayed a prayer of faith and told God that he would be Jesus' disciple. Then I prayed for him as he embarked on this life of discipleship—and for his family and the camp of people who looked to him for leadership. Finally we rose to our feet, both so moved that we could not immediately speak. Finally I asked, "How is it that you came today ready and eager to follow Jesus? What happened?"

He replied with a rush of Bengali words, "You know that booklet you gave me some days ago? I read it through carefully several times, and each time the final words on the last page gripped me." He opened to that page to show me:

> Then they said to Him, "What shall we do, that we may work the works of God?" Jesus answered and said to them, "This is the work of God, that you believe in Him [Christ] whom He sent. . . . Most assuredly, I say to you, he who believes in Me has everlasting life."[7]

"These words were like a great light in my mind. All my life I have done all kinds of good works. But it became perfectly clear to me that I had failed at the most important one—to deeply believe in Jesus the Messiah, which gives a person everlasting life. Immediately I began explaining all I had learned to the people in the camp. And now I have become a disciple of the highly respected Jesus. I feel very happy."

Then he told me more: "Doctor, as a result of my teaching at our camp, thirty-three families have decided they want to be disci-

Mr. U. teaching his people in the refugee camp

ples of Jesus." I was flabbergasted. He continued, "I hope you will train me and some of my lieutenants so that we can properly teach the members of these families how to be good disciples."

Astounded by this news, I agreed to provide the training Mr. U. requested. After he departed my head was still spinning from all that I had learned about developments in the refugee camp—and I marveled at the power of the remarkable Prophet.

The next week we heard the good news that Jalal Ahmed's nineteen-year-old daughter, Bitu, had obtained her student visa for the United States on the strength of my recommendation and statement that Joan and I would be her sponsors. Bitu had already reached Tucson, Arizona, where she would study for the next several years. She was an attractive, intelligent, sensible girl, and we were confident she would succeed in her studies and life in the United States.

During the second week in June President Zia traveled to Great Britain to attend the Conference of Heads of Governments of Commonwealth States. There he held two valuable private meetings with India's new Prime Minister Desai. Zia complained about Tiger Siddiqi's pro-Mujib Bengali dissidents who were continuing to infiltrate Bangladesh from sanctuaries in India to carry out sabotage operations. Desai promised to shut down these attacks from Indian territory. Two weeks later the Indians turned over six hundred Bengali guerrilla fighters to military authorities in Bangladesh. Later, two thousand pro-Mujib civilian refugees also were eased out of India back into Bangladesh. Clearly, the new Desai government in India was a boon to the Zia government.

In July the figures for fiscal 1976-77 were published. The news was not good, for the overall performance of the Bangladesh economy during the fiscal year had been poor. Because the rice harvest was down one million tons from the year before, the price of rice in the bazaars was already beginning to climb. Bad weather had caused the poor grain crop—drought during the fall, followed later by damaging floods.

Also in July we started on a 'round-the-world journey. Joan, Nancy, and I flew the Pacific route to Los Angeles. There we happily linked up with Lynne, then took Nancy to visit the colleges that interested her. She decided on Biola University, partly because she would be near to Lynne and Mark. Then we enjoyed weeklong visits with Wendy and Mark, my parents, and Joan's mother; those delightful days passed all too quickly. We also visited Bitu Ahmed and were impressed with her good academic record and her mature adjustment to life in the United States.

Bitu Ahmed in Tucson

Olsen family:
Back row—*Mark, Lynne, Vic;* Front row—*Nancy, Joan, Wendy*

While in the Midwest we decided that it was time for a new family picture, since we would not all be together in the same place again for at least two years. This required the last-minute purchase of some new clothes, especially for Mark, who had only "grubs" in his suitcase. In fact, we purchased Mark's suit twelve minutes before the picture appointment; fortunately, his rolled-up pant-legs were not visible. The picture turned out just fine, and each one of us treasured his or her copy, especially during the months of separation.

After our final good-byes Joan and I flew from New York out across the rainy, dark Atlantic in an aircraft that was showing its age. But in Frankfurt, Germany, we picked up a bright, new, beautiful Thai International wide-bodied jet for our long flight to Bangkok; the flight was smooth and elegant. In Bangkok I enjoyed giving an address to the large Field Conference of the Christian and Missionary Alliance Mission team, a well-known group, which had worked effectively in Southeast Asia for many years.

In Dacca we updated the Ahmeds on our time with their daughter Bitu and assured them that she was doing very well in the United States. Then we learned that most of the Bangladesh Biman planes were grounded because of maintenance problems and lack of spare parts, making it impossible to get an early flight to Chittagong. Jalal thoughtfully arranged a microbus to drive us the seven hours to Chittagong, then three more hours to Malumghat. We were home!

Just before our return to Bangladesh an American physician had become ill in Dacca; he was Dr. Bucky Greenough, director of the Cholera Research Hospital. Another American physician serving in Dacca as an administrator had examined him, then advised, "Bucky, I think you may have a bowel obstruction which should be operated on. You must find a way to get to Malumghat."

Because a high-ranking air force officer owed the ill physician a favor, he and his wife were soon flying south in a military helicopter flown by two senior air force pilots. The noisy, dramatic landing at Malumghat drew an instant crowd. While the patient was being moved to the hospital the puzzled pilots asked, "Why in the world were we told to fly Dr. Greenough from Dacca [the capital city with several large hospitals] to this smallish hospital on the distant rural countryside?" Dick Stagg replied that he was not sure why the decision was made, but possibly it was because operations done at Malumghat have a high success rate.

Surgeon Donn Ketcham examined Bucky Greenough, concurred in the diagnosis, and soon had him in the operating room. During surgery Donn successfully relieved the obstruction. Soon Bucky and his wife were ambling about our Malumghat campus enjoying the beautiful flowers and the lush greenery. By his ninth postoperative evening we had returned to Malumghat and were able to enjoy dinner with the Greenoughs and the Staggs. Bucky spoke warmly of the fine treatment he had received and the friendships they had made during their time with our team; the next day they returned to Dacca.

Two days later I operated on Debapriyaw Roy who had developed three large bladder stones. After removing the stones I very carefully sutured my incision in the bladder wall. I expected him to recover quickly. But apparently the suture material was defective; four days later Deb suddenly hemorrhaged so severely into his bladder that I had to give him blood transfusions and reoperate to stop the bleeding. Because this emergency operation worked out well, Deb then made an uneventful recovery. Fortunately, that was the first and last time I have ever encountered that particular complication. Once was quite enough. That unusual and frightening experience caused Deb to examine his life and seek new ways to please God and serve Him.

By the end of August we were elated to receive printed copies of our special Bengali Gospel of John and New Readers' Selections fresh off the press. Wonderful! To show my gratitude to Dr. Bud Hurst, the fine short-term surgeon who had been relieving me for the last several weeks, I presented to him the first copy of the Gospel of John. It was an appropriate gesture because he, as well as Dr. Ross Gillman, had played an important part in freeing me to continue the translation project. From that day on these pieces would be purchased by tens of thousands of interested people throughout the land.

Early in September Dr. Richard Trinity with his wife, Lois, and their children arrived at Malumghat to spell me for the next several months. Rich was a surgeon in training who performed excellent service, working side-by-side with Dr. Donn Ketcham. Later he was succeeded by short-term surgical resident Bob Cropsey, who came with his wife, Shirley, and their children. He, also, was an immense help to us and to the hospital team.

In mid-September in a meeting of the Malumghat Tribal Committee we decided to bring into our team Ray Phrue, a fine young educated Mogh who had become a follower of Christ; he was eager to share his Master's good news with members of his own tribal group.

Joan, Samuel, and I continued to work long hours on the special Bengali New Testament project; it was a godsend to have surgeons to cover for me. Samuel and I also taught the Burmese refugee leaders and some young men involved in a study program. It was a killing schedule. But I did my best to encourage Samuel, who also gained support and encouragement from translator Mrs. Dass; she had much affection for Samuel and mothered him in a loving way.

In September I flew to Dacca to give Lynn Silvernale and Mrs. Dass a hand. After more than eleven years of work they had finally finished their task—they had checked the final page of the printed proofs of the standard Bengali common language New Testament. Because the manuscript was so precious and because there was no second copy, using my macro lens I photographed every page. This was a safety measure to provide backup in case the manuscript went down at sea or was otherwise lost or damaged during its travels. On September 20 a friend hand-carried the manuscript to those who would arrange and supervise the printing in Hong Kong.

Although I was in Dacca during September, I heard nothing about the simmering discontent of the army troops. But that month a rumor spread through the military cantonments of the country that the new pay scale being proposed would give the officers a substantial increase in salary, while the sepoys (enlisted men) would gain very little. The leftist revolutionary soldiers used this rumor to drum up bitterness and resentment among many sepoys and noncoms. During the previous ten months Zia had already faced five mutinies or attempted coups—an average of one every two months. Now there were whispers among the sepoys that it was time to try again.

In late September President Zia was meeting with Egypt's President Anwar Sadat in Cairo; Sadat had some disturbing information to pass on to him. Egyptian intelligence agents had picked up secret information about a communist plot to attack and kill Zia and the top Bangladeshi army and air force generals and commanders; they would then install a revolutionary communist government. This attack was scheduled to take place three days hence (September 28) during an Air Force Day celebration in Dacca very near where our friend Jalal lives.

This would be the ideal time and place to strike, for all the army and air force brass would be congregated there that day. Furthermore, President Zia would be present as the chief guest. The sepoys could keep firing into that room full of officers until no one remained standing. Understandably, Zia was appalled to hear this secret information. And President Sadat had one last jolt for him —possibly the Soviets and the Libyans were working behind the scenes to support the assassination scheme.[8]

On September 27, just one day before the scheduled attack, President Zia coolly flew back to Dacca. There he immediately sent to the air force chief a short handwritten note stating he would be unable to attend the Air Force Day reception as chief guest. That message really complicated life for the air force head. Should he cancel the reception, or should he select a new chief guest?

Actually, the air force chief need not have worried about what to do, for a startling, unexpected emergency would take the decision completely out of his hands. On that exact day a Japan Airlines DC-8 took off from Bombay, India, heading for Bangkok. Suddenly the 156 passengers and crew were terrified when five Japanese hijackers took over the flight; they were members of a notorious communist terrorist group known as the Japanese Red Army Faction. The hijackers forced the plane to land at Dacca airport. There they threatened to begin executing passengers unless nine of their members were released from jail in Japan and unless they received a ransom of $6 million. This drama created an immediate commotion throughout Dacca and automatically canceled the next day's reception at which the coupmakers intended to wipe out all the senior military officers.

On President Zia's orders the air force chief took his position in the airport control tower, where he began to negotiate with the hijackers by radio. Those nerve-wracking negotiations continued for four days.

Either because of this crisis at the Dacca airport or in spite of it, some of the sepoys in the faraway Bogra Cantonment became restless, itching for another mutiny. Three days later (September 30) they gave it a try.[9] But, because they were few in number and because they failed to persuade enough other troops to join them, their minimutiny collapsed. They did, however, kill two young army lieutenants and take some other officers prisoner. Then they rampaged awhile in Bogra City, where they robbed banks, looted stores, and freed from the Bogra jail seventeen fellow soldiers who were doing time for the previous year's Bogra coup attempt. This relatively minor mutiny was quickly quelled by troops loyal to the government.

Despite the successful outcome in Bogra, Zia reasoned that the Dacca mutiny, which had been frustrated by the cancellation of the Air Force Day celebration, could take place at any moment. So he called his senior officers together, told them there might be a coup attempt very soon, and ordered them to remain on the alert and to keep their troops under tight control.

A few hours later in the early morning hours of October 2 the uprising began. When the fully dressed and ready sepoys and noncoms of the Army Field Signals Battalion heard the agreed-upon signal—a burst of firecrackers followed by a single rifle shot—hundreds of them charged out of their barracks. Once they had looted the weapons from their battalion armory, they began firing in the air and shouting, *"Sheepai biblob* [sepoy revolution]!"[10]

They quickly raced to nearby military units where they excitedly began trying to rally other troops. Then, according to plan, they were joined by several hundred air force enlisted men from the nearby air base. By 3:00 A.M. seven hundred army and air force men in jeeps and trucks had successfully looted guns and ammunition from the main Central Ordnance Depot. Simultaneously, other sepoys were passing out leaflets throughout the cantonment listing their demands and calling for the elimination of President Zia and continuing armed revolt.

In the meantime, at the airport the rebel leftist airmen turned their doctrine of "class war" into vicious, bloody reality. They went on a savage officer-killing binge; this was possible in the early morning hours because many air force officers were present at the airport in connection with the Japanese Red Army hijacking incident. Just as the negotiation with the hijackers was reaching a critical point, the mutineers stormed into the air terminal, shooting down every officer in sight. In those brief moments they slaughtered half the air force's pilots, plus a number of other senior air force officers—and the sixteen-year-old son of one of the pilots.[11]

One report states that President Zia escaped with a few aides to a secret hideout just before his house was attacked, which may have saved his life.[12] Other observers stated, rather, that Zia's house was attacked by the rebels, but that the Forty-Sixth (Dacca) Brigade intervened in time to prevent the mutineers from killing him.[13] If in this final desperate attack on President Zia his enemies had succeeded in assassinating him, all the infantry troops might have joined the mutineers, brought down the Zia government, and replaced it with a communist revolutionary government. It was a close call.

About dawn rampaging sepoys took over the Dacca radio station. After they shut down the programming then in process, a sepoy seized the microphone. Next, in quite substandard Bengali, he announced the sepoy revolution. After shouting some slogans he then introduced their leader, Sergeant Afzar of the Bangladesh Air Force.[14] Taking the microphone, Afzar declared himself the new head of state and leader of the Revolutionary Council that he had formed to govern the country. But a moment later he was haranguing into a dead microphone, for the radio transmitter twenty miles away was suddenly switched off to abort his speech.

By this time the generals had ordered loyal infantry units to withstand the mutineers and counterattack them. By 6:00 A.M. the radio station had been recaptured and an infantry company was fighting its way into the airport terminal. By 7:00 A.M. this company had overcome the air force mutineers, killing twenty of them and capturing another sixty. By 9:00 A.M. the mutiny was history.

In all, several hundred officers, troops, and airmen had been killed at the airport and in the cantonment. This was a far more significant and dangerous coup attempt than the one in Bogra two days earlier.

By then the Japanese hijackers had also prevailed. They had gained the release of their fellow Communists from the Japanese jail and received the $6 million just a few minutes before they were to kill the first hostage. Amazingly, however, they missed a package of diamonds worth nearly $2 million lying in plain sight on a seat.

President Zia was seriously shaken by the bloody uprising right under his nose in the capital city. In response he took several wide-ranging and draconian measures:[15]

- He disbanded the regiment and battalions responsible for the mutiny.
- He sacked the heads of the military and civilian intelligence agencies for not warning him of the coup.
- He immediately banned three political parties: the radical leftist JSD party, the pro-Soviet Communist Party of Bangladesh, and former president Mushtaque's Democratic League.
- Over the next two months Zia and his government allegedly executed more than eleven hundred men and imprisoned several hundred others. Bypassing the usual legal procedures, special military tribunals were set up, which quickly disposed of case after case in an assembly-line fashion. The government's retribution against these mutineers was swift and terrible.

In mid-October Burmese refugee leader Mr. U. brought to me a man fresh from Burma. This young man, dressed in the garments of a priest, at midnight had clandestinely crossed the wide Naf River (which divides Burma and Bangladesh). He was sent by Mr. U.'s cousin, a senior priest on whom I had operated three months earlier. This older priest, now fully recovered from his surgery, was the head of a large religious school in northern Burma. He had sent the young man to obtain from us all available portions of the Holy New Testament. I agreed to provide what he wanted, then asked, "Why did he make this request? How did he know that we had available any portions of the New Testament?"

The young man replied, "When he came to you for his severe sickness some weeks ago, you told him he would require an operation. Although he was very fearful of this surgery, he trusted your words and agreed to the operation. While he was waiting to be operated on, he purchased a copy of a booklet called *The Remarkable*

Prophet. This small booklet had a great effect on him. He was impressed by the mighty power of the Prophet Jesus and the fact that He is still alive. Also, his mind was captivated by the fact that Jesus the Messiah is a Prophet who gives a *guarantee* of salvation. And he was reminded, too, of what he had always known—that Jesus is the miracle-working Prophet and the Healer of difficult diseases.

"So, while he was being wheeled into the big, frightening operating room, he talked from his heart to the Living Jesus and asked for His protection throughout the operation. He got that protection and survived the surgery, then returned to Burma as soon as he regained his strength."

"That's an extraordinary story," I exclaimed. "He told me nothing about all this while he was here. Now what is he doing in Burma? Has he resumed his work at the religious school?"

The young man replied, "No, he has appointed another priest to be acting principal in order to allow him more time for a special work. He now spends his time making handwritten copies of *The Remarkable Prophet,* then gives them out to priests and students to read. When he hands them out, he explains, 'This is from the Holy New Testament about the Prophet Jesus. That Holy Scripture contains a marvelous teaching: the Prophet Jesus is able to give you a *guarantee* of salvation and a place in Paradise. Here, read and study it.'"

So we loaded up the midnight messenger from Burma with copies of the Scripture portions and other literature that he had requested. Again, I was struck by the power of the remarkable Prophet—and His amazing Word.

By this time Chakma prince Debapriyaw Roy had gained further strength. Some months before, he had carefully crafted a three-phase program to introduce his Chakma tribe to Christ. The linchpin of phase one was translation of the New Testament into the Chakma language. So we were teaching him theology and techniques of translation to prepare him for his important task.

At that point Debapriyaw and we had been invited to the capital city of the Hill Tracts (Rangamati) for the formal, colorful coronation of the new king of the Chakmas. The new king, by hereditary succession, would be Deb's younger cousin Devasheesh Roy. But at the last minute the government decreed that no foreigners would be allowed to travel to Rangamati for the occasion. So Debapriyaw went alone to share in the royal pageantry of this highly significant occasion in the life of the Chakma tribe. Later, however, we would develop a valuable friendship with the young king.

In another area of the Hill Tracts, a unique problem had erupted. The Shanti Bahini guerrillas, fighting against the Bangladesh government, were putting pressure on the new Murung Christians. "Forget about this religion stuff," they urged. "Religion is useless and won't gain freedom for you. You should join with us, because we are the ones fighting for your freedom." Some of the aboriginal Murungs, intimidated by these men and pressured by other problems, resumed some of their old animal sacrifices along with their Christian worship. Thus it became necessary for our tribal teachers to fan out to the Murung villages to explain the uselessness of animal sacrifices (in the light of their Lord's final and all-sufficient sacrifice), and to teach them that "if the Son makes you free, you shall be free indeed."[16]

Also in October, we began to receive complaints from students studying at Malumghat that Samuel, their direct supervisor, had become increasingly severe with them and harsh in his discipline. They were deeply offended at this martinet-style supervision. I carefully investigated the complaints and found them valid. The project's supervisory committee then decided that not only was correction required, but also it was essential to decrease Samuel's impossible workload. So the committee closed the department responsible for teaching these students and suspended Samuel from all work for a month to give him a chance to rest up and think things through. He accepted this painful decision, but I wondered how long it would be before I received his next resignation notice.

During our October Field Council meetings an ongoing drama—a matter of life and death—took place at the hospital. Two weeks earlier Joan and I and other co-workers had enjoyed dinner at the home of a church member named Badol. Although his wife was more than eight months pregnant, she and her aged mother had served us all a fine rice and curry dinner. While we were eating Badol reminded us that neither his wife nor his mother-in-law had yet become Christian believers; they were all from a Hindu background. So in the afterglow of that pleasant meal we talked for a long time with the two women, answering their questions and telling them about some of the wondrous benefits that we had gained by becoming followers of Christ. The ladies listened attentively and seemed to enjoy the give-and-take of the discussion.

Now, during our marathon meetings, Badol's wife had gone into labor and delivered a lovely baby. But shortly thereafter she fell into deep shock and was suddenly at death's door. At first Dr. Joe DeCook was puzzled about what could have caused this abrupt, unexpected catastrophe, but he soon diagnosed an extremely rare condition. He reported these disquieting developments to the assembled Field Council and explained that the outlook was grim.

Because our members are people of prayer, the team immediately began praying for the dying young woman, then set up an ingenious program by which someone would be praying earnestly for her at all times throughout the day and night—if she should survive that long. I took my turn from 1:30 to 2:00 P.M. and Joan from 2:00 to 2:30 P.M. Later we learned that she sank so low just before two o'clock that the doctor and nurses gave up hope and decided to just make her as comfortable as possible as she faded away. But then, marvelously, about 2:00 P.M. she began to rally and, against all odds, hung on the rest of the day and through the night and was a bit better by morning. During those hours, while her friends Linda and Chinu were at her side, she made the great faith decision. From that point onward she made steady progress and a fine recovery. We all rejoiced with Badol and his family in this spectacular answer to prayer. "Thank You, Father!"

Representatives of Bangladesh and India had been meeting over several months to work out the fine points of the basic agreement the two nations had reached on sharing the Ganges River water. Finally on November 5, 1977, the appropriate officials signed the formal documents in Dacca. After a quarter-century of deadlock this was a momentous and historic moment. The five-year agreement (with provision for extension) specified that during the five months of dry season, when water was in short supply, Bangladesh would receive approximately 60 percent of the Ganges

We rejoiced with Badol

water, leaving India about 40 percent. In the beginning both sides had demanded more water, but finally they both agreed to compromise on their demands. The agreement also stipulated that the Joint Rivers Commission would be reactivated to study possible ways to bring more water into the Ganges during the lean period. At last reason had prevailed.

At the same time the government was apparently becoming less reasonable about the granting of visas. For several months we had been hearing that foreigners were having increasing difficulty in obtaining visas for Bangladesh. Prior to this time the Directorate of Immigration and Passports had handled visa applications in a routine fashion. They simply followed the guidelines laid down by their supervising ministry, the Ministry of Home Affairs. But during the last few months the Home Ministry had made the guidelines more stringent and had become more actively involved in the process of approving—or denying—visas. By early November we had learned that several missions' requests for visas had been denied—and, on appeal, rejected again. We decided that I would have to investigate this problem during my upcoming trip to the capital city.

In mid-November I traveled to Dacca. Within two days I completed my business and confirmed that some foreign organizations were, in fact, having serious visa problems. That afternoon I ran into an old friend, an experienced missionary from another mission agency. Immediately he explained their particular problems—the visa applications for three new couples had been turned down and appeals had failed. Also, one of their active couples in Bangladesh had been ordered to leave the country within a few days. "Vic," he asked, "is there anything you can do to help us with this problem?"

I replied, "Phil, I really don't know. I am scheduled to leave the city tomorrow, but let me get right to work on it and see what I can do." Immediately I proceeded to Jalal's house, where he and I discussed the problem in detail. I asked, "Jalal, why would anyone in government decide to reject foreigners' visa applications and begin throwing out dedicated workers who have done so much to help the country? It makes no sense. These foreigners come mostly from Western nations which have given Bangladesh hundreds of millions of dollars and greatly helped to rehabilitate the nation. Besides that, President Zia has always been quite pro-Western. Why would he want to offend these helpful nations now?"

"We will have to seek the answers to those questions," Jalal replied. Then we focused on what I might do to influence the situation in the short time I had left in Dacca. We decided that it would be prudent to approach the American ambassador, brief him, and request him to help out in this crisis. Even though it was an awkward hour—9:00 P.M.—it was the one thing I could do that might pay dividends.

Jalal's driver took me immediately to the home of American ambassador Edward Masters. The houseboy ushered me into a drawing room. Very soon, the ambassador came down a long staircase, still tying his black bow tie; he and his wife were just going out to a formal reception. "Good evening, Vic," he greeted me warmly.

I responded, "I'm sorry to bother you this time of night, but what I have to say is important, and I return to Chittagong too early in the morning to meet you in your office."

"Oh, that's no problem; what's on your mind?"

"The leader of another mission has just told me about the rejection of the visa applications of three new American families; also the government has ordered another of their American families to leave the country. This is quite an extreme step, and it seems to signal a distinct change in the attitude of the government toward foreign organizations."

"Vic, I'm very glad you came. This is the first I have heard about this. You know I will do anything I can to help, but the problem is this—I leave the country in a week to become ambassador in Indonesia. But I promise you that I will tackle this situation immediately and do whatever I can to help. Please tell your friend to come to my office tomorrow morning."

So far, so good; we had the ball rolling. I returned to Jalal's house, briefed him, then called Phil to update him and request him to see Ambassador Masters the next morning. Early the following morning I flew to Chittagong, then drove to Malumghat.

Arriving home, I learned that Samuel had indeed decided to resign as soon as his month of suspension was over; the suspension and the loss of the student department were both bitter pills to swallow. I suggested that he reconsider his decision, because much was at stake in his own life and in the translation project.

A few days later the Medical Committee decided that Samuel must shift his translation office to his bedroom because that hospital office was urgently required for other purposes. Another heavy blow—a jolt that further strengthened his decision to resign. "Samuel, it might be a wise idea to decide nothing for a few days until this latest shock wears off," I suggested.

A few days later on December 1, Samuel's decision to resign had not wavered. I talked with him about the principle of "cross-bearing"; day by day we must take up the crosses—those painful things we must bear in order to serve God—and follow our Lord.

Samuel replied, "But this cross [the lost office] is too heavy for me to bear. Even Jesus found His cross too heavy; someone had to help Him carry it."

"Yes, Samuel, you also need help. We appreciate you and love you, and we'll help you to bear this painful cross."

But these words of encouragement seemed like chaff in the wind; they did not seem to sway Samuel one iota from his decision to quit. This was the fifth time that Samuel was on the verge of resigning. Would we ever complete this all-important special Bengali New Testament? So many problems, so many obstacles!

When Samuel arrived the next morning he seemed more relaxed with a hint of a smile on his face. His first words were these: "I have decided not to resign."

"That's good news, Samuel! What made you change your mind?"

"First of all, two men I know dropped in yesterday evening to stay overnight with me. They insisted I should not quit because this translation must be done and there is no one else with the qualifications or experience that I have. They pressed me very hard about it. Then, this morning, I opened up my New Testament and my eyes fell on these words:

> Then He [Jesus] said to them all, "If anyone one desires to come after Me, let him deny himself, and take up his cross daily, and follow Me."[17]

"This verse dealt with the very subject we discussed yesterday. It told me that I must deny myself—and my hurt feelings. And it reminded me that I had to pick up my cross today and every day. But the verse did not say I would have to carry it all by myself. So if you and the Lord will help me carry it day by day, then I should be able to finish up the New Testament project." We prayed together, and I thanked the Father for giving him insight and strength to make this difficult decision.

That problem was resolved just in time, for two hours later a messenger arrived from Chittagong with a letter requesting me to go to Dacca. The secretaries of the Home Ministry and the Foreign Ministry had requested a meeting with several mission representatives regarding the visa situation. And preceding this meeting leaders of all the mission societies would gather for an emergency Intermission Meeting.

A little later word reached us that our friend M. R. Siddiqi, Bangladesh ambassador to the United States, was in Bangladesh and would be visiting Chittagong (his home town) in a day or two. So we decided that four of us would meet Ambassador Siddiqi in

Chittagong to discuss the visa crisis with him, then I would fly on to Dacca for the Intermission Meeting and the meeting with government officials.

Jay, Donn, Dick, and I enjoyed our ride together to Chittagong. There we first met with David, a British missionary who updated us on his mission's visa difficulties. When he had approached officials of the Home Ministry about his organization's visa problems, these officers reluctantly admitted that there was a new rule—that foreigners who had been in the country longer than three years would not have their visas renewed. "Three years is a long time," they asserted, as though that were some justification for throwing people out of the country. What shocking news! This meant that our busy hospital and the rest of the mission would have to be operated by four new language students, who knew nothing about medicine, as soon as our veterans were sent home. This, of course, would be unthinkable.

David further explained that Bill, a British missionary from another organization, had taken their visa problems to the British high commissioner (ambassador), Mr. Smallman, and the deputy high commissioner, Mr. Desmond Kerr. Smallman then tackled the Home Ministry, while Kerr approached the Foreign Ministry to express their concern about the new visa policy. The Foreign Ministry had then suggested that the foreign secretary and the home secretary should meet with a contingent of mission leaders. I was impressed with this solid cooperation from the British embassy; I would have to meet these men to thank them and learn more about why they were being so exceptionally helpful.

The next morning we met Ambassador Siddiqi in Chittagong City at the home of a noted industrialist of Bangladesh. It was a great pleasure to see him again, for he was a valued friend. We explained the visa problems faced by several organizations and "the three-year rule," which was the death knell for all of us. He seemed well aware of the problem and explained that it was an overreaction to some reports of "forced conversions."

We replied that such reports were almost surely false, for none of us in all of our years in the country had heard of any forced conversions. Then we requested his help in resolving the problem. He promised to do several things:

- Talk to President Zia that very week about our visas which would expire in less than three months
- Receive in Washington future visa applications from our members on home leave, then grant them at least three-month visas to ensure their return to Bangladesh

- Introduce Jay Walsh and me to all the other hands in the Bangladesh embassy in Washington so that there would be continuity when his time in Washington was finished

How grateful we were for such a good friend!

The next afternoon I flew to Dacca and obtained a thorough briefing from Bill, the British missionary. First, he explained that U.S. ambassador Edward Masters had made a splendid effort to help us before he left the country. He had expressed his displeasure about the new visa policy once to the secretary of the Foreign Ministry, twice to the adviser (minister) of foreign affairs, and once to President Zia. As a result, the government agreed that the missionary family that had been forced out of Bangladesh would be allowed to return. Then, at his own going-away party, Ambassador Masters had recruited several other ambassadors from Western countries to work together to attempt to overcome this new visa policy. Finally, just before he left Bangladesh, Ed Masters turned the whole matter of Americans' visas over to the embassy's political officer, Craig Baxter, whom he charged with the responsibility of keeping the ball rolling.

When I visited Craig I learned that he had been in touch with British, Australian, and Vatican envoys the day before. Also, he explained that the meeting between government officers and missionaries that I had come to attend had run into a snag. Although the Foreign Ministry was still eager to proceed with the meeting, the Home Ministry was now refusing to take part in the talks.

The next day my British missionary friend David and I went to the British embassy for discussions. Because the high commissioner (ambassador) was out, we were ushered into the office of the deputy high commissioner, Mr. Desmond Kerr. Introductions over, I noticed a quizzical smile playing about his lips. He looked at me very directly, then announced, "Before we discuss your business, Doctor, I think I should first tell you something."

"Fine," I replied.

Then, pointing a finger directly at my chest, he astounded me by declaring, "It is because of *you* that I am here in Bangladesh!"

After a long moment of puzzled silence I finally responded, "I don't understand. You will have to explain that to me."

"I'll be glad to. You'll remember that your book *Daktar* was published in Great Britain as well as in America. I was posted in London at the time. Your book had a strong influence on me in two ways. First of all, I was deeply moved by your descriptions of the people of Bangladesh and the many crises they face year after year. Secondly, I was fascinated by one of the appendixes at the end of the book—the one about gaining divine guidance. In fact I taught that material to my adult Sunday School class in London. Like you, I am also a believer in Christ.

"Later I was notified that it was time for my next foreign assignment; one of the options presented to me was Bangladesh. From the point of view of my professional advancement it was not the best choice for me. But I could not get Bangladesh out of my mind; something about the things you wrote had hooked me. At that point it struck me that it was time to put into practice the principles of gaining guidance outlined in your book. When I did so I became even further convinced that I should take the posting in Bangladesh. And so here I am—because of you."

"What a fascinating story," I replied. "Now you are here just in time for this serious visa crisis. Perhaps you have 'come to the kingdom for such a time as this.' It may be that you were directed to Bangladesh because you are greatly needed at this critical point in the history of the country."

Then Desmond replied with much feeling, "I have thought that might be the case. And you can be sure that I will do my best to help resolve this crisis."

The next day, as good as his word, Desmond Kerr appeared at the meeting of leaders of the various mission societies (Intermission Meeting). He gave the assembled group valuable background information and recommended that we choose delegates to attend the upcoming meeting the government had requested. We took that as prudent advice and selected a committee of five men; two of us were from the United States and the other three from Great Britain, Germany, and Australia. The group also began calling Jalal a code name—Peter—because they feared he might get into trouble if it were widely known that he was favorable to our cause. That seemed quite unnecessary to me, for Jalal had every right, as a senior government official, to speak up against a policy that he was convinced would damage his nation's interests.

When I told Jalal he was now code-named "Peter," he laughed and replied without a missed beat, "I hope it is not Peter Pan." That same night he attended a reception at the German embassy; for two hours he discussed the problem with the German ambassador and encouraged him to take a forthright stand. And the German ambassador did just that.

The next day our committee of mission delegates met together to discuss strategy and get used to working together. We tried to anticipate some of the questions the government officials might ask us. I was elected to be spokesman for the group, perhaps because I had been deeply involved in tackling the earlier visa crisis in 1966.

By this time we had diagnosed that the focal point of our problem lay in the Ministry of Home Affairs (Home Ministry). The secretary of the Home Ministry (home secretary), supported by one of his subordinate officers, seemed eager to rid the country of as many foreigners as possible. He had a unique opportunity to do so, for at that time there was no adviser (minister) of home affairs to whom he reported—the secretary reported directly to President Zia himself. And somehow he had convinced the president that foreigners had to go.

I had heard conflicting reports about the ominous "three-year rule." The home secretary had said there was no such rule, but other officers insisted that the three-year rule existed. To try to resolve these inconsistent reports I went straight to the director of immigration. At first he was not eager to discuss the subject. But I continued, "Sir, I have a truly legitimate need to know the policy. You well know that we are responsible for the treatment of many hundreds of seriously ill patients. We must know the current visa rule so that we can plan ahead for adequate staff to care for these patients. This is not a minor concern. It is a matter of life and death."

"That is certainly true," he acknowledged. Then he called for the written order from the Home Ministry. And, there in front of me, he reread it carefully. Lifting his eyes from the paper he explained gravely, "The directive is very clear. I can grant your members renewal of their visas each year for their first three years in the country. Thereafter I cannot grant them any further visas. So when your current visa expires, I cannot renew your visa." There it was—crystal clear! The Home Ministry had officially ordered the director of immigration to implement a three-year rule.

Feeling disheartened, I returned to Jalal's house, where I was staying. Despite our hard work and despite the outstanding support of Jalal and the ambassadors, we were making no progress. The Home Ministry was like a rock against us and refused even to meet with our mission representatives, although the Foreign Ministry kept pressing them to do so.

There was no levity around the dinner table that night. We all went to bed early, feeling depressed about the seriousness of the situation and about our lack of progress. Before falling off to sleep I prayed earnestly, "Oh Father, You know we have done everything we know to do. Yet we are failing miserably. Jalal and all these fine ambassadors are helping us, yet we are making no headway. This is an extreme crisis! Oh Lord, please step in and do something special; otherwise, our cause is lost, and we will be forced to leave the country and our patients."

We awakened the next morning still disheartened. Jalal and I sat in the parlor not saying much, each of us casting about in his mind for any new approach we might make to impact the visa crisis. A newspaper boy threw the morning paper into the parlor, but we did not stir. Minutes later Jalal absentmindedly reached out, picked up the paper, then opened it to check the headlines. Suddenly I heard the newspaper crackle and an electric sense of excitement filled the room. Jalal, his eyes dancing, looked up over the paper and declared, "Allah has begun to answer your prayers!"

"What do you mean, Jalal?"

"I didn't know this was going to happen, but last night there was a cabinet shakeup. Some advisers [ministers] were dismissed and some new ones brought into the cabinet. And listen to this! President Zia has selected a new deputy adviser of home affairs. And out of all the people in this country, he has selected a man who considers himself my disciple—who thinks of me as his guru! I once read his palm and predicted what would happen to him. And that exact thing did happen!"

Instantly I was sure in my heart that Jalal was correct, for this man would be in a higher position than the difficult home secre-

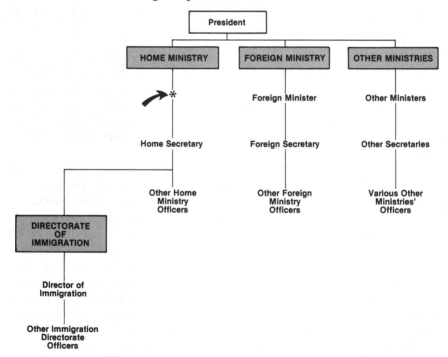

Figure 27. Simplified table of organization of a part of the Bangladesh government. Foreign ambassadors usually interact with the Foreign Ministry. Missionaries and relief and development workers relate to the Home Ministry—and to the Immigration Directorate, which is supervised by the Home Ministry. ✱ = the empty slot where the new deputy adviser (minister) of the Home Ministry was placed; here he was in position to convince President Zia to reverse the devastating new visa policy.

tary (see figure 27). God had indeed begun to answer our prayers. A half-hour later, with this fantastic news echoing in my heart, I left for the Sunday morning service of the International Church. My worship that morning was filled with an immense joy and an outpouring of devotion and praise to the Father who had been listening—and working—all the time.

Jalal would meet the new deputy minister as soon as he began his work, but in the meantime he would continue to talk with other officials. That afternoon at a reception, Jalal took the director general of foreign affairs aside and spoke to him quite directly: "This new visa policy of the Home Ministry is not only poor policy, but it also has far-reaching international implications. The Western nations have been great friends to Bangladesh and they have been extremely generous to us. Why should we harass their citizens who have come to help us and who have sacrificed so much for us? We have nothing to gain by this policy, but much to lose. The ambassadors of these nations are up in arms over this high-handed policy. We must take this seriously and somehow bring reason to bear on this crisis." The director general promised to keep pressing the home secretary to meet with the mission delegates so that the whole issue could be discussed openly.

The next day I brainstormed with Jalal about other arguments that we and the ambassadors might use in our approaches to the government. That same afternoon he used some of these points and other key arguments during a long discussion with the minister of foreign affairs. This cabinet-level officer, who already had been bombarded by the American and British ambassadors, agreed wholeheartedly with Jalal's assessment.

Over the next three days I met several times with our friends in the American and British embassies. When they reported that the Home Ministry officials were still refusing to meet with the mission representatives, I suggested that we meet the Foreign Ministry officials anyway; all agreed to this proposal. I also discovered that we would soon have to take a long break from our frenetic activities, because President Zia and the Foreign Ministry officers would be gone on a ten-day tour of the subcontinent to visit Nepal, India, and Pakistan. Then Jalal wisely suggested that I call for a meeting of our mission committee with the involved ambassadors; I set the wheels in motion for that meeting.

In the meantime, I learned about two other men whose requests for new visas had been denied; they were told to leave the country within fourteen days of the expiration of their present visas. One was an American worker of a charitable organization. The other was a Roman Catholic priest from Great Britain who had served for sixteen years at the highly regarded Notre Dame College in Dacca. And we picked up word that a whole flood of visa rejections and quit-the-country notices would soon be issued.

In mid-December I attended the beautiful International Church Christmas feast. There I spent time with our dear friends Mark and Ida Tucker who were suffering. Their beloved son, Brian, a U.S. Air Force flight officer, had been killed in a plane accident. We talked and grieved and prayed together about the untimely death of that precious son.

The next afternoon our five-member mission committee met with the ambassadors of nine Western nations; also present was Britain's Desmond Kerr, who summarized the overall situation from the diplomatic perspective. Then our mission delegates and I briefed the group on Peter's initiatives and new facts that we had uncovered. Next, the British ambassador reported on his very direct discussions with the minister and secretary of the Foreign Ministry; he had pointed out to them that the proposed drastic action against British nationals in Bangladesh would unquestionably damage relations between Bangladesh and his government. The next day he learned that his message had been conveyed directly to the president.

One thing had become clear to me. President Zia was definitely involved, so our strategy would have to touch the very top; no lesser official would be able to reverse the new visa regulations. Finally, we laid out a plan of how to proceed after the Christmas break when Zia and the Foreign Ministry officials would return to Bangladesh from their ten-day trip. In the meantime, each embassy would attempt to help any of its own nationals who were told to leave the country—and they would keep careful records of all these cases.

That night, my last night in Dacca, Jalal attended a Victory Day reception at President's House. There he talked with his friend and "disciple," the new deputy minister of the Home Ministry —who would be elevated to full minister as soon as he gained a little experience in his post. There Jalal gave him a bare-bones briefing about the serious problem that had been created by the Home Ministry, the ministry now under his control. They agreed to meet again very soon to go into the problem more deeply. That night I worked feverishly until midnight compiling all the cases of visa rejections for Jalal to present to the new deputy minister.

I was up at 5:00 A.M. the following morning to fly to Cox's Bazar, then on to the hospital by road. During my ten days at Malumghat, while President Zia and his entourage were touring the subcontinent, Joan and I enjoyed the many Christmas festivities and the Christmas Day church service, which climaxed the holiday season, giving it a warm spiritual flavor. Yet every day my mind vaulted northward to Dacca. What was happening in the visa crisis? How many were receiving fourteen-day notices to leave the country? Was Jalal making any headway with the new deputy minister of home affairs?

At the end of the ten-day break, as soon as I returned to Dacca, I went directly to Jalal's house for an update on the situation, then on to meet Bill. From them I learned the fascinating story of what had transpired during the ten days I had been away.

On day one of the ten-day period several more visa rejections had been announced. They included an American Catholic priest who had worked in the country for forty-four years—and two French Roman Catholic sisters who had served for forty-two and thirty-seven years, respectively. They were ordered to leave the country within fourteen days.

The next day Jalal visited the new deputy minister of the Home Ministry in his office. Because of his respect for Jalal, he listened with close attention to his briefing. For an hour Jalal explained the weaknesses of the new visa policy and the dangerous ramifications of it for the future.

The deputy minister replied, "I agree with you completely. But one thing confuses me; my own secretary of the Home Ministry told me that no letter containing a three-year-rule clause was sent to the director of immigration."

"Then why not set up a meeting with the director of immigration to clarify this point?" Jalal responded. Later, during that meeting, the director confirmed that he had indeed been given a written order from the Home Ministry stating that he could no longer renew the visas of foreigners who had been in the country for three years. At that point the American embassy's Craig Baxter also had a valuable meeting with the new deputy minister in which he conveyed the viewpoint of the U.S. government.

The next day the deputy minister visited Jalal's home as an intimate family friend; this was their third meeting. For three hours they discussed the issue in further detail, and Jalal reviewed with him our eight or ten strongest arguments against the new restrictive visa policy. Then Jalal advised, "You'll have to get to the president immediately to convince him of the folly of this new visa rule."

"But that will be impossible. The president will be out of the country for more than a week, so I will be unable to talk with him until he returns from his journey."

"But I have learned that he has changed his schedule," Jalal replied. "He is on his way back to Dacca now and will sleep tonight in his own bed, then tomorrow proceed to Pakistan. You must reach him at his house tonight, convince him that the visa policy must be changed, then act immediately before more foreign people are forced out of the country."

That evening the new deputy minister headed for the home of President Zia. This was the crucial hour! Everything was hanging on the outcome of that meeting—the fate of Christian missions in Bangladesh. He had no difficulty getting in to see the president, for they had been army buddies.

After greeting his old friend the deputy minister explained his misgivings about the visa policy, then began to spell out the reasons for his concern. The president was not easily convinced. But as the deputy minister presented reason after reason why the policy was ill-conceived, Zia listened more and more thoughtfully. At last he acknowledged, "Until now I have heard only one side of this issue—the other side. But what you are saying seems reasonable; maybe it is unwise to risk upsetting these Western nations." Then more questions and answers. Finally, Zia exclaimed, "You're right! We are making a mistake. So we must reverse what we are doing and go back to the previous visa regulations for foreigners. I will be out of the country, so you must take care of this in my absence."

The next day the new deputy minister informed his secretary of the Home Ministry that a new policy decision had been made canceling the new visa regulations—including the three-year rule. He further instructed the home secretary to send messengers to those under orders to leave the country, telling them they could remain and that their visas would be granted. He also ordered that letters be sent to those who had actually left the country, notifying them that their visas would be granted so they could return to Bangladesh. What a difference a day makes! What a stunning turnaround of the whole critical situation!

Although he was dismayed by this sudden turn of events, the home secretary could only comply with this policy decision. Consequently, on the day after Christmas he had passed the word to all the offices and officers down the line that the three-year rule was out and visas would be granted as they had been in former years. The deputy minister kept Jalal advised of all these developments and asked him to inform us that he himself would meet with our committee of mission delegates in a few days.

Then I reached Dacca from Malumghat on December 28 and learned about this fantastic series of events. This dangerous crisis in the history of missions in Bangladesh had come and gone. When all seemed lost and when our every effort had failed, then the Creator of all stepped in and placed the one person out of 80 million who considered Jalal his guru figure into the key position where he could resolve the problem. As spectators on the sidelines we could only marvel at this exceptional stroke. "Oh, thank You, Father!"

On December 29 I called the delegates of our mission committee together to brief them on the remarkable developments. We all rejoiced together and thanked the Father who had brought it all to pass. Also, I announced that we were invited to meet with the new deputy minister of home affairs the following morning, when we would receive official word about the turnaround in the visa crisis.

Accordingly, the next morning at 9:00 A.M. our mission delegates met with the deputy minister in his office; also present was the director general of the Ministry of Foreign Affairs. The meeting was warm, positive, and very pleasant. The deputy minister reassured us that we would have no more worries about our visas; the three-year rule had been rescinded, and visas would be granted as they had been before the restrictive policy. Both current staff and new workers would be granted visas. He thanked us for all the help that our missions and their institutions were providing for the people of the country. And he expressed his concern about the personal safety of our members because, as he explained, a certain extremist segment of the population was "ignorant and fanatical."

At the end of the meeting the deputy minister thanked us again and gave us these words of advice: "If and when your organizations dispense relief goods to our people, please do not give them to just one religious community; rather, distribute them to everyone in the area so that people do not think you care only for the Christians. Also, I want you to move about carefully and discreetly, keeping in mind the ignorance and fanaticism of a certain section of our people."

We left the Secretariat rejoicing. Then we met with national church leaders at a place called the "Archbishop's House." These national leaders also seemed pleased by the spectacular developments. That afternoon we reported our good news to the leaders of the various mission societies. More prayer—more praise—more rejoicing!

The following morning our mission delegates, along with four national Christian leaders, returned to the Secretariat where we participated in yet another official meeting, this time with the secretary of home affairs, the officer who had initiated the whole problem in the first place. With him were his joint secretary and, again, the director general of the Ministry of Foreign Affairs. This, then, was the long-delayed meeting that the government had called for in the beginning.

Despite his natural disappointment over what had happened, the secretary was cordial. He asked whether or not we had been facing any problems. I replied, "The new visa policy with the three-year rule, plus mission personnel receiving fourteen-day notices to leave the country has caused us deep concern." The home secretary responded that we should forget about that, for the whole problem was now straightened out.

"Also," I continued, "personnel coming as replacements for those no longer serving in the country have been denied visas." The secretary replied that we would have no further problems on that score. I pressed on: "Sometimes we require new hands, in addition to replacements, and these people likewise have been denied visas." The secretary answered that even these new hands would be allowed if the work could not be done by Bangladeshi nationals.

Then the four national Christian leaders in our delegation mentioned some of their problems. The home secretary said "yes" to some of their requests and denied others. Finally he spoke in a conciliatory way, declaring, "Muslims and Christians are meant to be special friends, for we share some of the same holy books. Why, we are even called 'books brothers.' Also, we Muslims are so favorable to Christians that we are allowed to marry Christian wives. And you would be interested to know that when I was posted in Rome I took the opportunity to meet the Pope."

"We appreciate your good words about special friendship," I replied. "We feel that ourselves, as we have come to serve and help the people here. No doubt you have noticed that even your Holy Koran speaks of what motivates and compels us to come from the other side of the world to be of help." Then I referred him to a verse in chapter 57 of the Koran, which states:

> And we caused Jesus son of Mary to follow, and gave him the gospel, and placed compassion and mercy in the hearts of those who followed him.

The home secretary thanked me warmly for the quotation, and a few minutes later the meeting broke up.

Our mission delegates then went immediately to one of the embassies to meet with the ambassadors; this time there were ten, for the Dutch ambassador was also present. Most of the men looked rather glum, for they had not yet heard about the dramatic developments of the last few days. They were gathering with us after the Christmas break, as scheduled, to gear up again to resume the battle of the visa crisis.

When the moderator turned the meeting over to me, I had the delicious opportunity of telling these ambassadors of the great Western nations the good news: "Excellencies, in our last meeting two weeks ago we were disturbed about this severe visa crisis and disheartened that we could not seem to make headway against it. Then we decided to take a Christmas recess and resume the struggle after this meeting. During our Christmas celebrations we were reminded that the Creator of all gave to mankind a wondrous Gift—His best gift—on that very first Christmas. And I am happy to report that He has given us a special gift this Christmas as well. While our backs were turned the visa crisis has been fully resolved! So we have cause to thank the Almighty for this gift, too."

Then I explained the cabinet shakeup, Peter's three meetings with the new deputy minister, the deputy minister's critical meeting with the president, the president's decision to cancel the restrictive new visa policy, and our two warm, positive meetings in the Home Ministry. As I spoke the frowns turned to smiles.

"Gentlemen," I continued, "we want to thank you from full hearts for all you have done to help resolve this visa crisis. The fact that all of you were up in arms over this issue was a powerful weapon in Peter's hands to convince the new deputy minister—and ultimately President Zia—that this visa policy was a serious mistake."

At the end our mission delegates and the ten ambassadors rejoiced together. It was a never-to-be-forgotten moment and a dynamite way to close out 1977. Some of the ambassadors never learned Peter's identity, but one who did said quietly to me at the end of the meeting, "Your Peter told me he supported our viewpoint—and that he had much affection and appreciation for you and your co-workers."

Key Events of 1977: Summary

January
- We spend the day with the new U.S. ambassador, who visits Malumghat and other beauty spots in our area.
- Ex–lieutenant colonel Farook flies to Dacca where he is imprisoned.

February
- The church purchases beautiful land near Malumghat, while the mission buys an excellent plot in Chittagong City.
- I fly to Dacca to put out a fire involving the special Bengali translation of the New Testament.

March
- India's Indira Gandhi is replaced by a new prime minister more friendly to Bangladeshi leaders.

April
- A valuable literacy workshop is held at Malumghat.
- General Zia negotiates successfully with Indian leaders regarding the Farakka Barrage dispute.
- Zia becomes president—and retains his other posts.
- Zia amends the Constitution: secularism is muted, socialism is redefined, and the importance of women is emphasized.

May
- Referendum: nearly 99 percent of the voters support Zia.

June
- The first of six short-term surgeons arrives to free me for the special Bengali New Testament translation project.
- New Indian leaders force pro-Mujib, anti-Zia Bangladeshi guerrillas out of India back to Bangladesh.
- We travel to the U.S. and settle Nancy at her university.

August
- The special Bengali Gospel of John goes on the market.

September
- The Egyptian president warns Zia of an impending coup.
- Japanese Red Army gunmen hijack a JAL plane to Dacca.
- An abortive mutiny by leftist sepoys in Bogra is put down.

October
- A similar, more dangerous coup attempt in Dacca is crushed.
- A cousin of Debapriyaw Roy becomes king of the Chakmas.

November
- Bangladesh and India finally sign an amicable official agreement on the Farakka Barrage problem.
- The British deputy ambassador informs me, "I am in Bangladesh because of *you*"; he was influenced by *Daktar*.
- A severe visa crisis brings foreign missions to the brink of disaster in Bangladesh.

December
- At the eleventh hour the crisis is miraculously resolved.

Figure 28

11
1978: More Crises—More Refugees

The new year dawned cool, bright, and clear in Bangladesh. I was still in Dacca, and the instant I opened my eyes I was wide awake, for there was a chance this could be a banner day. Although the old year had closed on a joyous note because of our stunning victory in the visa crisis, I still had one concern. The home secretary, who had initiated the visa crisis and who had lost out in the end, would certainly be feeling negative about the outcome.

Then, again, the unusual and unexpected happened. A Dacca businessman close to us came to me, saying, "My friend the home secretary is requesting you to see his daughter as a patient. Would you kindly grant his request?"

"Yes, Giasuddin," I replied. "I will be happy to see this patient." At the same time I thought, *Maybe helping the home secretary's daughter will give me an opportunity to ease any negative feelings he might have.* The appointment was set for New Year's Day.

At the designated time I appeared at the home secretary's house. His daughter showed me in and we chatted awhile; she was an attractive, cultured young woman. Soon the home secretary appeared, and we began talking about various subjects—everything except the battle royal we had just been through, struggling against each other behind the scenes over the visa crisis. Our discussion was a bit stiff at first but quickly warmed up. Soon we found ourselves talking about vital spiritual issues. I explained to him my own conversion from agnosticism to Christian faith and shared with him some details of Christ's good news message, which had so powerfully influenced my life. Then he, in turn, told me about his visit to the tomb of a famous Muslim saint; this pilgrimage had made a deep spiritual impact on his life.

Later I met his hospitable wife and examined the daughter. The diagnosis was straightforward, and I gave her and the parents careful instructions about her treatment. By the time I departed a warm relationship had developed and any bitterness the home secretary might have felt was considerably eased. The next day he thoughtfully sent me a thank-you note written on a New Year's card. If the resolved visa crisis was the cake, then this New Year's Day event was the frosting on the cake. "Thank You, Father!"

By then President Zia was back in Dacca after successful visits to Nepal, India, and Pakistan; in each country he had received a warm welcome from the leaders and the people. It was clear that they had accepted him as a significant leader who was bringing a degree of stability to the troubled nation of Bangladesh. In Nepal and India he had discussed working together in a cooperative effort to harness the major rivers that flowed through the three countries. Then, in India, on January 2, America's president Jimmy Carter in a speech to the Indian Parliament promised that the U.S. would share in any cooperative effort to control those great rivers for the benefit of the three nations. Perhaps this generous offer would stimulate India, Bangladesh, and Nepal to get together on a long-range solution to their water problems.

That first week in January Joan was out of commission and hidden away in our darkened bedroom. She was suffering a flare-up of a recurrent eye disease called iritis; this was her most severe recurrence in ten years. Iritis causes pain in the eyes, greatly aggravated by bright light.

One day, while translator Mrs. Dass was visiting Joan in that darkened room, a car drove up outside, and we heard voices. Our gardener, who was standing in the hall, glanced out through the front door. Then, looking puzzled, he asked Joan, "Isn't that Wendy?"

Scarcely looking up, Joan replied, "No, she's in America"—then resumed her conversation with Mrs. Dass. At that instant the front door burst open and in stepped our oldest daughter, Wendy! With tears streaming down her cheeks she gave me a big hug and kiss, then headed for the bedroom where she threw herself into Joan's arms. Mrs. Dass, a loving mother herself, quietly slipped out to allow the family to revel in this joyous surprise reunion.

When we finally calmed down a bit Wendy explained, "Dr. Kempton told me that the government was expelling foreigners from Bangladesh, and if I ever wanted to see Bangladesh again I'd better do it now before you were forced to leave the country. So I traveled with Dr. Don and Doris Jennings, who were on their way here so Don could speak at the mission's Spiritual Life Conference. Now I am home again. I'm so happy!" And, because the visa crisis had been resolved, Wendy was able to remain and serve as a short-

Wendy home again—and "so *happy"*

term worker at the hospital for the next year and a half. Happily, Joan's iritis later relented, allowing her to resume her normal activities.

By February it was clear that President Zia, more confident all the time, was moving in the direction of allowing more freedom to political parties and ordering democratic elections. He even encouraged his vice-president, Justice Abdus Sattar, to launch a brand-new political party to be called the National Democratic Party (English) or the JAGODAL (Bengali). The new party, of course, reflected Zia's views.

While the country was buzzing about the new developments in politics, Joan and I flew from Dacca to the beautiful island of Bermuda in the Atlantic Ocean. There I would give three messages to those gathered for a unique conference. For the first time, our mission hosted a conference in the most beautiful hotel in Bermuda for people who wanted to enjoy a lovely vacation in idyllic surroundings, be informed and challenged by missionaries and other speakers, and also be entertained by outstanding musicians.

Not long after we arrived a crisis suddenly erupted. A telephone call from a conference member alerted me to the sudden sickness of her friend. Hurrying to the stricken lady's hotel room, I found a patient who knew all about us and the work of Memorial

Christian Hospital. In fact, she had come to the conference particularly to hear the update on our team's efforts in Bangladesh. But now she was in danger. A sudden heart attack had begun to steal her breath away.

Fortunately, the ambulance came fairly quickly in response to my call, for her condition was deteriorating. Inside the ambulance, she soon began thrashing about wildly in mounting heart failure and shock as the vehicle careened wildly around the curves leading to the distant hospital. Just as we wheeled her through the Emergency Room door, her breathing ceased—then instant CPR, endotracheal tube, oxygen! After an hour of intense work by the Emergency Room crew, she lived. And she was still hanging on by a thread when we left Bermuda a few days later.

A second crisis surfaced later in the week. We had enjoyed the outstanding music and various presentations. My own messages to the conference had featured our outreach to the tribal people, our interaction with Bengali patients and friends, and the thrilling outcome of the most severe visa crisis we had ever faced. I thoroughly enjoyed those opportunities to tell of the "wonderful works of God."

Then, on the last morning a message boomed over the hotel loudspeaker: "Doctor Olsen, Don Trott wants to see you in the dining room right away!" I found Don, a former ABWE field missionary, in earnest conversation with a new Bermudian friend named Mark. Don was calling for a "consultation" regarding the spiritual danger his newfound friend was facing. As we talked together over breakfast the diagnosis became more clear, and we explained the necessary treatment. After an hour of intense work this patient also lived. But this was an altogether new kind of life, for Mark had bowed his head and put his trust in the Great Physician. Then he went off quickly to tell his aged father, who had prayed for this son for many years.

From Bermuda we flew to the U.S. and proceeded to our mission headquarters in Cherry Hill, New Jersey; there we linked up with our co-worker Jay Walsh. Jay, Joan, and I represented our Bangladesh team in a series of round-table discussions aimed at updating the principles and practices of the mission. Other field personnel also attended from other parts of the world. The discussions were profitable, and the interaction between headquarters staff and mission workers fresh from the foreign fields was stimulating. The principles and practices were refined on the basis of these discussions, then sent to every member of the mission for any further suggestions.

Our next stop was Washington, D.C. There Jay and I met our good friend, Bangladesh ambassador M. R. Siddiqi. He introduced us to the key officers in the embassy staff and told them always to do their best to assist us because we had a long history of sincerely helping the people of Bangladesh. These introductions were important, for Mr. Siddiqi's period of service as ambassador to the U.S. would soon be completed and he would be returning to Bangladesh. At lunch we expressed our gratitude for his many kindnesses.

Then Joan and I flew on to Toledo where we enjoyed a visit with her mother and other family members. Next, after a delightful week with my parents and family members in Nebraska, we proceeded on to the Los Angeles area where our Lynne, Mark, and Nancy lived and studied. During that never-to-be-forgotten ten days we reveled in the special treat of being together. In addition to the family gatherings, we took each of the children to dinner individually so that we could discuss each one's situation in more depth and learn how we could help in the best way. At the end of March we flew directly back to Bangladesh, taking the transatlantic route.

At Malumghat I resumed seeing my share of the unending flow of patients. On the last day of March two infants with identical congenital problems were brought to the hospital. Diagnosis: imperforate anus. This meant that their intestinal tracts were completely blocked, since they had no anal openings. The eight-day-old baby had a massively distended abdomen and was much too ill to tolerate a full-scale repair of the defect. So we merely opened the colon onto the baby's abdominal wall (colostomy); this relieved the obstruction and saved the child's life. Later, when he was stronger, we would do a complete repair of the anomaly.

Fortunately, the parents of the second infant brought their son to us promptly; this handsome little boy was only twelve hours old. I helped surgical resident Bob Goddard carry out the repair; the case went smoothly. When the operation was nearly finished I left the operating room to keep an appointment. But in a minute I heard Wendy's voice behind me calling, "Dad! Dad, come back. The baby's in trouble." I raced back to the operating room to find the infant had turned blue, respiration had stopped, and the pulse was very slow. While Bob rapidly completed his operation I quickly restarted the tiny patient's respiration, gave oxygen, and suctioned out the obstructing mucous. The ugly blue color became a beautiful, healthy pink, and the vital signs soon returned to normal. The little tyke made a good recovery, and the final result was excellent.

By April Fool's Day it was clear that something foolish—and serious—was taking place in northern Burma, for literally hundreds and thousands of Burmese Bengalis were suddenly pouring across the border into Bangladesh. They were running from persecution and oppression. How long this influx would continue was anyone's guess. The startled Bangladesh government began to organize itself to receive this endless stream of refugees, to house them, and to feed them. And our patient load immediately began to escalate because we were the only hospital in the area to care for refugees who became seriously ill.

Meanwhile, a different kind of invasion was taking place near the hospital and Cha Bagan Village, where many of our staff reside. A herd of elephants had migrated from the deep interior jungle to our neighborhood. The dozen or more elephants would ransack the fields and fruit trees at night, then rest in a nearby forest area during the day.

After eleven o'clock one night a ward nurse, accompanied by a night watchman carrying his flickering kerosene lantern, started out from the hospital on the mile-long hike to her Cha Bagan house. But partway there they were suddenly aware of the massive bodies of elephants towering very near them. As the watchman hoisted his lantern they could see elephant trunks lifted like eerie, undulating serpents to catch their scent. Fortunately, the giant tuskers decided to ignore the two scurrying figures and their pitiful little light. Many in Cha Bagan spent three sleepless nights—or had nightmares about elephants lumbering through their houses —until at last the herd moseyed back to the deep jungle.

In late April President Zia made a surprise announcement that an election for the president of Bangladesh would take place on June 3, and a few days later he lifted all restrictions on political parties. Because they had only five weeks to work, the various party leaders then began a frantic scramble to select their candidates and launch their campaigns. This presidential election would be the biggest news of the year to the people of Bangladesh.

President Zia quickly chose Jalal to be the secretary of the Election Commission, for it would take an immensely competent person to organize and pull off a free and fair election in the short time available. I could tell that Jalal was feeling the squeeze when he exclaimed, "You had better pray for me. This is going to be a very tough job!"

Back at Malumghat Joan, Samuel, and I continued working flat-out on the special Bengali New Testament project. The trial edition of the special Bengali Gospel of John had been so popular that it quickly sold out around the country; another large printing was ordered. Also in April, the special Bengali New Readers' Selections No. 2 and No. 3 came off the press and were put on sale. Soon New Readers' Selections in Chakma (translated by Debapriyaw Roy) and Tippera (translated by Jay Walsh, Oncherai, and Robichandro) would also be printed and reach the marketplace.

New Readers' Selections in special Bengali

But the translation was not the only matter demanding our attention. For months we had been under pressure from our old friend the Kutubdia carpenter. Sadly, he had to be sent away from Cha Bagan Village for falsifying a document and defrauding the hospital. Reacting angrily, he then sent letters and telegrams to the deputy commissioner, the chief of police, the martial law authorities, the court, and President Zia. This explosion of letters created quite a furor in official circles.

Some of his charges were fantastic. He claimed that we had held a loaded revolver to his head and had stolen his property. He further claimed that I was the head of the American CIA for fifteen countries—and that I would communicate with my agents in those countries each night at 11:00 P.M. by my secret wrist radio. Those fanciful allegations brought down upon us a martial law investigation, a judicial investigation, and a police intelligence investigation. When the police intelligence officer asked to see my secret wrist radio, I showed him the suspect alarm wrist watch and demonstrated that the noise that came from it was a wake-up alarm, not a radio message. He dutifully recorded the name of the maker of the watch and its serial number.

As a result of these three investigations we were finally declared innocent and the Kutubdia carpenter was judged to be acting maliciously. Shortly thereafter I ran into the carpenter in Cox's

Bazar. I felt sorry for him, despite all the trouble he had caused us, for he had been a friend for several years and he and his family had been doing very well before his dishonest act. He asked whether there might be any way that he could reestablish our friendship. I replied, "Surely. You will need to admit that you were wrong in making all these untrue charges against us, ask for forgiveness, and then go before a judge and withdraw the complaints which you officially filed against us. In fact, you could approach the judge right now, for the courthouse is just a stone's throw away."

Because this sounded reasonable, and because his conscience had been stabbing him unmercifully for days, the Kutubdia carpenter capitulated. With bowed head he affirmed, "You are right; I did make charges that were untrue, and I will go right now to the judge and withdraw them all." Then, falling to the ground he clutched my feet and cried out piteously, "Now, please forgive me —forgive me—forgive me!"

Lifting him to his feet I replied, "As soon as you complete your duty at the court you may be sure that you are forgiven." On the spot he engaged a paralegal, who helped him draft his official statement withdrawing all the charges. The judge, who already had heard something about the case, registered the document according to the law of the land. Then he said a few words to the carpenter: "You have done a wise thing, getting yourself reconciled with the hospital authorities. I have heard that they did many things in the past to show kindness to you, so you made a big mistake by making a false case against them. Now go out and try to live your life in a better way."

In mid-May Jack Archibald, our mission administrative officer, and I traveled to Dacca to work together on several accumulated problems. The new income tax officer in Chittagong was refusing to honor our agreement with the government; he was withholding our workers' tax clearances, making it impossible for any of us to leave the country for vacation or furlough. To tackle this problem we approached upper-echelon tax officials of the National Board of Revenue (NBR), reminded them of the provisions of our agreement, and ultimately gained their support. They then ordered the income tax officer in Chittagong to grant the necessary clearances without further delay.

Second, our workers returning from home leave were running into difficulty getting their import privileges reinstated; this matter of reinstatement after furlough had not been covered in our official agreement. To solve this problem, Jack and I would have to approach another branch of the NBR. But, unexpectedly, in the hallway of the NBR Building I ran into the chairman himself. He seemed very happy to see me and called me into his private office. There he requested consultation and advice about the treatment of his recently diagnosed heart disease. I examined him and gave the appropriate advice. He seemed extremely grateful—and he saw to it that our members' import privileges were quickly reinstated. Our unplanned meeting in that hallway had been clearly providential.

Third, we hoped to obtain for the Walsh family multiple-entry visas to Pakistan. They expected to visit their children studying in Pakistan three or four times during the following two years. But we ran into a snag. A senior Pakistan embassy official called us in to say that he would grant only a single-entry thirty-day visa, which could be extended for two more weeks after the Walshes reached Pakistan. "Sir, are you a family man? Do you have children?" I asked.

"Yes," he replied, " I have a wife and children."

"Then put yourself in the Walshes' shoes for just a minute. If your precious children were studying in another country, wouldn't you want a multiple-entry visa to visit them during their vacations or when an emergency came up?"

The Pakistan official was quiet for a minute, then replied with a smile, "I am always open to be convinced—and you have convinced me. I am granting the Walsh family a two-year, multiple-entry visa." Great!

Our fourth urgent problem was the need for immediate Bangladesh visas for two of our ladies, Linda Short and Joyce Wilson, whose visas had expired and who could not leave the country without valid Bangladesh visas stamped in their passports. So Jack and I began to visit various government offices to track down their visa application papers.

We went first to Central Police Headquarters where we had an unusual interview with a senior police intelligence officer. Somewhere he had obtained a copy of our *Muslim Bengali to English Dictionary,* and he seemed quite taken with it. For fifteen minutes he extolled the virtues of the dictionary and insisted that it must be in all the libraries and institutions of higher learning in the country. Because of his keen interest in literary matters I gave him copies of the special Bengali Gospel of John and the English *The Agnostic Who Dared to Search*; he expressed his thanks for these books. At the end, we got down to business and learned that the visa applications for our two ladies had been forwarded to the Home Ministry. That was fortunate, for I already had an appointment to go to the home of the deputy minister of the Home Ministry for tea and medical consultation.

Later that day at the deputy minister's residence I enjoyed an elaborate and delicious afternoon tea. And I thanked him again for his outstanding intervention to resolve the visa crisis. After the refreshments I examined his wife, then her brother who had a rather complicated illness. After writing up their cases and the necessary prescriptions, I told the deputy minister about the two visa applications in his ministry and our need to get them approved on an emergency basis. It was a good day, for I had the pleasure of helping these valued friends, and the two visas were granted the next day.

During those few days we also started the ball rolling on two other problems that were ultimately resolved in our favor. Looking back at our forays into the corridors of power of the Bangladesh government, and remembering how everything had fallen into place each step of the way, Jack and I could only say, "Thank You, Father!"

At Jalal's house I observed that he, in his capacity as secretary of the Election Commission, was working at top speed to ensure that the upcoming presidential election would be carried out smoothly. Unwilling to risk a possible shortage of paper for ballots, he had arranged a special train with sixty cars to bring a hundred tons of paper from the paper mill in the Hill Tracts to the capital city.

Then he ordered a huge supply of indelible ink; this would be used to mark the hand of every voter to make sure that no one could vote twice. Unexpectedly, the vice-president called for Jalal to come and answer some questions that had been raised about the efficacy of the indelible ink. As they talked, Jalal suddenly exclaimed with his mischievous smile, "All right, let's test it!" Then, over the vice-president's protests, Jalal grabbed his thumb and plunged it into a bottle of the suspect ink. Four days later Vice-President Sattar still could not get the ink off his thumb. End of rumors about defective indelible ink!

Before I left Dacca three Christian organizations came to me and donated money with which to help the Burmese Bengali refugees. They recognized that we were in the best location to assist these tragic people. These gifts were a great help, for we were rapidly running out of funds caring for the many refugees who were too destitute to pay anything toward their care.

Soon after I returned to Malumghat we ransacked our hospital storerooms for warm sweaters, skim milk, high-protein biscuits, and other useful items. We were able to donate two truckloads of these materials to the government refugee camps and still have adequate supplies for the unofficial camp located near our hospital. We had not seen camp leader Mr. U. for weeks; he had visited Burma and was finding it difficult to return to Bangladesh. The camp subleaders, however, continued to come on their appointed days to receive the Scriptural teaching that they had requested. Memorizing important passages of Holy Writ continued to be a key part of their program.

One of the subleaders had been absent for many days, for he had been seized by the police for alleged involvement in a robbery. A local child had identified him as the thief, although the refugees all insisted that he had been in the camp at the time of the robbery. Later in May this refugee subleader was released from prison on bail. He came as soon as possible to Malumghat. He looked gaunt and pale—and when I reached out my hands to him he fell to the ground and sobbed. After we helped him to his feet and comforted him, he told his story.

He explained that he had not taken part in the robbery, but the police had seized him anyway and taken him to an out-of-the-way police station in the Hill Tracts. He said they tried to get a confession out of him by force. Even though he feared that he might die, he felt that he must not lie, so continued to declare his innocence. Later, in prison, experienced fellow prisoners told him that he should have admitted guilt, then withdrawn the confession later in front of the judge on the grounds that the confession was obtained by torture.

During those many days in prison he had repeated over and over again to himself the passages of Holy Scripture that he had memorized. Somehow this refugee man had survived his ordeal with a triumphant spirit; his faith seemed stronger than ever before. Clearly, God's Word tucked away in his memory bank had helped to sustain him.

One night Joan and I enjoyed a lovely dinner at the home of Dick and Carol Stagg. After dinner, when Joan returned home, I remained behind to attend a meeting. Soon she came racing back with the news that there was a snake in our house. "I need you," Joan explained. "The snake is stuck between the door and the door-jamb in the front room, and it keeps making a horrid spitting noise."

On the way home we picked up a watchman and his stick, then entered the house. With a knife I stabbed at the hissing, spitting cobra, which promptly slithered to the floor and faced us with head high and hood expanded. I shouted to the guard, *"Maro! Maro!* [Hit it! Hit it!]" But the hefty watchman just stood there motionless, speechless. As the hiss became louder and the cobra prepared to strike, I snatched the watchman's stick and smashed the snake's head.

But the watchman just shook his head and repeated reprovingly, "You shouldn't have done that. You shouldn't have done that."

"Why not?" I asked.

"We never strike a cobra's head inside a house, because it has a tiny, almost-invisible poison tooth. If that tooth gets knocked out onto the floor and someone comes along and steps on it, that person will die." Although I explained at length that a cobra's venom enters only the two large fangs, both quite visible, I suspect that he continued to believe the local superstition.

As May wore on the pace of electioneering for the presidential elections picked up. Two broad coalitions engaged each other in the debate. Supporting President Zia was the Nationalist Front made up of six disparate parties. In addition to the JAGODAL, the new party based on his own ideology, the patchwork included leftist parties, rightists, and a Hindu minority party.

Several other parties, anchored by the Awami League, formed the opposition alliance. This opposition front, which was also a duke's mixture, selected General M. A. G. Osmani as their candidate for president. General Osmani had been the commanding general of the Bangladesh freedom fighters during the war of liberation and later a minister in Sheikh Mujib's cabinet. During his active campaign Osmani emphasized again and again that his one great aim was to restore parliamentary democracy in Bangladesh.

Popular President Zia began his campaign at the shrine of a famous Muslim saint in the northeastern district of Sylhet.[1] From that point he toured the whole country, making speech after speech, emphasizing his now-famous nineteen-point program. His campaign was effective; massive crowds came out to hear his speeches.

By June 1 Jalal had the whole electoral process well organized. He had done everything humanly possible to ensure a free and fair election. Then on June 3 more than 20 million Bangladeshis trudged to the polls and cast their votes. They gave President Zia a massive victory (77 percent) over General Osmani (22 percent), a greater than three-to-one margin.[2] Several minor candidates obtained a few thousand scattered votes.

Why did Zia win so convincingly? Probably for several reasons:

- On the day in 1971 that he announced the independence of Bangladesh on the Chittagong radio station Zia became a national hero with instant charisma and nationwide name recognition.
- As a sector commander in the 1971 liberation war he led his troops (the Z-force) valiantly and well. He was soon promoted to general.
- Because he was appreciated and respected by the army enlisted men, they had made Zia their commanding general during the sepoy revolt in 1975.

- As chief martial law administrator and then president, he had proved himself to be an attractive, forceful leader who had improved the law-and-order situation, controlled smuggling, brought a degree of stability to the country, and improved the nation's economy.
- Zia had charmed the rural people (90 percent of the population) by making innumerable trips to their villages and initiating development schemes to help them.
- The business community voted for him because he had championed private enterprise.
- The military backed Zia, not only because he was one of them, but also because he had increased the defense budget and strengthened the armed forces.
- Bangladeshi intellectuals supported him because of his pragmatic approach, his success in bringing order out of chaos, and for raising the prestige of the nation around the world—and especially because he was moving toward democracy.
- The Islamic right cast their votes for Zia because he had made the Constitution more Islamic, strengthened Islamic religious education, and developed a close relationship with other Muslim nations.
- Most of the women voted for him because he had taken concrete steps to promote women's rights.
- Finally, President Zia was acclaimed throughout the country for his honesty and personal integrity. And he had promised to hold elections for a parliament (congress) that would make the nation's laws and even have authority to remove an unworthy president.[3]

Joan and I had reached Dacca three days before the election took place. There we found Jalal busily contacting the deputy commissioners of all the districts of the country; he ordered them to have the police out in force at the polling stations and to take stern action if any cases of vote fraud were discovered. Although there were unpreventable irregularities at a few polling stations, those sporadic incidents had no influence on the outcome of the election. Not a single citizen was killed during the voting—a considerable accomplishment in itself. Jalal and the Election Commission had succeeded in running a peaceful and fair election that clearly reflected the will of the people; no wonder the election gained the respect of the international press.

Three days after the election, while President Zia was still celebrating his victory, we met our children Lynne and Mark at the Dacca airport. Despite the fact that they had slept on the floor of the Calcutta airport the night before, they looked great to us. We missed seeing Nancy step off the plane, but she had responsibilities that kept her in the U.S. that summer.

Back at Malumghat the three children were excited to be reunited for the summer vacation. Wendy was working afternoons in the hospital business office and mornings in the Outpatient Department as a medical assistant and interpreter for a short-term physician. Lynne served as a ward nurse, while Mark supervised Burmese refugees in a land-clearing project and did storeroom work and office work. Throughout the delightful summer, together as a family we served God and man in the People's Republic of Bangladesh.

As soon as Dr. Bob Goddard departed, my own medical-surgical load increased until the next short-term surgeon arrived. During that interval I shared the load with Drs. Ketcham and DeCook and spent less time on our translation project. Because Dr. Dick Stagg was skillful with figures and comfortable with accounting, he stepped in to take over hospital business manager Bob Nusca's work when the Nuscas departed for home leave. That's what I call flexibility.

In mid-June our family enjoyed a day and night at Cox's Bazar. While the children went shopping, Joan and I "spiffed up," and I took her out to dinner to celebrate our thirtieth wedding anniversary. When our waiter learned of the occasion he thoughtfully slipped out into the night, then returned with a sprig of night-queen blossoms for our table; the small white petals gave off a beautiful jasmine-like scent. After our romantic dinner, we exchanged some gifts we had been saving for the event. When I opened an attractive Cross pen and pencil set, Joan explained, "In view of the fact that wives don't come with a 'lifetime mechanical guarantee,' a man should at least have a pen and pencil set that does."

The next day Samuel mysteriously requested us to be present in his quarters at 5:00 p.m. We arrived to find him with the pastors and other church leaders who had gathered to celebrate our wedding anniversary. Samuel presented to Joan her own thirty-year-old wedding Bible, which had been redone in a fresh white cover with her name imprinted on it in gold. And he presented to me a carefully-arranged bouquet of violet and orange flowers. In his presentation speech he stated that our contribution to the hospital and medical-surgical work was a small thing compared to our greater and more important work—preparing the Holy Scriptures in special Bengali for multiplied millions of Bengalis in Bangladesh and India. No doubt some of our patients would disagree with his assessment, but Samuel had a point. What could be more valuable than providing the revelation of the living God in the heart language of 100 million people?

Next the Bengali church leaders had prayer and Bible reading; because they were students of the Scriptures they found appropriate passages for a wedding anniversary. At the end we enjoyed Bangladeshi sweets and an animated conversation. What fine, thoughtful men these are!

Maintaining adequate supplies of vital medicines is often difficult in Bangladesh—and sometimes impossible. The medicine insulin is a case in point. NPH insulin, the type of insulin required by Awjit Sardar, one of our male nurses, was not even available in the country. Although we had imported a good supply and still had plenty in stock, we had placed an air freight order for more. When that order did not come, we placed a second air freight order—but it, too, was delayed. By then our supply of NPH insulin was dangerously low. So Dick Stagg and his family traveled to Calcutta to find some of this special insulin and to purchase various other essential medicines. After a full day of shopping he had found none of the insulin. Later, he finally located two vials of NPH insulin and returned to Malumghat—just in time, for Awjit was down to his last dose.

But by the end of June we were in trouble again. Once more, Awjit took his very last dose of the special insulin. Now what were we going to do? Three hours later that question was answered for

Awjit Sardar needed NPH insulin

us. A messenger arrived from Chittagong bringing many vials of beautiful NPH insulin; one of the air shipments had finally arrived and been cleared through Customs—and just in time, for that afternoon part of the road between Chittagong and Malumghat washed away in the monsoon floods, isolating us. But we had the precious NPH insulin, and Awjit was safe. "Thank You, Father!"

We continued to see patients with Chittagong perihepatitis. Surprisingly, some of the cases during that period showed additional disturbing symptoms—mental disorientation and an unsteady gait. Our staff began to call this variety the "*pagol* hepatitis [crazy hepatitis or cuckoo hepatitis]." Apparently the Chittagong perihepatitis virus had somehow changed in such a way that it was now affecting the brain as well as the liver capsule. During that last half of June four new cases surfaced; some of those patients were disoriented for days and otherwise ill for several months. A strange disease, indeed!

In early July I admitted to the hospital a forty-year-old Muslim woman with chest pain and an impressive chest X ray; the X ray showed a shadow the size of a cannonball in the center of the chest, sitting astride her heart and projecting toward the left. The cannonball, of course, was a tumor. In the operating room I opened her chest and stared the six-inch-by-six-inch cannonball in the face; it was a round, lumpy, irregular mass affixed to her heart, great blood vessels, and other vital structures. Slowly, steadily, carefully I dissected the tightly-attached tumor from all these structures. As I separated it from the membrane around her heart, the heart's muscular wall hammered a steady tattoo against my fingers. It was necessary to clamp and tie many blood vessels, for bleeding was substantial; she required four units of blood during the operation. Then, with a final stroke, the tumor was removed; the lady made a good recovery.

The next weekend our family drove south and visited some of the government refugee camps. By now the eleven camps contained *more than two hundred thousand* Bengali refugees from Burma. These people testified that they had crossed the border because they had been subjected to beatings, rape, and murder by the Burmese military and police, assisted by their own Burmese Buddhist neighbors; "Operation Dragon" they called it. Why did the authorities and people of Burma let loose a reign of terror on this Bengali minority? There were several theories:

- The Burmese wished to take over the farms and businesses of the Bengalis in northern Burma.
- The Burmese were fed up with Bangladeshis' migrating to northern Burma to become residents there.

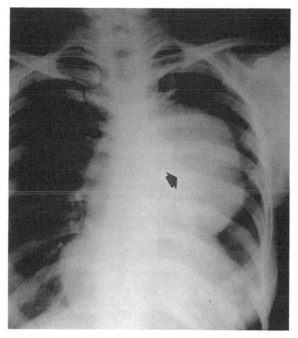

Cannonball-sized tumor in chest

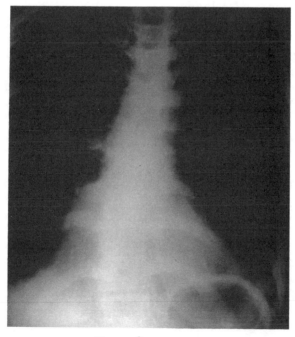

X ray after surgery

- The Burmese feared that the Bengalis were disloyal and were planning to conquer Burma's Arakan District and secede from Burma, possibly joining with Bangladesh. Indeed, one Burmese citizen, who advocated just such an overthrow, had been convicted of treason and sentenced to prison.[4]

Whatever the reason, the attack upon the Bengali people in Burma had been so cruel that tens of thousands of them had raced for the border and crossed into Bangladesh. Bangladesh could not long endure the pressure of this instant "population explosion," so hurried negotiations began between the two countries. Even though the international community of nations continued pressuring Burma to put a stop to Operation Dragon, the Burmese turned a deaf ear to such pleas. So the United Nations sent funds and a team to help relieve the suffering of the refugees.

As we entered each camp we saw great crowds of people, some looking adequately nourished, others very thin. Many children were pot-bellied from the load of worms they carried. The refugees lived in long barrack-type rows of bamboo rooms covered with sungrass roofs; some of these roofs were reinforced with long sheets of black plastic to keep out the pelting monsoon rains.

In addition to this shelter, the Bangladesh government provided the refugees with food and a physician for each camp to look after the ordinary medical problems. These medical officers would refer the seriously ill patients to our hospital. Although we saw plenty of human misery, we were impressed that the Zia government had done a good job of providing the essentials to keep most of these people alive. The refugees were pleased to see us, for they had heard that we treated their patients with kindness and compassion.

Although we did not know it at the time, the negotiations for repatriating the refugees to Burma reached a crisis just as we were visiting the camps. Burma at last capitulated and on July 9 signed an agreement to receive the refugees back to Burma. That was impressive, for most of the world's refugees still languished in primitive camps with no hope of repatriation to their homelands, all negotiations having failed.

Also in July, the government looked over the figures of the fiscal year 1977-78 and liked what it saw. Because the climate had behaved throughout most of the year, there was a record crop of rice and other food grains. And industrial production had increased by more than 10 percent. Despite these favorable developments, however, there was worrisome double-digit inflation (15 percent). Apparently that sharp increase in the cost of living oc-

Bengali refugees from Burma

Shelters in a government refugee camp

curred because the government had printed a large amount of new money and pumped it into the economy.[5]

With the advent of July the government's first Five-Year Plan was also completed, giving those in power an opportunity to face the music on the accuracy of the planning. This is what they discovered:

- The government had hoped to mobilize substantial revenue from its people, but it fell far short (realized only 13 percent of the anticipated amount).
- Because the income fell far below the expectations, so also did the outlay for development of the country (nearly 50 percent short of target levels).
- The goal of maintaining stable prices could not be achieved. In fact, prices rose more than 70 percent over the five-year period. Worldwide inflation was one of the culprits responsible for that rise.
- One of the objectives of the first Five-Year Plan had been to reduce foreign aid from 62 percent down to 27 percent. Instead, the quantum of foreign aid increased to nearly 75 percent in the fifth year of the plan.[6]

President Zia was determined to improve these figures in the years ahead.

In mid-July Malumghat was the scene of another church wedding. Pastor Gonijan had applied to the government three years before for his authorization to perform legal Christian weddings, but no response had been forthcoming from the government officials. During my last trip to Dacca I had contacted those officers and succeeded in stimulating some action. Just two days before the wedding Pastor Goni finally received his authorization.

The groom was Manik, the schoolmaster's son. The bride was Gita, who selected her friend Lynne Olsen to be her maid of honor. Pastor Goni conducted the ceremony with aplomb, and the bride was very pretty; she managed to look suitably sad, as is the custom in Bangladesh. Sari-clad Lynne also looked beautiful and seemed quite at ease in her attendant's role.

A few days later our family traveled north to Chittagong City to have some fun. There the children browsed and shopped in various stores and bazaars for mementos to take back to the U.S. Then, with special permission, we traveled deep into the Chittagong Hill Tracts to the capital city, Rangamati. We had been invited by the new young king of the Chakmas and the Chakma royal family for a three-day extravaganza in appreciation for our care for Debapriyaw Roy, a fellow-member of their royal family. We ar-

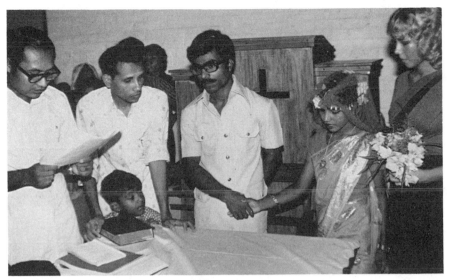

Wedding ceremony

rived in town after dark and met Debapriyaw's sidekick, our friend
Babul, who was the "secretary of the Reception Committee." He
took us to one of the new, attractive tourist cottages overlooking
Kaptai Lake, the immense body of water that had formed behind
Kaptai Dam. Babul presented us with a detailed, typed program
for our three-day stay.

The first morning we visited a tribal hand-loom factory and
sales room. The skillful weavers knew how to make their shuttles
fly incredibly quickly. We enjoyed a cup of tea at the sales room
where Joan and the children made purchases. Next we had tea at
the home of a friend. I had removed an ugly birthmark from the
forehead of her beautiful baby daughter some months earlier. So I
did a follow-up examination on the baby and was pleased with the
surgical result.

At midday we crossed a channel by boat and arrived at the
rajbari (king's house). The previous rajbari had been unexpectedly
submerged when Kaptai Lake was allowed to rise behind Kaptai
Dam. We wondered who had been responsible for that miscal-
culation.

We were greeted warmly by Raja Devasheesh Roy, a teenager
wearing jeans and a plaid shirt to make our teenagers feel comfortable. We were also greeted by the young king's grandmother,
Queen Mother Benita Roy, the member of the president's cabinet
who had come to Malumghat originally to request us to care for
Debapriyaw. We were also introduced to the young king's mother
and other members of the royal family.

Babul,
secretary of the Reception Committee

The young Chakma king,
Raja Devasheesh Roy

While we enjoyed an extravagant meal, royal family members thanked us for treating Deb, for saving his life, and for training him in laboratory science. These Buddhist tribal leaders seemed unruffled by the fact that their Debapriyaw had become a follower of Christ, because one's religion is a personal matter and because many members of a number of tribes in that region of Bangladesh and India are Christian people.

After lunch the young king led us on a hike to the closest Chakma village. Then we returned to visit the royal Buddhist temple; there the Queen Mother prostrated herself before the great brass image of the Buddha in an act of devotion and respect. Back at the rajbari we talked the afternoon away. Also I examined two family members as patients and presented inscribed copies of the brand-new standard Bengali New Testament to the Chakma king and other members of the royal family. They seemed pleased to receive this Scripture and talked of the day when Debapriyaw would complete the New Testament in the Chakma language. That night, after dinner at Deb's home, we presented four more standard Bengali New Testaments at that gathering; again there were warm expressions of appreciation.

The next day we visited the shop of a craftsman who made bracelets, rings, and other items out of ivory, then enjoyed tea at two Chakma homes. I had operated on one of these wives, and this home visit gave me an opportunity to check up on her progress. She presented to Joan a beautiful hand-woven Chakma sash, while her attractive daughters paid attention to our teenagers—especially Mark.

That night at the Tribal Cultural Institute we were the guests of honor at a tribal cultural show that had been prepared expressly for us. Tribal girls approached and gave us flowers. Then Babul made the opening speech, recounting Debapriyaw's terrible injury, his hospitalization, and the care given him by our medical staff. After the speech several musicians sang and played their numbers. In one sequence four attractive Chakma young women sang while four others in full costume danced a classic Chakma dance. Then someone sang a newly composed song about Debapriyaw and his physician. Next a hilarious comedy skit panned doctors and their foibles. The finale was a fascinating "bamboo dance" in which Chakma girls danced intricate patterns, somehow avoiding long bamboo poles clashing about their feet. The whole cultural show was outstanding and very enjoyable.

As the next day was Sunday, we worshiped in the morning with a small band of Christian people on the verandah of one of their homes. After the leader finished directing the Bengali hymns and giving his message in Bengali, he requested me, also, to minister to the people. So I selected a text from the standard Bengali New Testament, gave a brief exposition of it, and applied it to our lives as people living day by day in the nation of Bangladesh. After-

Vic presents a copy of the New Testament
to the queen mother, Mrs. Benita Roy

Chakma girls performing the bamboo dance

ward we all enjoyed tea together, and I treated members of the group who required medical attention.

Later, by request, we went to the Buddhist temple so that I could examine the chief Buddhist priest. He was an elderly man with an enlarged liver and spleen. Among other things I prescribed a high protein diet and explained that the best sources of protein are meat and fish. This caused some consternation, for these Buddhists were not accustomed to killing or eating any living thing. They finally decided, however, that it would be acceptable within their rules for the old priest to eat meat because he was sick and the meat could be viewed as medicine. I was happy for the chance to help the old gentleman, and we had a worthwhile talk.

We finished our last morning in town by enjoying more teas in Chakma homes. Finally, after lunch with Debapriyaw and his family we departed for home. But not far out of town we encountered two elephants, with mahouts on board, ambling along the roadside. So we stopped long enough for Lynne and Mark to enjoy elephant rides, then resumed our journey. It seemed that we reached Chittagong, then Malumghat, more quickly than usual, for there were so many events of our unique weekend to discuss and relive in our absorbing conversation along the way.

At the end of July Lynne and Mark said good-bye to their friends, packed their bags, and we flew with them to Dacca. There we participated in a Bangladesh Bible Society-sponsored dedication service for the new standard Bengali common language New Testament. After the president of the Bible Society opened the meeting, the general secretary gave a well-deserved eulogy of translators Lynn Silvernale, Mrs. Dass, Mr. Dores, and Samuel.

Lynne and Mark took elephant rides

Dr. Sam and Karen Logan

One of the other three addresses was my responsibility; to introduce the translation to the Christian community, I spoke on "Why a Standard Bengali Common Language New Testament for Bangladesh?" After the singing of some classic hymns of the faith and a dedicatory prayer, the general secretary formally presented inscribed New Testaments to leaders of various Christian denominations. It was our hope and prayer that the translators' labor of love would have wide use and influence throughout the land. At the same time Joan, Samuel, and I were further inspired to press on with our work on the special Bengali version of the New Testament.

Two days later we said our good-byes to Lynne and Mark, then put them on their flight back to the United States. Upon our return to Malumghat we greeted Dr. Sam and Karen Logan, who had come to provide short-term surgical and nursing help for a full year. And we read Dr. Donn Ketcham's freshly written newsletter with much empathy. Here is part of what he wrote:

> I am still dripping from the shower and I haven't combed my hair yet, but I've just gotta sit down and write this while I'm in the mood. Do we give you the impression that missionary life is ALL victory and roses and light? Well, then just let me describe to you the last twenty-four hours.
>
> This run of testings started with a case in surgery yesterday. The patient was a sixteen-year-old refugee from Burma. She had surgery in Burma and came to me with a severe respiratory problem. I took a look down her windpipe yesterday and discovered she had a very weird disease which caused airway obstruction about which I could do nothing. The stress of the exam itself caused her to go into heart failure and she died. Still feeling the sense of frustration of that case, I made rounds this morning and found Oncherai, our beloved Tippera evangelist, quite ill, and I can NOT figure out what's wrong with him.
>
> My wounded medical ego was joined by a whole bee's nest of stings this afternoon. My car battery went dead. I put in another battery. It wouldn't charge. . . . [Finally I got] the car started. The thing wouldn't go into gear. With the offer of help from two others, we opened up the clutch to find that moisture from the monsoons had swelled the plate until it simply split in two. In order to get a good look at it, we needed a flashlight. We own six. Not ONE would work. We needed a ratchet wrench. I own TWO—not one could be found. I then went to the storeroom to get a spare clutch plate. The door was locked. Whoever was there last broke off the key in the lock. I broke the lock. I discovered termites in the storeroom. I also discovered that when I had ordered a spare clutch plate, they had sent me a pressure plate and not a clutch plate.

Then the storeroom door wouldn't close without repair. I hopped on the motorcycle to head back to the house and the cycle ran out of gas.

We chuckled and remembered a few such days in our own history.

We learned from Donn and Wendy that Oncherai, the "apostle" to the Tipperas, was now seriously ill. Each day while we were gone Wendy had brought him milk and other special foods to help him try to gain strength. By then Donn had diagnosed an unusual, exceptionally severe intestinal infection; despite powerful medicines his condition was deteriorating at an alarming rate.

That night, at Wendy's request, she and I visited Oncherai, prayed with him, and I read to him from the Bengali Bible the beautiful Psalm 103. That wonderful smile of his played about his lips as I read about the gracious benefits and unique promises of the Father, who "crowns you with lovingkindness and tender mercies." I went on to read about His forgiveness of our sins and failings, the fleeting nature of life, and the stunning truth that "the mercy of the Lord is from everlasting to everlasting on those who fear Him." He loved those words and our moments together.

In the early morning hours Oncherai's intestine perforated and his consciousness faded into stupor. Donn took him to the operating room and made a valiant attempt to repair the damage; during the operation he had to bring him back from a cardiac arrest. Despite these herculean efforts Oncherai sank lower, and the next day he died. We delayed the burial as long as possible, hoping that Jay Walsh would return to Malumghat in time, for Jay was Oncherai's teacher and the two men had been very close. But in Bangladesh, where there are no embalming facilities, deceased persons must be buried within twenty-four hours. Sadly, Jay could not get back in time for the funeral.

The following morning, church leaders lovingly placed Oncherai's body in a plywood box covered with a blue cloth. The homemade coffin was lashed to two wooden poles to help the men carry it to the cemetery a mile or so away. Under a black sky and in drenching rain a party of about a hundred people accompanied the coffin across the highway, through a forest area, across a bridge over a rushing stream, past numerous rice paddies, through the Muslim village, on through the Christian settlement, and up over a hill to the church's new graveyard.

The stark hole in the ground was obviously too small for the coffin, so we watched as men chopped away at the slippery earth until the hole was big enough. As the crowd huddled together against the driving rain Tippera tribesmen sang great hymns of the faith in their own minor-key style; the rest of us then sang Bengali

Crossing the bridge with Oncherai's casket

Robi's farewell to Oncherai

hymn songs. Robichandro Tippera especially grieved the loss of his "big brother." Next Pastor Dewari preached an uplifting and comforting graveside sermon. After his message the thoroughly soaked crowd looked on as the coffin was lowered by ropes into six inches of dirty water at the bottom of the grave; tears mingled with rainwater on many cheeks. Then I worked with Tipperas and others to fill in the hole with mud. Finally we erected a crude wooden cross at the head of the grave. We had laid to rest a great soul, one of God's special servants. Despite the darkness, the slashing rain, the mud, and the tears, there was light and life and hope in the message we heard and the songs we sang.

That night I spent time with Oncherai's family. The youngest son was out of his head with grief. His mother, a rock of stability, said to the boy, "Daniel, there is no need to cry for your father, since he has gone to a far better place. But it is all right for you to cry for us, because we will miss him so—and because now it will be very difficult for us to live." I comforted the family the best I could.

The next morning I attended the tribal Sunday service. Robichandro Tippera, who had been studying the Bengali literacy course, astounded me by reading from the new common language Bengali New Testament; he had at last become literate! He proceeded to preach in Tippera from his text, which was the passage about the raising of Lazarus. Oncherai's wife and eldest son were composed enough to follow the victorious message, but the youngest son was still so dazed by grief that he could not concentrate. My heart ached for him.

There was other hopeful news, as well. On August 3, while Oncherai was still struggling for life, just before midnight Samuel had finished writing out the final verses of draft one of the whole special Bengali common language New Testament. Wonderful! Over the next months we would analyze, refine, test, and complete drafts two and three prior to publication.

During the first half of August the two political alliances that had contested the presidential election were crumbling, and President Zia's main opposition, the Awami League, split into two factions. However, the split did not prevent the AL from agitating vociferously against the Zia regime. The AL leaders continued to demand an inquiry into the murder of the father of the country, Sheikh Mujibur Rahman. And on August 15, the third anniversary of the assassination of Mujib, the AL organized a noisy demonstration and demanded that Mujib's assassins be put on trial.

Back at Malumghat Wendy continued to get much pleasure out of her work at the hospital. One evening she came home quite excited—and a bit unnerved. As she was walking home a majestic leopard had exited from some underbrush on our grounds and walked slowly and silently across the road in front of her, then disappeared into the forest beyond our boundary line. What a sight! She was also busy several evenings a week teaching English to Shantosh, a teenager from a Hindu family who was also Mark's good friend. Those lessons helped Shantosh pass his final high school English examination with good marks. Later, at a church camp, he decided to become a follower of Christ the Lord. Dr. John Bullock ultimately took him under his wing and trained him to be a capable orthopedic assistant.

About that time the church was preparing for annual elections of church leaders. Samuel somehow got the idea that missionaries had become improperly involved in those elections, which were purely the national church's business. In fact, he made an angry speech on that subject in a church meeting and exploded about it to me; we had a long discussion about the problem—and his rather extreme reaction to it. He finally decided that he had overreacted and made appropriate apologies. A few days later he was elected as one of the three pastors of the church. He would have to learn a great deal to carry out his new responsibilities in a wise and mature way.

Wendy tutored Shantosh

While the church election drama was taking place a short-term surgeon was settling in. A note came around to all of our houses asking if anyone had any size 12 rubber thongs to give or loan to him. One wag had written on the note being circulated, "Sorry, we left our skis at home in the States."

In late August Joan, Samuel, and I traveled to Chittagong for a meeting on translation matters. After the meeting, while Joan and I were driving to the guesthouse, suddenly a rickshaw driver began pounding noisily on the back of our car to get our attention. Pulling over to the curb I stopped, and out of the rickshaw stumbled the Kutubdia carpenter—with bandages encircling the stump where his right hand had been severed at the wrist. His face contorted with grief, he cried piteously and came to me with his bandaged stump outstretched. What could have happened to him? I embraced him, comforted him, put him into the car, and drove him to our mission office. There we heard his story.

After he had stood before the judge in Cox's Bazar and had withdrawn his complaints against the hospital and mission, he returned to Kutubdia Island. There his four brothers and some other extremists castigated him and told him to leave the island because they disliked his religious views—and because he kept pressing two of his brothers for the 6,000 takas they owed him.

On the other hand a local official, the Union Council chairman, defended him, saying that the brothers should pay what they owed, and explained, "According to Bangladesh law, a person's religious views are his personal and private matter and a citizen is free to follow any religion and live where he wants to live." The chairman voiced the views of the great mass of the law-abiding citizens of the island.

Despite the Union Council chairman's accurate ruling on the law of the land, in mid-August the carpenter's several enemies decided to take matters into their own hands. They drank enough liquor to give them "courage," then seized him and beat him with sticks and iron rods; they also beat his wife and children and threw them out of the house.

The assailants then took the carpenter's money, gagged him, tied him, and beat him harder. After a smashing blow to the base of his neck, one attacker shouted, "Don't kill him. Let's just cut off his right hand so he can never work again!" So the six drunken men held his arm down on the boards of a wooden bed, then began chopping with a heavy *da*. The first blow cut off his fingers, the second cut partway through his hand, and blow number three severed his whole right hand at the wrist. While blood spurted from the ragged stump his enemies quickly tied his arms around a leg of the heavy bed, then fled.

The carpenter was sure he would die from blood loss if he did not get help quickly. So, with a superhuman effort, he wedged a shoulder under the massive bed and lifted it just enough to pull the rope underneath the leg. Then he ran from the house trying to scream through the gag in his mouth. A helpful neighbor came to his aid; he bandaged the stump tightly enough to stop the bleeding, then took him by rickshaw five miles to the nearest police station. The carpenter begged the police to send him to Malumghat Hospital, but the police told him, "No, you have caused the people of that hospital so much trouble they probably wouldn't even accept you as a patient." So they sent him by motor boat to a hospital in Chittagong City.

After two weeks, in utter discouragement he had signed himself out of the hospital, hired a rickshaw, and started riding, sick and dizzy and not sure just where to go. Just then, remarkably, the rickshaw came up right behind us, and the driver began pounding on our car. Our hearts ached for this poor carpenter, whose means of livelihood had been destroyed by a chop of the *da*. We comforted him, fed him, prayed with him, arranged a room for him that night, then sent him to the hospital early the next morning for an operation to improve his stump.

Like the carpenter whose life was crumbling, the alliance of political parties that had helped Zia win the presidency was also coming apart at the seams. So on the first day of September President Zia officially launched a new political party named the Bangladesh Nationalist Party (BNP); this new party replaced the several parties of his alliance. The BNP was a wide-spectrum nationalist party based on the ideology contained in Zia's nineteen-point manifesto and open to rightists, leftists, and centrists. Because he appealed to members of other parties to join him, some of those parties began to split over whether or not to unite with the BNP. With the splintering of various parties and realignments of many politicians, the political scene was becoming increasingly chaotic.

Back at Malumghat, some days later, I received a note from a Bengali Roman Catholic priest located in a town named Bandarban in the Chittagong Hill Tracts. The thoughtful note said that he was sending a monkey to us in appreciation for our service to patients from his area. A few days later a man appeared with a brown short-tailed monkey on a rope. Because it was gentle, cuddly, and very cute, Wendy was thrilled to have it. And so we added to our family the perky little monkey named "Lambray," a Tippera name given by his original owner.

The perky little monkey named Lambray

The next day Wendy and some of her friends tried to give Lambray a bath—with zero success. He seemed to be highly "allergic" to both soap and water. Later the girls gave him a sedative from a sleeping capsule dissolved in Koolaid and attained partial success in the bath routine. Lambray was quite proud of himself when he got his own little house on top of a wooden post in the backyard. His high perch gave him a nice view, shelter from the rain, and safety from the jackals that sometimes ventured into our yard at night.

The next Sunday we arrived home from church to find a man squatting on our porch, sobbing piteously. He was a friend, a very poor man from a nearby village, whose daughter had just died in the hospital. He did not even have the few takas needed to bury her. We comforted him as best we could and gave him the money for her burial. The extreme poverty of so many of the people of Bangladesh is a heartbreak we never get used to.

In early October Jack Archibald and I again flew to Dacca to solve a new problem. We urgently needed some short-term workers from the United States who were champing at the bit to come, but the government had notified Jack that it would require four months to process their visa applications. In Dacca at each involved ministry we were able to approach upper-level officers who kindly expedited their ministry's approval, then allowed us to hand-carry the papers to the offices of the next ministry. This seemed to work out each step along the way, so that in short order the visas were approved; the short-term workers could come immediately. The four months had somehow shrunk to four days. "Thank You, Father!"

A few days later Dr. Joe and Joyce DeCook departed for the United States. Joyce had been troubled for more than two years with the most severe case of Chittagong perihepatitis we had seen. The DeCooks had decided that a change of climate and scenery, plus some sophisticated blood tests, might be useful. The four De-Cook children would remain behind at Malumghat to continue their studies; Mary Lou Brownell and Linda Short would move in to mother the children and keep the household operating. If Joyce improved, they would return in a few weeks to complete their term of service. Otherwise, Joe would return at the end of the school semester, pack up, and take the children back to Michigan, where they would settle. Our prayers were with them.

During the second week in October I had a fascinating plastic surgery operation to perform. Mrs. K., a noted radio vocalist, had first come to us as a private patient several months earlier with a tragic story. When the eczema on her foot did not respond to creams and ointments, a radiologist had given her X-ray treatments. Sadly, the dose of X rays had been so extreme that her foot was horribly damaged. A huge ulcer on the upper surface exposed dead tendons, while another deep ulcer on the bottom of her foot also extended nearly to the bone. She was greatly agitated because an amputation had been recommended. "Oh, Doctor, can you save my foot?" she cried.

"I think so," I replied, "but it may require a year of treatment. Are you willing to cooperate with several operations over such a long period of time?"

"Oh, yes, I'll do anything to save my foot!"

So the treatments had begun. In several sessions I trimmed away dead tendons and tissues until the ulcers were clean, but by that time the bone was exposed on the upper surface of the foot. This meant that an ordinary skin graft would not suffice, for it would not take on bare bone; a "cross-leg flap" would be necessary. So, a month earlier, I had mapped out on her good leg the flap of skin I would need to ultimately bring living tissue to her damaged foot; in the operating room I cut this rectangular flap on three sides and underneath, leaving it attached only on the fourth side. Then I sutured it back in its bed; it had remained this way for a month to allow the blood supply of the fourth side to increase.

Now it was time to go back to the operating room for the main operation. I recut the flap mapped on her good leg on the three sides and underneath, then brought this flap across to cover the exposed bone on the damaged foot and sutured it in place. Finally, I placed ordinary skin grafts on the raw area of the good leg and applied plaster casts and rods to hold her legs firmly in position so they could not possibly move and destroy the grafts.

After she had lain a month in this awkward position, the cross-leg flap had "taken" and nicely covered the ulcer and bone. I could then cut the base of the flap from the good leg and get rid of all the plaster and rods, to Mrs. K.'s great relief. Only time would tell whether the ulcer on the sole of her foot would continue responding to ordinary treatment, or whether it, too, would ultimately extend to the bone and require a second cross-leg flap.

One day in October, while Mrs. K. was lying in the hospital, Mel Beals and his daughter Kim took a walk in the nearby forest. Near the path they found three baby wildcats with big, pointed ears nestled in the grass; delighted, they carried these tiny orphans home. Kim and Wendy fell in love with the soft, helpless wild kittens and worked out an arrangement whereby Kim would keep them all day, and Wendy would keep them at night. Soon the baby wildcats' eyes began to open, and they seemed to thrive on non-mother's milk.

A few days later more than a dozen Murung Christian leaders emerged from the jungles of the Hill Tracts and hiked to Ma-

Two baby wildcats

lumghat. They had been invited by Jay Walsh to come and discuss their latest problem. They explained that a number of Murung Christian women were afraid to participate in the Christian ceremony of baptism. As the leaders discussed this matter back and forth, they were able to put their fingers on two major reasons behind the problem. First, the young Christian women were told that if they were baptized they would never find marriage partners. And, secondly, animistic Murungs had warned Christian women that if they should be baptized, then commit any sin, they would die on the spot. What a fascinating cultural problem! Jay guided the Murung leaders in a study of the Scriptures to combat the misinformation that was making these Murung women of the jungle so frightened. The leaders were greatly relieved when this teaching produced results.

The Bengali Bible training program at Malumghat, although beset by many obstacles, continued to function effectively. Not only did every course have to be written from scratch, but for each course a new textbook had to be created or an English language text had to be translated into Bengali. And the most recent course had a special twist: it was written as a "programmed instruction" course. This meant that the course could ultimately be studied by new leaders in outlying areas with much-reduced teacher involvement. Mel Beals and Linda Short played key roles in preparing and organizing the teaching of this first programmed instruction

Murung woman and child

course. Four mission men and three national women (trained by mission ladies) did the teaching; more than a hundred Bangladeshi men and women completed the course.

By the end of October the short-termers whose visas we had obtained arrived at Malumghat. Bob Anderson, a young man with mechanical skills, would work in the hospital Maintenance Department. Hal and Chick Youmans and their two children would also serve at Malumghat; Chick began supervising the guesthouse whereas Hal, an accountant, immediately phased into running the hospital's business office. This freed Dr. Dick Stagg to resume his medical work and teaching in the men's Bible training program and also allowed Linda Short to return to her work with the women and their Bible training program. At the same time, the Bullocks returned to Malumghat to begin their second term of service. John would resume his orthopedic surgery practice, which would help many and further enhance the reputation of the hospital.

Just at this time a new and different kind of crisis struck. A faithful employee came, called me out of a meeting, and breathlessly exclaimed, "I am afraid that some hospital employees have secretly formed a union. I accidentally saw some of their letterhead paper, which even lists a government registration number. That means that it must be an established union, officially registered by the government. I have learned that they plan to spring the union on you in a day or two—on payday. I can tell it is going to be a very bad union, not a helpful one."

This timely warning was a great help, for it gave us time to think through what to do. We decided to give our staff the opportunity on payday to sign the new, updated employment policy we had produced and refined over the preceding several months; that might give us an idea whether or not some of the employees really were enemies bent on causing trouble. So the next day we mimeographed copies of the new employment policy and the signature sheets. The following morning, payday, an announcement was made to the staff that the time had come for them to read and sign the updated employment policy when they picked up their pay.

Then pandemonium broke out. Because some of the new rules worked against them, the union leaders lost their composure and began to shout and threaten the employees. "If you sign that policy paper, we'll beat you senseless—we'll kill you!"

Another screamed the communist slogan "Workers of the world, unite!" Others shouted insults against the hospital authorities. This furious demonstration was so intimidating that only ten employees came to pick up their pay that day and sign the employment policy; a few others later came secretly to say they wanted to do so but feared for their lives.

The raging union leaders insisted that employees must not come to work the next day, and one sneered at a missionary supervisor, "If your employees come to work tomorrow, the pathway to the hospital will run red with their blood!"

This outburst was so fierce and broke so many provisions of both the old and new employment policies that we suspended a half-dozen ringleaders on the spot. It turned out to be providential that these men lost their composure, reacted so violently, and had to be suspended. We certainly would not have suspended them for forming a union, but we had to do so for their dangerous, threatening behavior. And once they were suspended they were no longer on the inside, receiving wages and creating inner dissension.

The next day some of our employees showed up for work, but others were too frightened to come. We soon learned that the head of the union group was an out-and-out Communist; paradoxically, he was one whom we had treated with special kindness, for when his job had been phased out we bent over backward to find a place for him in another department. He and the other union leaders were non-Christian men who were determined not only to force drastic changes in salaries and working conditions but also to shut down the mission's spiritual work. Had the union been led by honorable men who had come together to carry out normal and reasonable collective bargaining, we would have reacted in quite a different way. But now we found ourselves locked in a real struggle.

Hospital watchmen collected their pay

The next few days were marked by ongoing tension and more threats, like "You'd better stay inside your house at night if you want to stay alive!" and "We might not hurt you—but then there are your daughters." One employee was cruelly beaten. On a showdown day we had the police present so that fearful staff members could pick up their pay and sign the employment policy.

During that period our Medical Committee was meeting every day, sometimes for hours, to deal with new union problems that erupted daily. Because of the great blocks of time required to deal with the ongoing crisis and because of the loss of the suspended staff members, we finally had to close the hospital down to "emergencies only" status.

Then we learned that some of our Christian staff members were rather sympathetic to some of the union ideas. So we had long discussions with many of them to understand their concerns and complaints. Many expressed one particular fear—inadequate job security. We discovered that in this area our compassion had backfired. Previously, whenever we had to discharge an employee for theft, immorality, or inability to do the job, we considered the reason for dismissal the employee's private matter and never publicized the person's fault; we did not want to ruin his or her reputation. But, we learned, dismissed employees usually told everyone that they were fired for no reason at all. So the impression gained ground that anyone could be discharged without cause; they concluded that they had no job security. We reassured our employees, whom we valued so highly, that their jobs were indeed secure as long as they did their work and followed the rules of employment. And, from that point forward, we posted on the employees' bulletin board the exact reason for any employee's dismissal.

To overcome our lack of experience and knowledge about union and labor laws, we searched for resource materials and persons. Donn Ketcham traveled to Dacca to learn what he could about whether charitable hospitals such as ours were subject to or exempt from union activity; the officials he met in Dacca could not give him a clear-cut answer on this.

Then we learned that one of the foremost labor lawyers in Bangladesh, Mr. Rashiduzzaman, had his offices in Chittagong City. Three weeks into the crisis Joan and I traveled to the city for a lengthy meeting with this attorney. He was an intelligent man who had a thorough knowledge of all the labor laws. We found that he also knew something about our hospital by reputation. We filled him in on many more details of how we operate as an organization, how our policies work for the benefit of our employees, the unexpected registration of the new union, and the harsh developments since that day. Then he exclaimed admiringly, "You have done amazingly well in a very difficult situation; there are several places you could easily have gone wrong." And I thought, *Thank You, Father, for hearing our prayers and guiding us amateurs aright!*

Then Mr. Rashiduzzaman, in turn, briefed us on the relevant laws, the strengths and weaknesses of our hospital system in relation to those laws, and the additional steps we would need to take to overcome the problem of the hostile union. Joan took careful shorthand notes throughout the morning-long interview. But only after she read her notes back to him was he satisfied that we had grasped all the complexities of his information and advice. We thanked this gracious man for all the time he had given us and for his wise suggestions.

We then returned to Malumghat to report to the team and put into play what we had learned. To consider the suspended employees for actual dismissal according to Bangladesh law, we would have to issue "charge sheets" to them, receive their written defense, then allow them to give their verbal defense before a council made up of mission personnel and other employees; the council would then hear any witnesses for and against, then recommend to Medical Committee what action should be taken. So we proceeded along those lines.

Soon the suspended employees were threatening and terrorizing the eleven witnesses who could give damaging testimony against them. To their credit, the eleven remained firm and, because of their courageous testimonies, the suspended men were finally discharged from employment according to the laws of the land.

Although threats and demonstrations continued, the union's strength seemed to be waning slightly—at least for the time being. But we continued the struggle on three fronts:

1. Continued working with Mr. Rashiduzzaman to see if the union could be legally deregistered through the Chittagong Labor Court
2. Began negotiating in Dacca with the Department of Labor and the Ministry of Law regarding the legality of forming a union in a charitable institution
3. Set up a council to hear our employees' complaints and suggestions on a regular basis

In mid-November in Dacca the Bangladesh government had a fresh surprise for us—a new law entitled The Foreign Donations Regulation Ordinance, 1978. This ordinance was designed to regulate the donations that we and other voluntary organizations received and to monitor how this money was spent. In addition we would have to gain a new registration from the government to carry on our work. Furthermore, the government could at any time send officers to examine our account books and other documents. It was clear that the government would be keeping mission societies and other voluntary organizations under a much tighter rein than ever before. We could not predict whether we would encounter any difficulty obtaining this new registration. Time would tell.

A few days later Bangladesh gained some further prestige on the global stage. Despite being a poor third-world developing nation, Bangladesh was elected to a two-year term on the powerful Security Council of the United Nations. The majority of the world's nations preferred to elect Bangladesh rather than wealthy and powerful Japan, which also was competing for this important position. Apparently Bangladesh obtained most of the votes of other Muslim countries and other nations of the nonaligned block.

By mid-November most of the Burmese Bengali refugees in our unofficial camp had transferred to one of the government camps so that they could be processed to return to their homes in Burma. Only one subleader remained, and he continued to come faithfully for instruction in the Scriptures he had come to love.

Then one day Mr. U. appeared unexpectedly on the scene. He looked well, and we were delighted to see him again. He had finally been able to return from Burma to Bangladesh and was now staying in a government camp with many of his former flock. He was faithfully teaching them and others the Scriptural truths he had learned. When he departed our good-byes were poignant, for we were unsure whether we would ever meet again in this world. "Father, watch over Mr. U. and shower him with your mercy and lovingkindness," was my prayer, "and help him to get his property back in Burma and to steadfastly continue his teaching there." If he did continue his teaching in northern Burma, he would be sharing Christ's good news message in a closed area where no foreign missionary could possibly go.

In late November Joe and Joyce DeCook returned from the U.S. Joyce's Chittagong perihepatitis was considerably improved by the rest and change of climate. What a joyful reunion they had with their four children! Our prayers had been answered and a weight somehow lifted from all of our hearts.

On the first day of December President Zia announced that in late January 1979 elections would be held for a 300-seat Parliament (with thirty additional seats reserved for women). Very soon a dozen major opposition parties threatened to boycott the election unless Zia agreed to their five demands. Meeting them halfway, Zia accepted some of their points:

- He amended the Constitution to repeal the "undemocratic provisions" of Sheikh Mujib's much-criticized Fourth Amendment, which was still on the books.
- He promised that the new Parliament would be sovereign and have substantial powers.
- He gave up his post as army chief of staff.

With these concessions, after much haggling, a few of the opposition parties finally decided to take part in the elections.

Also in early December, I had more plastic surgery to do. The patient was a nine-year-old boy from another district. He had been born with a double cleft lip and a cleft palate; the lip had been repaired in infancy by an inexperienced doctor with a very poor result. Not only was the upper lip badly deformed, but the left nostril was far larger than the right. With two incisions I opened up the lines of the original two clefts, evened up the nostrils, then trimmed, fit, and sutured the two cleft areas. There at the operating table I was satisfied with the result—and even more pleased two months later after healing was complete. Soon the boy would return for repair of the cleft palate.

The next day the discharged union leaders attempted to launch a wild demonstration in front of the hospital, but the effort fizzled. By this time our employees were reassured about their job security and convinced that we were sincerely doing the best we could for them. But still the union leaders were not ready to give up. Off the hospital property they continued to periodically harass our employees.

Although the union problems had upset the work of Malumghat Hospital, they did not deter the church people from working steadily on the new church building near their homes in the Cha Bagan Christian village. In the early weeks we had all labored together, carrying building materials from the roadside for nearly a mile to the construction site. Men and women, adults and children, Bangladeshis and Americans, Bengalis and tribals again and again made the long hike with building materials in their hands, on their backs, or atop their heads. I have a vivid mental image of a two- or three-year-old toddling down the path holding a single brick on top of his head. Some of the men worked out ways to carry heavier loads by wagon, bicycle, motorcycle, and jeep. It was a great mass cooperative effort that made a tremendous impression on the community.

Once the materials had reached the church site Pastor Leslie, who was also head of construction at the hospital, expertly supervised the men in the laying of bricks and the wood framing. Now the workers were making a great effort throughout December to

Roofing the new church building

The new church—finished by Christmas!

finish at least the walls and the roof by Christmas. And they succeeded. The Christmas worship service held in the new building was a time of immense satisfaction and great joy. What a triumphant way to close out 1978 after a year of crisis and struggle!

Our family Christmas celebration was also a special delight because our Nancy had arrived just before Christmas with a friend. On the first weekend after Christmas we traveled again to the refugee camps, which were still jam-packed with the Bengali refugees from Burma. Despite the agreement between Burma and Bangladesh to repatriate the refugees, these displaced people were afraid to return to the land of Operation Dragon. Only a few refugees had returned to Burma and the rest were waiting to see how they fared. Perhaps their fears would be put to rest in the upcoming year.

Joyous Christmas service

Key Events of 1978: Summary

January
- The home secretary requests treatment for his daughter.
- President Zia returns to Bangladesh after a successful tour of Nepal, India, and Pakistan.
- We rejoice when our eldest daughter, Wendy, appears unexpectedly at Malumghat; she serves in the hospital.

February
- Zia encourages his vice-president to establish the new JAGODAL political party; it later disintegrates.
- Joan and I attend a unique conference in Bermuda.
- We participate in our mission's round-table conference in the U.S.
- Jay and I meet with Bangladesh's Ambassador Siddiqi in Washington, D.C.

April
- 200,000 Bengali refugees from Burma pour into southern Bangladesh; the government sets up eleven refugee camps.
- Elephants invade the Cha Bagan area near our hospital.

May
- We send food and supplies to the Burmese refugee camps.
- I kill a cobra in our house.

June
- Presidential election; Zia wins a landslide victory.

July
- I operate on a woman with a cannonball tumor in her chest.
- Burma finally allows the Burmese refugees to return home.
- Fiscal year 1977-78 statistics are better than usual.
- But figures for the first Five-Year Plan period are poor.
- Our family visits Rangamati in the Hill Tracts at the invitation of the Chakma king for a three-day extravaganza.
- In Dacca the Bangladesh Bible Society hosts a dedication service for the new standard Bengali New Testament.

August
- Our team completes draft 1 of the special Bengali NT.
- Tribal leader Oncherai Tippera dies.

September
- Zia launches his own Bangladesh Nationalist Party (BNP).

October
- A hostile hospital employees' union is formed; the union leaders create an ugly scene and threaten our staff.

November
- The government enacts the worrisome Foreign Donations Ordinance, requiring us to be registered all over again.

December
- The church at Cha Bagan completes the walls and roof of their new church building in time for Christmas services.

Figure 29

12
1979: New Parliament—New Scriptures

On New Year's Day a middle-aged man was admitted to the hospital with a surgical emergency that we did not often see in Bangladeshis—acute appendicitis. He had been suffering for five days, so was extremely ill. At the operating table I opened his abdomen and found double trouble. Not only had the inflamed appendix perforated but, in addition, infection had spread throughout his abdomen. To set things right I had to remove the appendix and clean up his whole abdominal cavity.

The next day a twenty-year-old woman arrived with the same symptoms—lower abdominal pain for five days. Sure enough, at the operating table we discovered a nearly identical case of appendicitis with perforation that required the same treatment. Quite unusual! Despite their serious conditions both patients finally recovered fully.

Although we would wait months for the next case of appendicitis in a Bangladeshi, within a few days American teenager Joanie Eaton developed the same disease. But what a contrast! She came for help immediately, not five days later. And the operation was neat, clean, and simple.

A few days later Donn and I operated on the brother of the Deputy Director of National Security Intelligence (NSI), the CIA of Bangladesh. Presumably NSI has detailed files on all of us foreigners who live and work in the country. There must have been something good in those files to influence this senior officer to select us to operate on his own family member. At the operating table we opened the patient's chest, diagnosed cancer of the lung, and carried out the appropriate procedure; he was soon able to return home.

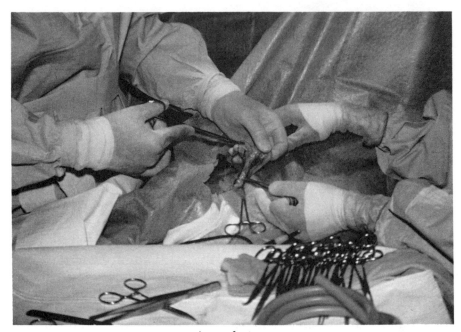

Appendectomy

While we were busily operating at Malumghat a hopeful President Zia opened up his political party's election campaign at a mammoth public meeting in Dacca. He not only extolled his new BNP party but also reiterated the concessions he had made to the opposition parties to encourage all of them to participate in the electoral process. Within a few days several more of these recalcitrant parties decided to take part in the parliamentary elections. Because time was short, they had to work frenetically to select candidates to stand for election in the 300 electoral districts.

During the second week in January septuagenarians Harold and Marie Wolters, after an eight-month absence, returned from the U.S. to Chittagong to complete the construction of the new literature/translation/administration building. During their absence the project had been stalled for months because of a legal dispute over the title to the land. After that problem was finally cleared up, our co-worker Reid Minich capably supervised the construction project until the Wolters returned; their return freed Reid to proceed to the U.S. on his regular home leave.

At Malumghat Dr. Dick Stagg, our team's most disciplined jogger/weight lifter/physical fitness buff, went down for the second time with infectious hepatitis; he turned nearly as yellow as the saffron robes of the local Buddhist priests. Our Bangladeshi staff members were sure they knew the cause of the problem: "If Dr.

Stagg would stop doing all that harmful heavy exercise, he would be more healthy."

By this time two new career workers had completed language school and settled in at Malumghat. They were Edie Phillips and Joyce Rudduck, both capable, well-trained school teachers. Edie would focus primarily on teaching upper grade children of the American staff; during some periods she would also act as a Field Council secretary. Joyce would teach American children and also provide training and counseling for Bangladeshi women and young people.

During January we continued to take our visiting children on weekend trips. First we traveled to Cox's Bazar by road to enjoy the beach, the ocean, and shopping for Burmese handicrafts. The next weekend we traveled by boat up the twisting Matamuhuri River to explore Hebron Station.

Finally, on their last weekend in Bangladesh we obtained permission to revisit Rangamati, the capital city of the Hill Tracts. Again our friend Babul organized for us a delightful weekend. We found the annual *mela* (county fair) in full swing and enjoyed the many colorful booths and the small zoo. At night there was a major cultural show featuring the fascinating songs and dances of several tribal groups. On our last day we hired a speedboat and driver to take us across Kaptai Lake and back; we reveled in the forest- and jungle-covered hills rolling down to the shoreline, for they were verdant and beautiful.

Very early the next morning we drove to Chittagong City to put Nancy and her friend on their flight to Dacca and the United States. What a delightful month we had enjoyed together! The only blot on their vacation was that a suitcase filled with Christmas presents was missing upon their arrival in the country. All were disappointed that the airline had been unable to locate it during the subsequent four weeks. As we checked them in for their Dacca flight an airline staff officer hurried over to announce, "The missing suitcase arrived in Dacca two days ago." As soon as Nancy

Edie Phillips teaching high school student Tim Golin

Joyce Rudduck working with Shantosh Master

Nancy in a sampan on the river trip

Nancy and Wendy at Rangamati

Tribal dance at Rangamati

reached Dacca she cleared the bag through Customs, then sent it to us on the evening flight. So everything worked out in the end—and we enjoyed an extra Christmas celebration.

Not long after we received the suitcase full of Christmas gifts, we were able to give another kind of gift to a poor village child who had never heard of Christmas. He arrived at the hospital at night, carrying a kerosene lantern, with a cow and a newborn calf in tow. The little calf had the same abnormality that plagues an occasional human newborn—imperforate anus. Wendy, who happened to be at the hospital, hurried home to implore me to try to help the poor little boy—by helping his poor little calf. Although I was a bit skeptical, we headed for the hospital to have a look.

We left the cow with its owner standing outside the hospital and took the calf to an inside verandah. As I tried to examine the skittery little guy it kept bawling loudly; outside, the worried mother continued to moo back even more noisily. Their stentorian calls ringing out through the quiet hospital halls seemed loud enough to wake the dead; they certainly did abruptly awaken all our sleeping patients. As quickly as possible I gave the calf an anesthetic injection; soon its frightened cries became weaker, then ceased.

Next, surrounded by amused hospital personnel, I examined the now-quiet calf more thoroughly and discovered that the defect was a type which did not require a major abdominal operation; a more simple operation would suffice. So I carried the patient, with its long legs sticking out in all directions, to a table in the plaster casting room. There I called for suitable instruments and began the procedure. After opening the blocked anal outlet, I carefully sutured the raw edges. The staff people looking on thought the whole affair was hilarious. Yet they well knew that the death of a calf is a major loss to a poor family.

A little later, when my small patient with the long ears and twitching tail awakened from the anesthetic, it immediately picked up where it had left off after the injection. It resumed bawling to its mother outside the hospital. Again, sleeping patients on the wards sat bolt upright in their beds, wondering drowsily whether they were in a hospital or a barnyard. Then we took our postoperative patient outside and explained to the boy that his calf should be all right now. One look at the lad's smiling face made the hour's work completely worthwhile.

The next week trouble struck our mission team—and our translation project received a shattering blow. Samuel, so capable and competent in his translation work, yet so mercurial and unpredictable, had allegedly slandered two mission men and some Bangladeshi nationals. The slander was serious enough that the whole Field Council gathered together, heard the evidence, and dismissed Samuel. Joan and I were in shock. As we moved numbly

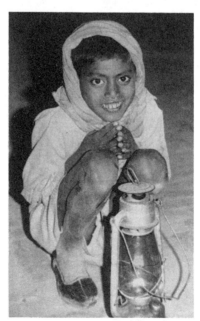

"One look at the lad's smiling face . . . "

toward the door to go home, wondering how to rescue the special Bengali translation project, our co-worker Lynn Silvernale stepped across the room and offered, "If there is anything that Mrs. Dass and Mr. Dores can do to help, you can feel free to make use of them." What a thoughtful, helpful offer to ease a painful moment! Although they did not speak the special Bengali of the translation, there was one aspect of our remaining work for which we could use translators Mrs. Dass and Mr. Dores to excellent advantage.

By early February the hospital workers' union was further weakened by internal strife. The communist leader had split with the other union leaders and returned to his own village near Chittagong City. Shortly after he reached home his baby boy had become ill and died; despite his enmity we, too, felt the pain of his loss.

I next traveled to Chittagong and Dacca to pursue the question of the legality of the union. I found the Labor Department officials in Chittagong City strongly pro-union; although I could make no headway with those men, I was able to be of help to their director, who was ill at home. When I visited him there I discovered that he was suffering from infectious hepatitis and depression; I was happy for the opportunity to lift his spirits and prescribe for him.

On to Dacca. There I made more than one visit to the Ministry of Law to ferret out any legal precedents that might bear on our case. Fortunately, I picked up some clues that there had been a case or two in which unions formed in charitable institutions in Dacca had later been disallowed by the Dacca courts.

With this information in hand I approached the minister of labor, Mr. Shah Azizur Rahman. Neither he nor I knew during that interview that in just a few days he would unexpectedly become the prime minister of Bangladesh. He listened carefully to my pitch, noted the material I had uncovered in the Law Ministry, and agreed wholeheartedly that there should be no trade union in our hospital. He then ordered the officials of his ministry to track down the legal precedents and set the wheels in motion to have the union deregistered; he sent me to those officers to work out the details.

I learned from these men that the Labor Ministry would locate the previous court actions, then order their labor director in Chittagong (my patient) to petition the Chittagong Labor Court for permission to deregister the hospital workers' union. Only this particular court had the authority to grant that permission. Time would tell how long this complicated procedure would require, but it appeared that we could possibly succeed—even though the Chittagong Labor Court had never before granted permission to deregister a union.

While in Dacca I was acutely aware of the political fever gripping the city. After President Zia's long parleys with opposition leaders, making further concessions to them, and twice postponing the elections to give them more time, almost all of the opposition parties had finally agreed to take part in the parliamentary elections. That would give the elections real legitimacy.

Arrayed against Zia's BNP party were the Awami League (two factions) and three alliances of multiple parties—a far right alliance, a left-leaning group, and a mixed coalition. Now more than 2,000 candidates put up by thirty parties were campaigning vigorously for the 300 seats in Parliament.[1] It was quite inspiring to see and feel it happening—and to remember that an army general holding dictatorial power had organized this democratic election. Quite unusual!

The other person who was making it happen, on the practical level, was Jalal, who was still secretary of the Election Commission. He and his officers worked long hours allotting election symbols to the various parties, designing the ballots, and caring for a hundred other details. Early on, he sensed that radical leftist trade unions might try to frustrate the election by taking the workers of the government presses out on strike; if this ploy were to succeed there would be no printed ballots on election day. Cannily Jalal met with the government printing press workers, gave them a motivational speech about the importance of the election, appealed to their patriotism, and promised a big bonus for good work on their part. What a wise move! A few days later the labor unions did try to convince those same workers to strike, but failed miserably. The workers liked Jalal's proposal far better.

February 18—election day at last! More than 19 million Bangladeshis made their way to the polling stations and cast their votes. Here are the results of that election:[2]

Parties	Seats
BNP (Zia's party) (207 + 30 = 237)	237
AL (Awami League—main faction)	39
ML-IDL (rightist coalition)	20
JSD (far left party)	8
Other parties	10
Independent candidates	16
Total	330

Several things were clear from the election results. Hitchhiking off President Zia's popularity, his BNP party had gained 207 seats, more than two-thirds the total. Because the thirty so-called "women's reserved seats" were elected by the Parliament, not the public, the dominant BNP obtained all thirty of those seats for BNP women. This gave them 207 + 30 = 237 seats (more than 70 percent).

But that left a significant opposition with some strong, articulate opposition leaders in the new Parliament, who would be able to keep the BNP on its toes. The Awami League (main faction) gained the most opposition seats. They were followed by the rightist coalition; its parties were making a comeback after being barred from elections during the Mujib era. Jalal was relieved and pleased that the elections had taken place quite smoothly. And we were happy for him—and for the fresh buds of democracy sprouting in the People's Republic of Bangladesh.

On March 4 many of us gathered in Chittagong City for a special occasion—the dedication of the new literature/translation/administration building to be known as the Bible Literature Centre. The occasion was especially meaningful for Jeannie Lockerbie, head of the mission's Literature Division, who had been the sparkplug behind the building. Her vision and promotion had initiated the project; then many others became involved in praying, fundraising, and actual construction.

Literature Manager John Sircar opened the dedication service, detailed the history of the Literature Division as it outgrew its facilities three times, then showed samples of old and new pieces of literature that had been produced. The ABWE Literature Division

The new Bible Literature Centre

had become the largest producer of Christian literature in Bangladesh.

Then it was my turn to represent the translation work and explain the high importance of the two new common language translations of the Holy Scriptures. These translations in the heart language of the people would be foundational to every phase of our future work in the land of Bangladesh. Because they were so readily understandable, these Scriptures would bring God's Word to the minds and hearts of the multitudes with new freshness and vitality.

Engineer Harold Wolters then told of his sense of God's call to twice cross the seas to supervise the construction of the building; he called the whole experience "the highlight of my life." All this was spiced with hearty singing, salted with dedicatory prayers, and sweetened with Bengali candies and cakes. Thus the beautiful new building was joyously dedicated to the glory of God.

Two days later I received a repentant letter from Samuel, who had returned to his home. He spoke of a spiritual experience that had taken place that very day. He referred to the Biblical episode of Christ opening the eyes of a blind man. He then explained that the Lord had likewise opened his spiritual eyes and continued:

> Now I can see clearly. Now I can see how deeply I hurt you! Just because of my conduct you suffered much because you love me. In many ways I caused you trouble. Sometimes you groaned in the spirit because of my rude nature. In many ways I was unfaithful to the Lord. Several times I told you that I loved the mission—but I failed to love the missionaries. I was a hindrance to the Lord and now I see everything properly. I have committed myself to the Lord for the second time. But will you forgive me? Can you? Yes, I know you will. Please let me know your reaction.

As I finished reading the letter I remembered the words of Jesus:

> Take heed to yourselves. If your brother sins against you, rebuke him; and if he repents, forgive him. And if he sins against you seven times in a day, and seven times in a day returns to you, saying, "I repent," you shall forgive him.[3]

I wrote back words of forgiveness.

To try to compensate for the loss of Samuel we decided to make several major adjustments. We upgraded two men, Hassan and Shamshul, who had long been involved in the project, to share in vocabulary decisions and proofreading chores. We used Shantosh Master, a Malumghat-based translator of Bible Institute

We upgraded Hassan

Translators Mrs. Dass and Mr. Dores

courses, to help produce the first Bengali draft of the glossary and introductions to the New Testament books. Also, we utilized Chittagong-based Mrs. Dass and Mr. Dores in our checking and refining of these sections. And, of course, Joan and I picked up much of Samuel's work ourselves.

Providentially, I could again work full-time on the translation project, for our doctor coverage had suddenly improved remarkably. Donn Ketcham's and John Bullock's vacations were over, short-termer Sam Logan had come, and Joe DeCook had returned from the U.S. Dick Stagg, after two back-to-back episodes of ordinary hepatitis, had just resumed his medical work, and a senior medical student would soon arrive to help out.

During this period Jesse Eaton was teaching a particularly popular seminar on "family life" from the Scriptural perspective. At Hebron Station he had taught the seminar in a concentrated way over several days. Now at Malumghat ten young Bangladeshi church couples were taking the classes at Jesse and Joyce's home at a more leisurely pace and profiting greatly from them. Ultimately, Jesse's notes were upgraded from a seminar to a course in the Bible Institute program at Malumghat.

But for Gonochandro, an old friend and respected Tippera leader, family life was only a memory; for two months he had been languishing in a prison at the town of Alikadam deep in the Hill Tracts. He had been accused of aiding and abetting the Shanti Bahini guerrillas who were fighting for the independence of the Hill Tracts. "No," he insisted when questioned by the police, "I have never given them anything unless forced to do so by their armed men." But they did not believe him. So, in the ancient apostolic tradition, he used his time behind bars to share Christ's good news message with other prisoners.

Meanwhile, the members of the mission and scores of congregations in the hills and on the plains prayed earnestly for his release. More than once he faced special dangers, but each time at the last instant he escaped them. Finally, he was pardoned and released; soon he arrived at Malumghat with that big, warm smile of his intact, and his faith strengthened by the ordeal. Then he traveled back to his home in the hills, where he talked in a kindly way to the enemy whose lies had been responsible for his imprisonment. This foe was so moved by Gonochandro's faith and sweet spirit that he, too, became a follower of Christ.

By that time Menshai Murung, like Robichandro, had completed the Bengali literacy course and could read the standard Bengali common language New Testament. An impressive accomplishment! This greatly facilitated his ability to feed his own soul and minister to his people.

*Malumghat doctors Donn Ketcham, John Bullock,
Vic Olsen, Dick Stagg, and Joe DeCook*

Jesse and Joyce Eaton

Also during that period, Jay Walsh was teaching theology to Debapriyaw to further prepare him for his Chakma Bible translation project. Simultaneously, a clinical laboratory was under construction on Deb's property in Rangamati; he would support himself by using his laboratory technician skills. Later in the year he moved back to Rangamati, began his work, and married a fine, educated Chakma girl who had responded to his teaching and become a follower of Christ the Lord.

In Dacca President Zia had his hands full. Very quickly he would have to hold key meetings of his political party, constitute the new Parliament, then select a prime minister and his cabinet. To set up the Parliament he needed a highly competent senior civil servant to be the secretary of Parliament; this man had to be someone who could command the respect of the elected members of Parliament and be able to organize all the rules and regulations and the physical arrangements for the first session of that legislative body six weeks hence. You guessed it—he selected Jalal for the post. Jalal began immediately to assemble the nuts and bolts of the brand-new Parliament to be known as the National Assembly.

During the final days of March President Zia met with his BNP party leaders to finalize the agenda for the upcoming session of Parliament and to select those who would be ministers in the cabinet. On the last day of the meetings Zia announced to the press

Mr. Jalal Ahmed, Secretary of Parliament

that his prime minister would be Shah Azizur Rahman, the former labor minister who had helped us deal with the union problem.

The Awami League and other opposition parties bitterly criticized this appointment, saying that Mr. Rahman was so pro-Pakistan that he had even been imprisoned for his sentiments. And they wondered how he could now become the prime minister of Bangladesh when he had so opposed its very existence.[4] Shah Aziz, a skilled debater and parliamentarian, had a ready rebuttal against these charges.

The prime minister in Zia's government would have quite a different job description from that of the prime minister in the original Awami League government of Sheikh Mujib. In Mujib's "parliamentary system" of government the prime minister's post had been the power post, so Mujib became the prime minister; in that system the president was but a figurehead. But Zia's "presidential" pattern of government was more like the French system, with a powerful president who was both the head of state and the head of government—and a less significant prime minister who was the spokesman for Zia and his government in Parliament, the "connecting link" between the president and the Parliament.

About that time I took a rough ten-hour train trip from Chittagong to Dacca because there were no plane tickets available. In Dacca I spent many hours with the leaders of the Bangladesh Bible Society, making decisions about the special Bengali New Testament cover, page size, margin size, type styles, and other key points. And I handed over to them the finalized manuscript for the first two books of the New Testament.

While I was in Dacca I examined a brand-new language student: nurse Ila Pechumer from Michigan. Her abdominal pain was severe enough that I sent her to Malumghat for observation and possible surgery; there she had an appendectomy. Later, despite a sharp case of Chittagong perihepatitis, she completed language study and served well in the hospital for some time. However, health problems finally made it impossible for her to remain overseas. But this did not keep her from continuing to help the people of Bangladesh. On the home front she began working with others to receive hospital supplies, then organize and ship them to us at Memorial Christian Hospital.

As I was leaving Dacca Jalal said to me, "The government is inviting you to attend the opening session of the new Parliament." I demurred on the grounds that it would be impossible to get a plane ticket to return to Dacca in time. Jalal replied, "We will arrange the plane ticket and send it to you. You must be present in Parliament for this historic occasion!" I gladly accepted.

Back at Malumghat I again plunged into our translation work. At that point Joan, Hassan, and Shamshul were checking the scores of details on page after page of the manuscript. While I shared in this checking process, my main focus was preparing the preface, introductions to each New Testament book, glossary notes, and maps. We reasoned that these reader's helps would play a major role in helping the understanding of Bangladeshis reading the New Testament for the first time.

As March was drawing to a close we received a welcome letter from the Ministry of Labor in Dacca. The letter officially declared that our hospital would not be subject to labor laws; this made us exempt from trade union activities. What great news! Still we hoped to see the union legally deregistered so there could be no possible confusion on this point in the future. And we wanted to win a pending lawsuit against the hospital that had challenged the dismissal of one of the union leaders.

On the last day of March I was notified that my airline seats were arranged. The following day I flew to Dacca to attend the inaugural session of the new Parliament; the next morning a government driver and car picked me up quite early to take me to the Parliament Building in good time. I entered the building very conscious that I was representing the staffs of our hospital and mission and the members of our Bangladeshi churches. A gloved officer resplendent in a white uniform looked at my engraved invitation, then showed me to my seat. I was astounded to see how we had been honored in the seating arrangement. The director of the United Nations and I were the only foreigners to be seated in the president's box to the right of the central dais. The dozens of ambassadors of foreign nations and other foreign dignitaries were seated in another gallery to the left of the central platform.

The dais, made of polished teakwood, was high, massive, and striking. On its upper level was a seat for the speaker of the House. At the lower level were the chair and desk of the secretary of Parliament (Jalal). The great auditorium was attractively appointed, and the 330 seats for the parliamentarians were ready for occupancy. The television cameramen and still photographers were busily working with their equipment, for this historic event would receive massive media coverage.

While the cameramen were finishing their final preparations in the main auditorium, Vice-President Sattar was administering the oath of office to the new members of Parliament in another room on the premises. But the vice-president was having his problems. Fifty-three opposition members were steadfastly refusing to take the oath of office, insisting that the oath should be given by the speaker of the House in the main auditorium. Obviously, the opposition was in a feisty mood.

Finally, when all those members of Parliament who had taken the oath of office filed into the main auditorium and took their seats, fifty-three opposition seats still remained empty. Jalal was at his desk up front, and the vice-president took the chair as temporary speaker of the House. But when he began speaking in English his voice was drowned out by a sudden uproar. "Speak in Bengali! Speak in Bengali!" shouted the congressmen. The vice-president then conducted the election for the speaker and deputy speaker of the House—in Bengali! The speaker chosen was M. G. Hafiz, a former minister and a friend who had visited our hospital along with his daughter, who was a physician. During a recess the speaker and deputy speaker were sworn in.

Following this recess the newly elected speaker took the chair. This time the fifty-three opposition members were present, but remained standing; they could not legally occupy their seats until they had taken the oath of office. The majority of them were obviously Awami League members, for over their white clothing they wore dark vests known as "Mujib jackets." And pinned on their jackets were large badges with Sheikh Mujib's picture on them.

The leader of the opposition was the Awami League's Mr. A. Khan; Jalal had seen to it that he was accorded, for the first time in the history of Bangladesh, the same rank and privileges as a minister of the cabinet. Mr. Khan loudly protested that the oath of office must be given in the main auditorium; therefore, he said, the swearing-in ceremony that had taken place in the other room was illegal. He demanded that the speaker give him and the others the oath of office there in the main Parliament auditorium.

Immediately pro-government members noisily objected to this irksome demand. Arguments and counter-arguments flew back and forth, and confusion reigned for at least thirty minutes, then began increasing in intensity; the speaker was unable to maintain proper order. Seeing no other way out of the dilemma, Jalal sent a note to the speaker advising him to declare a recess.

During that recess Jalal "talked turkey" to Mr. Khan and his colleagues; because they respected Jalal they listened to his words, then entered into the speaker's chambers and took the oath of office. Later, as soon as all the members took their seats, opposition leader Khan requested the floor, then demanded that a large picture of former prime minister Sheikh Mujibur Rahman be placed in the front of the auditorium. The speaker agreed to put that request on the agenda a day or two later. There were more arguments and counter-arguments, but this time they were less explosive and more short-lived.

Near the end of the morning session the body elected the prime minister and two deputy prime ministers. The new prime minister was Shah Azizur Rahman; one of the deputy prime ministers was attorney Moudud Ahmed, an acquaintance and the law partner of our legal advisor. The new Parliament had made a boisterous beginning but, I reminded myself, that was democracy in living color. We recessed for lunch.

After the midday meal we returned to hear President Zia's inaugural speech to the new Parliament. As his vehicle approached the Parliament Building a corps of trumpeters standing on the roof of the building sounded a bold salute in clear, piercing tones. Zia entered the dais from a door behind the speaker, then walked forward; we all rose to our feet. He stood there for a moment, ramrod-straight. Because I was standing very near him I could see that he was deeply moved as he looked out into the eyes of the members of his new Parliament; the muscles of his face tightened as he clenched and unclenched his jaw. After a band played the stirring tones of the Bangladesh national anthem we took our seats.

Then Zia proceeded to the microphone and gave a detailed and very significant speech, which lasted nearly two hours. He began with these words:

> *Bismillahir Rahmanir Rahim* [In the name of Allah, most gracious and merciful].
> MR SPEAKER AND HONOURABLE MEMBERS,
> On this historic occasion today I, on behalf of the eighty million people of Bangladesh, offer my infinite gratitude to Almighty Allah. It is only through His bounteous grace and the sincere efforts put in by all the people of the country, irrespective of caste, creed, party or opinion, that it has now been possible to hold this session of the second Parliament of the independent and sovereign Bangladesh.[5]

He went on to pay tribute to prominent Bangladeshi patriots of the past. He spoke of the three objectives of his own life and detailed the steps his government had taken to improve conditions in Bangladesh. Then he pointed out unfinished work to which the new Parliament must address itself. And he concluded with these words:

> Mr Speaker and Members of the Parliament, before I conclude, I would like to mention that the great responsibility which I had to shoulder as President for the last 23 months has been greatly unburdened with today's opening of the Parliament.
> Not only the people of Bangladesh but also of the whole world are observing your activities with keen interest, because this Parliament is the nerve centre of politics in Bangladesh.
> Let the beginning made by you today be auspicious and the constant welfare of the eighty million people be your noble mission.

Let us resolve to build up a democratic Bangladesh. Allah will help us. *Khuda Hafez* [God be with you]. *Bangladesh Zindabad* [Long live Bangladesh]![6]

His speech finished, Zia acknowledged the applause, then turned and walked out the door at the back of the dais. He spoke to only one person before entering his car; with much emotion he embraced Jalal just outside the door and exclaimed, "You have given me my dream!"

As soon as the afternoon session closed I spent some time talking with Vice-President Sattar. Then Speaker Hafiz collared me and took me to his office to have tea with him, his wife, and his physician daughter. He thoughtfully asked about the well-being of our hospital and staff. Later I enjoyed more tea with Prime Minister Shah Azizur Rahman, who also asked about the hospital and our progress in getting the workers' union deregistered. Others stopped in that office for tea, too, and we found the prime minister to be a highly entertaining person with a keen sense of humor. With his sharp wit and parliamentary skills, I suspected he would be able to handle whatever the opposition might dish out.

Although I returned to Malumghat the next day, the Parliament continued meeting for a week. Those sessions were marked by many more arguments, counter-arguments, verbal altercations, and repeated calls to order by the speaker. Opposition members staged three separate walkouts, but they were not carried out in a united way; smaller groups walked out over varying issues.

The Awami League continued to demand that Sheikh Mujib's picture be displayed at the front of the Parliament auditorium. Then the leader of the Muslim League insisted that Bangladesh be declared an Islamic republic based squarely on Islamic religious faith. And the far-left JSD party repeatedly demanded that the government release its members who had been imprisoned for revolutionary activities. But the government firmly resisted all these demands.

The Parliament did pass the substantive, but somewhat controversial, Fifth Amendment to the Constitution. The amendment validated all the martial law orders of the last three and a half years; that prevented a legal vacuum by giving the government an ongoing set of laws to use in governing the nation. The day after Parliament passed the Fifth Amendment President Zia, true to his promise, withdrew martial law and resigned from the army.

When I returned to Malumghat I learned that many of the staff had watched parts of the first day's session on the television set in the employees' club. Frequently the TV cameras focused on the president's box where the UN chief and I were sitting. That had brought great pleasure and a sense of pride to our whole staff; then in the evening some staff members had brought Joan and Wendy to the club to view the proceedings on the TV evening news. I made reports of my trip to the hospital staff and to our Field Council, which was then in session, and answered the many questions people asked.

During those Field Council meetings a special tribute was paid to the single women of our mission team. And what a wonderful group of ladies they are—so committed, so competent, so valuable to our work! Their citation read this way:

> Whereas: The single ladies on this field have proven to be the most congenial colleagues, and
>
> Whereas: The single ladies on this field have continued to make contributions to the work that are among the most important of all contributions made by our team,
>
> Therefore: The married members of this Field Council pass this resolution whereby we express to them our deep love and appreciation and our thanks to God for the honor of serving by their side.

I can think of no citation more deserved than that one.

Special commendation was also given to Jay Walsh for his new book, *Ripe Mangoes*.[7] The volume contains vignettes of the lives of a number of Bangladeshis who are true followers of Christ the Lord. Jay's chapters on their life experiences make fascinating reading. It had been a privilege for me to write the foreword to his fine book.

In early April a cataclysmic event took place across India in the country of Pakistan. Two years earlier the Pakistani people had castigated their prime minister, Mr. Bhutto, for rigging elections. Finally the army took over and, to control the upheaval, declared martial law. Later Bhutto was imprisoned on charges of complicity in the murder of a political enemy; the Pakistan High Court had convicted him on that charge and the Supreme Court upheld the conviction.

U.S. president Jimmy Carter and other heads of state from all over the world pleaded for his life—but to no avail. On April 4 at 1:10 A.M. guards informed Bhutto that the hangman was waiting. After shaving his ten-day growth of beard, he recited verses from the Koran while a guard was tying his hands behind his back. The court's so-called "black warrant" was read out, and Bhutto began the long, bleak walk to the gallows. There he climbed the steps to the ten-foot-high platform and cried, "Lord, help me, for I am innocent."[8] Then the hangman carried out his grim task. The execution of Bhutto reverberated across the subcontinent and around the world for many days thereafter.

In Bangladesh the people remembered that Mr. Bhutto had forcefully opposed their movement for autonomy and had refused to receive tens of thousands of non-Bengali Biharis who had opted for Pakistan. But they also recalled that Bhutto had released their Sheikh Mujib from a Pakistani prison. The Bangladesh authorities said little about the execution of Bhutto.

In mid-April the government's sizable forty-two-member cabinet was sworn in; during the following months this number was gradually increased to sixty-three. Apparently President Zia selected such a huge cabinet to reward the several blocs and groups within the BNP party; after all, it was an extremely broad-spectrum party and there was bound to be much competitiveness among its diverse factions.

About the time Zia's cabinent was being sworn in, at Malumghat a young woman with highly unusual symptoms was admitted from the Outpatient Department into the hospital. Sympathetic Wendy spent a long time helping and comforting this very ill young woman. Then a ward nurse learned from a family member the disturbing information that the woman had been bitten by a *pagol kukur* (rabid dog) several weeks earlier. The patient was suffering from rabies (hydrophobia)—a 100 percent fatal disease. Within a few hours the lady died.

We felt sad for this woman and her family, and we were concerned about Wendy, for she had an open sore on her hand and she had been in very close contact with the patient and her saliva. Unfortunately, we had neither the anti-rabies serum (for immediate protection) nor the latest vaccine (for long-term protection). So immediately Wendy and I headed for Dacca. After several frustrating experiences we finally found what we needed at the United Nations office; the UN doctor kindly supplied us so that Wendy's rabies exposure could be properly covered. "Thank You, Father!"

Wendy was further traumatized that week when her monkey, Lambray, became ill and died. Seeing that she was grieving, our Muslim gardener discreetly buried the pet, then consoled Wendy with the words, "Don't feel so sad. I took him out and buried him properly—the same way I would bury a Muslim person."

Across the subcontinent in Pakistan the government continued to be bedeviled by violent demonstrations in the wake of the Bhutto execution. In that troubled environment, in the city of Islamabad an unusual meeting of three men was taking place. They had in common that they were all Bangladeshis—and that all three had been majors who had taken part in the "majors' coup," during which Sheikh Mujib had been assassinated nearly four years earlier.

All three men—the "second team" of the mutinous majors —had been given excellent posts in Bangladesh embassies abroad. Dalim had come from China and Pasha from Turkey to meet with Huda who was serving in Pakistan. Apparently they were not satisfied with these comfortable assignments in their country's foreign service and still nursed a desire to someday take over in Bangladesh. This thirst for power had never slackened, but somehow time and circumstances had changed their political ideology; from right-wing militarists they had by then become left-leaning socialists. To capture power from Zia's government they decided to establish a political party supported by an underground organization and leftist cells in the Bangladesh armed forces.[9]

Next Dalim flew to Iran to meet former major Nur, the officer who had reportedly pulled the trigger on Mujib.[10] Dalim updated Nur, and together they devised a set of codes the four men could use to communicate with each other in the days ahead.

Dalim and Pasha then flew to Dacca, where they successfully recruited two lieutenant colonels to begin setting up the leftist cells in the army. Dalim and Pasha also enlisted two leftist civilians and held discussions with Communists from the JSD and Shorbohara parties. The two visitors from abroad insisted that it was necessary for leftist groups to put aside their doctrinal differences and start working together in a united way, or they would never plant socialism in Bangladesh. The conspirators would not meet again until the end of the year.

Oblivious of all this dark plotting in Dacca, in May our mission purchased two and a half acres of beautiful rolling hills between Malumghat and Chittagong for a campground; Bob and Barb Adolph had been the visionaries behind this project. In the years to follow many young people would go to camp, have fun, and also make life-changing spiritual decisions. About the same time, the church in Chittagong joyously held their first service led by their new pastor in a new church building on a new plot of land. These were powerful developments in the life of the church in our region of Bangladesh.

In mid-May at Malumghat we learned something about other kinds of power. Our brand-new generator, which provided electricity for both our hospital and housing areas, simply died; its breakdown was sufficiently serious that it could not be repaired by ordinary measures. We would have to live for some time with the erratic and inadequate electrical power produced by the nation's electrical company.

Bob Adolph with boys at camp

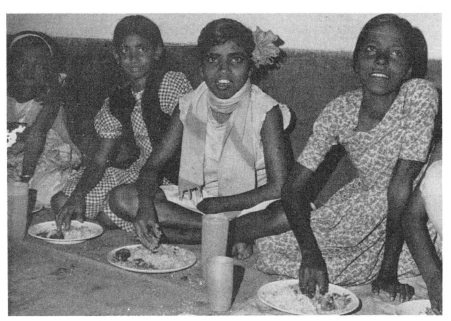

Chow time at the girls' camp

But a few days later we suddenly had more electrical energy than we wanted. During a monstrous evening thunderstorm a bolt of lightning streaked across the dark sky and struck a tall, stately tree standing ten feet from our carport; the tree was deeply gouged down two sides and chunks of wood covered the ground and the carport. The lightning traveled along a root of the tall tree, damaged the concrete carport slab, and blew the screens out of our nearby kitchen verandah, knocking the breath out of the startled cook and houseboy. Because the lightning surge also exploded the light bulbs in that half of the house, the men were plunged into instant darkness.

The strike also sent sparks dancing along the wiring to the ceiling fan of the room at the far end of the house, where it sizzled and spat sparks at Joan sitting there under the fan. At the same time a second bolt of lightning hit the wiring to the Bullocks' house and actually melted one of the burners in their electric range.

Much later, a large fireball popped out of the supercharged wall of our bedroom, leaving an acrid smell behind. Fortunately, no one was injured in either house, but the surge burned out our housing area water pump, creating a water shortage on top of the electricity shortage. Days later the generator, water pump, and electric range were finally repaired. But the danger and shortages reminded us to be thankful for safety, water, and electricity—"ordinary" things we so often took for granted.

By this time the special Bengali Gospel of Luke had been completed and was selling very well. And the Bangladesh Bible Society had hired Samuel to supervise the typesetting of our full New Testament manuscript in Dacca. Once or twice a week he would send completed material to us on the Bangladesh Biman airline flights to Cox's Bazar. These "formas" were very large pieces of paper, each of which contained eight pages of text. As soon as our messenger brought them to the hospital we would proofread them with care, mark our corrections, and send them back to Dacca on the next flight. It was essential to keep this revolving process moving quickly, for the press had only a limited number of lead type pieces to use. As soon as the type was perfectly set on a forma, it was printed out on beautiful white paper; then the type was reused by the typesetters for the following pages.

At that point our daughter Lynne was on the verge of graduating from her five-year nurse's training program in the U.S. Of course, we were eager to be there on that very special occasion to support her and be a part of that graduation. She had done an outstanding job. But, with the presses rolling inexorably in Dacca, we could not both leave the printing/proofreading process. So we decided that I would be the one to go for the graduation.

A few days later I headed for Dacca to pick up my overseas flight. But somehow I left my suit coat behind. Joan sent it up to me on the next flight, hoping that it would reach me, but that flight was delayed in Chittagong. I kept on checking until the last moment, but no coat came through. There was nothing I could do but clear outgoing Customs and walk to the boarding line. But as I was about to enter the plane, an airline staff officer came running up with a box containing the coat—just in the nick of time! I was relieved, for I had brought only the one suit to wear at the graduation. In a few minutes we were winging our way toward Bangkok en route to California.

Lynne, Mark, and Nancy met me at Los Angeles International Airport; it was wonderful to be together again. Lynne's graduation was lovely, and she was a radiant graduate. I was so proud and happy to be there for her special occasion. My few days in the U.S. were soon over, and I flew back out across the Pacific to return to Bangladesh.

But in Bangkok I ran into a snag. Because of a tragic DC-10 crash in Chicago during the last week of May, DC-10s around the world had been pulled out of service for inspection; due to this complication my Bangkok-Dacca flight had been canceled. So I was stuck in Bangkok until I could obtain a seat on another airline's flight to Dacca. Meanwhile, unaware of all this, Joan and Wendy drove to Cox's Bazar to meet my flight due there on June 9, but of course I did not arrive. So they remained two more days, meeting each day's flight from Dacca; still I did not come in, so they returned to Malumghat. On the fourth morning, Joan again traveled to Cox's Bazar, and this time she was relieved to see me step off the plane. After her welcome she handed me an American greeting card. On the front a snappy-looking girl was saying, "We can't go on meeting like this. . . " and inside were the words, "You never show up!"

Driving home, I noticed the weather was oppressively hot because of a country-wide drought that was seriously damaging the rice crop. Back at Malumghat I updated Joan and Wendy on my adventures and told them all about Lynne's graduation. Then Wendy took me to the roof of our house to show me how quickly her most recent pets were growing. They were a wild boar piglet ("boarlet"?) and a kitten who played, ate, and slept together, blissfully unaware that they were not of the same species. They had grown visibly during the time that I was away; they must have been "eating like pigs."

On one particularly suffocating day Wendy had brought the kitten off the roof into the cooler rooms below, but our Siamese house cat, the imperious Munchkin, was indignant at this invasion of her turf. She hissed and spat and switched her tail at the intrud-

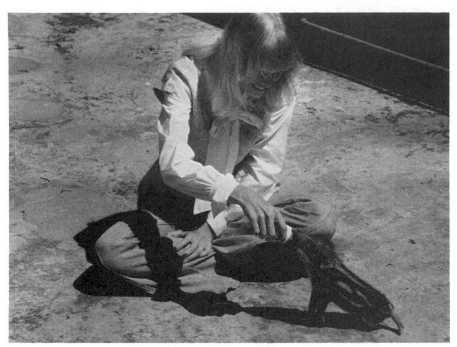

Wendy feeding her "boarlet"

Baby boar and "roof kitty"—eating like pigs

er. Oblivious of this fury, the roof kitty, who had never seen an angry cat, ambled innocently up to her and lovingly rubbed her nose. And she got away with it. Joan exclaimed, "What a great animal-kingdom illustration of the Bible verse that says, 'Do not be overcome by evil, but overcome evil with good'!"[11]

In mid-June Wendy traveled with the Ketcham family to Pakistan to revisit her high school alma mater, Murree Christian School, in the Murree Hills. With Donn Ketcham gone, Dick Stagg and I were the only physicians on deck for the next three weeks. Because my major assignment was to focus on the New Testament translation, Dick extended himself heroically to protect me for that urgent work. He took care of the outpatients, the inpatients, and although he was a family practice physician he handled 95 percent of the surgical cases. I was amazed at the fine surgical skills Dick had developed over the previous year or two—and very grateful for all the time he gave me for the translation project.

One of my few cases during that period was a twenty-one-year-old Hindu woman whose husband had attacked her with a sharp da. On examination we found a deep laceration of her neck. Also, one forearm was cut two-thirds through; the blow had cut through a bone, a major nerve, and a number of muscles. Furthermore, the wounds were filthy because some "helpful" soul had poured a black substance into them. At the operating table I care-

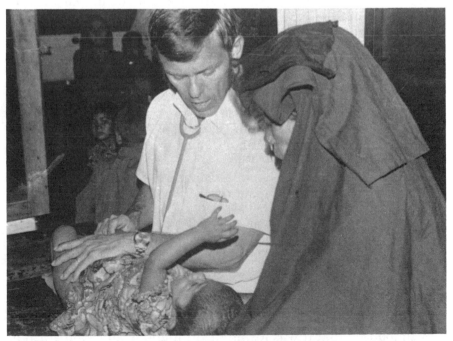

Dr. Dick Stagg examining a child

fully cleaned out the black gunk, inserted a rod down the broken bone, and with exquisite care sutured the filmy envelope around the nerve, bringing the ends together with the finest imaginable sutures. By filling her system with powerful antibiotics we minimized infection in the badly contaminated wound and she healed nicely.

We continued to suffer from the exceptionally hot and enervating weather. Clothing was saturated with perspiration in an hour's time. The days were miserable, and the nights were insufferable. When the monsoon rains finally did arrive they were too late to save the bulk of the drought-damaged crops. Already rice prices had doubled, and if the government did not obtain rice from abroad, famine would surely strike in the fall. This was a bitter blow to President Zia's plans to accelerate the rate of development of the country, for now he would have to spend the precious development dollars to purchase and import food.

Dr. John Bullock was keeping busy with the many fractures and other orthopedic cases that poured into the hospital. But one problem continued to plague his department. Many of the chronic orthopedic cases were not only time-consuming, but also relatively expensive to treat; yet many of the sufferers could not afford even the cost of the plaster or surgical supplies. So John, with the support of the Medical Committee, set up the HOPE Fund. HOPE stands for Hospital Orthopedic Patient Enablement. Those who donated to this fund have enabled many orthopedic patients to receive the plaster casts and operations they needed, as well as braces and artificial limbs. Incidentally, in mid-July the Limb and Brace Shop, which had produced many artificial legs, turned out its first artificial arm. Although the home-made double hook was a bit crude, it proved to be quite effective.

During July I visited labor attorney Rashiduzzaman in Chittagong. He had nothing new to report about the union situation but hoped the Chittagong Labor Court would take some action within the next two months. I was surprised to hear him say, "You may not know it, but your book *Daktar* and the work of the hospital team have made a great impact on me. You all are doing so much for my people and my country, while I am doing nothing. So I have decided to establish a fund and organize some projects to benefit my own people. Oh yes, when you get back to Malumghat, send me any other literature that you might have." I commended him on his generous plan to organize some worthy projects, and I did send the literature he requested.

A few days later the big news in Bangladesh—and around the world—was the American *Skylab* space station. American officials had announced that it was losing its orbit and would soon crash to earth. This news about Skylab affected people around the globe:

Some heart patients died in the Philippines, several villages in India were evacuated, [and] quacks in Sri Lanka made quick money selling remedies for *Skylab* fallout effects. Astrologers, of course, did roaring business dishing out predictions.[12]

Skylab made its mark in our locality, too. Somehow, people got the idea that *Skylab* would surely fall in Bangladesh. When our gardener sent his small son to bring the cow home, his wife refused to let the boy go out. "Our family must all be together when *Skylab* falls," she insisted. Our co-workers Hassan and Shamshul also were concerned that Wendy and I were away in Dacca; they, too, felt that families should be together under such dangerous circumstances. Everyone was much relieved when *Skylab* finally crashed to earth on July 11 far from Bangladesh.

At the end of July the wife of Shahabuddin, whose fourth wedding anniversary we had celebrated, went into labor. Because her baby was large and passing through the birth canal in an abnormal way, the mother was completely unable to deliver the child. The situation called for that excellent, life-saving operation known as a Caesarean section. Halfway through the surgery we happily presented her with a strong, healthy baby boy—to her great delight. Months later we learned that this son had turned out to be a very strong-willed child. His mother explained that this was so for two reasons: "all C-section babies are hot-tempered," and he was born on a Monday which, as everyone knows, also causes babies to be strong-minded.

While Wendy was visiting her old high school in Pakistan she had decided rather suddenly that it was time for her to say good-bye to Bangladesh and resume her college education. She had spent an outstanding year and a half at Malumghat, enjoying her Bangladeshi friends and serving our patients well, but now it was time to get on with her studies. With the return of the Bullocks and the Ketchams, there were enough surgeons on board that we could accompany Wendy to Dacca on her way out of the country. After emotional good-byes she flew off to London to visit friends, then on to the U.S.

By mid-August we were hearing that three missions were again encountering severe visa problems. This was disquieting information and would have to be investigated. At that point Jalal sent word from Dacca requesting me to come to assist the minister of the Home Ministry (previously the deputy minister), who was finding it impossible to get his son admitted to Notre Dame College in Dacca. So a friend and I started driving toward Chittagong in the pouring rain. At one place we had to push the car through calf-deep water covering the road. Fortunately, we were able to obtain seats on the evening flight to Dacca.

There I learned from Jalal, the minister, and his son several key points: despite the immense clout a minister has in Bangladesh, the home minister had been unable to get the boy admitted to the prestigious college because his marks fell just short of the required scores. But there were definite extenuating circumstances. Because the young man had most of his education in English medium schools, he was not as strong in Bengali as some other students. Despite this disadvantage he had done amazingly well. And as I interacted with the boy I found him to be alert, very bright, and highly motivated; I was sure that he could make good.

I decided against going directly to the college principal. Instead, I went to see the Roman Catholic archbishop, who had always been a friendly, reasonable person. I explained the situation, spoke on behalf of the boy, and reminded the archbishop that their missionaries and ours would have been forced out of Bangladesh except for the intervention of the very helpful home minister.

The archbishop picked up the telephone, talked to the college principal for a while, then said to me, "We agree with the points you have made, and we are allowing the boy to sit for the entrance exams; unless he does really badly he will be admitted to the college." I thanked him, then went to report the good news to Jalal and the home minister. They, too, were overjoyed. And I felt pleased that we could do something for the minister who had done so much for us and the whole missionary community.

On August 15, the fourth anniversary of the assassination of Sheikh Mujib, his Awami League party geared up to observe a day of public mourning for the first time since Mujib's death. Arrayed against the Awami League, however, were six right-wing parties, which also had organized to celebrate the historic August 15—as a "day of deliverance." But all these extensive preparations went down the drain when heavy monsoon rains throughout the day washed out all the demonstrations.

August was also the month in which the Biharis (non-Bengali Muslims), still moldering in Bangladesh, decided on a novel gambit to remind the peoples of the subcontinent about their sad plight. Eighty thousand of them started on a so-called "long march" that would take them fifteen hundred miles across Bangladesh and India to Pakistan, where they so desperately wanted to be. Although Indian and Bangladeshi authorities aborted their long-distance hike by closing the border, the Biharis did make a big enough splash to gain extensive media coverage. They hoped that would pressure Pakistan to make some positive decisions in their behalf.

But Pakistani leaders would not budge. They had previously received 110,000 of these people and later agreed to accept another 25,000 "hardship cases," but that was the end of it. That left in

Bangladesh some 200,000 despairing Biharis who longed to leave and migrate to Pakistan.

Back at Malumghat the hospital workers' union was falling apart. One union leader criticized another leader (the Communist whose son had died) for misusing the 19,000 takas they had collected for paying bribes. He charged that the leftist leader, instead of properly using the money to pay bribes, kept much of the money for his personal use. This was viewed by the other union leaders as being "dishonest," although it did not seem to occur to them that there was anything wrong with offering bribes to officials. By then the union was so disorganized that it failed to send representatives or an attorney to the court hearings on the two pending cases.

In September labor lawyer Rashiduzzaman wrote to inform us that the lawsuit against the hospital for dismissing a union leader had been decided in our favor. A few days later I received another letter from him, which contained the message we had been waiting for:

> I have very good news for you and the Medical Committee. On 26 September 1979 the Labour Court has finally . . . accorded permission to the Registrar to cancel the registration of the Union. I am enclosing a copy of the Court's order. You must feel great about it. It was your show all the way. Congratulations!

At last the lengthy, time-consuming, harrowing struggle with the hostile union had been fully resolved. "Thank You, Father!"

By mid-September the printing of the camera-ready copy of our special Bengali common language New Testament was really rolling. Because we and our Bengali co-workers had completed the introductions, maps, and glossary notes by then, Joan and I moved to Dacca to facilitate our proofreading operation. There we were warmly received by Mark and Ida Tucker; they insisted that we stay with them, no matter how many weeks our project required. That was real friendship!

The press was housed in a decrepit building down winding alleys and a narrow lane. What ancient methods they used! Every letter had to be set by hand. Despite using this centuries-old system of typesetting, the result was excellent because we had selected a particularly beautiful type style. The typesetters numbered as few as two and as many as eight at a time, and the output was directly related to the number of typesetters working on any given day. They were not very accurate, so we had to keep on checking proof after proof until they had each page exactly right; that often meant proofreading a page as many as eight times.

The press—down a narrow lane

"Every letter had to be set by hand"

By the end of September we were about half through. It was then time to design the cover; that job fell to Joan, the one on our team who had artistic skills. That day, as we ate lunch at the Intercontinental Hotel, she spied some beautiful archways that were part of the decor. In short order she sketched out one of the arches, then penciled in the title and an appropriate border. We turned this sketch over to a Bengali artist, who inserted the fine pen work for the background design. The final result was striking.

Then Joan produced copies of the cover using various color combinations so that we could test the public to determine which colors they preferred. The test results were quite conclusive. The people definitely preferred dark green; bright red and sky blue tied for second place.

All along during the typesetting and printing process, we had to overcome an immense number of obstacles. Often the owner of the printing company could not find enough typesetters to keep the formas coming. Then when he did have enough typesetters, the electricity would go off for hours or days, shutting down the lights and the presses. Several times the foundry was unable to produce enough type, or the type their operator produced was defective. I diagnosed the foundry problem to be the main operator, a hypochondriac. Several medical examinations and varied prescriptions kept him going until he finally provided the typesetters with enough lead type to complete their work.

Despite the obstacles, day by day and week by week we were completing formas. Samuel had the most killing job, for he stayed all the time at the hot, dingy press, overseeing the typesetters and proofreading the formas again and again. Joan and I did the final proofings because something about our background, training, and temperament made us quite accurate proofreaders.

At the end of October I flew to Malumghat for a day or two of Field Council meetings. That gave me an opportunity to make a final report on our New Testament translation project and offer our thanks to the many who had helped bring it to a successful conclusion: to Lynn Silvernale and the standard Bengali translation team; to Donn Ketcham, Jay Walsh, and Reid Minich, who constituted our special Bengali translation subcommittee; to the main Translation Committee; to all of our doctors and nurses who had graciously shouldered a heavier load to free me for the translation project; to the six short-term general surgeons who had come especially to relieve me.

Then our Field Council thoughtfully made a generous statement of appreciation for the record and for me to carry back to Joan in Dacca. This citation was especially meaningful, for there had been many hard times throughout the long, difficult process of checking the SBCL translation and completing the special Bengali translation. There were differences of opinion about the renderings of certain passages. During one period there was tension between the two translation teams, which took time and goodwill to resolve. Then there was Samuel, again and again on the verge of resigning. And his behavior had aggravated many Americans and Bangladeshis; that left us in hot water much of the time with co-workers, because he was part of our team.

In addition, the civil war and our furlough had combined to shut the translation project down for three years. And on a number of occasions I had to drop the translation work to provide medical/surgical coverage at the hospital. Yet at last it had finally worked out, and the special Bengali common language version of the New Testament was now on the verge of completion.

As soon as I returned to Dacca we became like a team of horses that pick up their pace and begin to gallop when they catch sight of the barn. With adrenaline flowing, we all operated like a well-oiled machine because the end was in sight. Then we discovered breaks in some key letters caused by defective type; Joan, undaunted by this catastrophe, put on my surgeon's magnifying glasses and, with an ultrafine engineering pen, touched up more than 7,000 letters!

By the last week of November we finally completed the camera-ready copy of the New Testament. Our decade-long grind was finished. How wonderful! "Thank You, Father!" In a few days the manuscript would be sent to Hong Kong, where it would be printed and bound.

We then returned to Malumghat and began packing furiously and closing up the house, for we had a deep desire to reach the U.S. in time to spend Christmas with our children. But we never would have made it without the support and help of several of our co-workers. Bless them! During that ten-day period we had a final meal with each of the families, including the Nuscas, who had recently returned as career workers.

When we said good-bye to the church leaders we learned about Pastor Leslie's recent activities. He had befriended a group of Hindu neighbors, who later expressed interest in learning about the Christian Scriptures. So, by appointment, he began holding Bible studies in their homes. Fascinated by what they were learning, ten of them had become followers of Christ. Not content to be the supervisor of building and maintenance at the hospital, Pastor Leslie reached out to build spiritual truth into the lives of church members—and his neighbors.

Our third term of service was now complete, and it had been a long one—nearly five and a half years. In high spirits we flew off to Dacca, then on to Hong Kong to meet officials representing many of the world's Bible societies, which would finance the printing of

Joan touched up more than 7,000 letters

Pastor Leslie

the New Testament. We also went over the manuscript carefully with officers of the Hong Kong Bible Society, for they would be shepherding the volume through the press. With all these details cared for, we flew out of Hong Kong to reach California five days before Christmas. We made it! And our Christmas celebration was especially joyous, for we were together again as a family.

During November and December, while we had been focused on producing God's Word for the multitudes in Muslim-majority Bangladesh, cataclysmic events were taking place in other Muslim nations; those events had their inevitable impact on our lives in Bangladesh. In early November fifty-two American embassy personnel in Iran were taken hostage, blindfolded, imprisoned, and insulted. This stimulated Islamic fundamentalists in Bangladesh to start agitating against Americans. The situation became tense enough that the U.S. embassy in Dacca evacuated scores of their personnel during November, then evacuated all their dependents some days later. They suggested that we would be wise to leave the country. But our work was far too urgent to consider evacuation and, as it turned out, we were never in any serious danger despite the tension in the city.

Later in November, Saudi Arabia also became a flashpoint. A band of heavily armed zealots attacked and invaded Islam's holiest shrine, the Grand Mosque in the city of Mecca. They occupied it for two weeks before they were finally driven out. A rumor out of Iran blamed this sacrilege on America's CIA. This false report had its inescapable ripple effect in Bangladesh; again, anti-American feelings began to escalate, especially in Dacca where we were working.

At that point our friend the home minister diffused the situation with cool precision. He invited the Saudi Arabian ambassador in Bangladesh to worship at Dacca's central mosque, then give a speech about what was really happening in Saudi Arabia. When the ambassador cooperated and explained that Saudi radical Islamic fundamentalists, not the American CIA, had caused the trouble, the tension quickly eased.

Christmas dawned on a shocking situation in yet another Muslim land; the Soviet army was murderously invading Afghanistan. That, of course, created a strong wave of anti-Soviet feeling among the Muslim people of Bangladesh, for they naturally sympathized with their Muslim brothers and sisters in Afghanistan.

And in Muslim-majority Bangladesh other people were on the move in December; I speak of the Burmese Bengali refugees. Their repatriation to Burma was by then proceeding smoothly and rapidly, for the Burmese government really was receiving and rehabilitating them. By the end of December the eleven government refugee camps in southern Bangladesh had all emptied out. Just a handful of refugees remained in the unofficial camp near our hospital.

In Dacca during December simmering discontent among the BNP members of Parliament broke out openly during the BNP par-

Dacca's central mosque

ty meetings. These members, led by attorney Moudud Ahmed, complained that the party was not being run in a democratic way; rather, it was a one-man show revolving around President Zia. These men enshrined their demands in a twelve-point resolution. Added to the dissatisfaction of the BNP members of Parliament was the ongoing feuding among the leftists, the right-wingers, and others in this extremely broad-based political party. A few weeks earlier this divisiveness had touched the student wing of the party—two factions of BNP students at Dacca University had engaged each other in a blazing gun battle. Zia was finding it as difficult to keep his fractious party under control as it was to deal with the aggressive opposition.

During the last week of December some of the players in the 1975 "majors' coup" again met together, this time in the capital city of Turkey. They all flew in from various Muslim nations: Rashid came from Libya, Nur from Iran, and Huda from Pakistan; Pasha lived there in the city of Ankara. Dalim was unable to obtain leave to come, and the same was true of Farook—he was still behind bars in Bangladesh. With Rashid had come a senior Libyan intelligence officer, which raised immediate questions about Libyan involvement. Apparently, the band of conspirators furthered their planning to topple the Zia government, and Rashid guaranteed that the money would be available.[13]

The Bangladesh ambassador to Turkey, aware of the meeting, sent off a dispatch to the Foreign Office in Dacca about the clandestine gathering. He then received instructions from Dacca to keep a close eye on the situation. When Pasha intercepted these instructions, he lost control and reportedly manhandled the ambassador; for some reason he was not disciplined for this gross violation of protocol.[14]

So 1979 ended on a note of intrigue. The year would, however, be long remembered as a year of free and fair elections, a new Parliament, the impressive repatriation of 200,000 Bengali refugees from Burma—and the completion of the special Bengali common language New Testament, our gift of love to the Bengali Muslim multitudes of Bangladesh and eastern India.

Key Events of 1979: Summary

January	• After losing translator Samuel, we make adjustments to try to save the special Bengali NT project.
February	• Parliamentary elections; Zia's BNP party wins big.
March	• Dedication of the mission's new literature/translation/administration building in Chittagong.
	• Zia selects Jalal to be the new secretary of Parliament.
	• The Ministry of Labor decrees that our hospital is not subject to labor laws = is exempt from union activities.
April	• At the government's invitation I attend the inaugural session of the new Parliament; Zia makes a strong speech.
	• I have valuable discussions with the vice-president, speaker of the Parliament, and the prime minister.
	• Parliament passes the Fifth Amendment to the Constitution; Zia then cancels martial law and resigns from the army.
	• Three of the majors involved in the 1975 "majors' coup" meet to plan a fresh coup in Dacca.
May	• The mission purchases beautiful land for a camp.
	• The Bangladesh Bible Society hires Samuel to shepherd our New Testament through the press in Dacca.
	• I travel to the U.S. for our daughter Lynne's graduation.
June	• A severe drought causes heavy crop damage.
	• Dr. John Bullock establishes the Hospital Orthopedic Patient Enablement (HOPE) fund.
August	• The "long march" of 80,000 Biharis from Bangladesh to Pakistan is frustrated by closure of the Indian border.
September	• The Chittagong Labor Court formally approves deregistration of the hospital workers' union.
	• We complete the special Bengali NT and its introductions, maps, etc., then move to Dacca to speed the proofreading.
	• Joan designs the cover for this unique NT; later she touches up more than 7,000 defective letters.
November	• The press completes the camera-ready copy for the special Bengali NT, and we send it to Hong Kong for printing and binding—our decade-long task is finished.
December	• All the Burmese Bengali refugees are finally repatriated to Burma from camps in southern Bangladesh.

Figure 30

13

1980: Troublesome Book— Troubled Missions

On the second day of January two events created fresh waves in the fledgling National Assembly (Parliament). In the first place, President Zia dismissed Moudud Ahmed from his post as deputy prime minister for attempting a so-called "parliamentary coup."[1] This was a matter of interest to us because Moudud, law partner of our attorney, had always been friendly and helpful to us. The president held him responsible for rallying Zia's own BNP members of Parliament to demand a more democratic system of making decisions within the BNP party and additional powers for the Parliament. So the power struggle between the legislative and executive branches of government, a struggle common to democracies everywhere, had surfaced within a few short months in Bangladesh.

Also on January 2, a new ten-party alliance of left-leaning opposition parties began to stir the same kettle; this pro-Indian, pro-Soviet coalition led by the Awami League also demanded increased powers for the Parliament. After President Zia rejected most of their twenty-four-point charter of demands, these opposition members refused to attend meetings of Parliament; some of the parties actually maintained this boycott throughout the rest of the National Assembly's eight-week session. President Zia was discovering that democracy was no bed of roses.

Back in the U.S., in early January Joan and I traveled from California to Nebraska for a happy reunion with my beloved parents. They updated us on my father's troublesome illness and told us a fascinating story. During the previous year, when Dad's respiratory problem had flared up, he was hospitalized in the small Nebraska City hospital. When he failed to improve after a full month of treatment, his physician shifted him by ambulance to a major hospital in Omaha, a large city boasting two medical colleges. There he would be seen by the most highly reputed chest disease specialist in the region.

At the appointed hour the specialist arrived and introduced himself to my father. But when he noticed his name was Viggo C. Olsen, he stopped short. "Isn't there someone in your family with this same name who is involved in mission work overseas?" he inquired.

"Why, yes," my father replied, "my eldest son is a medical missionary in the country of Bangladesh."

Putting the chart down, the doctor continued, "Then, before I examine you, I think I should tell you something. I am well aware that your son wrote a book called *Daktar*—and it was through his book that I was converted and became a Christian. I owe him a great debt of gratitude."

Despite his surprise at this unexpected revelation, my father smiled and responded, "Thank you for telling me about that. Now let me ask, have you followed through on your important decision and joined a church?"

"Oh yes, I have become deeply involved in a fine church," he replied.

After a little further discussion the doctor again picked up the chart, studied it, examined his patient, and provided such expert treatment that my dad was soon feeling much better and able to return home. A few days later I met this physician and, at his request, gladly wrote on the flyleaf of his copy of *Daktar*—including words of gratitude for his wise and successful treatment of my father.

On the other side of the world in mid-January the first of several severe blows struck our mission team. One unforgettable day the local police chief ordered the Weber family to leave Hebron Station within seventy-two hours and informed them they would be expected to leave Bangladesh within six months, before their current visas expired. No reason was given. What a shock! Was this the work of some individual stirred by the American hostage crisis in Iran, or was something else behind it?

The order seemed like a colossal mistake, for the Webers are extremely sincere, devoted, and law-abiding workers. Immediately, the whole Hebron Station team lent a hand to help George and Shirley pack up, then all came downriver to Malumghat Station. In the meantime, Dr. Donn Ketcham headed for Dacca to discuss the problem in depth with our friend Jalal. Hopefully, some way could be discovered to get this harsh order reversed.

A different kind of surprise shook the foundations of neighboring India that same month. Against all the predictions of the political pundits, the Indians voted the formidable Indira Gandhi back into power as their new prime minister. It was an extraordinary political comeback, for less than three years earlier the voters had vigorously repudiated her—and her authoritarian "emergency rule." Now she was being touted in *Newsweek* magazine as the "Empress of India."[2] This stunning development would, predictably, create new problems for the government of Bangladesh because there were long-standing points of tension between President Zia and Mrs. Gandhi.

By this time Joan and I had reached the Chicago suburbs where we were reunited with our eldest and youngest daughters, Wendy and Nancy. They were purposely studying at Trinity College in Deerfield, Illinois, so that we could be near each other during our year of furlough. Soon our son, Mark, arrived from California to bring some of our belongings and spend a few weeks with us. How delighted we all were to be together again!

In late February Joan, Mark, and I drove to Chicago's O'Hare Airport to meet a young friend arriving from Bangladesh. Riaz was the home minister's son whom I had helped gain admission to No-

We drove Riaz to his university in Indiana

tre Dame College in Dacca. He would now complete his university studies in the U.S. Because of our association with Riaz and his parents, it was a pleasure for us to receive him and drive him that evening to Tri-State University at Angola, Indiana.

Later, soon after our return to the Chicago area, we selected a house in the suburban city of Wheaton, signed the papers, and moved in. We made sure there was plenty of room for our children to stay with us on weekends and during vacations.

Meanwhile, in distant Bangladesh our mission administrators continued dealing with the Weber family's disturbing problem. On Jalal's advice they appealed the case to the home minister and to another minister who hailed from the region where Hebron was located. These helpful officers launched an immediate investigation into the case. Because George and Shirley had notified their supporting churches in the U.S. about the crisis, their church people discussed the situation at length and prayed earnestly that the ruling against them would be canceled and that the new visas would be granted. A child in one of those concerned churches, a bit puzzled about the problem, asked, "If they are having so much trouble getting Visa, why don't they try for Master Card?"

Also in February, the Totman family left Malumghat and returned upriver to Hebron Station, followed a few days later by nurse Alice Payne and schoolteacher Shirley Harkness. That same night most of the group were rudely awakened at midnight by the nearby ominous rat-a-tat-tat of automatic weapons fire. The Shanti Bahini rebel tribesmen first made a bold assault on the neighboring paramilitary camp, then attacked the adjacent army camp and the bazaar area. After all this scary military action, sleep did not come easily—and our Hebron team wondered whether they would be able to remain at Hebron Station for long. Two weeks later the police intelligence branch officially requested the mission to bring all the Hebron workers out of their station, at least for the time being. The mission complied, and the Malumghat team received the Hebronites and housed and cared for them.

While the Hebron Station crisis was playing out, other pressures were also squeezing our mission team. Three of our American women had developed such troublesome cases of Chittagong perihepatitis that they returned to the U.S. on medical leave. At the same time the electrical rates at Malumghat suddenly tripled. This, of course, created immense pressure on the hospital budget. Then word came from the U.S. that Joyce DeCook and Marge Beals were still so affected by Chittagong perihepatitis that these two families would be unable to return to Bangladesh as planned. Furthermore, the Walsh family would remain in the U.S. another year or more because Jay had been requested by the mission to employ his proved fund-raising skills on the home front to help finance some key mission projects.

In addition to these stresses, the mission continued to face the problem of obtaining registration under the rules of the 1978 law that required fresh registration of all organizations receiving funds from abroad. The powerful government "Standing Committee" was empowered to decide which organizations would be registered and which rejected. Already, several mission agencies had been refused registration and ordered to "wind down" their operations. Most foreign organizations, including our own, were still in limbo, hoping that the Standing Committee would grant them registration but fearing that they, too, might be ordered to leave the country.

While the mission was dealing with these problems, the government continued to struggle against mounting challenges to its authority. In early February in the northern city of Rajshahi a severe prison riot forced the guards to open fire; three prisoners were killed and thirty-seven wounded.[3]

The opposition alliance seized on this unfortunate incident, and soon the streets of the capital were rocked with fierce protest meetings. This violence in the streets made a tremendous impact on the public, for the city had been more or less peaceful during the previous four years of strict martial law. Furthermore, the students who had been much quieter than usual during the martial law years were again in the forefront of riots and heated protest. Similar disturbances soon exploded in other major cities beyond Dacca. The prison riots also proved contagious, for later in the year they broke out in other prisons around the country. All these upsets were compounded by a shortage of food and rising prices.

President Zia, responding to the explosive problems confronting him on all sides, first flew to India to talk face-to-face with the new prime minister, Indira Gandhi, in an effort to ease the strains between Bangladesh and India. At the end of their meetings, however, there was no indication that any of the points of tension between the two nations had been resolved. Soon after Zia returned to Bangladesh he was confronted by further defiance—a prisoners' hunger strike at Dacca Central Jail, strikes of industrial and dock workers, and a massive strike of 700,000 lower-level government employees.

Zia matched these challenges with a concession here and a concession there to quiet the strikers and the opposition. Then on March 24, just before the ninth anniversary of independence, he released 1,600 political prisoners, including some prominent leaders like former president Mushtaque Ahmed and former lieutenant colonel Farook. Interestingly enough, those released were either

right-wingers or pro-Chinese leftists, all of whom were antagonistic to Zia's main opposition, the Awami League and its pro-Soviet
ten-party alliance. Then, a week later, Zia changed course and
again began arresting people—Awami League leaders and forty
top personalities of the pro-Soviet Communist Party of Bangladesh.

During February and March, while riots and protests were
stalking the streets of Dacca and other cities on the plains, violence
also mounted in the hills and jungles of the Chittagong Hill Tracts.
The Shanti Bahini tribal insurgents continued to escalate their
guerrilla warfare against the government forces. They succeeded in
killing scattered sepoys and policemen in several areas. Then, later
in March, they ambushed and wiped out a patrol of twenty-two
soldiers.

During this period, while the Shanti Bahini was stepping up
its attacks, leaders of the government made two conciliatory
moves. They formed a "tribal convention" of leading tribesmen
whom they considered to be more moderate and amenable than
the guerrilla fighters. But, because the government remained firmly in charge of this convention, the tribal people looked upon it as
flawed and would not support it. The government also released
about a hundred imprisoned tribal men, including Shantu Larma,
brother of the head of the Shanti Bahini movement.

Despite these conciliatory gestures by the highest level of the
Bangladesh government, the Bangladesh media one day reported
that a tragedy had taken place in the Chittagong Hill Tracts on
March 25, 1980. U. L. Chakma, himself an educated tribal man and
a member of the Bangladesh Parliament, in his press conference
reported a disaster called the Kaokhali massacre.[4] He described to
the press how troops from the army camp located at Kaokhali Bazar in the Chittagong Hill Tracts had attacked a peaceful gathering
of tribal people, killing an estimated two hundred men, women,
and children. This member of Parliament claimed that the troops,
aided by armed Bengali settlers, then fanned out from that point to
attack and burn houses in some two dozen surrounding villages.
He also complained that even Buddhist temples, monks, and nuns
were not spared. The people were stunned by these charges. Again
Bangladesh seemed to be *rawktodesh*—nation of blood.

Back in the U.S. we utilized March and April to settle in and
prepare messages, visual aids, and slide presentations for reports
to our supporting churches. Our middle daughter, Lynne, came
from California to be with us for a month and also to have medical
attention at the Mayo Clinic. After successful treatment and a delightful family time together, Lynne returned to her nursing duties
in southern California.

In May we began our traveling about the country to report to our generous supporting churches, who had loved us, prayed for us, and sustained us during our previous term of service. There were also opportunities to give addresses at schools, Christian colleges and universities, and meetings of clubs and other groups. The first college on my schedule was Ohio's Cedarville College, where I gave several addresses during a three-day preaching/teaching/counseling conference. Several years earlier I had encouraged the college leadership to consider establishing a professional Bachelor of Science in Nursing (B.S.N.) program, as there was a great dearth of such programs in Christian colleges in the U.S. They followed through, did a feasibility study, recruited an excellent head of department, then launched the new B.S.N. program. I was pleased to see that the course had become extremely popular and was filling an important need.

During this period some of the original majors responsible for the 1975 killing of Sheikh Mujib continued to plot and plan how to take over the government of Bangladesh. At the end of May, five of them met again in Turkey. This time in Rashid's place came Farook, who had been released from prison in Dacca a few weeks earlier and returned to exile in Libya.

The group reviewed the progress of the plans for the current coup that they were sponsoring in Bangladesh. Their man in Dacca, Lt. Col. Didarul Alam, working hand-in-hand with Marxist JSD party leaders, had successfully organized secret revolutionary cells among army troops in the Dacca, Savar, and Comilla cantonments. They planned that the leftist sepoys would imprison their officers, kill General Ershad (the commanding general of the army), seize the radio station, then set up a revolutionary council to run the country.[5] All of this was scheduled to take place on June 17. They would not have to worry about President Zia, for he would be away in London at that time.

But even as the plan was being concocted, military intelligence got wind of it. Suspecting that their plot was compromised, Didarul got cold feet and tried to call off the coup attempt. But by then the preparations had gained so much momentum that the sepoys insisted on going ahead with the plan. When they did so, their attempt failed miserably, because army units loyal to the government were well prepared for them. Four rebel lieutenant colonels and a number of soldiers were taken into custody. Lt. Col. Didarul Alam and some of the sepoys escaped, only to be captured later, court-martialed, and imprisoned. Thus another coup attempt had fizzled, and again Zia's government was preserved.

Side by side with the June military violence in Dacca, civilian agitation and violence also exploded. Early in June, after the gov-

ernment had convicted and executed four Awami League supporters, prisoners rioted in Dacca Central Jail in protest against
these executions.[6] Two days later the Awami League successfully
shut down the city of Dacca for hours with a general strike. When
the strikers clashed with police some were injured and dozens
arrested.

A few days later, a mere seventy miles east of Dacca just
across the border in India, another tragedy took place and made
headlines around the world. The background of the event was easy
to understand. Just as poor, landless Bengalis had been entering
the sparsely populated tribal areas of the Chittagong Hill Tracts as
settlers over many years, so other Bengalis had slipped across the
border and settled in tribal areas of India's neighboring Tripura
District. This escalating encroachment had infuriated the tribal
people in India as it had in Bangladesh. So in June 1980 angry
Indian tribesmen viciously attacked Bengali settlers in the village
of Mandai near the town of Agartala, India. More than three hundred Bengalis were killed by spears, bows and arrows, machetes,
and gunfire in the Mandai massacre.[7] The people of Bangladesh,
India, and other nations were sickened by this tragedy.

During June the Bangladesh government's powerful Standing
Committee was busy interviewing foreign organizations. Our own
mission's administrators were given six minutes to explain the
various phases of our work to the committee members. They left
that meeting without any indication of whether or not we would
gain registration. This, of course, led to more weeks of suspense
while everyone waited for the fateful notification.

Since the Weber problem was not yet resolved, George and
Shirley decided they should comply with the government's order
and go to the U.S. on home leave. Then, if the problem were later
solved and new visas granted, they would return to serve in Chittagong City rather than Hebron Station. The Field Council concurred
with this plan.

Jack Archibald continued working to obtain the Webers' visa
approval, but progress was agonizingly slow. He even made a final
attempt the morning of their departure. But, at last, he had to go to
George and Shirley and tell them he had failed to obtain the visas
that would ensure their later reentry into Bangladesh. Then, an
hour before they departed for the airport, while Jack was eating
lunch with them he was called to the telephone. A few minutes
later he returned to the table, with a broad smile on his face, to
announce, "The Webers have been granted permission to return to
Bangladesh!" It had been another cliff-hanger—with a beautiful
ending. "Thank You, Father!"

Then, out of the blue, another serious crisis struck the hospital and the mission at Malumghat. Momin, the hospital's public relations officer, and Dr. Matin, a friendly local medical practitioner, brought the first word that some people in the area were seething with anger about a Bengali book being sold in our Malumghat book store. The people, they said, were offended by anti-Islamic statements in this book, which was entitled *There Is No Fear in Death*.[8] The book was a biography of a Christian physician who lived a century before in the Muslim country of Iran. To do battle with the mission over this hated book local extremists, emboldened by the imprisonment of American hostages in Iran, had formed an organization named "The Islamic War Committee" or "Islamic Action Committee."

At the end of June posters appeared on the trees, tea stalls, and general stores near the entrance to the hospital. The posters, put up by some radical students, contained harsh anti-mission, anti-American slogans. When one of the mission men asked the local shopkeepers if there would be any objection to his taking two of the rain-soaked posters for his file, they replied, "Go ahead. It's all right." But after he removed the posters, a great hue and cry arose from the zealous students.

The first Friday in July several thousand men and students were scheduled to march in a procession to Malumghat in protest against the offensive book. But, providentially, the monsoon rains poured down in torrents that day and washed out the procession. Of course, the hospital staff was greatly relieved that the threatened procession did not materialize.

The next week newspaper articles against the hospital and the mission began to appear in various Bengali newspapers. At the same time, the Action Committee sent their written petitions of complaint to President Zia, the prime minister, the Ministry of Religion, the Home Ministry, and the American ambassador.

The following day leaders of the mission and the Action Committee were called to meet with the local chief of police. Both sides gave information and answered questions to help the police chief properly evaluate the conflict. Finally, he advised the mission men to avoid any actions that might provoke the other side. And he told the Action Committee leaders that they would not be allowed to carry out any demonstrations or riots and that they should quietly await the response of high government officials to their petitions.

The extremist leaders of the Action Committee left, angry at this "interference" by the police. They were determined to ignore the police order—nothing would keep them from marching on the hospital.

The next day word reached the hospital staff from all sides that a massive procession would take place two days hence, at midday on Friday. Later that morning two college students railed at the hospital gateman, "You have received your last pay. After Friday there will be no hospital!" These were obviously the words of radicals, for the great mass of the population was made up of decent, reasonable, law-abiding people who might join a peaceful procession but would never condone damaging property or hurting people.

Later that day the church pastors came to the American staff with further information that extremists were fanning the current agitation. The pastors were visibly upset and exclaimed, "The word is out that Friday's demonstration will not be peaceful. In fact, the radicals will turn it into a riot. We are told that rioters will burn buildings and beat and stab people. Not only that, we have also heard that the main targets will be the Americans because anti-American political elements will join the procession."

The next morning, Thursday, Bangladeshi and American Christians were diligent about their morning prayer and Bible reading. Some of them located passages of Scripture that eased their fear and gave them a never-to-be-forgotten peace of mind. The hospital staff went about their work of caring for the patients. Later that day the police chief insisted that the Action Committee leaders promise there would be no procession. But no one really knew what would happen that night or the next day.

The worrisome night passed without incident, and the sun rose on the fateful Friday morning. Shortly after 7:00 A.M. about forty policemen, who had come all the way from Cox's Bazar and Chittagong City, arrived on the scene. An hour later a helicopter flew over to land at the neighboring military camp and disgorge army officers and troops who had been away on a training mission. The helicopter continued to fly back and forth until all the military men had been returned to their base camp. Then the subdivisional officer (SDO) from Cox's Bazar appeared. He was the government officer in charge of the whole Cox's Bazar Subdivision (southern one-third of Chittagong District). With him came the subdivisional police officer. They had come to make sure that everything remained under control.

All this movement of the police, the army, and civil officials ensured that the Action Committee kept its promise and did not march on the hospital. The day passed uneventfully, and the staff thanked God for the authorities who had conscientiously extended themselves to keep the procession and riot from occurring.

During the next week Shahabuddin, our friend who formerly lived in his ancestral home near the hospital, came from his new home in Chittagong City to help further evaluate the local situation. During that week the Action Committee finalized its document entitled "Seven Demands," then sent copies to high government officials and to all the members of Parliament. Two days later the subject of Christian missions explosively hit the Parliament floor, the daytime radio news, and the evening TV news. Things were not going well.

However, the Parliament and the government did not have much time to focus on the issue of Christian missions just then, since nation-building was currently at the forefront of their attention. Upon the completion of the First Five-Year Plan, the planners had not been ready to launch the official Second Five-Year Plan. So, to give themselves time, they had prepared an interim Two-Year Plan to cover 1978-80. Then in July 1980 the Second Five-Year Plan finally went into effect. By then President Zia was making speeches about carrying out a "peaceful revolution." His talk of revolution was a bit confusing to people because he was firmly in control of the country; usually those pressing for a revolution are those striving to gain control.

Some of the main features of Zia's revolution and the nation's Second Five-Year Plan were these:

1. Canal digging—if millions of people could be motivated to dig hundreds of miles of canals to store monsoon season rainwater, irrigation (and food production) could be greatly increased. The goal was to make the country self-sufficient in rice and wheat production so that no more precious dollars would have to be spent on importing those food grains.
2. Literacy—in February 1980 the government had launched a massive literacy campaign to teach illiterate multitudes how to read.
3. Family planning—the government would increase its already considerable emphasis on slowing the rapid rise in the population.

On the last day of July at Dulahazara the Action Committee bombarded President Zia and other key officials with yet another petition. At the same time, our mission leaders had a meeting with Jalal, who was on tour in nearby Cox's Bazar. After the meeting they returned to Malumghat to report to the mission team, "In our meeting with Jalal Ahmed, secretary of Parliament, he urged us to request Vic Olsen to come out to help the entire missionary community in the growing, boiling crisis within government circles. He explained that Vic's long years of negotiating experience and his many friends and contacts in government circles will be invaluable in trying to save the day for Christian missions in Bangladesh." A meeting was scheduled to deal with this request as soon as possible.

In early August 1980, through the mediation of Shahabuddin from Chittagong City, the two sides to the conflict finally sat together at Cox's Bazar in a formal meeting refereed by the SDO. The point of the meeting was to discuss the seven demands of the Action Committee and settle the dispute. The meeting got off to an uneasy start, but eventually there was some discussion on each of the points. One demand called for the chairman of the mission to ask the forgiveness of the Action Committee for creating tension by taking down some of the protest posters put up by the students. He did apologize, which nicely cared for that point.

However, differences of opinion continued on some of the demands. Then the discussion got stuck over the question of documentary proof that the mission was authorized to carry out religious work as well as medical treatment. The SDO brought the meeting to an end by requesting the mission representatives to provide copies of the relevant documents to him. Sadly, the negotiation had failed to resolve the burning issues.

A week later our mission leaders visited the SDO in Cox's Bazar to hand over to him copies of the papers he had requested. Among these were two main documents of approval for our project, plus a dozen pages photocopied from the book *Daktar*. These pages explained that the government had originally thought to withhold freedom to do religious work. But after we had reminded them about the very strong clause in the Bangladesh Constitution that granted complete religious liberty, they had reversed their stand and allowed the mission this full religious freedom. Later in the day our men reported to the team, "The response of the SDO was beyond our fondest expectation. The thing that seemed to impress him most of all was the historical record of the developments in the book *Daktar*. Thank the Lord for this book!"

Suddenly, after a week or two of relative calm, the Action Committee again began to distribute handbills in the bazaars and on all the buses plying our end of Bangladesh. In these leaflets they criticized not only the mission and the hospital but also the SDO, the subdivisional police officer, and the local chief of police. And they bemoaned the fact that the government had paid no attention to their grievances.

While these unsettling events were taking place, our Hebron team complied with the government order. They spent a week working long hours at Hebron Station packing up all their movable items for transfer to Malumghat. On the day the handbills were being distributed the crew came downriver. It required forty-one

Loading the boats at Hebron

boats to transport all their suitcases and fifty-five-gallon drums filled with materials and supplies. Of course, they were all exhausted when they piled into bed at Malumghat that night.

During that same week, on the U.S. side of the globe, we received an urgent letter from our team in Bangladesh. The major point of the letter was explained in these words:

> Actually, the main purpose in writing is to communicate an *urgent appeal to you.* Our Field Council has unanimously voted to invite you (Vic and Joan) back to Bangladesh to spearhead government high-level negotiations at this moment of extreme crisis. Vic and Joan, the need is for now! . . .
>
> In a private session with Jalal he came quickly to the point and said, "The general picture for Christian missions is bad. It is very important that you get Vic to come back now. To delay may be too late. . . ."
>
> We are confident that you will believe our words and accept our Field Council's 100% decision. In addition, you will surely consider the intense request (probably better stated as an order/demand) made by Jalal and the sentiment of the evangelical missionary community as significant factors in coming out as soon as is practically possible. . . .
>
> [May God] give you the inner peace to heed this impassioned appeal to come over and help us. However untimely it may seem to you, perhaps you can call it your *Bangladesh Call.* Surely your supporting churches and pastors will understand when you tell them that this is really a "do or die" situation.

It didn't take long to determine that we had to drop everything and respond to our co-workers' request. Quickly we canceled
a full schedule of meetings and sent out an instant newsletter to all
our supporters. Next, we providentially encountered a friend who
needed a house for her family to live in for just the period we
planned to be away. Then we moved unneeded personal belongings into the garage, drew up new wills, and otherwise put our affairs in order. When we received all of our immunizations at once,
we were unavoidably sick for the next two days.

Then I telephoned the current U.S. ambassador to Bangladesh, Mr. David Schneider, who was in Washington at the time.
We discussed at length the emergency regarding the registration of
American mission societies, and I reviewed the valuable part
played by a previous U.S. ambassador in the 1977 visa crisis. He
replied that he would not feel free to become involved this time
until the mission community had exhausted all other approaches
—and unless they requested him directly for assistance. I made a
mental note of these two key points.

Finally we drove to Indiana to visit Riaz, the home minister's
son. We had dinner together, took snapshots, and received his
handwritten letter to his father and mother. Soon we were winging
our way toward Bangladesh.

In Bangkok, Thailand, we were happy to meet our field chairman, who was beginning a much-needed vacation; he gave us a
quick update on the situation and a list of projects for us to tackle.
Heading the list were three key assignments:

1. Obtain the registration of the mission required by the 1978
   law
2. Assist other missions in their quest for registration
3. Solve the simmering problems in the hospital locality
   caused by the book *There Is No Fear in Death*

The next day (September 14) we flew into the brand-new,
beautiful Zia International Airport in Dacca. In 1975 coupmaker
Major Rashid had deployed his artillery pieces at this airport,
which was then only partially built. Mark Tucker warmly received
us and a few days later Ida Tucker also returned from the U.S. As
usual, they took very good care of us.

That afternoon Joan and I went to Jalal's house. It was a delight to see him and be with the family again. He updated me on
the situation and emphasized that the continuance of Christian
missions in Bangladesh was in jeopardy. He advised that we make
every effort to calm the agitation around the hospital as soon as
possible, hopefully before the next session of Parliament, which

would begin in late October or November. We departed that evening sobered by his assessment.

The next morning, despite jet lag, I appeared at the well-attended Intermission Meeting. It was great to see Jack Archibald, our mission's administrative officer, and representatives of eighteen other mission societies. I was saddened to learn that ten of them had already been rejected for registration by the government. The majority of these rejected groups were relatively new in the country. Unless these rejections could be reversed there would be a great loss of valuable mission work in Bangladesh.

After the meeting Jack briefed me and handed over a voluminous file about the problems at the hospital and the larger national issue. That night I devoured this material and confirmed that the controversial book did, in fact, contain a few statements that compared Islam unfavorably with Christianity and maligned Muslim people. Although the actual amount of negative material was small, any earnest Muslim would naturally be offended by it.

Over the next two days I met the Bengali leaders of two large Bangladeshi church groups. The Roman Catholic archbishop explained that they were attempting to have their churches exempted from the troublesome registration requirement, but, despite approaches to the Home Ministry and the president's office, they had failed to make progress. Then, when I met the head of the National Council of Churches, he remembered with much emotion how we had received him at Malumghat and helped him when he was fleeing from the horrors of war in 1971. He confirmed that the government continued to demand that their churches be registered if they expected to continue receiving funds from abroad.

Neither of these men said much about the problems their groups' foreign missionaries were facing. Later I was surprised to learn that they both had informed government officials that they had no objection to the government's limiting their missionaries. This meant to these officials that there was no unity in the overall "Christian community" about the rejection of most of the personnel of foreign mission societies. I knew that this would make it much more difficult to convince the government to reverse the rejections. What a complex issue!

I also spent time with Frank Patterson, the head of Baptist Mid-Missions (BMM); many of the U.S. churches that support our workers also support BMM personnel. My own colleagues and I had worked with Frank to help him get settled in the country. We also assisted him in making the appropriate applications to the government for approval of the hospital his organization hoped to build in northern Bangladesh. Jalal, also, was impressed with their commitment to the task and often gave Frank wise counsel. I was sorry to hear, however, that BMM had already been rejected for registration. But Frank, who had not lost hope, showed Jalal and me the first draft of his letter of appeal. At his request, we made suggestions about refining the letter.

The next evening Joan and I made a social call at the residence of the home minister. He and his wife were hungry for news about their son studying in Indiana. They relished every word Joan and I could tell them about our recent time with him. Then they oohed and ahed over the photographs we had taken of him, his room, and his university. Of course, they were overjoyed to receive his handwritten letter. Having had our own four children study in universities and colleges across the sea, we deeply empathized with their feelings.

Two days later I met the home minister in his office. There was a tenseness about him, and he confirmed this impression with the words "There is so much pressure in this job! I am an absolute mental wreck." But he went on to indicate that we needed to talk and face the issue at hand. He then opened a file marked "URGENT." Inside was a copy of the controversial book and some papers stamped "SECRET." Then he said wearily, "I don't have very good news for you. The public is in an uproar over this book purchased from your bookstall. Not only that, the deputy commissioner of Chittagong District urges that the visa of your mission's chairman be canceled. And, because the joint meeting of intelligence agencies confirmed that his visa should be withdrawn, it would be very difficult for me to go against all this official recommendation."

"Please let me respond to this matter," I replied. "First, I want to make clear that we did not write this book, publish the book, or even have the book printed. Presuming that it had passed the normal government censorship procedures, we merely purchased it from the market and stocked it in the bookstore. None of our people were aware of any negative statements in this book against Islam or any other religion. To learn that there were anti-Islamic statements in the book was a shock to us, because one of our first principles is that we do not criticize another person's religion. So the whole matter of the book is simply an unfortunate misunderstanding. Besides, our mission chairman is a fine man who has given years of devoted service to the people. It seems to me that cancellation of his visa is unnecessarily severe. Please try to think of some way to avoid such a drastic penalty."

After deep thought the home minister replied, "All right, I accept the points of your argument. Write a letter directly to me stating all of those extenuating factors. On the strength of your letter I will decree that the visa should not be canceled at this time. Then if there are no further problems over a six-month period of probation, his visa will be secure."

I thanked him for this generous decision, then asked about the matter of registration and the 1978 law that required it. He explained that there had been a haphazard proliferation of too many organizations in the months following the birth of Bangladesh. So one of the intents of the 1978 ordinance was to "lop off some of the newer organizations."

I expressed concern that there did not seem to be clear-cut criteria for acceptance or rejection and that organizations such as BMM and others had much to offer, yet they had been rejected. He agreed that there was a lack of clear guidelines and that probably some mistakes in judgment had been made. I spoke further on behalf of the mission societies engaged solely in religious and church work. He responded that some large national Christian groups had no objection to such missionaries being sent home, and said, "We are surprised that the overall Christian community is not united on this point."

Before we left Dacca, Jack Archibald and I had the immense pleasure of walking into the Department of Social Welfare, having a congenial talk with the deputy director, then walking out with the paper stating that our mission had been registered. "Thank You, Father!" The only negative was a short clause attached to the approval that read, "Expatriates should be reduced." Because we had new young men and women preparing to join us in Bangladesh, we would surely have to appeal that clause.

Now that our mission had been registered, Joan and I felt free to leave Dacca and head for the hospital. So on our ninth day in the country we traveled by air and road to Malumghat. It was a great joy to see everyone. After dinner Momin, the hospital public relations officer, appeared to brief me on the local situation. He explained what had gone wrong in the beginning and how the Action Committee had escalated the confrontation. He felt the Action Committee had greatly overreacted but also that the mission had made some mistakes. Because the problem was not at all resolved, he said, public discontent continued to seethe just below the surface and could again explode into open confrontation at any time. I could see that this problem would not be easy to resolve.

The next morning we had a visit from a Murung tribesman who worked at Malumghat and who could speak a little Bengali. His son attended our Bengali-medium school. Beaming, the tribesman told us that his son could now read the Scriptures. This allowed him, his wife, and their other children to hear God's Word read in their own home every day. "This is very profitable for our family!" he exclaimed. Joan asked which class the boy was in. He responded that his son was in class five. Then Joan inquired about the boy's age. With great pride he replied, "He's nineteen years old." Although not many American parents would be button-popping proud of a nineteen-year-old boy in the fifth grade, our Murung brother was thrilled. "Instead of attending school, my son could get a job and bring in some money," he explained, "but his learning reading and writing is much more gain to us."

We settled in quickly, and I got my feet on the ground by interacting with co-workers, pastors, friends, hospital staff, and others. I could see that our Muslim neighbors had a right to be upset about the anti-Islamic statements in the book. After all, Bangladesh was a Muslim nation, and we were guests in the country. Also, we could learn from the most famous missionary of all time, the apostle Paul, and his companions, who had been careful not to blaspheme the deity revered in a city where they were teaching.[9]

So I decided the most important thing I could do over the next few days would be to apologize to key people for stocking and selling the troublesome book. I had learned long before from my association with many dear Muslim friends that they could be expected to respond positively to a sincere apology. In fact, their religious convictions require this.

So on the last day of September Dr. Dick Stagg (Malumghat Station Council chairman), Momin, and I drove six miles to the local police headquarters to talk with the chief of police. He was a man of strong feelings, and it soon became clear that he was still angry with the mission as well as the Islamic Action Committee. On the other hand, he did not agree with the SDO's decision to require the mission to provide documentary evidence of our permission to do religious and church work. He declared, "Foreigners or any others have a right to preach their religion because our Constitution gives that right. And the Constitution was developed from Islamic principles."

I thanked the police chief for his wise and courageous work in protecting our patients, our hospital, and our mission. And I apologized for our mistake in selling the book that had so greatly wounded the feelings of our local friends and neighbors. He accepted the apology and immediately showed a new warmth toward us. And he promised to continue to protect all the foreigners under his jurisdiction.

The next morning I was scheduled to meet with a leading man of the community. He was an old friend, the president of the nearby Dulahazara mosque and, interestingly, had recently become the honorary president of the Action Committee. Although he was a pious and orthodox Muslim, he was certainly not an extremist. The fact that he had consented to become the president of the Action Committee told me volumes. It meant that the antagonism against

He was an old friend, president of the nearby mosque

the mission had spread beyond the radicals and was felt by reasonable, thoughtful people as well.

At 8:00 A.M. that morning the old gentleman arrived at my house. We embraced each other, enjoyed tea together, and each inquired about the other's family. Only then did I raise the question of the controversial book. I expressed surprise that he, who had always been a well-wisher of the hospital and mission, had now become head of the Action Committee. Squaring his thin shoulders he replied severely, "But your mission has offended us. Your people distributed a book containing statements against the holy Prophet of Islam and against our religion. Then, when we brought this to the attention of your mission, there was no good response, and the public became more and more angry. Only then did the situation become dangerous."

"I am very sorry to hear about all of this, my dear friend," I replied, "and I do want to explain that when our people obtained this book from the market they were completely unaware that it contained these negative statements. They assumed that it was all right because it had passed the government censorship procedure. But, although we did not write or publish this book, we should have checked it, for it is our principle not to criticize the religion of another person. So I want to tell you how sorry I am about our mistake, and I want to beg your forgiveness."

The result was powerful, deep, moving. With tears coursing down his cheeks the old gentleman reached over and embraced me. He said, "Oh, you have said the words I wanted to hear and needed to hear. *Now*, my friend, I can work for you and try to help you!" It was a dramatic moment. And I wondered for an instant if those then negotiating for the release of the American hostages in Iran understood this facet of Islamic theology and this generous capacity of the Muslim heart.

The next morning Dick Stagg, Momin, and I drove thirty miles south to Cox's Bazar for another critical meeting, this time with the subdivisional officer (SDO). He greeted us warmly and served us an elaborate tea with cookies, cake, and Bengali sweets.

At the beginning of our conversation he reminisced about medical advice I had once given him and his physician-wife about their small daughter's rather severe eating problem. He reminded me that I had asked many questions and considered their problem in depth. Finally, I had given this prescription: "There is only one solution to the problem. You must try many different foods to finally hit on two or three that your daughter will like so much that she will eat them. Then she will begin growing again, and this will finally stimulate her appetite so that one day she will begin eating other foods, too." Chuckling, he explained, "Because that was the most unusual prescription we had ever heard, I told dozens of people about it, so that now everyone in town knows about your prescription. Not only that, it worked." We were off to a good start.

I thanked the SDO for his excellent effort in successfully maintaining law and order and in keeping the agitated people under control. Obviously pleased, he talked for a while about how he had managed to calm down the more difficult leaders. Then he told us frankly that he was also upset at the mission for selling such an offensive book and for not finding some way to quiet the furor in the days that followed. This statement gave us the opportunity to explain again that we would never intentionally offend our neighbors and that we had been unaware that this book contained these negative statements. Presumably it had passed the government Censorship Board, and no one had ever complained before, although the book had been on the market for nearly ten years. "Despite these facts," I continued, "we should have read the book ourselves. We are extremely sorry that our mistake has caused so much dissatisfaction and trouble. And we do beg your forgiveness for this."

The SDO responded warmly and generously, then thanked us for coming. He expressed confidence that the problems would be solved and encouraged us to continue to meet and talk with key people.

That afternoon Joan and I drove to Chittagong City for two important meetings the next day. The following morning Jack Archibald and I went to the office of the deputy commissioner (DC) who is the government officer in charge of the whole Chittagong District. He is the direct superior of the SDO in Cox's Bazar. He had a crystal clear recollection of the whole problem that had created the uproar, and he was well aware that a serious incident involving American nationals could have created an international furor. He went on to express his dissatisfaction with the controversial book, the mission, and the progressive escalation of the problem. He stated forthrightly that he was the officer who had requested the Home Ministry to revoke the visa of the mission chairman.

I told him how sorry we were about all of these problems and explained the steps we had taken so far to resolve the tension. Continuing on, I explained, "I agree that there are offensive statements in this book. If we had known that, we never would have stocked and sold the book. I do beg your forgiveness for the mistakes we have made."

The DC graciously accepted our apology. Then, after we enjoyed the refreshments he served, he arranged for us to see the divisional commissioner, whose office was nearby. He was the main government officer over the eastern one-fourth of the whole country. It was good to see the commissioner again. We were well known to each other, for he had visited us more than once at Malumghat. I repeated our apology to him; he, too, responded in a positive way.

The next day I had a long session with our friend Shahabuddin, who lived in Chittagong. Because he was a very tactful person and because he and his family were highly respected in the Dulahazara/Malumghat area, the mission had earlier requested him to come from Chittagong City to help calm the storm. He went twice but was now disillusioned because the meeting he helped to set up between the two sides had failed to resolve the smoldering problem.

I thanked him for his efforts and detailed the various people we had met and the positive response we had obtained from each one. Then I apologized to him, as a previous long-standing member of the Dulahazara community, for our error in selling such a controversial book. He responded to that apology warmly, then asked, "Why is it that you haven't met with the two ringleaders of the agitation?"

"Shahabuddin," I answered, "I felt that I wanted to talk to you and other involved people first and make things right with everyone. Then we would have their backing if we run into trouble with the two ringleaders."

These two extremist leaders of the Islamic Action Committee were:

1. Mr. S. "Light" (English translation), vice-president of the Action Committee. He looked up to Shahabuddin and was well known to me. For a decade he had worked behind the scenes against the mission. In more recent years, however, I had finally developed a friendship with him and consulted him on several occasions as an expert on terminology for our translation project.
2. Mr. S. "Merciful" (English translation), secretary-treasurer of the Action Committee. Fiercely antagonistic to the mission, he had traveled about raising money to support the Action Committee's battle against our group. He was the type of fanatical person who greatly worried the government officers. In fact, not many weeks later the indignant SDO had to issue a warrant for the man's arrest for leading another Action Committee in Cox's Bazar to attack and burn a row of stalls at a government-sponsored fair and exhibition. A number of people had been injured in that vicious attack.

If we could finally gain the support of one or both of these men, we should be able to resolve our problems with the local community.

A few days later Joan and I were again in Dacca for another Intermission Meeting. After we all shared our new information at the meeting, we began discussing strategy. There was agreement that the rejected mission societies should appeal vigorously to high-level officials, including President Zia. I was put in charge of a drafting committee to prepare a letter to the president. We produced the first draft of the letter, then had it typed and photocopied for appraisal by each mission society, by some diplomats, and by Jalal.

The next day, as I was reflecting further on approaches that might help the disapproved mission societies, it came to me that it was now high time to request the American ambassador and other ambassadors to become involved. After all, the remarkable cooperation of ten ambassadors in the 1977 visa crisis had played a useful part in the happy outcome. And Ambassador Schneider had told me in our telephone conversation in the U.S. that he would consider becoming involved if we had exhausted all other avenues of approach—and if we requested him directly.

The next morning I met with a well-known war hero and author who was currently the director of an important government agency. Over the previous few days I had been examining and prescribing for him, his wife, and other family members. After our medical discussions were completed, he asked how we were progressing on our work with the government. I told him the good news that our mission had been registered and that we were building up a strategy to attempt to save the mission societies which had been rejected. He then offered some sage advice: "You must analyze the personality of the top man, President Zia. As a very pragmatic person he is sensitive to anything that would increase or diminish his popularity and power. You should get some powerful persons to help you convince Zia that his reputation at home or abroad will suffer if his government throws the mission agencies out of the country."

His comments resonated so perfectly with my previous day's strong impression about the American ambassador that something clicked. So I went immediately to the American embassy to set up an appointment with Ambassador Schneider. That afternoon I had a long session with him. I reported on recent developments and then directly requested him to become involved, as his help was now needed. He responded, "That's interesting! I will be glad to hear the reasoning behind your request because today is the very day I am facing this issue. Already I have called for information about what other embassies are doing, and now I want to hear what you have to say."

I pointed out my reflections of the day before and the reinforcing insight that I had received that morning from my knowledgeable patient. I continued, "Our mission committee was able to do a great deal in the 1977 visa crisis because of Jalal's influence and the providential selection of his intimate friend to be the new home minister. This time, however, you who are diplomats might be able to accomplish more with a direct approach to the government."

"But the same home minister is still there," he reminded me.

"True," I replied, "but his viewpoint may have changed somewhat, for he told me that one purpose of the 1978 ordinance was to 'lop off some of the newer organizations.'"

The ambassador said that he was sorry to hear that. Finally, he stated, "The things you have told me have been very helpful. These points would seem to indicate that I should get involved. I will keep you informed." As I was leaving it struck me that the timing of my meeting with Ambassador Schneider was clearly providential. And he did effectively go to bat for us.

The next day Joan and I returned from Dacca to Malumghat. There we learned that a patient, the ten-year-old son of an influential local family, had hovered at the brink of death for days. Several times the violent tetanus spasms had caused complete respiratory arrest—but each time an alert staff member had successfully restarted his breathing. Finally the deadly disease began to relent, and the boy was now out of danger. I found the boy's father and mother simply overwhelmed with joy and gratitude. They had already sent telegrams praising the hospital staff to the U.S. ambassador in Dacca and to President Carter in Washington.

Then Momin briefed me on a disturbing development. Nine days earlier, the day after Joan and I had left Malumghat, Momin had picked up word that there would again be fiery speeches in Dulahazara bazaar, followed by a potentially dangerous procession to the hospital. Momin immediately telephoned the SDO in Cox's Bazar and requested him to be present the next day.

The following morning, Friday, the SDO and the subdivisional police officer had appeared in nearby Dulahazara, approached two leaders of the Islamic Action Committee (the friendly president and the extremist Mr. Light) and told them that the procession absolutely must be canceled. And he warned them that the police, who would be stationed between Dulahazara bazaar and the hospital, had orders to prevent any procession. Then the SDO charged these two leaders with the responsibility for keeping the peace. The two men agreed to comply with the SDO's order, putting themselves in direct opposition to the other top leader of the Action Committee, the radical Mr. Merciful.

After the midday mosque prayers the three prearranged special speeches were given. The first and the third were relatively mild and reasonable, but the second was an angry tirade against the mission and against those mosque members who had become "traitors" to the Action Committee. By the end of the speeches thunder was rolling across the leaden skies and sheets of rain began slashing down. Because of the heavy rain, the strong order of the SDO, the police deployed against them, and dissension within the Action Committee itself, again no procession materialized. "Thank You, Father!"

Later we learned that it had been doubly important that the procession be blocked. First of all, one or two of the radicals were prepared to convert the procession into a riot. In such riots anything can happen, as the SDO and the police well knew. To make matters worse, leftist political elements were working behind the scenes to create trouble. We were told that these antigovernment, anti-American elements wanted to embarrass the Bangladesh government in the eyes of the U.S. government by wreaking havoc at the only American institution in the area. Under cover of the procession they allegedly intended to set fire to the hospital and to injure hospital people with heavy sticks. Those with daggers would cut and stab Americans and Bangladeshis alike. Reportedly, the cudgels had already been hewn from the forest and those assigned to cut-and-slash duty had been chosen.

I learned, further, that Momin, the SDO, and the helpful old president had done a terrific job of preventing this calamity. Even extremist Mr. Light, who had confided all this inside information to Shahabuddin, had supported canceling the procession, for he did not agree with the burning-beating-stabbing scenario; he is a man of conscience.

Having made all the necessary preliminary contacts, and having gained the backing of the chief government officers and police, I was now ready to approach the Action Committee for a final settlement of the problem. But the leaders steadfastly declined to meet unless either a government officer was present or Shahabuddin came from Chittagong. So I sent a message requesting Shahabuddin to come. Three days later he arrived, confident that he could easily arrange the meeting with the Action Committee so that we could try to reach agreement with them. At 6:00 P.M. he met with the six top leaders of the committee at his home. Only later did I learn what an extremely difficult time he had.

After a few moments of conversation, he was shocked to find that some of these men were more angry and resistant than ever before. They flatly refused to meet with the mission representatives. So he just let them blow off steam for twenty minutes until they wound down a bit.

Then Shahabuddin launched into a long, inspired lecture, later described by Momin as "eloquent." Softening a little, the leaders suggested that Shahabuddin could talk to both sides as an intermediary. He refused, and argued further that Dr. Olsen had

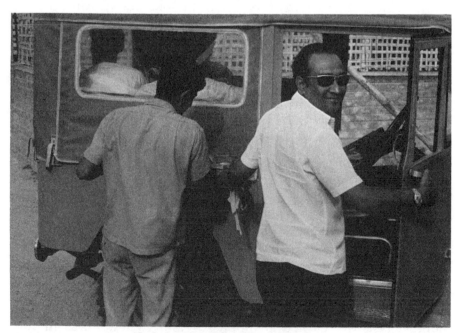

Shahabuddin came from Chittagong

interrupted his home leave, leaving his children and aged parents behind, just to return to Bangladesh to talk with them in an effort to solve this painful problem. How, then, could they so ungraciously refuse to meet with him? Further subdued, the leaders finally agreed to the meeting, but only if the SDO were present.

Again, Shahabuddin refused their suggestion. He reminded them that he had worked hard to set up the previous official meeting with the SDO, which was supposed to settle everything. But the meeting had failed and that, he declared, had damaged his prestige. This time there must be a preliminary meeting to deal with all the points before the final official meeting with the SDO. Bowing to this telling point, the leaders finally reluctantly agreed to talk, but only with Dr. Olsen alone. When? Right now!

About 8:00 P.M. a breathless Shahabuddin arrived at our house to report what had happened. He said the Action Committee leaders were sitting at his family home waiting for me to come. Dick Stagg and I had planned to go together, but we quickly decided that I should go alone to cooperate with the Action Committee's stipulation. So Shahabuddin and I stepped out into the dark night.

Entering his house a few minutes later, I greeted the waiting men one by one and embraced the aged president and Mr. Light, referring to the latter as "my former *ostad* (teacher)." I was pleased that at last the fateful night had come to talk with this roomful of proud, tough, bearded leaders of the Action Committee, each wearing a white prayer cap as a badge of his orthodoxy. After a little preliminary conversation we got down to their demands.

The first one had to do with the hated book. I earnestly apologized to them, as I had done to various government officials. They nodded their approval and began to move on to the next point. But I demurred, saying that although I had made a sincere apology I had not yet heard any words of forgiveness, the usual response in Muslim faith as well as Christian faith.

A bit embarrassed, they explained that they would be happy to grant forgiveness, but not until the group would meet in the presence of the SDO during the final settlement meeting. They explained that, if they were to grant forgiveness prematurely in the absence of the government officer, their own people would criticize them as weak and claim that they had taken a huge bribe to give in to the mission. I could see their point.

Next, we entered into a long, intense debate on their second demand, which had to do with the religious work of the mission. We went back and forth on this point for an hour. The committee men spoke forcefully. Feeling as though I were skating on thin ice, I spoke carefully lest I force anyone into a corner or abort the discussion. At last, we reached an impasse—and I knew I was in very serious trouble. Then, in my predicament, I silently cried out, "Oh

Father, I am in a real fix now. Please do something to get me out of this tight spot." Very soon the debate took a more favorable turn and somehow came to a very satisfactory conclusion. Simultaneously, the extreme tension in the room, little by little, eased. "Thank You, Father!"

The discussion of the remaining demands proceeded more smoothly and the do-or-die meeting finally ended on a surprisingly upbeat note. Afterward Shahabuddin served tea and Bengali refreshments, and everyone was smiling and friendly. I was given the assignment by the group to schedule the final official settlement meeting with the SDO during the following week after the holy month of Ramzan (Ramadan) was over.

The next morning Shahabuddin came to report that the Action Committee members were informally discussing the previous night's meeting with the people. Nothing unfavorable seemed to be happening. He was still marveling over the sudden, unexpected turn of the confrontation in our favor just when the situation had appeared so dark. Then I confided to him about my silent crisis prayer just before the tide turned.

Later he told Mr. Light to do everything in his power to make our tentative agreement hold solid. He warned him that, if the agreement broke down and trouble should again develop causing the government to close the hospital, the people of every village and town in Bangladesh would curse the people of Dulahazara for being so foolish as to cause the loss of precious high-quality medical care.

Soon after this in a Station Council meeting, the group discussed and ratified the tentative decisions I had to make under fire during the fateful gathering. After the meeting one of our newer career nurses, Dorothy Adams, came over to talk with Joan and me. Dorothy is a competent nurse and an outstanding pianist. Thoughtfully, she thanked us for our willingness to drop everything and come at this time of crisis. She explained that she felt comforted and safer with us there to be able to devote ourselves full-time to the complex problems. She also mentioned that, in the recent difficult and dangerous days, a particular Old Testament chapter had helped and strengthened her. That was the chapter that contains these fitting words:

> The Lord is my rock, my fortress and my deliverer;
> The God of my strength, in Him I will trust,
> My shield and the horn of my salvation,
> My stronghold and my refuge;
> My Savior, You save me from violence.[10]

Nurse Dorothy Adams

Next, all members of our Field Council met for the usual prayer meeting that preceded the annual Field Council meetings. The emphasis that morning was on praise and thanks to the Father, who had done so much for us. Dr. Hank Ottens, a fine visiting orthopedic surgeon, told a moving—yet hilarious—story about what had happened to him and his wife, Sharon, just a few hours earlier.

The previous evening one of their children had captured a frog and imprisoned it in a pail in their house. But in the middle of the night the irrepressible creature had escaped from the pail and began practicing its high jump around the house. Trying for a new world record, it landed—plop!—right on sleeping Sharon's chest. She awakened with a gasp and energetically brushed it onto the floor. Then Hank stumbled groggily out of bed, chased the frog down, and finally reincarcerated it in the pail.

But twenty minutes later, the irritating amphibian began jumping so vigorously and noisily around inside the pail that sleep was impossible. Exasperated, Hank and Sharon both got up to take the pail to the farthest end of the house where the pesky thing could jump around to its heart's content. Suddenly—just then—a large glass globe lamp hanging over the head of their bed crashed heavily down on the headboard and the empty pillows where their heads had been resting a minute before; it shattered into dozens of razor-sharp shards of glass. Because of the frog and the remarkable timing of its provoking them out of bed, they had narrowly escaped serious injury. "Thank You, Father!"

Three days later the morning of the final settlement meeting with the Action Committee dawned. I had no way to predict whether the meeting would proceed smoothly because of the tentative agreements reached in the previous meeting, or whether there would be some new obstacle or problem to face. Feeling the need for immense wisdom, I focused on a short but beautiful passage of Scripture in my morning meditation:

> But the wisdom that is from above is first pure, then peaceable, gentle, willing to yield, full of mercy and good fruits, without partiality and without hypocrisy.[11]

That was the kind of wisdom I needed—and asked for—that morning.

At the meeting the Action Committee was represented by its three officers. The mission was also represented by three men— Drs. Olsen, Stagg, and Bullock. The government was likewise represented by three men—the SDO, the subdivisional police officer, and the local chief of police. And representing the local elite of Dulahazara were Shahabuddin and Momin.

After greetings all around, the SDO took the chair and began the meeting, which would focus on the seven demands of the Action Committee. The first demand had to do with the troublesome book. As before, I apologized for our mistake in selling the book and begged the forgiveness of the members of the committee.

The SDO then moved on to the next point. But I stopped the proceedings, saying, "Gentlemen, from the depths of my heart I have honestly requested your forgiveness. How can I continue on in this meeting, not knowing whether or not you have forgiven us? Do you forgive us or not?" The Action Committee members looked at each other for a moment while the SDO urged them to give an answer to my question. Suddenly, our old friend, the elderly president of the Action Committee, jumped from his seat to shake my hand, embrace me, and offer official words of forgiveness. A tear trickled down his cheek. By then the other Action Committee men were on their feet, embracing and shaking hands with Drs. Stagg and Bullock. It was a never-to-be-forgotten moment, which brought sighs of relief from those looking on.

We proceeded through the other six points without a hitch— except one. Mr. Merciful, the most unfriendly one, again raised the question of the apology. He said it was certainly satisfactory, but he would like to see it repeated before a larger representative group of members of the community. Because the government officers suspected this was some kind of ploy, they reacted negatively. But, after considerable discussion, we finally decided to grant Mr. Merciful's request and set a time two days later when the gathering would take place. At the end of the meeting all were in good spirits and seemed to be happy and relieved that the misunderstandings had finally been overcome. Photographs were taken, and we all drank tea together.

At the opening of our official Field Council meetings later that day I was able to give an upbeat report on the developments of recent days, culminating in the climactic meeting that very morning. What a way to begin a Field Council meeting! All those present stood and sang the "Doxology," that majestic hymn song which begins, "Praise God from Whom all blessings flow."

Later that afternoon I headed for Chittagong. That wondrous day—and my elation—were topped off by one of the most glorious sunsets I have ever seen. It set my soul aglow. The following morning I was up at 4:45 A.M. to fly to Dacca for another Intermission Meeting. There I discovered that the letter to the president we had drafted had been through the mill and watered down a bit, so that all the different groups felt comfortable appending their names to it.

At Jalal's suggestion our British missionary friend Bill had contacted some British members of Parliament visiting in Dacca. He found them very cooperative. They encouraged the current British ambassador, who was much less helpful than his predecessor Mr. Smallman, to become more involved in the mission registration crisis. They also promised to get London to react to the Bangladesh government's pressure on British missionaries.

Vic gave an upbeat report to the Field Council

I flew back to Chittagong that same evening and enjoyed another spectacular ride to Malumghat. It was the time of a major Buddhist festival marked by *phanushes* in the sky. These were kite-paper and bamboo contrivances, each with a flickering fire inside, that floated upward-upward-upward. Literally dozens of these picturesque illuminated phanushes dotted the night sky. They were still in my mind later as I fell into a deep, exhausted sleep.

The following morning I was wide awake in an instant. The day of the final ceremonial apology had come. But soon Shahabuddin and Momin arrived with unsettling news: Mr. Merciful had come to Momin and, uncharacteristically, talked to him in soft, silken tones. He said, "There is no need to be in such a rush about this apology meeting. Besides, I am busy today. So I will not be able to bring the larger group of men to the 1:30 meeting, and I will not even be coming myself." Shahabuddin and Momin felt that this was another of the man's tricks.

Later they brought the chief of police to discuss the situation further. He saw no point in our attending the meeting, since the other parties would not be there. But I replied, "Regardless, we will be present according to the order of the SDO." There was a difference of opinion on this point for some minutes, but I felt that we had to stick to our guns and respect the SDO's order, even though we would be making a useless trip.

So at 1:30 P.M. Dick Stagg, John Bullock, and I arrived at the appointed place. Soon Shahabuddin, Momin, the police chief, and the president and vice-president of the Islamic Action Committee also appeared. Momin excitedly said to us, "You were very wise to insist on coming today! Mr. Merciful did not notify the other officers of the Action Committee that he was not bringing the larger group of men. If you had been absent as well, the two officers who have appeared would have been angry, thinking you did not care enough to come. Also, I heard that Merciful has been speaking against the agreement."

Confirming this point, Mr. Light explained, "After the congregational prayers and sermon at the mosque a while ago, after three-fourths of the men had left, Mr. Merciful harangued the rest of them against the mission and against the agreement. But he gained support only from his three leftist politician friends. The rest of the people just returned to their homes."

The police chief promised to notify the SDO that the mission representatives, out of respect for his order, had appeared at the appointed time to give the final apology to the larger representative group, as requested by Mr. Merciful. And he emphasized he would also report that Mr. Merciful had not appeared, but instead had agitated at the mosque against the official settlement. What a marvelous finale! Not only did we look very good, but the radical

Vic and the chief of police

Mr. Merciful lost the support of the mosque congregation, angered his fellow committee officers, and made himself look insincere to the government officers. This was a far more positive outcome than I had even hoped to see. "Thank You, Father!"

The following morning I brought Shahabuddin into our official Field Council session and presented him to the group. Then Medical Director John Bullock read a letter of commendation to him and officially thanked him for so effectively helping to resolve the local problem. Shahabuddin testified that, although he had worked hard from the human viewpoint, all credit must go to Allah Himself who had helped us very much. Before leaving, he went around the circle and shook the hand of every member of the Field Council. Several days later we had a similar ceremony and presented a letter of commendation to Momin, who had also worked wisely and efficiently to help achieve the settlement. Both men were quite pleased by these official expressions of appreciation.

Two afternoons later a messenger arrived from Cox's Bazar bringing our copy of a letter from the SDO to the DC in Chittagong, which stated that an amicable settlement had been reached. Most of the letter was fine, but I was stunned to read one paragraph that committed us to three things definitely not a part of the agreement. I quickly ascertained that no other copies of the letter had yet been distributed. That meant that we had to get to Cox's Bazar at once and deal with the problem before any other copies could be sent out. So Joan and I, Dick Stagg, and Momin left immediately for Cox's Bazar. We had no idea how the SDO would react, but if we failed to obtain a revised letter we would be in real difficulty. We did some serious praying.

Fortunately, the SDO was at home and available. We soon learned that the other copies of the letter were to be delivered the following morning. Then I mentioned that there were two or three problems in the letter that needed to be straightened out. He responded quickly that he had added a point about having all our new books checked by the Action Committee and asked if it should be deleted—since it had not been discussed in the negotiations. I replied that it ought to be deleted. After a little further discussion the SDO not only was kind enough to make all the necessary adjustments, but he sent someone to bring his secretary to the office so that the letter could be retyped right then. Since it was after 8:00 P.M., we four went out for dinner, then returned to pick up the excellent revised and retyped letter—with great relief.

Joan and I stayed overnight in the motel at Cox's Bazar and the next morning headed for the Cox's Bazar beach, said to be the longest sand beach in the world. It was a beautiful day, and the water was as lovely as I have ever seen it. With our minds free at last from concern about the troublesome and dangerous problem, frolicking awhile in the surf was simply delightful.

Back at Malumghat the next morning we had the special pleasure of having in our home for tea the elderly president and the vice-president of the Action Committee, Momin, and Dr. Matin. While drinking tea and eating good things we talked, reminisced, and rejoiced together that the problems were solved and that our long-standing friendship had been restored. They reported that Mr. Merciful was attempting a power play to take over the Action Com-

LEFT TO RIGHT: *Dr. Matin, Momin,*
the elderly president, Vic, and Mr. Light

mittee. As we talked, it was decided by consensus that the committee should remain intact with the same president and vice-president at the helm. That way, the Action Committee could act as a guarantor of the agreement that had been reached.

This local settlement had come none too soon, because in just four days we were scheduled to face the high-level inquiry into the matter in Dacca. On the last day of October Joan and I traveled to Chittagong and visited the DC and his wife in their home. She served us delicious refreshments and introduced their small son to us. As the DC had not yet received a copy of the SDO's letter about the local settlement, I provided a copy for him. He read it through with satisfaction. Then, to ease our way in the upcoming high-level inquiry, he promised to send a copy of the letter by special messenger on the late train to Dacca that very night.

Also, the DC told me that he had notified the upper levels of government that our hospital was a very fine institution, highly regarded by him and the people of the district, and that it must be protected and helped to remain open at all costs. I was pleased to know that he felt that way.

Finally, we discussed the two remaining possible danger points in the hospital locality. The first was Mr. Merciful who, although he was a party to the settlement, was speaking against it to the people. And second, closely connected with him were local anti-government political elements. The DC explained that he was aware of those people who were not only anti-government but also anti-American. He knew they would like nothing better than to close down the American hospital, which would bring great embarrassment to the government of Bangladesh.

On to Dacca. On November 2 Bengali and English language newspapers throughout the country contained the news that the book *There Is No Fear in Death* had been officially banned and that all copies were to be handed over to the government.

The next day the high-level inquiry into our problem with the troublesome book reached a climax. Our mission chairman and I had to face the secretary of the Ministry of Home Affairs about the book and the cancellation of the chairman's visa. As he opened the secret file before him the secretary's manner was brusque. "This book has caused trouble and injured the sentiments of the people of Dulahazara," he stated.

I explained the whole thing one last time, told him about the actions we had taken to resolve the problem, and apologized to him about the book and the problems it had caused.

I went on to explain that we had reached an amicable settlement with the Dulahazara Action Committee and asked him if he had received his copy of the SDO's letter on this point. When he

Joan with the DC's wife and son

Vic with the Chittagong DC

replied that it was probably in his office but he had not yet seen it, I handed him a copy of the important letter. That helped.

Then he raised the question of my colleague's visa, which had come within a hair's breadth of being canceled. Looking up at him from the file, the home secretary said gravely, "We were going to cancel your visa—but we have now withdrawn the cancellation order." We both thanked him for this welcome official news. It had all worked out just as the minister of the Home Ministry had promised.

Even though an attendant had brought in tea and cookies, the tenor of the interview had continued to be strictly business and very heavy. Smiling, I said, "Maybe we can look on these refreshments you have kindly served us as a celebration of the fact that this visa problem is now history and that the misunderstandings at Dulahazara have been cleared up." For the first time the home secretary cracked a minute smile, then changed the subject. For the final fifteen minutes we chatted about other things, then we walked out rejoicing that the whole complicated mess was finally behind us. "Thank You, Father!"

The next day, the first anniversary of the seizing and holding of American hostages in Iran, made me pause and think about the differences between various governments. In some countries the whole leadership and millions more seemed to be quite radical in their views. In Bangladesh, however, we had encountered only a very few extremists who had wanted to burn the hospital and hurt people. But the Bangladesh government officials, both upper-level and local, stood resolutely against those few radical people and prevented them from causing mayhem. Furthermore, with the exception of Mr. Merciful, I did not encounter a single government officer or member of the public who did not willingly grant forgiveness when I apologized to him about the offending book.

That same day my thoughts were also on another far-off nation, the U.S.A., for presidential elections were then in progress. Republican Ronald Reagan won a decisive victory.

With our mission registered and the disturbing agitation around the hospital finally resolved, I could now devote myself more fully to trying to help the rejected mission societies, including BMM led by Frank Patterson. Frank had recently received a severe blow; the Ministry of Health had sent him a letter stating that the ministry no longer approved his medical project. Without this approval, he knew the government's Standing Committee would never grant registration to his mission.

At this point another strategy, which we had been implementing to help BMM, reached a climax. We had learned that a recommendation from a powerful deputy prime minister from the northern part of the country, where BMM hoped to build their hospital, would be a great help to Frank. Fortunately, Jalal's sister and nephew knew the man well, for they lived in that same area of the country. When illness struck, both of them had come for surgery all the way from that northwestern corner of Bangladesh to Malumghat in the distant southeast. I had operated on the nephew, and Donn Ketcham had done an extremely complex operation on Jalal's sister. Jalal and I requested these two patients to contact the key deputy prime minister, tell him that they needed a hospital like ours in northern Bangladesh, and explain that the Ministry of Health was standing in the way. When they did this, the deputy prime minister was not only sympathetic but also contacted the chairman of the Standing Committee to tell him that he wanted to see BMM registered. Further, he obtained an appointment with the Minister of Health for Frank in an attempt to get the objection of that ministry overturned.

Frank and I went together to that immensely important appointment to talk with the minister of health, Dr. Matin, whom I had known for a long time. Smiling, he told Frank, "You should have no difficulty succeeding because your friend Dr. Olsen is a very powerful person." I chuckled at that, because none of us who are foreigners has any power at all. We are in the country as guests, our every project must be approved by the government, and the government has complete control over our visas. But, although we have zero political power, we are graciously allowed the opportunity to reason and negotiate, and perhaps we have some moral influence because of our love for the people and the good work we have come to do. And, more important, the Father seems to hear our prayers and answer them; that's where the real power lies.

Frank explained his problem and showed the health minister the relevant documents, including the disturbing negative letter issued by the minister's own subordinates. The minister looked at the material, then observed, "This letter that you are so worried about is not the *Al Koran*, so it can easily be changed." What music to our ears!

Then we learned in another government office that fifteen rejected missions had finally applied for reconsideration of their cases. We also picked up information that another of the strategies of our intermission group was bearing fruit. Some prominent Americans in the U.S., including some senators and congressmen, had been notified about the rejection of various missions and other voluntary agencies in Bangladesh. Some of those influential men had been bombarding the Bangladesh ambassador in Washington about this problem. His worried Telex messages back to Dacca placed additional pressure on the Bangladesh government to reconsider the rejections they had issued.

At 1:00 P.M. I drove to the Dacca home of M. R. Siddiqi, the previous Bangladesh ambassador to the United States. I went there for dinner and to examine the son of an acquaintance of his. The patient was a teenager who had been injured by shrapnel as a child during the 1971 war. The damaged artery in his leg had enlarged to become a fist-sized pulsating bulge (aneurysm) requiring surgery. I agreed to operate along with Dr. Khan, a well-trained cardiovascular surgeon in Dacca.

While eating a lovely dinner, Mr. Siddiqi and I had a pleasant time reminiscing about past experiences. I learned that he was then for the most part out of politics and working full-time in business. Although he had been a distinguished member of Sheikh Mujib's first Awami League cabinet, he explained that he had been "kicked out of the Awami League" because, during his tenure as Bangladesh ambassador in Washington, he had signed the agreement allowing American Peace Corps volunteers to serve in Bangladesh. Some AL leaders insisted that these volunteers would all be U.S. spies. He further explained that the Awami League, previously a broad middle-of-the-road party accepting rightists, leftists, and centrists, had become more left-leaning and out of alignment with his own rightist views.

When we talked again a few days later, Mr. Siddiqi laughingly told me that a Bengali newspaper had reported that I was in Dacca and had criticized him for fraternizing with me, an American, and again denounced the Peace Corps agreement.

Later that afternoon, representatives of other American mission agencies and I met with the U.S. ambassador in his office at his invitation. He wanted to report to us the results of his contact with the government on behalf of those American missions that had been denied registration.

The ambassador first explained that he made his primary approach to a branch of government that had a strong voice in deciding whether or not registration would be granted. This branch was the External Resources Division (ERD) of the Finance Ministry. ERD was also responsible for obtaining foreign aid and administering all funds that came to Bangladesh from other countries. Ambassador Schneider had talked to the ERD secretary and to the joint secretary (who was also chairman of the powerful Standing Committee).

The ambassador said he had first inquired about the criteria for registration. The joint secretary replied that it had been very difficult to establish criteria because they had to evaluate, not only mission societies, but relief organizations and other kinds of organizations receiving funds from abroad—240 in all. As he continued on, however, little by little in the free flow of the discussion four unwritten criteria gradually emerged:

1. Newer organizations that came after 1971 were usually denied registration.
2. Organizations having very high overhead expenses, with relatively little going into services, were usually refused registration.
3. Organizations that did work fitting into the government's overall development plan were being granted registration.
4. Organizations that worked wherever the government assigned them tended to gain registration.

The U.S. ambassador went on to explain that, at this point, the secretary had stepped in and promised that ERD would draw up a set of written criteria for registration in order to help the agencies in their applications and appeals. Also, he assured the ambassador that the mission personnel whose cases were pending would be allowed to remain in Bangladesh until the appeal process was complete and final decisions made.

At the end of their meeting Ambassador Schneider had warned the two men that there was every likelihood of a bad reaction in the U.S. if mission organizations were to be expelled from the country. First, he emphasized that missionaries are dedicated men and women and that they provide genuine services to the people. Periodically they return to the U.S. on home leave and travel widely throughout the country meeting many people in many churches and groups. In this role they are excellent ambassadors for Bangladesh as they speak highly of the country to large numbers of Americans. This strengthens the U.S. State Department's appeal to Congress to grant foreign aid for projects in Bangladesh. He also reminded them that just then foreign aid was a very sensitive topic in America. Many in the U.S. Congress were not favorable toward granting foreign aid. If missionaries were sent out of Bangladesh, this would become known immediately in Congress and could easily upset the future of U.S. aid to Bangladesh.

Having explained to us what had happened, Ambassador Schneider asked for our reactions. We thanked him and congratulated him on doing an excellent job. Not only had he obtained an assurance that written criteria would be provided but also the promise that those who were appealing rejections could remain in Bangladesh until the results of their appeals were known. We requested him to follow up with ERD in case time passed and the written criteria were not forthcoming.

Then the ambassador suggested that, if we desired, he could also make a single approach to the home minister to plead the case. He asked whether we would like to see that done soon or saved for an emergency somewhere down the line. This was not an easy question, because it could be argued either way. After we chewed on it for a while, I suggested that we must pursue a go-for-broke strategy. If the mission societies were again rejected, there would be no opportunity for further appeals. Therefore I thought he should contact the home minister soon so that he, too, would be aware of a probable negative reaction in the U.S.A. Furthermore, as the home minister was very close to President Zia, he would no doubt explain the risk of that negative reaction to the president. Perhaps the ambassador could, in this meeting with the home minister, also arrange to keep the door ajar for another meeting in the event of an emergency. There was general agreement that this would be the best way to proceed.

Finally, Ambassador Schneider stated that there seemed to be no possibility of strong collective action by several Western embassies, as had happened in 1977. Some current Western ambassadors, he explained, had declined to contact the government on the subject, whereas others had made a one-shot approach, not intending to make a second one. His words underscored the fact that the enthusiastic assistance given us by ten Western ambassadors in 1977 had been highly unusual.

The winter session of Parliament had been delayed—fortunately for us, as this had given us more time beforehand to reach a harmonious settlement of the problem in Dulahazara. The Parliament session finally began on November 23. Jalal felt that Joan and I should remain in the country until that session of Parliament was completed several weeks later, just in case reaction against Christian missions should again flare up on the Parliament floor.

To redeem the time I spent the first week in December tracking down our application for a food ration shop for our hospital's patients and employees. I shuttled back and forth several times between the Food Ministry (where policy decisions are made) and the Food Directorate (where policy decisions are carried out). The directorate officer was prepared to recommend ration shop privileges for our patients but not for the employees. But I gave several reasons why our employees should be considered. Convinced, he wrote a letter to the Food Ministry encouraging them to approve my request as a special case.

The first officer I met in the ministry asked me to examine his heart, which was giving him trouble. I promised that I would bring my stethoscope and check it. As we discussed the application he meticulously wrote all my positive arguments in the file. Then he sent me to the deputy secretary, a Mr. Chakma from Rangamati, who knew our hospital well because he had once served in Cox's Bazar. He said he would do his best to help us.

Two days later I finally met the secretary of the Food Ministry, who would actually make the decision. During the hospital union crisis, he had been serving in another ministry and had opposed our stand. After looking at the file he stated, "I can easily approve a ration shop for the patients of your hospital, but I cannot give your staff ration shop privileges. There is simply no precedent for granting this to a private hospital."

I stood, walked across the room, then showed him on the huge map on his wall how we were serving as a district hospital for the southern halves of both Chittagong and Chittagong Hill Tracts districts. I explained, "You see, in the absence of a government district hospital in these areas, we do the work of such a hospital. As the staffs of government hospitals enjoy ration shop privileges, it seems reasonable that our staff should enjoy the same benefits. Furthermore, every one of your food officers out in the subdivision, in the district, at the Food Directorate and also in your own ministry, have favored the idea of our staff enjoying these privileges."

Feeling the pressure of these arguments and all the supporting reports in the file, he suddenly changed the subject. He confided that he was under great stress because the Parliament was demanding from him written answers to various questions. Not only that, a certain parliamentary committee was holding him responsible for the shortcomings of some of his subordinate officers. At that moment the telephone rang. It was the secretary of Parliament himself—Jalal! He put in a good word for us, explaining to the secretary that ours was a very worthy organization. Just then Mr. Chakma came in with papers for the file and showed him his own note recommending the case.

Exasperated, the secretary burst out, "But how can we agree to this when there is no precedent for it?" Mr. Chakma answered that we could be allowed this privilege as a special case, considering that we were doing the work of a government district hospital. "Not only that," he added, "but I think that we may have discovered a precedent—a private hospital at Mirzapur." These arguments, plus the mounting pressure squeezing him from all sides, turned the trick. The secretary suddenly picked up his pen and scratched, "Approved," on the application. I was delighted, for this would be a great boost for our dedicated staff and our patients. "Thank You, Father!"

Two weeks later our friend Frank Patterson was in real trouble. He was about to face the government's Standing Committee, but the health minister had not yet provided the all-important Health Ministry letter of clearance. Without this key document the Standing Committee would never approve Frank's mission (BMM) for registration. Because he had to have that letter the next day, and because it was past office hours, drastic action was necessary. I asked Jalal to call the minister of health at home and somehow persuade him to meet us at Jalal's office, where Frank could talk with him face-to-face and convey to him the urgency of the situation.

Jalal picked up the telephone, and I listened to his end of the conversation. "Please give me the minister. Of course he's there! I know he is there! Tell him that the secretary of Parliament is calling." The houseboy then went and called the minister out of bed. Jalal requested him to come to the Parliament Building immediately, as we had an urgent matter to discuss with him. The minister wearily agreed to come. Then, turning to me, Jalal said, "You will have to take the blame for calling the minister out of his bed so that I don't get into his bad book." So when the minister arrived I told him I was the culprit behind the telephone call and apologized for causing him this inconvenience. Then I explained, "The last possible minute has come for Mr. Patterson to obtain the letter you promised him; he must have it in his hands tomorrow morning." Frank went on to explain the reasons he needed the letter immediately. The minister kindly asked us to meet him in his office at 8:45 the following morning. Wonderfully, Frank obtained the essential letter in time for his meeting with the Standing Committee.

We enjoyed Christmas Day in Dacca, but our joy was turned to shock and sorrow when we learned that Karolyn Kempton, wife of our mission president, Wendell Kempton, had just died of a sudden brain hemorrhage. What an immense loss to Dr. Kempton, their children, and the whole mission! We grieved for this precious family from afar.

The next day the letter we had drafted to President Zia paid off. The chairman and the secretary of the intermission group had a quite positive meeting with the president. He told them that he did not want to see any mission personnel leaving the country, adding that anyone with any problems could work them out with the minister of religion, who was also present at the meeting. It appeared that the pressures applied by the U.S. ambassador and other diplomats in Dacca—plus pressure on Bangladesh diplomats from various nations' senators, congressmen, and members of Parliament in Washington and other world capitals—were paying off.

Throughout the year, President Zia had been very much involved with foreign policy and trips abroad. To the United Nations General Assembly he spoke vividly of the immense problems of the thirty-one least developed countries (LDCs). Further, he made everyone sit up and take notice when he requested the developed nations to double their aid to the LDCs and also asked the OPEC oil-producing countries to cut the price of oil in half for the LDCs. And he proposed a further massive transfer of resources from developed nations to the developing nations through a special tax on international trade and purchases of arms. His bold speech created quite a stir at the UN and in the world press.

Shortly thereafter he traveled to Washington, D.C., where he had a warm meeting with President Jimmy Carter. President Carter commented favorably on Zia's forthright speech in the UN and emphasized that the open and free election process in Bangladesh had been an inspiration to the world. Pretty heady stuff!

By year's end we returned to Malumghat just in time for some excitement. Our newest nurse at the hospital, Nancie Dellaganna, one evening walked off the end of a sidewalk into the grass, nearly stepping on a highly poisonous five-foot snake, a yellow-banded krait. At the nearby guest house, we and the Nuscas heard her sudden call for help. Bob and I went running, and Bob made short work of the creature with a powerful shotgun. Nancie, a capable nurse, had trained at Biola University, where our Lynne had studied. Along with her nursing duties she was working on the translation of a health book in Bengali to help us get across basic health information to our patients and the general public. Nancie also became an expert anesthetist, which has been a great help to those of us who perform surgery.

Nurse Nancie Dellaganna

Nineteen eighty had been a traumatic year for us and for the government and people of Bangladesh. The riots around the country, the aggressive stance of the opposition parties, and severe economic problems had created intense pressure on the fledgling democracy. Maybe next year would be a little easier for all of us.

Key Events of 1980: Summary

January
- A new leftist pro-Soviet ten-party alliance is formed; when Zia rejects their demands they boycott Parliament.

February
- Military action occurs near Hebron Station; at the government's request our Hebron workers transfer to Malumghat.
- The government "Standing Committee" refuses registration to some foreign missions and other organizations.
- The worst strikes, student protests, and street violence in four years assail Dacca.

March
- Violence also escalates in the Chittagong Hill Tracts.
- Report of Kaokhali massacre of tribespeople in the CHT.

June
- Report of Mandai massacre of Bengalis by tribals in India.
- In Dacca an attempted coup by army personnel fails.
- A crisis in the hospital area is caused by a book that offended the public; Action Committee is formed.

July
- Two processions against the hospital are stopped.
- The Action Committee sends complaints to the government.
- Christian missions are criticized on the Parliament floor.
- Zia promotes his "peaceful revolution" while the Second Five-Year Plan begins.

August
- A meeting between mission and Action Committee officers fails to clear up the misunderstanding about the book.
- Our mission team requests us to return to help resolve the crises (mission registration and the book problem).

September
- Joan and I reach Dacca; I meet Jalal, other senior government officials, mission leaders, and church leaders.
- The Standing Committee grants registration to our mission, but rejects others.

October
- I request the U.S. ambassador to help the rejected missions.
- We proceed to Malumghat. I apologize (for selling the controversial book) to local government officers and influential members of the public; they grant forgiveness.
- We meet three times with the Action Committee officers; they accept our apology, and the tension eases.

November
- The government bans the troublesome book.
- We meet the home secretary; he also accepts our apology.
- We meet the U.S. ambassador; he has done well in his approach to the government regarding the rejected missions.

Figure 31

14

1981: President's Parley—
President's Peril

Nineteen eighty-one was the final year of Bangladesh's first decade. And it started out just fine. The key leaders of the Islamic Action Committee invited our men for a friendly tea to be held at Momin's house near Dulahazara bazaar. We enjoyed the warmth of our time with the elderly chairman, Mr. Light, Dr. Matin, and Momin. They explained proudly how they had been working since our last meeting to preserve the settlement. Delegations had come to them from three distant areas, complaining that according to the bamboo telegraph the Action Committee had settled the dispute for a 200,000-taka bribe from the mission. This rumor was started by Mr. Merciful, who had by now completely broken with the other members of the Action Committee.

The committee officers had replied that such a report was completely false. In fact, they assured these delegations, an amicable settlement had been reached satisfactory to the Action Committee, the SDO, and the mission. We thanked them for standing behind the settlement so steadfastly. Our time together was simply delightful. I would have been happy just to see the original difficult situation improve from strong-negative to neutral, but it had actually advanced to strong-positive.

The next day Joan and I were packing furiously to leave Malumghat and return to the U.S. I took time out, however, to hear Mr. Light's symptoms, examine him, and obtain the necessary X rays. Finally, I explained the diagnosis and prescribed for him. He was grateful, for he knew that I was seeing no other patients during the rush before our departure. His final words were these: "Please forgive me for all the troubles I have caused you."

During our final three days at Malumghat we completed a minidictionary containing the key vocabulary used in the special

Bengali common language New Testament. Joan had done the lion's share of the work on this project—several hundred hours—while I was busy dealing with the various problems. This small dictionary would be a great help to foreign and minority community people who needed to understand these beautiful and important words used in the translation.

We then proceeded to Dacca for our final two weeks' work before flying out to the U.S. Frank Patterson met us with the report that the clearance letter provided by the minister of health had smoothed the way for him in his meeting with the Standing Committee. The previous rejection of BMM had been canceled and registration granted. We rejoiced with Frank and his wife, Vanza, over this great news.

On January 18 Joan and I had an unusual personal summit meeting with President Ziaur Rahman. At the palatial President's House we were received cordially by a very pleasant lieutenant colonel, then taken to a special reception room. Soon President Zia, dressed rather nattily in a gray suit, came in and greeted us; he readily agreed to our recording the interview. I explained who we were and that we had come to Bangladesh enough years before that our children had grown up in the country. Thoughtfully, he asked about the children. Then I continued, "I remember that I last heard you speak at the inaugural meeting of the Parliament."

"That was two years ago," he replied. "It was a very stormy time, wasn't it?"

"It was stormier in the morning than during your appearance in the afternoon; everything was quite calm by then. I appreciated your speech. What did you think when you walked out on that plat-

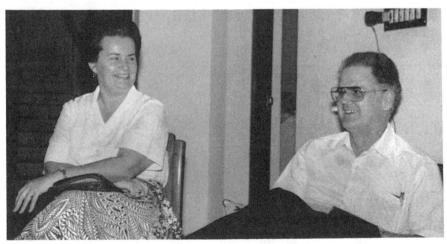

Frank and Vanza Patterson

Gate to the palatial President's House

form for the first time and looked into the faces of those 330 members of Parliament?"

"Oh, it was a great day!" Zia exclaimed. "It was a great day for this country, because it wasn't easy to do the whole thing. You know all the background—after 1971 what all happened. We were sucked into the whole matter. And gradually the responsibility came on me. Bangladesh is a very difficult country, I tell you," the president emphasized with a chuckle. "It's a small area, yet there are ninety million people now. There is poverty, underdevelopment, no system. The worst thing is that we did not have a system in the government or in the political realm. We did not have law and order; it must have been bad in your area. It was just fighting against impossibilities. . . . There are two ways of doing it, of meeting the situation. One is to say, 'Impossible,' and run away. The other is to say, 'Nothing has happened, so get moving.' So we decided to say the latter, and we kept moving."

Then I took the president back to his early days. He had been born and reared in a village in the district of Bogra. His father became a "small government officer, a chemist who worked in a testing laboratory." At age seventeen Zia had joined the army and been successful in his military career. He went on, "In 1970 I was posted to Chittagong in the 18th Bengal Regiment; I was second in command. And on the twenty-fifth night [of March 1971] all these things [the Pakistan Army attack] started. Around midnight we knew the whole thing. Early in the morning of the twenty-sixth I took out my battalion and proceeded toward your side to Patiya, because first we had to withdraw in order to reorganize—a lot of boys were killed, you see. To begin with, I had about 220 fellows.

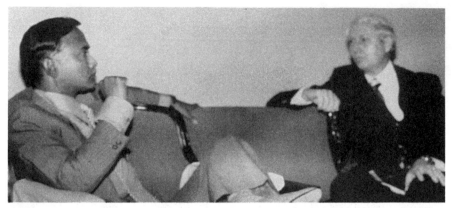

President Zia and Vic

We went to the hills, reorganized, and came back; after that the whole thing spread."

Then I asked President Zia what had happened four years later after the assassination of Sheikh Mujib in August 1975. He replied, "After August there were coups and countercoups. In 1976 there were a lot of coups; in 1977 there was a lot of trouble also. And in October 1977 there was a big problem. But during that whole period, irrespective of what was happening, we were pushing the country toward democracy. Although there was martial law, it was more or less in name. Armed forces officers did not administer much except in a few small places, only a few courts."

"What were the main steps of progress in 1976?" I asked.

"Right from the early days of 1976 what we tried to do was just dig up all those previous [government] schemes and plans to find out what had been done so far. Then you will remember that I did the finance minister job for three years. Oh, it was terrible! There was no money, no foreign exchange. But still we had to get things moving. And it is surprising how much can be done without having anything. It was a great experience for me. In any case, I was neither a student of economics nor of finance. But we made a decision to up the annual foreign exchange and also increase the local earnings, the revenue. And we started a number of projects which now are getting completed; a good number of projects have already been completed which we started in 1976."

To my questions about the presidential and parliamentary elections Zia responded, with the lift of an eyebrow, "In early 1978 I started contacting all the politicians. It was very difficult to reach an understanding. The whole thing in democracy is a matter of compromises. Night after night, the whole night, I kept them sitting in my house or in this room. And then, gradually, after quite a few months we managed to get over the difficulties.

"The people then asked, 'What are you going to do?' Then we formed a political party, because unless we have a party for ourselves we can't make a front [alliance] with others. So we made a party. Then we made a front, and with the front we went for the presidential elections. For that we made some changes in the Constitution so that it was democratic. This gave anybody in the opposition enough [opportunity]. Because if there is no opposition—good opposition—then democracy will not work. And I never thought that I would get so many votes; I just kept working.

"Then after the election we set a timetable for the parliamentary election; it was to take place in December. I was bent upon it. But the opposition, they thought that this was a bluff. When they found that the dates were declared and that I was serious about the whole thing, then they said, 'Oh, you can't do it so quickly.' Because they raised so many problems, it had to be delayed by about two months to February 1979.

"I was very sure what I was going to do in my capacity as president. We blocked out a time program. We were determined to get back the democratic process—that was the singular objective. Around that we built up everything else. [We said,] 'The election has got to be held! Democracy has to be got back! Martial law has to be lifted!' In fact, we lifted the martial law earlier than when it was agreed upon. . . . It was a big risk to do politics at this level without knowing people. And I didn't know anybody. But, as God willed it, the thing succeeded.

"Then the Parliament sat, and people said, 'It's not going to last. It will not last for three months. And surely it will not last over six months.' But two years have passed, and it lasted. So the whole thing boils down to purpose and sincerity. And I find that problems, one after the other, have been overcome. Things are happening; good things are happening.

"During those two [election] years the development program, although it suffered, we managed to carry on reasonably well. But it was most important to get back democracy; it was most important to have elections, even if the economy suffered a little."

In response to questions about the results of democracy and the various development projects President Zia responded, "You cannot expect miracles to happen in this country. Right now it is terribly hard work; it has been the worst nightmare. We did not have any organization; you know that. Now we have organized the villages, and I can assure you we are going to develop. Right now we don't have enough storehouses to keep all the food we have. The prices have gone down so much. And the way the people are digging canals now is fantastic. The canals are much better now with better engineering, you know, and very long. The other day in Rangpur they were digging one canal twenty-six miles long." The water collected in these canals would be used for irrigation during the dry season, ensuring three crops per year.

I asked about his new village government program. Zia replied, "People have got to be organized and, because of our long two hundred years of colonial past, we do not have organization —neither political nor social organization. So, *swarnivar gram sharkar* [self-reliant village government] is our new socioeconomic organization. Now we have people at the village able to say, 'Look, this is what you should do, and we know something about it because we have some experience.'

"We are decentralizing and restructuring the government. You know, there are a lot of strikes among the government officials. We said, 'We have got to change the system; otherwise, it just won't work.' And we changed it for the better and now it will work. . . . It is necessary to sort of arouse people politically and to arouse them economically and socially. And that is what we are doing. And we are finding opposition. So wherever we find opposition, we know this is the right place to work.

"The people have tremendous energy. There are ninety million people, and they were not being utilized. They were getting wasted, there was no direction set, and they were not organized. So, by the grace of God, henceforth I think the country will move forward—in spite of all these heavy burdens that have come upon us because of inflation and oil prices."

By then our time was up, but President Zia asked, "Are you very busy right now? Why don't you have a cup of tea in the next room until I finish up with the next gentleman? Then we can talk some more." So we slipped out to enjoy tea and conversation with his military secretary, General Choudhury. He told us about the president's recent visit to New York City to address the United Nations—and his rather late-night look at the city.

Later, back in the reception room with President Zia I continued, "We just heard from General Choudhury that you had an interesting night on the town in New York City."

"Oh, yes, yes. I didn't get time to look at the city during the daytime, so from midnight we went around, and we got on top of the tallest building. It was quite funny—everything was closed. But the guard was very nice and said, 'I will open it up.' So we got a good look around." Then Zia talked about his visit to Washington, D.C., and his meeting with President Carter. "Oh, yes, we had a very fine talk. He is a very pleasant person."

"And as I recall, your parting comment to him was that you appreciated his stand on human rights," I remembered aloud.

"Yes, yes. I made that comment. It's true, you see. What is true must be expressed."

He had quite a lot to say about the women of Bangladesh. "The womenfolks are coming forward nowadays, you know. And we are trying to utilize them for useful work. Initially we were under great pressure from the people who are conservative, and they think that our religion does not allow women out. I said, 'No,' and I quoted from the Holy Koran, and I kept on quoting. I said that in our religion men and women are equal and in no other religion. . . . Now womenfolks are coming forward—and the men are very afraid."

Then he spoke about controlling the burgeoning population: "Family planning—you [Americans] always hit us on that. But we are going to be one country where family planning will succeed."

"Why is that?" I asked.

"Because we have to succeed. There is no way out. During the last few years we have been a little slow because we have a lot of maulvis [fundamentalist Muslim priests], you know. So now we have got them with us. Now we can force everybody to cooperate. Since last week I have started saying in public meetings, 'One child!'"

That was a change, for the official government position had long been "Two children are enough." The president continued, "And the womenfolks—the girls—they all agree. It is the building

Zia: "Good things are happening"

of the mental attitude that is most important. That's what it takes; the actual doing is nothing. On the canal digging I have been working since 1976. It took me three years to convince the people. Now it's just like that!" he exclaimed, snapping his fingers.

I asked him how many days he worked each week. He replied, "I virtually work every day. Today I am back from Chittagong. Last night I stayed at Teknaf and the previous night at Bandarban in a tribal village. It was pretty cold, you know. They made a hut for me—just a hut with those bamboo walls. And they gave me some blankets which were too small in size. I am not a tall man, but those blankets were too small. I pulled them up—and my legs were out; all night I couldn't sleep."

Smiling, Joan commented, "My husband has that problem, too."

Zia replied with a laugh, "Yes, he is tall even for an American."

Then I thanked President Zia for his decision to reverse the 1977 visa policy, which had required foreigners to leave the country. He replied, "Listen, I tell you no country can survive by itself. I just told the Swedish TV the other day, 'We are all interdependent.'"

I thanked him, also, for voicing his support for registering the various mission societies that had been rejected for registration. He responded, "I said, 'If anybody is doing a good work, why should he go away?' We need a lot of help, you see. If anybody is doing even a small piece of good work he is valuable."

Then I mentioned the order to us and others that the number of our expatriates must be reduced. I explained that we, too, are stimulated about the development of the country and feel that we have a part to play in it. And I added, "Then suddenly when an order comes along saying, 'Well, you'll have to leave,' or, 'Your numbers will have to be cut down,' it's like a knife in the heart."

"Right. If you have a problem, we'll ask into it," President Zia replied. "I'll look into it!"

I thanked him for this promise, then congratulated him on somehow managing to convince the Burmese to take back the Burmese Bengali refugees. I asked him how it had been accomplished. Although part of his reply was not for publication, I can say that direct negotiations took place with the highest political leadership of Burma—and those negotiations were successful. The president reminded me, "Every refugee is now back. And this was the only success of its type in the whole world. But it didn't get the proper publicity." I certainly agreed with that point; the *un*solved refugee problems around the planet were the ones hitting the headlines.

At the end, President Zia thoughtfully said, "I wish you had come earlier. You have stayed in the country for such a long time that you have a right to know many secrets which others do not. You are not a foreigner anymore. You have a right to know. You are leaving the country tomorrow, I am told. When you come back you come to see me again." We appreciated his invitation and agreed to do so. As we stood to leave he continued, "I do not look on you as an American. You'll be my friend, OK?"

"I like that idea," I replied.

Joan suggested, "Maybe he could be both."

"No," Zia responded, laughing, "you will be my friend." The meaning was clear; a person had to get beyond being a foreigner and become one with the Bengali people before he or she could be considered a true friend.

We departed, stimulated by this lengthy, fascinating discussion. The media had often commented on the president's charisma and his work ethic; we sensed both of these qualities as we talked with him. He also seemed to have the ability to analyze a problem, organize solutions, motivate friends, and negotiate with opponents. And he showed a curious mixture of patience and impatience—he was impatient to see results happen on schedule, but patient enough to keep plugging away when that didn't happen. He seemed to be far more tuned in to the common man—and woman—than the leaders of some countries. And he was young enough that he would be able to serve his country for years if he could continue to win elections—and survive the mutinies and coup attempts that periodically threatened him and his regime.

On our last day in the country I worked with two Bangladeshi surgeons to operate on the teenage boy referred to us by former ambassador M. R. Siddiqi. The large pulsating lump in the boy's leg was difficult to remove, but finally the job was done. At the same time our five-month emergency stint in Bangladesh was also completed.

The next day, January 20, 1981, we flew out of Dacca on our way to the U.S. On that exact day Ronald Reagan was inaugurated as the new American president. Twenty-four minutes later, while he was still delivering his inaugural address, the fifty-two American hostages were flown out of Iran.[1] Finally, after a 444-day nightmare, they were free again, and Americans, wherever they were located around the globe, rejoiced at this thrilling news.

During the last week of January we enjoyed a happy reunion with our children and prepared for Lynne's marriage. What a pleasure it was to be together again! The last day of the month was memorable because of Lynne and Harry's lovely wedding in a beautiful garden chapel in California.

When we had departed Bangladesh earlier in the month we could see looming on the horizon a severe personnel crunch, especially of administrators. This would pose a serious problem because of the ongoing negotiations with the government about the "expatriates should be reduced" order. President Zia had agreed to look into the problem, but some experienced person needed to follow up on that. So we had requested speedy notification if the mission had any thought of recalling us from home leave again. In mid-February that word came from the new Field Council chairman:

> I would like to take this opportunity to again express the official thanks of the entire Bangladesh Field Council family to the two of you for interrupting your plans to come out here and give us some very valuable and timely help when it was so vitally needed. Certainly the Lord used you again in accomplishing His purposes for His work in Bangladesh.
>
> You know, of course, the delicate state of negotiations concerning both the number of personnel we will be allowed and the necessary visas for them. . . . The Field Council has voted to ask you to return in time for the next Field Council session beginning March 22, 1981, and to handle the work now being done by the Chief Administrative Officer until a suitable replacement returns to the field.

It was clear that we again had to respond to the emergency need of our team in Bangladesh. After cabling them that we would be coming as requested, we spent the rest of February preparing for the trip and visiting loved ones.

When we traveled to Wheaton, Illinois, we discovered that the family occupying our house was delighted that we would be returning overseas, since they had not yet sold their house in another city. How convenient for both our families! In Wheaton we stayed with dear friends of long standing, Roger and Alice Dauchy. They were wonderfully hospitable, and their lovely home was always open to us. Alice also sacrificially undertook to mail out our books to those who ordered them; that was an immense help. Another much-appreciated lady, Margaret Nendick, also spent long hours for a year or two mailing out our books. How fortunate we are to have such generous, faithful friends!

February was also a significant month for our team in Bangladesh. The local Malumghat theological training program had been upgraded into a full-fledged fieldwide theological school named the Baptist Bible Institute of Bangladesh (BBIB); the institute offers a three-year diploma program and a four-year degree program. Dave Totman became the head of this new theological institute, and Dr. Dick Stagg taught the initial course, first to church leaders at Malumghat for two weeks, then for two weeks to

BBIB class

those in Chittagong City. Because some of these leaders at Malumghat were male nurses or technicians in the hospital, our American nurses and technicians put in an immense number of extra working hours to free the students for their studies. That was true teamwork in action.

During that same February, thirty miles away in Cox's Bazar, the armed services carried out "Exercise Ironshield," a major military maneuver that involved amphibious landings on the beach. President Zia and other top military and civilian VIPs were there to observe the exercise. According to an investigative reporter, a secret plot was operating simultaneously behind the scenes. A group of Chittagong-based army officers led by their senior general planned to assassinate President Zia, the prime minister, other ministers, and the top army brass, then take over the country. At the last minute, for unknown reasons, General Manzoor did not give the fateful signal to open fire.[2] Again, Zia had narrowly escaped assassination.

In mid-March, after our final good-byes, Joan and I flew out of California across the Pacific Ocean to Dacca; this was the fifth time that I or both of us had interrupted our furlough to return to help out in Bangladesh. At the Bangladesh Bible Society office in Dacca we found everyone buzzing with excitement. They had received the first 40,000 copies of our special Bengali common language New Testament from Hong Kong. These Scriptures were selling so rapidly that another 40,000 already had been ordered. There were large and small vinyl-covered editions, each available in a choice of three colors. The mid-sized edition, also available in three colors, was the most important because it was an inexpensive paper-

back. The printing and binding were simply beautiful. We noted
this development in the life of the nation with immense satisfaction.

In Dacca we also learned that all except two of the fifteen rejected mission societies had finally been approved for registration.
And those two were allowed to continue their work under the aegis
of other organizations. The long hours of devising strategies in the
intermission meetings, the outstanding cooperation of the American ambassador and a few other diplomats, the pressure of irate
senators, congressmen, and members of Parliament on Bangladesh
ambassadors abroad, the intervention of sympathetic government
officials, volumes of prayer, endless negotiations, and the positive
response of the president had finally turned the trick. "Thank You,
Father!"

During our days in Dacca we learned that President Zia had
continued to gain stature on the international stage. Two months
earlier he had played a sufficiently prominent role in the Islamic
Summit meetings to be elected one of the three vice-presidents of
the Organization of Islamic Countries. And another of his recent
ideas was beginning to gain recognition; I speak of his formal proposal to establish a forum of the seven nations of South Asia (India,
Pakistan, Bangladesh, Sri Lanka, Nepal, Bhutan, and the Mal-
dives). Even India's prime minister Indira Gandhi called this a
statesmanlike vision. This proposal ultimately developed into a
significant organization, the South Asian Association for Regional
Cooperation (SAARC); in this forum the seven nations explore a
wide range of issues of mutual concern.

On the home front Zia and his government continued to stress
the establishment in every village of *swarnivar gram sharkar* (self-
reliant village government). Each "self-reliant" village council was
given four major tasks:

1. Stop the village's population explosion
2. Double the local rice and wheat production
3. Teach the people how to read
4. Maintain law and order

We reached Malumghat in time to participate in our annual
Field Council meetings. During the two days of reports and discussion of business matters a decision was made to change the title of
the chief administrative officer to director of administration—
DOA. As I would be wearing this new title for a while, I had to
speak to the point: "No physician could be happy with the title
'DOA,' for to us it means 'dead on arrival.'" So we decided that the

director of administration would be known as the DA. In addition, I was elected Field Council chairman. One person is not supposed to hold both of these offices simultaneously, but we would be so short-staffed over much of the next six months that we were forced to double up. In fact, I also had to become the acting chairman of Chittagong Station Council, for we would be living in personnel-starved Chittagong City during this period.

On March 23, during these Field Council meetings, two seriously injured patients were brought to the hospital from Cox's Bazar; they had sustained their injuries in a riot at a government-sponsored exhibition. One patient angrily exploded, "Some religious priests led a huge, noisy procession to the exhibition center because they thought the cultural dances were anti-Islamic. Suddenly they got ugly and began throwing stones and bricks—and they set some of the stalls on fire." In fact, the newspapers reported that fifty stalls had been gutted by fire and twenty-two people injured.[3]

The main leader of the four-thousand-strong procession turned out to be good old Mr. Merciful. By this time he was in hiding because there was a warrant out for his arrest; the SDO was furious with him. Although the first phalanx of the procession had been composed of Islamic fundamentalists, they had been joined by hooligans, by thieves interested in looting, and by leftist political elements who aimed to embarrass the government.

After the conclusion of the Field Council meetings we began to prepare for our move to Chittagong. We were looking forward to living in bustling Chittagong City, but we knew we would miss beautiful Malumghat—it was home. So we savored the lovely foliage, the tall, stately trees, and the songs of the forest birds. One of them seemed to be saying again and again, "Oh, wow! Oh, wow!" Just then the first "jackfruit bird" (Indian cuckoo) began singing its piercing four-note song, which is said to be announcing, *"Katal paka* [The jackfruit is ripe]!"

On the last day of March we were shaken by the news that U.S. President Ronald Reagan had been shot by a demented young man. On our side of the world we added our prayers to those of his family members and the American public. We were greatly relieved when news broadcasts began announcing that he was on the mend. It struck us as ironic that President Reagan and three others had been seriously injured by the first attempt of an amateur civilian assassin, using only a small handgun, while President Zia had never been scratched in more than twenty mutinies and assassination attempts by experienced military men with tanks, artillery, rockets, and automatic weapons at their disposal. He seemed to be leading a charmed life—but could he continue to be so fortunate indefinitely?

We spent two weeks at Malumghat, packing up things that we would need for our stay in Chittagong City. After a final tribal curry with Tippera friends we departed from Malumghat to set up housekeeping in Chittagong City. By the end of April I had taken over the DA work from Jack Archibald.

Living in Dacca for language study at that time was a new family, Larry and Nancy Allen and their four children. Larry was a theological teacher who had also been a medical technician in the armed services; he ultimately devoted himself to establishing and building up churches in and around Chittagong City. Nancy, a busy homemaker and language student, had noticed a small lump in her neck, which she asked me to examine one day when I was in Dacca. On examination I found the lump to be a tumor in her thyroid gland. I recommended that the Allens go to the United States for the necessary operation because the surgeon would need to have a pathologist in attendance during surgery. The pathologist would immediately freeze the removed tumor, prepare slides, and examine the tissue under a microscope while Nancy was still on the operating table. He would then tell the surgeon whether the tumor was completely removed and whether it was malignant or benign. This procedure is called "frozen section control."

Because we did not have a pathologist available at Malumghat we could not provide this necessary control, so the Allens flew to the U.S. Fortunately, the tumor turned out to be benign and the operation successful. And, in another fascinating twist of this incident, there in the U.S. Larry was able to help his slowly dying father make the great faith decision before he left this world. The timing of their unexpected trip had been ideal. "Thank You, Father!"

During that period, while the Ketchams and Staggs were in the U.S. and while I was tied down in Chittagong with administrative duties, short-term surgeons were an immense help to us at Malumghat. Dr. Jim and Mae Teeter, who had done a fine job, were departing, being replaced by Dr. Jim Shane. Jim, a friend of many years' standing, with his wife, Janet, had supported us and our work for many years. It was a delight to see him again. A few days later Dr. Bill and Barbara Barrick and their four children arrived in Chittagong. Bill was a highly trained Hebrew scholar who would effectively plug into our Old Testament translation projects. Barb would be a busy homemaker, primary school teacher, and capable guesthouse supervisor.

As I settled into my new office in Chittagong City I was oblivious of the fact that behind the scenes there was skulduggery afoot. Two army lieutenant colonels stationed in the Chittagong sector not only had a burning hatred for President Zia, but they were

Translator Dr. Bill Barrick

determined to act on it.[4] Lieutenant Colonels Moti and Mehboob (their nicknames) had fought as freedom fighters against the Pakistan Army during the 1971 civil war. They felt that Zia, himself a freedom fighter, should be giving the best army posts to freedom fighter officers because they had fought for their country. Instead, Zia seemed to favor the repatriates, those officers who had been held in Pakistan and returned only after the fighting was over.

M. and M. (Moti and Mehboob) also complained that Zia's lifting of martial law and civilianizing the country had caused the high prices, riots in the streets, and all the other problems afflicting the nation. So, like Majors Farook and Rashid six years earlier, they had been plotting for a long time to do away with the president —and also some top army generals—then take over the country. In fact, they and three other officers had been behind the aborted plan to assassinate Zia and others three months earlier at Cox's Bazar during the military drill code-named Exercise Ironshield.[5]

Unlike Majors Farook and Rashid, who had utilized no top-level officers in their assassination of Sheikh Mujib, M. and M. were in league with the powerful commanding general of the whole Chittagong sector, Maj. Gen. M. A. Manzoor; the general was also Mehboob's uncle. The ambitious, imperious Manzoor hated President Zia for a reason. During a 1977 coup attempt he had reportedly saved Zia's life and hoped to be rewarded with the top position in the army command structure. Instead, Zia had given the coveted post to General Ershad, a repatriate officer, and had assigned former freedom fighter Manzoor to Chittagong; General Manzoor looked on this as the equivalent of being shipped off to Siberia.[6]

These angry men even had a Dacca accomplice in President's House itself at Zia's right hand. He was Lieutenant Colonel Mahfuz (his nickname), the president's personal staff officer.[7] This conspirator was the pleasant lieutenant colonel who had welcomed Joan and me to President's House a few weeks earlier.

On May 25 Moti traveled to Dacca and made contact with his friend Lieutenant Colonel Mahfuz. Mahfuz tipped off Moti that within a week Zia would be transferring General Manzoor from Chittagong to Dacca to become the commandant of the Army Staff College; this meant that for the first time in his career Manzoor would not be in command of troops. This news deeply disturbed Moti because he knew it would be extremely difficult to assassinate Zia and the top army brass if General Manzoor were in Dacca with no officers or troops at his disposal.

Then Mahfuz further confided that President Zia would be traveling to Chittagong four days later. Moti could see immediately that this would be their last chance to exterminate Zia before Manzoor shifted to Dacca in just six days.

The following day Moti returned to Chittagong to update his inner circle on the disturbing developments—and also on the golden opportunity that would be theirs when Zia came to Chittagong. Although they could not agree on an exact plan of action, there was a consensus that they must try to erase Zia during his one-day stay in Chittagong.

Then, to drum up the support of all the former freedom fighter officers, Moti began to spread the word that President Zia was coming to Chittagong to activate a secret plan to eliminate the freedom fighters.[8] He backed up this tall tale with a false list of Chittagong-sector officers; there were stars on the list by the names of those who, purportedly, would be killed. As Moti expected, this created such turmoil among the freedom fighter officers that they were easily recruited for the assassination attempt.

Then on Friday, May 29, President Zia flew from Dacca to Chittagong, arriving just before 10:00 A.M. He did so against the strong advice of the directors of the nation's three main intelligence agencies; they insisted he should delay his trip to Chittagong until the angry General Manzoor had shifted to Dacca. But Zia was adamant that he had to go to Chittagong then to reconcile two warring factions of his BNP political party. At this, the director general of the top military intelligence agency pleaded with him, saying that at least he must not remain in Chittagong overnight. Surprisingly, the usually cautious Zia ignored this sensible advice.

Zia's entourage included military staff and senior members of his BNP political party. They were met at the Chittagong Airport by prominent military and civilian leaders who then accompanied them to the Circuit House where Zia and his group would be staying. The Circuit House was a classical piece of British colonial architecture utilized by the Bangladesh government as a guesthouse for top-level officers; it is located about two miles from our mission office.

Before Zia partook of the refreshments awaiting him, they were first tasted for poison content by a military doctor. He had the unenviable duty of being not only Zia's personal physician but also his official food taster.

After two hours of political discussion with BNP party men, Zia donned white garments and prayer cap to join the Friday midday congregational prayers at the elaborately ornamented Chandanpura mosque; this well-known mosque was located less than a mile from our mission office in a section of the city known as Chawk Bazar. The excited mosque congregation felt honored to have their president worshiping with them, so after the prayers and sermon they crowded happily around him. He conversed easily with the people for a while before returning to the Circuit House for lunch. In the afternoon he rested an hour or two, then gave a talk in a room filled with the upper crust of Chittagong society. After his address he chatted with the people for a long time before finally excusing himself.

That night Zia had two hours of very frank discussions with his BNP party men in an effort to resolve the conflict between the

The Circuit House in Chittagong

The Chandanpura mosque

two warring factions of his party. Only after these strenuous talks were finished at 11:00 P.M. did he finally eat dinner, phone his wife in Dacca, then retire. As he climbed into bed a driving rain was pelting furiously on the Circuit House roof, and the blackness of the stormy night was punctuated by brilliant flashes of lightning and cracks of thunder. Of course, the weary president was completely unaware that his enemies in the Chittagong Cantonment were even then carrying out a ritual that involved touching the Koran—and making grim preparations to launch a commando raid on the Circuit House.

Fourteen hours earlier in the Chittagong Cantonment, even as Zia had been flying from Dacca to Chittagong, General Manzoor was filled with fury. Not only had Zia ordered him to move to Dacca within three days to take up his new duties, but he had instructed Manzoor not to meet him upon his arrival at the Chittagong Airport—a major put-down and humiliation for Manzoor.

At midday, while the white-clad Zia had been chatting amiably with the mosque congregation, General Manzoor was assembling his co-conspirators in his office. Then he gave the fateful order: "Now is the time to act. How you do it, with what you do it, I don't know. No troops [enlisted men] are to be deployed. Only selected persons will go to the Circuit House to lift the Head [seize President Zia]."⁹

That afternoon Lieutenant Colonel Moti telephoned the president's principal staff officer, Mahfuz, at the Circuit House. According to later testimony, Mahfuz promised his help and that night withdrew the two armed policemen standing guard outside the president's room.¹⁰

About 6:00 P.M., M. and M. and five other lieutenant colonels and majors met to work out the detailed plan of attack. They argued back and forth on whether to simply assassinate Zia or to kidnap him and use him as bait to lure the vice-president, the army commander (General Ershad), and the rest of the army brass to Chittagong where they could all be eliminated. The meeting finished with this point still up in the air.

Despite General Manzoor's order not to utilize enlisted men, the conspirators tried three times to muster a number of regular troops to increase their firepower. But each time the troops refused to have anything to do with the operation. Enlisted men had suffered too much already in the wake of previous coup attempts.

At 11:30 P.M. that stormy night, M. and M. assembled a half-dozen majors and captains behind closed doors. Placing a copy of the Koran on a table Moti asserted, "Whatever we are doing we are doing in the interest of our country, our people, and for justice. Those of you who are with us will touch the Holy Koran and promise to do what is necessary."¹¹ This, of course, was the equivalent of "swearing on the Bible" in Western societies. All six officers swore on the Holy Koran to commit themselves to the operation, then armed themselves with their automatic weapons.

About midnight a repeat performance took place in another part of the cantonment with five other majors, captains, and lieutenants. The leader explained only that they would go to Zia, talk to him, and emphasize certain points to him. With one accord the officers consented and touched the Koran.

After midnight, when May 29 had dissolved into May 30, members of the strike team by twos and threes began slipping out of the cantonment. This went unnoticed because night training exercises were then in progress, providing perfect cover for the operation. By 3:00 A.M. eighteen officers and two junior commissioned officers had rendezvoused at a place outside the city limits called Kalurghat. This assembly point was near the Chittagong radio transmitter from which Zia had boldly announced the independence of Bangladesh a decade earlier. We know Kalurghat well, for we always pass through it on our way to and from the hospital.

Lieutenant Colonel Moti, who commanded the overall strike force, next divided the group into three teams:

1. Assault team—six officers who would attempt the attack on Zia's room
2. Backup team—six officers who would follow up the assault team
3. Cutoff team—four officers who would seize anyone trying to escape out the back door

The desperate men then loaded their automatic weapons and rocket launchers, again touched the Koran, and renewed their vows of allegiance to the cause. Soon their short caravan of vehicles began moving inexorably through the blinding sheets of rain toward the Circuit House—for a date with destiny.

The conversation in the packed vehicles revealed that some of the officers still mistakenly thought they were on their way to abduct the president. But those in the inner circle had made up their minds—they would kill Zia or die in the attempt. With pulses pounding they reached the Circuit House around 4:00 A.M. Surprisingly, the main gate was open, and the four sentries meekly allowed them to pass. Almost immediately the marauders fired two rockets into the building, followed by a withering stream of more rockets, grenades, and automatic weapons fire. This barrage quickly killed one policeman and four soldiers and injured five other policemen and soldiers on the ground floor. Forty-one other policemen were taken by surprise and offered no resistance at all.

Two members of the assault team also were shot—not by the defenders but by their own backup team. The remainder of the attack team and the backup team then stormed up the staircase to the second floor and immediately cut down three military guards who burst out of their rooms in courageous attempts to protect Zia. Expecting to find the president in room 9, the rebels kicked open the door, only to find a badly frightened lady officer of the BNP party inside. Then the killers deduced that their prey must be in room 4, so they began to kick in one of the two doors to that room. At that moment the other door opened and Zia, wearing white pajamas, stepped out. In a commanding voice he uttered three Bengali words: *"Tomra ki chao* [What do you want]?"[12]

A young lieutenant, still thinking they had come to abduct Zia, replied comfortingly, "Don't worry. Nothing to be afraid of, Sir."[13] But before those reassuring words could sink in, Lieutenant Colonel Moti, at point-blank range, emptied his automatic weapon into Zia's torso and face—and the president of Bangladesh was gone![14] Our friendship with Zia had been the shortest friendship we had ever known—and Bangladesh was still *rawktodesh*, nation of blood.

The attack force immediately withdrew, taking their two wounded officers with them. They reached the cantonment before

5:00 A.M. and reported immediately to General Manzoor that the operation had succeeded and the president was dead. Manzoor, bent on taking over Bangladesh, began issuing orders to protect Chittagong from troops who might advance against him from the north by road, air, or sea.[15] He then addressed the senior officers under him, pointing out the failures of Zia's administration and explaining that he had formed a Revolutionary Council to rule the country. He would, he said, stop the widespread corruption and build up Islam in Bangladesh. Each one present touched the Koran and swore allegiance to General Manzoor and the new Revolutionary Council.

Later in the morning Manzoor summoned to his office civil officials, including our friends the divisional commissioner and the DC. They saw on the general's desk a revolver and a copy of the Koran. So the commissioner and the DC touched the Koran and swore that they, too, would support General Manzoor and his Revolutionary Council.

Then Manzoor made a rambling speech on Chittagong Radio, explaining why he was taking over the country. He spoke of widespread corruption, high prices, shortages of food and clothing, and anti-Islamic practices such as drinking alcohol and gambling. In the hours that followed, various orders from his Revolutionary Council were also announced on Chittagong Radio.

Of course, all of these orders from Chittagong were a bit of a farce, since both the main military power and the seat of government were located to the north in Dacca, the capital. At 5:30 A.M., long before General Manzoor's radio broadcast, one of the dead president's surviving military aides had put a call through from Chittagong to Dacca to General Choudhury at President's House. He was the general who had served Joan and me tea and chatted with us several weeks earlier while we were waiting to resume our talk with President Zia.

General Choudhury immediately notified key officers, and within forty-five minutes the commanding general of the army (General Ershad) and other top generals were skillfully orchestrating their response to the Chittagong rebellion. General Ershad had a golden opportunity to put down the coup attempt and take over the government himself, but instead he faithfully followed the procedures laid down in the Constitution of Bangladesh.

Years later General Ershad told me directly that he went almost immediately to the hospital where Vice-President Sattar was a patient. Ershad explained, "I went to him in the morning and I said, 'Now you are the president. You take over.'"[16] Then the general promised the elderly, ailing vice-president his full support and took him to President's House where he was sworn in as the acting president of Bangladesh.

Afterward, the new head of state made a short but important broadcast from the Dacca radio station, then convened a cabinet meeting. The cabinet proclaimed a "national emergency" and ordered the Chittagong rebels to surrender. Later, General Ershad also addressed the nation on Dacca radio and television. He encouraged the people and ordered army units around the country to remain loyal to the government, explaining that the rebels who had killed President Zia in Chittagong were a relatively small group who would soon be crushed. Further, he also shrewdly offered amnesty to the officers and troops in Chittagong who would defect from the rebel forces.

The next day, May 31, General Ershad threatened an air strike on the Chittagong Cantonment by the Bangladesh Air Force unless General Manzoor's group surrendered by a specified time. But when stormy weather made it impossible for the air force planes to fly, the deadline was extended to 6:00 A.M. the following morning. By then hordes of rebel troops and officers were defecting to the government's side to gain the promised amnesty.

At about 3:00 A.M., three hours before the deadline, General Manzoor could see the handwriting on the wall—his coup attempt had failed. Hurrying to escape, he and his family, plus a second family, M. and M., the two injured officers, and six other officers began driving to the northeast in four vehicles. M. and M. and two other officers were driving rapidly ahead of the other cars when they suddenly encountered a group of soldiers loyal to the government. The major in command of these troops promptly placed M. and M. under arrest. Seeing that their attempt to talk their way out of the arrest was failing, Moti grabbed an automatic weapon and began firing. But the loyal soldiers instantly returned the fire, killing M. and M. on the spot.

At the sound of firing up ahead General Manzoor turned his small convoy back toward the south for a few miles; then, abandoning the vehicles, he began hiking with the two families and two majors toward the Chittagong Hill Tracts. Exhausted, they finally stopped to rest at a tea garden; there they were soon surrounded and easily captured by the police. They were immediately taken by their captors to a police station a few miles distant.

Within a few hours some 30,000 people had gathered around the police station ready to kill Manzoor with their bare hands, so enraged were they by his murder of their president. Finally, the prisoners were turned over to army officers who drove them in jeeps back to the Chittagong Cantonment where they were to be incarcerated. But, once they were inside the cantonment, roving troops spotted the jeeps, dragged General Manzoor out of one, and sent the jeeps away. There on the cantonment street the troops mercilessly executed Manzoor, their erstwhile commanding general.[17] Yes, Bangladesh was still *rawktodesh*—nation of blood.

About the time Manzoor was being apprehended, the bodies of President Zia and two of his fallen security officers were recovered from shallow graves outside of Chittagong beside the road to Kaptai. After autopsy by a military pathologist his specially prepared body was flown by helicopter to Dacca where it lay in state. The next day, June 2, a million grieving people attended his funeral; he was buried at a lovely site near the new Parliament Building. When it was discovered that Zia, because of his legendary honesty, had no savings to leave to his wife and children, the cabinet generously gave the family a million takas cash, a beautiful home, and other lifetime "perks."[18]

During May, while this incredible series of events had been incubating, Joan and I were dealing with a personal problem; I discovered a worrisome skin cancer on the edge of her nose. Over the years she had had a number of minor facial skin cancers caused by X-ray treatments to her face during her college years. This tumor, however, looked different from the others we had removed, and it was located in a pesky spot. It would have to be removed with frozen section control. So I set the wheels in motion for her to proceed to the U.S. for this surgery.

Just then Joan was stricken with severe abdominal pain. Although her symptoms did not fit the diagnosis of infection by the amoeba organism, the results of the laboratory tests brought that possibility to mind. Acting on that hunch, I started her on anti-amoebic treatment—and it worked; she then packed for her trip to the U.S. John Bullock, also, needed some special medical examinations abroad. So in early June, after the airports were reopened following the quashing of the coup attempt, Joan and the Bullocks flew out of Dacca to the Mayo Clinic in Rochester, Minnesota. We were acquainted with Dr. John Woods, chief of the Plastic Surgery Division of that institution. In fact, he and his wife, Janet, thoughtfully insisted that Joan and the Bullocks move out of the motel and into their home until the surgery and investigations were complete.

In mid-June Dr. Woods took Joan to the operating room, removed the skin cancer on the rim of her nose, and began to close the remaining defect. Just then the pathologist reported on his frozen section examination that the tumor was not fully removed. To Dr. Woods's surprise, this happened three times before the pathologist finally reported that all the cancer had been removed. When I read Joan's letter about this surgery I was glad that we had not tried to remove this insidious cancer in Bangladesh without frozen section control.

Just after Joan, John, and Tense had left for Minnesota, nurse Jan Wolfe also flew to the United States. Shortly before her departure for regular home leave she had discovered a breast lump; on examination I judged it probably malignant and advised her to go directly to the U.S. for expeditious surgery. There the operation confirmed the diagnosis of cancer; it had already spread to the adjacent lymph nodes. So dedicated, conscientious Jan had to begin a long series of X-ray and chemotherapy treatments. Our hearts ached for her and for her family. Now Jan is in glory enjoying the company of Oncherai, Dr. Peter, and others, for within a year she succumbed to her disease. How we miss her!

After Joan's surgery she visited her family in Toledo, Ohio. There, unexpectedly, the severe abdominal pain returned. Fortunately, Toledo was Dr. Dick Stagg's furlough headquarters. Because of his years of working in Bangladesh he, too, was experienced in the treatment of amoebic disease and ordered the appropriate medicine. When her pain eased Joan flew to California to spend time with our children. But soon the news came through that my dear father had died, so Joan flew to Nebraska for the funeral and to encourage and support my grieving mom.

Nurse Jan Wolfe—how we miss her!

During Joan's two-and-a-half months in the U.S. the Bangladesh government and people were slowly recovering from the murder of President Zia and the attempted coup. The opposition parties deserved commendation, for they took the high road, condemned the assassination of Zia, and supported the government's steps toward recovery. President Sattar, backed by the powerful General Ershad, continued to run the country along constitutional lines.

Interestingly enough, in late May I was seeing as a patient the sister-in-law of General Ershad. She had a rather complicated problem, which finally required surgery at Malumghat some weeks later.

In June I contacted our various mission committees and station councils about the fact that our long-standing plan to begin systematically determining our objectives, goals, and measurable standards had bogged down. It was now time for each committee and station council to focus on this important exercise, which would enhance our mission's overall strategic planning.

Also in June I shifted to Malumghat, returning temporarily to the field of surgery. This would tide the hospital over until the next short-term surgeon arrived. I loved every minute of my time on the wards and in the operating room as we cared for the many fascinating cases that came our way.

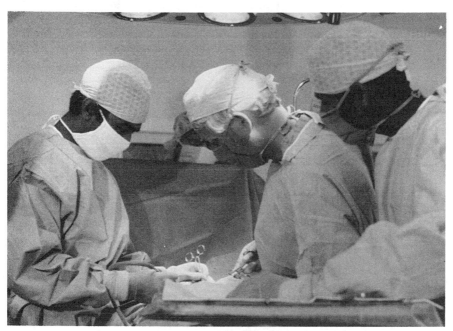

I loved every minute of it

Then short-term surgeon Dr. Harold Adolph, brother of our own Bob Adolph, arrived at Malumghat. Because he had long experience as a missionary surgeon in Africa he settled in quickly, leaving me free to return to Chittagong. There I made immediate arrangements to fly on to Dacca where I had several days' work to do.

But before my departure I received an urgent note about a problem in our Bengali-medium children's school at Malumghat. The note said in part:

> It is impossible to brief you by letter, but the situation is SERI-OUS! Our present decision is that we are closing the school until further notice. We need you down here immediately. We understand that the Dacca trip is important, but we feel we have an emergency on our hands. Thus we are asking you to come as soon as you can.

The note was signed by Linda Short, Becky Davey, and Mary Lou Brownell. What to do? That was easy to answer. If those three experienced, highly competent women assessed the problem to be serious, I had to go. So, canceling the Dacca trip, I departed for Malumghat at 5:30 the following morning.

There I soon learned that the school situation was indeed explosive and feelings were running high. An overly aggressive teacher had flared up in open rebellion against the school headmaster, completely disrupting the school. A concerned Bengali parent wrote in a note, "A cyclone has erupted in the school." I brainstormed with Mary Lou, Becky, and Linda; we finally decided to leave the school open, but to suspend the firebrand teacher. This, we reasoned, should calm the situation until we could assess it further.

I spent the next three days, full-time, interviewing about twenty-five parents, teachers, and others. This extensive investigation uncovered other underlying problems in the school as well. In the end we decided to separate the primary school from the high school, leave the current headmaster as the primary school headmaster, and make Mary Lou both high school headmistress and English teacher. The result was excellent. Discipline was restored, the long-standing problems were uncovered and resolved, the parents were delighted, and both principals did fine work in their new assignments. For Mary Lou, being a high school headmistress in the Bengali milieu became a real adventure.

On to Dacca. Now how could I obtain visas for eight new workers in the face of the government's statement that our "expatriates should be reduced"? As we were in the process of appealing that order, I reasoned that we were not yet bound by it; I decided

Mr. Roy,
primary school headmaster

Mary Lou Brownell,
high school headmistress

to "go for broke." I would attempt to obtain visas for our appointees, not as replacements, but as "new hands." But I knew that simply making a routine application would doom my effort to failure.

So during the first week of July I met the home minister in his office by appointment. I reminded him of his promise to mission leaders three years earlier that, if we could make a convincing enough argument for our new people, the Home Ministry would grant visas to them as new hands. Then I made a case for each one of them verbally and in writing. He assured me that he and his ministry would study the applications and let us know their decision. Some days later I learned that my request had been granted —each appointee had been given a visa as a new worker. That was fabulous news.

While in Dacca I learned that the divisions in the BNP party had not been overcome. A minority group, still led by attorney Moudud Ahmed, continued to promote a more democratic party structure.[19] This group also insisted that in the upcoming elections the vice-presidential candidate should run side-by-side with the presidential candidate, as in the United States—rather than being appointed by the president or cabinet or Parliament. Acting President Sattar resisted these demands.

Also the political scene had been enlivened in Dacca by two intriguing women who had become leaders in the two largest political parties. One was Sheikh Hasina Wajed, daughter of Sheikh

Mujib, who had returned to Bangladesh several weeks earlier after six years of self-exile in India. She had been elected head of the Awami League party and had arrived in Dacca to a tumultuous airport welcome. She demanded that the officers and soldiers who had assassinated her father be "brought to book."

The other woman then attracting attention was the widow of President Zia—Begum (Mrs.) Khaleda Zia. She was described as a charming and graceful homemaker who had conducted herself with dignity following her husband's death. Some of those who had supported Zia now supported her, and she was quickly gaining stature as one of the leaders of the BNP party.

Shortly after my return to Chittagong I was asked to see the wife of the manager of the American Express Bank. Despite her upper-class life-style, she had contracted malaria—and she was pregnant. After careful research in my medical journals I selected the antimalarial medicine least likely to induce premature delivery or cause any other harm to her unborn baby. The signs and symptoms of malaria were soon gone, and we were all pleased several months later when she gave birth to a lovely, healthy baby. While she was under my care, the grateful bank manager had thoughtfully offered me the use of the bank's Telex system. That was a godsend to me, because just then I needed to carry out some urgent, high-speed correspondence with Joan, who was still in the United States.

For the government July was a turbulent month filled with intrigue. The newspapers made the most of the Soviet embassy's bungled attempt to smuggle sophisticated electronic gear into the country—obviously intended for espionage.[20] The equipment and two Soviet officials were sent back to Moscow posthaste. Also well publicized was news of the arrival of a known Soviet KGB intelligence agent in Dacca and stepped-up KGB activity.[21] Some theorized that the KGB was trying to organize yet another coup in order to bring pro-Soviet people into power.

Simultaneously, some newspapers reported that India's central intelligence agency, RAW, had chalked out a plan to destabilize Bangladesh. One report specified, "The scheme includes disruption of the country's communications network, train and bank robberies and attacks on police stations."[22]

In mid-July our Chittagong City team began to reevaluate and reorganize the work of Chittagong Station. We had been forced to postpone this important task because of the lack of personnel. At one point the Station Council consisted only of the Olsens and Gail Hopkins, a competent trained teacher of team members' children.

But then a threesome of experienced Chittagong workers returned: theological teacher Reid Minich, translator Lynn Silvernale, and literature specialist Jeannie Lockerbie. In addition, we were happy to welcome helpful short-termer Bonnie Hilton. Later in July George and Shirley Weber and family, according to plan, returned to join the work in Chittagong City.

When our group began to meet together, as Station Council chairman I asked each one to express his or her ideas, suggestions, and dreams for the future. Little by little, through hours of interacting, sharing, and praying together, we developed a spirit of oneness as a newly functioning team. We analyzed the previous and ongoing programs and went on to think about future projects. Then, for a little comic relief, the time seemed right for me to present to the group the "Six Stages in the Development of a Project": (1) Enthusiasm (2) Disillusionment (3) Panic (4) Search for a guilty party (5) Punishment of the innocent (6) Praise for those who did little or nothing to promote the project.

We soon learned that the existing church (located in an area of the city named Dampara) had fallen on hard days and was in need of assistance and renewal. It was decided that I would meet with the leaders of the Dampara Church to delve into the problems. After three meetings with those conscientious church leaders, I was up to speed on the issues, and they were encouraged. I assured them of the mission's continuing interest and suggested they request us to provide a church adviser. They decided to do so, and Reid Minich assumed that position. Then, with the church leaders' blessing, Jeannie and Lynn pitched in to help revitalize the Sunday school, girls' meetings, and women's meetings.

Meanwhile, in Dacca, the secret court-martial trial of thirty-one army officers implicated in the Zia killing continued. The opposition parties, freedom fighters, and Amnesty International condemned the secret nature of the court-martial and demanded an open trial, but the new government would not budge on this point. Then a separate army commission set up to inquire into Zia's killing and the attempted coup issued a report placing the blame squarely on General Manzoor.[23] Later a government "white paper" came up with the same conclusion.

In early August the military court found twenty-nine of the thirty-one officers guilty and officially blamed General Manzoor for the killing of President Zia and for the coup attempt. Of the twenty-nine convicted officers, twelve were given the death penalty, including Lieutenant Colonel Mahfuz, Zia's personal staff officer. Twelve others were sentenced to prison terms, and the remaining five were discharged from the armed services. These cases were immediately appealed to the Supreme Court.[24]

By then Dr. Harold Adolph had completed his helpful stint as a short-term surgeon at Malumghat. Next came Dr. Dick Furman with his wife, Harriet, and three children. After he had worked two weeks at Malumghat I received a note from Dick saying, "I am having a tremendous time here; so is the family. It is exciting to be a small, small part of the work here."

Because Dick and I both had training and experience in thoracic surgery we decided to operate on a pretty little five-year-old girl whom I had examined in Chittagong and diagnosed as a case of congenital heart disease. Her enlarged heart and congested lungs were caused by an abnormal connection between two large blood vessels just where they emerged from the heart (patent ductus arteriosus). On the appointed day I traveled to Malumghat, and we opened up little Ruma's chest. There, big as life, was the abnormal connection; it was a particularly large one. We clamped the ductus connection with special vascular clamps, cut it, then sewed up the two ends.

After the successful surgery we shared in the happiness of Ruma's father and mother. But a few days later, although this family was still rejoicing, the Furman children began crying—because they had had so much fun at Malumghat and it was now time to leave for their return trip to the United States.

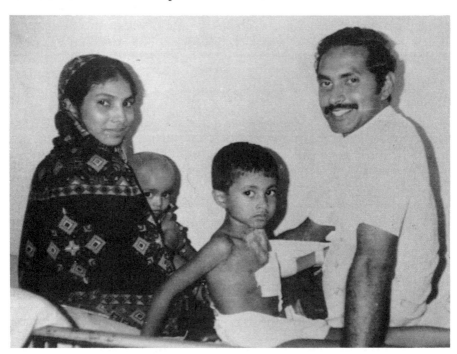

Little Ruma and her family

Back in Chittagong City we continued our stimulating strategy meetings. George Weber hoped to establish a new church and was searching for the most suitable location. He studied maps, talked with local pastors, and consulted men in the city planner's office. Then, when he learned about a group of Christians in a far northern suburb of the city by the Dacca Trunk Road, he met with their representatives. He found them eager to start a church in that area, since they were located so far from the Dampara church. The Station Council happily concurred with this proposal, and George immediately began his church-planting work.

The rest of us accepted other assignments to different phases of the work in Chittagong City. One of my duties would be to help revitalize the Bible Correspondence School and obtain or produce a series of courses written in special Bengali; this would make the studies more interesting and meaningful to the millions who spoke that form of the language. This goal was achieved with the help and cooperation of George and Jeannie.

There was also another concept that I was particularly eager to promote during our meetings. I was convinced that we needed a whole new approach to church establishment in the urban environment of Chittagong City. There were others who shared that view, and the time seemed right to pursue this matter.

In the past the mission had required members of national church groups to provide all the funds to buy land and build their church buildings or to borrow part of the funds from the mission. They could borrow only a limited amount, depending on the total sum collected by the congregation. Then they would have to pay back every last cent, no matter how long that took. Although this system had worked in the Hill Tracts where land was inexpensive and building simple, it had proved to be unworkable in this urban context. Land and construction costs were extremely high in the city, so it would require a substantial outlay of money to obtain a plot of land in a good location and build a reasonably attractive and functional church building. Because of these high costs and the poverty of most of the people, it would be impossible for a church to pay back that whole amount even in a hundred years.

Recognizing all these factors, it seemed right to us as a group to expect the churches to collect all they could in the beginning. Then the mission would provide the remainder of the needed funds as available. Of this, the churches should pay back into our revolving loan fund a stipulated portion over a reasonable period of time, but we should consider the balance a brotherly donation from donor churches abroad. We decided to present this new policy proposal to our Field Council Church Formation Committee and, with their approval, to the whole Field Council. If this policy were adopted we would then need to raise funds to activate the plan and assist the churches.

Late in August life took on new meaning for me—Joan returned home from the U.S. Loneliness became togetherness, and we were happy again. Her plastic surgical incision had healed, her amoebic disease was eradicated, and she was back up to her normal weight and strength. So we plunged back into our mutual work together.

About that time a British physician requested me to come to examine Sue, a British nurse at a hospital in another town. The young woman was seriously ill with high fever and worrisome abdominal tenderness. After putting all our data together we concluded that she was suffering from typhoid fever. We prescribed the proper medicine, and I returned to Chittagong. Knowing that the intestine sometimes perforates in this disease, I couldn't get Sue out of my mind. So two days later I drove again the thirty or so miles to the British hospital and found that our patient was considerably improved. After a pleasant cup of tea with my physician friend I then returned to Chittagong with a freer mind and lighter heart.

But this good feeling was dispelled a few days later when two people came to my office. One was the SDO of a subdivision located between Chittagong City and Malumghat Hospital. These two were relatives of an imprisoned brigadier (brigadier general in U.S. parlance); he was the highest ranking officer to be convicted for complicity in the recent assassination and coup attempt. He was one of those who had been given the death penalty and whose appeal was up before the Supreme Court.

The two visitors pleaded with me to approach the government and demand that the brigadier's sentence be commuted to a lesser penalty. And they urged that I do this immediately because he would be executed as soon as the Supreme Court handed down its judgment. Sadly, I had to refuse their request since we, as guests in the country, have no right to become involved in political issues; our mission rules do not allow such involvement, and the government would not tolerate it. The law would have to take its course.

On September 22 the Supreme Court confirmed the death sentences for the twelve officers; the next day they were executed —and I felt pain in my heart for the grieving loved ones left behind.[25] Immediately riots exploded in Dacca, and Awami League leaders insisted that the assassins of their Sheikh Mujib also must be tried and punished. It seemed to them grossly unjust to take a hard line with Zia's killers but allow Mujib's assassins to continue enjoying plush government foreign service posts abroad.

During September and October Shanti Bahini tribal insurgents also vented their rage in the Chittagong Hill Tracts, where they stepped up their assaults on police outposts, an army camp, and Bengali villages. In those hit-and-run attacks they killed and injured a number of Bengalis. In response, the Bangladesh Army and police fiercely counterattacked the tribal guerrilla forces. Again, the simple noncombatant tribal people were caught in the middle. In their fear and distress nearly 19,000 tribespeople poured across the border into India.[26] The Bangladesh government charged that India had harbored the Shanti Bahini fighters, while the Indians blamed Bangladesh, in turn, for the reprisals that had caused the exodus of thousands of tribal refugees into India. Later, after passions had cooled, the Bangladesh government readmitted and resettled the refugees. By the year's end about three-fourths of them had returned home.

As DA I was dealing almost every day with some aspect of the comings and goings of our career and short-term personnel. In early October we received a cablegram stating that a short-term surgeon would be arriving in Dacca on a certain date and flight. The cable continued, "You arrange internal trouble." I guessed that they meant "internal travel," so obtained reservations for a flight from Dacca to Chittagong—the "internal trouble" could be tackled as it appeared.

A few days later I received an urgent summons from Jalal to fly to Dacca because the home minister had suffered some kind of attack. I arrived to find that he had sustained a coronary-occlusion-type heart attack of moderate severity. His Dacca physicians had made the diagnosis and ordered appropriate treatment. There was little additional to suggest in the way of treatment, but I was able to spend time with the minister as a friend, encourage him, and discuss some spiritual issues of interest to both of us.

Back in Chittagong Joan and I focused on an important decision—to pack or not to pack. We were scheduled to return to the U.S. in November, but we had been requested by the Bangladesh Bible Society to cancel those plans and remain another year to provide some Old Testament Scriptures in special Bengali. They were so euphoric about the reception of the New Testament that they were eager to follow up with something from the Old Testament. So in October we revved up our heads and hearts into high gear, discussed the proposal with our co-workers, made pro and con lists, and prayed earnestly for guidance to make the correct decision. We soon had peace of mind that it was right to remain the extra year. So we fired off cables to the family and to the mission, canceled a speaking engagement in Bermuda, and settled in for the long haul. This would be our sixth furlough-interrupting assignment.

We weren't sure where we would obtain the toiletries and other necessities for the upcoming year, but after a late-night meeting I received from smiling nurses some spray cans of Arrid Extra Dry—to tide us through, they explained, the long hours of late meetings in the coming year. By this time our newest nurse, Carol Baldwin, had completed language study and settled in at Malumghat. She served expertly on the women's/children's ward, specializing in obstetrical cases.

For several months the Literature Division in Chittagong had been making progress on planning an in-house printing operation. Jeannie Lockerbie had been in contact with printing specialists who were eager to help. And she made application to various organizations and foundations for funding. To everyone's delight one organization gave nearly $60,000 for a computerized phototypesetter and other equipment. Another organization donated a small press, a special camera, and a mammoth paper-cutter. Because this equipment would be a great help in the printing of hospital forms, charts, public health booklets, and so on, I was able to negotiate successfully with the joint collector of Customs for concessional clearance of the shipments. It took several months for all the items to finally reach the country and be installed.

In late October we traveled to Malumghat again for our annual Field Council meetings. During our first meeting we paused to consider the words of a great Biblical character named Joshua. In his farewell message to two-and-a-half tribes of ancient Israel, he encouraged them "to love the Lord your God, to walk in all His ways, to keep His commandments, to hold fast to Him, and to

Philip operating phototypesetter

serve Him with all your heart and with all your soul."[27] We took that as great advice for our two-and-a-half station councils.

During those meetings I was able to report that, at long last, the objectives, goals, and measurable standards of our FC stations, committees, and projects had been completed and approved. This major accomplishment would allow our team members to better establish their personal objectives/goals/standards. Also, for the first time, the Executive Committee had the information needed to carry out two of its heretofore neglected duties:

1. To carry out effective long-range planning
2. To present to new workers the mission's five- and ten-year goals

I was also happy to report that we were now free to reoccupy Hebron Station if we desired. The government had not only given us an official letter to that effect, but also had issued identity passes to all of us who might have reason to live or visit there. In addition, I had applied for permission for us to travel to Hebron via the new Alikadam Road. If this should be granted we would be able to reach the station much more quickly and easily.

I also updated the Field Council on my yearlong negotiation for lower electric rates. This had involved repeated meetings with the pertinent minister, the Power Development Board, and engineers of WAPDA (Water and Power Development Authority). The long hours of intense negotiating finally had paid off. In Chittagong we had been granted a 60,000-taka ($3,000) rebate on the Bible Literature Centre electric bill. For Malumghat Hospital we had been given a "high tension bulk rate" and for the Malumghat housing area a "special colony rate"; these concessions cut our Malumghat electric rate nearly in half. "Thank You, Father!"

In this context, Dr. Donn Ketcham then told us a personal story involving WAPDA, the term we had come to use for government-supplied electricity. The lights went out one day while he was writing a letter to his mother, so he put a note in parentheses, "Dear old WAPDA just died," then went on with the letter. Some days later his mom wrote back, "Donn, you mentioned in your letter the death of someone named WAPDA; I assume he was an old friend. I am so sorry to hear it, but I trust he was a believer and you can be comforted that he is with Daddy in heaven." Donn's mother was one sweet lady, who is now doing what WAPDA could not do—enjoying heaven with Donn's dad.

The big news in early November was the upcoming election of a new president to succeed the fallen Zia. The Constitution required an election within 180 days of the loss of a president. Zia's party, the BNP, had selected elderly Acting President Sattar to be its candidate. The Awami League could not nominate its party head, Sheikh Hasina, because she was not quite thirty-five years old, the minimum age allowed by the Constitution. Instead, the Awami League ran a politically experienced former AL minister. Other opposition parties put up seven other candidates for the office of president; thirty independent candidates also joined the race. Imagine thirty-nine candidates on a ballot for president!

Finally, the last election speech was given, and on November 15 more than 21 million Bangladeshi citizens traveled to their nearest polling stations. The illiterate majority, unable to sign their names, gave their thumbprints instead; then each one stamped on a ballot the symbol of his or her party. The Awami League symbol was a boat and the emblem of the BNP party a sheaf of rice. When all the votes were counted the sheaf of rice had prevailed, making Acting President Sattar the big winner—he had garnered two-thirds of the votes.[28] And his big win was televised to the country in living color. For the first time, people were able to watch the election returns on color TV, a recent innovation in Bangladesh.

While the BNP party was celebrating its decisive victory, the leaders of the Awami League and other opposition parties declared that the election was rigged. However, neutral observers reported that the election was relatively fair and certainly conclusive, in spite of irregularities observed at a few polling stations.

The new president had long years of experience in government service. He had been a Superior Court judge, chief election commissioner, cabinet minister, vice-president, and acting president of Bangladesh. I remembered talking with him during my visit to Parliament. On another occasion Joan and I had greeted him at a reception; he was so pleased to hear an American woman speaking Bengali that a big smile broke out on his face.

Although the new president was elated by his landslide victory, he was also well aware that he was now in a tug of war with the army chief, General Ershad. Six weeks earlier the general had referred publicly to the numerous mutinies and coups that had hurt the country and assassinated two of its presidents. He believed that it would be wise to give the military a voice in government in an effort to stop these frequent recurring attacks. "To stop further coups," he explained, "if the Army participates in the administration of the country, then they will probably have a feeling that they are also involved, and they will not be frustrated."[29] At that stage, he did not specify whether he wanted to see military officers as vice-president, cabinet ministers, or in some other powerful council. But it was clear that he thought the military should have some say in running the country.

The day after the election President Sattar responded quite negatively to this proposition. He stated, "The Army has a role to protect the sovereignty of the country, and I don't think any other role is possible."[30] But two days later several army generals strode into the president's office to press him further about giving the military a voice in government and a share of the power.

Not long after this incident General Ershad again spoke out publicly. "It is true," he said, "that the Army's main role is to maintain the country's independence, but it has its own internal problems. It must be heard. The Army can also play other roles. Its point of view should be heard, its suggestions considered and its presence recognized before formulating policies and pro-grammes."[31] The president and the army general, who had been so close a few months before, were now becoming more and more divided over this issue. The year would end with this civilian-military conflict yet unresolved.

During those weeks of pulling and hauling between President Sattar and the military I was going back and forth with the government in another way, trying to help the advance man of the MV *Logos* gain approval to dock at Chittagong Port. The *Logos* was manned by an international Christian crew who presented an outstanding on-board exhibition of literally thousands of sacred and secular books. In addition, they held seminars to train Christian leaders and meetings to encourage church people. During a number of trips to Dacca we were shunted back and forth between various ministries that seemed reluctant to make a decision. Jalal, however, put us in touch with the really key decision-makers who, at the last possible moment, finally said yes to the proposal. Another cliff-hanger!

So in December the *Logos* steamed into Chittagong Port for a very successful several days. The immense book exhibition was impressive to the many hundreds of local people who visited the ship. Our own Literature Division provided most of the Bengali religious literature. The mission's two common language New Testaments were featured prominently and purchased by many. There were special days or evenings on shipboard for government and civic leaders, women, children, and mission personnel. Church leaders benefited from a two-day training seminar. All in all, the *Logos* made quite a splash at Chittagong Port.

Then came all the interesting and happy events of the Christmas season; we enjoyed them immensely. A few days later 1981 came to an end. Simultaneously, the eventful first decade of the new nation of Bangladesh also passed into history.

The MV Logos

Bangladesh's first ten years had been a turbulent period, spattered by the blood of recurrent coups and countercoups. Two strong leaders, Sheikh Mujib and General Zia, had been cut down by automatic weapons wielded by officers who had been freedom fighters in 1971. In fact, all of the decade's mutinies and coups had been launched by freedom fighter officers, those men who had fought valiantly for their country against daunting odds.[32] Perhaps their rebellion against the Pakistan Army had changed them forever, made them more insubordinate, radicalized them, and made them prone to resort to military force again and again in attempts to resave their country. By the decade's end there were few freedom fighter officers left; some had died in the coups—others had been executed afterward, imprisoned, or drummed out of the army.

During that ten-year period there had been some noticeable progress in the country. The size of crops and amount of goods manufactured had increased, but much of the gain had been consumed by the exploding population, drowned by the recurrent floods, battered by the periodic cyclones, or destroyed by persistent inflation. One Bangladeshi writer, in his overview of the nation's first decade, put it this way:

Drastic rise in prices has been the most devastating development of the last ten years. Prices of most commodities have increased several times. . . . Soaring price of essential commodities
has sapped the economic strength of the common man. . . .

Production has increased in most sectors of the economy,
maybe not enough, maybe below the rate of population growth,
but increased all the same. . . . The transportation network has
been reconstructed and expanded. The administrative and social
infrastructure is now stronger. . . .

However, foundations of the economy are still weak and
highly vulnerable to unfavourable weather or adverse swings in
trade and aid. . . .

The general economic situation remains one of pervasive
poverty. Due to faulty policies, imbalances in structure of the
economy have been heightened and poverty has deepened in rural
areas. . . . No significant progress has also been made in solving
the fundamental causes of our poverty—unrestrained population
growth, widespread illiteracy and malnutrition, poor physical
and social infrastructure, inefficient use of existing resources, low
productivity, inadequate expansion in employment and so on.[33]

Or, to put all this another way, at the end of its first decade of
existence Bangladesh continued to be one of the very poorest of the
world's thirty-one Least Developed Countries (LDCs). Eighty percent of the population lived below the "poverty line"—and more
than half of the people lived below the "extreme poverty line."[34]

Our mission, also, had its ups and downs during the first decade of Bangladesh. Like the rest of the population, we also were
subject to the same floods, cyclones, armed conflicts, and periodic
breakdowns of law and order. Although most government officials
and ministries of the government had been cordial and helpful to
us, an occasional official and ministry had applied heavy pressure
on us, even threatening our right to remain in Bangladesh. But,
even then, the government had always given us an opportunity to
state our case, discuss, and negotiate the issue at hand.

We had been pressed by a hostile union and an angry local
Action Committee, but with the aid of conscientious government
officers and fair-minded neighbors we were able to resolve these
crises—and learn a great deal in the process.

Memorial Christian Hospital at Malumghat had provided
competent and compassionate medical care to thousands of inpatients and tens of thousands of outpatients throughout the first
decade of the new nation. At the same time, we were able to teach
multitudes simple principles of hygiene and nutrition. Our highly

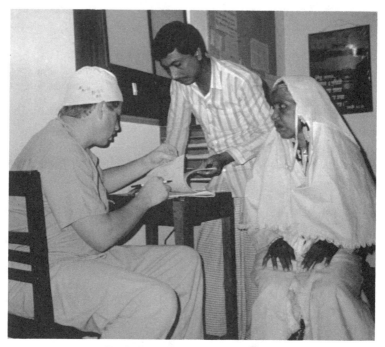

Dr. Bob Goddard with a patient

*Nurse Ila Bisswas
charting nurse's notes*

*Nurse Biren Bisswas
coming to work on a winter morning*

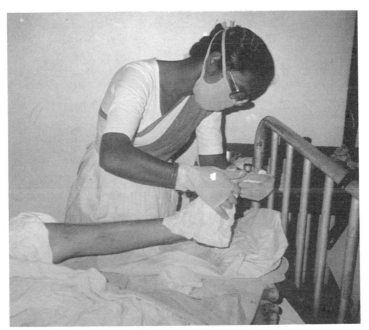

Nurse's aide changing a foot dressing

Medic Babul Dass taking a medical history

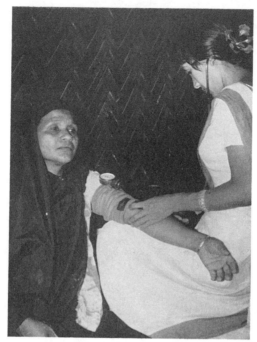

*Medic Kra Phrue Kyung
taking a patient's blood pressure*

Chief laboratory technician Khaite Phrue Kyung

trained foreign staff and immense patient load also helped us to train a number of outstanding paramedics, technicians, and nurses' aides, and to considerably upgrade the skills of our Bangladeshi graduate nurses.

For the churches in Bangladesh we had translated a brand-new common language New Testament, which the church people could readily understand and live by. Simultaneously, we had produced a special Bengali common language New Testament, our gift of love to our esteemed Muslim friends and neighbors—a sacred Scripture revered by both Muslims and Christians. And we had also created a Literature Division, which now produces most of the Christian literature in Bangladesh.

In addition, the mission assisted Bangladeshi Christians in establishing dozens of congregations and churches. The majority of these were among the Tippera and Murung tribes of the Chittagong Hill Tracts, but active churches were also planted at Malumghat, Hebron, and Chittagong City.

For years we had provided informal training programs for church leaders and members. The tempo of these efforts had gradually increased, especially at Malumghat Station, and near the end of the decade we had succeeded in establishing a more formal theological training institution for church leaders. All in all, it had been ten years of solid progress for the mission.

We were also pleased by the influence of our book *Daktar* during the first decade of Bangladesh. Moody Press published hardcover and deluxe paperback editions. Then three other publishers (two American and one British) produced mass paperback editions, which were followed by several foreign language editions and a Braille edition. But we were even more pleased to learn of many people's lives being changed for good through reading *Daktar* and *The Agnostic Who Dared to Search*. Some had overcome an icy atheism or agnosticism to make the great faith decision. Others had surrendered their lives into God's hands and were guided into fruitful service. Yet others sensed a call into foreign mission work and crossed oceans to serve the people of distant lands. "Thank You, Father!"

Key Events of 1981: Summary

January	• Joan and I have a fascinating meeting with President Zia.
	• We fly to the U.S. for a yearlong furlough.
February	• Our new formal Bible Institute (BBIB) begins.
March	• Due to a severe personnel shortage, we cancel our furlough and hurriedly return to Bangladesh.
	• Forty thousand special Bengali common language NTs have reached Bangladesh; thousands already sold.
	• Thirteen of fifteen rejected mission societies finally gain registration; workers of the other two agencies are allowed to remain under the aegis of other groups.
May	• President Zia is brutally assassinated in Chittagong by rebel army officers.
June	• Vice-President Sattar takes over. The coup attempt is crushed; General Manzoor and other rebels are killed.
	• Joan travels to the U.S. for special skin cancer surgery.
July	• Despite obstacles we succeed in obtaining visas for eight new workers.
	• Soviets attempt to smuggle in sophisticated electronic gear; they also increase their intelligence activities.
	• We reorganize the work of our Chittagong Station team.
	• The government blames General Manzoor for masterminding the army rebellion and the assassination of Zia.
August	• In a military trial twenty-nine of thirty-one army officers are convicted for complicity in the assassination and coup attempt.
September	• Twelve of the guilty officers are executed, twelve imprisoned, and five discharged from the army.
October	• Reacting to increased military action in the CHT, nearly 19,000 tribal people cross the border into India.
	• Army chief General Ershad states that the army should have a voice in running the country.
November	• In the election for a new president, acting President Sattar wins by a wide margin.
	• President Sattar declares that the army should have no role in ruling the nation.
December	• Bangladesh's first decade draws to a close.

Figure 32

Epilogue

15
1982-89: Evolving Problems—
Enduring Progress

Several years have passed since Bangladesh's eventful first decade faded from the headlines and drifted into history. The passage of these subsequent years has allowed the decade's dust to settle and given me an opportunity to assess the events and write about them with considerable accuracy. But time goes by each day, painting a few more brush strokes on the ongoing wall-mural of life. So it seems right that I should now update you on some of these more recent events.

During 1982 Joan and I and our Bangladeshi co-workers focused single-mindedly on the special Bengali common language translation of the Pentateuch section of the Bible, that is, the first five books of the Old Testament. Both Muslims and Christians in Bangladesh respect these five books of Moses as true Holy Scripture in the same way that they revere the New Testament. We succeeded in completing draft two of these five books and the final draft of the first one. This allowed the early publication of several attractive booklets on the lives of various prophets.

Simultaneously I continued working to reverse the "expatriates should be reduced" order. The negotiation was exceedingly complex, the most difficult I have ever attempted. Each month the obstacles seemed to increase and the prospects of success to fade. Everything was going wrong. Then toward the end of the year the whole situation suddenly and dramatically changed. Through an unforeseen series of events I became acquainted with the powerful chairman of the Standing Committee. Because of that relationship he and his committee developed a heightened appreciation for our medical work, then made a stunning decision to reverse their decree that our numbers must be reduced. In fact, they granted us a substantial increase. "Thank You, Father!"

Special Bengali translation team

The chairman of the Standing Committee

While I had been struggling with this complicated issue, another struggle was making headlines in the Bangladesh newspapers. The army generals, dissatisfied with the performance of President Sattar and his civilian government, demanded reforms. The government made some changes, but they were too little, too late. So in March 1982 the army commander, General H. M. Ershad, toppled President Sattar in a bloodless coup. He then suspended the Constitution, instituted martial law, and became the head of the new military government. The general explained his reasons for taking over the country in these words: "The economy was on the verge of collapse, the nation was threatened by conspiracy of internal enemies, and an all-pervasive corruption was ruining the society."[1]

General Ershad began immediately to institute various reforms to cure the nation's malaise. During the year he also changed the English spelling of the name of the capital city from "Dacca" to "Dhaka." This new spelling pleased the people since it better reflected the correct Bengali spelling and pronunciation.

In addition, General Ershad began a step-by-step process to reinstitute a democracy headed by civilians—and simultaneously to convert himself from a military head of government to a civilian president. This was no easy process with the opposition parties snapping at his heels every inch of the way.

The two most prominent opposition leaders continued to be the two strong women who had come into the limelight the year before. Mrs. Khaleda Zia, the wife of former president Zia, was now the head both of his BNP political party and of an alliance (including the BNP) of several like-minded opposition parties. Similarly, Sheikh Hasina, the daughter of Sheikh Mujib, was president of the Awami League, as well as the leader of a coalition of several other opposition parties.

Here are some of the steps General Ershad took to work with these antigovernment parties in an effort to reestablish a civilian, democratic government:

1983 • He allowed the political parties freedom to operate and announced that elections would be held in 1984. But the opposition parties imperiously refused to take part in these elections. The military government then appointed General Ershad the president of Bangladesh.

1984 • Despite generous concessions by President Ershad, the opposition parties again boycotted the proposed elections. He then made other concessions and began to relax certain aspects of martial law to further accommodate them.

1985 • When the fractious opposition parties still refused to take part in the elections, in exasperation President Ershad abruptly reimposed full martial law and held a referendum instead. More than 94 percent of the voters endorsed his presidency and his policies.

1986 • That year the opposition parties were somewhat subdued. Most of them finally agreed to participate in the elections. President Ershad also retired from the army so that he could run as a civilian candidate in the presidential election. In the parliamentary elections Ershad's party gained a modest majority, but in the presidential election he celebrated another landslide victory (more than 83 percent of the votes).

1987 • Although President Ershad as a civilian had won the presidency by democratic election, the opposition parties were still determined to bring him down. They took to the streets and vigorously demanded his resignation. The violent rallies and processions reached a peak in November on "Dhaka Siege Day" when opposition party workers from around the country converged on Dhaka to besiege the city and confront the government forces. The result? Downtown Dhaka looked like a war zone with bombs exploding, tear-gas canisters erupting, weapons firing, and buildings burning. Several people were killed and scores injured. For the next two weeks, strikes and rioting continued until the government at last reluctantly declared a state of emergency, suspended the people's fundamental rights, and dissolved Parliament.

1988 • A new Parliament was elected and the state of emergency lifted. The violent protests remained muted during the rest of the year, partly because of an exceptionally devastating flood. The overpowering deluge inundated most of the country, diverting public attention from political matters.

In the last quarter of 1988, I raced to Bangladesh on behalf of MAP International to organize medical relief for thousands of flood-afflicted people. During that trip I had a fascinating meeting with President Ershad.[2] Accompanying me was photojournalist Phil Craven, who recorded and videotaped our meeting. Someday I hope to write a full report of our discussion, but in this short epilogue I can give only the gist of it. President Ershad was friendly, pleasant, easy to talk to. In the beginning we discussed the inaugural meeting of his first Parliament. I had a vivid memory of the day because I had attended that session. When I spoke appreciatively

1988 flood—living on the rooftops

Surviving on a rooftop

President Ershad was friendly, pleasant, and easy to talk to

of his speech, he responded, "Thank you very much. Also, martial law was lifted [at that time]."

We discussed his sister-in-law, who had been my patient in Chittagong. Later Dr. Donn Ketcham and I had carried out the operation that she needed. The president remembered all about it—and he recalled her words of praise for our staff.

Then President Ershad spoke about our care for the more needy members of the society: "I must say that you have done a wonderful job here in our country, looking after the poor people. And I should say it is a total commitment, what you have done for the people, what you have done as a doctor—not only as a doctor but as a human being. I very much appreciate it! I have wanted to meet you."

He seemed particularly impressed that our highly trained physicians and surgeons had elected to work in the rural countryside. In Bangladesh most trained doctors gravitate to the cities—or to foreign countries where salaries are high.

He went on to explain, "Most of our doctors who are qualified have left the country for Iran, Iraq, or other places—for Saudi Arabia." That was disturbing to him since the Bangladesh government highly subsidizes the education of every physician. He continued, "These doctors are not serving the people for whom they have been trained. It is by [the people's] money they have been trained. This is the unfortunate part. Very unfortunate. Because of this I feel very, very sad."

The president then detailed his progress in decentralizing the government. Although Mujib and Zia had not lived long enough to put their decentralization plans into effect, President Ershad had succeeded in converting the 64 subdivisions into full-fledged districts, then building up the 469 subdistricts (counties) into important centers of local administration.

He spoke of the subdistrict health complexes that were designed to improve the medical care available to village people. We were well aware of this system, for the subdistrict health complexes in our area usually refer their serious cases to our hospital. He went on to point out that Bangladeshi physicians were not very happy about being assigned to these countryside complexes.

Next President Ershad explained how and why he had placed the country under martial law. Then he added, "After we took over we brought many changes. First the decentralization of the administration, then the new drug policy. Our drug policy is now very much praised and appreciated." This policy certainly had made a positive impression around the world. It involved assisting the local pharmaceutical companies to expand enough to produce all the primary drugs needed in the country. Locally based large international companies would manufacture certain more complex medications, and a few other essential medicines would be imported.

"After we took over we brought many changes"

All other drugs were banned. This prevented wasting money on the manufacture or import of expensive drugs with limited usefulness.

The president went on to speak of other reform measures, including the steps he and his government had taken to control the population explosion. Sometime during 1985 the population had *crossed the 100 million mark*, although it had been only about 50 million when we first arrived in the country in 1962. Since then the Ershad government had made significant progress in reducing the birthrate, but he was eager to further intensify family planning efforts. He explained, "I am not trying to praise myself, but the country has been benefited because of some of the strong measures we took."

He also spoke of the heavy pressures brought to bear on him and on his government by the opposition political parties. He expostulated, "What they thought, you know, was that they would take the country to such a place, or to such a situation, that I would not be able to hold the elections. But God has been kind. We could hold the election in the face of threats from the opposition political parties, bombs, and things like that. And now you can see there is total peace prevailing and stability in the country."

We talked about many other subjects. At the end he said, "Thank you for coming. I very much appreciate what you are doing. And I wish some doctors from our country would take an example from you. I wish I were a doctor and could go sit there in the jungle like you and treat people."

It was an enjoyable interview. I found President Ershad to be a strong man imbued with a dogged determination to make his plans and projects succeed. At the same time, he possessed a certain gentleness and deep sympathy for the sick, the poor, and the hungry in his country. I appreciated that.

During the years of the evolving Ershad era, Jalal continued to serve his government as a senior civil servant. For some years he was the nation's secretary of education, during a later period the secretary of defense. Meanwhile, he remained a friend and well-wisher of our hospital staff and mission team. We grieved with him when his wife, Shakina, died of a heart attack. To this day Joan and I have many precious memories of her warmth and hospitality.

As for former lieutenant colonels Farook and Rashid, the masterminds behind the 1975 coup, they remained for years as exiles in Libya. Finally, President Ershad allowed them to return and live freely in Bangladesh. Farook then ran against Ershad in the 1986 presidential election. When the votes were counted he achieved a distant third place. Later, Farook and Rashid established a unique new political party named the Freedom party. I found it heartening that these men had progressed from organizing military coups to utilizing political action to achieve their purposes.

In late 1988, to find out what made Farook tick, I had a five-hour marathon discussion with him in Dhaka.[3] He was a direct, forceful man, the paradigm of a military officer. From his lips I learned exactly what had happened that fateful night of August 14-15, 1975, when he launched the coup in which Sheikh Mujib had been assassinated and the Mushtaque government installed. Because of his vivid, detailed explanations, I was able to refine my chapters on this subject and make them much more accurate and thorough.

During that interview I inquired about his new Freedom party. He replied that it was a party based on Islamic principles and would have an Islamic constitution. I looked through his early draft of that constitution and could see that it quite clearly described an Islamic religious state. I noted that this was somewhat different from his previous political philosophy. Farook explained, "Certain obligations and rights are given by God to man, and nobody else has the right to throw them out. If there is an Islamic government, the Sovereign is God, not the president. God rules, and in God's rule emergencies and war don't change things. These principles must be kept up, and they must be active laws."

Lt. Col.(Rtd) S. Farook Reehman

Although the Ershad government had never promoted making Bangladesh an Islamic state, in 1988 it did strengthen the Islamic orientation of the nation. It did so by enshrining Islam as the state religion. The Constitution was amended to read: "The state religion of the republic is Islam, but other religions may be practised in peace and harmony in the republic."[4]

Speaking on this subject, President Ershad declared that Islam protects the rights of people of other faiths. He also explained, "My government does not subscribe to [Islamic] fundamentalism, and we are not anti-progress. We are not dogmatic or reactionary."[5]

During the parliamentary debate on the subject, ministers of the government also emphasized that Bangladesh would continue to be a secular state and not an Islamic republic. The prime minister wound up the parliamentary discussion of the subject in the same vein. Interestingly enough, the prime minister was by then Moudud Ahmed, the friendly law partner of our attorney.

Some of the problems of the first decade have continued to haunt the country. Although many of the non-Bengali Biharis have integrated with Bangladeshi society, tens of thousands still consider themselves Pakistanis and long to move to Pakistan. They are an unhappy, miserable community of people, since Pakistan to this day refuses to receive them.

After the expiration of the original Farakka agreement in November 1982, the Farakka Barrage and the supply of Ganges River water to Bangladesh again became a thorny issue, causing tension between Bangladesh and India. Although President Ershad succeeded in negotiating two additional temporary agreements with India, the second one will soon expire. There was no agreement of any kind to cover the dry season of 1985.

The lack of a permanent agreement on sharing the Ganges water is a matter of grave concern to the government and people of Bangladesh. Furthermore, there has been no meeting of the minds about a long-term approach to increasing the overall amount of water flowing into the Ganges—or how to share the waters of a number of other important rivers. It is Bangladesh's misfortune to be on the downstream end of all these rivers.

The Shanti Bahini tribal insurgency in the Chittagong Hill Tracts also has continued to challenge the government. President Ershad has given his personal attention to the problem, and the Parliament has enacted a law on the Hill Tracts issue. In April 1989 President Ershad, addressing the Grand Peace Conference in the CHT, again offered amnesty to Shanti Bahini fighters. Elections have been held for the three district councils in the Hill Tracts. About two-thirds of the new members are tribal men and one-third Bengalis. Only time will tell how the tribal people in general and the Shanti Bahini in particular will respond to these new developments.

The American people and government continue to have a soft spot in their hearts for the people of Bangladesh. Since its birth in 1971 the U.S. government has poured in more than $2.5 billion in assistance to the nation. Diplomatic relations between the two countries are warm and friendly, and the U.S. government has consistently assigned excellent ambassadors to Dhaka. We salute these diplomats who have represented their nation so ably. Recently, for the first time, Bangladesh is exporting more goods to the U.S. than the U.S. exports to Bangladesh. That is due to the mushrooming exports of ready-made garments manufactured in Bangladesh.

Over the last few years our special Bengali common language New Testament has found favor with the people of Bangladesh. The sales record is phenomenal. Several times we have seen a priest with prayer cap and flowing white beard pick up a copy, recognize it as a true Holy Scripture he has never before seen, kiss it, and hold it reverently to his heart. Students read it and marvel at the exalted teaching and remarkable life of Jesus the Messiah. Thousands all around the country have been drawn closer to this remarkable Prophet, whom they have always revered and admired from afar.

New church south of Chittagong—Pastor Shapan with Vic

Service at Dampara church

In 1982 George Weber and I presented to the mission's Church Formation Committee our new proposal for financing the establishment of churches. After an animated discussion and the infusion of some additional ideas, the program was approved by the committee and ultimately by the whole Field Council. Since then the tempo of effective church planting has perceptibly quickened.

The efforts at renewal of the Dampara church in Chittagong have also succeeded. The growing church now has a good spirit and a fine leader, Pastor Anup. There in the city the Literature Division continues to produce valuable new titles each year, with a good share of the work being turned out on the in-house presses. The standard Bengali translation team has made steady progress in the translation of Old Testament books.

In connection with our tribal outreach, the government finally did grant our request for permission to travel via the new Alikadam Road through a section of the Hill Tracts to our Hebron Station. The trip, which used to take a day by river, now takes only an hour by road. What an improvement! At Hebron, resident national teachers now teach seventy-five tribal students. In addition, there are smaller schools in more than a dozen Hill Tracts villages. At last we are doing better in conquering the curse of tribal illiteracy.

The tribal churches are stronger now, and, because of the Tribal Bible Institute program, they have increasingly capable leaders. The translation of the New Testament into the Tippera language is in progress. And in far-off Rangamati, Debapriyaw Roy

Chittagong Hill Tracts from the new Alikadam Road

Tribal Bible Institute at Hebron

has successfully completed the New Testament in his Chakma language, a major accomplishment. "Thank You, Father!"

At Malumghat the medical personnel continue their compassionate work of caring for the multitudes who pour into the hospital like an unending river of sorrow and anguish. The patients are touched by caring, competent hands that administer modern treatments and carry out complex surgical operations. These hands are strengthened by the earnest prayers of the staff and thousands of supporters the world around.

The church at Malumghat has grown and matured. Its special services are attended by literally hundreds of members and visitors from the neighborhood. Pastors Gonijan, Shorno, and Leslie are now very experienced shepherds who teach and lead their people well.

We continue to place increasing emphasis on training. The new Bible Institute is effectively teaching national church leaders. Also, two men have been sent abroad for advanced education. Dr. Babla is studying medicine and theology in the U.S. He is a fine young man who grew up in our church in Chittagong, then completed medical college and served as a physician at Malumghat Hospital. John Sircar, manager of the Literature Division, has earned in the U.S. assorted master's degrees and a doctorate in theological studies. What an asset he will be in educating national

Dr. Babla

church leaders! At the other end of the age scale, our beautiful camp and a new program for training young people (named AWANA) have fostered the children's love for God and strengthened their characters.

Translator Samuel has married and now has two pretty daughters. He has become somewhat more settled, more serene, and we hear that he faithfully continues his work of teaching the Holy Scriptures to interested people.

Robichandro Tippera, bewildered for a while by the death of his wife, has now regained his focus. Although he rarely treks into the Hill Tracts now, he daily teaches his people who come to Malumghat for treatment and training. His newly acquired ability to read is an immense help to him in this ministry. Menshai Murung, also newly literate, continues trekking to the Murung villages to tell his people about Jesus. And he plays an important part in training new Murung church leaders.

Mr. U., the leader of the Burmese Bengali refugee camp near Malumghat Hospital, was repatriated to Burma where he regained his house and property. Soon he entered into a program of explaining Christ's good news message to his relatives and neighbors. After quite a number of them became His disciples, they constructed their own house of worship. There Mr. U. began leading them in a weekly service of praise to the true and living God. "Thank You, Father!"

We and the Dulahazara Action Committee continue to honor our mutual agreement. And the friendships that we cemented with the Action Committee leaders during the tense negotiations are to this day a source of much pleasure. One of the first things I plan to do upon our return to Malumghat is to spend some time with these men, enjoy their company, and hear about their sons, daughters, and grandchildren.

During these few years our own family has grown up. Wendy, Lynne, Mark, and Nancy have all married mates who love the Lord, and they now have their own children. Joan and I have had a much longer than usual home leave because a new skin cancer appeared in the neighborhood of her previous operation. This has required a number of additional operations to remove the disease and reconstruct the tissues.

The end of that process is now in sight, and we are preparing to head back to that green and golden lowland perched astride the Bay of Bengal. With an inner sense of joy and expectancy, we look forward again to serving God and man in the People's Republic of Bangladesh. There is so much more that needs to be done.

What a fine life our family has enjoyed helping and working side-by-side with the people of golden Bengal! What priceless experiences have been ours as we suffered with the people during their times of distress and rejoiced with them as they gained their independence and began a new nation! We rejoiced with them, too, when their harvests were bountiful, when their new babies entered the world, and when they recovered from myriad illnesses that had taken some of them to death's door.

And all these great life experiences came to us because of those three simple words: salvation, surrender, and service. The day Joan and I placed our faith in Christ the Lord was the day of our *salvation,* the point in time when we received forgiveness and life everlasting. Months later, in an act of *surrender,* we placed our lives into the Father's hands so that He could use them for good and spiritual purposes. Then guidance came that our *service* would be to love, to heal, and to teach the people of a land we now call Bangladesh—land of the Bengalis.

To me, the best illustration of this three-fold rule of life is that razor-sharp knifelike instrument, the surgeon's scalpel. My scalpel was not always a shining, stainless steel precision instrument. Once it was a lowly, brown, dirty, misshapen piece of iron ore buried in a hillside. One day, however, a miner dug it out—rescued it, saved it—from that hillside for a more useful purpose.

Just as the miner did his work (for a salary), so Christ the Lord worked on our behalf (for love's sake). Entering into humanity, He lived a perfect life, then gave that life on a rough wooden cross —not for His sins, but rather to pay for ours. As the iron ore was impotent to save itself, so we were incapable of saving ourselves. In a sense, the miner became the savior of the iron ore. Similarly,

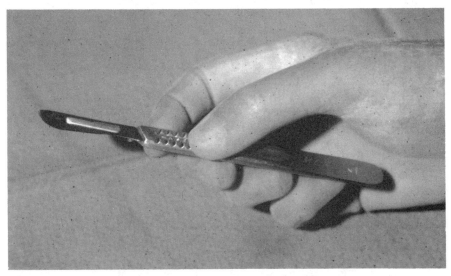

The surgeon's scalpel

Christ the Lord becomes the Savior of all who put their faith in Him. And the *salvation* He provided became ours the instant we believed this good news message and personally received Him by faith as our Savior. Then, just as the piece of iron ore was changed into something more valuable and more effective, so we were changed into people far more worthwhile and useful.

And what about *surrender?* Listen, my scalpel is the ultimate picture of surrender. It is 1,000 percent surrendered to my hand. Although I have picked it up multiplied thousands of times, it has never once cut north when I told it to cut south. In fact, it has never varied one hair's breadth from what I have told it to do. It has no will of its own; it is there to do my will perfectly and exclusively. And, according to the Scriptures, that is to be our stance, too. We are told,

> . . . present [surrender] yourselves to God as being alive from the dead, and your members as instruments of righteousness to God.[6]

Once we made that commitment, a new contentment settled in and guidance began to flow. We soon discovered that divinely directed lives were more satisfying and productive than self-directed lives.

And third, what is the purpose of the scalpel? It was created to be used by a caring surgeon to help the sick and the injured in their agony and distress—and sometimes to save their lives. And doesn't this perfectly picture what our *service* should be? We are to be instruments in the Master's hand who show His love to others and who aid them in their pain, confusion, and grief, and, in some instances, help them gain new life.

In this matter of service our model is, of course, that Man from Palestine we unexpectedly encountered so many years ago. He instructs and motivates us by His example—and by His words:

> Yet I am among you as the One who *serves.*[7]

> For even the Son of Man did not come to be served, but to *serve*, and to give His life a ransom for many.[8]

A final question about the surgeon's premier instrument. When a complex operation is successful, where does the credit go? No headline ever featured "Scalpel No. 2459." Rather, the noted surgeon who so skillfully uses it receives the accolades. Similarly, our accomplishments are motivated, directed, and implemented by the Great Physician—so *He* is the praiseworthy One.

As for the analogy of the scalpel, true as it is, the comparison can only be taken so far. This is so because the Creator has endowed us with will and capacities unknown to cold steel. Whereas the scalpel has no choice about responding to the surgeon's touch, we can either accept or reject our calls to salvation, surrender, and service. And if we do decide to serve, we have the capacity to relish the rich rewards of inner joy and satisfaction. Ours the challenge, ours the choice, ours the joy—but the glory His alone!

Appendix
Two Concepts

If you are a Muslim, Hindu, or Buddhist person reading this book you will find it easy to follow—except for possibly two concepts. One is calling God "Father." I do it sometimes because I have found this special title frequently in the Holy Bible and because it is beautiful to me and full of deep meaning. He is like a human father in that He loves His own people, protects them, provides for them, disciplines them, cares for them, and guides them along life's pathway. I mention this because during my many years of living in Bangladesh I have observed that calling God "Father" sounds strange to most Bangladeshi ears. That is understandable, for the concept is not taught in Islam, Hinduism, or Buddhism.

The second point that could cause confusion for you relates to another title—calling Jesus the "Son of God." What does this unusual title mean? Some years ago we ourselves were confused about it, so we studied this question carefully and learned several facts:

First of all, we cannot take all titles or expressions in a strictly physical or literal sense. For example, does the expression "son of the soil" mean that the earth (of Bangladesh or some other land) married a man, became pregnant, then nine months later gave birth to a son? No, the phrase merely identifies a person as native-born rather than foreign-born.

Second, as in the example above, the title "Son of God" cannot be taken in a strictly physical sense. It does not mean that the Creator God entered into marriage with a young woman named Mary, and through a human physical act caused her to become pregnant. After all, God is a spirit and is not restricted to our human ways of doing things.

Third, as educated Christians and Muslims well know, the holy God did, in a pure, holy, and miraculous way, place a life within the virgin Mary's womb. No human father was involved.

This is one reason Jesus is called the Son of God. In the Bible we read these words spoken to Mary by an angelic being:

> ... the power of the Most High will overshadow you; and for that reason the holy offspring shall be called the Son of God.[1]

Fourth, this unusual title "Son of God" was established and used for Jesus the Messiah long before His unique conception and birth; thus it is also a title from eternity past. We read in the Psalms of David, the writings of the prophets, and the New Testament that God used this title for His Messiah (His Christ) hundreds of years before His birth. And after He was born God Himself, the angel Gabriel, the prophet John the Baptist, and the companions of Jesus all called Him the Son of God. And, of course, He claimed and used the title for Himself.

Finally, we recognized that Christ the Lord was a remarkable, composite Person—a unique combination of humanity and deity. We found that we could diagram His composite nature in this way:

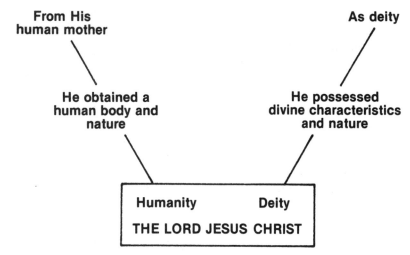

The Holy Scriptures beautifully attest to this dual nature. Because of His humanity He is often called the Son of Man. And because of His deity He is frequently designated the Son of God.

These several facts make clear that the name Son of God should no longer be a point of confusion; rather, we can all understand and appreciate the deep significance of this rich and beautiful title.

Notes

Preface

1. Viggo Olsen, M.D., with Jeanette Lockerbie, *Daktar/Diplomat in Bangladesh* (Chicago: Moody, 1973).

Chapter 1. Three Majors with a Plan for a Coup

1. Anthony Mascarenhas, *Bangladesh: A Legacy of Blood* (London: Hodder and Stoughton, 1986), p. 2.
2. Lt. Col.(Rtd) Sayyed Farook Reehman, interview with author at the Reehman residence, Dhaka, Bangladesh, on October 14, 1988; Mascarenhas, pp. 69-70, presents a somewhat different version of the deployment of the artillery pieces.
3. Lawrence Lifschultz, *Bangladesh: The Unfinished Revolution* (London: Zed, 1979), p. 98.
4. Lt. Col. (Rtd) S. Farook Reehman, interview with the author in Dhaka on October 14, 1988.
5. Mascarenhas, p. 70.
6. Ibid., p. 71.
7. Lt. Col. (Rtd) S. Farook Reehman, interview with the author in Dhaka on October 14, 1988.
8. Ibid.
9. Mascarenhas, p. 72.

Chapter 2. Three Decisions by a Couple Named Olsen

1. The Holy Bible *(New King James Version)*, Romans 6:13. All Scripture quotations in this book, unless noted otherwise, are from *The Holy Bible, New King James Version* © 1982; *New King James Version, New Testament and New Testament with Psalms*, © 1980, 1979 by Thomas Nelson, Inc.
2. Ibid., Romans 12:1.

Chapter 3. Three Meetings with a President Named Khan

1. Viggo Olsen M.D., with Jeanette Lockerbie, *Daktar/Diplomat in Bangladesh* (Chicago: Moody, 1973), p. 350.
2. *Statistical Pocket Book of Bangladesh 1978* (Dacca: Bangladesh Bureau of Statistics, Government of Bangladesh, 1977), p. 74.
3. Muhammad Ishaq, *Bangladesh District Gazetteers: Chittagong Hill Tracts* (Dacca: OSD, Establishment Division, Incharge, Bangladesh Government Press, 1971), pp. 39, 44. Because the population of the CHT increased about one-third between 1951 and 1961, I increased the 1951 figures for each tribe by one-third, then rounded them off to arrive at the 1961 figures.
4. *Statistical Pocket Book of Bangladesh 1978*, pp. 90-91.
5. Stephen Neill, *The Story of the Christian Church in India and Pakistan* (Grand Rapids, Mich.: Eerdmans, 1970), pp. 66-69.
6. *Encyclopaedia Brittannica*, 15th ed., s.v. "Judson, Adoniram."
7. Viggo B. Olsen, *A Muslim Bengali to English Dictionary* (Chittagong, East Pakistan: V. B. Olsen with the Pakistan Cooperative Book Society, 1967).
8. Moudud Ahmed, *Bangladesh: Constitutional Quest for Autonomy 1950-1971* (Dacca: U. Press, 1979), p. 133.
9. Zillur R. Khan, *Martial Law to Martial Law—Leadership Crisis in Bangladesh* (Dhaka: U. Press, 1984), pp. 12-13.
10. The Holy Bible (*New King James Version*), Proverbs 21:1.
11. Ahmed, pp.132-62.
12. *The Man Jesus* (Wheaton, Ill.: Tyndale House, 1966).
13. The Holy Bible (*New King James Version*), 2 Corinthians 5:19.
14. Ibid., Luke 2:11 (emphasis added).
15. Ibid., Romans 5:8.
16. Ibid., Titus 3:5 (emphasis added).
17. Ibid., 2 Timothy 1:9 (emphasis added).
18. Ibid., Acts 16:31.
19. Ibid., John 1:12.
20. Ibid., Romans 10:13.

Chapter 4. Three Attacks in a Province Called East Pakistan

1. Craig Baxter, *Bangladesh, a New Nation in an Old Setting* (Boulder, Colo.: Westview, 1984), p. 46.
2. Rafiq-ul-Islam, *A Tale of Millions* (Dacca: Bangladesh Books International, 1981), pp. 98-99.
3. Moudud Ahmed, *Bangladesh: Constitutional Quest for Autonomy 1950-1971* (Dacca: U. Press, 1979), pp. 254-55.
4. Viggo Olsen M.D., with Jeanette Lockerbie, *Daktar/Diplomat in Bangladesh* (Chicago: Moody, 1973); Jeannie Lockerbie, *On Duty in Bangladesh* (Grand Rapids, Mich.: Zondervan, 1973).
5. Ahmed, pp. 264-66.
6. Moudud Ahmed, *Bangladesh: Era of Sheikh Mujibur Rahman* (Dhaka: U. Press, 1984), p. 10.

7. Lawrence Lifschultz, *Bangladesh: The Unfinished Revolution* (London: Zed, 1979), pp. 113-16.

8. E. Peer with J. Friedman and L. Jenkins, "Final Frame," *Newsweek* (May 19, 1975): 45.

Chapter 5. 1972: Relief and Reconstuction

1. Viggo Olsen M.D., with Jeanette Lockerbie, *Daktar/Diplomat in Bangladesh* (Chicago: Moody, 1973), pp. 306-46.

2. Sanford J. Ungar, "Secret Texts Raise Lid on Kissinger Policy Against India in War," *Chicago Sun-Times*, January 5, 1972.

3. "Text of Remarks at Secret Meeting on India-Pakistan," *Chicago Sun-Times*, January 5, 1972.

4. "Second Document: Text of NSC Unit's India-Pakistan Talk," *Chicago Sun-Times*, January 5, 1972.

5. Lawrence Lifschultz, *Bangladesh: The Unfinished Revolution* (London: Zed, 1979), pp. 158-59.

6. Anthony Mascarenhas, *Bangladesh: A Legacy of Blood* (London: Hodder and Stoughton, 1986), p. 5.

7. Ibid.

8. Ramendu Majumdar, *Bangladesh My Bangladesh* (Dacca: Muktadhara, 1972), p. 135.

9. Ibid., p. 138.

10. Ibid., pp. 139-44.

11. Moudud Ahmed, *Bangladesh: Era of Sheikh Mujibur Rahman* (Dhaka: U. Press, 1984), p. 10.

12. *This Is Bangladesh* (Dhaka: Department of Films and Publications, Ministry of Information, 1985), p. 2.

13. U.S. Congress, Senate Committee on the Judiciary, *Relief Problems in Bangladesh, Hearing Before the Subcommittee to Investigate Problems Connected with Refugees and Escapees of the Committee on the Judiciary*, 92d Cong., 2d sess., February 2, 1972.

14. *The Chittagong Hill Tracts* (London: Anti-Slavery Society, 1984), pp. 46, 56.

15. Ibid., pp. 46-47, 56-57.

16. Ahmed, p. 19.

17. U.S. Congress, Senate Committee on Foreign Relations, *Recognition of Bangladesh: Hearings Before the Committee on Foreign Relations*, 92d Cong., March 6-7, 1972, p. 2.

18. Ibid., p. 5.

19. "25,000 Cheer Mujib's Opponent," *Chicago Sun-Times*, April 3, 1972.

20. "Constitution of the People's Republic of Bangladesh," *Bangladesh Gazette, Extraordinary*, Part 1 (December 14, 1972): 10 (emphasis added).

21. Ibid., p. 11.

22. Ibid., pp. 18, 21.

23. "Bangladesh: One Year After," *Newsweek* (December 11, 1972): 60, 65.

Chapter 6. 1973: Elections and *Daktar*

1. Moudud Ahmed, *Bangladesh: Era of Sheikh Mujibur Rahman* (Dhaka: U. Press, 1984), p. 157.
2. Talukder Maniruzzaman, *The Bangladesh Revolution and Its Aftermath* (Dacca: Bangladesh Books International, 1980), p. 176.
3. Ahmed, pp. 139-40.
4. Khan, *Martial Law to Martial Law—Leadership Crisis in Bangladesh* (Dhaka: U. Press, 1984), p. 118.
5. Ahmed, p. 144.
6. Ibid., p. 146.
7. Jeannie Lockerbie, *On Duty in Bangladesh* (Grand Rapids, Mich.: Zondervan, 1973).
8. "Pakistan: The Other POW's," *Newsweek* (April 16, 1973): 38.
9. Ahmed, pp. 199-200, 205; "World Court Begins Hearing Pakistan's Case on POWs; India Boycotts Proceedings," *Pakistan Affairs* 26 (June, 16, 1973): 3.
10. Information taken from Abdus Samad, *Bangladesh: Facing the Future* (Dhaka: A. Samad, 1983), pp. 17, 24, 35.
11. Richard F. Nyrop et al., *Area Handbook for Bangladesh* (Washington: Foreign Area Studies, The American University, 1975), p. 230.
12. Ahmed, pp. 160-77.
13. Ibid., 202-06; "Indo-Pak Accord at Delhi," *India News* 12 (September 7, 1973): 1; "Solution of Humanitarian Issues: Agreement Signed," *Bangladesh* 3 (September 7, 1973): 1.
14. Ahmed, pp. 149-50.

Chapter 7. 1974: Floods and Famine

1. "National Religious Bestsellers," *Bookstore Journal* (January, February, March, April, 1974).
2. Anthony Mascarenhas, *Bangladesh: A Legacy of Blood* (London: Hodder and Stoughton, 1986), pp. 45-46.
3. A. L. Khatib, *Who Killed Mujib?* (New Delhi: Vikas, 1981), pp. 45-47.
4. Talukder Maniruzzaman, "Bangladesh in 1974: Economic Crisis and Political Polarization," *Asian Survey* 15, no. 2 (February 1975): 122-23.
5. The Holy Bible (*New King James Version*), John 3:16.
6. Dr. and Mrs. Richard Stagg, newsletter, March 1974.
7. Maniruzzaman, p. 124.
8. "Tripartite Agreement of India, Bangladesh and Pakistan," *Bangladesh* 4 (April 12, 1974): 2.
9. "Return of POWs Enables Reordering of Relations Among S. Asian Neighbors," *Pakistan Affairs* 27 (May 16, 1974): 1.
10. Zillur R. Khan, *Martial Law to Martial Law—Leadership Crisis in Bangladesh* (Dhaka: U. Press, 1984), p. 123.
11. Mascarenhas, p. 47.
12. Ibid., p. 48.
13. Ibid.

14. Lawrence Lifschultz, *Bangladesh: The Unfinished Revolution* (London: Zed, 1979), p. 139.
15. Mascarenhas, pp. 49-50.
16. Ibid., p. 50.
17. Lifschultz, pp. 169-71.
18. Ibid., p. 142.
19. Ibid., pp. 132-36, 177-84.
20. Mascarenhas, p. 50.
21. Ibid., p. 51.
22. Nurul Momen, *Bangladesh: The First Four Years* (Dacca: Bangladesh Institute of Law and International Affairs, 1980), p. 126.

Chapter 8. 1975: Mrus and Coups

1. "The Emergency Powers Rules, 1975," *The Bangladesh Gazette* (January 3, 1975): 9.
2. Charles Peter O'Donnell, *Bangladesh: Biography of a Muslim Nation* (Boulder, Colo.: Westview, 1984), p. 171.
3. Moudud Ahmed, *Bangladesh: Era of Sheikh Mujibur Rahman* (Dhaka: U. Press, 1984), pp. 235-44.
4. Anthony Mascarenhas, *Bangladesh: A Legacy of Blood* (London: Hodder and Stoughton, 1986), p. 53.
5. Ibid., p. 52.
6. Lt. Col. (Rtd) S. Farook Reehman, interview with the author in Dhaka on October 14, 1988.
7. Mascarenhas, p. 54.
8. Lawrence Lifschultz, *Bangladesh: The Unfinished Revolution* (London: Zed, 1979), p. 103.
9. Ahmed, pp. 245-47.
10. Mascarenhas, p. 54.
11. Ibid., p. 55.
12. Ibid.
13. Ibid., p. 57.
14. Asoka Raina, *Inside RAW: The Story of India's Secret Service* (New Delhi: Vikas, 1981), pp. 61-62.
15. Mascarenhas, p. 60.
16. Ibid.
17. Ibid.
18. Ibid., p. 63.
19. Ibid., p. 2.
20. Ibid., p. 66.
21. Ibid., p. 68.
22. Ibid.
23. Ibid.
24. Ibid., p. 69.
25. Lt. Col. (Rtd) S. Farook Reehman, interview with the author in Dhaka on October 14, 1988.

26. Ibid.
27. Ibid.
28. Ibid.
29. Ibid.
30. Mascarenhas, p. 72.
31. Ibid., p. 73.
32. Ibid.
33. Bachchu Rahman, *Latenight Massacre* (Dhaka: Privately published, 1985), p. 4; A. L. Khatib, *Who Killed Mujib?* (New Delhi: Vikas, 1981), p. 38; Lt. Col. (Rtd) S. Farook Reehman, interview with the author in Dhaka on October 14, 1988. Farook explained that the outer perimeter soldiers would not have allowed Risaldar Moslemuddin to cross their line to go to Mujib's house; they had been given irreversible orders to kill anyone who tried to pass through their outer perimeter.
34. Lt. Col. (Rtd) S. Farook Reehman, interview with the author in Dhaka on October 14, 1988.
35. Ibid.
36. Khatib, pp. 6, 20; Mascarenhas, pp. 77, 81.
37. Khatib, p. 13.
38. The Holy Bible (*New King James Version*), Matthew 27:54.
39. Ibid., Matthew 26:53-54.
40. Ibid., John 10:17-18.
41. "Pakistan Recognizes New Dacca Regime: Gifts 50,000 Tons Rice, 15 M. Yards Cloth," *Pakistan Affairs* 28 (September 1, 1975):4.
42. Mascarenhas, p. 94.
43. Ibid., p. 96.
44. Ibid., pp. 85-86, 96-98.
45. Ibid., p. 95.
46. Ibid., p. 101.
47. Ibid.
48. Ibid., p. 111.
49. Ibid., p. 115.

Chapter 9. 1976: Militant Majors and Ragged Refugees

1. Anthony Mascarenhas, *Bangladesh: A Legacy of Blood* (London: Hodder and Stoughton, 1986), p. 138.
2. The Holy Bible (*New King James Version*), Ephesians 2:8-9 (emphasis added).
3. Mascarenhas, p. 139.
4. Ibid., pp. 139-40.
5. Ibid., p. 139.
6. Ibid., pp. 75, 96, 140-41.
7. Ibid., p. 141.
8. Ibid.
9. Ibid., p. 142.
10. Ibid.

11. Ibid.
12. Lawrence Lifschultz, *Bangladesh: The Unfinished Revolution* (London: Zed, 1979), p. 58.
13. Ibid., pp. 90-92.
14. Ibid., p. 60.
15. Talukder Maniruzzaman, "Bangladesh in 1976: Struggle for Survival as an Independent State," *Asian Survey* 17, no. 2 (February 1977): 196-97.
16. The Holy Bible (*New King James Version*), Isaiah 41:10.
17. Ibid.

Chapter 10. 1977: Translation Triumphs and Visa Crisis

1. Talukder Maniruzzaman, *The Bangladesh Revolution and Its Aftermath* (Dacca: Bangladesh Books International, 1980), p. 229.
2. Anthony Mascarenhas, *Bangladesh: A Legacy of Blood* (London: Hodder and Stoughton, 1986), p. 122.
3. Abusadat Mohammad Sayem, *At Bangabhaban: Last Phase* (Dhaka: Hakkani, 1988), pp. 38-41.
4. Maniruzzaman, p. 217.
5. Ibid.
6. Ibid., pp. 217-18.
7. The Holy Bible (*New King James Version*), John 6:28-29, 47 (emphasis added).
8. Mascarenhas, p. 145.
9. Ibid., p. 146.
10. Ibid., pp. 146-47.
11. Ibid., p. 147.
12. Ibid., pp. 147-48.
13. Zillur R. Khan, *Martial Law to Martial Law—Leadership Crisis in Bangladesh* (Dhaka: U. Press, 1984), pp. 175-76.
14. Mascarenhas, p. 147.
15. Ibid., pp. 148-50.
16. The Holy Bible (*New King James Version*), John 8:36.
17. Ibid., Luke 9:23.

Chapter 11. 1978: More Crises—More Refugees

1. Golam Hossain, *General Ziaur Rahman and the BNP* (Dhaka: U. Press, 1988), p. 45.
2. S. R. Chakravarty and Virendra Narain, *Bangladesh: Domestic Politics* (New Delhi: South Asian Publishers, 1986), 2:103-5.
3. Ibid., pp. 105-7.
4. Daud Majlis, "Disturbances on the Border of Peace—The Exodus Reversed," *Far Eastern Economic Review* (May 19, 1978): 36-37; "A New Blight on the Border," *Far Eastern Economic Review* (June 9, 1978): 35-36.
5. Abdus Samad, *Bangladesh: Facing the Future* (Dhaka: A. Samad, 1983), pp. 48-50.
6. Ibid., pp. 50-56.

Chapter 12. 1979: New Parliament—New Scriptures

1. S. R. Chakravarty and Virendra Narain, *Bangladesh: Domestic Politics* (New Delhi: South Asian Publishers, 1986), 2:81-82.
2. Talukder Maniruzzaman, *The Bangladesh Revolution and Its Aftermath* (Dacca: Bangladesh Books International, 1980), pp. 226-27.
3. The Holy Bible (*New King James Version*), Luke 17:3-4.
4. Marcus Franda, *Bangladesh: The First Decade* (New Delhi: South Asian Publishers, 1982), pp. 230-31, 329-30.
5. *Address by President Ziaur Rahman at the Inaugural Session of the Second Parliament of Bangladesh, April 2, 1979* (Dacca: Department of Films and Publications, Government of Bangladesh, 1972), p. 1.
6. Ibid., p. 29.
7. D. Jay Walsh, *Ripe Mangoes* (Schaumburg, Ill.: Regular Baptist, 1979).
8. "Lord, Help Me, for I am Innocent," *Asiaweek* (April 20, 1979): 12.
9. Anthony Mascarenhas, *Bangladesh: A Legacy of Blood* (London: Hodder and Stoughton, 1986), p. 150.
10. Ibid., pp. 74, 150.
11. The Holy Bible (*New King James Version*), Romans 12:21.
12. "It's Everyone's Space," *Asiaweek* (July 27, 1979): 13.
13. Mascarenhas, p. 151.
14. Ibid., pp. 151-52.

Chapter 13. 1980: Troublesome Book—Troubled Missions

1. "Bangladesh—Cabinet Changes—Other Internal Political Developments, November 1979 to October 1980," *Keesing's Contemporary Archives* (January 9, 1981): 30657.
2. "The Empress of India," *Newsweek* (January 21, 1980): 45-46.
3. "Bangladesh," 30658.
4. English translation of the written statement of Upendra Lal Chakma M.P. made in the press Conference held on April 1, 1980, in the no. 2 Committee room of Sangsad Bhaban [Parliament Building].
5. Anthony Mascarenhas, *Bangladesh: A Legacy of Blood* (London: Hodder and Stoughton, 1986), pp. 151-53.
6. "Bangladesh," 30658.
7. "Entire Bengali Village Wiped Out in Two Days of Carnage," *The Register*, Orange County, California, June 16, 1980.
8. James M. Rosooli and Allen, *There Is No Fear in Death* (Calcutta: Evangelical Literature Depot, 1966).
9. The Holy Bible, (*New King James Version*), Acts 19:37.
10. Ibid. 2 Samuel 22:2-3.
11. Ibid., James 3:17.

Chapter 14. 1981: President's Parley—President's Peril

1. "The Hostages Return: Who Won?" *Asiaweek* (January 30, 1981): 14.

2. Anthony Mascarenhas, *Bangladesh: A Legacy of Blood* (London: Hodder and Stoughton, 1986), pp. 158-59.
3. "Chittagong Exhibition Stalls Gutted: 22 Injured," *The Bangladesh Observer*, Dacca, March 25, 1981.
4. Mascarenhas, p. 157.
5. Ibid., pp. 158-59.
6. Ibid., p. 154.
7. Ibid., p. 159.
8. Ibid., p. 160.
9. Ibid.
10. Ibid., p. 162.
11. Ibid., p. 163.
12. Ibid., p. 165.
13. Ibid., p. 166.
14. Ibid.
15. Ibid., p. 168.
16. President H. M. Ershad, interview with the author at President's Secretariat in Dhaka, Bangladesh, on October 10, 1988.
17. Mascarenhas, p. 177.
18. Ibid., pp. 178-79.
19. "A Race for the Oldies," *Far Eastern Economic Review* (July 17, 1981): 18.
20. "Bangladesh: Politics on Trial," *Far Eastern Economic Review* (August 14, 1981): 23.
21. Ibid.
22. Ibid.
23. "Bangladesh: Ambition Plus Arrogance," *Far Eastern Economic Review* (July 24, 1981): 26.
24. Charles Peter O'Donnell, *Bangladesh: Biography of a Muslim Nation* (Boulder, Colo.: Westview, 1984), p. 232.
25. Ibid.
26. "Bangladesh: The Chittagong Tribal Revolt—Flight of Refugees to India," *Keesing's Contemporary Archives* (March 19, 1982): 31386.
27. The Holy Bible (*New King James Version*), Joshua 22:5.
28. "Bangladesh—Mr Sattar Elected President," *Keesing's Contemporary Archives* (March 19, 1982): 31385.
29. "Bangladesh: Conflict Between President Sattar and Army Leaders," *Keesing's Contemporary Archives* (March 19, 1982): 31386.
30. Ibid.
31. Ibid.
32. Zillur R. Khan, *Martial Law to Martial Law—Leadership Crisis in Bangladesh* (Dhaka: U. Press, 1984), pp. 225-26.
33. Abdus Samad, *Bangladesh: Facing the Future* (Dhaka: A. Samad, 1983), pp. 79, 85-87.
34. Ibid., pp. 218-19.

Chapter 15. 1982-89: Evolving Problems—Enduring Progress

1. "Bangladesh in 1982: Beginning of the Second Decade," *Asian Survey* 23, no. 2 (February 1983): 151.
2. Pres. H. M. Ershad, interview with the author in Dhaka on October 10, 1988.
3. Lt. Col. (Rtd) S. Farook Reehman, interview with the author in Dhaka on October 14, 1988.
4. "Islam Made State Religion," *Bangladesh News* 3, no. 18 (June 1988):1.
5. Ibid., p. 2.
6. The Holy Bible (*New King James Version*), Romans 6:13.
7. Ibid., Luke 22:27 (emphasis added).
8. Ibid., Mark 10:45 (emphasis added).

Appendix. Two Concepts

1. The Holy Bible (*New American Standard Bible*), Luke 1:35.

We would be happy to share with you in your spiritual pilgrimage by answering questions and providing information about intriguing correspondence courses. If you would like this type of input into your search for spiritual truth, please write us without obligation: Moody Press, c/o MLM, Chicago, Illinois 60610.